D/C

25. APR 98

A C5/96

C9/97

CFD 08/04

This book is to be returned on or before the date above.
It may be borrowed for a further period if not in demand.

063526740

HARLOW CENTRAL

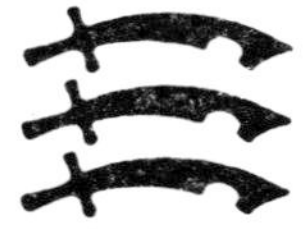

Essex County Council
Libraries

GW00776069

This is an exampl
County Special

Enquire at yo
for de...

30130 063526742

An Anthology of Russian Women's Writing, 1777–1992

◆

EDITED BY

Catriona Kelly

TRANSLATED BY

Catriona Kelly, Sibelan Forrester, Diana Greene, Elizabeth Neatrour, Brian Thomas Oles, Marian Schwartz, and Mary Zirin

ESSEX COUNTY LIBRARIES	
063526740	
J M L S	21/01/96
	£14.95

OXFORD UNIVERSITY PRESS · 1994

891.70809287

Oxford Unversity Press, Walton Street, Oxford OX2 6DP
Oxford New York Toronto
Delhi Bombay Calcutta Madras Karachi
Kuala Lumpur Singapore Hong Kong Tokyo
Nairobi Dar es Salaam Cape Town
Melbourne Auckland Madrid
and associated companies in
Berlin Ibadan

Oxford is a trade mark of Oxford University Press

Published in the United States
by Oxford University Press Inc., New York

Selection, translations, and
editorial material © Catriona Kelly 1994

All rights reserved. No part of this publication may be reproduced, stored in a retrieval system, or transmitted, in any form or by any means, without the prior permission in writing of Oxford University Press. Within the UK, exceptions are allowed in respect of any fair dealing for the purpose of research or private study, or criticism or review, as permitted under the Copyright, Designs and Patents Act, 1988, or in the case of reprographic reproduction in accordance with the terms of the licences issued by the Copyright Licensing Agency. Enquiries concerning reproduction outside these terms and in other countries should be sent to the Rights Department, Oxford University Press, at the address above

This book is sold subject to the condition that it shall not, by way of trade or otherwise, be lent, re-sold, hired out or otherwise circulated without the publisher's prior consent in any form of binding or cover other than that in which it is published and without a similar condition including this condition being imposed on the subsequent purchaser

British Library Cataloguing in Publication Data
Data available

Library of Congress Cataloguing in Publication Data
An Anthology of Russian women's writing, 1777–1992/edited by Catriona Kelly; translated by Catriona Kelly . . . [et al.].
Poetry, prose, and drama; poetry is in original Russian and English translation.
1. Russian literature—Women authors—Translations into English.
I. Kelly, Catriona.
PG3213.A57 1994
891.708'09287—dc20 93-26542
ISBN 0–19–871504–8
ISBN 0–19–871505–6 (Pbk)

1 3 5 7 9 10 8 6 4 2

Typeset by Datix International Limited, Bungay, Suffolk
Printed in Great Britain
on acid-free paper by
Bookcraft Ltd,
Midsomer Norton, Bath

To the memory of Anne Pennington
and of Halina Willetts

CONTENTS

Errata

p.299: last line omitted; should read:
in a piano shop, to her left, her great-grandfather on her mother's side, a

pp. 443 and 444 have been transposed.

INTRODUCTION

This anthology is meant as the companion piece to my *History of Russian Women's Writing 1820–1992*, and its origins lie in the preparatory work for that volume. As I gathered material for my *History*, I came to realize that many of the texts that I proposed to discuss were unlikely to be familiar even to those of my readers who had a reading knowledge of Russian; certainly, they would be quite inaccessible to those without such a knowledge. It became increasingly evident that critical discussion stood in danger of being effaced by quotation and synopsis, and that my book could only too easily become the modern counterpart of the deadly review articles in turn-of-the-century Russian literary journals, composed of pages of dreary synopsis, with a sentence or two of perfunctory critical commentary as afterthought. The sense of dialogue with the reader, of shared discovery, which a historian of women's writing in English is able to project, was likely to be replaced by a monologue with all the galvanizing potential of a lecture droned out at five o'clock on a Friday afternoon. The compilation of an anthology that might at once amplify the *History*, and lead its own autonomous existence as a sampler of Russian women's writing, indicating the vivacity and diversity of that writing's historical traditions, seemed not only desirable, but essential.

The present selection is by no means the first anthology of Russian women's writing that has been put together, whether in Russia or the West. Though 'women's writing', for reasons that I have discussed at length in the *History*, is a term that has little currency in Russian culture, recent years have seen the publication, in Russia itself, of several important collections of fiction and poetry by women writers. Such editions as *The New Amazons* (1991) and *She Who Recalls No Evil* (1989), as well as the ineptly entitled *A Very Pure Life* (1987), and *Feminine Logic* (1989), have made available a representative and at times impressive selection of recent fiction. A proportion of women's fiction before 1917 has also been republished, notably in V. V. Uchenova's useful three-volume edition, *The House on the Peterhof Road, The Assignation*, and *Only an Hour* (1986–9). A certain amount of material has also made its way into English. Several recent anthologies, such as Helena Goscilo's *Balancing Acts* (1989), and the American–Soviet collection *Soviet Women Writing* (1990), have assembled an eclectic and exciting array of women's writing from the past twenty years; occasional scattered publications, such as Temira Pachmuss's *Women Writers in Russian Modernism*, have given a tantalizing sampling of lesser-known writers of the past.[1] There are also numerous translations in existence (some of high quality) which have allowed Western readers to become familiar with work by individual Russian women writers. Amongst the important texts available in Western libraries and bookshops are Karolina Pavlova's important lyric novella *A Double Life*, some fiction by Zinaida Gippius and Lidiya Zinoveva-Annibal, and a number of important memoirs, including those of Nadezhda Durova, Nadezhda Mandelstam, Lidiya Ginzburg, Evgeniya Ginzburg, and Lidiya Chukovskaya.[2]

But such forays into the field, important as they have been, have still necessarily left huge areas almost untouched. When I came, in the *History*, to analyse the provincial tale (a kind of incentive myth showing an exceptional woman escaping from the constraints of the upbringing considered suitable for young ladies of the Russian gentry), I immediately realized that not even one such tale had been translated into English; yet this genre had dominated women's prose fiction for more than forty years, between the late 1830s and the early 1880s. Indeed, the whole of pre-Revolutionary women's fiction was almost uncharted territory in English; for their part, the selections of such fiction available in Russian had an emphasis on women's involvement with political radicalism that made their picture of women's writing reductive, if not falsificatory. Other gaps soon made themselves felt. Though the 1940s fiction of one important Parisian émigrée, Nina Berberova, was well represented in English, the years between

[1] *Novye amazonki* (Moscow, 1991); *Ne pomnyashchaya zla* (Moscow, 1989); *Chisten'kaya zhizn'* (Moscow, 1987), *Zhenskaya logika* (Moscow, 1989); V. V. Uchenova (ed.), *Dacha na Petergofskoi doroge* (Moscow, 1986), *Svidanie* (Moscow, 1987), *Tol'ko chas* (Moscow, 1989); Helena Goscilo (ed.), *Balancing Acts: Recent Writing by Soviet Women* (Bloomington, Ind., 1989); *Soviet Women Writing* (London, 1990); Temira Pachmuss (ed.), *Women Writers in Russian Modernism* (Urbana, Ill., 1978); Marina Ledkovsky (ed.), *Rossiya glazami zhenshchin* (Tenafly, 1989; in English, 1991). Adele Barker *et al.* (eds.), *Dialogues/Dialogi: Literary Cultural Exchanges between [ex] Soviet and American Women* (Durham, NC, 1993), and Elaine Feinstein and Cathy Porter (eds.), *Russian Women's Writing* (London, 1993), appeared whilst this anthology was in press. On translations, see also Diane Nemec Ignashev and Sarah Krive, *Women and Writing in Russia and the USSR: A Bibliography of English-Language Sources* (New York, 1992).

[2] Karolina Pavlova, *A Double Life*, trans. Barbara Heldt, 2nd edn. (Oakland, Calif., 1986); Zinaida Gippius, *Selected Works*, trans. Temira Pachmuss (Urbana, Ill., 1972); Lidiya Zinov'eva-Annibal, *Thirty-Three Abominations*, trans. Sam Cioran, *Russian Literature Triquarterly*, 9 (1974); Nadezhda Durova, *The Cavalry Maid*, trans. Mary Zirin (London, 1990); Nadezhda Mandelstam, *Hope against Hope*, trans. Max Hayward (London, 1971); *Hope Abandoned*, trans. Max Hayward (London, 1974); Evgeniya Ginzburg, *Into the Whirlwind*, trans. Paul Stevenson and Manya Harari (London, 1967); *Within the Whirlwind*, trans. Ian Boland (London, 1981); Lidiya Ginzburg, *The Writer at his Desk* (London, 1993); Lidiya Chukovskaya, *Conversations with Anna Akhmatova* (London, 1993).

1917 and 1970 were otherwise poorly represented in English translation; no Russian anthologies whatever had been dedicated to this period, and even reprints of individual authors were few and far between.[3]

A much richer selection of poetry was available, both in Russian and English, no doubt because the only two Russian woman writers ever to have achieved international reputations (with the exception of the theosophist Madame Blavatsky), Marina Tsvetaeva and Anna Akhmatova, are poets, a circumstance that has raised the profile of women's poetry in general. But even here, there were remarkable absences. The nineteenth-century poetic tradition was almost entirely unfamiliar to Western audiences; Russian selections, such as the indicatively entitled *A Hundred Pearls* and *Tsaritsas of the Muses*, had an unfortunate tendency to emphasize sugary love poetry, eschewing work that manifested a fierce and challenging subjectivity. Though Russian and Western selections dealing with the twentieth century had a greater catholicity, as was most especially evident in the case of a recent collection, *A Hundred Russian Poetesses*, the importance of, for example, religious and prophetic poetry had been insufficiently recognized; this was one reason why the poetry written by women of the Russian emigration between 1920 and 1950 had been almost entirely overlooked. And, though some individual poets, such as Natalya Gorbanevskaya and Irina Ratushinskaya, besides of course Akhmatova and Tsvetaeva, have been relatively well served by translators, others, such as Vera Merkureva, Anna Prismanova, Adelaida Gertsyk, and even Karolina Pavlova, are still very little known to Western readers.[4]

My work for the anthology began, then, with the recovery of historical material. Many of the texts here come from books, journals, or almanacs that are now scarce; they have been collected in the course of quite a lengthy period of first-hand research in Russia and in the West. But, though I could not have put the book together without research, indulgence of the recondite for its own sake was never my intention. The texts collected here are not presented as colourful items from an antiquarian cabinet of curiosities, but as material that illustrates the development of Russian women's writing, that communicates both the diversity of writing by women, and

[3] Nina Berberova's translated works include *The Accompanist*, trans. Marian Schwartz (London, 1990), and *The Tattered Coat*, trans. Marian Schwartz (New York, 1992).

[4] *Sto zhemchuzhin: Lirika russkikh zhenshchin XX veka* (Omsk, 1979); *Tsaritsy muz: Russkie poetessy XIX–nach. XX veka* (Moscow, 1989); *Sto russkikh poetess* (Moscow, 1993). On translations of Gorbanevskaya, Ratushinskaya, Akhmatova, and Tsvetaeva see Ignashev and Krive, *Women and Writing*.

that writing's special character, its recurring preoccupations, its pet themes, and its preferred linguistic strategies.

Read from the beginning, the anthology provides a brief history of Russian women's writing, both in its discontinuities and in its continuities.[5] We see the public, declaratory tone of neo-classicism, the earliest genre which fostered women's poetry, replaced, around 1840, by the intense poetry of self-contemplation that Romanticism had made available to men twenty years earlier. In prose, the earliest important pieces of Russian fiction, the 'society tales', witty and many-layered studies of metropolitan aristocratic life, have their authority challenged, around 1840, and ended, around 1860, by the single-minded polemicism of the 'provincial tales', which depict women campaigning for the right to education and employment. From the mid-1880s, the 'provincial tale' begins in its turn to be effaced by a new kind of feminist realism, whose political engagement is equally evident, but whose ideology is now more sophisticated, and whose range of artistic practices is broader, than those of the 'provincial tale' had been. After 1895, however, the social commitment of feminist realism begins to come under attack. Its first adversary is a 'decadent' libertarian individualism borrowed from France, which places a new emphasis on feminine sexuality, and on service to self rather than to community. From about 1905, a second, and more powerful, adversary is also evident. The mystical Symbolists introduce the notion that poetry is a vision of other worlds, a form of prophecy, and at the same time emphasize women's 'otherness', which among other things means their capacity to communicate with other worlds. This ideological coincidence leads to a new emphasis on feminine prophecy and on female prophets—an emphasis which is adjusted, but never repudiated, by the ironical and paradoxical productions of post-Symbolism, and which in some senses retains its potency right up to the present day.

The Bolshevik Revolution ushers in a new era of realist prose, in which incentive myths again become dominant: women prose writers now show women acquiring an education (especially a political education), doing responsible jobs, and taking an active part in politics. From 1935, Soviet policy on the family begins to become more conservative, and ideology calls for the appearance of a 'Soviet superwoman', able to combine a full public life, as worker and political activist, with the role of a radiant wife and

[5] The historical account that follows is a distillation of the argument that will be found in expanded form in the survey sections of Kelly, *A History of Women's Writing 1820–1992* (Oxford, 1994).

mother. If early Soviet literature saw women's bodies, attitudes, and behaviour as the battlefield of social change, high Socialist Realism presents women's lives as a metaphor for the vast changes already wrought by Soviet society. From outside official Soviet culture, individual feminine voices, many of which are self-analytical, independent, and idiosyncratic, rise to challenge these bland over-simplifications. At the same time, much unofficial women's writing asserts the woman in her collective and supraindividualistic role, as mother of the nation, just as insistently as the official writing that it challenges.

The years after Stalin's death have seen a reversion, in some senses, to the pre-Revolutionary tradition disrupted by the 1917 Revolution, with a resurrection of 'realist' and 'anti-realist' modes that resemble those that were predominant around 1900. As at the beginning of the present century, heroines have now become less monolithically virtuous: there is an urgent, anxious exploration of extreme psychological states. An intense preoccupation with women fallen from grace has replaced Socialist Realism's celebration of women who conform; in stylistic terms, a narrative manner that is at once lapidary and oblique has replaced the facile loquaciousness of Socialist Realism. Of course, the particular intensity with which women's falling from grace is often described can be seen as a bizarre perpetuation of the past, in the sense that women are never just what they seem: the demented alcoholic of the present is as loaded a symbol of national identity as the serene Madonna of the past. The late 1980s have, however, witnessed the emergence of texts which question women's status as national symbols: one example is Bella Ulanovskaya's story 'Journey to Kashgar', the tale of a war heroine that at once parodies the mythic manner of Socialist Realism and explodes the Socialist Realist myth of an ordered universe by means of an emphasis on chance and on human frailty.

Such are the discontinuities of Russian women's writing; what are its continuities? A pronounced interest in women's autonomy is one, even if sympathy for institutionalized feminism is most certainly not. Karolina Pavlova's story 'At the Tea-Table' shows us a woman whose social origins are far too grand for her to require the programme for women's liberation that Sofya Soboleva's tale 'Pros and Cons' (also included here) sketches out. But Pavlova's sceptical treatment of the notion that women are always victims of educational and economic discrimination—a notion that was canonical for the women's liberation programmes of the day—does not mean that she is any less concerned than Soboleva with the issue of women's intellectual and emotional independence in the absolute. Similarly,

Tsvetaeva's great narrative poem *Staircase*, for all the obvious ideological and technical differences, can be seen as a refraction, at a subtextual level, of the same questions about women's domestic enslavement that preoccupy the mainstream feminist writer Olga Shapir.

If a preoccupation with issues of autonomy, in however abstract a sense, is one force that binds Russian women, another is their tendency to realize this preoccupation by means of the representation of a heroine who is both outstandingly gifted and a social misfit. This tendency links writers as different, in terms of immediate social context, as Anna Bunina and Anastasiya Mirovich, or Elizaveta Shakhova and Marina Tsvetaeva, Zinaida Gippius and Ekaterina Strogova. United by their insistence on *some* women's right to decide their fates for themselves (an all-embracing gender solidarity is rarely advocated), Russian women writers are also united by the quizzical, critical, and often despairing eye which they turn on the behaviour of men. *Aficionados* of the persistent and irritating psychological categories beloved of Russian literary history (for which the term 'pedestrian' often suggests too dynamic a process of intellectual formulation) will find few 'superfluous men' here; rather than fatuously benevolent or shiftless, the heroes of these stories are selfish, self-interested, or at the very least self-deceiving.

All these factors give Russian women's writing a character that is markedly different from Anglophone women's writing (its resemblance to French women's writing is closer, but the distance is still a wide one). It might not be too outrageous a simplification to say that what distinguished pre-Revolutionary Russian women's writing from its Anglo-American equivalent was the huge interest that the issue of women's liberation aroused in all educated people in Russia (whichever way writers chose to react to that issue, they could not ignore it). Conversely, what has distinguished Russian and Anglophone women's writing *since* the Revolution—or at any rate since the 1930s—has been the huge *un*interest that the issue of women's liberation has aroused in all educated Russians. If the status of the women's liberation movement—prominent or invisible—often forms the abstract background to texts, rather than being directly appreciable in them, the distinction of tone between the Russian and Anglophone traditions can be sensed immediately. Russian women's writing (particularly prose writing) is more schematic, more inclined to generalization, often of a didactic kind, more insistent and more energetic than its English-language equivalent—at any rate in some of that English-language equivalent's manifestations. In Russia, the Charlotte Brontës, Emily Edens, and Maria Edgeworths greatly outnumber the Elizabeth Gaskells, Willa Cathers, or Edith Whartons. If the

Anglophone tradition, in the hands of its lesser practitioners, can on occasion seem smugly reasonable, or parochial, or cluttered with detail, then the Russian tradition has, at its worst, been marked by a tediously homiletic iteration of generally accepted beliefs in a spirit that suggests the writer supposed these to be daringly iconoclastic. These faults have, however, been most evident in large-scale works (there are almost no good novels by Russian women). The miniature to medium-length pieces here have taken some finding, given that Russian women (like their male contemporaries) have generally inclined to verbosity; but many of them show the Russian tradition at its best, radiating a sense that explosive material is tightly packed into small and friable vessels.

Apart from illustrating general affinities of perspective and tone, the anthology also throws up instances of incidental correspondences and overlaps. So, for example, we see both Elizaveta Kuzmina-Karavaeva and Anna Barkova write of themselves as barbarian princesses, though each orchestrates the motif in a quite different way; Evdokiya Rostopchina and Zinaida Gippius evoke sewing as an activity that gives free rein to fancy, and the same motif is treated quite differently by Olga Shapir. Readers will no doubt find many other instances of such affinities; I have mentioned only the most obvious and striking examples here.

If the first factor in my choice of texts was a consideration of how best to illustrate general historical principles, and to convey the essential flavour of Russian women's writing, a host of subsidiary, but equally important, factors also played a role in selecting material. I made a decision, on principle, against including numerous short extracts of long texts, preferring instead, whenever possible, to use texts in the form in which they had been published by their authors. This was because of my conviction that extracts give readers very little sense of how unfamiliar writers handle narrative. Nineteenth-century Russian women prose writers, like their British and American contemporaries, wrote at a more leisurely pace than their twentieth-century successors; I do not see how one can get any feeling of this pace unless one has a *whole* narrative by, say, Soboleva, to set alongside a short story by, say, Teffi or Petrushevskaya. As an exception to my rule, I have, however, included excerpts from three episodic texts that are not too much marred by being represented partially. The two central chapters from a memoir by Valentina Dmitrieva represent the late nineteenth-century memoir of female professional life, a very important genre that has been totally forgotten, but of which there exists no example short enough to be reproduced in its entirety. An extract from a Socialist Realist novel by Anna

Karavaeva stands for an enormously important direction in fiction that I would not have wanted to inflict on my readers in unabbreviated form. Finally, I could not resist including a section of Tatyana Esenina's delightful, and little known, short novel *Zhenya: The Wonder of the Twentieth Century*, a 1962 satire on Soviet life and on Socialist Realist art whose humour has not palled in the thirty years since it was written.

In order to stop the book from bursting at the seams, I have had to limit my selection of 'women's writing' to literary texts in the strictest sense: fiction, poetry, and drama, with the memoir making a token gesture of generic defiance. It would have been illuminating, but impracticable, to include, say, film scripts, domestic manuals, writing for children, letters, petitions, and journalistic essays, since such genres have attracted large numbers of women—at some historical periods, indeed, the majority of women.[6] Less exceptionably, perhaps, I have also excluded orally transmitted texts, such as the formal lament, which, in Russia as in Greece or Ireland, was very much a women's genre. Works by Russian women writers whose original language of composition was not Russian have also been left out. I regret these omissions, but I hope that later ventures may correct them.

Considerations of space have also meant that my selections have been guided by the availability of material in English. I have generally left out authors of secondary importance whose work is already well represented in translation (for example, Elena Guro, Elena Gan, Mariya Zhukova, Aleksandra Kollontai, or Mirra Lokhvitskaya).[7] My eye to what is already accessible has also meant that I have not, unlike most anthologists, funnelled out as I reach the modern period. In the case of Russian women's writing, the last three decades are already far better represented than any other era, and so I have preferred a corrective bias towards the past. But availability of material in English cannot be pressed too far as an argument for exclusion. Tsvetaeva, Akhmatova, and Gippius have, as I pointed out, already been translated. But these writers are so important that an anthology without them would be ridiculous; besides, the work of these, more familiar, figures appears to quite novel effect when set against the new and unfamiliar

[6] All reliable accounts suggest that pre-Petrine women's writing consisted entirely of letters, petitions, and suchlike; Russian aristocratic women may also have kept receipt books, as their Western counterparts did. In the Stalin years, film scripts, journalism, and writing for children, as well as translation, acquired an enormous importance for women who wished to publish their work.

[7] On translations of Guro, Gan, Lokhvitskaya, and Kollontai see Ignashev and Krive, *Women and Writing*; an extensive sampling of work by Elena Gan and Mariya Zhukova is to appear in Joe Andrew's anthology, *Russian Women's Fiction 1838–1855* (Oxford, forthcoming).

background of work by their lesser-known women contemporaries, predecessors, or successors. When dealing with well-known authors, though, I have been careful to select texts that are not customarily anthologized. This has dictated a preference for long poems over short poems, and for 'difficult' or unfamiliar material over the straightforward and obvious. Help with thematic, cultural, and linguistic problems is given in the annotations at the end of the book, the copiousness, or otherwise, of which depends on the level of such problems in the primary text. (For example, Tsvetaeva's *Staircase*, an obliquely narrated and linguistically demanding piece of work, is very heavily annotated, whilst Rostopchina's straightforward and accessible lyric 'The Unfinished Sewing' is hardly annotated at all.)

Every anthologist has at some point to negotiate the explosive area of personal choice. Most people would no doubt agree with Oscar Wilde's assertion that only an auctioneer can afford to like all kinds of art; the question of how much of an auctioneer the anthologist can afford to be is more contentious. The drive to be representative and the drive to be selective are at odds with each other (or are perceived so to be). I am certainly aware that these drives have on occasion conflicted in me. In order to be fully representative, I would have needed to include much more love poetry. However, love poetry, the genre with which Russian women have most often been associated, has also inspired in them poetry which I myself often find as short of original emotional currency as it is abundantly endowed with the false money of effusive cliché. The works that *are* of high quality (Tsvetaeva's *Poem of the End*, for example) have generally been translated and assimilated already. With the exception of love poetry, which I recognize *is* proportionally under-represented, the principle of representation according to a genre's relative importance has guided me. My selectivity has been exercised at another level: that of which text, or which texts, to choose as examples of a given genre. I have in general included only pieces that I personally found moving, convincing, or in some way remarkable or interesting. I can't pretend I feel the same degree of enthusiasm about every piece that I have put in. I would certainly not go to the stake in defence of the literary quality of, say, Karavaeva's five-year-plan novel *The Flying Start*. However, I would be prepared to argue that the luminous and piquant badness of her writing makes it in some senses more tolerable than competent mediocrity. And if this piece is included because it is strikingly bad, other pieces are included because they are striking in some other way: for their originality, their boldness, the power with which they transcend the predictable.

Two illustrations of what I mean will suffice here—I prefer to allow the selected pieces to speak for themselves. Amongst provincial tales, superficially a rebarbative tribe, I have chosen Sofya Soboleva's 'Pros and Cons'. Soboleva's story has the transparent didacticism that was characteristic of the provincial tale, schematically contrasting a virtuous and a self-serving heroine. But by making her self-serving heroine an embodiment of radical feminist chic, Soboleva achieves a crucial shift of emphasis (in most other provincial tales the virtuous heroine is a feminist). Shorter and livelier than most other provincial tales, the story is also—exceptionally for a provincial tale—a first-person narrative. Furthermore, the observations of Soboleva's narrator, Madame Lisitsyna, on contemporary Russian society are so sarcastically witty, and in some cases so studiedly partial, that the story reads more like a monologue than a sermon; certainly, it is a portrait as well as a polemic. To move on to another, and later, instance: amongst early twentieth-century fables of feminine identity, I have selected Anastasiya Mirovich's 'Lizards' and 'Elsa'. These two tiny stories raise an important, and in terms of the day original, point: that women's prophecy is all too easily effaced by men, and women's rebellion all too easily curtailed by men, if men have licensed these in the first place. Given that Mirovich's stories are only two amongst many philosophically interesting representations of women that appeared in the early twentieth century, however, I have chosen them for their imaginative strangeness, and for their compressed, suggestive style. Where other writers of the day are dry and diagrammatic, Mirovich manages to be both haunting and teasingly ironic.

The arrangement of texts, like the selection of them, is a compromise between historical and aesthetic considerations. The first piece in the book is also the earliest, the last the latest, and in between the order is roughly chronological: blocks of work by a single author have been kept together, each preceded by a brief biographical note; authors have generally been placed in an order that depends on the earliest date of the works by them that are included. But, rather than simply progressing, in the traditional anthologistic manner, from Anon. forward, in a sequence dictated solely by date, I have chosen to begin, in the correct classical manner, with an invocation to the Muses. I end with a poem, Olga Sedakova's 'Fifth Stanzas', which is at once sonorous and hesitantly analytical; it indicates the high achievements of recent writing, but also projects the sense that the breakdown of the old certainties has brought women's writing, like so much else in Russian culture, to a turning-point, and so brings the anthology to an appropriate culmination. Between the beginning and end, I have tried to keep a certain sense of variety in the alternation of material (prose follows poetry, avant-garde material stands next to more traditional pieces, provincial tale is placed where it may best contrast with society tale, and so on), which I hope will mean that the book can with profit be read straight through as well as dipped into.

A final aspect of the anthology which probably requires brief comment here is the principles behind the translation. The versions here are intended to be *equivalents* of the original, rather than cribs to the original. In other words, these are not absolutely literal translations, as anyone comparing the English versions of the poems with the Russian originals (which are given in the Appendix) will readily appreciate. Such a statement of position will not raise any eyebrows in itself, since any working translator—Nabokov in his most self-parodistically bigoted moods always excepted—is likely to accept the need to mediate between 'translation' in the sense of imitating a text from a different culture (and so stressing its exoticism), and 'translation' in the sense of interpreting it (which also means integrating it into the receiving culture). Disagreements, however, can and do arise at the level of which texts, and more minutely which precise words or phrases, should be reproduced in what way. Not everyone is going to agree with my assertion that, if a text's lexical and syntactical difficulties mean that it is hard work to read in Russian, a readily understandable and lucid English translation cannot be accounted its equivalent. To give a concrete illustration: Anna Prismanova's poem on Lomonosov is one of the very rare texts by a Russian woman in which intelligibility is almost subordinated to sound: if the English doesn't attempt to capture that aspect of the poem, it will give no sense of the text's interest or value, and won't even lend much help to the reader who is trying to pick his or her way through with a dictionary (since what something means is an elementary question compared to the problem of why it should have that meaning). If the obscure should not be made crystalline, the clumsy and irregular should not be made into bland perfection either. It would, for example, be misleading to translate Olga Shapir as though she were Chekhov, when part of the interest of her work lies in the fact that she, like many other Russian women writers, does not so much consciously manipulate the distinction between objective and subjective observation, between the authorial perspective and that of the characters, as blur these distinctions; the uneasiness that is projected by this blurring reflects an important conceptual uncertainty about the mechanics of identification, and the appropriate representation of identity. Is it better to adopt an involved, but critical, standpoint, or a standpoint that is tolerant but detached? Russian women writers have never settled this question, and that has given a peculiar flavour to their depictions of their characters' interior worlds.

I have, then, adhered to the principle that the right of texts not to say directly what they mean should be respected. Besides this consideration, decisions in the translations have been made on the basis of the conviction that an anthology needs to give readers a sense of the differences between authors, rather than smoothing these out in elegant and monotonous paraphrase. For that reason, I have allowed the pieces translated by American translators to retain a specifically American flavour, where this suits the nature of the original—as in the fiction of Lyudmila Petrushevskaya, for example, which has greater affinities with the work of certain modern American realists, such as Raymond Carver or Richard Ford, than with the work of any British writer that I can think of. In the poetry translations, this respect for differentiation has made me come down firmly on the side of retaining some form of metrical organization. The shock effect of Tsvetaeva's syncopated accentual metres can only be grasped if the metrical regularity and syntactical balance of the quatrains used by Gippius, Akhmatova, Kuzmina-Karavaeva, or Prismanova is represented by the English versions, in however remote a way. Without rhyme, too, the appealing naïvety of Ekaterina Urusova, or the wit of Anna Bunina, are lost.

Some measure of flexibility is, of course, also required. Exact reproduction of Pavlova's complex metre in 'Life calls us', would have imposed impossible constraints on meaning; assonance must anachronistically stand for full rhyme in the English, and the poem's nineteenth-century resonance be left to depend on the affinity of its lexicon and register with that of, say, Byron's *Childe Harold*. Indeed, full rhymes in Russian have nearly always had to become approximate rhymes, not only because the English reservoir of full rhymes runs relatively low, but also because current poetic taste is proscriptive about dipping into it. The standard metre of Russian poetry, the four-foot iamb, has often to be replaced by the standard metre of English poetry, the five-foot iamb; non-standard metres have been replaced by appropriate, rather than identical, non-standard metres. All this is simple enough; the real difficulties come with differences in English and Russian linguistic expectation. The pleonasm and repetition in which Russian writing, especially Russian poetry, rejoices, is lost on Anglophone readers, whose imprinted cultural associations do not embrace the mantric repetitions of Orthodox Christian liturgy. The rigid syntactical parallelism that twentieth-century

Russian poetry has borrowed from folk-song ('as runs the hare, as flies the bird, so sings the poet') cannot always be exactly reproduced, since the parallelism of English is more loosely structured, and more diffuse; and the tight grammatical ordering of Russian can tie together strings of subordinate clauses which the looser associations of English would send into incoherent fragmentation. The policy has been to allow oddities in English only where the Russian also sounds odd.

Such were the promptings behind the translations; the results, I leave readers to judge for themselves. It may be helpful to point out, though, that all significant deviations from the strictly literal are glossed in notes at the end of the book, for the convenience of those who are using the English to work through a poem in Russian.

Let me add a few final words as envoy. It has recently become rather fashionable to decry the composition of anthologies whose purview is defined by sociological criteria (gender, ethnic origin, sexuality). In genuinely egalitarian conditions, dedicated anthologies would without question be redundant: like the state upon the institution of true communism, anthologies of 'gay writing' or 'women's writing' would, upon the appearance of equality, simply wither away. In present circumstances, however, there is a striking under-representation of women or other so-called minority groups in anthologies and selections which purport to be general and inclusive; therefore, dedicated anthologies have as unassailable a logic as dedicated studies. So far as I am aware, none of the texts that I have included has ever been placed in a general anthology of Russian literature. If any of them find their way there in due course, I shall be delighted. But for the present I am equally delighted that they should take their place in a selection that, in my view, amply indicates just how much has been lost by other, supposedly more general and objective, anthologies when they excluded women writers, or included only token women. My readers need not expect to find a Tolstoy or Dostoevsky amongst the prose writers here, or a Pushkin amongst the nineteenth-century poets; they will, however, be able to make the acquaintance of a whole range of voices, many of them previously muffled or stifled, whose power, energy, and originality allow them to transcend both the spaces of lost time and the gulfs of cultural difference.

C. K.

ACKNOWLEDGEMENTS

LIKE my *History of Russian Women's Writing 1777–1992*, this anthology was funded by the British Academy through a Post-Doctoral Fellowship and grants for travel to Russia and Finland, and by Christ Church, Oxford, who provided a room and research facilities; the Taylor Institution, Oxford, made a grant through its Rochester Fund to help with permission expenses. I am very grateful to these institutions for their support. For allowing me to use work by them in copyright, I should like to thank Olga Sedakova, Elena Shvarts, Elena Chizhova, Nina Sadur, Lyudmila Petrushevskaya, and Bella Ulanovskaya. I am also grateful to Leuxenhoff Publishers of The Hague for permission to reproduce the three texts by Anna Prismanova which appear here; to Ardis Publishers of Ann Arbor, Mich., who kindly allowed me to use work by Sofiya Parnok; to M. L. Gasparov, for a poem by Vera Merkureva; to S. S. Vilensky and Virago Press, for work by Anna Barkova and Mira Linkevich. The vast majority of the translations have not previously been published, but in three cases where work has appeared before, in slightly different form, I have acknowledgements to make: to Rodopi Press, Amsterdam, for Vera Bulich's 'From my Diary', and Vera Merkureva's 'Grandmother of Russian Poetry' from Joe Andrew (ed.), *Poetics of the Text* (Amsterdam, 1992); to Natalia Perova of *Glas* magazine, in the case of Olga Sedakova's 'Fifth Stanzas'; and to Bloodaxe for Elena Shvart's 'Sale of a Historian's Library'.

Amongst individuals, I should particularly mention Charlotte Rosenthal and Mary Zirin, who were most helpful in suggesting texts for inclusion in this book. The efficiency and helpfulness of all my translators made the work of putting together this volume a positive pleasure; I should additionally like to thank Marian Schwartz and Diana Greene, both of whom supplied material for the notes. Those who gave aid on the more recondite sections of the commentary included Kseniya Kumpan, who gave me invaluable help in the search for biographical details relating to several of the lesser-known women writers included here; Mary MacRobert and Andrew Spira, who gave information on saints' lives and on icons; Frank Göpfert, for material on Pavlova; and Nigel Thompson and Helen Frink, who helped with translations from languages other than Russian. Adele Barker, Birgit Beumers, Adrian Boehler, John Crowfoot, Natalia Perova, and Riitta Pittman have all helped with permissions and other practicalities, whilst Glenys McGregor dealt cheerfully with an endless two-way stream of faxes, and Veronica Ions was a most able copy-editor. Finally, I am more grateful than I can say to the colleagues, relatives, and friends who have read the translations and commentary and made suggestions for changes and improvements: Mikhail Leonovich Gasparov, Barbara Heldt, Alexander and Margaret Kelly, Jim Naughton, Wendy Rosslyn, Biljana Scott, Gerry Smith, Bill

Swainson, Nigel Thompson, Neill Walker; and above all Ian Thompson, who put up with this book over the whole elephantine era of its gestation, and also, still more tryingly, with its author.

I have decided to dedicate this anthology to the memory of the two people from whom I learnt most about how to translate: Anne Pennington and Halina Willetts.

C. K.

A NOTE ON TRANSLITERATION AND OTHER CONVENTIONS

THE transliteration used is a modified form of British Standard, as follows:

а	a	и	i	р	r	ш	sh
б	b	й	i[2]	с	s	щ	shch
в	v	к	k	т	t	ь	(omitted)
г	g	л	l	у	u	ы	y
д	d	м	m	ф	f	ь	(omitted[3])
е	e[1]	н	n	х	kh	э	e
ж	zh	о	o	ц	ts	ю	yu
з	z	п	p	ч	ch	я	ya

1 As an aid to pronunciation, stressed *ё* appears as *yo*.

2 The surname suffix *-ский* appears throughout as *-sky*.

3 As an aid to reference (in dictionaries, library catalogues, encyclopedias, etc.), this letter is specified in the Notes: e.g. 'Vera Merkureva (i.e. Merkur'eva)'.

The dates of texts are given in the following forms:
(*1922*) indicates a date as specified by an author;
[1922] indicates a date of first publication;
[*c.*1922] indicates an approximate date of composition, where the date of publication is self-evidently unrelated to the date of composition (as in the case of posthumous publications, etc.).

The symbol ° in a prose text or drama indicates that an explanation will be found in the Notes. Notes to the poetry, however, are keyed to line number, rather than marked in the text.

Where not otherwise credited, all translations are by Catriona Kelly.

◆ EKATERINA URUSOVA ◆

Urusova (1747–after 1816) was descended from an aristocratic family with literary connections, her second cousin being the neo-classical poet Mikhail Kheraskov. She appears to have been well educated; many of her poems are based on classical topics, and her work includes an epic, *Pollion*, as well as lyric poetry. Besides publishing individual volumes, most of which appeared anonymously, Urusova also placed many pieces in magazines. Her date of death is unknown; her last published piece is a poem dated 1816 welcoming her 'seventieth year', which was published in *Syn otechestva* during 1817.[1]

[Invocation, from *Heroides: Dedicated to the Muses*]

(Russian text p. 397)

O Muses! I beseech you, fire my heart with song
And hear one who, like you, to the fair sex belongs.
In ancient times my native place, the Russian land
Was filled with ignorance, and lay in darkness' hand.
Your dwelling place all unsuspected lay,
And thorny bushes choked the Parnassian way.
The Parnassian flame had not yet fired our hearts,
Unkindled was our genius' spark.
Then a great dawn lit Russia's endless night,
The beauty of the Lyre then came in sight.
And ignorance 'gan withering mightily,
Stupidity flew from Russia speedily,
All made obeisance at Learning's throne,
Your voice, your pleasant voice enraptured every one.
Soon all the Russian land burst into bloom,

[1] The biographical notes on authors are intended to give the briefest background information only; broader guidance may generally be found in Marina Ledkovsky, Charlotte Rosenthal, and Mary Zirin's *Bio-Bibliographical Guide to Russian Women Writers* (2 vols.; Westport, Conn., 1993). I have supplied patronymics and exact dates of birth only in the case of authors who are not listed in the *Guide*, or in other standard works of reference, such as Wolfgang Kasack's *Lexicon of Russian Literature*.

Racines and Pindars issued from her womb,
Singing in praise of CATARINA's day,
Giving her wise deeds immortality.
Upon the Russian land the planets fix their gaze:
Sing, then, ye beauteous muses, sing in praise!
Surely our times a golden age will prove,
Castalian waters flow to us from above!
Now, clustering about the sacred Muses' throne
The female sex begins to lift its song:
These ladies deck the virtues in their verse,
An overflowing tenderness rehearse:
Sweetly they sing of pleasurable things
And in those songs passion and feeling ring.
Russia has Sapphos now, and De La Suzes,
I would with them: O hear me, beauteous Muses!
To cheer me and lend beauty to my song
Scatter Parnassian flowers my way along!
You've bathed the Lyre in the healing waters' flow,
Hand it to me so I may play it now.
And I shall strive to tune my thoughts to yours,
Shall strive to lift my song unto your ears.
From the high hills turn now your eyes to me,
Strengthen my timid voice so far you may.
Listen with condescension as it sings:
Muses! it is for you I tune these strings.

[*1777*]

◆ ANNA BUNINA ◆

The facts of Bunina's early childhood were much as she states them in 'Though poverty's no stain'. She was born in 1774 on her father's estate in Ryazan province, but was packed off to live with various relatives after her mother's death; on reaching adulthood, she went to live in St Petersburg, where she moved in literary circles, attracting the sponsorship of Aleksandr Shishkov, the leader of the traditionalist 'Archaist' movement. Besides poetry, Bunina's works included short stories and a manual of versification for young women. In the 1820s, she became ill with breast cancer, which was eventually to kill her in 1829; this illness was to be the subject of her moving poem 'The Sick Woman's May Outing'. Bunina was perhaps the first genuine woman poet in Russian literature, but her reputation has suffered unfairly from the sneers of the 1820s Romantics, particularly Pushkin, who (partly because of their hostility to Shishkov, and partly for misogynist reasons) cited Bunina's work as a crying example of the worthlessness of poetry before Romanticism.

(Russian text p. 399)

Though poverty's no stain
On those who have a brain,
Still, everyone sees shame therein,
Concealing it as if it were a sin.
Drop in on one man's luncheon to enquire:
He's dining by the fire,
Some turnips in his bowl:
A little dish of cress,
Some water in a glass.
When you ask why, he'll say, 'Old chap, to save my soul!
It's Wednesday, I must fast!'
One blames the cooks for all
The dry food he must eat;
A second says, 'After a little I'm replete!'
A third man says, 'I cannot stomach meat!
'My doctor has prescribed a special diet.'

Not one will say, 'There's not a copeck in the house!'
They all try somehow to deny it.

Each one of us, no doubt,
Knows all about
The source of this odd habit.
So it will be, has always been:
The moneybag's a thing we all conceal.

And so I beg you not to leap to anger!
If someone who has naught to make a meal
Feels shame still stronger
Than all his pangs of hunger,
Then how may I, by feigning penury,
Do rightful honour to my parents' memory?
They knew nothing of such disasters,
But lived the life of wealthy masters!
Houses with wings stood on the entailed estate;
The demesne was ringed by walls of stone;
One corner held our bait—
Swings, the children's own—
The other held all sorts of little towers,
And toadstools built of wood,
And other decorations no less good;
Lemon and peach trees, tulips, lily flowers
In flowerbeds or in pots,
Blooming or bearing fruits,
At my papa's were common as the weeds!
Pine nuts and almonds too,
Everything was our own! We never even needed
To send away for prunes
In winter time!
It all grew round about, despite the hostile clime.
(The Province of Ryazan, Ryazhsk city was nearby.)
Pears, apples . . . thick as stars up in the sky!
And juicy all, as if in sugar steeped;
And even sweetmeats of our own;
For there were bees, you know—
Two or three swarms arrived upon one day alone!

The servants ran to catch them in their coats!
Darlings! I look at these sweet bees,
And the bees of long ago fly back to me!
A beauty flies! as if made all of gold!
With honey in her two back legs she wings;
First from the linden, then the rose she drinks,
Honey is in her mouth—her front leg up she brings,
And hands it to her back to hold.
Sometimes I see a crowd of the dear things,
And every last one sings!
And, lending an ear beside the branches,
I'd learn to buzz from them,
And then, in imitation,
Cluck like a broody hen!
I'd think, 'I've copied them just right!' and smile.
I was a child!
But still, that childish game has been of use to me:
For even in my later years, from bees
I've learned to sweeten labour with a song,
To work and sing along,
To sing until my grief is gone.
Once, I recall, I went to pick a leaf
That had a little bee hid underneath:
She stung my finger, just like that!
I started wailing like a little fool...
Nurse dabbed some mud on, nice and cool,
And offered me a piece of gingerbread.
An infant's wit is not too great, be sure:
For grief, for illness—gingerbread's the universal cure!
And to this day my wits are not much grown:
It's hardly decent, all the yarns I've spun,
Straying ever farther off the track!
It's my ill luck. Forgive me, please,
For this untimely flight of little bees!
Now I shall lead you back
To the first subject of our conversation!
My father and grandfather,
And great-grandfather, and all my relations
Lived not as I live now. But rather,

By God's all-powerful will
It was their fate to live in ampleness!
For they had grain aplenty in the fields
To feed themselves, their servants, and their guests.

Three brothers had I, of sisters I made three,
And I was the most small.
My mother died when she was having me;
And so I was considered least of all.
They nicknamed me 'plain Jane'!
My father felt such pain
He sent us all to live with relatives.
My two big sisters lived
Life at their whim—freedom without reserve!
But I, like a domestic serf,
Was parcelled to nine houses through the years,
I took on in turn their different ways,
And knew naught at all of play;
Led by the fate to which I had been born
Along a path of pricking thorns
Weeping salt tears!
The whole wide world grew tedious to me!
After attaining my majority,
I asked my brothers for my share of the estate
So as to live at my own will's dictate.
But then the Muses motioned their fair hands!
Since knowledge and sciences were my soul's delight,
To Petropolis, their capital, I hied!
In place of cavaliers and dandies,
I summon the pedantic,
And model myself upon their manners.
But alas! The sciences love silver here!
My little purse was quickly emptied!
Since I was paying dear
For each period of play,
Each movement of the lips,
For logic's reasoned words,
For all the quirks of physics,
And for my room and board,

I soon grew short of funds,
And I could hardly sing those songs
That satisfied your taste.
There, now my sin's confess'd!

I still possess my meadows in the air,
But my feet would be bare,
Were it not for our good Sovereign,
Who, like to the radiant sun,
In slender rays descends,
From grass to grain of sand,
Infusing lively strength
In all, from lap-dogs to elephants.
Even so does he my strength restore;
And the dear Muses favour me once more!

[*29 February 1813*]

Translated by Sibelan Forrester

♦ ANNA BUNINA ♦

Conversation between Me and the Women

(Russian text p. 403)

THE WOMEN

Our sister dear, what joy for us!
You are a poetess! your palette's able,
Holding all shades, to paint an ode, a fable;
Your heart must brim with praise for us!
A man's tongue, though... Ah, God preserve us, dear!
Sharp as a knife is sharp!
In Paris, London—as in Russia here—
  They're all the same! On just one string they harp:
Naught but abuse—and ladies always suffer!
We wait for madrigals—it's epigrams they offer.
Don't expect brothers, husbands, fathers, sons
  To praise you even once.
How long we've lacked a songstress of our own!
So, do you sing? Pray answer, yes or no?

ME

Yes, yes, dear sisters! Thanks be to Providence
I have been singing now for five years since.

THE WOMEN

And in those years, what have you sung and how?
Though few of us, in truth, have Russian educations,
And Russian verses make such complications!
Besides, you know, they aren't in fashion now.

ME

I sing all Nature's beauteous hues,
Above the flood the hornèd sickle moon;
I count the little drops of dew,
I hymn the sun's ascension in the morn.
Flocks gambolling in the fields enjoy my care:
I give reed pipes unto the shepherdesses,
Flowers I entwine in their companions' tresses,
  That are so flaxen-fair;
I order them to take each other's hands,
  To caper to a dance,
And as their fleet feet pass,
To trample not a single blade of grass.
Up to the heavens rocky crags I raise,
  I plant out branchy trees
To rest an old man in their shady breeze
  On summer's sultry days;
I search the roses for bright insects' wings,
  And, having summoned feathered birds to sing,
  I languish pale
To the sweet warble of the nightingale.
Or, all at once, freeing the horse's manes,
  I order them to race the wind;
And with their hooves dust to the clouds they fling.
I draw a corn-field crowned with ears of grain,
  Which, from the sun's bright rays
    Takes on the look of seas
Of molten gold,
  Sways, ripples, dazzles, shines—
    Blinding the eye,
As humble ploughmen their reward behold.
In fortifying my own timid voice
Through Nature's loveliness,
  I'm braver in a flash!

THE WOMEN

Fie! what balderdash!
There's not one word in this for us!

Tell us what good such singing does?
What use are all your livestock, polled and horned
  To us, who weren't as herdsmen born?
So, with the beasts you feel at home?
Well! ... if that's your topic, then,
    Hide in a den,
  Among the fields, pray, roam,
And never haunt the capitals in vain!

ME

O no, dear sisters, come!
People are also in my ken.

THE WOMEN

Commendable! but whom *have* you sung, then?

ME

At times I've hymned the deeds of mighty men,
  Who, when the bloody fight drew near,
Declared for faith and Tsar; they knew no fear.
Shaking with my lament the field of quarrels
  I bore them thence away with laurels,
    Dropping a tear.
At times I've left this grievous task,
And passed to those who keep the laws,
I've filled my soul with cheer,
And rested 'neath their aegis, free from cares.
  At times to poets I've inclined my ear
And bent the knee before their thunderous lyres.
    At times
  Moved by esteem,
I've made the chemist or astronomer my theme.

THE WOMEN

And here again we're missing from your rhymes!
  You do us quite a service!
So what good *are* you? Don't you make things worse?
  Why did you bother learning to sing verse?

You ought to take your themes from your own circle.
'Tis only men you honour with your lays,
As if their sex alone deserved your praise.
You traitress! Give our case some thought!
  For is this what you ought?
Are their own founts of flattery too few,
Or can they boast of more than our virtue?

ME

It's true, my dears, you are no less,
  But understand:
With men, not you, the courts of taste are manned
  Where authors all must stand,
And all an author's fame is in their hands,
And none can help loving himself the best.[1]

Translated by Sibelan Forrester

[1] May I be forgiven for this jest in deference to the merry Muses, who love to mix business with idleness, lies with truth, and to enliven conversation with innocent playfulness. [Author's note.]

♦ ELISAVETA KULMAN ♦

Kulman, who was born in 1808 into a large family of Russified Baltic Germans settled in St Petersburg, was perhaps the most talented of several early nineteenth-century girl prodigies (others included the polyglot Sarra Tolstaya, and Elizaveta Shakhova, on whom see below). Before her death in 1825 from a consumption resulting from catching cold in the Great Flood of 1824, she had acquired a knowledge of French, German, and the classical languages as well as Russian, and had written poetry in Russian, German, Italian, and French, much of it composed in neo-classical odic forms.

To Diana

(Russian text p. 407)

We greet you now, Diana,
The sister of Apollo,
In these your shady thickets,
And on the lofty mountains!

Forth from your golden quiver
You take the long sharp arrows
Of vengeance, so the oak woods
May be purified from monsters,

Whether from wolves that raven
And thirst for blood each moment,
Or from the sharp-tusked wild boar,
An insatiable aggressor.

The earth rebounds and trembles
As the mighty beasts are brought low,
The oaks shake with their wailing
Their death-throes rend the air,

Yet when the young doe shyly
Runs to you, and caresses
Your fierce palm with her soft nose,
You caress her in return;

She follows you to Delphi,
Your temple, where you set down
Your bow and empty quiver
By the sacred temple gates;

Sometimes you join the thronging
Camenae, sweet-voiced maidens,
And dance to the sounds of music
Played on Apollo's lyre,

Then golden-haired Latona
Comes down from high Olympus,
She looks at you in wonder,
And sheathes her fiery gaze.

As we, your timid maidens,
Haste to your woodland feast-day:
Protect us now, Diana,
In this, your sacred grove!

[*before 1824*]

♦ ZINAIDA VOLKONSKAYA ♦

Princess Zinaida Volkonskaya was born in 1792 into one of the richest and most distinguished families in Russia, and married into another one. Her father, Prince Beloselsky-Belozersky, was a landowner and connoisseur, and her stepmother came from a wealthy family of industrialists; Volkonskaya's husband was a diplomat and courtier. Volkonskaya spent much of her youth abroad; her first language was French, and this was also the language in which she produced her earliest literary works. Settling in Moscow in the early 1820s, Volkonskaya became the moving spirit of one of the most brilliant Moscow salons; she also began making a serious study of Russian, and from about 1824, started to write in the language. The author of poetry, prose fiction, and travel memoirs, Volkonskaya also wrote the libretto (in Italian) and music for an opera, *Giovanna d'Arco* (1821); her tutelary genius was Madame de Staël, to whom she had addressed a paean on the occasion of the latter's visit to Russia in 1814. In 1829, Volkonskaya, who had converted to Catholicism, was pressurized by the sectarian policies of Nicholas I's government into leaving Russia. She spent the rest of her life in Rome, devoting herself to religious philanthropy (she was to join the Franciscan Tertiaries) rather than to writing, though her drawing-room remained a social centre for Russian expatriates, such as Nikolai Gogol. She died in 1862. Her Roman villa survives as the British Embassy.

The Dream: A Letter

I have read your letter, my dear Gulyanov.° And imagine where I read it: in the house under whose roof I was born, my father's house, that haunt of elegance, where I grew up in the shade of Greek, Roman, Egyptian, Italian works of art, my youthful gaze becoming schooled to ideal forms. The pictures, antique bronzes, marble sculptures, are all as dear to me as brothers, as friends, belonging as much to my father's family as I do myself. And imagine, too, the trembling reverence with which I approached the Mummy, with its outer garment all decked in the ancient script, calling to mind as I did your studies of the Hieroglyph! For long I gazed in incomprehension, with the same rapt attention and blind admiration with which an unlettered, but pious, villager will drink in the eloquency of the Eastern prophets; sharing, too, his feeling when he quits the temple, I made my departure from the pagan relics of mysterious Egypt. Withdrawing to my room, I began musing; but then, I am sorry to say, I fell asleep over your friends the hieroglyphs.

. . . And now I find myself sitting on a purple couch in the Ancient Greek style; my son is with me. A lamp burns over my head; above it rises a verdigrised bronze of the Ephesian Diana, her arms spread out; a little way off is the Medici Venus, in the full glory of her charms and her modest coquetry; all around are bas-reliefs, inscriptions, urns for tears, tears which have long dried up and vanished, as the cause of them has; here is the Medusa with her petrifying glance, her parted lips, and her snaky locks, and there a Faun in ecstasy, crowned with vines, with a merry, tormented face. Looking at him, I wonder aloud: 'Why should it be that inner joy is always mingled with sadness?' But suddenly I see a figure approaching: it is dark and upright as an ancient, dried-up tree-trunk; it has neither arms nor legs, yet the form is surely human. The vision pauses; but surely those are fingers gently putting back the narrow, dark veil; a sweet aroma fills the air... Suddenly there is a flash of light... It is glancing off those large rings, with their black stones in settings of such pearly whiteness they resemble coals on snow. But now the veil falls to the ground: before me stands a majestic woman, dark of complexion and strange! 'Fear not,' she says, 'I have come to converse with you.' Then, turning to me, she adds: 'Often your curious gaze has rested on the many-coloured signs which figure my mysterious covering. Often indeed did you ponder their secret meaning; yet that meaning remained closed to you and all others; now I shall reveal it to you. But you should expect no long and intricate tale of some tempestuous life; no, my days were spent in contemplation, I lived peacefully as water flowing over the moist lotuses. See that Isis in the mirror, with her silver face: she is the very image of my life, the reflection of my earthly existence. My father belonged to the sacred Caste; he dwelt with four other priests on a quiet, lonely river-bank opposite a noisy city,° a city which I never visited. But do not ask me at what time, and in what place, I made my home on this earth. Now that I have lived out my days, everything is grand and infinite to me, without name or boundary. Only what was imprinted on my spirit remains with me now. My father would speak never a word to me of my mother—and I never saw the person who gave me life.° Like a stream running out of its native source, I flowed ever onward, never returning whence I came. Surrounded by old men from my earliest days, I grew like a pink lily in the shade of sycamores; at an early age I became used to grey hairs, to soft, weighty words; I loved old age as I loved hope, sweet sleep, and peaceful evenings. From afar I would glimpse the merry youths and maidens at their games and dances; I could not understand why they should move about so quickly, speak and sing so eagerly: for after all, they were not honouring the immortals. Wherefore, I asked myself, those words, those movements, those sounds? I felt pity and horror, looking at their insane joy. All I knew of youth was what I heard the old men recall of theirs, and how pleasant those recollections seemed to me, like the sound of the holy harmonies as a sacred procession approaches; but a worldly youth I supposed worse than the sun beating down on the bare desert, worse than a lashing sandstorm.

'O, I thought, will the roses of my youth never fall? Will the green, fresh leaves never drop from the tree of life? How long I would have to wait before the time of wisdom and peace should come upon me! And then I began to look for ways in which I might anticipate my longed-for old age, and make the years of my bloom, which to me were so threatening, run forward. In the temple, before the image of the fearful god,° the enemy of smiles and cheerfulness, I would bow down, and compose my pent-up yearning in a cycle of melancholy songs, so that no one should distract me from my stern thoughts of death, the best guide on the path to wisdom. I would crown my locks with the leaves of the banana, a tree dedicated to the making of coffins. Now I remained day and night in the dwelling of my parent; I was determined to wait there until the old age I had so long desired overtook me. When I had cast away the transient garment of youth, I would go forth again into the light, clad now in the robe of divine wisdom. And then, I would tell myself at such times, my words would cut themselves into hearts as deeply as the magic signs carved on the pyramids; but, like those signs too, their meaning would remain closed, except to initiates. And now hear the tale of what I did during the long period of my novitiate! From my earliest youth I had, under the supervision of my father, often practised writing the many-coloured hieroglyphs on the walls of the temple and on the shrouds of the dead; and now I decided to make ready my own last garment. I began to spend all my days in painting those signs.'

And here the daughter of Ancient Egypt unwrapped her many-coloured *epitrachilion*° for us, and, running her dark-complexioned finger over the bright signs with which it was covered, said: 'This circle signifies the sun; it is dark as the morning of my youth was dark for me... For my sun did not once shine out, being covered with a dark cloud to the end of my days! These secret signs, marked lower down, are symbols of the heat in my soul, which never burned free under an open sky; the wind of the outside world never fanned this inner heat; it burned quietly, as the holy, pure fire of all-powerful Ptah° burns under the silent vaults of the impenetrable temple; and, like that fire, my sacred flame lit and transfigured the feelings and thoughts in my soul. Look: here I have represented the sacred gaze of the god of gods; it is fixed on each one as he walks about the earth, it follows him as he goes amidst the multitude, in the storm of the vanities; as it looks on mortals, this gaze also studies the universe, counting the moments and the centuries... But the firmament of Ptah's gaze is eternity. Look at me, eye of the stern divinity! Look at the maiden who, crowned by leaves of the tree of death, walks her lonely path, striving to approach you!

'And here below is the snake, winding her two-headed coils; in her you see a power higher than all powers, save those of the gods. Death, like that snake, long writhes near her prey; scarcely has she chosen the spot where her venom will be unleashed, than corruption overtakes all that is living. But the earth sloughs its skin; and thus death, taking unto herself what is spoilt, is transformed into eternity.

'Yet the powers of life in nature are perpetually bubbling next to the powers of death—bubbling in excitation, as the noisy waters swirl over the wide-jawed Crocodile. How swiftly this monster swims; the populous bank is soon behind him, giving way to new banks where he may wreak his destruction; but not for long is he away; his eye can never have enough of gazing, and his hunger is never sated.

'And here I have drawn the temporary dwelling of man; under this his fragile covering he hides from the vast spectacle of nature, complacent in his own insignificance. What is a great building, what is the shadow of the Pyramids, compared with the extent of the firmament?

'The triumph of man lies, rather, in the word! This sign here shows the opening of the lips; from this hot spring rush thoughts, feelings, anger, prayers, passions—all flowing in a torrent of picturesque words—making man as much a creator as the gods. He at one and the same time imagines, confers form, describes, inspires, and rules over life and nature.'

But here the strange maiden fell a-trembling. 'Our conversation', she said, 'is drawing to a close. I must return to my narrow sycamore grove, to the skiff in which I roam the abyss of eternity...' Uttering these words, she hid from my curious orbs a thousand other signs, whose meaning I longed to learn, and gently wrapped herself in her dark shroud once more—and once more the aromatic scents filled the air beside us.

'Young man!' she continued, looking at my son. 'Sink yourself in study, and may the Genius of Egypt be with you! May you rise from the earth like an obelisk, and like the obelisk, may you hold your secret within you—the secret of deep feeling and learning; do not communicate it to any but initiates, for the sounds of your heart and thought must not strike on unresponsive ears. These sounds must only ring out when other, sibling, sounds rise in response to them. Bear in mind my life of solitude, remember this my last garment, and follow me; live within yourself, keeping the sacred flame cherished in your soul. And may your youth be crowned by fresh and pure lotus! And may your life be decorated in imperishable colours! And may all the lineaments of that painting be noble, agreeable, and pure, and may your soul breathe the air of these colours as the heavenly harmony does!'

And then her face was once more hidden from us; she began to withdraw into the distance—and at that moment, everything vanished...

Forgive me, my dear Gulyanov, for occupying you at such length with my delirious fancies; forgive me, if my dream should contradict your opinions of the Hieroglyph in some manner which I do not suspect. For what system does not vanish in a dream, where imagination alone triumphs over the mind, over Logic and Reason? In very truth I was not thinking of you, nor of Champollion,° at the time when I conversed with the Mummy come to life. But in my waking hours, as you well know, I am always in agreement with you, recognizing that you are my one true guide to the labyrinth of signs; I resign all my own suppositions about the Hieroglyph before the power of your genius.

Forgive this *amatrice* of antiquity her fantastical aberrations, and be always persuaded of her most cordial feelings for you.

Princess Zinaida Volkonskaya

(1829)

◆ EVDOKIYA ROSTOPCHINA ◆

Rostopchina (1812–58) was a native of Moscow; after her mother's death in 1817, her father moved from the city, but his daughter remained, being sent to live with her maternal grandparents, the Pashkovs. She was educated at home, and began writing as a child; later, her beauty and liveliness made her a salon favourite. In 1833, she married Count Andrei Rostopchin, from a wealthy and prominent literary family; a man of refined taste, he also proved a capricious spendthrift. In 1836, the couple moved from Rostopchin's country estate to Petersburg. Here Rostopchina continued writing poetry, but after 1840 she was to turn increasingly to prose. As a young girl, she had written some fiery anti-establishment poems, and she continued to associate with liberal 'Westernizing' political circles in adulthood; this was one factor behind the well-publicized split between her and Karolina Pavlova in the 1840s. Rostopchina's anti-traditionalist political views were not, however, reflected in the form or lexicon of her writings, which remained high-Romantic even in the 1850s. However, her work is often informed by a Romantic self-consciousness too; Rostopchina's manipulation of perspective in the manner of the 'society tale', and her exact sense of detail, make her in some ways the 'grandmother' of Akhmatova.

The Unfinished Sewing

(Russian text p. 409)

Freudvoll
Und leid voll,
Gedankenvoll sein...°

(Klärchens Lied, *Egmont*)

No! put the work down! No, not another stitch!
No! I shall not complete this tapestry!
The assiduous needle never shall return
To the task I interrupted; this white fabric
Will never be enclosed in patterned wool!
These intricate knots here, and these glowing flowers
Were made by me in other times and moods...

So many sweet and lively memories
  Return when I survey them,
So many feelings, meditations,
Were worked into this gaudy cloth,
As I disburdened here my soul!

The hour when woman sews her modest seam
Brings silence, peace, and space for sweet reflection;
Far from the worldly crowd, she's sunk in contemplation;
Enjoys a rest from parties, carriage rides;
Has respite from the world, from visitors, from strife;
Then she may read her soul, may gaze upon herself.
Full work-table to hand, she sits at her round frame,
And stitches rapidly, absorbed in what she sews.
But be assured, winged spectres, fluttering shades
Play all about; her secret, favourite dreams
All dance before her, beckoning her on;
Perhaps this is the time when feelings speak,
Perhaps she feels a trembling of the heart;
  Or nurtures some vain hope
Within her breast, like a soft dove...
The harmless witness of her thoughts,
A true and silent confidante,
A friend she treasures and she loves,
Her sewing shares her secret life.

Unfinished tapestry, memorial to the past,
I sat with you during my leisure hours,
And often glimpsed with my interior eye
Moments of radiance; nor has my faithful soul
Forgotten these; not so, they stay with me!
  Alas! that round of brilliance,
Of happiness, is gone for ever now!
Past troubles and past hopes are fled for good;
  My cherished thoughts will not return
Bringing their past delights; no, they are flown!
Now, as I work, I do not think with joy
Nor even anguish, of sweet *yesterday*,
Dreams of *tomorrow* do not visit me;

I wait for nothing, and my days are grey!
My heart is cold; in this new, hopeless mood,
Of vain remorse, how can I sew once more?
I do not want the flood of gloomy thoughts
To dim that glow! No, let my work remain
An image of past days! So, when I look at it,
Once more I hear the confessions of my heart,
With dreary joy, and forget the years that pass!

(*October 1839*
Anna Village)

◆ KAROLINA PAVLOVA ◆

Of mixed German, English, French, and Russian descent, Pavlova was born in 1807 in Moscow, into the family of a physics lecturer; she grew up trilingual, and received a good education at home. An early romance with the Polish poet Mickiewicz was blighted when the Jänisch relatives refused to allow the marriage; in 1837, Karolina married the minor prose writer Nikolai Pavlov. The Pavlovs' residence was soon to become a literary and political salon, which at first operated on cross-party lines. Pavlova herself, who was already the author of translations and of poetry in French and German, began writing original poetry in Russian in the late 1830s; she was soon enjoying a considerable reputation. From the mid-1840s, however, Pavlova's position began to be increasingly isolated and embattled. The formal inventiveness and linguistic austerity of her mature work was poorly understood; the polarization of the intelligentsia into 'Slavophile' and 'Western' groups led to Pavlova's increasing identification with the former group, perceived as reactionary by the Westerners; and in the early 1850s, Pavlova's marital conflicts with her husband began to attract general censure, she being alleged to have 'mistreated' him. In 1853, Pavlova left Moscow for Dorpat, where her son was being educated; in 1858, she took up residence in Dresden, where she was to remain until her death. The whereabouts of her grave is unknown.

The Crone

(Russian text p. 411)

I

'Young man, do not hurl yourself
Along the road so wide,
Do not rush to gallop so
Past me, horseman bold!

Cease to stare in impudence,
Be sure to mark my words:
For I know that silently
A thought gnaws at this youth.

I know he sits night after night
Sunk in a cancerous gloom;
I know the beauties' glinting eyes
Shine in vain on him.

Amid the salon's riots and joys,
Or in the forest's wooded calm,
I know his mad delirium,
The sadness of his noble heart.

Yes, if you will, give a forced sneer,
Clap your spurs to the horse's sides;
You shall not always easily
Dash past me, as you ride.

Loud though your horse's hooves may beat
You shan't blot out my words;
Gallop and hurry as you may,
You shall not outrun those,

But you shall come into my hut,
My handsome youth, in time,
And listen to an old hag speak,
Nor dare to turn your eyes.'

Eddies of dust rose up afar,
In a trice the youth was flown;
But the old woman laughed aloud,
Clapping her window to.

And hardly did the hoof-beat sound,
On the air, of that fleet steed,
Than the old woman once again
Was waiting, window wide.

Like an arrow plunging deep
Straight to his heart's sore wounds,
She flung her gaze after the youth,
She snared him in magic rope.

Soon enough the time was come,
When from morn till night
At the broken fence his mount,
Nimble and coal-black, neighed.

What is the old woman doing
With the black-browed, brave young man?
Rumours are flying, people talking,
Talking of strange things going on.

2

Beside the one and only lamp
The young man sits and stares;
Into the deep dusk of her room
His eyes gaze, set and wild.

What dreams are charming his young heart?
What is he waiting for?
The door grows pale: then something stirs:
The crone walks in the room.

Grey-haired, decrepit, in she comes,
And takes her seat again,
Enrapturing, enraging him at once
Her whispered speech begins.

The stormy rage of youthful grief,
All fancy's sacred things
Are dressed by her in tenderness,
And decked in innocence.

And she tells him of a maid
So fair belief's defied.
Taking such words, God knows from where,
He cannot hear enough:

How languorously her scented cheek,
How beautifully, it glows;
How those her lips no man may touch
Are sealed by her chaste thoughts;

How the abyss of those blue orbs
Has glowing, azure depths,
How, like the stars above the world,
They shine on pettiness;

How her majestic gaze is calm,
How a soft mist of curls
Is wrapped like a dark cloud around
Her clear and sober brow.

How, loving her, he loves in vain,
Since her powers have no bound;
Her beauty is irresistible,
But so cold that hope must end.

The chamber has grown quiet and cold;
An hour strikes, then another;
Seductively the old woman still
Whispers her tale, and whispers.

And she tells him of a maid
So fair belief's defied.
Taking such words, God knows from where,
He cannot hear enough.

3

The horseman does not hurl himself
Along the road so wide;
No longer is the steed hard pressed
And spurred by the youth so bold.

In winter's frost, in summer's heat,
He stays both night and day,
Behind the locked doors of that room,
With the crone for company.

Shrivelled and motionless he sits,
Like one whose will is gone;
Gazing at her wrinkled face,
Possessed by greed, and dumb.

(*February 1840*)

♦ KAROLINA PAVLOVA ♦

(Russian text p. 415)

Life calls us, and we go, massing our courage;
But in the short hour when grief's thunder stints,
And passions sleep, when the heart's strife is mute,
The soul takes breath awhile from the world's troubles,
And suddenly the far-off Edens shine,
And meditations come to power again.

Sometimes when he is half-way up a mountain,
A traveller stops to cast his eyes around;
Flowers and May sunshine in the vale behind him,
Before him, granite and a wintry chill.
Like him, I now abjure a forward look,
More often now than not my eyes turn back.

How many things I shall not see again:
The charms of joy, likewise misfortune's charms;
How much that I once loved, and once held sacred,
Was smashed by the hand of Fortune, and is gone;
Yet how could my soul forget all this,
How could it pass, leaving no trace?

And can you all be lifeless ghosts for me,
Who took from me, in my own vernal years,
Gifts of hot tears and gifts of bitter pain?
Ones who have perished! Can you now be strangers,
And be remembered, in my heart's indolence,
Infrequently and darkly, as if I dreamt?

O lady of whom I, weeping, took my leave,
Whose path the merciless Creator turned:
The youthful champion of sacred love,
You submitted, and you took your crown of thorns;
But the bare wastelands of the deadly North
Swallowed alike your saintly deeds, your death.

I see the place whither you took your anguish
And faded in suffering words could not express:
Even there, perhaps, no heart recalls your torments,
Perhaps your gravestone does not bear your name;
The years have passed—your ring is on my hand:
I see it, yet do not mark it in my mind.

Yet at the moment when I parted from you,
It seemed to me that I could best endure;
That I could love, that I would not forget you,
That twenty years of grief would speed like hours.
But now I see another shade before me,
One seeming sadder, lady, even than yours.

O unknown grave, o grave that lies far distant!
The years have galloped past that grave as well!
The devastating force lives on in fancy,
And in my struggles senseless pride persists;
For, child, the futile dream that murdered you
Waits on the time when it can kill me too!

In the stillness of the night your life was ended,
Let it not be me who now forgets that death!
Two or three friends, in agony, were clustered
That night, around the sinking exile's bed;
Scarce audible his breath, it came so quiet:
Yet his mother, and his motherland, were rapt.

How young you were when destiny assailed you!
The sacred feelings were still quick and warm;
In the coming gloom your gaze had long been seeking
Virtuous paths and deeds that would live on:

The cruel lessons of advancing age
You did not learn; how blessed you were in that!

Blessèd! although you closed your eyes in exile!
You still advanced towards that single end;
So, with a cross upon their warlike garb,
Did knights of old go to Jerusalem;
When thunder rolled, and hope's destiny was dust,
The pilgrim had long fallen on the road.

Here's yet one more! O, torture to my feelings,
How light they sleep! Yes, yet another comes!
Childe Harold, alas, was right: there are too many,
Yes, though so few—and who from time to time
Has not gone pale, and covered up his face,
On reading through the melancholy list?

How many are the poets that we buried,
Culled in the flower of youth by envious fate!
He was the first—can I forget those tidings?
And others were to come, more painful yet:
Yes! Once again a pistol shot had triumphed;
But another death smote deeper in my breast.

Can it be true, favourite of inspiration,
Who vanished like a dream's sad paling ghost,
Can it be true the land where you were born,
Grieved not for you, and paid no last respects?
And is it I, Evgeny, who must name you,
Do only I give you the gift of verse?

But take my gift now, in this fateful hour,
But take it now, since others say no word.
Alas! will-o'-the-wisps of former feelings,
Why do you glow amid the lightless gloom?
Wherefore this feeble, meaningless combustion?
Who called you forth, days of my vanished youth?

Why, distant face, do you too fix your eyes
Unswerving on me, staring pallidly?

I am calm now; years have gone past without you;
You went off long ago: why are you here?
Let me alone! in the East the pale day rises,
Begone, sad phantoms' chorus, let me go!

The pale day rises, the diamond stars are fading,
Day calls to work, demands that things be done;
It is high time this dreary road was ended,
Time to forget what life has overcome,
And sober up intoxicated fancy,
Cast off the trace of daydreams from my brow.

(July 1846
Gireevo)

◆ KAROLINA PAVLOVA ◆

At the Tea-Table

Die Gräfin spricht wehmutig:
'Die Lieb' ist eine Passion!!'
Und präsentiret gütig
Die Tasse dem Herren Baron.

(Heine)

I would prefer there to be no finished stories: it is the ending that spoils everything. If you storytellers have been able to show me living people and make me feel for them, why should you all without fail do something that makes those people uninteresting to me? Why this desire to leave me with nothing to dream about? A finished tale—why, that's like nothing so much as a garden with a high stone wall that keeps me from seeing into the distance—

(A madman's ratiocinations)°

The conversation had turned into an argument. Bulanin, seized by all the ardour of a 25-year-old's convictions and by the heat of the debate, had forgotten the proprieties so far as to raise his voice.

The Countess glanced at him and smiled.

'No,' he continued, tossing his long hair back off his face, 'I admit no such necessity. I find the social position of women improper, even indecent. My heart shrinks to see it.'

'Won't you have some tea?' asked the lady of the house.

'Please. No, it's simply barbaric! I see no moral reason why a woman should blindly obey her husband and bear his insults; that is the most painful kind of dependency. Why should they not be equals?'

The Countess glanced at him again, but without smiling this time. 'It would certainly be hard to find any justification in logic for the situation,' she muttered under her breath.

'*Vae victis*!'° said the man of about 40 sitting next to her.

'What does that mean?' asked his other neighbour, a charming brunette in a pink dress. 'See how happy I am to admit to you that I understand no Latin!'

'It means a great deal,' he replied. 'It means, among other things, that if France declared war on China, none of us would be surprised to discover that the French had beaten an army led by some Li or other.'

'*Tant de choses en deux mots*,' said the pink lady with a laugh; '*c'est une belle langue que la langue turque*!'°

'French can also express all that in a single word,' he added. '*Parceque*.'

'Don't you think', asked the lady of the house quietly from behind her silver samovar, 'that the Chinese would be different if they were brought up differently?'

'Even so,' he replied, 'it would be next to impossible for them to turn into Frenchmen, I think. And what would be the point of remaking them? I have visited China, and I assure you that the Chinese are very charming, and especially the women, with their broad faces, slanted eyes, and bound feet, their indolent mannerisms and childish amusements. I find it all most appealing.'

She cast a quick glance at him and bit her lip.

'But surely, Aleksei,' objected Bulanin, who had caught a few words of this sally, 'you have to acknowledge the influence of a good education? Or do you place no value on upbringing? Do I understand you as asserting that it is impossible to make a person behave more nobly, to inculcate a serious outlook on life in him, or even to correct his shortcomings?'

'All I say', Aleksei Petrovich said calmly, 'is that you can't transform a feminine nature into a masculine.'

'But what *I* think', Bulanin continued vehemently, 'is that all the shortcomings of women depend on their upbringing. Under other circumstances they would probably be much closer to perfection than men, but we develop only the most childish proclivities in them, and then most courteously damn them as children.'

'There's some truth in that, after all,' observed the Countess, turning to Aleksei Petrovich. 'You must, surely, admit that the education of women is absurd in the highest degree—no, it is more than absurd; it seems designed to fly in the face of common sense. One might suppose that women, or most of them, were brought up by their worst enemies, when the conduct of those who take care of them is so strange. A woman cannot acquire wealth in the way a man can, and the law almost entirely deprives her of her patrimony;° and so a craving for luxury and the habit of considering wealth a necessary condition for existence are instilled in her. She cannot propose to a man; so from her very childhood spinsterhood is held up before her as a shameful misfortune; she is made incapable of independence, and taught to regard it as something indecent. A frivolous decision can make her wretched for life; so she must be schooled to frivolity and whim. A single moment of passion is enough to ruin her irrevocably; knowing that, her guardians foster in her coquetry and a proclivity for dangerous games, and remove everything that might direct her towards serious occupations. Is that not so?'

'You are very eloquent,' replied Aleksei Petrovich with a smile, 'and your outburst is well-founded; but permit me to remark that it none the less upholds my opinions concerning the charming weakness of the feminine nature; after all, you yourself affirm that your sex can withstand no negative influence. You talk about the upbringing of women, but is not the upbringing of men, in general, a thousand times worse? Are men subjected to fewer harmful influences? Do we not undergo many more dangerous temptations and opportunities for ruining ourselves than you?'

'Whilst remaining steadfast?' interrupted the Countess ironically. 'That would be rather a bold assertion.'

'And a thumping falsehood to boot,' he added.

'So where does the moral strength of men lie; wherein are their advantages?'

'You answer that question yourself, Countess, when you choose to seek the company and even the friendship of a man whom you know to have taken part in drinking-bouts with his friends. You would not allow a woman about whom that was said to cross your threshold.'

'And so what do you conclude from that?'

'The same thing that you do: that a woman is not a man, that it is more difficult to ruin him than her, and that his moral nature, as well as his physical nature, is sounder than a woman's.'

'At any rate,' Bulanin said, raising his voice once more, 'we have to admit that women are superior in the matter of mankind's best quality: feeling. A woman is always moved by a noble act; her heart will always respond to honest candour, to a confidence.'

'I dare not take exception to that in the presence of so many ladies,' Aleksei Petrovich pronounced.

'What? You question even that?' exclaimed Bulanin.

'God forbid!' replied Aleksei Petrovich. 'I agree that one can on occasion move a woman by dint of magnanimity and candour, assuming that one has the skills to do it. But by no means always.'

'Always! Always!' the other repeated.

The sceptic was silent.

'Prove the opposite,' went on Bulanin. 'Prove it with an example.'

'There are very many such examples.'

'Share at least one with us.'

'Splendid!' the Countess said, turning to her neighbour. 'You have led yourself into a story. Let that be your punishment. Kindly begin. Give us, as Monsieur Bulanin has demanded, a convincing example that might support your heretical views.'

'And not one that you have just invented,' added the lady of the house.

'I can tell you a true story, if you would like to hear one,' said Aleksei Petrovich; 'I can recount a factual case, of which I heard from a most reliable source.'

'Excellent! We're listening.'

'You will permit me not to use real names?' Aleksei Petrovich continued.

'We will,' replied the lady of the house, 'but perhaps you will whisper them in our ears later on.'

Smiling, Aleksei Petrovich began:

A few years ago, if a newcomer to Moscow happened to be in company, and, having his curiosity stirred by a name that he frequently heard mentioned, to ask, 'What sort of fellow is Khozrevsky?' one of two answers would be sure to follow, depending on whether he had addressed the question to a lady or to a gentleman. A gentleman would usually say unceremoniously, 'An arrant fool!' A lady, however, would answer, '*C'est un excellent garçon.*'°

At one of those Moscow salons where a number of guests will gather on certain *jours fixes*, these two different opinions happened one day to be advanced in two opposite corners of the room; in one corner, a stiff and proper Muscovite said to the man he was standing next to, a man of about 35, with a striking appearance, and a swarthy expressive face, 'Khozrevsky—*c'est un rien du tout.*° He has no estate, no decent family connections either, no looks, and he's an utter blockhead. Yet he is received everywhere, and he seems to be a great favourite with the ladies, God knows why.' At the same time, in the opposite corner, a lady whose appearance was still very attractive, despite her mature years, was saying to her cousin the Princess, a graceful young widow who had come to Moscow for the winter from her Tambov estate, 'Khozrevsky, *ma chère amie*, is a fine man, and, believe me, he is not nearly as stupid as people will tell you. The attacks on him are unfair. Of course, he's no brilliant salon conversationalist, no dandy, *c'est un homme sans prétentions*, but he has some unusual qualities, and he is not so much simple as merely shy; *et puis, il a une si haute opinion des femmes!*° I shall present him to you now; he's sure to be here. But don't judge by your first impressions; you have to get to know him well to appreciate him.'

During this conversation, a new guest came into the salon, a young man whom there was absolutely no reason to notice. 'There he is,' said the lovely widow's cousin. 'There he is,' said the very proper Muscovite to the man he was talking to. 'See what a figure he makes; nothing to envy, you'd think. But just watch how the ladies receive him.' They moved out of their corner, and the swarthy-faced man stopped opposite the Princess's armchair. If her marvellous black brows quivered slightly, there was no reason why that barely noticeable movement should have been attributed to his appearance. Meanwhile, her cousin was responding to a polite bow from the approaching Khozrevsky. 'Good day, Trofim Lukich. I am delighted to see you, just as always. Now I am going to give you cause to thank me; I shall present you to my cousin, about whom I've told you so much. *Ma chère Aline,* Trofim Lukich Khozrevsky. Be sure not to frighten him too much.'

'*Suis-je si formidable?*' asked the Princess with a laugh.

'Sometimes,' replied Nastasya Pavlovna. 'When you take a notion to amuse yourself with someone, you become quite inhuman.'

'A fine introduction,' interrupted the Princess, 'and a proper encouragement to the timid. Is that not so, Monsieur Khozrevsky?'

'I am not frightened, Princess,' replied Khozrevsky in a quiet voice. 'I doubt that I shall be your victim.'

'What makes you so sure of that?' asked the bewitching widow, resting her dangerous gaze on him.

'A nice understanding of myself,' replied Khozrevsky.

'Really?'

'Of course, Princess. Who lowers himself to attack the fallen?'

'Sit down next to me,' she said, indicating a chair, 'and imagine that we have known each other for ages; that is the best way of avoiding the unbearable formality of a first meeting, and talking without constraint.'

Khozrevsky settled in the chair she had indicated, but with such a meek look that, when seated, he seemed much more respectful of the Princess than those who were standing in her presence.

'Do you live here in Moscow?' she asked.

'Ever since I came back from abroad.'

'You spent a long time there?'

'Three years.'

'Mostly where?'

'Longest of all in Paris and in Italy.'

'Italy is the best place, don't you agree?'

'Italy is a country just like any other.'

'In some respects, of course,' she said with a smile. 'However, it is also the land of elegance, the land of the arts.'

'I am no artist, and I have no appreciation of art,' replied Khozrevsky humbly.

'One cannot help feeling art's influence, whether one knows how to appreciate it or not,' the Princess went on. 'Were you in the Vatican?'

'I spent a morning there.'

'Can it really have made no impression on you? Impossible. I have seen many visitors to the Vatican, and I have never seen anyone leave there unmoved; all of them, if only unconsciously, recognized the force of genius; all of them felt that strange fatigue which is also a proof of the power that elegance has over us. We are not capable of looking at beauty for long; it overwhelms us with its majesty. The soul gets tired.'

'My feet got tired,' said Khozrevsky.

The Princess burst out laughing.

'Your candour will do you irrevocable harm in Alina's mind,' remarked Nastasya Pavlovna. 'She is utterly devoted to art; why, she is a very fine painter herself.'

'I would admire the Princess's pictures', pronounced Khozrevsky modestly, 'only because it is she who painted them.'

'And not because of their own merits?' asked Alina ironically.

'I make so bold as to remark', Khozrevsky objected bashfully, 'that there are many good pictures.'

'But few women like Alina,' added Nastasya Pavlovna. 'I have guessed your thoughts, have I not?'

'I would not venture to speak so directly,' replied Trofim Lukich.

'And how do you know whether there are many women like me or not? And how, in five minutes flat, have I managed to demonstrate to you my superiority over others?' rejoined the Princess in a lightly mocking tone.

Khozrevsky raised his eyes to her and lowered them again.

'Princess,' he replied, 'you are trying to force me into another absurdity. I know my own stupidity; and in any case, why should I be ashamed of it? Are we not all more or less on a level? After all, compared with you everyone is stupid,' he added, getting up to yield his chair to an approaching lady.

'*Au revoir,*' the Princess said to him. '*Je suis toujours chez moi dans l'avant-soirée.*° I shall be expecting you, and you are too courteous to make me wait for you in vain, *n'est ce pas?*'

Khozrevsky gave a silent bow, then walked away.

The Princess armed herself with her lorgnette and began inspecting the salon so intently that her behaviour seemed less than entirely natural.

'Will you excuse me if I take advantage of the unexpected chance that brings us together here?' A question brought her to herself.

The Princess glanced around. The swarthy man who had been a witness to her conversation with Khozrevsky was sitting in the seat that Nastasya Pavlovna had just vacated.

'*C'est vous, Monsieur Wismer*!' she said. 'I didn't recognize you just now.'

'I should not have been surprised if you had not recognized me at all, Princess,' replied Wismer. 'It would be no more than natural. But when I noticed the animation with which you were talking about Italy a moment ago, I dared to hope that you had kept some memory of even those circumstances of your time in Rome that were least important to you.'

All this was said with extreme courtesy; only the Princess detected a certain underlying intonation. She gave a small, unfriendly smile.

'You are no doubt unaware,' she said, 'that I am gifted with a most enviable and rare ability: I remember only what has given me pleasure.'

'In that case, Princess, I must rank as a stranger, and must ask your permission to introduce myself. My name is Yury Wismer. Having noticed just now your amiable indulgence of a new acquaintance, I am myself emboldened.'

'But in order that one should become acquainted, one condition is surely necessary?'

'May I know what that might be?'

'A mutual desire to make friends, which I have no sound reason to assume applies in our case.'

'On my part, Princess, desire is very keen. You do not know me: I am an eccentric person, and like everything that is extraordinary, that stands out from the usual order of things.'

'Excellent. But if you do not find my complete indifference to eccentric people outside your order of things, then I must warn you that there is nothing about me that could possibly interest you.'

'You cannot be your own judge, Princess. What amazes others seems simple and easy to your exceptional intellect. You do not understand that others do not even dare think about the things that you do in jest.'

The responses followed one another as swiftly as the sword-thrusts of two antagonists. Those present observed only light-hearted salon banter; but in fact a merciless duel was taking place.

However, the Princess now began to retreat.

'Your opinion is very flattering, but you must realize that I cannot share it,' she said.

'Your modesty only affords new proof that I have made no mistake in your extraordinary gifts,' Wismer went on implacably. 'Like all great artists, you are dissatisfied with yourself, realizing that you have the power to achieve incomparably more than you have already.'

The duel was continuing; Wismer now had the upper hand.

'You, it seems, claim to divine all the thoughts and feelings of those you meet?' The Princess, resorting to extreme measures, raised her eyes to her opponent, accompanying her reply with a glance that served as an unexpected commentary to her curt speech.

But her opponent would not surrender.

'Providence has granted every creature some means of self-defence,' he replied with a laugh. 'Why should you wish that I alone should be unarmed? My capacity to guess the secret motives and thoughts of the people I deal with is the only defence I have.'

'But if we suppose there is no danger?'

'Hm!' said Wismer.

'However,' she went on, now in a half-jesting tone, 'you must admit that every person—except of course the Pope, if you happen to be a Catholic—is capable of mistakes.'

'Certainly.'

'*Et vous n'êtes pas le pape.*'°

And she made a light, graceful, almost affable gesture of her shapely hand; at that minute her white glove had a hint of the flag that a besieged fortress runs up when it desires to begin negotiations.

'Princess,' said Wismer, half-ironically and half-seriously, 'permit me to congratulate you on your successes in the art of war. I see that you have been refining your skills, although they were no less than superb before; but you must remember that I am a seasoned warrior myself. I know that there are cases where all means of destroying the enemy are permissible, even those which you are now using. Forgive me, though, if I do not yield.'

The Amazon drew herself up under this blow.

'Monsieur Wismer,' she said, 'it would be much more to the point, I think, if you were to congratulate me on something else, and namely on the accuracy of my instinct, which appraised your abilities and sensed in advance the degree of development they would reach. You have fully justified my expectations, and attained a degree of perfection even beyond that which I anticipated. I see that it is impossible for any woman to deal with you. But whether you are entitled to be proud of that, I cannot say.'

She stood up.

'Princess,' said Wismer, also standing and lowering his voice, 'I understand all the enormity of my guilt; I know that I have inflicted on you the sole insult for which all a lady's generosity can find no excuse. I know that a woman can forgive a man who wounds her, even one who betrays her, but never one who sees through her. I have no right to your mercy and must bear your anger resignedly.'

Their eyes met. For a full minute, a mute battle, a last fierce clash, took place between them.

'Bonsoir, Monsieur Wismer,' said the Princess easily, showing the stoicism that only a society woman is capable of attaining. '*Sans rancune*,'° she added, extending her hand to him.

Wismer's fingers touched the cold kid leather of her gloves, and an ambiguous smile flashed across his lips, contradicting the amiability of the gesture.

'Who was that talking to you? A foreigner, I suppose,' an elegant old lady observed to Princess Alina, who had just joined her.

'No, a Russian,' replied the Princess. 'It was Wismer, the painter. I met him in Rome. He is a talented man.'

'Ah!' said the old lady, who would have reacted with the same profound spiritual composure to the report that Wismer had no talent at all.

The next morning Nastasya Pavlovna came out of a dressmaker's on Kuznetsky Most, and ran into Khozrevsky.

'Trofim Lukich! Where can you have been?'

'Visiting your lovely cousin,' he replied, with a most respectful bow.

'A charming woman, isn't she?'

'Very. But a woman should be charming; that is what pertains to her.'

'Yet some women are particularly charming, even more so than others,' said Nastasya Pavlovna.

'Yes, without themselves being aware of the fact,' Khozrevsky said, as if this were a novel observation.

'Be careful, though,' she added with a laugh. 'Don't fall in love *pour tout de bon*° with Alina. You're in danger.'

'Why should you care whether I am in danger or not?' he replied. 'Whom can that interest?'

'Good-bye!' she said with a benevolent smile and, having seated herself in her carriage, gave a nod of farewell.

A few days later found Princess Alina in her study, with a small group of men sitting round her. She had just given them an excellent dinner, and servants were handing round the coffee. The conversation was lively, and the Princess had little work to do in keeping it going. Everyone there knew the conventions of life in society. Nobody dines anywhere for nothing. In a princely home one pays for dinner just as one does in a hotel; the difference is that the payment is of a more demanding kind, namely, as witty a conversation as one can manage, full of anecdotes and *bons mots*.

The Princess seemed even more attractive than usual that day. It was no coincidence that she liked to receive visitors in her study; the setting suited her, and she it. It is always a pleasure for me to remember the Princess's study; so much in it was eloquent of her taste and *savoir-faire*; it was at once so elegant, and so natural and unaffected, so luxurious and so simple, giving unforced proof of an artistic talent, and a knowledge of art, that are rare in a woman. None of the remarkable objects drew attention to itself or obtruded on the eye.

The company that day was appropriate too: guests *à deux fins*,° aristocrats posing as artists, and artists posing as aristocrats. Even Khozrevsky was there, though Heaven knows why. The discussions and arguments flowed on all kinds of subjects. Finally, the talk turned to a certain incident that was preoccupying all Moscow: an engagement which had suddenly been broken off, for reasons that no one could discover.

Someone remarked, 'And they say that they love each other.'

'That is, they claim to,' said the Princess.

'How so, claim to?' asked two or three guests with one voice.

'Have you ever seen', she replied, 'how children play at buying and selling, giving one another pebbles that they arbitrarily call money? In the same way, we arbitrarily substitute words and tokens for the love that is denied us. But sometimes we are stupider than children, and get more carried away, so that we begin believing that our pebbles have real value; until we come to our senses again, and are shamed by our behaviour. I have seen any number of cases of love in that arbitrary sense, but never even one case of genuine love, and nobody else seems to have seen one either. But what do you think, Monsieur Khozrevsky?'

'I don't know, Princess,' was the reply, 'only it seems to me that if there is a name for something, then that thing must exist.'

'On the contrary,' she rejoined sharply, 'where a word exists, the thing itself very often does not, and vice versa.'

'I don't understand that,' said Khozrevsky, 'and I think it would be difficult to prove.'

'It's not difficult at all,' the Princess went on. 'You'll notice that a nation often has no name for its most fundamental trait. There is no word for *ennui* in English, and so Miss Edgeworth had to use the French word for the title of her novel.° And the French, for their part, have no word for "one-sidedness". The entire nation is so naturally one-sided that they don't even notice it and give no thought to having a word for it.'

A very grand gentleman sitting next to the Princess began applauding with his fingertips, and a young man said, 'Here's another proof of the correctness of your opinion, Princess: Russian has no word for "gracefulness", the prime attribute of Russian woman.'

'But on the other hand,' she replied, 'the Germans have no fewer than *two* words for gracefulness.'

There was a burst of laughter.

'Where are you going?' the Princess asked the grand gentleman, who had just risen from the armchair next to her.

'I am expected over at my club. *Bon soir, chère Princesse.*'

And the other guests took their hats too.

'You're all going to the Elskys,° I suppose?' asked the lady of the house.

'Of course. You too, Princess?'

'No.'

'Where are you going to spend the evening, then?'

'Here, in this room. I don't feel like going.'

'You can't mean that! It would be a crime for you to keep away. Everyone will be there.'

'*Raison de plus*,'° she replied. 'I wish you a splendid evening.'

They went out, and Khozrevsky, making to follow them, bowed to the Princess.

'I expect that you are going to the Elskys' too, Monsieur Khozrevsky?'

'I feel ridiculous in admitting to any resemblance between us, Princess, but if it were not for that, I would tell you that I have no desire to go there either.'

'Then stay here a while. We can have a nice conversation.'

He obeyed. An hour and a half later, when the Princess rang for tea, Khozrevsky was still sitting alone with her in her beautiful study.

If you were to ask me now what Princess Alina liked in Trofim Lukich, I would be forced to reveal a truth that ladies themselves wish to conceal, though I cannot say why, since it can hardly be unknown to anyone. Begging the pardon of members of the fair sex, both present and absent, I have to say that no one is less inclined to feelings of equality than a woman; nothing bores the ladies so much as being on the same moral level as us. Every woman admits to herself that, when she becomes intimate with a man, she wants him to be either much higher or much lower than she; it is only genuinely agreeable to meet a man who surprises her, or one whom she surprises. On the evening when she remained alone with Khozrevsky, the Princess enjoyed the latter pleasure to the full. She had never encountered such naïve wonderment, such simple-minded veneration. And besides, after all the egotistical strivings, the indefatigable ingenuities of her guests, her companion's complete lack of pretension was both soothing and gratifying. The conversation (actually, it consisted almost entirely of a monologue) ran along smoothly. Before her modest listener, the Princess flaunted her talents, her learning, her views on philosophy, her mental profundities, her convictions, her emotions, the strength of her character—the whole of her diverse arsenal. She overwhelmed the poor fellow, bombarding him with her intellectual abundance, blinding him with her brilliance, and stunning him with her enormous superiority. She spoke extremely well, and he sat listening with the same unconditional faith with which pagans would harken to the dicta of the Pythia° or, to be more accurate, with which a child will listen to a fairy-tale. When he emerged on to the street from the Princess's house, Trofim Lukich was smiling complacently.

From that day on, Khozrevsky began to visit the Princess's house as of right; but he made such modest use of that right that a servant would often arrive with a message such as, 'The Princess ordered me to invite you to pay a call this afternoon'; or, 'The Princess ordered me to inform you that she will be at home this evening and wishes to see you.' In the latter case Khozrevsky, appearing in response to the invitation, would usually find the Princess alone, and they would converse just as they had on that first occasion. Once more he would sit before her like a schoolboy in the presence of his teacher, listening as raptly as if he took the lovely widow for one of those strict tutors who keep repeating to their charges, 'Be quiet when you're talking to me!' In the presence of the naïve young man's limited intellectual abilities, the Princess's genius was in the happy position of a beauty at the looking-glass; she saw in Khozrevsky only her own reflection. In this way, several weeks passed. The talk in society was that Princess Alina had been seized by a fit of melancholy. Certainly, she was less often to be seen at the most fashionable balls and receptions. The Princess's doctor said that her nerves were distraught. Since her maids were gossiping in their attics that for some time there had been no pleasing the Princess, a situation that often does symptomize distraught nerves, the doctor was probably right. The Princess herself said that she was terribly bored, something that Moscow society could readily understand. And so everything dragged on as it always does, continuing to continue, with cold and snowstorms outside, and dinners and receptions and rumours and gossip in.

But everything in this world comes to an end, even the Moscow winter. In only two weeks, the whole aspect of earth and sky changed completely. Suddenly, in the way that is typical for our city, the wet snow vanished from the streets and the grey clouds from the sky, and spring, that marvellous improvisation of Northern nature, entered the white stone capital.°

Along with this general transformation came a change in Moscow society's own pastimes; the first warm days were greeted by that time-honoured ceremony, promenading upon the Tverskoi Boulevard.°

One fine morning, the boulevard was bright with the colourful apparel of the fair sex, and the dark vestments of the other, whilst equipages bearing loads of ladies and misses streamed continually towards the long avenue. A marvellous pair of black horses came dashing up, drawing Princess Alina's carriage behind them. Five or six young men who were standing in a knot nearby made haste to bow as her widowed Highness, accompanied by Nastasya Pavlovna, went past their scout corps. Even less than any other woman could the Princess pass without attracting looks from, and stimulating rumours among, these stiff and proper young men.

'How elegantly she dresses!'

'What does she not do elegantly?'

'I'll wager it's all nonsense.'

'What's nonsense?'

'That she's interested in that fool Khozrevsky.'

'Maybe it's nonsense, but it may not be.'

'For Heaven's sake, what could she possibly see in him?'

'That's exactly it. Nothing.'

'That's no reason for her to like him.'

'On the contrary, it's a very good reason: she's been fed on nothing but spiced cake and sweets, and Khozrevsky is like a piece of black bread to her.'

'Bah! The usual Moscow fairy stories!'

'Wismer! Wismer! Come over here. We're quarrelling about a subject close to your heart.'

'And what might that be?' asked Wismer, responding to the call.

'We were talking about your rival.'

'What rival?'

'Khozrevsky.'

'Why should I have the honour of being that gentleman's rival?'

'No pretences. Everyone knows that you're an admirer of Princess Alina!'

'Who does not admire her?'

'They say that she prefers Khozrevsky to you.'

'I say as much myself.'

'But you're chasing after her as hard as you can all the while. You seek her out everywhere; yesterday, at the concert, you never once left her side, and you've certainly come here today hoping to find her.'

'That may be. Is the Princess here?'

'Yes, see, there she is, standing with the Elskys. Holding the pink parasol.'

'Well then, in my character as her devoted admirer, I will go and pay my respects.'

'You're head over heels in love with her, Wismer.'

Wismer smiled, and walked off towards the pink parasol, beneath which the Princess's white hat and light grey dress could be glimpsed.

The scout corps had also begun moving forward, blending into the colourful crowd. Not long afterwards, the glorious dress with its silvery tint, in company with that superb and most conspicuous of hats, the white *chef d'œuvre* of a Parisian milliner, and the pink parasol, could been seen approaching from the opposite end of the boulevard. Beside them, Wismer's swarthy face stood out clearly. He was leaning towards his elegant companion, and conversing animatedly; laughing, she answered him, whilst all the while toying impatiently with her lorgnette, using it to scan the crowd on all sides as though she were seeking or expecting something—deliverance, perhaps.

On one of the numerous little green benches that are set out in rows for the comfort of the public, Khozrevsky was sitting, next to a little old man who belonged to the aristocracy of Moscow, as anyone could see immediately by the way he was leaning on the cane positioned between his legs, nodding to acquaintances, and adjusting his gold-rimmed eyeglasses, and by the arrogant curl of his lips when he spoke. When the Princess first appeared, Trofim Lukich hastily rose from his seat and, as she passed, gave her a bow filled with the most infinite respect. Now the two cousins, with their persistent companion, appeared once more near the benches occupied by the spectators. Wismer was still deep in conversation with the Princess; her eyes, glittering restlessly, suddenly lighted on Khozrevsky, who was approaching her, diffident as always. He was not the man who could help her, if indeed she needed help; if she was looking, at that moment, for a man clever enough to guess that she needed rescue, and capable of rescuing her, the innocent Trofim Lukich had certainly appeared at the wrong moment. She continued to sweep her eyes about as Khozrevsky murmured, in his customary humble tone, 'Excuse me, Monsieur Wismer. I must tell you that I have done something foolish that may displease you.'

Wismer glanced at him, and smiled involuntarily. 'How is that?'

'Excuse my asking,' Khozrevsky went on, 'but did I not hear you say yesterday that you would like to see the Dürer painting that Count Semyon Ignatevich has just brought back with him from abroad?'

'No, I said no such thing.'

'Then I really have done something foolish, and I do beg your forgiveness. I was sure that I had heard you express that wish, and I told the Count so just now. He has sent me to tell you that he would be extremely glad to have your opinion as to whether his painting is in fact an original; the Count is setting off for his Oryol estate later today, and so he begs you to go with him this minute, and take a look at it. The Count is sure that you will agree to give him and yourself that pleasure.'

Wismer went over to the bench, from where the old aristocrat was gazing at him affably, and the Count stood up and took his arm.

Princess Alina looked at Khozrevsky with a strange expression in her lovely eyes, as if his speech to Wismer had outdone the efforts of the world's greatest orators; and she smiled so affectingly that Heaven knows what Nastasya Pavlovna must have thought.

Trofim Lukich, who no doubt had failed to notice the Princess's look of amazement, and did not suppose himself the object of her charming smile, took two more turns along the boulevard with the bewitching cousins, then helped them into their carriage. As he did this, the Princess gave his hand an involuntary squeeze.

He walked home deep in thought. Was he perhaps pondering the reason for that unexpected pressure?

Outside the house, a bright torrential spring rain, as sudden and short-lived as a woman's whim, was pouring merrily. The door from the Princess's study on to her balcony was open, and inside, near the door, the Princess was once again sitting alone with Khozrevsky; this had become an almost daily occurrence. She had seriously applied herself to the task of developing and re-educating him. To be an instrument of enlightenment was for her a new, and therefore an amusing, occupation; and she had begun to see some success in her efforts: Trofim Lukich really was becoming more alert; the education was doing him good. Little by little, the Princess's pedagogical exercises had become as necessary to her as the cigarettes she smoked. If a sluggish Hollander can fill his whole life with fussing over tulips, it is not surprising that the impressionable Princess should have become more and more engrossed by her concern for Khozrevsky. But someone skilled in psychology might have suggested that she was following a direct route to a result that she could not foresee. A certain tender predilection for the works of one's own hand is characteristic of mankind: Pygmalion, that prototype of authors, serves as an example of how far such a natural attachment can go. And ladies, those pre-eminently sentimental beings, are still more gifted with the capacity to acquire a violent interest in the objects of their labours; experience compels us to believe, indeed, that no lady has engaged in the praiseworthy labour of perfecting those around her with impunity. The performance of good deeds is an activity that is fraught with peculiar dangers; not for nothing do the perspicacious French say that 'the road to hell is paved with good intentions'. Was there a degree of danger, in this instance, for Princess Alina? The question apparently never entered her head. Was there any danger in the matter for Khozrevsky? She probably never asked herself this second question either, but that was for another reason; because she had already answered it in her mind *a priori*, and in the positive. That Khozrevsky could not obtain enlightenment without paying a price for it, the Princess considered to be in the natural order of things, indeed inevitable; and certain indications allowed her to assure herself that she was not mistaken in this assumption. At the same time, it would be difficult to say in what way her later conversations with Khozrevsky differed from her very earliest; but in such cases precisely what can *not* be defined is what can be seen most clearly. With each passing day that indefinable thing became clearer, and not only to the experienced Princess, but even to any accidental witness of these sessions. When Khozrevsky's lovely mentor spoke, eloquent as always, the eyes of her student were more attentive than his ears; at times he followed her so assiduously with his gaze that he scarcely heard her at all, and replied completely at random. But the Princess indulgently forgave him his erroneous answers, and took no offence at his distracted state.

Distraction was indeed excusable during the Princess's instruction, and

Trofim Lukich had a worthy object of his admiration. Here she was again, sitting so gracefully amidst her lovely surroundings. Beside her rose a bank of many-coloured, sweet-smelling hyacinths; exotic plants arched their broad leaves over her head. Reposing on a small divan, she was toying with a Chinese fan. She was discoursing on certain strange things that had happened during the reign of Louis XIV, and speaking, in particular, about the terrible Marquise de Brinvilliers.° She recounted the whole of that monstrous history, and the innumerable evil deeds committed by the Marquise, who had used a subtle poison furnished to her by her lover, the depraved Sainte-Croix, in order that she might murder her father, brothers, and sister, and so inherit their estates; the Princess described how the woman had developed a terrible passion for murder, and how she had begun poisoning people for no reason at all; she told Khozrevsky of the death of the villainous Sainte-Croix, and the execution of the Marquise—and of how, suddenly, after her execution, the mysterious poisonings had inexplicably begun again, occurring now in all strata of society, so that fathers began to fear their own sons, and brothers their brothers; and she told him how at last they had tracked down the old woman who had sold the poison, and found, at her home, a register filled with the names of noble personages who had resorted to her terrible art. The Princess recounted her tale masterfully: how well she developed her frightening theme, the capacity of those in cultivated circles to turn to bestial savagery, to feel a growing inclination for evil-doing, and to commit their crimes for pleasure's sake. Khozrevsky sat before her, giving her his deepest attention; he saw how the lace triangle thrown over his teacher's black hair emphasized the marvellous oval of her face, how charmingly she would knit her fine brows from time to time, and how beautiful was the hand that rested on the dark velvet of her pillow.

'And what is most striking in the history of these vile murders', the Princess went on, 'is the view of them held in the society of that time. They called that poison "inheritance powder", *poudre de succession*, which to my mind is a most repulsive manifestation of the national character; and, in exactly the same way, I hold that the most terrible of all the cruel deeds committed during the first French Revolution was the fashion of appearing in society with one finger smeared in blood, not to speak of the establishment of balls *des victimes*. The organization of festivals for the wives, children, brothers, and sisters of those who have been guillotined is an indication of a national character in comparison with which cannibals are to be praised for their morality, is that not so?'

The Princess glanced enquiringly at the motionless Khozrevsky, awaiting his opinion. It was slow in coming. He was deep in thought.

'I think', he said at last, 'that I should spend less time here.'

And he took his hat and went out, forgetting his bow. But the Princess was not offended even by that lapse in good manners.

Later that same evening or, to be more exact, early the following morning—that is, between the hours of two and three—Princess Alina's porter, who had been dozing, was woken by the loud clatter of a carriage, which broke off suddenly just by his own *porte-cochère*. He jumped up from his chair and rushed to open the door. The Princess flashed past him, throwing down her hooded cloak, which the footman who was following her failed to catch before it reached the floor, and ran up the wrought-iron staircase. In the ante-room upstairs, another servant, rubbing his eyes like the first, jumped up as his mistress appeared and, still half-asleep, struggled to grasp her order: 'Light a fire in the study!' The Princess's maid, Marfa Terentevna, who had also been roused by the carriage's noisy approach, hurried into her mistress's bedroom to undress her; but her haste was in vain. The Princess had not gone into her bedroom. The zealous maidservant found this so curious that she ventured to creep up to the study door several times in order to peer at what her mistress was doing. Still in her gauzy evening gown, the Princess was pacing back and forth across the room rapidly, a scowl etched deep on her face. Finally, she seized a candle, went over to the desk, picked up a pen, and started to write. A few minutes later, Marfa Terentevna was almost bowled right over, as the Princess got up, then rushed through the door into the bedroom, and flung the note down on the dressing-table, saying abruptly, 'Have this sent first thing in the morning to Yury Petrovich Wismer. Find out where he lives. They know at the Elskys. Undress me.'

Now more than ever, the course of Marfa Terentevna's duties was to offer her ample and unpleasant proof that her mistress's nerves were distraught.

The spring sun seemed to sense that an interesting scene was building up in the elegant study, so great were its efforts to peek in under the drawn pink curtains. The Princess sat alone, in her usual spot, by a small malachite table.

'Yury Petrovich Wismer,' announced the servant, pulling aside the *portière*.

'Show him in,' said the Princess, and turned to face her visitor.

He came in slowly, and made her a sedate bow. The Princess gestured with her hand in greeting, indicating to him an armchair opposite her *chaise-longue*. He sat down in silence.

'I was forced to ask you to come and see me,' she began by saying. 'You will have received my note.'

He nodded his head in reply.

'Monsieur Wismer.' (This normally so practised society lady was feeling some uncertainty about how best to set in motion the plan that she had worked out in advance for this conversation.) 'Monsieur Wismer, I wanted to ask you how long you intend to go on persecuting me.'

'In what way?' he enquired.

'When I ask a direct question, it would appear to require a direct answer. Intelligent people have no need to pretend; we cannot talk civilly in that way.'

'Civilly!' Wismer repeated, with a strange smile.

'Well, uncivilly, then, if you wish,' she said, looking him straight in the eye. 'But if we are to be enemies, let us at least be honourable enemies.'

'Which is to say?'

'You understand me perfectly well. I cannot take a step without running into you; I have to defend myself from you everywhere, bear your importunate gaze, your indecent meddling in my conversation with others, your oblique insults. Can such behaviour be worthy of a noble person? Is this really what is done in good society?'

'You are right, Princess,' replied Wismer in his pleasant voice. 'In good society things are not done that way. No: barefaced lies, hypocrisy, and innuendoes, shameless manipulation of others' emotions, vile treachery, cold-blooded crime—that is is how things are done in good society, is that not so?'

'Let us put aside Byronism and high-flown rhetoric. I cannot bear phrase-mongering. Let us speak and act simply. I am asking you what your purpose is? What do you want from me?'

'Nothing, Princess, except what I am already achieving.'

'Monsieur Wismer!' Then she checked the angry tide that was rising in her soul. A minute of silence followed.

'You hate me.' And in what a masterful tone this was said, with what skill and grace did she lean back, stretched out in her armchair, so that her whole figure became an expostulation, seeming to end her speech with the words, 'Can you really hate me?'

Wismer cast a glance over that marvellous figure, as he might have looked at one of his models.

'How mistaken a man can be,' he said. 'I assumed that you had invited me to come and see you, Princess, so that you could thank me.'

This was so unexpected that she made an involuntary gesture, something that happened to her extremely rarely.

'To thank you? ...'

'I imagined that you might value all my acts of courtesy towards you.'

The Princess's anger flared; again, she came very close to giving free rein to the feelings that were raging inside her.

'Go on,' she said bitterly. 'Why shouldn't a man insult a woman in every way that he can, why shouldn't he pour mockery and rudeness on her, especially when he knows that he can do so with complete impunity? Go on, I'm curious to learn how far you will go. Take advantage of your opportunity.'

Wismer got up, took a quick turn around the room, came over to the Princess again, and sat down. The ironic smile had disappeared from his face. He bent forward a little, meeting her gaze with a hard gaze; then he began speaking in a different voice, coldly and curtly.

'So it pleases you to settle accounts with me? By all means. Four years ago, the brilliant Princess began toying with the poor artist; she, having nothing better to do, began performing her experiments on him; and all for a simple reason: to amuse herself. It was dull in Rome. There were few people with whom she cared to associate. She seized on the diversion that she had come upon by chance, and gave herself up to the pleasant exercise of driving a man from ecstasy to despair ten times a day, disenchanting him and enchanting him all over again. It's all quite easy to understand, I'm sure you'll agree. She was a mistress in the art of enchantment; besides, she derived enjoyment, and amusement, from practising that art. Then one day he came to see her, pale and in distress, carrying a letter. His mother in Russia was lying on her death-bed, and asking for her son. The Princess sensed an opportunity to make her sport even more amusing, and set about performing new experiments. After all, why give up a game when it becomes most interesting? Perhaps the aristocratic lady would have valued the amusement less had she not received the news that a relative of her own had died; now she must keep to the house for three weeks, and give no parties. However, she found a way to pass the days of her involuntary seclusion without suffering from boredom. She took an oath that she would not permit the son to go to his dying mother—and she kept that oath.'

Wismer paused to draw breath. He spoke with a strange calm and, as he spoke, seemed to become steadily more composed.

'She kept her oath. He was not a bad son; but she was practised in her arts, and applied her utmost efforts to her task. Her artistic inclinations were well developed; the harder the task, the more she enjoyed it. And it was hard; day after day she had to exert all her skill, charming away hour after hour, fascinating him, deceiving him, making a fool of him, driving him mad. But the very effort of it all entertained her. She made scenes, employing every available effect; she swore oaths on all that was sacred. Then, one evening, returning home from a visit, the son found a telegram on his table informing him that his mother had died. The next day, the Princess had trouble handling him, but she was still determined to have her own way. She had to resort to strong measures: she wept (which she could do superbly), she fell to her knees before him and insisted that he must do as she said. But excuse me—there is something else I should mention. Just then, a friend of the man with whom she was toying so charmingly, his only friend, happened to arrive in Rome. His arrival was opportune: the Princess had begun to tire of her game. A new scheme had presented itself, and not a moment too soon. One can easily understand why she did not let that chance slip either. In any case, how can you demand that someone should not make use of his talents? You see, I don't blame her in the least, on the contrary; I find her actions very natural. As I said, she had highly developed artistic instincts, and the drama in the idea of making rivals and enemies of two intimate friends attracted her. Her contrivances were so masterful that only a few weeks later the two friends found themselves standing face to face with pistol in hand, aiming at each other's breasts.° The Princess had reason to be proud of her success. So, the two men came closer and closer, terribly close, and the man who had abandoned his dying mother—it was he who had challenged the other to the duel—fired his pistol at his friend.'

And again Wismer fell silent for a minute, then went on speaking, neither raising nor lowering his voice. The cold intonation of his words made them peculiarly effective.

'The shot found its mark; the friend fell to the ground. But the Princess had made a small blunder: she had failed to grasp how a man may be affected by shedding the blood of a friend, by the very sight of that blood. The murderer flung himself on his fallen antagonist, and his antagonist embraced him closely, clasping him to his wounded breast. God had mercy on the criminal; his friend lived, he was given medical treatment and saved from death; and through his salvation, his murderous rival was saved in his turn. The shot had broken the enchantment; the evil spell was dissipated, as if the thunderous voice of God had spoken. The two friends left Rome together.—But permit me to finish. The first man and the Princess met again. By chance, that man had come into possession of a certain thing that might cause the Princess unpleasantness: a trifling thing, a brief note in her handwriting. Oh, no! not the sort of note that one might suppose... The Princess could never have been accused of lack of caution; she would never, under any circumstances, have been capable of writing anything that might harm her reputation even in the slightest degree. The letter of which I am speaking is a most innocuous document, only four lines of spiteful gossip, in which the Princess very wittily ridicules an old aunt, relating all kinds of hilarious things about the lady. The Princess's ridicule was caustic, since at the time she could afford to laugh at her aunt with complete impunity; after all, even her superb intellect could not have foreseen that this witch, this dried-up old maid, as the letter has it, would turn out to be a person of importance to the Princess; that both the old woman's bachelor brothers would die of cholera and that, as a result, the old aunt would come into possession of a huge estate, which stood to be inherited by the Princess after the death of the aunt. Now, given those entirely unexpected circumstances, one can see that the old letter might become rather dangerous for its author. One could almost guarantee, in fact, that if it were handed over to the aunt, the witty niece would be deprived of her inheritance. But why should the niece be reproached? She hardly deserves it; after all, she could not be expected to guess the future. Now the letter is in the hands of the very man with whom the Princess formerly chose to amuse herself. So permit him to allow himself some small amusement in his turn. You and I have completely exonerated the pastimes of a certain aristocratic lady; let us admit that even a plebeian may occasionally have a fancy for a pleasant diversion. A patrician lady was once seized by a whim to torment a poor man; should that poor man not now be entitled to a whim of his own? His whim is a very modest one: he permits himself to be a small inconvenience to the brilliant Princess, a slight unpleasantness for her, something on the order of a pebble in her shoe. He gets satisfaction from forcing her to endure his presence, his gazes, his respectful bows. She enjoyed the sight of his torments; now he enjoys the sight of her vexation. It is all quite natural. Now I make so bold as to ask what you wish from me.'

The Princess had heard all this out looking directly at Wismer and, frozen in her lovely pose, was leaning against the back of her *chaise-longue*, her arms folded, and half-bared by the broad lace sleeves that cascaded from them. She sat quite motionless; certainly, her little foot may have clenched convulsively in its velvet slipper, but it was hidden by the long folds of her *peignoir*.

'You are not only a good painter, but a remarkable story-teller as well,' she said in well-restrained tones. 'Your story is very effective; indeed, it might vie with the best works of fiction. However, I have the impression that you were attempting more than a display of your talent for authorship; in so far as I can tell, you seem to have had the intention of recounting true facts. If that is so, I am permitted to demand that there be no embellishments. And if I am to suppose that we are not joking...'

'I fancy that we are not,' Wismer said.

'If,' she went on, 'we are now bringing our case to judgement, and are speaking unconstrained by the considerations of propriety, then permit me to ask you this: who made you the judge of another's conscience? Who gave you the right to rummage in another person's thoughts, to interpret his actions? Have you looked into the soul of the woman that you described? Yes, she would not let a son go to his mother; for that, certainly, she may be indicted. But who can know, except she herself, why she tried to hold him back? Was it really a game, or was she swept away by her emotions? Who can decide? You can say: this is what she did, but how dare you say; this is what she thought, what she desired, what she felt? How dare you say that her tears were a lie? She could not resolve to relinquish the company of, the daily meeting with, a man whom she considered her friend. Call that egotism if you like, she will not quarrel; reproach her for behaving thoughtlessly, she will accept your reproach. But what justice is there in making her answer for another's deeds? Shifting one's guilt to someone else is simply a convenient way of appeasing one's own conscience.'

The Princess's voice had altered, become uneven. She was sitting differently in her chair, no longer leaning against the back now; she had lowered her arms, and her eyes glittered.

'You dwell on what she did. She does not expect that you will excuse it; she admits her feminine weaknesses, perhaps she is atoning for them. Did you see her after the duel? Do you know whether she suffered or not? Are you sure that the memory does not torment her to this very day? Are you sure that she does not reproach herself? That she is incapable...'

Wismer rose, picked up an embroidered pillow from the sofa, and placed it at the feet of his interlocutor. 'You will see, Princess,' he said, straightening up again, 'that I am no longer the boor that I was in Rome. I let you fall to your knees before me then, and did not attempt to find a pillow for you.'

She shuddered. The cautious, calculating, sly being of the past had disappeared, leaving only a woman who had been cruelly insulted.

'I did not suppose,' she uttered with trembling lips, 'that you could make the thought that I am partly in your hands a pleasant one for me. But now I wish that not only my wealth, but my life depended on you, for that would allow me to express to you even more effectively how repulsive you are to me; I would find it even more pleasant to prove to you that my repulsion for you outweighs any sense of danger; I would tell you to your face that a man who behaves to a woman as you do to me is worthy of contempt. I can only thank you for so debasing yourself in my eyes.'

'I regret, Princess,' replied Wismer, 'that you have betrayed your usual character, and have let yourself get carried away by anger and impetuosity. Your words are premature, you must acknowledge; you should not have permitted yourself to utter them when you did.'

Saying that, he put his hand in his pocket, and laid on the Princess's little table a thin piece of paper covered with writing.

'This is what you should have waited for. Now you can give free rein to your hatred of me, in perfect safety. I will listen in silence.'

Even before the paper had reached the table, the Princess had recognized the writing; her head drooped involuntarily. They were both silent.

Wismer picked up his hat.

'*Je vous salue, Monsieur,*'° said the Princess indistinctly.

Standing before her, he looked down on the proud aristocrat, who was trying in vain to collect herself; with a formal bow he answered, '*Nous sommes quittes, Madame*!'°

Since this tale is not my own invention, but a true occurrence, which I am relating just as I myself heard it, I must regretfully manage without the convenient omniscience of novelists. I cannot, as they do, read through my characters' fleshly covering into their souls, or see through walls into their locked chambers, or disclose events to which there are no witnesses. What the Princess's thoughts and actions were, alone in her study after Wismer left, I cannot say, and so I am in no position to reveal it to you. I only know that when Khozrevsky came to see the Princess later that same morning with a book he had promised her, he found her pacing rapidly back and forth about the room. On seeing him, she came up to him with such alacrity, and took his hand in such a firm grip that he raised his eyes to look at her, and could not restrain the question, 'But Princess, what can be the matter?'

'Nothing. My nerves are distraught. Sit down,' and she flung herself into her armchair.

'I have brought...' began Trofim Lukich, setting the book down on the table.

'*Merci*,' she interrupted.

Silence followed.

'It is a very clever book, they say,' Khozrevsky began again. 'Not that I have read it myself...'

'Never mind the book!' said the Princess abruptly. 'There's no getting away from cleverness.° It becomes unbearable, a punishment for us!'

'You would not say that, Princess,' her modest visitor permitted himself to object, 'if you sensed a lack of cleverness in yourself.'

'What help is my intellect to me?' she answered brusquely. 'Why should I prize it? No matter how clever I was, would I find any source of support in it? Will it protect me against insult? What benefit do I get from it?'

'That everyone is amazed by you, Princess.'

'And respect me so much the less.'

'How can that be, Princess!'

'Do you really not know that to praise a woman's mind is to abuse her? Is everyone not convinced that where there's cleverness there's no heart? Has it not been decided that a clever woman is a sort of monster who can feel nothing? Ask anyone, they'll all tell you so.'

'But surely no one would dare hold an unfavourable opinion of you, Princess?'

'Indeed? You should try listening to them. Try this: tell them all that I have never known any prompting of the heart, any rush of passion; that I am incapable of disinterested feeling, that I do not understand how anyone could perform a noble act, that I am always and in every thing calculating, that I am a creature without soul and without conscience. Just see whether anyone disputes it. They are all ready to tell me so to my face. Who can prevent them?'

Silence fell again. The Princess tore at the silk tassel of the cord that held her *peignoir* around her slender waist. Khozrevsky looked at her in surprise. She was making a strange impression on him, a new impression; at that minute his liking for her changed in character, becoming, if anything, stronger than before. In her face, her gestures, in the bitter intonation of her voice, there was something attractive and unfamiliar—naturalness. Perhaps for the first time in her conscious life, the Princess was no longer in perfect control of herself; she was no longer observing herself. And for the first time in her life she felt herself to be helpless. The young man—whether he understood the nature of his feelings or not—kept his eyes fixed on this new woman, of whom he knew so little, who was suffering, weak, and in need of his protection.

'Princess,' he said at last, 'you are distraught, and so you are seeing everything in a gloomy light. You cannot complain of your fate; your position is enviable.'

'Very!' she interrupted with a nervous laugh.

'You have everything that can be desired: beauty; all possible gifts and advantages; wealth; freedom.'

'Yes, complete freedom to die from boredom and vexation. Nobody cares a straw about that.'

'Everybody longs to claim you as an acquaintance, a friend.'

'Yes, everyone who enjoys parties and good dinners.'

'All the celebrities in Moscow, all the remarkable and talented people, all the artists, gather around you; and you enjoy their company.'

'Yes! Yes! I do,' she replied, becoming more and more unable to restrain her irritation. 'I enjoy myself tremendously!'

Observing the failure of his efforts to calm her angry Highness, Trofim Lukich fell silent.

'And you hold the same opinion yourself,' said the Princess suddenly, glancing at him; 'you too think that pride and egotism are my only emotions, don't you?'

'Why should you care about my opinion, Princess?' enquired Khozrevsky. 'Can I be your judge?'

'But you do think that. You too find me repulsive,' she went on, gazing into his eyes, though in them she read a clear refutation of that assertion.

'Princess! You cannot mean that seriously,' objected Khozrevsky. 'You know—'

She gave him no chance to finish. 'Oh, God! Yes, I know. You value my talents, my erudition, my intellectual capacities, everything that all the others value; but you too look on me as a brilliant monster, and cannot admit that I have a heart or affections, or anything that distinguishes a woman. Well? Admit it.'

Khozrevsky remained silent. Tears sparkled in her eyes.

'Isn't that so? Tell me, tell me like an honest man.'

'Princess,' he replied, 'you command me to speak according to my conscience: I must obey. I must forget the fact that you will be angry with me, and the effects that anger will have on me. I am not so stupid as to be mistaken in myself; I know that the opinion of a man like me can mean nothing to you; I understand that only a momentary whim has made you demand that I should tell you my honest opinion of you now. Your whim will cost me dearly, but I must submit. Princess! You know my awkwardness;

you know that I cannot express myself as I should. When you require me to speak the truth, I can only do so directly. And so I admit I assumed the general notion about you to be correct.'

'Ah!' exclaimed the Princess.

'You did seem to me too clever,' Khozrevsky went on haltingly. 'It seemed to me that every other quality in you must surely be suppressed by your inordinate cleverness; that, finally, you could not possibly be endowed with all the virtues, could not be perfection itself; that it would be quite impossible to expect in you warmth of feeling, or the customary blind magnanimity of womankind; I thought that you were capable of acting only according to the dictates of intellect and reason.'

'So that is what you think?' asked the Princess, not lowering her gaze.

'I did think that, yes.'

'And now?'

'And now I think that I was mistaken.'

'In what respect?'

'Princess, you understand me perfectly as it is. Do not force me into explanations; I lack the gift of words.'

'But you can at least tell me what you think of me now.'

'To speak of that would be uninteresting for you, Princess; for me it would be painful.'

'But suppose that I want to know?'

'You do know.'

The Princess thought it over. 'And so,' she said after a short silence, 'you assumed that I could only act by calculation, and that I understood only my own advantage?'

'Princess... Of course, I should not have thought it; but people said such things so often in my presence...'

'Yes, all my good friends, my admirers; that's their delightful opinion of me. But you needed no other proof?'

'It is notorious that your marriage was not a love match, Princess.'

'No, I married because I wanted a title,' she replied with a bitter smile. 'That was the general verdict; and also that I toy with everything and everyone, and that anything in me that appears to come from the soul is false! And, as a result of that general verdict, everyone has the right to insult me and abuse me.'

She fell silent again, and settled back in her armchair. The unhappy Khozrevsky did not dare break that menacing silence.

'Princess!' he said at last.

She ignored him.

'Princess!' repeated the young man, not daring to look directly at the angry lady. 'I have ruined myself; I knew what would happen; but you wanted that, and I could only do your will. You ordered me to cut my throat, and I did as you wished.'

The Princess rested her penetrating gaze on him in silence, lost in thought; then suddenly she got up from her armchair.

'Very well,' she whispered. 'I'll show them. They'll see, they'll see, perhaps it won't be what they expected... and then perhaps... we'll see.'

Trofim Lukich took his hat, not knowing what he should do. 'Princess!' and, raising his humble eyes to her, the poor man added, 'I see that you cannot forgive me; I understand that. I am banished from your house. It is all over for me.'

'Khozrevsky,' she said, extending her hand to him, 'come and see me this evening.'

As he approached the Princess's house that evening, Trofim Lukich stopped, then turned down the next street along, needing to calm his throbbing heart. He walked up and down the pavement ten times from end to end; his abstraction was so striking that passers-by turned to look at him. But the numbers of passers-by on Moscow streets are not large, and Khozrevsky was not distracted by them. The Princess's words, 'Khozrevsky, come and see me this evening', could mean something extraordinary; but they could also mean nothing, as was infinitely more likely. The poor man had not spent time in the best society for nothing. He had suffered many cruel insults and bitter experiences. In the early days of his intimacy with the bewitching Princess, he had kept telling himself, with no hint of vexation, as something completely simple and natural, that he could never mean any more to her than the parrot, his rival, which, like him, also occupied her idle moments, and which she petted with as innocent an affection as she did Trofim Lukich; no, Princess Alina could never, even for a single moment, have the feelings for Trofim Lukich that woman has for man. One may suppose that he was telling himself the same thing now, but in a spirit of utter dejection. Between those early days, when he had serenely recognized his insignificance in the eyes of the proud beauty, and this present hour of timid recollection, had any sense of dazzling possibility ever flashed through his mind? Had he ever dreamed of a wealthy home where he might be master, freely entering the study of its lovely mistress, calling her by name, 'Alina'? Had a sly imp ever whispered in his ear that axiom of Prince Talleyrand's, '*Tout arrive*'?° It was difficult to tell.

But it was easy to guess that Khozrevsky was not listening to some imp's insolent mephistophelean whisper now; he was hearing the naïve speech of a young heart, afraid to read meaning into that fateful phrase, 'Khozrevsky, come and see me this evening'; a heart that was trying to stand firm, not daring to comprehend that the Princess might be in that state of mind in which women carry out astonishing acts and reckless exploits.

In a high state of agitation, Trofim Lukich mounted the stairs of the princely home; some two hours later, down he came again, still more agitated now, and with the appearance of a man to whom Heaven knows what has happened.

What had happened was that the Princess had said, 'Khozrevsky! You love me and dare not show it. You are a good man—I am yours.'

And along Tverskoi Boulevard, through the salons and the clubs, ran the rumour that Princess Alina was betrothed to Khozrevsky, greatly engaging Moscow society, for want of any other news. The rumours were various; but the joy at finding something to talk about was unanimous.

'Alina has acted splendidly,' Nastasya Pavlovna replied in answer to an old lady whom she had met in a shop selling Russian wares. 'She has demonstrated that she knows how to value the love of a worthy man and that she places deep feeling above all else. I approve her action without reservation; this is her reply to the accusation that she has no heart. Her passion is a noble one, and she will not repent it. Khozrevsky deserves his happiness.'

In another room of the same shop, three young ladies were buying embroidery thread and whispering. 'You know that she's marrying him because her aunt ordered her to?'

'Yes, I heard that too. So it's true?'

'It's true. The old woman is absolutely mad about Khozrevsky; she told the Princess that she would disinherit her if she chose another husband. So what could she do? They say she's looking very thin.'

'Well, she's certainly found herself a fine catch, I must say!' exclaimed a young husband, sitting at dinner tête-à-tête with his wife, and helping himself to a large slab of rare roast beef. 'Just imagine, she's head over heels in love with him; they say she even proposed to him herself. Well, it's a remarkable choice she's made! There's feminine genius for you!'

'She couldn't be acting more cleverly,' was the view of a rich tax collector, expressed over cards at his club. 'There's a double advantage in it for her: she gains a fool of a husband who won't interfere in anything she does, and an estate manager who won't steal, at one and the same time. She's a woman of astonishing judgement!'

'It is a real romance,' a lady in her middle years informed her guests as she poured the tea. 'They say that Khozrevsky came into her study with a loaded pistol, and threatened to shoot himself before her very eyes, and she was so delighted that she agreed to become his wife on the spot!'

'I can't believe it,' said one of her guests. 'A vulgar trick like that would never fool Princess Alina; she could never have yielded to it.'

'But listen,' replied his hostess, 'suppose that Khozrevsky really did mean to shoot himself? Can we rule that out?'

'I would not put it past him at all,' remarked another guest. 'He is quite stupid enough.'

'His stupidity has served him well, though, when you think how he's come up in the world,' a clever man put in.

'*Mon cher*,' cried a haughty dandy, in the midst of lighting a cigar as he left the Troitsky tavern with a bevy of companions, '*C'est tout simplement une envie de se jeter par la fenêtre; maladie de femme*.'°

On a warm May evening, Marfa Terentevna was in the Princess's dressing-room, filling trunks and boxes with superb *toilettes*. The Princess had decided that she should be married at her estate; they were due to leave for there on the following day. Marfa Terentevna, as she busied herself with the necessary preparations, was quite out of sorts; having an aristocrat's soul lodged in her serf's body, she disapproved of her mistress's *mésalliance* more fiercely than anyone else, and now she was giving vent to her disapproval by muttering under her breath. The worthy serving-woman was in the bitter grip of an *idée fixe*; she saw herself, thanks to the Princess's ignoble whim, reduced from a silk dress to a peasant sarafan.° Meanwhile, the object of Marfa Terentevna's grumbles was sitting in her study, alone with Khozrevsky. Trofim Lukich appeared to be deep in thought; certainly, he was even more silent than usual; but no doubt that was how the feeling of happiness manifested itself in him, as it does in many lower organisms. The Princess was reading aloud, as she did in almost every tête-à-tête with her betrothed. That evening, she was acquainting him with George Sand's novella *Simon*,° which also concludes with a rather eccentric marriage. She read with animation, admiring the energetic character of Fiamma as if it were her own portrait.

'What a masterful sketch of a woman!' said the delightful bride-to-be, interrupting her reading, 'and what a true understanding of noble, honest love, of respect for oneself and for another! What are you thinking about?' she asked the silent Khozrevsky.

'About a great deal, Princess.'

'Can you not confide in me even a little of that great deal?'

'I am thinking about you, Princess.' (She smiled.) 'I am thinking', he went on, 'that you may be much better than I am.'

'In looks?' she asked, laughing.

'In every way,' he replied, quite seriously.

'If that's the way things are,' she retorted gaily, 'there's nothing to be done. You must bear your misfortune with fortitude.'

He rested his gaze on her; at that moment she was so charming.

'Princess,' he said suddenly with resolve, 'I have a duty that I must carry out.' He fell silent, then began speaking again. 'Once before, you demanded that I speak the truth, and I saw that you were capable of hearing it. I must not hide it from you now.'

The Princess gazed at his face, then set the book down on the table.

'We must be perfectly honest in our relations with each other,' Khozrevsky went on.

Once again there was a moment of silence.

'I am listening,' she said.

Khozrevsky gazed at her with a strange look on his face. 'You have done what was was not expected of you,' he said, and his voice had an unusual note. 'You chose me, who had none of the qualities that make people distinguished in the world: neither wealth, nor noble birth, nor influence in society. You showed much unselfishness in that. But that is not all; you acted in a still more extraordinary way when you decided to become the wife of a man whom everybody called stupid. You yourself must be convinced that I am a complete simpleton. But you are mistaken in that, Princess, just as everyone else is. I myself decided that I would pass for a fool; I have made every effort to encourage that opinion of myself, and it has taken a good deal of cleverness to do it.'

The Princess fixed a gaze of astonishment on him, and he went on.

'Hear me out. I must tell you about many things of which you are unaware. For you, the word "need" suggests an idea at once vague and fluid. You cannot grasp the exact meaning of the word; indeed, only those crushed under its weight know that. There are a great many such people. The plight of those who must struggle day after day, and exhaust themselves, finding no help anywhere, is a stale topic—one which cultivation makes us consider shameful—and we talk as little as possible about such things, the more so since talking about them is quite useless; it simply bores people. As a child, I racked my brains over the business of finding daily bread for me and my widowed and impoverished mother; with that idea always in my head, I sat in school from morning until evening, then worked all night at my books, applying myself to my task with an iron will, and sacrificing my health, to gain knowledge that proved useless to me. My situation was utterly banal, no different from that which overtakes hundreds of thousands of others. Everything followed its natural order; gifted with intelligence and understanding, with an education that had developed my abilities, and a readiness to work until I collapsed, to take up any kind of thankless and painful work, at 20 I stood face to face with destitution, and could see no salvation.

'I don't know how I can make you understand, even in part, the inner state of a man for whom, day and night, waking and sleeping, at work or at rest, the same question is always buzzing in his head: "How shall I manage? Where can I turn?" Just imagine being told, on the very day of a magnificent ball to which you have been looking forward for months, that the marvellous gown that you had ordered, and which had been meant to eclipse the apparel of all your rivals, will not be ready; imagine that you have no other gown that you could possibly wear to the ball, and that it is essential to you that you go; imagine how you would ask yourself ceaselessly, "What am I to do?" Of course, I hope that you will never suffer any such misfortune, but I have to invoke such a possibility, since that is the only means of making my story at least partially comprehensible to you.

'I was born in a *guberniya*° capital, and in all probability should have expected to die there, having no relations who could smooth my way for me, and no other source of support. It was imperative that I find such a source; I had to seek patronage. See, Princess, every minute I have to use words that you must find mysterious. You only know how to give patronage, how it is sought, Princess. But how people wait in the ante-rooms, then haltingly make their pleas, to hear always the same curt answer, that, "regrettably, there is nothing to be done"; and then, after receiving that answer, how they must make their bow, and then leave the room, walking past the insolent footmen sprawling on chairs in the hall, forced to bear their impudent smiles, and then return to their poor hovel, to face their expectant mother, who has still not broken herself of the habit of hoping—this is what *I* know.

'By now I had begun to understand where the problem lay, and what my greatest misfortune was—a misfortune to which I had been condemned from birth. In my first school, the boys, their spite inspired by the fact that I was a better student than they, would grin and call me "the bright boy". That was my nickname at school, too; everyone picked it up and used it as a term of abuse. I could not conceal my disdain for my schoolmates' ignorance; it gave me pleasure that I, the poorest of all, should be first in every class. And having forced them to yield to me, day after day, over several years, having, by dint of my diligence and good behaviour, compelled my teachers constantly to hold me up as an example and to praise me, having conclusively demonstrated my intellectual and moral superiority to everyone I knew—I then, in my naïvety, would go and petition their fathers to be my protectors, to put in a good word for me, to give me a place.

'An elderly bachelor whom I often went to see, a lawyer, was the first to make me understand all this. My late father, in the days of his prosperity, had helped this old man a great deal; and now he in his turn considered it his obligation, should he ever run into me, to invite me over to visit him, and to take tea with him.

'"You know, my boy," he said to me once, on an occasion when he was carrying out the duty that his conscience had laid upon him (this was a day when I had, incidentally, said farewell to yet another hope for the future), "you'd best not fret yourself so. Nothing will come of all this; you'll never have any luck."

'"It does seem so, Matvei Artemevich," I said sadly.

'"You'll never make it, my dear fellow," he went on. "You're not the right sort, you know. You're very clever, and you flaunt your brains. More brains than sense, that's you; or you'd have guessed what to do by now."

'"So what should I do?," I asked.

'"Remember that fairy-tale?" he replied. "The one that starts 'Once upon a time there were three brothers; the elder two were clever boys, but the third was a fool'?"

'"Yes," I said bitterly, "and the fool was the lucky one. When I was a child, I would get angry when I listened to that story, and I never believed what it said; but now I've been forced to."

'The old man looked at me from behind the samovar, with a cunning look in his sharp old eyes.

'"But was Ivanushka really such a fool? He was making fools of other people, but he had sharp enough wits himself, didn't he? He was only pretending to be stupid, surely? He'd caught on that that was the surest way, hadn't he? That's no idle tale, my boy; if you once took its moral into account, things would start to go better for you, and you could get yourself off the rocks. Cleverness is all very well for the rich, but it doesn't become us poor fellows. I tell you, my boy, that's how it is."

'I took his words to heart. I thought things over for a few days, and came up with an irrefutable axiom: when a man demonstrates he is cleverer than most people, he also demonstrates that most people are stupider than he. And that helped me grasp something rather simple and obvious—that this demonstration of superiority is unlikely to inspire most people with any great enthusiasm, or any particular affection for the man who has contrived it. Discovery followed on discovery; I grasped that, if it is unpleasant for us all to feel that we stand lower than others, it is, conversely, more than moderately pleasant to feel that we stand higher; we cannot say to ourselves, "Why, the poor man is so stupid!" without satisfaction, since that proposition is inevitably accompanied by another: "That means that *I* am clever." And at that point I realized that people are instinctively well disposed towards those who afford them that satisfaction, and feel an involuntary benevolence for them; and I repeated to myself the old man's words, "That's how it is."

'But all these discoveries and logical conclusions led nowhere. For me everything was over. No matter what I might do, no matter to what boundless humility I might condemn myself, no matter what vow of unconditional obedience I might impose on myself, matters could not be mended; the general opinion of my character was firmly fixed. There is nothing more unshakeable in the entire universe than public opinion in a small city. Khozrevsky was an insufferable, an unworthy, a dissolute, a malicious, and a dangerous man; so much was decided, so much was immutable. Everyone pitied the mother to whom God in his wrath had given such a son.

'There is nothing strange and nothing new in all this. It is a question of variations on the plot of *Woe from Wit*.° The chief variation was a dispiriting one for me, however. No matter how people cursed Chatsky, he never went hungry; and that seemed to me a significant difference between him and me. He left his enemies behind; I had nowhere to go.

'And so a year went by—that's quickly said! I had to find some way of avoiding imminent disaster, I had to think of something: there was nothing to be thought of. As I sat at night in my dark cubby-hole, straining my wits to futile exertions, a certain old fable became a terrible truth; I saw before me the living Sphinx, as she appeared to Oedipus; her eyes glared ferociously into mine, as she insisted: "Solve the riddle, or I shall tear you to pieces!" The riddle was this: how might one find some reliable way of furnishing an indigent man with sustenance? That is the riddle over which our entire generation labours in vain, and over which successive generations will labour in vain.

'One morning, Matvei Artemevich came to see me with a proposal: would I like to make a little money for myself by carrying out a simple commission? The errand in question was that I should take a stack of papers to a rich landowner at his nearby estate; I was to acquaint him with their contents, and explain anything else that might need explaining, and then bring back the landowner's reply to Matvei Artemevich. At the time the old man had nobody at hand capable of the task except me, so I could do both of us a good turn by undertaking it. I agreed joyfully, and set out that same day.

'You will know the name of the man I was going to see; it was Count Nikanor Glebovich Kholkovsky. You may have run into him abroad. You will know that he was brought up in Paris, and spent his youth there, and that he married a Frenchwoman. He visits Russia only occasionally, when he cannot avoid it. On this occasion, he was repaying his debt to his native land by appearing there in order to collect the quit-rent from his three thousand souls,° and was hoping to spend the shortest possible time in the country before leaving for Paris once more. He had left his wife in Petersburg, and was making a tour of his estates in the company of his 10-year-old son, Count Kholkovsky, a most amiable child, who, though he could not pronounce his own name, looked with great pity on all the unhappy souls deprived of the right to call themselves, as he did, *le comte Kolkonsky*.

'I arrived at the count's estate late one evening, and reported to its owner the next morning. Count Nikanor Glebovich is known for his exquisite sense of good form, and for his impeccable manners. He treated me most affably and, having glanced briefly at the papers I had brought, asked me if I would leave them with him for the moment, and do him the honour of spending two or three days at his house, so that he would have a chance to make a thorough study of the matter, before giving me his considered answer. Then he invited me to share his luncheon, and began discussing all kinds of subjects. I noticed that he had something of a passion for oratory, and realized that it would not at all become me to interrupt the flow of his eloquence. He was evidently very pleased by my modesty, asked me about my studies, putting me through my paces a little, and ended the conversation by announcing that he greatly liked my turn of mind, and that, if he had only made my acquaintance a few days earlier, he would have asked me to agree to act as his son's tutor and travel abroad with the family; but, unfortunately, he could not offer me the position now, since he had already come to an agreement with another young man, whom he was expecting from Moscow at any moment.

'When I had left the Count's study, I wandered for a long time around the vast park, deep in painful meditation. Another failure, another malicious trick of fate! If only I could have received that commission and met the Count a week earlier! It would have been my salvation, it would have given me the opportunity to provide for my mother, to lead a life of ease, to go abroad, to see Paris and Italy! It all could have happened so easily! But now this was never to be, because I had come five or six days too late! I could not shake off these bitter thoughts; they stirred in me anew with each step that I took, with each glance that I cast around: what a park! what a house! Comfort, a life amidst all the appurtenances of wealth, all the things that I had never dared to imagine for myself—and all this, as it now seemed to me, had been taken from me for ever! I spent a sleepless night.

'The next day, over dinner, I was to encounter the innocent cause of my sorrow, the new arrival with his degree from Moscow University, the happy man who was to travel with the Count's family. I have rarely met anyone with such an attractive appearance, such a clever and pleasant face. He and the Count struck up a very lively conversation, touching on all kinds of learned topics. The tutor spoke exceptionally well; he refuted the Count's opinions to great effect, whilst brilliantly demonstrating the correctness of his own. I was in no mood to compete with him, and sat listening in silence. I was ashamed that I was giving such an unfavourable account of myself; I tried to suppress the thoughts that weighed on my mind and take part in the conversation, but with no success.

'In the evening, sitting with us on the terrace, the Count once again tried to prove to us that Hamlet could not have been speaking of him when he affirmed that there were more things in heaven and earth than are dreamt of in philosophy. Count Nikanor Glebovich's hobby-horse was his own exact understanding of everything in the world. From psychology he turned—with amazing deftness—to politics, and from there to differences in national characters, and thence to the innate hatred that nation feels for nation. Speaking of the hostile feelings that all Frenchmen nurture for the English, he pointed to the song "Malbrouck s'en va-t-en guerre" as a remarkable manifestation of that feeling. Such mockery of the Duke of Marlborough was a most characteristic manifestation of the spirit of the French rabble, and was totally in accordance with the national character. And to this the Count added a few remarks about the profound meaning and significance of folk-songs.

'When he had finished speaking, the young Muscovite replied that he would permit himself only to object that the song "Malbrouck s'en va-t-en guerre'' was in no sense French, not at all ironic, and that it had nothing to do with the Duke of Marlborough; that, as had been recently demonstrated, it was derived from an ancient Spanish poem borrowed from the Moors, a song about a knight who had received the popular nickname "El Mambru", in Old French "Le Mambru", a word signifying a strong, powerfully built man, which had later become corrupted to "Malbrouck". He referred to the content of the forgotten ending of the song, and to the fact that a Spanish woman, Louis XIV's wet-nurse, had lulled him to sleep with it and so made it known in France; only the textual distortions that had come with time, and the ignorance of the French themselves, had caused this simple Moorish poetry with its mournful tune to be taken, later on, at the court of Marie Antoinette, for a Parisian satirical song—which might, of course, be described as something of a blunder. All this the young man explained superbly well, with great tact and propriety. But, having heard him out, the Count said offhandedly, "*C'est bien possible,*"° and rang for tea, after which we went our separate ways.

'I spent the hours until midnight walking up and down the dark avenue of limes and along the terraces. This was the last time that I would be able to enjoy this lovely garden and breathe the clean air freely. Tomorrow I would have to go home, back to my stuffy back street, to my crowded room, to constant worry about every crust of bread, and all the other aspects of my unbearable existence. And to cap it all, I was nagged by the overwhelming awareness of how close I had come to having a chance to escape from all this. My heart grew heavier and heavier. Good Lord! some people really were lucky, and not just fools. That young man was one; his studies, his hard work, had not been in vain, his labour had not been wasted, nor his cleverness proved useless; he had found people who appreciated him. And what a stupid fellow I had seemed beside him, and all at the very moment when I could least afford a false step! If I had displayed a little of my own learning, perhaps the Count would have recommended me to his acquaintances; that had been my only chance to get somewhere, and I had let it slip—there would be no other. It was painful to think of.

'I spent the next morning alone with the Count, having a final discussion of the business on which I had been sent to him. When everything concerning the affair had been said and all had been decided, the Count suddenly turned to me and said, "Do you want to come with me? I've dismissed the young man we had dinner with yesterday. I can't bear gentlemen who know everything better than others and want to be cleverer than everybody else. People with such a high opinion of themselves are unbearable. I noticed your modesty, and it pleases me; in fact, you please me very well on the whole. I can offer you a life of ease and a salary of a thousand silver roubles a year, which, I may say, is more than I intended paying. Think it over, then give me your answer. I shall be most grateful to you if you agree." And with that he shook my hand, and I left the study, stunned by the thought that everything I had dreamed of had suddenly fallen into my hands, and all thanks to the ditty "Malbrouck s'en va-t-en guerre".

'I walked without heeding where I was going, feeling the need to escape to some distant spot, away from other people. I crossed the entire park, a field, a copse; there, in the wilderness, I sat down and began to come to my senses, and ponder the course of events.

'I understood what had happened; it wasn't difficult to grasp. The Count, like many others, Counts and non-Counts alike, wanted to employ as tutor for his son a man without gifts, without character and opinions, without talent or abilities. The Count wanted to be a Count in an intellectual sense as well as a social sense; he could not bear the thought that those who surrounded him might be superior, and he felt an innate repulsion towards cleverness in others, as some people are repelled by cats or spiders. I understood what I was condemning myself to if I decided to remain with him. The condition was to renounce an essential right of humanity, the right to the expression of my thoughts; I would have to deny myself intelligent communication with other people; I would have to hide, as if it were something disgraceful, all that was best in me, everything of which I could be proud; I would have to display myself to all I knew as an ignoramus, and bear their flagrant disdain; I would have to buy myself a secure existence at the cost of my moral dignity. I had been given a few hours in order to think about this proposition, and decide whether to accept it or not.

'You already know that I did accept it; to confess this to you is perhaps no less painful to me now than it was to decide on my humiliation in the first place.

'In that moment, one on which my entire future depended, my thoughts became strangely lucid, as happens in times of great danger. I grasped all life's practicalities; I pondered everything, weighing it coolly and dispassionately. Could I subdue misfortune by my own efforts and make my way in the world? Yes, you can be born in the provinces, without social advantages, with an outlandish name such as Trofim Lukich, you can be an impoverished orphan without a single protector, and yet despite all that win yourself a reputation and prosperity, forcing people to make way for you against their will. A man of genius can do that; many such men have done so, and many are doing so now. But I was no genius; I had only my intellect, and a reasonably good education. That is not enough; if you are to rise to the top, having only those qualities, you must also abandon your honour. I could not bring myself to become a rogue. There remained only poverty, poverty lasting until the end of my life, as I had known it from the beginning. The gentlemen who make a pleasant pastime of talking about those in need soothe their sensibilities with the consolation that habit eases the most painful situations. But those compassionate gentlemen are mistaken. One cannot become accustomed to torment; the longer it continues, the worse it becomes. You have no doubt heard that a drop of water falling every second on a man's head is the most terrible torture that exists. Need dripped constantly, unbearably, on my head. There are, certainly, examples of people who have borne torture without weakening in spirit; but the strength of others gives out, their will grows exhausted, and at last they give in. Galileo renounced his convictions; I renounced my intellectual significance. I agreed to cut out the tongues of my thoughts and feelings. I thought of my mother; I was being offered a way to save her, and give her a life of tranquillity. She was never to realize what I had traded for that life.

'I spent three years in the Count's home, without my resolve once wavering. At first things were difficult; later, though, they became easier. I became adapted to my role, and began to act it with skill. I disciplined myself so that I could see on the the face of everyone who spoke to me the imprint of the thought: "How stupid he is!"—and see it without vexation. I found it amusing to dupe others, and mislead them into complacent smiles. I realized that the people who live in Paris and London were just like the people in the town where I was born, and that it pays to give way before others' self-esteem, wherever you are. I learned by experience that people extend a helping hand only to those whom they can look down on. The Count continued to be delighted with me, and became a tireless protector to me. When his son had moved on into the care of others, he obtained me another position, and procured me the patronage of influential people. From the moment when I ceased to distinguish myself, I began to gain a reputation as a man distinguished by his amiability. I became convinced of the truth of Matvei Artemevich's opinion, that this was the "surest way"; and so I continued to play Ivanushka the fool.

'I am not making excuses for myself. Perhaps I would have found another means of salvation if I had had the firmness of character to wait for it. It would have been more worthy of a man who respects himself to refuse the comforts of a humiliating life, to refuse to give in, and to struggle manfully with misfortune; it would have been nobler to take up day-labour, to break rocks on the highway. More than once I have felt so much, and I feel it more bitterly now than I ever did before; I never expected that I might have to stand before a woman who was prepared to sacrifice to me all the advantages which she had been taught to value. No, I did not foresee that. You must understand what it costs me to admit to an act that borders on the shameful. I have condemned myself to this admission, to this most difficult, but most honourable act; this confession is a great punishment that I have laid on myself, by means of which I settle accounts with my conscience.'

Khozrevsky fell silent, and remained sitting as he had been before, trying to master himself; he glanced at the Princess as if there were something else he wanted to say, but he said nothing. The Princess also sat in silence. Two or three long minutes passed. The Princess raised her head.

'I will give you my answer tomorrow,' she said, and stood up; then she rang the bell.

A servant came in, and Khozrevsky left.

The next morning Khozrevsky was given a narrow pink note which contained only two lines: 'I cannot bring myself to be the wife of a man who is so skilled in the art of deception.'

He read those words once, then again, and then burst into loud laughter.

'It serves me right,' he said, throwing the letter down on the table. 'For once I have committed an act of stupidity; rather than keeping my intellect on its leash, I have directly expressed what was in my heart.'

Having got to the end of his long story, Aleksei Petrovich contentedly sipped the dregs of his cold cup of tea.

'So what happened after that?' enquired the lady of the house. 'We're all waiting for the ending.'

'I regret that I must leave your expectations unsatisfied,' said Aleksei Petrovich. 'I cannot give you any ending; neither Khozrevsky, nor Wismer, nor Princess Alina went to an early grave, nor did she marry either one of them.'

'So what is your story supposed to prove?' asked the Countess.

'Absolutely nothing,' he replied.

'Do you think', she went on, 'that if it had been the other way around, and a woman had been in Khozrevsky's place, and a man in the Princess's, he would have acted differently?'

'I don't know,' said Aleksei Petrovich.

(*September 1859*
Dresden)

Translated by Diana Greene and Mary Zirin

◆ SOFYA SOBOLEVA ◆

Soboleva, who wrote under the androgynous pseudonym 'V. Samoilovich', was born in 1840 at Schlüsselburg, near St Petersburg, where her father was an engineer working on the construction of a lock. Until she was 8 years old she was educated at home, but the formative period of her life was spent at Madame Kamerat's *pension* in St Petersburg; she was later to remember both the school and its owner with great affection. She began publishing in her early twenties. 'Pros and Cons', one of her earliest stories, was written whilst she was employed in the editorial offices of *Otechestvennye zapiski*. Forced to support herself after the breakdown of her marriage to a middle-ranking civil servant, Soboleva worked as a private teacher. From 1867 she turned to writing for children, and involved herself in the publication of several early children's journals, including *Semeinye vechera* and *Detskoe chtenie*. Although her children's fiction enjoyed the esteem of critics and readers alike, Soboleva's financial circumstances remained difficult, particularly since she spent every available copeck on caring for and educating a large brood of poor children whom she had adopted; she died in 1884 almost penniless.

Pros and Cons: The Thoughts and Dreams of Madame Court Counsellor Lisitsyna°

I

Before I begin, I should warn my readers that I am generally considered an emancipated woman, a progressive in fact. I ought to say a few words to try to explain how I might have come by that title. At one time of my life, I appeared to be nothing more or less than a run-of-the-mill Russian noblewoman, the wife of Monsieur Court Counsellor Lisitsyn... but, no, that is not what I should be saying, I had better begin at the beginning, and tell you everything that happened in the right order.

I was born on the family estate belonging to my *maman*; with (as an old-fashioned novelist might have put it) all the good fairies in attendance. My papa was a man of substance, and the moment of my arrival was one at which fortune smiled on the world at large: for in those days, the fairy of propriety and order held unchallenged sway. What marvellous times those were! Girls were not brought up at all in the way that they are now. It would have been considered quite improper enough to have ideas in the first place; to get excited about ideas, or perturbed by them, would have been unthinkable. Why, I myself never heard my mother give voice to a single idea which she had not picked up when reading some novel or other; and I have more than a suspicion that even my father's intellectual life largely subsisted on material which he had gleaned in the course of his brief duties in the public service (as a young man, he had held a post as an excise officer in the section dealing with duty on alcohol).

No, indeed, things were very different in those days. The literary magazines were full of fictions distinguished by a most exquisite refinement,° in which one might learn of the adventures experienced by noble ladies and officers of the guards, or make the acquaintance of countesses and dark, handsome young princes. It was not then at all the thing to write of *moujiks russes*;° the usual story would have run something like this. Vladimir and Olga, two delightful young people living somewhere or other, are madly in love with each other. But for some reason or other, there are obstacles to their marriage, which unravel themselves in the course of three instalments. The fourth and final instalment concludes with their joyous nuptials, or else with one of the partners dead as the result of some tragedy, and the other left inconsolably lamenting his (or her) demise for the rest of his (or her) life. In order to ensure that the novel shall be properly instructive, some material from Russian history is also woven into the story—usually in an artfully distorted form, of course, as befits a work of *belles-lettres*. The ladies occupy themselves with embroidery, the latest fashions, and with various household occupations; the gentlemen are all engaged in the public service. The young ladies have their days taken up with fashions, as well as their beaux in the Guards; occasionally they find time for a little playing of the pianoforte, or singing; or perhaps they may do a little embroidery. Every self-respecting *maman* thinks it proper that her daughter should wear tight stays.

Well, as I told my readers earlier, those were the days when propriety held sway, and when everything kept to its place. The men wore their hair neatly cropped, and no duty constable dared to set foot outside his booth. Each man kept serenely to his own business, and none of the women had anything to do with talk of emancipation, God forbid! Why, if I had undertaken to compromise myself in that manner, my papa would have been the first to cast me off, and then I should never have married my present husband, Monsieur Court Counsellor Lisitsyn.

I spent all my childhood in the country, surrounded from my earliest days by a veritable regiment of little Matryoshkas, Katyushkas, Varyushkas, and Dashkas.° I now find it difficult to guess at the purpose of my own existence in those days; but from the moment I could reason at all I knew very well what Katyushka, Dashka, and the rest had been put on this earth for. My nurse, Astafevna, indoctrinated both me and them with the belief that the entire purpose of their lives was to keep their young mistress amused; they were to make sure that she was never bored, or tearful; they were to stop her from throwing tantrums, or trying to bite and scratch other people. And Nanny Astafevna herself believed, the simple soul, that God had made her, too, to do her young mistress's every wish, and cater to her every whim. So strongly did she believe this, in fact, that she had not one possession in the world which she accounted her own—she believed that her shoes, her clothes, her thoughts, her feelings, the cups of tea of which she was so fond, were all the property of her masters, which they most graciously allowed Nanny to use; even her very devotion to them was their property...

My early upbringing took place according to a system of the most elegant simplicity. I was allowed to do whatever I liked; and I needed no encouragement to make use of my rights in this matter, as you may well imagine. Nanny Astafevna's sole instructions were to make sure that I stayed in one piece, and that nobody tried to thwart me. The rest was left to nature. And nature was treated by me with no particular ceremony; in summer I would feast on cucumbers, gooseberries, and raspberries in the garden—without, it should be said, any apparent detriment to my health. In winter, I stayed in my nursery, with my suite of Dashkas and Katyushkas in tow, playing all kinds of silly games, and giving free rein to my temperament, which inclined in any case to boisterousness and egotism.

My *maman* had no time to concern herself with me. She was still quite young in those days; her looks were rather handsome, and she played a not inconsiderable role in local society. Our village was around twenty miles from the chief town in the *guberniya*;° we had a large acquaintance, who were for ever holding parties, dinners, and balls. My mother expended untold efforts on ensuring that her *toilettes* would be smarter and more fashionable than any other lady's in the *guberniya*—most particularly, than those worn by the wife of the governor himself. I can leave you to judge for yourselves the trouble which my mother had to take over her appearance; and then there were her domestic duties, to which she had to devote some part of the day, whether she liked it or not. Where should she have found the time to occupy herself with me? There are no more than twenty-four hours in a day, after all! However, I am quite persuaded of the fact that she loved me both warmly and deeply; later on, indeed, she was to show me as much, to the best of her abilities. The point is, you see, that there were quite different attitudes to many things then, not least to upbringing. If a child had no obvious bruises and was not complaining of headaches, then he must be doing well, and praise the Lord for that! What more could one expect for him?

But all the same, when I reached the age of 8, my mother did come to the conclusion that I probably ought to be given some schooling. In those days the done thing was for wealthy people to employ a foreign governess; and so they sent away to Moscow for one, and soon a big fat Swiss woman, looking for all the world like a drum major from the army, rolled up on our doorstep. For all her height and weight, though, she found me more than she could deal with. Here I ought to confess that I was a wilful and boisterous young chit, who was not above being spiteful at times. But I did have one saving grace: never, from my earliest youth, did I ever lie or attempt to deceive anyone, no matter what the provocation. I simply did not understand the meaning of the words 'lies' and 'deceit'. Even now, when I look back over a long life, during which I have often had occasion to make the close acquaintance of the human heart, I feel a terrible sense of oppression as I scrutinize the sad comedy of human manners. Why is it that people strive to deceive each other, to cheat, to abase themselves before others, to act the hypocrite? It seems high time, in this age of progress, for us all honestly to acknowledge that others are no more stupid than we are ourselves, and to grasp that everyone whom we deceive understands perfectly well what is going on, simply affecting to believe us either out of the weakness or out of the sweetness of their natures. I have so firm a belief in this point that I shall only begin to credit the reality of progress once my casual acquaintances cease cross-questioning me about my health with affected concern as soon as they see me (when all the time I know that they have not the slightest interest in the matter), and instead show that they are prepared to come to my aid in moments of crisis; when they stop treating me as men of the world treat a woman of the world, and begin treating me as one human being treats another. For all that I am Madame Court Counsellor Lisitsyna, I have a secret dream, to which I love to surrender myself from time to time. I know that it is a dream, because if such a thing had been possible in reality, then it would long ago have come to pass somewhere or other, at some time or other. My dream is this: I often muse on how wonderful it would be if three bright angels were to make their homes on this earth, and protect us all with their wings: the angels of truth, sincere fellow-feeling, and rational labour.°

Excuse me, however! I run off the point. Many were the reasons which caused me to take a dislike to my fat Swiss governess, but there were two things in particular which put me against her. I hated her for forcing me to come to lessons at fixed hours, according to a set routine: the pattern was one repellent to my rebellious and unbridled nature. But I hated her still more because she was a liar. She lied to my mother, assuring her that she was perfectly satisfied with her position, whilst I knew that in the schoolroom, the nursery, the maids' room, the pantry—anywhere, in fact, where my mother was out of earshot—she would grumble incessantly, complaining that she had never experienced anything one-half so uncivilized as what she was witnessing in the houses of *les pométchiks russes*. The food was disgusting, her collars and cuffs were most sluttishly ironed, and as for the coffee! that was brewed '*d'une manière barbare*!' She told lies to my father too, saying that I was a most industrious pupil, whilst in fact I did nothing at all. Certainly, I soon learnt to chatter away in French, but for that I had my own good memory to thank, and also the loquacity of my governess; I did not acquire the skill by dint of my own effort or desire.

I treated my Swiss lady rather rudely; at first she tolerated this behaviour from me, since she was being paid a good salary. But at last even she had had enough, and complained to my papa of my behaviour. Though I was absolutely to blame for what had happened, my *maman* and papa took my side; neither of them had any liking for fuss and argument; and besides, both of them held that, in saying that she could not deal with the behaviour of the child in her care, my governess had simply proved that she was unworthy of her own position. Nevertheless, the memory of my governess's complaints rankled with me. My suite of Dashkas had been driven from my nursery; but whenever I was allowed free time from lessons, I would rush out to play in the garden or the courtyard with my little friends. I gave them my word that I should see the Swiss governess dismissed; and I kept it. I began to be impossibly rude to her, making faces, tipping her coffee over, spattering her dresses, so that in the end she herself considered it wise to give in her notice. Nanny Astafevna also helped my cause in her own way, by constantly grumbling about the governess to my *maman*.

When my Swiss lady had left, my parents talked things over amongst themselves, and then decided that I should have an Englishwoman. My *maman* was persuaded that Englishwomen were steadier and more reliable than others; in consequence, they were certain to make good governesses.

And so they sent off to Moscow for one, and in due course Miss Turling arrived. She did indeed prove very steady: she was so earnest in her demeanour, indeed, that at first I was afraid to look her in the eyes; however, this happy situation did not last. In a matter of three days I had thrown off my timidity; and then I began acting the same comedy with Miss Turling as I had with my Swiss lady. I had not the slightest wish to learn anything; whilst lessons were in progress, I would study Miss Turling's every move, so that I might have a better idea of how to tease her later. The unfortunate woman was a cripple, lame in one leg. I got all her various poses by heart, then in secret I taught my Akulkas and Dashkas to limp just as she did. Then, one fine day, when I was especially bored with my governess—who might as well have been dumb for all that I could understand of what she said to me in English!—we staged the *coup de grâce*.

Miss Turling's bedroom was on the ground floor, and its windows looked out on to the inner courtyard of the house, which had a patch of grass in the middle. We had just had luncheon, and Miss Turling had sent me out to play, with my nanny to keep an eye on me, whilst she herself went to sit by the window in her room with her coffee. I lined up my Dashkas and Katyushkas on the grass, counted to three, and clapped my hands. On hearing this prearranged signal, all the little girls went running off round the grass, one after the other, limping exactly as Miss Turling did; except that for variety's sake half the team limped with their right legs, the other half with their left, whilst I brought up the rear, limping with both. I can leave you to imagine the fury of Britannia's daughter when she saw the show that we had put on. She rushed to the drawing-room, dragged my parents to the window, and harangued them in English at the top of her voice. As a result, I was made to go and kneel on the floor as a punishment—for the first time in my life, I should say—whilst my nanny was commanded to administer a well-deserved thrashing to all the little Akulkas and Dashkas. The next day Miss Turling left for Moscow, in high dudgeon.

This incident made my parents see that they would have to adopt stronger measures to make me behave. They pondered the problem, sought advice amongst their acquaintance, and then packed me off to boarding-school. 'You are sure to be taught some obedience and respect for others there,' my father told me.

Why my parents should have assumed that a boarding-school was the equivalent of a house of correction, I do not know. But in August that year I was indeed sent off to an institute for the daughters of the nobility, where I was to spend the next six years. I think that I must lack inborn intelligence, for in those six years I learnt nothing thoroughly, not even my own native language—but no, not so fast! That is a lie: there was one thing of which I *did* acquire a detailed knowledge: how to make perfect low court curtsies. I cannot say that this accomplishment was to benefit me much in my later existence, however, for in all my considerable experience of life in society, I have never seen ladies drop curtsies of that kind. I grant you that actresses taking their curtain calls make obeisance in very much the same way; however, regrettably, fate and my parents did not have a life on the stage° in mind for me, and so my curtseying was all to go for nothing!

By the time that I had left my institute, my parents had taken up residence in Petersburg. My life moved in such a whirl of gaiety that I did not have the time, the inclination, or indeed the cause to think deeply about anything. My *maman* had given up her dancing career for my sake, as all good mothers should; and I now took her place in the quadrille. By day she and I would do a little shopping, or go out visiting. We soon had a very large circle of acquaintance. My mother was determined that I should become a lady of society; our set, the people with whom we spent all our time from noon till midnight, admired urbanity, elegance, good breeding, and wealth above all other things. I did not have a good singing voice, but a singing teacher was engaged to give me lessons; I had no ear for music, but another teacher was employed so that I could keep up my playing. I imagine that my parents were able to afford all this because their peasants were conscientious in the payment of their quit-rent.

We had a distant and impoverished relative living in Petersburg; his name was Grigory Vasilevich Temryukov. My father was acting as his patron: that is, he had made over a spare room in the house to him, and invited him to eat one meal a day at our table. Whilst Temryukov was dining with us, my father loved to read him lectures on morals and the ways of the world. Temryukov was an orphan, and he was as poor as Job, or at any rate a minor official on a pension. But somehow he struggled to get by in the wide world on his own, relying on his energy, which he had in abundance, and his talent as an artist, in which he hardly dared to be quite confident as yet. In those days he was a young man of about 22; he was a pupil at the Academy of Arts,° and passionately in love with all the great painters; he was shy and rather gauche in company, and his face, whilst not at all handsome, radiated intelligence. Even in those days, his usual manner was sarcastic to the point of bitterness, but he often made his points with subtlety and conviction. It was from Temryukov that I heard the first words of truth and justice—not that he took upon himself the high role of the champion of truth; it was simply that he was incapable of dissembling when people voiced opinions with which he did not agree. My *maman* used to call him (though not to his face, of course) an uncouth, boorish young man; and my papa would often predict that he would come to a bad end if he did not change his ways.

My father and Temryukov would always quarrel about the same thing. My father felt that Temryukov, as a Russian nobleman, should do his duty to society by performing some useful function; and to this end, he made several attempts on Temryukov's personal and moral integrity, by trying to do him the dubious favour of finding him employment as a clerk in some government office. My father's passion for philanthropy riled the young man beyond endurance.

I do not know why, but I cannot bear the word 'philanthropy'. I understand only too well, though, how bitter the bread from our table tasted to poor Temryukov, and how his heart sank as he mounted the steps leading to our front door. He was already in residence when I came back from the institute. At first I took a fierce dislike to him, and it took us a long time to make friends. His mockery of my upbringing, of our whole way of life, provoked me intensely, and we often had fierce quarrels. According to my view of the world at that time, he was a mere boy, a dauber, next thing to a nonentity. But then something happened which made me look at him with new eyes, and brought about a rapprochement between us.

An exhibition was in progress at the Academy. Everyone in town was going to see it, and so we went along too. We strolled through all the rooms, glancing at the paintings as we passed; if we saw a crowd by one of them, we would stop and look for five minutes or so—or even ten, if the crowd was a large one. On concluding our grand tour of inspection, we went back home. We had guests that evening, and conversation naturally turned to the exhibition. When he heard my comments about the paintings and the artists, Temryukov gave a hideous grimace (not that my judgements were intended for his ears, of course!) At last he could stand it no longer; he walked away and went into another room.

The next day, Temryukov and I happened to fall into talk about what he himself was up to. I had never seen any of his work, and said that I should very much like to see some of his drawings.

'I am sure the exercise would be of great benefit to us both,' he said, with an expression of deep contempt.

'But why will you not show me your drawings?' I asked.

'Because you cannot possibly be interested in a subject of which you know nothing. Still worse, you will probably voice opinions of the kind to which you gave vent yesterday, when you were discussing those unfortunate pictures at the exhibition.'

Like everyone else in the house, I had long grown used to hearing Temryukov talk like this; but for some reason this sally irritated me so deeply, or to be more exact, I was so hurt by it, that I burst into tears. He flushed deep red, and stood before me as awkwardly as a schoolboy, glancing at me from under his lids every now and then, and twisting his pencil in his hands.

'I have offended you, I see,' he muttered at last, half-apologetically and half-forgivingly.

'Not in the least,' I replied, wiping away my tears. 'I can only be offended by the opinions of those whom I respect. But if you had any drop of kindness in you, then instead of laughing at my views on art, you would explain to me where I am mistaken.'

'But would you listen to me?' he asked.

'Naturally I would.'

'I assure you that you would soon be bored with the whole business. In order to be able to make judgements about art, one must have at least a nodding acquaintance with its theoretical principles, and that is something that cannot be acquired in an hour or two.'

'If I choose, I shall find time enough,' I responded.

'Is that so?'

Temryukov's expression was sceptical.

'Why do you not try? Come, try giving me some lessons on art.'

'To begin with, you must go to the Academy again tomorrow, and take me with you. Then I shall try to explain which the good pictures in the exhibition are, and why they are good. Of course, that first lesson will be incomplete and superficial. There are some paintings which demand to be looked at for hours on end; and then one needs to go back the next day and look at them again, and it will still not be enough time to appreciate them. A good painting is no mere piece of canvas decorated with inanimate figures. No, it is the creation of a living human being; it is part of his thoughts, a piece of his life. An artist, a poet, a painter always shares his life, to a greater or lesser extent, with his paintings. If you only knew what a pleasure it is to cherish and nurture some secret, deeply buried idea and to represent it in living images, to convey it in such a way that another human being exactly like oneself should stop before it and be made to meditate by it!'

It was the first time that Temryukov had ever spoken to me like this; and I was astonished to recall that until now I had not found him handsome. He seemed so to me at this moment: his face expressed energy and will-power of a kind which it is hard to predict, and which it is still more difficult to imitate.

'Do you love the idea of glory?' I asked, when he had finished, and immediately realized that my question was out of place.

'Glory?' he repeated abstractedly. 'I cannot say. I think that in time I may come to love it, but I am prepared to do without it all my life if I can only be certain that I am following my true vocation, and not simply playing at being an artist, as one might play at blind man's buff. What others say of us is not important; it is our own consciousness of what is right that matters.'

From that day on, we became firm friends. My *maman* was horrified by the idea that Temryukov should be our cicerone at the exhibition—why, to be accompanied by a gentleman in torn gloves!—but I took care of that little matter, and soon we were all at the exhibition again. But this time the whole occasion took on a quite different significance; every picture now had its own meaning. How many brilliant paintings, though, now lost favour in my eyes! Temryukov poured vitriol on painters who lavished their labours on aping rich satins and velvets; but in compensation, he made me look at the unshowy paintings of the Russian genre painters° with a new appreciation, explaining their work with such enthusiasm, such love, and such concern for the tasks which they had set themselves that I too was infected with these emotions.

It is intriguing to recall the methods by which drawing was taught° in pensions and institutes in those days. First we were made to draw endless straight lines, then circles, and then we were set to copy the grandiosely arched noses of classical profiles. From these we progressed to studies of heads wearing helmets. When we had sketched a sufficient quantity of heroes and demigods in black pencil, we then moved on—quite illogically, for variety's sake as it seemed—to copying landscapes. When we reached the top class, we were all let loose on the boxes of watercolours, and quantities of roses, tulips, and poppies, adorned with fluttering butterflies, bloomed under our eager fingers. And that was the end of our induction into the fine arts. Our tutor had no time to explain or interpret what we were doing; he hardly had time to correct even a tenth part of the copies which we made. On our parents' name-days, we would present them with splendid bouquets of painted flowers; at examination time, whole tables would be heaped with our dainty sketches. But if we had been told to draw an ink-well or an apple from life, hardly one in twenty of us could have done it.

Temryukov, though, took me right back to the ABC, as it were: to the elementary rules of drawing from nature. My *maman* and papa were not at all pleased with my new passion for drawing, since it took up a great deal of the time which I had earlier spent going visiting and strolling round the shops. Still less were they delighted with the fact that, the closer I got to Temryukov, the more serious did I become, and the more indifferent to worldly chatter. It was not simply drawing in which Temryukov educated me. He and I often had long talks about other subjects; without making any particular effort, he made me start to think. Although he was so young, Temryukov had lived through a great deal of suffering; he taught me to place myself dispassionately in the position of others, and in so doing to forgive them, not judge them. Despite the bitterness with which he spoke, he had a kind, abundantly sympathetic heart; and our conversations gave me a lively respect for poverty. A poor man may be forgiven much: ignorance, irritability, envy. The rich have everything—he has nothing. They amuse themselves—he suffers. They oppress him with their superiority, and at the same time expect him to be grateful, not realizing the extent to which human nature—their own just as much as his—resists the emotion of gratitude. Of all the evils in our century, poverty is probably the most extreme; even disease can be tolerated more easily. There are only two things which cannot be forgiven a poor man: idleness and apathy.

It was now three years since I had left the institute. With each year that passed, my parents reprimanded me more and more often for my failure to observe the customs of high society. But then, one autumn day, Temryukov caught cold; his chill took a turn for the worse, and soon he was dangerously ill. During all the three months of his illness we did not see each other; but we exchanged letters. Then one day, the doctor told me that he was so ill that it was doubtful whether he would live till nightfall. At this I leapt to my feet and rushed into his room. Even my *maman*, that stern guardian of propriety, did not venture to stop me, though she gave me a look of consternation. Later on, in fact, she was to tell me that she had found my behaviour so extraordinary that she suspected I had gone quite mad.

Temryukov knew very well how serious his illness was: he had gone down with a galloping consumption, the result of overwork, and of life in the damp lodgings which he had been forced to inhabit during his earlier, nomadic existence. How hard it was for him to die now, by this too sudden and inopportune death; he was only 25, and he had just been awarded a gold medal on completing his studies at the Academy.° A few hours before he died, he said to me:

'Do not weep for me. Many times I wondered what was likely to become of us; and speaking frankly, I could anticipate nothing but suffering. What else were we to expect? Your parents would never have agreed to your marrying me, and I could not have borne it if you had married anyone else.'

This declaration was so sudden, so eccentric—made there on his deathbed—that the whole scene has stayed fixed in my mind, and often returns to me now. The dusk of the room with its lowered blinds; the flickering lamp in one corner, whose sputtering flame faintly illumines the invalid's pale and emaciated face. I shall never forget Temryukov's expression, which wordlessly narrated the whole story of his life: the memory of past sufferings, the determination to fight without ceasing, the passionate longing for the future that promised so much, and the inescapable despair caused by this hard fate, that had thwarted his resolute spirit—all this showed in him, appearing not by turns, not sequentially, but at one and the same time, as though all the dying man's spiritual powers had been brought to a final and extraordinary pitch in his last moments. But suddenly the tension in his face ebbed away. He turned a look of boundless love on me; and then that expression froze on his face, fixed now for ever...

He had gone, but I was still sitting by his bed and holding his cold hand in mine. It was the first time in my life that I had witnessed the mystery of death. I studied the face of the dead man intently.

Then the maid's voice cut through my oblivion.

'There's no use holding his hand now, miss,' she whispered. 'Can't you see he's dead?'

'Dead!' I repeated, putting down his hand, and trying to grasp the meaning of the word.

II

And so my one and only great love was cut off before the end of its first chapter. No; 'cut off' is not really the right way of putting it: the absurdity of circumstance caused that love to be frozen, petrified. In actual fact, I might as well have left the matter out of my narrative, since it is of no relevance to what follows. My readers can scarcely be expected to concern themselves with the question of whether I was ever in love or no; nor is the matter of whether the object of my affections be dead or alive likely to be of interest to them. But I am a woman, after all. Could I be expected to pass over the tale of my love affair in silence, having reached that point in my story? No; all the less so considering how much my being in love changed me. Days, years passed; I was now not so far off 30 years old. My parents were in desperation; they were persuaded that I should certainly remain an old maid. In truth, of course, there was no cause for desperation in that: for surely it is far better to remain an old maid, no matter what the ridicule one may attract by doing so, than to enter a loveless marriage? And in any case, if you once allow women to change their way of life, then old maids will no longer seem so useless and ridiculous.

I shunned society in the first years after Temryukov's death; the emptiness and frivolity of that life were loathsome to me. But art became ever dearer; I was moved not only by the aesthetic pleasure which it stimulates in all of us, but also by the sense that art was the bond between me and my beloved. My *maman* and papa, though, heartily disapproved of my love for art. My father fell into sulks over my behaviour; every Tuesday he would open the house to guests, and then I was forced to play the charming hostess and to entertain the company. My mother's reaction was different; it was clear that she felt pity for me. A woman like myself, she recognized the importance of romantic attachments, and approved them, so long as they did not overstep the boundaries of propriety; what she did not understand was how one could mourn a lost love all one's life. She grieved for me so sincerely and so inconsolably, she so constantly tried to persuade me that I must get married in order to assure my position in society, that in the end I could endure things no more, and I gave in. Out of cowardice, I renounced my own wishes and surrendered myself into my parents' hands, submitting to their oppressive and suffocating love.

Little by little I was drawn back into the maelstrom of society; but how low I had now sunk morally! My state was far worse than it had been when I left the institute; then I had been a mere doll, whose ignorance made her behaviour pardonable. But now there was nothing to excuse the triviality of my behaviour, as I myself well knew; and how I hated the society which fostered such triviality!

And then one day Monsieur Court Counsellor Lisitsyn visited my parents, and made a formal and ceremonious request for my hand in marriage and my dowry. I was informed of what had happened; my parents dwelt at length on the many virtues of my suitor, and then reminded me that I was, after all, now 27 years old. I agonized for some time, but in the end I gave my consent. I felt stifled in my parents' house; I was longing for freedom, freedom in the sense of repose, relief from harassment, but also in the sense of enhanced rights, since I firmly believed that a married woman was allowed more freedom by society than a girl. To the duties of a married woman I gave not one thought.

Lisitsyn was a perfectly presentable character. In company with other men, he comported himself with dignity; he said little, but he thought rather more. He treated women with the affectionate indulgence with which one treats children whom one, unknown to them, intends to deprive of a promised carriage-ride or trip to the theatre. In actual fact, to this day I have only foggy notions of my husband's character; I have never permitted myself to scrutinize it in detail. People tell me that he is a good man. I believe them, since belief is one of humanity's essential requirements. When I married, I did not trouble myself to discover much about my husband's profession. I knew that he was a member of the civil service, and that he was employed in some ministry or other. I had a very good idea of the various kinds of employment open to gentlemen in Russian society. I knew that a man who was in the army might be an officer in the Guards, or in some other regiment; that he might be an officer in the cavalry or in the infantry. I knew that an officer in the Navy had to spend the summer in the Baltic. I knew that engineers were supposed to mend roads and bridges. I knew that officers in the civil service spent their time signing pieces of paper. What precisely those pieces of paper said or meant was no concern of mine (no matter that it was my own husband who was signing them), and so I never made any enquiries about them. In any case, we did not live on the money which he earned from dealing with those bits of paper—it was too insignificant a sum to support us. We lived on the income from my own estate; accordingly, I was not in the least surprised when Lisitsyn severed all connection with his pieces of paper a year after we were married—which is to say, he retired from the service. At his suggestion, we then moved to the country. The future that stretched before me could not be described as brilliant, but I could make myself useful to society in many ways. I was going to turn myself into a landowner's wife, and organize my former playmates, the Akulkas and Dashkas of my childhood, to sit at their embroidery frames and produce fine work; I was to sit pouring out my husband's tea, whilst hour by hour I grew visibly rounder and plumper; I was to bully and patronize a shoal of companions from minor gentry families, and dress myself in breathtaking finery for every dreary ball which might be got up in the central town of our *guberniya*.

At any rate, that was what Lisitsyn supposed, in his innnocence. But this was one matter on which we did not agree. I was a patient, attentive, and obedient wife in all things save one: I had very firm and strong-minded notions concerning my own property rights. Poor Temryukov's history had given me a very good idea of what poverty meant. And in any case, it was more than possible that I should some day myself have children. I was determined that they should not grow up enduring want and hardship as Temryukov had, and that they should not be forced into a decline by damp lodgings and sleepless nights. So I stood by my own rights, and insisted on administering the income from my estate myself.

One day I came near to quarrelling with my husband about this. He tried to convince me that a married couple should share all they had.

'How can it be,' he said in conclusion of his argument, 'that you could be prepared to entrust me with your hand in marriage, and with your heart, and yet do not wish to share the work of managing your estate with me? Can you really value money more than yourself?'

I remained unconvinced by this logic.

'Yes, my dear, I did entrust you with my hand and heart. But that is not at all the same thing as sharing my money with you. The income from my estate is meant for me; it was made over to me so that it should support me in my own lifetime, and not so that I might cede it to anyone else whatsoever. In any case, village elder° Gavrila has proved himself more than capable of dealing with our peasants; so why should you trouble your head about it? You are a man whose life should be devoted to pleasure, not to hard labour. I want you to enjoy perfect happiness. And in any case, am I to suppose that you only married me for my money?'

'Of course not,' Lisitsyn hastened to assure me.

'I am sure that is true. If it were not, I should certainly hate you. Can a woman really be expected to love a man who marries her for her income, and not for herself? I could certainly not love such a man.'

'But do you really suppose that other women share your feelings?'

'I cannot say whether all of them do. But I am certain that fifty out of a hundred hold the same opinions as I.'

'So do you really suppose that a man has no right at all to be influenced to the slightest extent in his choice of a wife by any consideration of her income?'

'No, I think he has no right at all to such considerations.'

'But do you really think that such considerations are criminal?'

'They are worse than criminal; they are base. And baseness is more offensive to women than anything; they will avenge themselves more quickly on its account than for any other reason.'

'But what is a man to do, in your opinion, if he, let us say, loves a girl, but has not sufficient income to marry her?'

'Then he must find himself work. After all, that is what God gave him a brain and hands for.'

'But we all do work—that is, we all have a position in the service.'

'In that case, you must all have means as well.'

'But suppose that a man's means are insufficient, and yet he is head over heels in love?'

'Who told you that you should spend your lives signing papers? Are we to blame for the fact that you can find yourselves no other employment?'

'What else are we to do, then?'

'My dear, are there so few kinds of employment which are really useful and which are profitable at the same time? You could go into trade; you could invent different kinds of machinery or build them; you could plant market gardens. All those things would be more honourable than living on your wife's income.'

'So you want to turn us all into market gardeners, of all things, is that it?'

'All that I know is this. If a man loves a woman and wishes to acquire sufficient income to support her, and if he sets up a market garden—yes, even if he plants cabbages and turnips with his own hands—and if the woman whom he loves has an ounce of heart and a drop of common sense, then she will certainly show that she is capable of valuing and respecting her husband. But if a man marries in order to exploit his wife's funds, and to ensure himself a comfortable or a luxurious existence, then even the most limited woman will eventually realize that she is worth nothing in her husband's eyes, and nothing in the eyes of society at large. You can judge for yourself whether one is likely to enjoy being a nonentity. After all, women are capable of quite as much self-love as men. Suppose, for instance, I had married a man who had my income in mind rather than me. Should I not spend every minute thinking that I might as well be hunchbacked, foul-tempered, crippled, soulless, heartless, or even an out-and-out idiot, for all that he cares? And are not such incessant thoughts the worst kind of torture, the most intolerable humiliation, that any woman might experience? It is inevitable that one should start to detest the person who has prompted them.'

'How you do exaggerate!'

'Quite possibly. But if I exaggerate, so do women in general. As a result, marriages of convenience usually turn out to the inconvenience of both parties.'

'I assume, therefore, that this is the conclusion of your argument: a poor man must never marry a rich girl, no matter how much he may love her?'

'No, he certainly may. Why ever not? Such things happen every day, after all. But if he does marry her, then he should not make any attempt to lay hands on her fortune. He must regard his wife's money as her own, and accept that he has no right to it. If she loves her husband, then she will share with him all the things that money can buy. But he should still make every effort to earn her love and respect.'

I said this knowing very well that, so far as Monsieur Court Counseller Lisitsyn was concerned, the only guarantee of my rights was my money.

We spent that whole summer in the country, and in the autumn I proposed to my husband that we should spend some time travelling abroad. I was eager to visit other countries, to acquaint myself with other peoples, with different manners and customs. I felt that it would be an unpardonable waste of opportunity to spend one's whole life closeted like a snail in its shell, when one had the means to do otherwise. My husband was by no means unwilling to make new acquaintances, and to show himself off to new circles. I wanted to visit southern Europe; for my husband, however, like any true Russian gentleman, Paris was his Mecca. On this occasion I did give way, and agree that we should indeed visit Paris first. In fact, we spent the whole winter there; I could not drag my husband away. Once we were abroad, he developed his native Russian facility for adaptation to astonishing levels. The Lisitsyn I knew vanished absolutely. Once in Paris, he turned himself not merely into a Frenchman, but into a native Parisian. He rushed through life at top speed, full of fuss and excitement; he flung himself into society, mingling in every circle, and taking as great an interest in politics as any Frenchman; he plunged into furious debates about progress, and then dived just as enthusiastically into the frivolity of balls and parties. His fervour and enjoyment were so great that one would have thought he had grown up on Parisian soil, and sucked in the French national character with his mother's milk. I often had to suppress a laugh when I saw what was going on. If I had not dragged him out of the country, he would have been happy enough to spend the whole winter lying on his sofa in his dressing-gown, enjoying a well-earned rest after his efforts on behalf of society, flicking carelessly through the Russian papers, or exerting himself to have the odd game of cards with a neighbour; instead of paying court to *grisettes*, he would have flirted with Russian peasant girls in their sarafans. He would not have had a moment's interest in the Parisians who now inspired his ready sympathy.

As for me, once I had seen all that might inspire a visitor's curiosity in Paris, had had a taste of life in the capital, and had made the acquaintance of diverse representatives of the many different layers of Parisian society, I began to find life in that everlasting fun-fair distinctly tedious. There is a brittleness in the French character which I find uncongenial; and I cannot bear associating with people to whom I can extend no real sympathy. Most of the French are no more than empty phrase-mongers, and I have no time for that style of life; my opinion of such matters might be summed up in the Russian proverb, 'A good talker is a bad doer'.

The following spring, we returned to our Lipovki estate, and spent all the next summer and all the following winter there. I wanted to allow time for my experiences to sink in; I wanted to have space and quiet so that I could ponder and ruminate on all I had heard and seen. As you see, Temryukov had not taught me to think in vain. But at the beginning of the following summer, we again went off abroad, this time to Germany. The good honest Germans were a good deal more to my taste than the French. For his part, Lisitsyn found Germany less enjoyable than France; but he became as friendly with the Germans as his knowledge of the language allowed, and showed himself adept in picking up their customs and attitudes. He learned to drink beer and to love music; he was forever talking of how he would take up some serious activity so soon as we got back to Lipovki. And indeed, no sooner had we returned, than he set up a cabinet of antiquities, and developed such a passion for archaeology that I became quite anxious. However, I soon nipped this new enthusiasm in the bud by refusing to give him money for his purchases. Lisitsyn assuaged his disappointment by buying a carpenter's lathe, of which I was glad: this at least promised to be more useful than his dabbling in archaeology.

Time went by, and soon three winters had passed since our return from Germany. At length I went off abroad once more, but without my husband this time; he had been infected by the lassitude of landowner life, and had become too lazy to travel. So I went off to Italy on my own, taking my small daughter with me. This was another profitable era of my life; I could almost say that I felt happy. I was living in a country whose past is as remarkable as its present, and whose people, for all their backwardness, always inspire affection and sympathy—indeed, it may even be that it is their very backwardness which prompts the traveller's sympathy. And in Italy one lives surrounded by a landscape which would be sufficient in itself to ensure the happiness of anyone who loves nature.

On my return to Russia, I found many changes. The position of the peasants had been profoundly altered, and the tone of society in general had changed. I felt as though a healthy fresh breeze had begun to blow. Even in the drawing-rooms of our provincial town, the words 'the modern world', 'emancipation', 'progress' had become common currency. 'Thank God,' I thought. It felt as though a huge forest had woken from its enchanted sleep. Millions of voices had begun to mutter, to chatter, to make noises that might only be half-articulate as yet, but which were already distinct. And every now and then some fully formed note would sound amidst that disorganized racket, with the promise of a delightful harmony in time.

I was wholly on the women's side, since there is no doubt that men have vastly superior lives to ours. 'Progress is enlightenment,' I thought, 'and enlightenment is justice.' I leave it to the learned to determine whether society treats women justly—though I hasten to say that I do not number Monsieur Michelet° among these! Let us glance for a moment, however, at the level of development and education which is accessible to women. The only skills which society allows a woman to acquire are intellectually superficial accomplishments which are useful neither to her nor to others—playing the piano and sewing. Here I should observe that these comments on women's lot in no sense reflect the position of wealthy women. They have no cause to complain: if they wish, they can always use their fortune in order to enrich some young man whom they love by granting him their hand in marriage; and if any rich young woman feels the need for serious study and moral development, then so much the better for her and for society at large. At any rate, such women are not my present concern.

I am sure that we all agree that it is hard for a poor man to earn his daily bread. But society has placed all possible means at a man's disposal—always assuming, of course, that he is not constrained by prejudice. A poor man of the gentry classes may well feel that to take up a craft or a trade would not be fitting to his station; he may choose to endure want in order that he may follow in the footsteps of his grandfather and great-grandfather, and in order that he should not have to choose a path unsanctified by them. But his actions are the result of his own free will. However, when women endure deprivation—as they in fact often do—matters are quite different. Society does not accept that women are capable of serious work: it is generally supposed that the weakness of their constitution and health make them incapable of such work. But one thing is forgotten when arguments of this kind are advanced: that poverty forces a woman to work in any case, and that she must then labour from early in the morning until late at night, sustained only by that limited level of intellectual development which our society allows women to attain. The suffocating atmosphere of prejudice does not allow her to undertake really useful work, but only such work as will undermine her health all the faster, since the remuneration which she is able to obtain by it is less than what would be hers if she were properly educated.

In Russia, if a woman is so poor that she needs to support herself—and there are many women who must do not only that, but also support a mother, and perhaps also younger sisters and brothers—she has only three choices of career open to her. If she has had the usual lightweight and superficial education, and can chatter three or four languages (but probably not write grammatically in any of them), then she becomes a governess. Is it generally known what the life of a governess is like? It is the most back-breaking work, the dreariest trade one can imagine—and this thanks once more to the attitudes of society at large. There are households where it is stipulated that the governess is not allowed to read any books, apart from the Bible on Sundays, because reading might distract her attention from the children in her care. In other households, she must endure constant genteel humiliation, because her employers feel that they are entitled to treat her as they wish, since they pay her salary. Such households are by no means exceptional: one encounters them everywhere in Russia, the bulk of society here being underdeveloped in an intellectual sense. Even in households where every effort is made to ensure the governess's happiness, the conditions in which she lives usually make happiness impossible: for instance, if there are a lot of children in the family, she will hardly have a minute to herself all day. No wonder so many governesses detest their hard labour, and feel that their work hangs on them like heavy chains which they long to throw off at the first possible opportunity! And what does a governess receive in return for selling herself like this? Some twenty, thirty or at most forty roubles a month; there are many governesses who earn under twenty roubles a month. Just imagine how you are to keep a sick mother or your younger sisters on twenty roubles a month! If she has an attractive appearance, a governess does have one way out—to marry the first gentleman whose fancy she takes in sufficient measure that he is prepared to extend her his protection. Whether she likes him or not, whether he is young or old, clever or stupid, kind or unkind—no matter. She is a poor girl; she has no right to choose; she must gratefully accept the favour which this gentleman has graciously conferred on her. If she declines it, then so much the worse for her! Until her death she will be a slave in other people's houses—unless, of course, a still worse fate overtakes her.°

Everything which I have just said of governesses also applies to companions. But a companion's role is still more degrading: she occupies a position somewhere between that of a pet monkey and a caged parrot. The only other possibilities for women are to find work as a musician or as a seamstress.

Music is a miraculous thing; but to be a musician, you must have inborn gifts. Here in Russia, though, a piano is something close to a *sine qua non* in any household of substance; without any regard to whether their children have any talent for music or not, parents will hire a master or mistress to teach them the piano. The result of this fashion—for one cannot speak of society's genuine need for music—is that Russia is flooded with bad lady musicians and with incompetent music mistresses.

Let us suppose that some girl from a poor family has learnt to play the piano quite nicely. She fixes on this as a means to earn herself some money; our newspapers are full of advertisements for ladies who will give lessons for forty copecks an hour, or sometimes even for twenty-five. In downpours, gales, in all kinds of inclement weather, the poor music mistress must rush from one end of the town to the other collecting her twenty-five copecks. Yet all the twenty-five copeck pieces she can accumulate are not enough to keep her, especially if she has to support others as well as herself. And the sole result of her work is that one can visit any household in town where young ladies are in residence and listen to music being played in a manner that makes one regret the invention of the pianoforte.

A seamstress's life has nothing appealing about it. There are so many of these women at every turn that I am sure one-tenth of the number could keep all of humanity dressed in more fashionable bonnets and hats than it could ever require. More than half the seamstresses are employed by the day; they work from nine in the morning until late without a break, and get paid thirty copecks for their pains. Can this possibly be healthy?

So what, I wonder, will the philosophizing gentlemen who see women's health as the first obstacle to her further development say to all this?

I do not go so far as to say that, if women were allowed to develop their minds in the same way as men, we would see a rash of female Newtons, Hegels, or Copernicuses.° To this day there have been none such, nor could there have been. But that there have been, are, and will be women whose mental organization is exemplary is a fact which it is impossible to dispute. And the number of such women is greater than society would like to suppose. They are unnoticeable because they are oppressed by their environment—their abilities are not developed, but are blunted and dissipated amidst the common run.

Woman's role is not to shine in brilliance, but to be useful, to further as much happiness around herself as she can. But her present social position does not allow that idea to enter her head. Take a girl who is struggling to earn herself her bitter and insufficient crust, and whose education has left her mental capacities underdeveloped—how can such a girl acquire any sense of a higher moral ideal and found her whole life upon its principles? It is far more likely that she will take the first opportunity of finding someone else to take care of her—someone, no matter whom, who will free her from hard work and constant suffering.

There is an unassailable belief amongst us that if a woman devotes herself to scholarship or to the sciences, that is, if she takes up an activity 'not proper to women', as the usual expression has it, then this will stop her from being a good housewife and mother, will distract her attention from her family and her domestic duties. By your leave, ladies and gentlemen! Who has put about this unfortunate rumour that we Russian women are such zealous housewives, such devoted mothers? We are Russian aristocrats, and we thank God for it; who has ever supposed that we peel our own potatoes? Why, we prefer not even to darn our own stockings, no matter how poor we may be. And if some grim fate should force us, after we have got married, to take a casual interest in what is happening in the kitchen, then our husbands will get no great joy from that. Just try asking them! What we Russian women need more than anything is pleasure, luxury, and playing at being in love. This last occupation is one which we enjoy until we are 50 years old, at the very least. Our upbringing has ensured that all our dreams and desires are concerned with our own pleasures. If our husbands cannot afford to pay for those, then that is their fault. Who asked them to marry us? As for our children, we tend to treat them like amusing dolls—until they have the temerity to grow up. For when our daughters begin to cost us real money, and we, their mothers, grasp that we need to deny ourselves from time to time for their sakes, then we start to regard them as a burden, and one of which we cannot wait to be rid.

All in all, then, we have no reason to be afraid that development of our intellects will make us bad or careless housewives and mothers! So we hear that women's health and constitutions are obstacles to their development? But needs must when the devil drives, as they say. Are we not witnesses to daily cases of husbands who, for all their cries that women's sphere should be the home and only the home, make no efforts to feed their families, but leave the task to their wives? And since mothers do have hearts, after all, these wives will run through mud and slush, cursing their own fates, to give lessons, or will sit up until late at their sewing, or will open some ridiculous school, where thirty little ruffians riot and scream through every lesson—and all in order to drive themselves into a decline! Do we not see it every day?

One could mention other cases: where husbands, for all their own heartfelt wishes and deep attachment to their families, are unable to meet all those families' financial needs, so that their wives must help them to, whether it is injurious to health or not. And here is another question: does every woman marry? Do all women have families? Twist things as you like, the fact is inescapable: even in these times, so distinguished by humanism and progress, filthy lucre plays as important a role as it must have played in any other era. There are far larger numbers of poor women than of rich ones. How many cases does one see where a girl loves a man dearly, but the man has next to no earnings, and the girl no portion! Each has his own kind of poverty; but the girl's is the more extreme, of course. And if they do marry, then that does not always lead to joy. Whilst women who remain old maids condemn themselves to the most helpless existence: they sit doing their drawn-thread work and gossiping, making themselves a burden on their fathers and brothers; sensing their own frail position in the world, they become irritable and demanding. But suppose one were to bring knowledge of some kind into their world, an intellectual interest which might absorb their mental capacities and bring them some real benefit? Why, then they would be given the opportunity to become delightful beings, full of kindness and helpfulness to others! Nothing has such a beneficial effect on the heart as the chance of bringing some benefit to those around us—it is so much more worthy than simply avoiding being a burden on them. When a person's intellect is occupied in a serious way, it has no chance to dissipate itself on humdrum and possibly harmful trivialities. And apart from old maids, how many widows do you think there are, left to bring up their children without means? Such women are glad to sacrifice everything for their children; but they may be forced to part with them altogether, sending them to live with relatives, whilst they submit themselves to the hard labour of life as a governess or companion—though this work is torture for them, since every moment they feel the pain of separation, not seeing their children for weeks at a time, or sometimes even years!

In the name of all such women, whose genuine unhappiness is recognized by all who have studied their lives and who are closely acquainted with the circumstances of their existence, in the name of these I have decided to voice my thoughts. My ideas are not new, they are not original... but it still takes courage to remind our society of those ideas' existence. No doubt I shall be ridiculed and accused of intellectual pretension; but '*rira bien, qui rira le dernier*', as the French say.

Just suppose that a new experiment were tried, and that an institute of higher education were opened° to small numbers of women who wished to continue their education after leaving the *gimnaziya*°—where they could be taught the same subjects as men, modern and ancient languages, just as the men are taught them, so that women, like men, would be able to exist by the fruits of their own labours, not by the sweated efforts of work as a governess or companion?

What would happen if such a quasi-university were opened in Russia? At first the novelty would ensure that all women, both rich and poor, would rush to attend all the lectures they could—it would be quite the thing. No doubt society ladies would be the first to set an example—setting examples is their speciality. But most of them, having neither the inclination to serious work nor the necessity of engaging in it, would soon tire of their new pastime. The indolent would stop attending lectures. Only those driven by necessity would continue to attend. What would happen to them? I think that each one would study one subject in depth, and that her studies would not be in vain; in time they would help her to earn herself a proper income. One might ask: to what extent may a woman employ her skills in real life, and derive genuine benefit from them, on her own behalf, and on others' behalf? The answer is: try opening a university, and then see what happens. One should not condemn any plan untried and untested. Women would certainly gain in a moral sense from the scheme which I envisage. The better educated—I will not say 'brought up'—a woman is, the better things will be for her and all those around her. Not all women are granted the same gifts; but women who are gifted should not be forced to waste their talents. However, if education for women is to achieve its aims, then the conviction that education is valuable for its own sake, and not simply as a way of shining in society and drawing attention to oneself, must percolate amongst us, infiltrating the very air we breathe. Without such a conviction, education is better not even attempted.

But let me return to my story.

Circumstances had compelled us to return to Petersburg. I was delighted by this; I was longing to be back in the capital at the moment when Russia was preparing to 'be reborn'. On our arrival, I sought out old friends, made new ones, and began to take an interest in public life, taking note of everything I heard and saw, and keeping a weather eye open for any signs of progress. Lisitsyn was not entirely delighted with my behaviour: for him the words 'women's emancipation' meant much the same as 'immorality'. There had been a time when he saw things otherwise; but that had been in Paris, where it was necessary to affect a lively interest in progress if one was to seem a modern man of the world. Lisitsyn had realized in a flash that any gentleman who wishes to be a someone in French society has to bandy his opinions about—no matter whether they be his own or borrowed, impossibly wise or incredibly foolish—but opinions there must be: for they are the vital stimulus of Gallic life, with its phrase-mongering, oratory, pleasure-seeking. In France, the individual self peeks forth from its opinions as picturesquely and magnificently as the full moon from a thin veil of clouds.

At the same time, Lisitsyn knew very well that we were only visitors to Paris, that handsome phrases were no more than handsome phrases, and that things would return to their proper places the moment we got back to Lipovki.

But things were different again in Petersburg. The word 'emancipation', which he only half-understood, frightened him terribly. He was vain by nature, and in addition he believed that 'emancipation' meant the same in the case of a European woman as it might in the case of a Turkess, who had been walled up in a harem from the moment she could walk. Where he had got this wild notion from I cannot say. It is an idea that is terribly offensive to a Russian woman, since her sense of personal dignity is far greater than one might expect, given the circumstances in which she is forced to live.

My efforts to observe what was going on, the circle of friends in which I moved, our views, our discussions all troubled Lisitsyn terribly. Several times he remarked to me—though very delicately—that he was by no means enraptured with his own wife's emancipated behaviour. I, however, have little time for hints, preferring to speak 'straight from the shoulder', as they say—a habit that has often got me into trouble with my family, and indeed still does!—and therefore I decided to speak my mind on this subject once and for all.

'Let us suppose, my dear,' I said, 'that I *had* been inclined to be unfaithful; do you really imagine that I should have waited until it became fashionable to talk of progress? Believe me, even if we had lived in medieval Russia, and you had worn a long beard and kept me locked up in a high solar with narrow slits for windows°—even then I should have been unfaithful if I had wanted to be, not once, but on many occasions. An enslaved woman is as cunning as any cat. But you are my legal husband, and I have given you my word that I shall walk life's long path with you arm in arm; and so you may set your mind at rest; I shall never be unfaithful to you. Besides, I am 40 years old now, and the world is full of beautiful young women.'

Lisitsyn was struck by the force of this last argument, and stopped interfering in my business from then on.

There was one family amongst my Petersburg circle in whose doings I had lately been taking a particular interest. The grandmother was a lady of the old school; I suspect that she even dreamed in French. Every morning she would have herself laced into tight stays; her dresses were made of nothing but silk. She had her widowed son living with her. Now *he* was rather an eccentric: a mixture of the typical Russian landowner and the gentleman scholar. He had two great passions: archaeology and his daughter. This girl had been 14 years old at the time of my marriage; she had a delicate, clever face, which made one hope of great things in the future. Her father and grandmother had occupied themselves with her upbringing, each in his own manner. Andrei Osipovich Vetlyagin, her father, detested music and singing, and believed that women's education should concern itself entirely with the exact sciences. Zina was an able girl; she enjoyed her lessons and learnt quickly, and at 14 was already beginning to be spoken of as a prodigy. But as I have said, for all his learning, Andrei Osipovich was a typical Russian landowner, who did not consider that boasting numbered amongst the vices. He had only one reason for educating Zina. He was not concerned with the benefits which education might bring her, or with its effects on her own character; he was determined that she should make a show in society. As a result, Zina was given a very broad education—so broad, in fact, that there was nothing of which she had a more than superficial knowledge. When he had company, Andrei Osipovich loved to show off his daughter's brilliance, and Zina herself was not at all disinclined to act the prodigy. She was sharp-witted enough to have given herself a nodding acquaintance with subjects which would not generally interest girls of 14, and was adept at introducing some technical term or other into ordinary conversation every now and again, a habit which had her father and grandmother in raptures.

Zina's grandmother had at first protested against turning the girl into a scholar; she wanted her grand-daughter to have a glittering society upbringing, and no more. But when she realized what a furore Zina was creating amongst the family's acquaintance, she ceased her protests.

'It is clear that she has remarkable prospects,' the old lady would say. 'She will be a second Madame de Staël, at the very least. History has brought forth only a handful of such women, you know.'

Whether Zina would turn into a woman who could be really useful to herself and to society, who would be genuinely good, and educated in the proper sense of the word, was a question with which neither her father nor her grandmother bothered their heads.

On my return to Petersburg, Zina came into my mind again. I was certain that something exceptional must have come of the girl; I was particularly curious to learn what had been the results of her half-worldly, half-scholarly education. Had she turned into a pedant in skirts, an intolerable *bas bleu*, or had her feminine soul, allied to her sound common sense, enabled her to cut a straight path through the chaos of her contradictory and fragmentary influences, and come forth unscathed from the world of society, whose incongruous attitudes and pervasive flattery so often prove dangerously attractive to young people?

When I arrived in Petersburg, I asked my friends what had happened to the Vetlyagins. It emerged that they were away at present, but that they would return in the autumn. I heard very diverse reports of Zina. Some people found her delightful, others poked fun at her; a third group, amongst whom women were especially well represented, said that she deserved to take up a university chair—in the subject of coquetry. But what everybody agreed on was that she was a well-educated, thoroughly modern young woman. Some people asserted that she was even trying to convert her father to the cause of 'emancipation', and added that the spectacle of this Russian gentleman, torn between the new ideas with which he was being indoctrinated and the ingrained prejudices of his class (a struggle in which the latter elements were often victorious over the former), was a very amusing one. Of her grandmother I heard nothing.

So soon as the Vetlyagins had got back to Petersburg, I called on them and renewed my acquaintance. Zina must by now have been about twenty years old. The rumours, I found, were more or less accurate: Zina had turned into a 'progressive'° on a grand scale. She refused to occupy herself with needlework of any kind, she made regular visits to the public library (where, however, she spent her time reading an edition of Shakespeare that stood on her own bookshelf); she neglected her toilet, asserting that her time was too valuable to waste on such matters—though in fact she achieved nothing of real value by spending her days as she did.

I decided to make Zina and her circle the object of my intensive study, and began to call on the Vetlyagins at regular intervals. In the evenings a circle of young people used sometimes to gather there; all of them were as emancipated as Zina herself. The young girls, the young married ladies, and the young gentleman chattered long and loud about current affairs, about the arts and sciences, and other such serious matters. But none expressed his opinions so forcefully as Zina. She especially loved stating her views on human rights; so hotly did she defend these rights that one might have supposed she was ready to devote herself entirely to their cause. And meanwhile Zina's father and grandmother would listen admiringly to her clever speeches, not daring to put a word in edgeways, though Zina's grandmother was sometimes unable to suppress her raptures, and would gasp:

'*C'est un cœur d'or!*'

The young progressives would usually wind up the evening with some dancing; Zina, I noticed, was a great enthusiast for this too. Many of the young gentlemen were quite obviously paying court to her. The expression on her clever, intriguing little face was summed up by one seminarian (of whom more presently) in the following words: 'The seal of thought lies on it.'

Zina dressed simply and even carelessly, but her clothes always suited her perfectly. One suspected that such a nice choice of attire must have cost her much valuable time spent parading before her looking-glass. Her hair was dressed with great originality. She had it cropped short, and tossed back her locks carelessly as little girls of 8 will—but it curled beautifully, whether by the offices of nature or of art I do not know, so that the style purportedly invented to save time was in fact greatly becoming to Zina's looks.

There was one young girl who often attended the Vetlyagins' parties, whom it was impossible not to notice, because she made no efforts at all to attract attention to herself. She never joined in any of the conversations, and the only time when the young gentlemen took any account of her presence was when the dancing started. But actually this was a very attractive young person. She was only of medium height, but seemed taller, because she was one of those slender, willowy people, who look as though they might sway when the wind blows. Her face was pale, her features irregular, but her expression had an uncommon sweetness; at the same time there was a look of sadness, even of suffering, about her. She was dressed even more simply than the others.

One morning I came across this girl sitting in Zina's bedroom. She was very busy sewing.

'What is that you are sewing?' I asked her.

'A dress—for the lady,' she said, glancing at Zina.

When she had left the room, I asked Zina:

'Who is that girl, then?'

'Oh, that's my cousin,' Zina answered.

'Why does she always seem so sad? She hardly ever speaks when you have company.'

'That's because she has nothing to say. She's completely uneducated, you know.'

'But why should she not have been given an education?'

'Because her family have no money. Her mother had a dowry of five or six thousand souls,° but her father squandered the lot, and then he died. He hadn't been long in the service, and so they didn't let his wife have a widow's pension.'

'But why should her own mother not have educated her?'

'She was hardly capable of it. She did go to boarding-school, but she must either have had no talent for lessons, or have forgotten all she knew; at any rate, when she was widowed, she couldn't even find employment as a governess.'

'So how did they manage to keep themselves?'

'The whole family helped. Then eventually Lyubinka's mother did manage to find work of some kind, and Lyubinka got sent to the orphanage. They taught her to read and write there, and to sew.'

'The poor girl, one does feel sorry for her!'

'Certainly,' Zina agreed indifferently.

'Where do they live?'

'Very near here. Lyubinka's mother rents a room from a civil servant's widow, and Lyuba takes in sewing.'

'I shall be sure to make Lyubinka's acquaintance!'

'Do you really find her so interesting?'

'I certainly do.'

Zina gave me a rather peculiar smile, but she said nothing.

And in time I did get to know Lyubinka, and hear of the sad and difficult life which this young woman had led. Her mother was an invalid, demoralized and made irritable by deprivation and ill-health. If Lyubinka was unable to find work, and money was short, then her mother blamed it on her. Grim necessity often forced Lyubinka to petition her relatives for money—it should be said that she had large numbers of relatives, and that all of them were wealthy. Poor Lyuba would run from house to house trying to borrow money; her relatives would refuse to lend her anything, and would munificently present her with a rouble or two, or with a worn-out dress or a hat. For all her lack of education, Lyubinka was quite an intelligent girl, and a proud one, in the good sense of the word: she would vastly have preferred to earn her own bread than to have fallen back on charity. But she had no choice: her mother would badger her to go, shouting at her angrily and upbraiding her. So Lyuba tried to ensure that she always had work on hand; she would often take jobs at cheap rates just to make sure that there would always be some money in the house.

Lyuba and her mother lived very simply, in a room that was no more than fourteen foot square,° with a single filthy window looking out on to an inner courtyard. This place was where Lyubinka spent most of her life: a life without purpose, warmed by no feelings of joy, cheered by none of those hopeful thoughts that sometimes give people strength to endure still more difficult circumstances. When she had work to do, she would sit sewing from early morning till late at night; she had next to no leisure. When Zina needed sewing done, she would have Lyuba to stay for a week or two at a time, or sometimes even a month; she would pay 'family rates'—that is, whatever came into her head, without bothering to enquire the usual price for the work. Often this meant that Lyuba was paid very little; but Zina was as generous in trifling matters as she was mean in large ones. She would give Lyuba little presents of powder, scent, or a collar which she no longer wanted to wear, and her father would often add a gift of his own: a sack of potatoes, say, or something else which was useful, but inexpensive. A couple of times a year, one of Lyubinka's relatives would take her out to the theatre; every Easter and Christmas they gave her a length of cotton print for a new dress.

Lyuba was very shy of me at first; she had been cowed by Zina's educated friends, amongst whom she felt quite lost. But little by little, as she grew used to me, she lost her timidity. When I had sewing to be done, I would have Lyuba to stay. It was curiosity that first prompted my interest in the girl, but soon a genuine warmth took curiosity's place.

Lyubinka was tormented by her own ignorance more than by anything else.

'Don't you ever read?' I once asked her.

'How am I to find the time?' she replied. 'No, I can't think of reading at the moment; I'm in work, thank the Lord.'

But then after a few minute's silence she added:

'Do you suppose it's too late now for me to learn anything?'

'I doubt very much that it is. How old are you, Lyubinka?'

'Eighteen already.'

'Well, at that age one can still learn a lot. Indeed, at any age one can, if one wants to.'

'Is that really true?' Lyubinka asked, and her face lit up. 'That's what Yakov Ivanych° says too. Anyone would think you two had been talking.'

'So who is Yakov Ivanovich?'

'He's our landlady's nephew.'

'What has *he* been telling you, then?'

'He keeps pestering me to do lessons. He brings me these books, and reads aloud to me some evenings while I'm working, and then he makes me go over what I've heard, and if I don't understand anything, he tells me what it means.'

'But what does he do, this Yakov Ivanovich? Where is he from?'

Lyubinka gave a laugh.

'He arrived here last summer. He's from near Penza, his father was a priest there. He studied at the seminary himself, and did so well that they sent him to Petersburg.'

'So what does he do here?'

'He's in the service, but he doesn't get much of a salary, only twenty roubles a month. That's why his aunt took him in.'

And Lyubinka looked solemn again.

'Well, that is wonderful,' I said. 'Your Yakov Ivanych will give you an education.'

Lyubinka shook her head.

'If only I had more time...' she began, but left the sentence unfinished.

A month or two later, Zina called in on me one morning.

'I have good news for you,' she said.

'What might that be, Zina?'

'Your protégée is engaged to be married.'

'Your protégée' was the way that Zina usually referred to Lyubinka when speaking to me.

'I am delighted to hear it. Who is the young man?'

'A civil servant. He's far from stupid and not badly educated. I feel quite sorry for him, in fact, even if he is a bit of an oaf.'

'Why should you be sorry for him?'

'Because he'll never be happy with Lyuba.'

'Can you really be so sure of that?'

'Of course. How can an intelligent man be happy with a woman as limited as Lyuba?'

'Lyuba is not one-half so stupid as you suppose. She has plenty of native wit; all she lacks is education. If he is so clever, then he will be sure to give her that.'

Zina smiled sceptically.

'How did you meet this young man?' I asked.

'Lyuba's mother brought him to call on us yesterday. He is being taken to meet everyone in the family.'

'So is everything arranged for the wedding?'

'I reckon that they will have to wait until the pair of them have some money. And I should imagine *that* will take some time.'

'Will your family not do anything for Lyuba?'

'Of course they will! But anyway, if you want to meet this young man, you should call on us tomorrow evening, when we shall have company.'

The next evening I duly went round to the Vetlyagins'. There were only a few other guests. Two young ladies whom I had not met before; Lyubinka and her fiancé; a young man from the cadets, tall and slender as a poplar; and two other young gentlemen. I must say for the Vetlyagins that they had the gift of putting visitors at their ease; people did exactly as they liked there. It was not one of those dreadful households where the host and hostess make such efforts to amuse their guests that they conclude by tyrannizing them; in any case, I am glad to say, such Tatar customs° now seem to be on the wane, even in Russia.

Lyubinka brought up her young man, and presented him to me.

I have nothing against seminarians; on the contrary, I respect them, since they are invariably more or less educated and thoughtful people. But all the same, the seminary does leave its mark, and one can always recognize its products at a single glance. Take the way that a seminarian bows when he is introduced: stiff-backed, inclining his head and nothing else. Another characteristic is that they have a rather uncomfortable way of behaving in company, with what I can only describe as a kind of self-conscious deliberation in whatever they do. And their most typical qualities in a moral sense are suspicion and a fierce pride which sometimes reaches levels touching on absurdity.

Yakov Ivanovich was no exception to the general rule. He responded confusedly to my greeting and then shuffled off to sit in a quiet corner by the window. But Lyubinka was unrecognizable: she had become so much more lively and cheerful. Her happiness was as tangible as a breeze.

Soon some more friends turned up, and the party began in earnest. But I remained preoccupied with Yakov Ivanovich. I was eager to make his closer acquaintance, but knew that I must wait for the right moment if I were to avoid making him take fright; so I kept a close eye on him from a distance. A lady was persuaded to sing, and almost everyone went off to the music room to listen, Lyubinka along with the rest. I stayed in the drawing-room, and saw Zina sit down next to Yakov Ivanovich and begin making intent conversation to him. He replied almost in monosyllables; but Zina, no whit deterred, continued talking away. Then dancing began; but Zina said that she had no wish to dance, and stayed sitting next to Yakov Ivanovich. He gradually lost his timidity, and became more and more trusting. Seeing him become more involved in the discussion, I crossed the room and sat down not far away from Zina. They were talking about America, and Zina was speaking enthusiastically about American customs; Yakov Ivanovich was listening with some interest. Every now and then he would express agreement with what she was saying, or sometimes contradict her. From America they moved to the latest inventions, and from there to women writers, and from there to provincial young ladies. I could see Zina playing along with Yakov Ivanovich, and trying to impress him by the breadth of her knowledge and the radicalism of her views—something which it was not difficult for her to achieve.

Yakov Ivanovich was little used to the society of women. In the naïvety of his heart, he had no idea that there might nowadays be women who deliberately employed their fluency in conversation, and paraded their wide-ranging knowledge, in order to pull the wool over a poor seminarian's eyes, and make him fall head over heels in love with them. The evening left me feeling most uneasy, and fearing for the future.

As I left, I invited Yakov Ivanovich to visit me, saying that his fiancée's welfare was of great concern to me; and one morning he did indeed turn up, looking shy and awkward, and behaving as if paying a call on me were irksome to him. But I called all my social skills into play, and treated him as though he and I were old friends. At first he was so taken aback by this approach that I could get little from him, and conversation flagged. We spoke of Petersburg and its pleasures; then we began to talk of Petersburg society, and here Yakov Ivanovich did become more animated. He said that he did not find life in Petersburg entirely to his taste: people here lacked sincerity and cordiality, he found.

I had some framed photographs standing on an open-fronted bookcase, a portrait of Zina among them. Catching sight of it, Yakov Ivanovich began talking of women's education; then he began to speak of the matters which were closest to his heart. Zina had enraptured him, dazzled him. He talked almost reverently of her intelligence, said that her views of the world were almost as sound as a man's—forgetting, of course, that this was no surprise, since it was of course men who had evolved the views that Zina was so glibly parroting, and forgetting that it is, in any case, the easiest thing in the world to get a reputation for brilliance if you state borrowed opinions in a sufficiently confident voice.

'She is an extraordinary girl,' said Yakov Ivanovich. 'I have never met a woman with such well-developed intellectual powers.'

In vain did I try to convince him that girls with modern views were two-a-penny, and that those views were often half-baked. At last we began talking about Lyuba. Yakov Ivanovich said that she was a young woman of wonderful spiritual qualities, and that she had suffered much. But he appeared to be uncomfortable when speaking about her; I even spied a faint flush on his cheeks.

I spent most of the next three weeks ill in bed. I had no chance to visit anyone, and so did not set eyes on Zina. Whilst I was recovering, Lyubinka paid a call; the poor girl looked just as downcast as in the old days. More than that, she was quite obviously upset; it was clear that she had something worrying her which she could not make up her mind to communicate, though she was in sore need of reassurance.

'Well, what is Yakov Ivanovich up to these days?' I asked her, since she had failed to raise the subject herself.

'Oh! Nothing much. He's well, thank the Lord,' she said, with a heavy sigh.

'Has he met all your relations?'

'Yes, all of them.'

'Will you be married soon?'

'Oh, no, I hardly think so,' Lyubinka replied, with an oddly bitter smile.

'Why ever not?'

'He says we must wait until he at least gets a salary raise.'

'Is that what he said when he first started paying court to you?'

'No, he never said anything then about his salary. All he said was that he'd like my relatives to find a hundred and fifty roubles for me, so that I could have a trousseau of some kind.'

'Did your relatives agree to that?'

'Mama said they'd promised they would help.'

'But Yakov Ivanovich was quite right to say that you should wait until he gets a salary increase. You cannot possibly live on twenty roubles a month, after all.'

'*You* couldn't possibly, maybe, but we'd have managed somehow,' Lyuba said.

'How on earth would you have done that?'

'We'd have rented somewhere with plenty of space, and found a couple of lodgers, I could have done the cooking myself, and taken in work...'

'Did you talk to Yakov Ivanovich about that?'

'That was what we both wanted before. Now I don't know: probably it *is* better to wait.'

'Has he been visiting your relatives?'

'He's only been going to Andrei Osipych's lately.'

'How often does he go there?'

'Nearly every evening at the moment.'

'But you go with him, I expect?'

'No. I've got work to do. I was there last Wednesday, but not since.'

With that I had heard enough. So soon as I was well enough to be up and about, I went round to the Vetlyagins' for the evening, and immediately satisfied myself that Zina had Yakov Ivanovich in absolute thrall. He had come so far out of his shell that he had not only deserted his corner, but was talking louder and longer than anyone else. He agreed with everything that Zina said, and it was clear the two were in absolute understanding. Of Lyubinka there was no sign.

In the summer, the Vetlyagins moved to their dacha, and I began visiting them there. The open air and the free-and-easy atmosphere of dacha life mean that people are brought together faster than they would be in town; Yakov Ivanovich and I got to know each other better, and I succeeded in winning his trust. He had moved out of his aunt's flat, I learned, and did not visit his fiancée very often.

As for Lyubinka, she grew ever paler and thinner; but she never said a word about her fiancé or her cousin. She visited the dacha only twice that summer; in her presence Yakov Ivanovich became awkward, taciturn, and morose. And Lyubinka herself found things difficult, with Zina always at hand.

One evening in early September, I was in my sitting-room with my little daughter Masha, helping her to make dolly a new dress, when the maid announced Yakov Ivanovich. I was surprised, but delighted, to see my visitor; I had been wanting to have a heart-to-heart talk with him for some time. But when he came in, I saw at once that he was in a most peculiar and agitated frame of mind. He bowed to me distractedly, like a schoolboy who knows he has done wrong, but who does not want to confess it.

When we had exchanged a few empty pleasantries, Yakov Ivanovich fell into silent thought.

'I have come to ask for your advice,' he blurted out at last. 'You may well wish to condemn my behaviour, and I do not myself know whether I have been right or wrong to do as I have done. But I am the unhappiest man in the world, and you are the only person who can tell me how to extract myself from a very difficult situation.'

'Tell me what the matter is, and if I can give you any advice, then of course I will do so.'

Then Yakov Ivanovich told me what, of course, I knew already. Zina had so enchanted him, so bewitched him, that he had eyes and ears for her alone. He never wanted to be freed from her spell. But he was a man of conscience, and his relations with Lyuba were making him reproach himself every minute, were poisoning his life. She was a poor girl, with no possessions but her own good name. Yakov Ivanovich had been introduced to all her family. The voice of conscience could not be silenced, and it told him that he must marry her. Yakov Ivanovich was at the point of despair, but he was prepared to go to the altar with a bride whom he no longer loved. But before he did so, he needed someone else's advice. I suspect that his moral courage had given out, and that he needed someone else to tell him whether or not he was in the right.

When Yakov Ivanovich had finished his story, I began to feel very sorry for him. All his oddity and awkwardness had vanished, and I saw only a man who was very young, very inexperienced, but very honourable: a man of spiritual depth and firmness of character, who was readier to sacrifice his own happiness than to offend against the dictates of conscience.

'It is all a great deal less significant than you imagine,' I said. 'I will give you some advice; but first I want you to answer some questions as honestly as if you were in the confessional.'

'Confess me, then,' he replied, with a faint smile.

'Did you ever love Lyubinka?'

'Of course I did, or why should I have proposed to her?'

'You knew that she was uneducated, that she had no money, that it would take time and patience to turn her into a woman capable of your Zina's kind of mental activity. Yet you loved her. Why should that have been?'

Yakov Ivanovich was silent.

'You cannot answer that question, because you are not used to analysing your own feelings. But I can tell you why you loved her.'

Yakov Ivanovich gave me a questioning look.

'Firstly because she has a sweet face, which accurately reflects her kind heart; secondly because she has a sharp, though untutored, intelligence;

and thirdly because you sensed that she was sympathetic to you, and knew that you could bring some joy into her unhappy life.'

Yakov Ivanovich nodded gloomily.

'But now you love Zina, and I can tell you why that is as well. She has shocked you, she has numbed you. She is the first educated woman whom you have met, and so you think of her as perfection. You forget that such women are commonplace these days. You have fallen madly in love with her fashionable phrases, you believe in them so fervently that you fail to notice the gap between words and deeds. Forgive my frankness, but I must tell you that in my view Zina, for all her education, humanitarian ideas, and wise opinions, is worth less than Lyubinka's little finger.'

Yakov Ivanovich's head shot up, and he gave me a glance as if he had been bitten by a snake.

'No, don't be angry,' I went on. 'You are entitled to your own views on the matter, but they should not stop you hearing me out. Zina is worth nothing in comparison with Lyubinka, because Lyubinka has a real heart and soul, whereas Zina's heart and soul are made out of phrases. Lyubinka is certain to turn out for the best: whether she is educated or no, she will become a woman who is genuinely good, and capable of doing good, whilst Zina is likely to end up as nothing but a heartless coquette. She is a flower that will bear no fruit.'

'You assail her too cruelly,' whispered Yakov Ivanovich timidly, almost pleading with me.

'We shall see about that. Tell me this: could you love a woman who paid you no attention, who treated you so distantly that you could have no shadow of hope?'

'I think it would be hard to love a woman like that,' Yakov Ivanovich replied.

'I agree. She might attract you, but common sense and self-interest would not allow the feeling to develop into love. I do not think that you lack those qualities; and so we must conclude that if Zina had not flirted with you, you would not have fallen head over heels in love with her.'

'But why do you suppose that she was flirting with me? Can she not have been inspired by real feeling, as I was?' Yakov Ivanovich protested, coming back to life again.

'You promised that you would speak as frankly as you would in the confessional. I shall not ask you to go into any details, but answer this one question. Have you any reason to believe that Zina is sympathetic to your case, that she has any more feeling for you than for any other good friend whose conversation she enjoys?'

'Perhaps I do.'

'Good, in that case, your problems are at an end. You should put the matter to the test, and ask Zina whether she is prepared to link her life with yours.'

Yakov Ivanovich gave a start, and looked at me in astonishment. He had certainly not expected matters to take this turn. His face expressed fear, hope, and doubt in turns.

'Can I possibly do that?' he asked eventually.

'Why should you not? After all, do you not suppose that Zina is favourably inclined towards you?'

'But what of Lyubov Petrovna?'

'Lyubinka knows as well as anyone else what is going on. And in any case, she has plenty of self-respect, believe me. She will not make herself an obstacle to your happiness. If you marry her without loving her, then you will make her unhappy all her life. Don't take more on yourself than a man can stand; choose the lesser of two evils.'

'But will Zina Andreevna accept me?' Yakov Ivanovich still hesitated.

'Of course she will, if she is the remarkable woman whom you suppose her to be. She can see that you live and breathe only for her. If, on the other hand, it does turn out that she has only been flirting with you, then we will know that I was right, and that she is a soulless woman who has taken away poor Lyubinka's fiancé in order to satisfy her own vanity and tickle her own fancy.'

'That is not what I mean. What I am afraid of, rather, is that Andrei Osipovich will not give his consent to our marriage. What kind of husband will I make? I have no money or position, and they are a wealthy family. They are sure to want a better match for their daughter.'

'But what of progress? What of emancipation?' I rushed in, not without a modicum of malicious enjoyment. 'That whole family is emancipated, after all. Why, even the grandmother is! You know very well that she has learnt to find her footstool herself when it is missing, and not to bother Mishka for it—so that now he can stand in the hall chasing flies all day if he wants to. Besides, Andrei Osipovich will consent to anything his daughter wishes; I am certain that if she had taken it into her head to marry an Egyptian Pasha, her father would meekly dispatch messengers to take the proposal to Egypt.'

My talk with Yakov Ivanovich lasted for a very long time, but at length I managed to instil some decisiveness in him. What made him most anxious was the fear that Lyubinka might become ill with despair, or even die. I advised him to say nothing to her until he had spoken to Zina.

For the next week I had no news of what was going on at the Vetlyagins'. I was tormented by curiosity, but the bad weather prevented my visiting them. But then, after dinner one evening, I heard someone ring the doorbell so loudly that I sprang up from my chair in horror.

It was pouring with rain. Who could be visiting in this kind of weather, and ringing the bell so loudly? It must be someone in the grip of a terrible crisis. I immediately thought of Yakov Ivanovich—and sure enough, there he was, in the doorway of my sitting-room.

He looked pale and strained, and the expression on his face made me quite worried.

'What on earth is the matter?' I asked.

'You were right!' he said, gesticulating with his hat, from which a stream of water was pouring on to my carpet. 'What a cunning creature she is! Women!... They are nothing but deceiving coquettes, created to destroy the whole of humanity,' he continued, and began rushing around the room, still waving his hat about.

'Your compliments enrapture me, sir! Kindly put your hat down somewhere, and then tell me what has happened.'

Yakov Ivanovich flung his hat on to a chair in the corner and then began rushing about the room once more, eyes darting.

'Sit down and calm yourself,' I begged him. I was anxious that he should not stumble into some piece of furniture and knock it over. 'Is Zinaida Andreevna well?'

'She is very well,' he hissed, with a grimace of fury, coming to a halt right in front of my chair. 'What do you suppose might be wrong with her? I expect her to live at least another hundred years, and torment dozens of poor fools like me.'

'What should that mean?'

'Are you happy with the news?'

'What news?'

'She is engaged to be married!'

'To whom, to you?'

'No. Thank God, not to me.'

'To whom, then?'

'To the head of a department in the civil service.'

'Can this be true?'

'How can it not be, when she wrote to tell me so herself?'

Yakov Ivanovich tugged a thin, scented piece of paper from his pocket. It was a letter, written in a beautiful script and very elegantly phrased, which conveyed a most slippery and ingenious refusal of his proposal. Zina had written that she felt the deepest affection for Yakov Ivanovich, and that she was sure she should have been blissfully happy, had they been able to marry; but that society would rightly condemn her if she were to marry her cousin's fiancé. This led to a long digression on public opinion and the need to sacrifice personal happiness to it, and so on. In conclusion, Zina added that she had in any case promised her father that she would marry Mr Shestakov, who had made an offer for her hand some time ago; she had, however, not at first decided whether or not to accept him. 'But now,' Zina wrote, 'it is a matter of indifference to me. If I am to sacrifice myself, then the sooner the sacrifice is accomplished, the better! I should like you to know that I do not love him, that I shall never love him. I shall always treasure my recollections of you.' She ended by lamenting that she and Yakov Ivanovich had met too late.

'What do you say to that?' asked Yakov Ivanovich, when he saw that I had finished reading, and was twisting the paper between my fingers, sunk in thought.

'That it is exactly what I expected. I knew perfectly well that she would never marry you.'

'You knew that! In that case, why did you advise me to propose to her? Were you intending to make fun of me?' cried Yakov Ivanovich, brought to despair by this endless vista of feminine perfidy.

'There is nothing to make fun of; on the contrary, it is all very sad. I felt pity for you and Lyubinka, and so I wanted to open your eyes to reality.'

Yakov Ivanovich took several turns round the room, and began to calm down a little.

'Could anyone expect that Zinaida Andreevna would turn out to be so cold, so calculating?' he said at last, sinking into an armchair opposite me.

'Rather tell me why one should not have expected it!'

'By your leave! With her intellect, with her education, with her enlightened view of life, her sophisticated, elevated perceptions of humanity... What can one expect from other women after that? It is enough to drive one insane!'

And Yakov Ivanovich clutched his forehead.

At this I burst out laughing.

'Zina's conduct is not one-half so criminal as you suppose,' I said. 'There are dozens of women just like her; the point is that she is the first such woman whom you have met. What is really at fault is the ridiculous and ephemeral education which Russian women are given. If you scrutinize the matter, what is the mainspring of social life here? Self-praise. Each one of us is an abyss of vanity; the result is that appearance is everything. Women are not educated for their own good; from childhood, they are taught to show off, to parade their talents, their brains, their beauty, their wit. It is not women themselves who are to blame; it is those who bring them up. Most people in society here are shams from their toes to the tops of their heads—and beyond. We are nothing but pathetic imitations, with our 'progress', our 'emancipation'—all words which we have picked up somewhere, and which we have started bandying about because otherwise we might fall behind the fashion, get stuck in the mud! We are not remotely interested in really bettering ourselves, or our society. 'Progress!' 'Emancipation!' Right back to the time of Peter the Great, the Russian language has been stuffed with words like that, with their superficial intellectuality, superficial glitter. And if all that applies to society at large, what can you expect from women? How can you expect a woman to realize that real education has to begin in her own soul, that all her fancy knowledge, her mental development will be fruitless unless they facilitate her progress in a *moral* sense? Just look at Zina. She is a clever girl, I'll grant you, but what does she ever do but chatter? Her sense of the decorum incumbent on an emancipated, contemporary woman means that she would never dream of picking up a needle; she would consider herself dishonoured if she so much as opened the door of a kitchen. And she is by no means unusual. She has a disease which has taken hold of many, many fashionable young women—as the result of ideas which have been half-understood, or not understood at all...'

'She will pay for this!' Yakov Ivanovich suddenly broke in. 'I shall write to her. May I?' he went on, sitting down at my writing-desk. 'I should like you to read it first.'

'Certainly,' I said. I was curious to see what he would write.

A quarter of an hour later, Yakov Ivanovich handed me the following epistle, written in an elaborately curlicued script:

What have you done to me? What have you done to yourself? Your letter cast me into an abyss of despair. I do not know what will become of me; I think that I shall go insane. My head is spinning, an infernal flame gnaws my innermost being, my heart is tormented by suffering. O, Zinaida Andreevna! You, that most elevated, most emancipated of women, can you have taken fright at the thought of public opinion? What is the world to you, when you yourself stand so far above it? Let its fatuous rebukes be ground in the dust before you! O, my heart is breaking to pieces! And to think of the future which I had planned for us, of which you knew nothing!

If you had loved me—as I had sufficient reason to think that you did—if you had united your life with mine, we should have travelled the world together, discovering new truths hitherto unknown as we voyaged, we should have departed to some far-off corner,° and there we should have made the Golden Age come to life again, and made all of humanity follow in our path! The world would have bowed at your feet, wondering at your glory. You would have placed Woman on the high pedestal—that pedestal which you now surrender of your own will. And what will become of you now? To be Madame Shestakova, the wife of a head of department, what a paltry fate that is! And as for me, unhappy man! You have destroyed me too! You have destroyed a man who might have been a genius! Blow, windy tempest! Blow my anguish away! Let the whole of nature tremble, let all humanity burn in the hellish conflagration of perfidy and hypocrisy! Flow on, fast rivers, and swallow all living creatures, the wide world is loathsome to me now! Darkness is in my soul, darkness all around me! The sun of my life has set!

I remain, Madam, Your most humble servt.

Yakov Peresvetov

'Why on earth have you written this?' I asked Yakov Ivanovich, when I had got to the end of this nonsensical effusion.

'I want her to know that I find her ridiculous. That will at least relieve my feelings. Do you think that I should send her the letter?'

'If it really will relieve your feelings, then I suppose that you might as well send it.'

Yakov Ivanovich sealed the letter and rushed to post it. I would dearly have liked the chance to prefix a title to his epistle: *The Seminarian's Revenge*. But not all good ideas are destined to come to fruition, alas!

A few days later, I visited Lyubinka, and we talked of her cousin's forthcoming marriage.

'Does Yakov Ivanovich still visit you, Lyubinka?' I asked her.

'He was here yesterday,' she said reluctantly.

'Are you expecting to be married soon?'

Lyubinka showed a flash of temper.

'I don't want to marry him,' she said. 'Bother him, I say.'

'But Lyubinka, why this change of heart?'

'He needs a clever, educated wife, like he is himself. He'd never be happy with me.'

'Are you angry with him, Lyubinka? You have a right to be, there is no doubt of that! But can you not forgive him? He is only young, after all, and young men are so unstable in their affections!'

'There's nothing to be angry about,' she replied calmly. 'He's not to blame for seeing what's better than what, when it's as plain as the nose on your face. But it's still not right I should marry him. You say yourself he's young—let him sow his wild oats, I say, but I don't want to be made unhappy myself, nor for him to be neither.'

'So you never really loved him, then, Lyubinka? You were mistaken in your own feelings?'

Lyubinka gave me a long stare, and tried to say something. But her eyes filled with the tears that her pride had held back for so long, and she could not speak. I tried to persuade her to be magnaminous, and forgive Yakov Ivanovich, but she refused to be swayed.

'How could I marry an educated husband like that?' she asked. 'He'd blush for me at every step. I'll battle through on my own somehow, you see if I don't, with God's help. There's an end to everything, after all. And even life on earth doesn't last for ever—thank the Lord.'

[*1863*]

◆ ELIZAVETA SHAKHOVA ◆

Like Elisaveta Kulman, Shakhova, who was born in 1821, made her name as a child prodigy; the publication of her first book of verse in 1837 led, as she records herself, to a flurry of enthusiasm, and the expression of many flattering opinions. In 1849, Shakhova took the veil as a nun, but she still continued to write. Her later output includes devotional verse, plays on religious subjects, retellings of saints' lives for the common soldiery, and biographies of prominent nuns, as well as occasional verse, and confessional or autobiographical pieces such as the one anthologized here. Many of these remained unpublished until after her death in 1899, when they were collected in a three-volume edition, *Sobranie sochinenii* (St Petersburg 1911), edited by Shakhova's nephew.

Autobiographical Response from a Provincial Wasteland (in Reply to a New Year's Greeting Sent with a Bouquet)

(Russian text p. 419)

to Sofya Mikhailovna Gogel

Through the small opening in the boarded wall
Of the hut that serves as cell here in the waste,
A golden shaft of sunlight glittered bright,
Shining in the pallid January frost
Like these roses in my blue glass jug,
Whose petals on their thin green stalk
Burst into life, a miracle
Of buffy silk and cloth-of-gold.
A gift in all ways miraculous,
This thin pale sheet reflects gold light,
It speaks to me of making new songs,
It prompts new sounds to wing their flight.

'This does not suit my character
Nor yet my age—I should learn sense!
But all the signs here indicate

That love has seized my soul again!'
In the afternoon of his short life
Thus the Immortal Pushkin spoke,
A poet's strength of intellect
Could not subdue his raging heart.

It is time for me too to cease my dreams
Of sounds not heard, of fresh new powers;
To pass the winter of my life
Sternly reviewing my past years;
Time to hang up my rusted lyre
Upon a birch here in the North,
So the wind may play upon the strings
And sing a lament for fancy's death!

Long ago, when I first dared
To touch the lyre's forbidden strings,
The infant melodies I shaped
Sang of far more than childish things;
The world allowed me my first taste
Of fame, first glimmer of renown;
Russia's most high and glorious sons
Deigned to commend my youthful songs;
The poets hailed me as their sister,
Heaped panegyrics on my head;
Greeting 'Elisabeth the Second',
They boldly named me Kulman's heir;
The bard of *Svetlana* and *Lyudmila*
Declared the laurels would be mine,
And the sweet chorus of fair ladies
Lifted their voices in my praise.
The scholars and the connoisseurs
Commended me, lent me their aid;
The only fault found in my verse
Was a too lively modesty.

It was not to be! The hand of fate
Drove me to live behind this wall,
To dwell on the fringes, in the shade.

I would never don the bridal veil.
On the day I entered on that path,
And saw the distance open wide,
In the flush of youth and innocence,
Of love and other earthly joys,
I stood at the bridal chamber's door—
But heard the voice of Christ resound—
Surrendering myself to my Lord's call,
I took my cross and followed Him!

I have survived. My heavy lids
Are swollen and reddened by my tears.
And all the hopes others expressed
Have borne no fruit upon this earth,
My sweet and melancholy lyre
Belied all the grand prophesies,
And I shall go into my grave,
In a crown of thorns, not wearing bays;
Dressed in black crape, a flowing cloak,
Wrapped up in garments like a shroud,
Unspotted by sin, beyond reproach,
I am no poet, but a nun.
But I nurtured the talent I was given
Through half a century and more;
Although my path was long and hard,
I have not betrayed the gift of song!
And if that gift hides in the wasteland,
As a seed will hide inside its fruit,
And if the world casts stones towards me,
I'll defend myself before my Judge!

My life has changed—so have my songs!
But I have never ceased to sing,
And now you, madam, call to me,
Alone you approach my wasteland here.
Yours is the key to the chest of tunes,
Songs may be summoned by you alone;
May the blessing that God alone can grant
Come down on your sons, and on their sons!

You have not lost the power to share
Those high emotions, you love them still;
You heard this voice cry in its wasteland
Through the chatter of the multitude;
You caught the music it did not hear,
You sensed the questions surging up
In this singing soul, you caught these sounds
You heard, you sensed, you comprehended!
In existence severed from the world
This voice sings other songs, I say;
But the world despises songs like these,
Its language and theirs are not the same;
Its worldly aims, worldly debates
Are directed by its worldly priests;
They cloak catastrophe, disaster,
In fateful clouds of flattery.
The world is deaf to cries from heaven!
It would silence all beyond the earth;
Its cry is '*Panem et circenses*!'
In many-tongued cacophony.

Though He seems superfluous to our 'age of reason'
Christ can plunge this world back into chaos;
But He will renew the earth, and then
Will make a better world for us!

[*c.*1865]

♦ OLGA SHAPIR ♦

Olga Shapir, who was born in 1850, came from a cross-class family: her father was a former serf, who had managed to make his way up to the position of estate manager by dint of hard work and force of personality, whilst her mother came from a family of Swedish aristocrats. In her early twenties, whilst attending the Courses of Higher Education in St Petersburg, Shapir became involved with the Nechaev movement (the radical circle led by the charismatic revolutionary terrorist Sergei Nechaev, which was later to be portrayed in Dostoevsky's *The Devils*). Shapir's husband, Lazar Shapir, was an active member of the circle, and was expelled from medical school as a result. Shapir herself got him reinstated; when he qualified, and was posted to the Russian provinces as a *zemstvo* (local authority) doctor, she went with him. She produced her first stories in the late 1870s, but her best work dates from the 1890s, after she had returned to St Petersburg, and had begun to be involved with the Russian Women's Mutual Philanthropic Society, a feminist group holding moderate reformist views. Shapir remained a feminist all her life, and played a prominent part in the First All-Russian Congress of Women, in 1908. A popular and well-regarded writer during her own lifetime, she has suffered from almost total neglect since her death in 1916; like Anastasiya Verbitskaya, she has been unfairly branded as a writer of pulp romantic fiction, but her best work in fact typifies late nineteenth-century feminist fiction in its broad range of political and social concerns, and its impassioned critical-realist standpoint.

The Settlement

Morals live on bread, not air.°
(*Russian proverb*)

A single lamp was burning late in Kuzma Portnyagin's cottage. The Settlement° inhabitants all knew that lamp well. They would see it whenever they came back at night after a long day in town, and dawdled back through the village to their homes, their feet as uncertain as their hearts were light.

The low, wretched cottages of the Settlement straggled untidily to one and the other side of its muddy, unmade streets, which were unlit by any street-lights. To a befuddled gaze and an inflamed fantasy they resembled distorted and hideous figures lying in ambush, which might rush out at any moment, and reveal the frenzied face and bony fists of an outraged mother, or let fly the howls and rebukes of an indignant wife. It was at such moments that the glimmer of a ten-copeck lamp would suddenly cut through the gloom, and dispel the nightmare visions. The unsteady wanderer would recognize his own crooked alley, and know whither he should direct his disobedient feet.

'Look at that... The poor lad at his books till late again,' he would mutter, squinting at the light. And he would smile without knowing why, and be filled with a vague sense of well-being, closeness, family warmth.

Well, it *was* family, or very near so! There weren't far off a thousand people living in the Settlement, and that Fedka Portnyagin stuck out like a sore thumb. He was the only lad you'd see going about in a *gimnaziya*° uniform, dressed up in fancy cloth with silver braid and shiny buttons, whilst his cousins and all the other lads his age either went barefoot, or were pleased enough with their blacked boots and plush jerkins. Even ruddy-cheeked and saucer-eyed Mitka, who was forever up to monkey tricks, who was the son and heir of the richest man in the settlement, Isaiah the shopkeeper, and who swaggered about togged out up to the nines every time there was a holiday, his parents' pockets having no bottoms when it came to presents for him, so that he got given the sort of stuff the other lads had as much chance of seeing as their own ears, even at Easter°—even Mitka, the apple of his fat, puffed-up, turkey-hen mother's eye, would shoot glances of involuntary admiration at Fedka's old navy-blue uniform coat, for all that it was too short in the waist and threadbare, and at his well-worn cap, which, despite the efforts of his sister Dunyasha the seamstress, refused to sit up straight on his brainy head, but instead crept down over his ears like a collapsed pancake. Seeing Fedka, Mitka would bare his teeth, or else he would recite the whole catalogue of the wretched uniform's stains and darns to the sound of catcalls from the barefoot fraternity. But Fedka would fail to rise to these taunts, and would walk coolly past the garishly painted porch of the shop, buoyed up by a quite genuine sense of his own superiority. Avoiding the schoolboy's eyes, Mitka would stare pointedly at the satchel hanging at his back. But then all of a sudden the expression on his plump, impudent face would turn serious, and a look of something very like envy would show in his bulging eyes. His ma and da would have done better than that for *his* uniform!

The whole Settlement followed the progress of its one *gimnaziya* pupil closely, vesting its trust and its pride in this small being, who, with God's help, was destined to take his family's hopes 'into the big wide world', to leave this Settlement mired in poverty and ignorance, and become part of city life, that city life that weighed down on the Settlement with its educated ways, its stone houses, its clean-swept broad streets, its gaslights, and its well-fed inhabitants. But such had by no means been the Settlement's initial reaction when Fedka's schooling first started; the novelty had by no means been accepted straight away in this tight-knit, hard-bitten world.

It might not seem much to send a boy to school, but clearly there is some hidden meaning in the action, for it had stirred up the whole of this backwater. An explosive mixture of feelings had been on show: every woman in the village had added her mite, and every tongue had wagged, making this timid, thoughtful small boy the hero of the hour. It was Fedka's sister Dunyasha who had decided to send him, and she had to snap back at attacks from all sides, defending herself against mocking hostility and venomous criticism. Got too good for her place, had she. Nose so far in the air she could hardly see where she was going. Getting above her station. Too much of a fool to realize she'd pay for all this in time. It made no difference that she was doing it all with the sweat of her own back, that she was working her own fingers to the bone to give Fedka a better start in life. Well, she'd give him his education, but then what? He wouldn't want to know. He'd get shot of all of them as quick as he could. His drunken father, who trawled the taverns offering his services as a scribe. His seamstress sister, who hauled her loads of mending up the service staircases of rich people's houses, and was rewarded for her efforts by the odd rag 'for the children' on top of her few copecks' pay. No wonder that little Lizka, the younger daughter, had swanned round in the crumpled and faded wrecks of fancy children's clothes from the moment she was out of nappies. No doubt this was how the famous uniform had been come by as well. You could tell at a glance it was second-hand; everyone in the Settlement knew it, and all Dunyasha's attempts to hide from the neighbours how things stood were in vain.

Dunyasha, or 'elder sister', as Fedya called her° when he was little, using the customary honorific title, had had to listen to all this dozens of times. She had worn her voice hoarse shouting at the stupid old women, trying to convince them they were wrong. Her irritation and anger had mounted as she had to 'fight like a dog' day after day, defending an action which went against the grain of her whole world—something that could wear out the energies even of someone more fortunate than a seamstress in a workers' settlement.

But time went on and on.

The poisoned arrows fell harmlessly at the feet of this energetic, unsmiling woman, who gazed at the world angrily and suspiciously with her intelligent eyes. Her youth was now past, and still she worked unceasingly, frenziedly, on behalf of her whole family. The schoolboy moved from class to class in a smooth, uninterrupted progress, and the Settlement gradually got used to his situation. Kuzma Portnyagin no longer moaned so often to his cronies about his 'spiteful' daughter, about how she would be ready to see her old pa off the face of the earth if it only gave her an extra copeck to spend on the lad. He had stopped beating up his son when he was drunk, and threatening to use his books as fuel in the stove. In fact, he now often turned to Fedka for help as a peacemaker in disputes with Dunyasha. The schoolboy could not stand the quarrels and fights which his energetic sister so eagerly initiated. And even the most critical of the neighbours, who had mourned Dunyasha's likely fate in advance, had to admit that there were no signs that Fedka's schooling was making him spoilt or demanding. Having taken off his uniform coat and folded it carefully, he would fetch water from the well, chop wood, or herd a pig that Lizka was too small to deal with—all just as before.

Time passed. Often, Settlement lads would pause thoughtfully as they passed the schoolboy, whose still childish frame was belied by an adult steadiness and seriousness of gaze. And, as the other lads listened to Fedya's excited and exciting stories about 'what they teach us in their *gimnaziya*', they would sometimes swell out their massive chests in a sigh.

Some hefty youth whose beard had hardly broken through, but whose hands were already coarsened by heavy work, might start up a lament:

'E-eh now! Well, it's us will pay for our sins. We've lived like moles, we'll die like moles, heaving earth in the dark. But, Fedya, lad, don't you dare forget, if it wasn't for your sister Avdotya Kuzminishna° you'd be no better off than us.'

'Fair enough,' Fedya would reply, scowling. 'Leave me be, will you. It's your fault, you should take care of your own wits, not pour them down the drain in the tavern.'

'What's the difference? We don't have to go to school, do we?' the Settlement sage would grin.

The whole Settlement knew what Fedya's school looked like too. Every boy there had run to stare at the big handsome building with its huge windows and its splendid doorway, this last guarded by a magnificent retired corporal, his chest bright with the medals of long-ago campaigns.

'Look, that's our Fedka!' the boys would nudge each other as Fedka Portnyagin appeared amongst the rich people's children. Before their very eyes Fedka, his manner quietly dignified as usual, would shake the hand of a handsome young rich boy, before the latter leapt into a dashing droshky° standing at the door.

But all that was long ago; by now the Settlement had got used to the fact that Kuzma's Fedka was a hop-out-o'kin. Their former mockery now vanished, folk would ask from time to time in a neighbourly way how the boy was doing, and whether he had got through his 'examinations'° all right. (That word had now passed into the vocabulary of almost the whole Settlement.) Here and there someone would even say: 'It's all a fuss about nothing. If things had been different, maybe our Senka, or our Petka, could have done just as well at the studies. What's so special about that Fedka, is what I say.'

But it was more the women who were inclined to such speculations, an inclination in which their sex's notorious capacity for vanity and envy no doubt played a role. For their part, the fathers stuck to their principles, and put any fanciful notions about schooling to flight in the directest possible way.

Fedya didn't just work hard; he worked obsessively. He didn't merely love the *gimnaziya*; he worshipped it.

But time flew on and on.

It was a dull spring night, and Fedya's lamp was shining alone once more in the dark of the Settlement. The cocks had already crowed twice in the stockyards; the paraffin was burning low, but Fedya was still turning the pages of his exercise books. His head back, his eyes closed, he was letting out a stream of rapid, incomprehensible sounds. Or now and again, to save time, he would raise his hand and use one finger to trace some strange word in the air.

An onlooker might have supposed the poor boy was touched in the head. There was a greenish tinge to his face, and his red-rimmed eyes shone with an unhealthy glint, or gazed dully and fixedly at a single point. Every so often his whole body would shake with a fit of nervous yawning, or he would shiver as the bitter night chill cut into his bony shoulders under his faded print shirt and well-worn waistcoat. For minutes at a time the boy would sit slumped in exhaustion, the grey paper exercise book slipping from his knees. Until roused by the sound of the book slapping on the ground, he would lose track of his thoughts altogether, dreaming that he was on his bunk above the stove, warmly wrapped in the printed cotton quilt which Dunya's skilled hands had made him.

Bang! went the book. Fedya shook himself, picked it up, rubbed his eyes—which felt as though they were full of sand—and walked up and down the room for a few minutes to wake himself up. He'd taken off his boots a while back to avoid making any unnecessary noise. The others, snoring sweetly behind the thin partitions, would have heard nothing had they woken but the occasional almost inaudible whisper, or a faint rustle of paper... And even these modest sounds of all-out mental effort were often blotted out by the monotonous chirp of a cricket behind the stove.

But all the same, not all was tranquillity behind the partitions. Every now and then a door papered with generously flyblown prints of what had once been the latest fashions would be pushed open gently, and Dunyasha's head would appear round it. Blinking and screwing up her eyes in the light, she would watch her brother for a few seconds; then, without saying a word, she would close the door carefully, and go back to her bed, at whose foot Lizka was soundly sleeping, curled up into a little ball. And every so often, from a dark corner in the hall, screened for privacy by a wardrobe, would rise the thick, drunken snores of father Kuzma, triumphing alike over the cricket's song and the sounds of his son's tense wakefulness.

'One more try through this and I can go to bed,' the schoolboy muttered to himself, scrabbling for his escaped exercise book.

The lamp had long grown sooty, and the sky at the little windows was turning pale. Suddenly the door with the fashion-prints on it swung wide, and Dunyasha came in wearing her dressing-gown. She would have died rather than been seen in this garment before visitors, but how well Fedya knew it. Her dishevelled hair was hidden by a scarf; her expression was grim, but she was wide awake. She came up to the table and sat down on the bench by her brother.

'Fyodor, what do you think you're up to? Have you lost your wits entirely, to try taking your examination on no sleep?'

'I was just going to bed anyway. Can't find my book... Where the devil is it...'

'That's enough now, I'll find it for you. Can't you see it's getting light? You'll get in to school tired out again, and you swore yourself you wasn't going to stay up late after last time, you said it just got you all muddled.'

Without saying anything, and forgetting all his efforts to keep quiet, Fedya flung his books on the table. As his brows moved low and narrowed into a frown, he began to look more and more like his sister, who herself was staring at him, screwing up her forehead.

'You did say that, you said so when you had the Russian literature one.'

'So if I did? So what? Think I don't know myself, is that it?' Fedya suddenly snapped. 'Yes, I did say that, and you know as well as I do I wasn't up half so late then as now.'

Dunyasha sat immobile, arms folded under her shapeless old woollen shawl. She had them crossed over the edges of her bodice, from which almost all the buttons were missing.

'The bigger you grow, the harder you seem to find it,' she said darkly, forcing the words out one by one.

Fedya threw his head back and flashed his eyes at her.

'It gets more difficult, doesn't it... But, then, how would you know that? After all, you just sit sticking your needle in and out, in and out, year after year, and if you lived to 200, still nothing'd change. But studying in the second form and the fourth, now that *is* different.'

'Well, you didn't need to go to the *gimnaziya* to know that much,' his sister said scornfully. 'You're not 10 years old now. Indeed, I do believe it was your fifteenth birthday a few days since.'

And now a faint patchy flush was beginning to show on Fedya's cheeks.

'That's right, just you start nagging... That's all I needed.'

A high childish note sounded in the boy's uncertain, forced bass.

Dunyasha released one of her hands and began to fiddle at her scarf.

'So I have started in on you... Well, I've got reason to. Working all night as though the devil was in you! One thing if you'd been slacking in the winter or been off sick, but as it is, you've been up to midnight night after night, and you never missed a day's school. You'd think you might know your stuff by now!'

'But I *do* know it! How come you think I don't?'

'So if you do, what's this nonsense for?' Dunyasha got up from her bench with an air of finality.

She seized the lamp, blew it out and shoved it on to the shelf below the table.

A dreary half-light filled the room. The chirp of the cricket and the snores of Kuzma resounded still more triumphantly in the gathering silence. Dunya shivered and put her hand back under her shawl. Fedya fixed his weary gaze on the muddy street; not even a dog was abroad yet.

'Well, get to bed, then.'

'You've got no cause to say harsh things to me,' the boy suddenly said. 'You don't know it all. You think that if I know the subject I've got nothing to fear. To you an exam is a word you've heard me use, that's all. You've never dreamt what actually happens *at* one...'

Fedya had put on his usual 'grown-up' manner again, but that only sharpened his bitterness, brought it further to the surface. Dunyasha measured him with her shrewd eyes.

'I'm not making less of an effort now; I can't try any harder. Before, I used to look forward to my exams... I never felt worried, never felt I couldn't do it... You know that, don't you?' His speech rose to a shriek, and tears shone in his darting eyes.

Dunya slid her hand from under her shawl again, and pressed her clenched fist into the table-top.

'What was I just saying? When you were little you had it easier, I see that, but there's still no call to sit up nights.'

She stared at him suspiciously, heaving her shrunken chest, and flaring the nostrils of her sharp hooked nose.

'So what is it, Fyodor?'

'I don't know,' he muttered dully.

'Well, who is supposed to know, if you're not? You know, I think you're scared. The last time you just scraped through, and you was so pleased you was crossing yourself. You stopped thinking about top marks long ago.'

'Top marks!' Fedya was close to desperation. 'What use is hoping for them now?'

Dunyasha leant closer and closer to him, tipping her body so far forward that it seemed she might fall off the bench. Her eyes spoke volumes.

'Well?'

'I've racked and racked my brains, and I still can't see what's going on. It's all changed so much. I was always supposed to be so good at it! Cross my heart, I can't see that I've done anything wrong. What I said just now was rot, about how the fourth form's harder, in fact I was keeping up easily just as usual—not that you could really say "easily", of course, since I don't get any help with my lessons, there's no one I can ask. But I *was* keeping on top of things, I wasn't worried...'

'We-ell?' Dunyasha simply repeated.

'Well... Suddenly they start telling me I'm no good! The inspector says to me every time he passes me, "So, Portnyagin my good fellow, having trouble are you?... No wonder, the fifth form is no joke, you know... And given your home background..."' (All this in a venomous hiss, as Fedya mimicked the inspector.) 'But I've been mugging up for the exam as usual... They always used to praise me and hold me up as an example to the slackers: look at Portnyagin, they'd say—and when you think of the problems he might have with that family, no peace, no one to lend a hand...

Then it was all "good work and an example to the others", and now... All of them just frown whenever I go up to the front... The maths master put me through it for a whole half hour the other day... After that you're damn glad to scrape a pass, I tell you!'

'So what'll you do now?'

Fedya paused.

'Well, if I flunk Latin, then they'll keep me down for a year.'

'Keep you down for a year? For a whole year? For God's sake, Fyodor! I'm not a cart-horse, even my strength won't last for ever! I've two mouths to feed besides yours, and where can I expect help from if you get stuck in the fourth form? And to spend all winter chewing over old stuff!'

Dunyasha was on her feet now, her breath coming in rushes—indicating the extremity of anger and distress.

'But it's not my fault!' shouted the boy desperately.

'Yes it is... Look here, boy, it can only be you! They don't push people around without just cause. Don't you tell me fairy stories! I know all too well what you boys are like, you little rascals. I bet it's some mischief you've cooked up between you, to put one across on the powers that be. So don't try spinning me no fibs. You know full well you can't take me in! You'd be better to own up straight. What is it you did?'

'I don't know of anything like that. I've been working harder than ever. I know my work hasn't got any worse, but as soon as I have to answer their questions, my heart just turns over! I can read it all in their eyes.'

Both were silent for a few seconds. Then Dunyasha sank heavily down on the bench again.

'Well, Fyodor... I feel like you've hit me on the head with something—pole-axed! I've always been sharp-witted, I've known just what to do all my life, but I can't bend my wits round this. I can see myself that you are studying... I've seen it with my own eyes. You used to boast that they thought such a lot of you, but now you think they might even keep you down... I've been wondering myself what's happened, why you aren't like yourself any more. It's not your first examination by a long chalk, but suddenly the stuffing seems to have gone out of you... You even look different, off your food, not getting enough sleep. What good can that do?'

'None... I don't suppose,' Fedya muttered gloomily.

'Nor me, nor me!' Dunyasha began. But then she broke off suddenly, tearing the scarf from her head. 'But what are we up to now, in God's name? Flying in the face of the Almighty! You must get a mite of sleep; there's no use in wearing yourself out once and for all.'

She got up from the bench and laid a heavy hand on her brother's shoulder.

'You've forgotten God, Fyodor, that's what it is. Haven't even time to cross yourself, what with this examination. You've lost the way to the Church. Tell you what, you should drop in to vespers tomorrow, and pray as hard as ever you can, and I'll give you five copecks for a candle, then things will take a turn for the better, you'll see. Your fright will disappear as though you'd never felt it, and things turn out all right again...'

The seamstress's stern eyes were fixed on Fedya in a clear, firm gaze; even her voice radiated a power of some kind. The boy stared hungrily at her.

'If I'd only done it yesterday... Tomorrow will be too late!' he gabbled tearfully.

'Stop that nonsense!' Dunya was frowning again. 'Get to bed quick, or have you quite lost your wits? It's time for me to light the stove. You hear?' she commanded, and hauled back the table.

Fedya said nothing more. Dunya went off to the kitchen, and he took his roll of bedding from the corner, spread it out on the bench, and rolled himself up, head and all, in the quilt. Soon there was silence.

It was still very early. A few minutes later Dunyasha glanced in at the door again, checked that Fedya was asleep, then shut the door tight and hurried to get things in order.

She moved with almost incredible deftness, seeming to manage everything at once. Whilst the fire in the stove was catching, she swept the room, cleaned Fedya's boots, and inspected his uniform coat carefully, holding it close to the window. She mended it in one or two places, picked off every scrap of dust, and scraped at almost invisible spots of dust with a fingernail. Then she stopped in mid-task, rushed to the stove, and began moving the pots and pans about. By the time the old uniform coat was back on its hanger, spotless now, and protected from the dust by an old apron, there was only a minute or two left before the big kettle came to the boil. But Dunya did not waste even this time. Squatting down beside a big padlocked trunk, she unlocked it and drew out a roll of bright green wool. Spreading this out over her knees, she began to think and calculate aloud. As the water boiled, she made haste to push the material back to where it had come from, but continued muttering ideas and figures all the while.

Finally she took a jar from the cupboard and began to make the coffee.

Having sprinkled in two teaspoons of grounds, she paused a few seconds, thrusting the teaspoon in the coffee jar, then taking it out again. ‘Oh, come on… Today of all days! It’ll give him more strength to go on,’ she finally whispered, then with a firm hand heaped a third teaspoon, before adding it ceremoniously to the pot.

She could not get her talk with Fedya out of her head. Her final and unexpected attempt to rally him had been caused by the sense that it was better to build the lad up in moments like this, not grind him down for nothing. Dunya had long ago realized that something was not right, although Fedya did his best to seem cheerful and hide his worries. This was by no means the first time that she had administered a stinging rebuke to this ‘hard worker’ who now seemed pleased enough even when he scraped a bare pass. Once a particular fit of annoyance had nearly made her go so far as to take the neighbour’s wife into her confidence.

The woman had asked her the habitual question: ‘Why now, Avdotya Kuzminishna! What has your lad brought back home to you today?’

‘Same as ever! I can’t get over the new fashions we have: growing downwards, not upwards…’

But the next minute Dunya had come to her senses, and turned her back on any further questions, before slamming the door violently, as if shutting it on her own tongue.

‘The boy’s not like that, he’s no lazy-bones,’ she now thought sombrely, gritting her teeth. ‘And no flibbertigibbet neither, not one to get above himself for no reason…’

Dunya respected Fedya, seeing in him her own traits of stubborness, energy, and pride. He wasn’t cut from the same cloth as that little idiot Lizka, who lied and boasted easy as breathing, and who had a way of getting out of what she was told to do… Enough said! We’d have to hope she lasted long enough to sort the little chit out and cure her of her rotten ways. Took after her da… Just let her wait till Fyodor really got down to his books with his pupils, then she’d have no time to hang round idling with the other girls, nor to think of boasting either…

Lizka was the subject that provoked her sister more than any other. Strict though Avdotya Kuzminishna was, she had still never managed to instil in her sly young minx of a sister that abject fear and trembling which she herself had felt in the presence of her mother, and even her father, in the days before the latter had descended to his present wretched condition. No matter how you looked at it, it was clear a sister was no substitute for a mother. Lizka even had the nerve to argue with her sister, and accuse her openly of favouring Fedya. Lizka was a good reader and knew several prayers by heart. By dint of hanging round her brother all the time, she had learnt several poems and many *bon mots* off by heart, and she made good use of these when showing off in front of her little friends.

Leaving the coffee to brew, Dunyasha went to get Lizka up. The little girl was sprawling voluptuously over the whole bed, making the most of the short time she had it to herself. She took a long time to wake up, despite Dunya's vigorous kicks in her side. Dunya made use of the next few minutes in order to change into her own black dress and run a brush through her hair.

'Enough lounging about... You're no fine lady! Get up, will you, there's plenty to do... Lizka, get up, d'you hear? Will you look at that seam still lying there waiting, am I supposed to unpick it for you? If we went on like that you'd have nothing to eat, if I wasted time on that sort of lousy work. Will you look at the time, girl? Lizka!'

'Yes, aw' right then!' Lizka shouted aggressively, flinging her long skinny legs to the floor. 'Is Fedka up?'

Not deigning to reply to this, Dunya rushed off to make the breakfast. The cries of 'Lizka! Lizka!' began coming from the kitchen when the little girl was still hauling herself into her dress.

'She ain't half bad-tempered today... No peace for the wicked, I can see!' Lizka grumbled to herself.

'God in Heaven, Lizka! Are you doing this on purpose or what? Here, take this twenty copecks and run along to the shop. Get me a quarter-pound of butter. Do you hear? I thought I'd stretch what we have to last today, but there isn't enough for Fyodor's breakfast. A quarter-pound, got it? But be sure to try some first, so's to check it's not rancid... As for bread, get the usual... And two copecks' worth of salt. Don't forget the basket!...'

'Where're my galoshes?'

'Where you put them.'

'*That's* where I put them.'

'Well in that case one of your chambermaids must have picked them up for you, mustn't she?'

Lizka flashed her eyes angrily.

'So I'm supposed to wade through the mud with no galoshes, am I?'

'Well, make the effort to find them then. Use your hands, like a normal human being, if you can manage it! Get down on your knees then, it won't kill you! Why should I spend my life crawling round the floor instead of you? You can trouble to do it yourself for once, madam.'

Lizka squatted down to look behind the trunk.

'Here they are! I said you'd put them there—I told you so.'

'Lizka!' Just then Kuzma's hoarse voice was heard calling from the hall, followed by a long choking fit of coughing.

'Eh! I wish you'd all... Will you get along when I tell you to?' yelled Dunya, by now really angry. 'Else I'll be late with the breakfast. You'll never manage to run in that mud. Leave your dad—it won't kill him.'

'Lizka!' bawled Kuzma through his coughs.

The little girl went out. Dunya went round behind the wardrobe. On seeing her, the old man was silent.

'What's the matter?' asked his daughter repressively.

'Eh... What's the time? My chest's bad... Can't get up.'

'Time for honest folk to get to work. But it's not even coffee-time for the likes of you,' snapped Dunya contemptuously and went straight back to what she had been doing.

She got out a piece of dried-up boiled beef and began cutting it carefully into slices. When put between two doorsteps of bread with a scraping of butter, a slice of this beef served as Fedya's 'emergency rations'—that is, something he got only on exam days, when he did not get back home till late. But Lizka and the butter had 'gone astray', and so breakfast wasn't ready by the time Fedya came out of the next room. Dunya scanned his pale face suspiciously.

'Did you get any sleep?'

'Why didn't you wake me?'

'No reason, I just didn't. Sit down and I'll get your coffee.'

But whilst she was pouring it, Fedya went back into his room and she had to call him once more. The boy drank his glass of coffee listlessly, and ate only part of the slice of bread his sister gave him.

'Off your food again? Eh, Fedya, don't mess about! It's only a little slice, you won't choke on that much bread and butter!' she nagged at him.

'I can't force it down when I'm full, can I?'

'How can you be full, don't talk nonsense... What are you getting up for? I'll give you some more coffee... Fedya, will you listen to me? How much sleep did you get? Just look at yourself in the mirror—you look like nothing on earth! They'll fail you so soon as they see your face!'

'Let them, then,' muttered the boy through his teeth, shoving the glass away stubbornly.

'But I put a whole extra spoonful in to make it stronger for you... That's real coffee for you—put hairs on your chest!'

'Lizka can drink it for me.'

'Lizka can get along very well without coffee. It's time I stopped running round after them all, made an end of it! You put every ounce of your strength in, you're at your wits' end, and then he tells you, "I don't want that" or "I won't". Stubborn as a mule!'

But Fedya wasn't listening. He was abstractedly walking from room to room collecting his things, making haste so that he should not be late. The blessed coffee was cooling in his glass untouched. Dunyasha herself had had nothing to eat; she was gazing at the door and cursing Lizka. Now Fyodor was getting into his coat.

Losing patience, Dunya rushed out on to the street. In the distance she glimpsed a scarf unknotting itself in the wind. Lizka's, and there she was, walking side by side with another little girl.

'I knew it... Slacking again, the shameless hussy. Today of all days, the wretch!' Dunya was stamping in indignation, but she did not venture out over the mud in her broken shoes.

'You wait! You wait!' she forced out, gasping for breath, as the little girl, catching sight of her, deserted her friend and made for the house in the nearest to a run she could manage. 'Oo-oo! Legs not dropped off yet? So you can walk, can you, when you smell what's coming to you? So you realize your brother can't get off to his examination till you've finished gossiping?'

Lizka nimbly shoved the basket into her hand and darted under her elbow into the kitchen.

Fedya was in his coat and at the door.

'But what about your lunch?' wailed Dunyasha. In anguish, she flung the basket to the floor and grabbed the butter from it.

A shower of coppers shot all over the floor and the paper screw of salt burst open. Fedya refused to wait for his lunch, insisting that he would be in no fit state to eat it anyway. Lizka kept up an incessant howling, for Dunyasha lost no opportunity to clip her round the ear whenever she was in reach. She was crawling all over the floor in an attempt to recapture the change.

At last, so as to pacify Dunya, the schoolboy gave way. He perched on a corner of a stool which had somehow found its way into the kitchen and sat waiting. From under the table Lizka asked him between her sobs when he expected to be back.

'When I do, you can be sure I'll come straight on in,' Fedya muttered between his teeth. Usually he treated his little sister kindly, but today even he was reacting coldly to her tears.

Kuzma was coughing behind the partition. At last he too crept into the kitchen, shivering and pulling his greasy old dressing-gown round him. His wrinkled face with its stubbly grey beard, rheumy eyes, and scarlet nose looked so bilious that it almost did seem likely he had a pain somewhere.

'E-eh! So you're still here, Mr Scholar, sir! Then your old dad will have to wait a while longer before he's allowed to wet his whistle,' the old man wheezed, studying the family group from the doorway.

'What's this! Do you think I have time to bother with you?' Dunyasha snapped straightaway. 'I was up before dawn, and I still haven't had time to wet *my* whistle! Besides, I'd be surprised if yours had had a chance to dry out since last evening.'

Fedya levered himself off the stool, took the bread firmly from his sister's hands, and wrapped it quickly in a piece of paper, dropping the beef, her pride and joy, on the table.

Dunyasha said nothing more. He made to go. But at the door he stopped:

'Goodbye, then.'

Dunya rushed forward, and, following him into the porch, seized him by the shoulder right on the threshold and kissed him.

'God go with you. Remember: don't lose heart, Fyodor!' she said, breathing heavily and making a hasty sign of the cross over him.

Fedya put his best foot forward, stepping neatly over the mud. His expression softened and his eyes brightened as he took a last look round the unprepossessing, crooked alley.

Dunyasha went back into the kitchen. She was too abstracted to feel bothered by the chaos reigning on her table. The dropped beef and spilt salt caused her no annoyance; she was even left unmoved by the two coins which Lizka had been unable to track down, however hard she scoured the floor. The sharp-witted little girl had grasped straight away that her sister had better things to think about now than what she was up to.

Dunyasha never lost her temper if she had her mind on important things. She would suddenly go all quiet and absent-minded, drained, seemingly, by the perpetual rows...

In silence she poured coffee for her father, topping it up liberally with water, then poured the dregs into a little teapot with no spout and hid them in the cupboard. She then filled cups for herself and Lizka with some peculiar, light-brown tea, whose entire virtue lay in the fact that it was hot.

Lizka burnt her mouth as she drank and looked enviously at the milk, which was kept for the coffee-drinkers only.

'Well, now you can wash up and clear away, properly, mind, and I'll get down to work—but don't you laze about or pester me, I'll be cutting a pattern,' Dunyasha announced, rather than giving Lizka 'what was coming to her', as she'd threatened before Fedka left.

'Barmy! You never know what she'll do next,' Lizka thought, cheering up now, as the seamstress took the green material from the trunk and set off with it to the parlour, to sit at the big table where Fedya worked in the evenings.

Kuzma stayed sitting at the kitchen table. He was great friends with his younger daughter; they always backed each other up against the stronger members of the family. As for Lizka, she got to work with a grown-up air of bustle but at a far from brisk pace. In this mood Dunyasha usually failed to notice the time and would forget to chivvy her on.

The little girl picked up the bits of beef which had been left by her brother, and looked at her father hesitantly.

'Why don't you eat it?' asked Kuzma.

'Shouldn't we leave it for Fedya?'

'Go on, eat it!' shouted Portnyagin suddenly, bringing his fist down on the table. 'You know, it's a disgrace! Why should he be treated like this? Let him turn himself into a young gentleman first, then he can have all the delicacies he fancies. Did you hear me tell you to eat it?' he added, by now losing his temper in earnest.

'But what about you?'

'You think I want that rubbish when my head's splitting? I have to get my strength back first, and I haven't the ten copecks to do it.'

Lizka looked pityingly at her father. Poor old man! Why should he have to put up with this? If she was in Dunya's place, she'd never yell at her father, nor her own sister neither. What good did it do in any case?

'What're you snivelling for this time?' Kuzma asked morosely.

'Belt you again, did she? E-eh. Well, love, you and I aren't doing too well. If she treats me, her own da, like a dog, then you can hardly wonder at what she does to you. Grin and bear it, Lizka, you're still young.'

Lizka poked her snub-nose in the air impudently.

'*And* I'm going to school this autumn. This summer I've only to learn to write and do my sums. I know nearly all the prayers and scripture stories.'

'Good girl, good girl. Yes, you do your studies. If your da had got through the seminary all right, then he wouldn't be out of work in his old age and having to stand for all this from his own children. Learning is light, ignorance is darkness... That's what Kuzma Portnyagin's always said, and that's what he's taught his children too. Whose son is at the *gimnaziya*? Kuzma Portnyagin's! Who can help any poor man out and show him how to write a petition in the best style? Kuzma Portnyagin! Because Kuzma might have been a deacon, or even a priest, if fate hadn't been harsh to him. You're too little, Lizka, you can't understand that.'

Lizka threw the towel over her shoulder, took the ends in her fingers and looked at her father, eyes alight.

'I understand *everything*! I'm going to study just as well as Fedya, and he told me... he told me... that if I'm top of the class, the best pupil in the whole school, then afterwards maybe I can even... go to the *gimnaziya* too! Fedya told Dunyasha that himself, I heard him!'

Portnyagin winked at his daughter ironically.

'Well, there now! The *gimnaziya*, eh!'

'It's true, it's true, no fibbing! Fedya told me, you know: when he gets his matric,° then he'll open a real school here in the Settlement, and I'll do my studies and come and help him.'

'A schoo-ool?' Kuzma drawled. 'He's a fool. He can do better than that for himself; what was the point of sending him to the *gimnaziya* if that's all he wants to do?'

Lizka looked at him, eyes round.

'That's a mug's game, running a school. That's no job for him,' Portnyagin said, suddenly filled with pride. 'So long as his da stays in the land of the living, there's someone can tell him things like that, can look out for him a bit. You listen to your sister too much. Your old da may take a drop too much now and again, but when push comes to shove, you can bet it won't be her will get your brother his place. You women should keep to your place, then things'd be simple enough, but she's a great one for the fights and she has a heart as hard as iron.'

Kuzma frowned again and looked at Lizka morosely.

'So what does she screw out of folks for those dresses of hers? Two, three roubles apiece—everyone knows so, I bet. So, what a joke, eh—two or three roubles for a woman's dress, it's money for old rope! And so what does she give her old da? Ten copecks every now and again, that's all. You've only got one father, Lizka; you'll never have another, however long you live.'

'Maybe *I'll* ask her,' Lizka said suddenly.

Kuzma screwed up his eyes in distress.

'What's the use?'

'No, I mean it! It'll work today, I know it will!'

'My head aches, Lizka, that's what the problem is. How can I think straight with that going on? Eh? You'd think she could see that, wouldn't you, when she's so proud of being sharper than anyone else?'

Lizka took the towel off her shoulder and walked boldly into the parlour. But as she approached the table covered in green cloth, the little girl began walking slowly, hesitantly.

'Well, are you finished?' Dunyasha threw her a glance.

'Nearly.'

'What are you doing in here, then, if you haven't finished?'

'Well, me da's not well,' Lizka said uncertainly.

'How do you mean, not well? Aha! I know very well what you mean. *That* old trick again. How many times do I have to tell you not to come running errands like that to me?'

But Lizka could tell from her sister's tone that the threatening words masked no real anger. Dunya had not even put her scissors down. She only said irritably, 'Get on with you!'

'But he *isn't* well, Dunya. You see... he's getting old, you know so. It's the damp, too,' Lizka concluded, pleased with her own resourcefulness.

'If he's not well, then he should take some medicine, like other folks, not drink vodka. Get out of my sight! If you can find some change on the table, give him that, why not, I suppose. To hell with him! It's the church he should be going to, to say a prayer for his son.'

Dunyasha bent closer to the table, and Lizka rushed hotfoot to the kitchen.

'She said yes! Yes!' she cried, waving her arms.

Kuzma was on his feet watching for her, pulling his dressing-gown round him every now and again.

'Did she now? How much?'

Lizka deftly tracked down two three-copeck pieces, then handed them over proudly.

'There was a couple of twos as well, but they rolled off somewhere, under the trunk, most like, when she flung the basket on the ground.'

'On the ground, is that it? Throwing money on the ground, when she's for ever moaning... But now she's feeling generous! Six copecks, eh! What good does that do anyone? But you're a sweetheart, Lizka—you'll be a hit with the lads when you're older! Don't be too scared of her, you'll be bigger than she is soon. You'll look after your old da, I know, not like her.'

Bobbing his head and pulling at his dressing-gown, Kuzma rushed off behind his wardrobe at a smart trot.

Lizka looked drearily at the pile of washing-up which she would now have to deal with all on her own...

Sitting over the pieces of fabric, with the big scissors in her hands, with hanks of cotton wound round her neck, and the bosom of her dress stuck with pins—now that was Dunyasha's real life, the life she loved. Housework tired her out straight away and made her irritable. She couldn't think standing up; every thing out of joint, every misfortune would rise unbidden to her notice, and provoke her spleen.

But over her sewing Dunya would become calm; it was not irritating trifles which filled her thoughts now, but huge, compelling images of the past and future. She had pondered all the most important decisions and questions of her life over her sewing. Whilst running the gathers and ruffles destined to adorn some wealthy merchant's wife through her hands, she had come without particular effort to the conclusion that marriage was out of the question and that she must turn down a man who was courting her, attracted by the idea of having such a tireless and skilful worker as his wife. Other stupid girlish weaknesses had been dealt with in their turn. She had persuaded herself that it was hardly an enviable lot to work all her life in order to support a coarse, drunken husband, and on top of that endure his beatings and saddle herself with a second family.

As she darned quickly and deftly, Dunya could see clear as day all the evils afflicting her own family and the whole of this sprawling, noisy, quarrelsome, drunken and poverty-stricken Settlement. For as a seamstress she had access to another, more ordered and prosperous, world. Looking at her beloved brother, who would often be sent by his father to fetch vodka when he was still holding himself together somehow, and work wasn't so short—looking at the child's bright, bold eyes, Dunya could see his whole future laid out on the palm of her hand. Was she going to have to watch him turning into a Settlement lad like any other? Watch him starting to swear, drink, and get up to mischief? When their grandfather had been a deacon, and in a cathedral—they weren't just any old peasants!

And gradually the brazen notion of 'sending him out into the world', and thus ensuring a better future for the whole family, had began to form in her head. She made some enquiries, followed them up in the right places, and secured the enthusiastic support of an energetic young lady from the town. One fine day, Dunya announced what she had in mind, and demanded that

Kuzma should teach his son his letters straight away. It was the first time that the word *gimnaziya* had ever been heard in the Settlement. Everyone saw it as some sort of mad insolence which had got into Dunya's head; they even thought the girl was touched. No one knew how long, how agonizingly, she had thought the problem over on her own, how often she had prostrated herself before the altar at Saturday vespers, till at last she attained spiritual peace and the insuperable righteousness of true conviction. Only then had she gone into battle with the whole Settlement...

And all this as a result of her sewing! But at the same time, any problem would swell to huge proportions as she wielded her needle. Dunya could see into the future; more than that, she was tormented by remote contingencies, concatenations of possible circumstances, by things that would probably never come about, and which, even had they done so, would most likely not have bothered those, the majority of people, with less inclination to the inner life than she had. How many times, and in how many different ways, had Dunya foreseen the course of her own life—and not only hers, but the lives of her whole family!

In this, too, Fyodor was like his sister. His favourite occupation was spending a winter holiday evening, or a summer one, out in the vegetable patch, sitting by his sister. Watching her nimble fingers, he would sink into endless dreams about how they would have a 'decent' life when he'd finished his studies. There would be no rows, no fights. His father would be allowed so much a month, but he wouldn't be allowed to hang round pubs. Dad had been ordered about enough: let him have his tipple at home. He hadn't so long left now, you couldn't teach him any better. As for Lizka, she could study too—the more she studied the better. She'd have it easier: there was someone to help her now, thank the Lord. And Dunyasha would keep house in place of their mother, just as she did now. Only she wouldn't have to wash the clothes and scrub the floors, and she wouldn't have to wear herself out making other people's clothes—he'd earn enough to keep them all himself.

For hours at a time Fedya would paint such imaginary pictures, speaking seriously, with conviction. He would fix his sharp eyes on this cherished vision of the future, and nervously tap his knee with a clenched fist. Raising her head from her sewing, Dunyasha would look lovingly at her 'hope for the future', as she secretly thought of him.

But schooling at the *gimnaziya* was a long-drawn-out business. It was no wonder the dark, ignorant Settlement felt such respect for it. Everyone knew that Fedya had been going into town for five years already with his satchel on his back, and that it would be nearly another five before he was through.

'But suppose... but suppose it really is a whole five, and not four and a bit? Suppose they really do make him repeat the year?' Dunyasha agonized. 'What's the time? Nearly time to get dinner. Thank heavens, we've still the cabbage soup left from yesterday, that means there's only the kasha° to fuss with.'

There was nothing for it; Dunyasha had to fold up the green dress and go into the kitchen, where, inevitably, she had to find fault with Lizka, who'd spent the whole morning doing nothing. And so again Dunyasha began to shout and scold (but it still seemed to Lizka she 'wasn't really herself'). She shoved the pans about angrily, making a din with the heavy steel door of the stove, but inside she was preoccupied with one and the same fateful question. 'What's happening in the *gimnaziya* now?'

In the *gimnaziya*, the examination was drawing to a close. The examiners and pupils, red-faced and exhausted to a man, had spent six hours sitting in the hot, stuffy classroom. It was Fedka's turn, going by alphabetical order, but he had still not been called up.

'It's a bad omen,' the boy thought superstitiously.

He had felt quite cheerful when he reached the *gimnaziya*, and all during the first half of the exam session. He'd actually made himself eat half a bread doorstep and a sliver of beef. But when they didn't call him up in order, his courage left him suddenly. He noticed the Inspector looking at him again and again, then flicking his eyes away as they met Fedya's anxious gaze...

The examiners were being very strict. Sometimes in Fedya's fright it seemed to him that they were asking questions on subjects the boys had never been taught. 'You should know *that*, sir!' the dry voice of the assistant examiner rang out every now and again. The Latin master, a thin middle-aged man with gold-rimmed glasses, let out a piercing sound like a squeak every now and again and flapped his hands helplessly. Many of the boys who had been examined were crying quietly. Those awaiting their turn sat blankly, heads hung.

'I'll flunk,' Fedya thought each time he heard one of the boys give a bad answer. He even thought he might not be able to answer at all.

When his turn finally did come (only two boys were left to come after him), the Inspector said his name quietly, hunched over the list, and the boy had only one feeling: to live through this ordeal. He had no hope of being saved any more.

The Inspector looked up and looked at Fedya's pale face and trembling lower jaw. Fedya took the exam paper and looked at it, not making out a word.

'Well, sir, what paper have you?' the assistant enquired.

A master lent towards the Inspector and whispered something.

'That's about me,' thought the boy in agony, and forgot that he was supposed to reply.

'Are you feeling unwell, Portnyagin?' asked the Inspector.

Fedya raised his eyes. And again, when he glimpsed the Inspector's face, he had the sense that his fate was being decided, and that seemed to paralyse his will.

'Are you ill?' the Inspector repeated sternly.

'No, sir,' the boy whispered.

They began to question him. He gave the answers as memory dictated; his conscious mind played no part at all. Sometimes they corrected him, sometimes they sat in silence, and he had no idea whether that meant he was making a mess of things or doing all right. When the fateful, dispassionate sentence, 'Take your seat, please' fell on his ears, Fedya had no idea whether it had been a reasonable effort, or a disaster.

'How did I do?'—he took the schoolmate nearest to him by the hand.

But it turned out the boy had just been called himself; he snatched his hand from Fedya's angrily.

When at length the crowd of boys was released from that dreadful room, Fedya's usual cheerfulness returned to him. So soon as the danger of being called out vanished, he felt himself again, but still with that dull sense that his fate was being decided.

Thinking about the paper on which he had just answered, the boy realized in a flash that he knew it perfectly well; it was in fact one of the easiest papers, and one he'd always hoped to get in the draw. Surely he couldn't have hashed up the answers completely!

Fedya began to pester his schoolmates, insisting that he could have answered on that paper any time with no prompting.

'So why were you standing by the table looking like you'd just pinched something?' shouted one boy rudely and cheerfully. He always got bad marks himself, but it never seemed to bother him.

Fedya said nothing. But involuntarily he thought of how the Inspector's face had followed him all spring.

There are things one can't explain, but simply knows for oneself without any question.

Prince Charsky, the tall, good-looking boy who had been Portnyagin's faithful protector from his first minute in the *gimnaziya*, now took him over to the window and tried without success to get him to say why he'd been in such a funk today, so that he'd made a real mess of the questions. He'd never done that before.

'I don't know,' Fedya insisted dully.

'Poof! my good fellow, this exam's certainly had a bad effect on your brain,' the good-hearted young Prince said eventually, losing his patience.

Only a few boys were allowed through to the next form without re-examination that autumn. The future of these boys depended on that examination, though by no means on it alone. Many boys would have to repeat the year. The Inspector called these in separately and spent much time assuring them of the benefits this measure would have if they were sensible and made use of the extra year to their own profit.

'You're not children any more!' the pedagogue hectored them. But the 'adults' all had tears in their eyes as they listened.

Fedya was not one of them. Nor was he with the group that had gone straight through, nor with the one being re-examined.

'So where am I? What on earth's going on?' he wondered, growing more and more anxious.

Charsky had also noticed that something strange was happening. He edged over to Fedya, glanced at his white, distressed face, and whispered:

'Hang on. Pyotr Andreich must have forgotten you.'

There was a ringing sound inside Fedya's head and his hands and feet were icy. He stayed by the window, apparently apathetic, back slumped against the frame.

The class broke up; the boys exchanged talk and good wishes. Only a few looked happy. Charsky fixed his burning eyes on the Inspector, trying in vain to catch his glance. First the Inspector was busy talking to someone, then he started getting ready to go.

But at last he came up to the window, the expression on his drawn face becoming markedly more sombre.

'Well, Portnyagin, my good fellow... I am most sincerely sorry about this, but I have bad news for you.'

Fedya gave him a look like a bound sheep, and said nothing.

'You live with your sister, is that not so?'

'Yes, with my sister,' the boy parroted dully.

'And his father,' Charsky added.

'Oh yes, now I remember! No, it is your sister whom I should like to meet. I think that she made the arrangements for him to come here, did she not?' the Inspector said, turning his back on Fedya.

No one answered.

'Tell your sister to come and see me at home tomorrow. At home, is that clear?'

'Pyotr Andreich!' Charsky burst out, but the Inspector interrupted him testily:

'Well, what do you suppose can be done? D'you think it's my responsibility? All year he's had to struggle to keep up, it's been obvious. What else do you expect? The *gimnaziya* course is hard enough in any case, very few boys can cope without extra help, or at the very least reasonable conditions at home. Of course, it was a ghastly mistake to send him here in the first place!'

'I've been doing my best,' Fedya said suddenly.

'Yes, yes, I know that! I've always said that, I've always been on your side, you know that.'

'Pyotr Andreich, people don't get expelled from the *gimnaziya for no reason*!' Charsky's voice rose to a shout.

'We are not expelling him, nothing has been said about that. He has done no wrong. We simply advise him, or rather his parents, to collect his documents and to apply for a transfer to another type of educational establishment, one more appropriate to his abilities and family circumstances.' The Inspector was bright red in the face, and his forehead was perspiring. 'His sister must come and see the headmaster. I shall review the position with my colleagues and think what advice I may best give her. I am most sincerely sorry, Portnyagin, but I am only a *gimnaziya* inspector, not a miracle worker!'

He turned on his heel and walked to the door.

'You know where he lives, Charsky, I think?' he asked without looking in their direction.

'I shall see him back.'

'Well, then you know how things stand. It must be the best part of six miles to the Settlement...'

'Yes, and he's done it on foot every day since he was 10 years old,' Charsky said rudely.

At that the Inspector walked through the door.

Charsky took Fedya to the cloakroom and helped him put on his coat.

'It's all nonsense! We'll sort it out, I promise you!' the boy said hotly. 'Your sister must go and see him straight away, and the headmaster, and the district curator! And be sure you go and see the headmaster yourself. I'll tell my father to pay a call on the headmaster, and my uncle will write some letters, he knows all the right people in Petersburg. Don't despair, Portnyagin, and for God's sake take that twittish expression off your face!'

Fedya said nothing. Only once, as they were half-way down the stairs, did he stop and turn to his companion.

'So does that mean I'm not to come here any more?'

'I told you, it's all nonsense!' yelled Charsky, going bright red in the face. 'If they do that to you, then... I'll leave here myself! I don't want to stay somewhere where they behave like that!'

Fedya followed him obediently, out to the smart droshky.

The family dinner was long over, though Kuzma was in fact not yet back from town. Fedya's dinner was keeping warm in the oven. Lizka was unpicking her hem at a snail's pace, gazing out of the window at frequent intervals. Dunyasha was pacing from room to room nervously, fiddling with her bits of green cloth, then flinging them down and going out on to the porch.

For the first time in Fedya's school career, the word 'examination' had grown to its real dimensions for Dunya. Till now she had had absolute faith in her clever, steady, much-loved brother. He wouldn't let her down. Dunya knew very well that study was hard work, but if others could manage it, then he could. Depression was something foreign to her nature, and Fedya's calm self-confidence had put all possible worries to flight.

'Is it an important subject you have tomorrow?' she had often asked in worried tones during his first year.

'Poof, important! Anyone who did enough in the winter term is sure to get through,' would be the little boy's dignified reply.

He hadn't flunked even once... Why should he, if he did his best? And he *had* been doing his best, for God's sake!

There is no occupation more oppressive than to ponder questions which go beyond the bounds of logic. The less sophisticated one is, the greater the torture.

'Something isn't right!' Again and again the thought rose into Dunyasha's head. 'He's no liar, he doesn't go in for empty talk. Should I go myself and find out?'

Fedka's studies had gone so well up till now that his sister had never even imagined having to visit the *gimnaziya*, especially since they'd given him a full scholarship in his second year.

'I'll go if they keep him down,' Dunyasha decided, staring with fierce impatience at every passing human shape coming round the corner down the far end of the street.

But then something extraordinary happened, something unheard-of. Something that made all the neighbours' wives lean out of their windows or rush into the street, whilst Dunyasha herself shook with a vague sense of foreboding.

The prince's droshky drew up at Kuzma Portnyagin's, and the tall, handsome schoolboy almost carried down his sheet-white friend.

Charsky said the same to Avdotya Kuzminishna as he had to her brother. She must go and see the headmaster and the district curator in the morning, she must put in a written petition saying how they were a poor family and how Fedya was their only hope for the future. The boy promised once again that his father would do his best for Fedya and that his uncle would send letters to Petersburg straight away.

Dunyasha listened to all this in a state of profound shock. The boy couldn't have been trying harder—what else did they expect, and now they were telling her to go and beg for mercy, write petitions... But perhaps they would take pity on him?

The seamstress's expression was chilly.

'Excuse me for asking, your honour,' she said, breathing heavily, 'we may be no peasants, but we're very little better! I'm not sure I quite take your meaning. Tell me the truth, for the love of God: did Fyodor know his Latin today or not?'

Her eyes bored into Charsky's white face.

'He did know it,' he said quietly.

'So why did they gave him a bad mark?'

'He had an attack of nerves... He wasn't himself and... He got into a bit of a mess. But he did know it, he had prepared it!'

'Why didn't he used to have any trouble, then?'

Charsky paused and looked at Fedya.

'They were terribly strict today. An awful lot got kept down for the year... Almost all the others have to go for another exam in the autumn...'

'And what mark did they give *you* today?' So this seamstress, whose work would never have been good enough for the prince's mother, interrogated him fearlessly.

'What, me? Well, for some reason I don't have trouble with work... I don't even do much homework. I'm second in the class,' the prince muttered in confusion, almost as though he felt guilty.

No sound came from Fedya. As soon as he came in, he had collapsed on the bench, and now he was just sitting there staring into space.

Charsky went out into the street. He wiped his forehead with his handkerchief; his whole body was shaking.

The plump, grey-haired coachman gave Charsky a quick glance and told him that the horses had stood around long enough. They had already waited three hours for him at the *gimnaziya*. Anyway, the carriage was all over mud, and if they weren't careful they'd break a spring, with the road all potholes.

'Will you shut your mouth!' the boy suddenly yelled at him.

Fedya had hung up his uniform and put the apron over it as he always did. When he finished, a cup of cabbage soup was waiting for him on the table. The boy blessed himself and picked up his spoon, but then frowned and put it down again.

Dunyasha sat on the bench and looked at him, hands folded under her shawl.

'Well, now... I'll... have... a see... tomorrow, won't I,' she began with obvious effort, then leapt up and shot through the door in her partition.

Lizka, face streaked with tears, crept out of somewhere in a corner.

'Would you like some kasha? it's your favourite!' she asked, staring closely at his face.

Fedya shook his head.

'Fedya... Will you go and see them tomorrow?' asked the little girl, her anxiety almost at an end.

'Yes,' he said listlessly.

'Me da can go too. He can put his best clothes on. They'll see he's an old man!' Lizka looked at her brother, then was suddenly choked by sobs.

'Leave off!' her brother said with a frown.

'All right... I'll leave off! But what's going to happen to you? You're 15 years old now!'

Fedya leapt up and, lifting his hand, gave her a blow on the head. Squealing shrilly, Lizka shot under the bench. Fedka staggered out on to the street.

As he appeared on the porch, several women who were gathered next to the neighbours' wicket gate stopped talking and stared at him greedily.

'See what I tell you! Look at his face!' one whispered; a moment later, she had appeared by the porch in some quite mysterious fashion, as if she had not actually walked, but been pulled forward by her own need to see the boy's face more clearly.

'Oh, poor little mite, just think how bad he must be feeling now!' another woman wailed. 'He's no layabout, everyone knows that.'

Fedka did not notice them at first; he was hanging on to the rails of the porch, breathing heavily, and convulsively squeezing the hand with which he had just hit his little sister for the first time in his life.

As he overheard the whispering, the boy made to go inside, but then thought better of it and vanished through the gates.

'Maybe they haven't really thrown him out yet? Maybe that's it?'

'How many times do I have to tell you? The coachman told me so himself. 'They've flung your boy out of the *gimnaziya*,' he told me, 'so out of the goodness of his heart his honour's come to see him back.' Those were his exact words. It's no gossip: I heard it with my own ears right on this very spot!'

'Jesus God! But why would they do that?'

'It all goes to show you should know your place! Do you think we didn't tell Avdotya so? But she had to know better than anyone. They're even trying to get that Lizka of theirs a schooling. Cheeky little minx! never leaves her friends alone as it is! Putting on airs like the gentry! And it's not even as if they was a real clergy family, her grandad was only a cathedral deacon. When you think that my uncle, my own uncle, was a real merchant, second guild.° And my son's apprenticed to a tailor, you know. What's Kuzma Portnyagin to that? A miserable drunkard, that's what!'

'It's all very well to talk like that, my duck, but he's 15 years old now. Never been in any kind of work. Well, Dunya's on her own now. Who knows what the old man will do when he finds out? Any case, the lad'll just be another burden. He's been studying five years! Five years, think of it! Hardly spent any time with the lads, forever at his books. Eh, girls, but I'm sorry for the poor little mite!'

News flew round the Settlement like wildfire. Anyone who had not gone into town that day to put in a day's work, who was working at home, or not working, was hungry for the smallest bit of juicy gossip to brighten the dreary round of routine.

Just as a few years back, Fedka Portnyagin's name was now on everyone's lips. Deep sighs of affected pity and hisses of envy were heard; malicious enjoyment was the order of the day. All the old objections stifled by Fedka's unexpected success now rose to the surface again.

The women were rushing from to house to house, and a troop of small boys had gathered outside Kuzma's house. Mitka Isaev, his cheeks red as coals in a stove, eyes shining with spite, had even scrambled up to a window so that he could see into the parlour.

Voices rose from the crowd. 'Where's he sneaked off to? Bet you he's down in the vegetable patch!'

'Eh, lads, let's go and look then, shall we? Let's see what he's got to say for himself *now*!'

The gang went round the backs of the houses, then one by one the lads squeezed through the wattle fence and set off at a canter over the fresh furrows, which were just showing a faint tinge of new green.

Fedka *was* there, as it happened. He was lying face down on the damp earth, between the fence and some tall bird-cherry bushes. In summer a wonderful thick shade would cover this whole area, but now Fedka's pale shirt was clearly visible between the bare black boughs.

The lads came to a halt at a respectful distance and began whispering together.

'Fedka! Fedka! Why are you hiding in the bushes? Scared your dad will find you, eh?'

'Look at that, what a coward! When you think how he boasted his dad didn't dare lay a finger!'

'We didn't get no schooling, but he turns up today in a fancy carriage!'

'Eh, Fedka, what you lying in the damp for? We're all the same now. Come over here, eh!'

'Nay, lads, wait a bit! Give Fedka a chance to tell us what's going on himself!' Mitka squeezed himself out of the crowd, glassy eyes shining at his own wit. 'Maybe our mums and dads would like to send us to the *gimnaziya* too, so he should tell us what goes on there! All right, so he doesn't give a tinker's cuss for us, but he's a Settlement lad too, look after your own, lads, that's the rule!'

A snigger of approval greeted Mitka's words.

'That's right! Good lad, Mitka!'

'That's it! You tell us, Fedka, we're all ears!'

'Here, lads! Leave him be, eh? Look, I'm off home now!' One skinny lad with a densely freckled face and sad dark eyes distanced himself from the crowd. 'Why should we bait him? It ain't right!'

'Shut yer mouth, will you!' Mitka yelled at him angrily.

'Well, what's it to us... He's in trouble...' the boy said timidly.

'Go to hell, then. See if we care!'

'Turned his nose up, didn't he?' the crude jokes continued. 'Do you remember how it used to be on Sundays? "Neow, I can't waste meh time with yew: I've got to study!" Stuck up, weren't he!'

'Didn't do him much good though, did it? By the look of it he just sat with the book open in front of him!' the smallest boy in the gang shouted happily.

'Or maybe he was just thick: they don't throw them out for nothing, rules are rules, lads! We was at school too, *we* know what's what!'

'It was all boasting. The whole family is like that. You should see the way that Lizka goes about...'

'Ha, ha! Lizka, now there's a one! We all call her "the young lady!"'

At that moment Fedka stirred. The crowd moved back a step or two.

'I'm going!' yelled the freckled boy. He sounded at the point of tears.

'I already told you—go to hell, will you?' Mitka moved threateningly towards him.

The boy ran off to one side, but then froze, staring unhappily at the bird cherries.

'Fedka, will you sell me your uniform? My uncle says I've got to go out herding° with him this winter, I'll need it to keep warm in!'

A yell of laughter greeted this show of wit. But suddenly the sound of a snapped branch came from the bird cherries. Two or three of the lads made off, but soon they rejoined the others.

'What's scaring you?' Mitka shouted commandingly.

But at that moment a big stone flew out of the cherry clump and clipped someone on the shoulder.

All the lads ran off, but soon they returned to a spot close to where they had been standing earlier.

'Jesus!'

'What a cheek! Could have smashed someone's head in!'

'Don't try provoking us, boy, if you want to stay in one piece yourself!'

'Bet he learnt that in the *gimnaziya*, throwing stones like that! Eh, hang on, I do believe he's coming out!'

And in fact Fedka had appeared beside the bushes. In one hand he held a stone, in the other a thick branch. His eyes were glittering wildly, his jaw shaking. Slowly he walked up to the gang.

'Maybe we should be off. Looks as mad as a wolf!'

'Lay off, lads! He's on his own, after all!'

'But he's really upset! He could do anything now!'

'Well, Fyodor, you're no feather, are you!'

'I'll thump anyone who runs for it now! You've just got used to being scared of him. You're like sheep!' Mitka raged.

God knows how all this might have ended, had Dunya's wiry figure not appeared at the wicket gate, threatening them with the poker.

'Be off with you this minute... And if... I catch a single one of you... You swine!' she panted.

By the time Kuzma Portnyagin got back from work, everyone, only excepting perhaps the inhabitants of the most far-flung streets, knew about the disaster which had overwhelmed Dunyasha and her brother. But Kuzma strode home with unfaltering steps, his hands thrust morosely into his pockets and his cap down over his eyes.

Kuzma was badly out of sorts. The six copecks which Dunya had given him had turned out, just as he had suspected, to be simply a mockery of fate. It had been a bad day: once again he had not managed to screw the rouble owed to him out of the corn chandler's assistant. Kuzma was due the money for composing a petition denouncing the man's brother, who had allegedly done him out of his share of some property.

Kuzma's head ached worse than ever. Against his will, his head was filled by those wretched, sober thoughts which he detested with his whole soul, and which he had only one way of keeping at a distance.

'Good evening to you, Kuzma Ivanych!' Isaiah the shopkeeper greeted him unexpectedly.

Naturally Kuzma had no idea that Isaiah had come out on the porch when Mitka told him that Kuzma was on his way home.

Mitka's feelings had not cooled in the least since the scene out at the vegetable patch. An irrational sense of triumph had begun to possess him more and more; the surprise of it all was intoxicating. Now there wasn't one lad, not a single lad in the whole Settlement who could be his rival as leader! Now he viewed the glittering prospect of being able to repay with interest all those moments when, against his will, he had been cowed and pacified by the mysterious force emanating from Fedka and his uniform. Now he could pay Fedka back for all those pricks to his own inflated vanity. From the first moments of his life, Mitka had been used to hearing that you can buy anything you like, and that a yardstick is the measure of everything. But Fedka had confronted him with something that couldn't be fitted into the village-shop system of values, with something that had transfigured the walls of the miserable cottage he lived in, fixing to those walls the hearts and minds of richer, more carefree and happier lads than him, as though they were glued.

Mitka danced impatiently by his father, like a cat on hot bricks, in anticipation of an amusing scene.

Portnyagin was rarely so honoured as to be greeted by the richest man in the Settlement. He lifted his cap and slowed his step.

'Why are you so late today?' Isaiah asked him.

'Why?' Portnyagin repeated glumly. 'Clear enough, why. We're not all shopkeepers like you, sitting at home and waiting for calls. I often have to go ten miles in a day.'

'Fair enough! But you ought to know that things haven't been right at home. Avdotya Kuzminishna must be waiting up for you...'

When Kuzma heard Isaiah's unusually civil tone, his heart missed a beat.

'What did you say? Things wrong at home? Is that a joke or what?'

'Off you go, lad! We don't make jokes like that here; we all know there's a God...'

By now anxious, Kuzma stared at him.

'Is it a fire? But no, I'd have heard in town, surely, if so.'

'A fire would be nothing, mate, I doubt whether you've got a hundred roubles of stuff to lose... But you've only the one son, Portnyagin, and it turns out it was a mistake for you to shove him up the ladder. I know the gospels say 'the first shall be last', but you can be sure they mean in the next world. In this one you must cut your coat to fit your cloth. Plenty of folks have done that, and ended up better off than your Avdotya Kuzminishna, and shown others the right way forward too.'

'Isaiah, what is all this, in God's name? Will you stop talking in riddles?' Portnyagin stepped closer to the porch. 'Is my lad ill, or what?'

Suddenly Mishka lost hold of himself. 'They've thrown him out of the *gimnaziya*!' he shrieked.

'Just you wait, you young dog! Who asked you to shove your nose in! In the house, quick march!' yelled Isaiah, booting him towards the door.

'Thrown him out? Who, Fyodor? No, you're messing me about. What would you understand anyway, you pop-eyed lout? Apart from jokes, that is. I was at a seminary myself. I know very well what "thrown out" means!'

And Kuzma made for home as quick as he could.

'You great yob!' Isaiah was muttering. 'Just look at you, not a rag to your back, running home to give him what-for. But then, you'd know, wouldn't you—for weren't you thrown out of the seminary yourself, out on your ear? Just like your son. Like father, like son. Brains run in that family, the Portnyagins, ha ha!'

Kuzma's word carried little weight in his own family. When he was drunk or in a bad mood, he would tell anyone who would listen how badly his daughter treated him. In circumstances where every last copeck is won through sweated labour, whoever earns it is boss. It was quite natural that the daughter's power should grow as the old man fell further and further under the spell of his own bad habits, leaving her to keep the whole family.

But clearly something else was going on now, something not determined merely by the power of the copeck, something which could be measured no better by that than it could by shopkeeper Isaiah's yardstick.

The hoarse, squeaky voice of old Portnyagin filled the house, boding no good. And Dunyasha, formerly all-powerful, was now slumped against the wall immobile, unseeing, apparently not hearing how her father, demented by grief, was laying into his son, who'd 'trampled on my honour before the whole Settlement'.

'Every last copeck spent on his books! Everyone knew how proud we were... We laughed in their faces. But the shameless layabout couldn't even stretch out his hand to take what was his for the picking. He was too idle even to sit and work in the warm indoors! Does he think we'd have kept him there all this time if he hadn't sworn he'd work till he dropped, that he'd do his very best, so's he could set his sister up later? When did they ever throw a boy out without just cause? You tell me that, you little skiver!

Should have kept a hold on himself! So he thought being at the *gimnaziya* would mean he'd be spared the stick for life, eh? Did he think he could get away without saying what really happened, the stupid little swine? Right, if he won't own up like he should, we'll just have to knock the truth out of him, won't we?'

Dunyasha could hear her father 'giving Fedka a lesson', threatening to beat him 'till he ended up in his box', to trample him underfoot, to send him out to earn his living as a herdsman. She could hear it, but she uttered no word, made no gesture in defence of her 'hope for the future'. By no word spoken in anger, intercession, or assertion of authority did she protect his proud head from the humiliating hail of blows.

And after all, Fyodor was nearly as tall as his father now. Why couldn't he turn his back, take his shoulders out of range of the trembling elderly hands? Why didn't he just leap out of the way, dodging his father's confused and aimless blows? Or there again, why didn't he give vent to some of his own despair, and so turn anger into pity, bringing tears to his father's eyes by his laments—not tears of disappointment and indignation, but tears of horror and pity for the sake of his wrecked life? Was his father no father to him, had Dunya not given him all the love of which she was capable?

Fedka was silent. He did not protest, or try to justify himself, or beg for mercy. He made no attempt to run or to deflect the blows. Only once did he open his mouth, and then to say: 'All right... Hit me, hit me then, if it makes you feel better.'

Everyone simply believed that this man, who had himself done nothing to bring about the realization of his son's now catastrophically disappointed hopes, that this man had alone the right to violent anger, merciless threats, and the vicious use of his fists.

'Am I your father or not?' Kuzma's tragic cry came again and again.

Only the hopeless wailing of Lizka, who had taken refuge behind the partition, rose in unconscious protest against what was going on...

The town was deep in sleep. No one dreamt of Fedka's terrible fate: neither the masters who had carried out their orders, whether in a spirit of indifference or racked by pangs of conscience, nor his thoughtless schoolmates, who were in any case entirely taken up by their own interests and had at most some vague notion that something peculiar had happened to poor Portnyagin, without knowing quite what that might be. Even hot-blooded, generous Charsky, who had succeeded that evening in rallying his entire family to the cause, did not dream of the horrible truth.

Worn out by excitement, at the point of total exhaustion, Charsky was sleeping fitfully. All night he dreamt of seeing Fedka happy, rescued by Charsky's father. Clutching his pillow, he dreamt that he was hugging his grateful friend.

Even in his dreams he did not see the dark, dirty attic of the miserable cottage, where, on a thick rope attached to the roof-beam, swayed the slowly stiffening, strangely distorted, bruised, and battered body of the only Settlement boy ever to study at the *gimnaziya*.

[1892]

◆ VALENTINA DMITRIEVA ◆

Dmitrieva (1859–1948), who came from a peasant family which had been enserfed until the Emancipation of 1861, was one of the first Russian woman writers whose origins lay outside the gentry or merchant classes. She was also a notable instance of social mobility; having taught herself to read, she was educated at a women's *gimnaziya* in Tambov, and the Women's Higher Medical Courses in St Petersburg (from 1878). As the memoir published here indicates, Dmitrieva worked for a year as a village schoolteacher before beginning to train as a doctor. Though she completed her training, she was to practise little, working more or less full-time as a writer, and producing a large number of substantial stories for the main thick journals of the day. She was actively involved with the populist movement, and this involvement is reflected in her fiction and memoirs, as well as in a series of revolutionary populist booklets which she produced in the early 1900s. Dmitrieva welcomed the 1917 Revolution, and remained in Russia until her death, but she wrote very little in her later years; though treated with respect by the literary establishment, she was considered something of a political dinosaur, since, as one Soviet commentator put it, 'the fog of [non-Bolshevik] populism continued to cloud her eyes'.

After the Great Hunger

Extract from 'Round the Villages: A Doctor's Memoirs of an Epidemic'

(In this memoir, Dmitrieva, who qualified as a doctor before becoming a professional writer, describes a trip which she made to the Zadonsk district about three years after the great famine of 1891, the worst of the repeated crop failures that plagued the Russian countryside in the late nineteenth century. The following extract shows her visiting two very different, but equally deprived, small villages in order to give ancillary medical help during an epidemic of diphtheria.)

The next day my driver Amelka and I left Kosikha, and made our way towards Solntsevka and Katerinovka, according to the 'timetable' which the village elder in Krivinsk had given me. The road went through bare open fields, diving now and then into pot-holed ravines; the way to Yarugino had been surrounded by mushrooming hamlets and villages, but this was quite empty of dwellings. We crossed fields, ravines, then more fields; the road was so narrow, so thick with snow, and so heavily rutted that even riders going in single file might have had trouble getting down it, and our sledge tilted crazily as it went, listing first to one side, then to the other. I found myself thinking of the empty steppes where I grew up, which I had so often had to struggle across, at first when I was on my way to school at the *gimnaziya*,° and then later when I was working as a teacher myself in a local village school. I recalled the peace, the space, the larks singing, the dreams and reveries of my youth—my surges of enthusiasm, my thirst for action, my longing to sacrifice myself for some good cause, with Nekrasov's verses running through my head all the while:

> Rye all around.° The steppe's alive,
> Though it lacks castles, hills, and seas...
> I give you thanks, land of my birth,
> For the magic of your endless plains!

Today was a holiday, and the weather could scarcely have been better: the sun shone brightly, the snow sparkled so vividly that it hurt to look at it, the shafts of the sleigh squeaked merrily. But Amelka was in a bad mood; he kept grumbling to himself:

'What d'ye call this, a holiday, and I've got to work! This is slave labour and no mistake—having to work till I sweat, whilst everyone else has fun!'

'What's the matter, Emelyan?'

'What d'ye think?' Amelka° replied crossly. 'Folks are off enjoying the holiday, but we've got to drag across country! I call this a dog's life, I do. And you should see what's up in Kozikha, too. The women have all been baking pies. The girls have got dressed up, they'll be out on the street singing songs...'

'Do you like going out and singing with them?'

'You bet I do! What d'ye take me for, a married man or something?'

He turned round to look at me, and his ugly, lumpy face lit up with a self-satisfied smile.

'I was a fool to go looking for work. I should have stayed at home, then I could have slept on the stove all day, and had a fine time stuffing myself and having fun with the girls every holiday! But then, I wouldn't have gone if I hadn't needed to, would I? There was nothing to live on at home, see? We mortgaged the land ages ago—if you call it land. Just over a third of an acre° a person. We've no horse, not even a cow, so my mother goes out cooking, and my father's got work as a shepherd. Fat lot of chance to stuff ourselves on pies there! Here, get along there will you?' he shouted at the horses angrily. 'Go-o on!'

He paused, then turned to look at me again.

'Well, that was a rumpus back there in the station, and no mistake! What a fuss and pother, eh! And now they make us hare about all over the place. How much longer is it going to take you, d'ye think?'

'As long as it does take: until people start getting better.'

'Well, how long will that be?'

'I really can't say. Patience, Amelka! We'll have a holiday ourselves when this is over!'

'Yes, if we last that long!' said Amelka; then he fell into gloomy silence.

What could be going through his rustic brain? Was he thinking of the pies, the warm stove, the girls singing? Or was he dreaming of his own house, his own farm, of freedom?

A speck of black appeared in the distance, to one side of the road, and then I saw a blinding flash of metal through the snow. We had reached the railway.

'That'll be the station,' Amelka said. 'I'll have to ask where we go from here. I've never been up this way before.'

We crossed the railway, passing the station standing empty amidst the wastes, with its water-pump to one side all forlorn; then we drove into a settlement of some kind. Some men were standing at a street corner; Amelka stopped to ask them the way.

'Keep going straight on!' one of the men said, gesturing vaguely with his hand.

I stared out at the expanse of snow in front of us, and glimpsed another black speck further up the road—from here it looked like a heap of manure. There was one heap to the left, another to the right. I tried to imagine the map of the district in my head; I seemed to remember seeing, amongst the vast expanses of open country, two black circles, for villages, marked somewhere in that direction. So this must be the road we wanted.

'Are we supposed to go that way?' Amelka asked in astonishment, raising himself on the box and peering into the darkness. 'Can't see the least sign of a proper road; how am I supposed to know where to drive?'

We ploughed on almost at random, the sleigh practically tipping over as the horses stumbled into drifts. The black specks grew ever larger and nearer, and at last we found ourselves caught up in someone's hurdle fence. Two small boys with toboggans leaped up from behind it, and stood staring at us in shock.

'This Solntsevka, then?' Amelka asked.

'Aye, 'tis.'

'How do we find the village elder?'°

The children exchanged glances.

'What will ye be wanting him for?'

'None of your cheek, just show us, will you?' Amelka snarled at them.

All of a sudden the two boys shot like lightning over the fence, and up on to the back of the sledge; here they perched as we drove, and shouted directions.

'Right here, right here, now go 'cross the threshing-floor... Down here... Here! See that cottage over there at the end? This one here, stop! Here, Fedot, come out here will you, there's a lady to see you!'

In response to their cries, out came a tall, stooping man in a torn jacket, whose thin yellow face bore the scars of gummatous syphilis.° He looked at us with alarm.

'Where are the sick people here?' I asked.

The old man stood without saying anything, opening and closing his lashless red eyelids.

'I was told that there are sick children in this village. Will you tell me where to go, please?'

The old man still said nothing, and Amelka lost patience.

'Come on, elder! Have you all gone deaf, or lost your tongues here? No need to stand there like you was stuffed—you heard the lady ask where you're keeping the sick childer!'

'There are lots here!' one of the boys rushed in. 'Three or more in that cottage there, and some in the house next door...'

'And all the Styopkin children too!' squeaked the other boy.

I got down from the sledge. At that the miserable, cowering elder at last took hold of himself, seeming to grasp what we wanted, and agreed to lead us around the village.

What the boys had said was quite true; every single house seemed to have three or four children down sick. I learnt that they had started to get ill back before Christmas, and that the disease had run through the village like wildfire. Five children had died; the rest were 'on the mend'. Only a few children had suffered relapses; when I had examined these, I realized that the epidemic which this village had suffered was one of scarlatina, not diphtheria at all. Most of the children were showing all the classic after-effects of the disease: bloated, puffy limbs, swollen stomachs, anaemia, adenoids, putrescent, suppurating ulcers... However, the disease seemed to have run its course without medical intervention.

The poverty of this village could only be described as appalling. The damp stone cottages in Yarugino were palaces beside these mud huts, these 'black houses'° with their churned-up earth floors and their tiny windows low in the walls. They had no chimneys, and the smoke from the fire had covered the walls in a thick layer of furry black soot. There were no calves, no sheep or lambs in the huts—no one in Solntsevka kept any animals—and when I asked why they had not sent for a doctor, they said, 'We haven't a horse in the village. They came and took them away long since.' One could only wonder that the mortality should have been so low; either the epidemic must have been a mild one, or the villagers' tenacity of life was truly extraordinary.

The elder had begun to recover from his alarm, and in between his flutterings and mewings one was able to make out the odd all but coherent sentence. He told me that a number children in Katerinovka were, indeed, already ill; he thought they had buried some there in the last few days. Other villagers confirmed this—a crowd of men, women, and children had rushed from all over the village to see me, and were following everywhere I went. I could see that my arrival was something of an event in this out-of-the-way place. In particular, my medicine-chest aroused a mixture of fierce curiosity and wondering reverence. They all pressed round to stare at what was inside, and I could hear the women muttering secretively:

'Go on.'

'No, ye first...'

'Ask her—she might give ye some.'

'Ooh, no, I couldn't...'

At last one woman with a bloated, puffy face pushed her way through the crowd. Coughing nervously, she touched my sleeve.

'Would ye ever give me some of that medicine of yours?' she whispered.

'What seems to be your trouble?'

'Well, ye see, I'm not so well... It's this water I've got everywhere: my belly's swole, and my hands, and just see how bad my legs are...'

She lifted her skirt to show grotesquely swollen legs, like tree-trunks.

'Have you had this trouble long?'

'Aye, must be a year now...'

'Why on earth didn't you go to the hospital? You could have seen a doctor there, surely?'

'How could I have done that, my lovey? We haven't a horse in the whole place, and I couldn't walk there like this, now could I? So would ye ever give me some medicine?'

I explained that I didn't have the right medicine for her at the moment, but that I would come back another time and bring it. I wrote down her surname.

Encouraged by this success, the crowd pressed round me still tighter.

'Write me down too!' croaked a bent, skeletally thin old man, seizing my hand and looking at me imploringly. 'It's my back... It's everything. Hear me wheeze... I can hardly breathe... I can't work any more...'

'Put me down too! See, will ye look at this rash I've got!'

'And me! Look, my gums are rotting, and now my teeth are falling out!'

'Have a look at my baby—his little belly-button's all swole up!'

'But I haven't got any medicine!' I protested.

'Never mind, have a look all the same!'

And they all fixed their eyes on me, gazing at me imploringly, wailing about their pains and illnesses, till I was stifled by the stench of their breath, made foul by scurvy and syphilis. There seemed not to be one healthy person in the whole village; I could see the whole panoply of destruction wrought by chronic hunger: the ulcers, rashes, bleeding gums, paralysed muscles, and putrefying bones... My head was spinning, there was black before my eyes... With difficulty I struggled back to the street, and began to recover myself only when I was safely back in the sleigh again. The crowd straggled after me, staring at me with a mixture of hope and desperation. And I realized my total impotence: all the medicine I could prescribe, the visits I could make, seemed pointless and ridiculous, reduced to childish games in the face of the rural poverty which was closing in on me from all sides...

'God in Heaven, that village!' said Amelka, as we drove out of Solntsevka. 'That village! I can't find words for it. I never saw nothing like that in all my born days.'

He seemed to be as shocked as I was; he spent the whole drive to Katerinovka shaking his head and muttering to himself.

Katerinovka was only a mile or so from Solntsevka. In the distance it looked as wretched a dung-heap as its miserable neighbour; but close to things seemed much more hopeful. Rather than being thrown down anywhere, the cottages here were set out in two lines, facing on to a tolerably broad and straight street; battered-roofed mud huts rubbed shoulders with big stone cottages, and these latter were furnished with chimneys, porches, and sometimes even with garden fences. Here and there on the streets were bright knots of people. The girls, lads, and men were out in their holiday best, and one could hear the sounds of songs being sung. Shouting and whistling like fury, the little boys flung themselves after the sledge, trying to hitch a ride on the back. But the gloomy impressions left by Solntsevka were still with me, and I could not help feeling that all these girls and boys, these adult men, must actually be diseased, with putrid ulcers hidden under their holiday clothes. The songs, the cheerful shouting of the little boys, seemed discordant and out of place.

I was conducted without delay to the elder. This man, too, could not have been more different from his Solntsevka counterpart. He was tall and stout, with a face which was intelligent, if not very attractive; he spoke fluently and circumstantially, accompanying his speech by well-rounded gestures. He was dressed in a good black stuff jacket, with a mauve scarf round his neck; on his head was a new fur hat. His actions proved to be just as sensible and well-considered as his words; he called up a young lad—the auxiliary policeman,° apparently—and sent him off round the village to find out where the sick people were, whilst he stayed by our sleigh so that he could 'inform us' (yes—that was just what he said, 'inform us', not 'tell us'!) how the Katerinovka epidemic had begun. The illness had come in from Solntsevka; his children had gone down with it first, and this was because, being the village elder, he had to do with all the visitors; later, other children had started to get sick as well. He had sent over to Krivinsk straight away, and an orderly had arrived from there yesterday.

'So your household was the first to be affected?'

'Yes, that's right.'

'Have you anyone there who is ill at the moment?'

'No, not no more we haven't, thank Providence.'

'Have they recovered, then?'

'No, we lost them both. A little lass 2 year old, and a babe in arms,' he said calmly.

The auxiliary policeman ran up, panting, and said that there were lots down sick. At Latubins, and Frolovs, and Vyakhirevs too...

'Vyakhirevs?' said the elder reflectively. 'Well, let's see, then. Yes, we'll begin that end, and work our way round from there, that makes sense. You run on ahead, Ivan, and show us the way, and I'll squeeze myself in here. Right, cabbie, my good lad, on you go, make for that big place there... Hey, here you go! Watch the drift, my lad! See that path there, that's where you want to be... That's right! Hey, budge up a bit... You don't expect the lady to get out in the snow, do you?'

We had drawn up by a big cottage. Crowds of people were gathered outside the windows and in the porch, and strange, prolonged sounds were coming from the house. The elder bustled past, scattering villagers to right and left, and we followed him in.

The scene which we met was so extraordinary that I stopped dead in my tracks. The cottage had been tidied and swept; there was a white cloth on the table, and a candle was lit in the icon corner. A bench had been placed below the icons, and something was lying on this, covered by a piece of bleached calico. A woman was sitting at table, her apron over her face, head propped on her hand; she was rocking herself from side to side, and wailing at full volume—keening, in fact. The cottage rang with the melancholy, heart-rending sounds of her lament; people were coming in and out all the time, but no one made any attempt to approach her or to address her. The setting sun was bright outside the windows, and you could see children standing outside, noses flattened against the panes.

My heart turned over, but I pulled myself together and went up to the woman.

'Good afternoon,' I said hesitantly, coming to a halt next to her.

She neither replied nor looked at me, but continued wailing just as before:

'My de-ear Vasinka, my grey-winged pi-igeon, why have you le-eft me?'

'Where is the master of the house?' I asked, turning to the other people. 'I must speak to him. I need to have a look at the sick children.'

'The master? He's not here,' a chorus of voices replied. 'He's gone off to Krivnya to get the priest... No, to get a coffin... A coffin, was that it?'

I turned back to the woman at the table.

'Where are the other sick children? Show me where they are, please.'

Once more she made no answer; her terrible cries went on and on, cutting straight to my heart. My nerves were giving way, and I knew that any minute I would start screaming myself.

'Here, you, will you listen to me, for God's sake?' I shouted roughly, trying to force down my mounting agitation. 'Can't you hear, I'm asking you a question?'

This absurd outburst did seem to make some impression on the woman. She stopped wailing, and looked up at me with dull, tear-reddened eyes.

'What's that?' she asked, speaking as though she had just returned to consciousness.

I was gripped by a terrible rush of pity, mixed with shame at my own behaviour; I felt humiliated before this woman, and the elder, and the silent crowd standing behind me, sensing their unspoken condemnation of what I had done. I should have left her alone, and gone away... But it was too late to think of that now; I must get on with my 'mission'. I repeated my question.

'Them two girlies there is sick,' the woman answered.

'Is that a boy there, then? Has he been dead long?'

'He went this morning... He wasn't sick long, only three days... Oh Vaasinka, how could you?' she burst out again, beating her head on the edge of the table.

'Now, now, Aksinya, what's all this!' the elder said gently. 'What can ye do? There are two of mine gone as well, ye know.'

'But she only had the one little lad,' said someone to him. 'She fretted over him like you wouldn't hardly believe! And he was such a good little lad, as well.'

I walked over to the bench and lifted the calico. The little boy was lying there serene and quiet in his new pink shirt, hands crossed upon his sash. His sweet little pale face with its half-open mouth had a calm, serious look. He really might have been asleep.

'You know, I think that we had better leave things at that for today,' I said, turning to the elder. 'But I will just have a quick look at the little girls whilst I am here.'

It emerged that the girls had gone running off to hide somewhere; but at last the elder tracked them down, cowering on the bunks over the stove. I managed to tempt two of them out with a promise of sweets, but the third refused to come down at any price. I did not persist; the whole business had made me feel thoroughly out of sorts. Even now I cannot forget that terrible scene; involuntarily I see, in my mind's eye, the picture of the little boy lying dead under the calico, with his mother sobbing and wailing over him, and then I see her dull, reddened eyes looking up at me, full of mute reproach...

We visited another eight houses after that. My medicine-chest became ever lighter; soon all I had left was some packets of dried mint,° which I handed out more to ease my own conscience than for anything else. But for some reason the mint made a tremendous impression on the villagers; people almost snatched it from me in their eagerness.

'Would you ever leave us some of that nice mint too, dearie!' old women would say, looking at me beseechingly.

'What do you want it for? You're perfectly healthy, after all!'

'Want to brew up tea with it,' they would mutter, darting secretive looks. 'I'll put a smidgen in the pot with some hot water, then drink some down. Got a wee bitty of sugar left, haven't I?'

And beaming with pleasure, they would carry off their little paper screws of mint as carefully as though they were eggshells.

'May as well make for Mareevs now, down the far end,' said the elder. 'I think we've done them all here now. No, wait a bit! Pyotr Kirsanov was in today, I think his little son is poorly. Hey, pull up here, boy!'

We had stopped by a low, untidy cottage, with manure piled right to the windows ('keeps the warm in'). There was no porch, only a narrow crack of a doorway; the lobby beyond was as black as a pit.

'Hang on a minute, lady!' the elder warned me, groping in the dark for the door. 'Here, take hold of my arm... Else you might take a tumble in the dark, not being used to it, like. The floor's a bit rough.'

Bending low to keep our heads from banging on the ceiling, we squeezed into the dim hut beyond.

'Hello there again, Petrukha!' the elder said, addressing someone in the gloom. 'I've brought the lady doctor for you. So who's the patient? Will ye show us?'

'It's our Andryusha's poorly,' someone said drearily.

I gazed about the hut. As my eyes grew used to the dark, I was able to start making things out. A tall man was standing in front of us; over in a corner by the stove, on a niche built out from the wall, lay a pale, puffy boy of about 8, bedded down on piles of rags. I went over and took his hand. He was burning hot, and his pulse was beating fast and irregularly, and his breath came in hoarse wheezes; his half-open lips were dry and crusty with the fever. His big blue eyes looked at me trustingly.

'Where does it hurt, Andryusha?' I asked, bending over him.

'It's me gullet!' the boy croaked.

'He was out playing yesterday, he even went to the school, but this morning he was took bad,' his father said. 'God in Heaven, what kind of an illness do you call this?'

The tone of the man's voice was so sad and bitter that I found myself looking at him with intense interest. He was still very young, not more than 25 at most, but his face, though handsome, expressed such hopeless anguish that it was awful to look at. His great blue eyes were full of the most profound melancholy, his lips were pressed together as though he were racked by internal pain: he looked the very personification of despair.

As I completed my examination of Andryusha, I felt something soft and warm stirring in the heap of rags next to him.

'Who's this here?' I asked.

'That's another wee lad, Fedka's his name.'

'Is he sick too?'

'He's got the bloody flux... but he's had it for days now.'

'Why on earth didn't you tell me? I'll have to examine him too. I've got all the medicines with me.'

'There's no point, is there? He's on the way out in any case,' said the man, with all the dreadful indifference of despair.

I began to unwrap the rags covering the child. It was a little boy of about 5. He lay with his face to the wall, and made no response when I addressed him. His pulse was so faint I could hardly feel it; his breath came in irregular gasps, seeming to tear at his chest; his eyes, blue like his father's, were fixed on the wall, wide open but unseeing; they were starting to cloud over. He was already in his death agony.

'Listen,' I said agitatedly. 'You're right, he *is* dying... But you really should find somewhere else to put him.'

'Should we now...' the man replied expressionessly.

A short dumpy woman of about 30 came into the cottage; she was terribly filthy and ill-favoured. Catching sight of me and the elder, she began bustling about anxiously: first she took a cloth, and rubbed at some mark on the table, then she seized a besom and began brushing the floor. I went up and stopped her; pointing at the dying boy, I asked her to find somewhere else to put him. Looking at me uncomprehendingly, she wiped her nose on her filthy fingers, and then said: 'well now... that's right... 'course we'll find him somewhere!'

I gave Andryusha a sweet. Suddenly I heard a high childish voice piping somewhere overhead.

'I wants one too!'

'Have you other children, then?' I asked.

'That's *my* boy there!' said the woman, smiling broadly to show her big white teeth.

'Aren't those two yours, then?'

'Nay, nay... they're his first wife's, I'm only their stepmother. Here, Petya, duckie! Come here, and the lady'll find a little something for thee, too!'

There was a rustling above the stove, and then a little boy of about 3 jumped down from the step as bold as brass. Smiling at me—he had a marked cast in the eye—he sidled up to me and held out his hand. I stroked his curly head and gave him a sweet; he snatched it like some young wild animal, then shot away to his lair over the stove.

'Ma, Ma, this tastes sweet!' came his voice in ringing tones.

'You wouldn't believe the run of bad luck that Petrukha had lately,' the elder observed when we were back in the sleigh. 'One accident after another, till he lost every stick he had. First the cow was took off by a murrain, then the hunger came and they had to sell their horse, then his wife took sick and died. So then he married that widow, so there'd be someone to look after the kiddies... You couldn't call her a bad woman, she's kind-hearted enough, but she's still not their real mother, and she's not much of a housekeeper neither. And now the lad's gone right off the rails. Soon as the kiddies went down sick, he says to me: "I'll see them buried, then I'll be off. The wife can see to herself. I'm going where the fancy takes me." He's a good lad too; doesn't drink or mess about, and he knows his letters...'

'I suppose that most people have a hard time making ends meet here?' I asked.

'No, no, things aren't too bad really... During the hunger, now, things weren't too good, but we get by mostly. The hunger really was something, though! You should have seen the difference that made! Take my da—he had eight horses before, now he has three. As for Solntsevka—thirty households there, you know, and not a horse to their name!'

'Yes, the poverty in that village is terrible.'

'You're not wrong there, God help us! They have to go round begging to get by.' The elder paused, and then added, 'Frankly, I shouldn't be surprised if they all get out soon, and there's an end.'

'Where do you think they'll go?'

'Somewhere or other, who knows? Lots around here already have. They go to the powers that be in the *volost*° to get their passport, then they're off—where to, who knows? Well, with that life, who can blame them? That's our school over there, by the way,' he said proudly, pointing at a fine smart little house with a fence, standing on a rise at some distance from the other houses.

'Did the *zemstvo*° build that?'

'No, it was the landlord did. What I mean to say is, that was where they lived themselves, the master and mistress, only the mistress doesn't live here any more, so she made it over for a school, God bless her, and she pays the teacher herself. The heating and the janitor, of course, that's communal. It's a good school we have here—they don't even have one like it in Krivinsk, you know!'

'Do many of the children go to the school?'

'All of them do, all the girls, and the boys too. They even send the kiddies over from the station, from the settlement there. It's ever such a good school. One of my own lads is there, 14 years old he is now, and doing ever so well at his studies. Why, I'm even hoping he might go to school in the town now, with God's help. The lady teacher thinks he should go. Well, who knows what it'll come to? But he's a good lad, he works really hard,' the elder said, smiling with pleasure at the thought. 'Soon as he claps eyes on a book, he starts shaking all over.'

'How do you get him books round here?'

'How? Well, he can borrow some down the school, and I buy him a few in town, every now and then. But he always wants more. Every time I go into town, he starts in on me. 'Dada, buy me a book, please buy me one, a nice fat one!' I've said a few bad words to him sometimes, God help me!'

'Why should you do that? Surely it's a good thing for him to like reading?'

'Well, I know there's no harm in it, but all the same... Well, if he's reading he can't be working, can he? I dunno! Ah, but that's Mareevs' over there, see! Nearly there now!'

[*1896*]

♦ ZINAIDA GIPPIUS ♦

Born into the provincial gentry, Gippius (1869–1945) was to move to St Petersburg in the late 1880s, after her marriage to the writer Dmitry Merezhkovsky. Here she soon became active in the literary world. Her earliest poems and stories were published in politically radical, but artistically conventional, journals such as *Mir bozhii*; however, in the late 1890s, Gippius and Merezhkovsky began to play leading roles, both as writers and as organizers, in the development of the Russian Symbolist movement. For almost two decades the two were perhaps the most powerful literary figures in St Petersburg; they also made frequent visits to Paris, and were on friendly terms with many prominent *littérateurs* in France. In 1918, their violent hostility to Bolshevism caused them to emigrate; eventually they settled in Paris for good, where they became the centre of an important, though smaller, coterie. Gippius was as talented as she was prolific, and her deft exploitation of decadent motifs made her probably the most famous and influential woman poet of the years before the Revolution. Her early poetry concentrates on themes of sin and transgression, juxtaposing an active hero and passive heroine. Her later work is denser and more sophisticated, developing a more abstract notion of androgyny as a multiplicity of spiritual qualities (in 'The Wedding Ring'), and linking decadent metaphors, such as blood-letting, to the new interest in the feminine as a conduit for the other-worldly (in 'Incantation').

The Seamstress

(Russian text p. 423)

For two days I have not said a word...
Spiteful thoughts gnaw me.
My back hurts; wherever I look
Blue spots are floating.

The church bell booms out for a while,
Then stops. I am left to myself.
The scarlet silk squeaks and slips
As it suffers my hesitant stitches.

All things flow into each other,
But each has a mark of its own;
I fasten on objects, and wonder
What may lie hidden beyond.

The silk flares up in flames,
Then turns to a pool of blood;
'Love' is our paltry word
For the blood language cannot name.

'Love' is a meaningless sound...
But I shall see no more now, it is late:
Not fire or blood, but silk
Suffers my hesitant stitches.

(1901)

◆ ZINAIDA GIPPIUS ◆

The Wedding Ring

(Russian text p. 424)

Although the lamp was out, above its darkness
I saw the bright reflection of a flame.
My soul is bare, stripped to the purest bareness;
It has escaped, transcended all its bounds.

A man, I held desire my dearest treasure,
But I give it, myself, my sacred pain,
My prayers, my ecstasies—all these, O Father,
I give with love to You, most loving one.

And so the hour of limitless surrender
Enclosed me in a cloak of flames like wings;
Empowered me with the power of Your commandment,
And clothed me in Your holy veil of fire.

So let me stretch my hand out to my brother;
I look in the Face of You, the Fount of Life,
And in the radiance of transfigured torture
I bear my cross, light as a wedding ring.

(1905)

◆ ZINAIDA GIPPIUS ◆

Incantation

(Russian text p. 425)

Get ye hence, rebellious spirits,
Get ye gone, enchaining fetters,
Split apart, stifling underworld!
Be still, black insatiable whirlwinds!

This secret is great and forbidden,
This vow must never be broken,
Human blood must never be shown,
Human blood must be kept from the sun.

Die away, what is bound by a curse!
Fly away, what is wrapped in a cloud!

Beat, heart, beat each heart in turn!
Rise up, each unshackled soul!

(*December 1905*
St Petersburg)

♦ ANASTASIYA MIROVICH ♦

Next to nothing is known of Mirovich's life, though letters preserved in the Moscow Central State Archive of Literature and Art make it clear that 'Anastasiya Mirovich' was a real name and not a pseudonym. She is thought to have been born about 1880. Apart from the two prose poems anthologized here, Mirovich was the author of two lyric poems, also published in the almanac *Severnye tsvety*.

Lizards

She was rescued from the bottom of a deep well. She could not remember when or how she had fallen in, or how long she had been there. The water had made her wet hair look still darker, her eyebrows and lashes still blacker; there was something seductive and startling in her gaze, which rested long on others, scrutinizing them deeply. She seemed to have forgotten how to speak; she seemed to have forgotten most things.

A sorcerer was brought to examine her.

Her parents hung near him, imploring him to restore the poor girl's consciousness and memory. He stood before her, in a chiton fashioned from creeping plants, in a crown of burdocks and feathers, and a serpentine smile slipped over his wrinkled face, extending his eyes to huge gulfs of light, or squeezing them narrow as slits.

'What memory, what consciousness shall I restore in you?' he said. 'It is your knowledge that has made you ill, is that not so? Your vision has become larger than you are, is that not so?'

She sighed and gave a long stretch, as though wearied by the necessity of answering him. Then she said:

'You have guessed right.'

Once more he gave his slippery smile.

'Certainly I have. Now tell me the difference between ash and wood.'

'Wood may become ash,' she answered, 'but burnt ash can never turn to wood.'

'And is it possible to count the birds who blacken the heavens in their shifting flocks?'

'Yes, but only by becoming a bird oneself,' she answered.

He held out to her a tray made of plaited rushes; on it were three necklaces. One was made of delicate wild flowers, one of pearls, and the third of live lizards.

'Which of these three necklaces draws your desire, tempts your hand, pulls your gaze and your will?'

She put out her hand to the third of the necklaces. With a faint groan, as though submitting to a power of which she was not conscious, she put the chain of green, pulsating lizards round her neck.

'There is nothing more for me to do,' said the sorcerer, turning to her relatives. 'Fear not. When she is once used to the lizards, she will become one of you.'

[1902]

♦ ANASTASIYA MIROVICH ♦

Elsa

'Silence,' said the pastor, closing his bible. 'If even the words of our divine Saviour cannot express poor Elsa's condition, what may human language say of her?'

Elsa's mother went on weeping; her tears came in such floods that she could not wipe them away. They poured from her eyes like floods from a great salty sea—oh yes! a salty sea!

'Elsa,' she said to her daughter, 'what time is it?'

'Cock-crow,' Elsa replied.

So they sat, the three of them, in the dark of the night, and it did not enter anyone's head that it was time they were in bed.

'Elsa, my child,' said the pastor, 'tell us what happened to you.'

The girl shook back her thick hair and laid her arms on the table. She began tracing her finger over the pattern on the tablecloth, and telling them what had happened. It was the third time already that night she had told them; had ten thousand nights been stretched end to end, they would have spent each one in the same way.

'We left in the early morning to search for waste land where we might bury those we had killed. They were all Saxon Guards; they were all wearing blue uniforms with gold braid. When one of them was dying he cursed me, saying I should give birth to vipers, not children. We hid our knives far away; we covered all the traces of our crime.'

'Elsa, my child,' said the pastor with a sigh, 'did you not think of us whilst you were murdering them?'

'No,' she replied. 'On the way back some people asked us if we knew anything about the murder of three sentries next to the prison. We said that we did not. The wind throbbed in our ears, the pavements trembled under our feet. When we reached town, someone had already been falsely accused of the murder. My friends were overjoyed, and made haste to leave town, saying it was dangerous to remain. They packed their suitcases and ate cheese sandwiches, staring at the clock all the time so they could be sure not to miss their train. The man we had freed when we killed the Saxon

Guards kept kissing me on the hands and the neck; he was muttering as though he were delirious, "I knew that you would follow me on everywhere. You abandoned your father and mother for my sake. You were not afraid to become a murderess.—See," he said, turning to his comrades, "here is a woman who knows how to love!" I fastened his bags; I could find no words to say.'

'They have gone away,' said the pastor, 'gone away down the Rhein. But you are still here.'

'You have been alone since ten o'clock,' her mother observed.

'I began to tidy the room, but nothing would take away the smell of blood, it would not stop clinging to me. I kissed my crucifix and went to bed.'

'So Christ was with you after all,' the pastor said.

'I no longer understand him.'

'You will understand him in time,' her mother said with conviction.

Dull patches of red showed on Elsa's cheeks; she was dry-eyed and staring fixedly.

'Amen,' said the pastor.

'Amen,' said Elsa.

But still they stayed where they were; dawn found them at the table, and the pale morning sun gave Elsa's flushed cheeks a desperate caress.

That was not how it ended.

The man who had been unjustly executed came back to earth, put on the clothes that he had been wearing, and went to find Elsa. He had something to say to her; for many years he searched for her tirelessly.

Late one night he came up to the house and looked through the lighted window; he saw Elsa sitting at the table and tracing the pattern on the cloth with her finger, and her parents staring at her in silence.

He knocked, and was let into the house. The pastor was on the point of saying 'Amen' when the door opened, and in came the man.

'Elsa, I greet you,' he said. 'I shall be with you always.'

And all three crossed themselves, obedient to the will of God.

[1902]

♦ NADEZHDA TEFFI ♦

Half-French and half-Russian, Teffi was born in 1872 into a distinguished St Petersburg family with many literary connections. Her father, Professor Aleksandr Lokhvitsky, was an eminent Russian academic; her great-grandfather had been a mystical poet, and Teffi's sister, Mirra Lokhvitskaya, was one of the most renowned turn-of-the-century woman poets. Teffi herself began by publishing poetry, and verse remained the literary interest which she herself perhaps took most seriously, but she is best known (and rightly so) for her humorous writings, especially her polished and laconic short stories. The pieces included here, the short play *The Woman Question* (first performed in 1907) and the short story 'Walled up' (1910), display different facets of her abilities. *The Woman Question*, a comedy of sex-role reversal, shows Teffi as a virtuoso of sparkling linguistic comedy. 'Walled up', on the other hand, is a piece whose treatment of two single women's absurd power games leaves the reader feeling battered as much as amused. It is an early example of Teffi's sour–sweet manner, which was to be extensively developed in the stories which she wrote when living in Paris after the Revolution.

The Woman Question

A Fantastical Farce in One Act

DRAMATIS PERSONAE

FATHER. In Scenes 1 and 3, wears ordinary gentlemen's clothes; in Scene 2, a long frock-coat in brightly coloured checks, with a shawl collar and a fluffy scarf tied under the chin with a ribbon.

MOTHER. In Scene 1, wears a house-dress. In Scene 2, a narrow skirt, frock-coat, waistcoat and a starched linen blouse.

Their children:

KATYA. Wears her hair up, like a lady; 18 years old. In Scene 2, dressed much like her mother.

VANYA. A 17-year-old boy.

KOLYA. A 16-year-old boy.

In Scene 1, Vanya is wearing a blazer and Kolya a cycling suit. In Scene 2, both are in long, brightly coloured frock-coats, one pink, the other light blue, with big, bright scarves and soft lace collars.

ANDREI NIKOLAEVICH. Dressed the same way as these two, but also has a hat with a veil, and a muff.

AUNT MASHA. A fat woman, in a knee-length uniform jacket, top-boots, grandiose epaulettes, medals. A ladylike coiffure.

PROFESSORESS. Tailcoat, narrow skirt, starched blouse, pince-nez. Skinny and balding, hair at the back of her head braided into a rat's tail with a blue ribbon.

PYOTR NIKOLAEVICH, her husband. A wide frock-coat, a lace scarf, a lorgnette, and a fan hanging from his belt at the side.

ORDERLYETTE. A fat woman, with greasy hair twisted up at the back of her head; in uniform.

ADJUTANTESS. In military uniform. Heavily made-up, with a fluffy hairdo, an *aigrette* pinned to her hair at the side; a fat woman of the people.

STYOPKA. Black trousers, pink sweater, an apron edged with lace, a maid's cap, with a bow around his neck. Very ugly.

CAB-DRIVERESS. A long scarf over her head topped by a cab-driver's hat. A long coat. Carrying a horse-whip.

GLASHA. A maid.

Scene I

[*A drawing-room. Against the wall stands a big, old-fashioned couch. Evening. Lamps are burning. Through the open door can be seen a table set for dinner.* MOTHER *is wiping the tea-cups with a cloth.* VANYA *is sitting at the table reading.* KOLYA *is stretched out in a rocking chair, wearing a cycling cap.* KATYA *is pacing round the room.*]

KATYA [*agitatedly*]. That's outrageous! Really outrageous! As if a woman weren't the same as a man!

KOLYA. That's just it. She isn't.

KATYA. But lots of countries do have equal rights for women, and no one there thinks that things are any the worse for that. Why can't we manage?

KOLYA. We just can't.

KATYA. But why not?

KOLYA. We just can't, and that's it.

KATYA. That's it—because you're a fool.

MOTHER [*from the dining room*]. Not fighting *again*? Do stop it! You ought to be ashamed of yourselves!

KATYA. He does it on purpose to tease me. You know how hard it is for me. I've dedicated my life... [*Starts crying*]

KOLYA. Ha, ha! [*sings*] She's dedicated her life, and she's been victimized! [*A bell is heard*]

MOTHER. Will you stop that, you two! That's someone at the door.

Enter Father.

FATHER. Well, here I am. What on earth is this? What's Katya bawling about?

KOLYA. She's dedicated her life, and she's been victimized.

MOTHER. Oh, for heaven's sake hold your tongues! Father's just got back, and he's tired... Instead of...

FATHER [*with a frown*]. Good God, whatever next! Your father rushes round all day like a mad dog, but he can't count on a moment's peace when he gets home. It's all your fault, Mother. *You* let things get out of hand. Katerina spends all day, every day running off to meetings, and this blockhead does nothing but loll about at home. Take off that hat! You're not in a stable. Father works like a horse, slaving over papers all day, and instead of...

MOTHER. Shurochka, dear, how about a nice glass of tea?

FATHER. I'm coming, Shurochka. I only want one, though. I've got to run again.

MOTHER [*passing him the glass, which he drinks down on his feet*]. You've got to run?

FATHER [*irritably*]. Yes, of course. Quite simple really. It's hardly the first time, is it? I spend my life running round like a mouse in a treadmill, and all for your sakes. The fact is, we've got a meeting this evening. Oh, yes, I nearly forgot what I dropped by for! Let me congratulate you, darling. Uncle Petya was promoted to general today. We must put on a dinner for him tomorrow. You'll arrange things, won't you? I'll buy the wine myself, of course.

MOTHER. So you're not coming home till late tonight?

FATHER. There's feminine logic for you! Well, of course not.

[*He picks up the briefcase by the wrong end, and out flutter papers and a long pink ribbon*]

KOLYA. Papa—you've dropped a ribbon.

FATHER [*stuffing the ribbon back hastily*]. Yes, yes, of course. Oh! The ribbon! That's a business matter! Well, goodbye, then, Shurochka [*pinching her cheek*]. Sleep well, Mama. [*Exit*

MOTHER [*Sighing*]. Oh, the poor dear. He's such a hard worker.

KOLYA. Hmmm, the ribbon—that's a business matter. Well, of course, if he says so.

MOTHER. What?

KATYA. I'm so bored, I think I'm going off my head.

MOTHER. That's because you never do anything, my dear. If you found yourself something to do, like sewing, or a little reading, or even helping your mother do the housework, then you wouldn't be bored, would you? [*Exit*

KOLYA. I'm off. I've decided to help Mother with the housework.

[*Exits through dining-room. Can be seen taking a spoon and eating jam directly from the pot.*]

KATYA. I don't want to help. I'm not a cook. Perhaps *I'd* like to work in an office too. Yes, sir. And maybe *I'd* like to go to meetings in the evenings.

[KOLYA *guffaws.* KATYA *jumps, then threatens him with her fist.*]

I hate you all! No, I've changed my mind. I don't want equal rights any more. What good would they do me? No! I'd like to see the men in our shoes for a while, then we women would boss them around like they boss us. *Then* we'd see what kind of tune they'd sing.

VANYA. You think that would be better?

KATYA. Better? Yes, we women would turn the whole world upside down...

VANYA. You've said enough! If you want a new life, invent a new breed of human beings. If people stay the same, so does everything else.

KATYA. That's not true! You're lying! You're saying that on purpose to spite me! And in any case, you can tell your Andrei Nikolaevich that I'm not going to marry him. I haven't the slightest intention of doing it. We'd get married, and the very next day he'd ask me what was for dinner. No, not for anything! I'd rather shoot myself.

VANYA. Now you really have gone off your rocker!

KATYA. I'll finish school, I'll train as a doctor, and then I'll have him as a wife myself. He'd better not dare do anything—except a little light housework. No need to worry, I can support the family on my own.

VANYA. But surely that's just the same?

KATYA. Of course it isn't. Life would be quite different if we were in charge. We women aren't the same as you men, you know: we're exactly the opposite.

VANYA. Which is to say, what? What do you mean, 'exactly the opposite'?

KATYA. Everything about us is exactly the opposite. You're all lunatics. You've gone insane from all that power. Take your Andrei Nikolaevich, for instance. How he dotes on that Professor Petukhov. Oh, what a scholar! Oh, how sweet, how absent-minded! Petukhov's nothing but an old dodderer, and he never takes a bath either. You all fawn on each other. You cheat on your wives, you play cards all day and night if you feel like it, and everything turns out just as you want. Could a woman get away with it?

MOTHER'S VOICE. Katya! I'm going to lie down for a while. If you hear Father ring the bell, wake Glasha up—you know how soundly she sleeps!

KATYA. All right! I won't sleep a wink all night in any case.

[VANYA *exits and locks his door*

KATYA [*banging on his door with her fist*]. So tell him I won't have him! Do you hear? I won't have him! [*Sits down on couch and starts crying*] Poor Andryusha... and poor me!... So what, we'll wait until everything's been turned upside down... I *will* be a lady doctor, Andrusha... [*lies on the couch*] I believe that everything will come true... won't it be wonderful?... [*yawns.*] I'll show him. It would be so nice... [*falls asleep*].

[*The lights dim slowly. For a few moments it is completely dark. Then immediately daylight blazes. Katya is sitting at the table going through some papers. Kolya is on the couch embroidering some slippers. Father is washing cups in the dining room.*]

Scene 2

KOLYA [*on a whining note*]. Bother, I've got to rip all this out! I'm a cross-stitch short again!

KATYA. Quiet, you're bothering me.

VANYA *enters, animated, throws his hat on a chair.*

VANYA. What an amazing day! I've come straight here from Parliament House. I sat up in the gallery; it was terribly stuffy. Deputy Ovchina was discussing the man question.° She said some amazing things. Men are humans too, she said! And a man's brain, in spite of its excessive weight and overabundance of grey matter, is a real human brain all the same. She cited history. In bygone days, men were allowed to hold extremely responsible jobs...

FATHER. That's all very interesting. But you'd better help me with the dishes.

VANYA. She cited examples of new experiments they're doing. For instance, if men work as cooks and nannies, why...°

KATYA. Shut up, Vanya, you're bothering me. [*A bell rings*] Oh, that must be Mama.

FATHER [*bustling about*]. Oh, Heavens, Styopka didn't hear it again. I'll have to open the door myself.

[*Runs out*

MOTHER [*coming in with* FATHER]. Really, my sweet, you shouldn't do it! Leave opening doors to the servants—that's what they're there for! Listen, children, I have some wonderful news! Aunt Masha has been promoted to general.

FATHER. What an impressive woman she is!

KATYA. Pooh! She's done nothing all her life except steal the regimental oats.

FATHER. Katya, really!

KATYA. She drinks like a fish and chases every pair of trousers in sight.

FATHER. Kolya, leave the room. Katya, you mustn't talk like that in front of the boy!

MOTHER [*to* FATHER]. Well, Shurochka, you'll have to organize a dinner for Aunt Masha today. Try not to let us down, won't you? I'll buy the wine myself, of course. But you're in charge of the food and so on. Kolya and Vanya, be sure to help your father!

FATHER [*timidly*]. Mightn't it be possible to postpone the dinner until tomorrow? It's a teeny bit short notice...

MOTHER. Wonderful! There's masculine logic for you! I invite guests for dinner today, and he says he'll serve it tomorrow! [*Exit*

VANYA. Oh, Ovchina made a tremendous speech! You should give men exactly the same education as women, not make slaves of them, and disgrace the name of human! We demand equal rights for men!

KOLYA. After all, Papa, why *are* things so unfair? Everything for women and nothing for us!

FATHER. Well, my child, at one time it was quite different.° Men *were* in control, and women were struggling for *their* rights. Finally the women revolted, and waged a bloody war. When the men surrendered, they were all shut up in towers and harems, and they're only just beginning to free themselves from slavery. In America, men are already studying medicine...

VANYA. Ha, ha! A man as a lady doctor! That's a good one!

KOLYA. And did men hold seats in parliament in those days?

FATHER. Yes, of course.

KOLYA. And all the chairwomen were men?

FATHER. It stands to reason.

KOLYA. Ha, ha! A chairwoman in trousers! Ha, ha, what a picture! A chairwoman in trousers opening a session of parliament! Ha! Ha! Ha!

VANYA. Oh! Stop! Don't make me laugh! Ha, ha!

FATHER. Stop that this instant!

MOTHER [*enters, fuming*]. Where *is* Styopka? I've been ringing and ringing. There's no water in the basin. What a farce! Your wife slaves like an ox all day in the office, and you can't even keep the servants in line.

FATHER [*anxiously*]. Right away, Shurochka, right away! [*shouts through the door*] Styopka!

Enter a young footman in a maid's cap and apron.

MOTHER. Why don't you answer when people ring for you?

STYOPKA. Beg pardon. Couldn't hear it, ma'am.

MOTHER. Couldn't hear it, ma'am, eh! You're always sitting in the kitchen with some firewoman.° *That's* why you can't hear.

STYOPKA. That's not me, ma'am, it's Fyodor who does that.

MOTHER. Bring some water for the washbasin.

[*Styopka exits*

FATHER. Shurochka, don't get angry. Whatever happens, we can't get rid of Fyodor now. Who would do the cooking? And besides, he's a good cook, as cooks go; it's so hard to find one, and a real woman cook is beyond our budget.°

KOLYA *enters*

KOLYA. Mama, Aunt Masha's orderlyette is here.

MOTHER. Send her in.

Enter a woman in a short skirt, boots, uniform jacket, and cap.

ORDERLYETTE. At your service, ma'am.

MOTHER. What's the matter?

ORDERLYETTE. The matter is that their Excellency have ordered me to inform you that they are on their way.

FATHER. Oh, gracious me! Kolya, Vanya! Quick, quick! Help me get ready!

MOTHER. Here, girl, have one on me.

ORDERLYETTE. Delighted to oblige, ma'am.

[*Does an about-face to the left and exits*

KATYA. Should *I* think about becoming an officeress, do you suppose?

MOTHER. Well, you do have all the right connections. Your aunt would take care of you. But in any case, you have excellent prospects. The boys are worrying me, though. I can see them both turning into old bachelors. With no dowry, who's going to take them?

KATYA. But Kolya is so pretty.

KOLYA [*poking his head round the door*]. Pretty, eh! Just you wait! I'll catch myself a councilloress or a mayoress yet. [*Vanishes again*].

[*A bell rings. Katya picks up her papers and exits. Mother follows her. Enter* AUNT MASHA. *She is in skirt, uniform jacket, hat, and elaborate epaulettes.*]

AUNT MASHA. Well! Everyone's vanished! [*Pulls out a cigarette case.*] Styopka, bring me a match! [*Enter Styopka.*] Why, there you are, Styopka, my petal! You look prettier every time I see you! Are you engaged to be married yet?

STYOPKA. How could I be, your Excellency? I'm a poor boy, a simple boy. Who would ask me?

AUNT MASHA. They say my adjutantess is courting you.

STYOPKA [*covering his face with his apron*]. Shame on you, ma'am, listening to men's silly gossip! I'm a good boy, I am.

AUNT MASHA. Bring me some soda water, will you, my love? I've the very devil of a hangover!

STYOPKA. Right away, ma'am.

[*Styopka exits.* AUNT MASHA *sits down, crosses her legs, drums on the table and sings military airs.*]

AUNT MASHA.

Run away, my sweeties,
Behind stones and trees,
Two by two, by two,
Too-roo-roo, roo-roo!

Enter FATHER.

FATHER. Good evening, Masha! My warmest congratulations!

AUNT MASHA [*Kissing* FATHER*'s hand*]. *Merci, merci,* my little friend. Well, how are you? Fussing about the housework, as usual? Well, what can we do? Such is you gentlemen's fate. Nature herself made you for family life. It's your instinct, you see—to bring forth and multiply, and coddle your offspring, heh, heh. And in return, we poor women are saddled with all life's burdens: work, worries about the family. Whilst you gentlemen flit about like butterflies, ha ha, like little moths, heh heh! And we're up working till dawn more often than not! But where are the children?

[*Enter* STYOPKA *with soda water; he puts it down on the table, then exits.*]

FATHER. Kolya, Vanya! Come here, will you! Aunt Masha has arrived.

Enter KOLYA, *with* MOTHER *behind him.*

MOTHER. Oh, your Excellency! Allow me to congratulate you! [*A bell rings.*]

AUNT MASHA. Thank you, my good chap! Only please don't on any account congratulate me! There was a joke going round about that in the regiment. We had this right-flank privatess in our regiment, you see, we all called her Sofya the Screech-Owl...

Enter PROFESSORESS *with her husband.*

FATHER. Oh, my compliments, dear Professoress! Good evening, Pyotr Nikolaevich.

PROFESSORESS. I am here to congratulate myself, that is, you, on your congratulation day.

PYOTR NIKOLAEVICH [*whispers*]. Lili! Lili! Great day. Not congratulation day!

PROFESSORESS [*continuing to greet people*]. *Merci*. I am so grateful to you, ladies and gentlemen, for honouring the fruits of my modest labours... I assure you that this day will never be forgotten...

AUNT MASHA [*angrily*]. Why 'modest'? I don't understand. What does my modesty have to do with this?

PYOTR NIKOLAEVICH. Oh, Heavens! Lili! You're all mixed up again. You're supposed to be talking about her, not her about you.

PROFESSORESS. Oh dear yes, I *am* sorry. I got a little confused. I was supposed to be talking about her, that is you, and not her, that is you, about me.

[*She sits down, missing the chair, and everyone rushes to pick her up.*]

FATHER. Gracious me! Did you hurt yourself?

MOTHER. Better lay her down on the couch for a moment.

PROFESSORESS. Ah, never mind! On the contrary, I rather enjoyed it!

AUNT MASHA. Ha, ha! We were just joking about that very thing in our regiment. It was quite a spicy story, you know, but if the gentlemen will permit... You see, it happened that two lieutenantesses were fighting, because their husbands had made cuckolds of them...

FATHER [*interrupting*]. *Finissez devant les garçons*!

AUNT MASHA. And, good God! but did Mariya Nikolaevna lose her head! The hullaballoo lasted for days! The skating parties, the celebrations, the dinners, and all with various gentlemen of easy virtue° in tow...

Enter STYOPKA

STYOPKA. Gentlemen and ladies, dinner is served!

PROFESSORESS [*jumps up quickly*]. Please, gentlemen and ladies, let us proceed to the table! I trust that you will enjoy what God has put before us!

PYOTR NIKOLAEVICH. Lili! Lili! You're at their house, they're not at yours! Oh, Heavens! This absentmindedness! [*Grabs her by the arm.*]

MOTHER. Ha, ha! Oh, that's these scholars for you! It's a dog's life with them!

PYOTR NIKOLAEVICH. All great people are absent-minded. And eccentric, too. I remember reading once...

AUNT MASHA. They were joking about that just recently in our regiment. One generaless has a young husband—you know, a real little rosebud...

[*Goes into the dining room. Through the door you can see them all taking their seats at the table. A bell rings. Styopka runs to open the door. Returns with the Adjutantess.*]

ADJUTANTEES. How on earth did you fetch up here, my drakelet?

STYOPKA. I'm working as a chambermaid girl now. Doing light washing. Fetching hot water, and that.

ADJUTANTESS [*pats him on the cheek*]. Bet the lady of the house is after you, eh?

STYOPKA. Eh, no, nothing like that. That's just men's idle gossip.

ADJUTANTESS. Good, good! Keep talking! Oh, you bad little boy! I do believe you're growing your beard! Give us a kiss, then, sourpuss! Well, hurry up about it! I haven't got all day! Why, you little devil!

STYOPKA [*struggling free*]. Let me go! Shame on you! I'm an honest boy. You just want to play around with me, and then you'll leave me.

ADJUTANTESS. Oh, you silly little sweetie! I love you, you know that! Mind you, you're not so bad-looking either...

STYOPKA. I don't trust you. You're all the same, you women! [*Starts crying*] First this lovey-dovey stuff, then you leave us holding the baby! You're taking advantage of my youth and innocence. [*Howls*]

KATYA *enters*

KATYA. What's going on here? [*Styopka runs away.*] Mariya Nikolaevna, shame on you! Your dinner's waiting.

ADJUTANTESS. Tra-la-la! Tra-la-la! You know, you should drop in to see us sometime, Katya. Yesterday we had some real fun. We put on this supper and did the honours for all the soubrets. Coco, Vanka the Cricket, Antipka°—you know the one, he used to be a launderer.° A whole bouquet of charming gentlemen, in a word. All naughty boys, of course, but real poppets too. [*Exit*

A bell rings loudly several times. STYOPKA *opens the door; a* CAB-DRIVERESS *rushes in. She has a long cloak, a woman's kerchief on her head with a cab-driver's cap on top, and a whip in her hand.*]

CAB-DRIVERESS This ain't on! It ain't on! She must have come here, there isn't nowhere else she could have come. I do have a right to me own money! That old janitor lady told me: be sure as you grab her by the tail, or she'll wriggle out by the back door before you know it. [*Makes for the drawing-room.*]

STYOPKA [*blocking the way*]. Where do you think you're shoving to? Talk sense, who do you want?

CAB-DRIVERESS. The fare who didn't pay. She said she'd pay me sixty copecks to drive over from Vasilievsky,° she beat me right down, then she even done me out of that.

STYOPKA. What does she look like?

CAB-DRIVERESS. Oh, eh. Well, that ain't hard: she looks a complete ragbag.

STYOPKA. Oh... That's Madame Professoress, for sure.

CAB-DRIVERESS. And, besides, the old janitoress says: be sure as you grab her, she says, by the tail, she says. ... she says...

STYOPKA. Just wait there, and I'll get her. [*Fetches* PROFESSORESS *from the dining room.*]

PROFESSORESS [*extending her hand to the cab-driveress*]. Good evening, ma'am. By the way, whom do I have the honour of addressing?

CAB-DRIVERESS. You don't have no honour, if you cheat someone...

PROFESSORESS [*to* STYOPKA]. I'm afraid that I don't understand the lady... What does she want from me?... Perhaps by your good offices, so to speak...

STYOPKA. That's the cab-driveress. She needs her sixty copecks.

PROFESSORESS. What? Sixty copecks? How peculiar! [*Hands over some money.*] Allow me... I am *so* sorry, madam... Does the lady mind having it in small change?

CAB-DRIVERESS [*looking at her*]. Looks like I made a mistake. [*Scratches her head with all five fingers.*]

PROFESSORESS. Did you make a mistake with me, or I with you?

CAB-DRIVERESS. Hard to say, ma'am. The one I wanted looks a complete ragbag, and begging your pardon, ma'am, only... don't take offence... and the janitoress says, be sure as you grab her by the tail, not you, your Honour, that is, but just giving you an example... suppose, bearing the mistake in mind, you was just to give me another ten copecks, because of the mistake, eh, as a sweetener, like...

STYOPKA. Get out of here, you filthy drunk, or I'll call the doorwoman! She'll sort you out. [*Pushes the* CAB-DRIVERESS *out through the door.*]

PROFESSORESS [*looking at* STYOPKA]. What a... tee hee hee. Look at that cute little ribbon round your neck, ha ha... You're such a little cutie pie, tyu-tyu-tyu...

STYOPKA [*going weak at the knees with fear*]. Madame Professoress... why ma'am... this very minute ma'am. Oh, Lord preserve us! Egyptian witchcraft!

PROFESSORESS [*rushes up to Styopka and grabs him by the chin*]. Tyu, tyu, tyu!

PYOTR NIKOLAEVICH [*running in*]. Lili! Lili! What's going on here? What did they want you for?

PROFESSORESS. Don't get upset, Petrushka. I just gave that cab-driveress some money.

PYOTR NIKOLAEVICH. Which cab-driveress?

PROFESSORESS. Hmmm... It's hard to say which one... a drunken one, it rather seems...

STYOPKA. That is, Madame Professoress paid the cab-driver who, I mean, brought you here...

PYOTR NIKOLAEVICH. What do you mean, the one who brought us here? We came on our own, that is to say, in our own carriage!

PROFESSORESS. Why yes, why yes... She herself said that she'd made a mistake. Don't get upset, Petrushka, it's all right now...

PYOTR NIKOLAEVICH. So why did you have your arm round this maid-fellow's neck?

PROFESSORESS. I... I... I... thought that... that you... He just came in from the right-hand side, do you see? And you often stand on the right and... it's all just turned out to be an illusion... a reflex illusion from the right hemisphere of the left frontal lobe of the brain... it's a phenomenon requiring further examination...

PYOTR NIKOLAEVICH. Oh, no, it's not necessary, not necessary! Don't examine it further, it's a waste of your time. Get one of your young assistantettes to do it.

[*Goes into the dining room.* STYOPKA *follows, through a different door. A moment later, the* ORDERLYETTE *enters through the same door.*]

ORDERLYETTE. Whoops! Wrong door! [*peering about*] The dining room must be there; you can hear the gentlemen and ladies in there eating. Oh, that's my Generaless chomping—you can hear it from here!

STYOPKA [*comes in with a dish*]. Eek!...

ORDERLYETTE. Stepan Ilich, greetings to you. Eyes... left! Where are you rushing to at such a pace?

STYOPKA [*waving the dish and dropping the cutlets*]. Leave off! How did you get here?

ORDERLYETTE. I drank a drop, and ate fit to pop! Dear little Fyodor did it all. Fyodor's a sweetie, but you're even nicer. [*Warmly*] You know, Ilich, you're a real peach. I'd love to make an honest man of you. You won't sully my good name, I'm sure, and I know you're certain to behave just as you should. As for me, I can look after myself. Do you know our soldiers' song? [*Singing and dancing*]

I am a soldieress,
I'm my own boss, yes,
So long as I'm far away
From where my generaless holds sway.

I treasure your sweet masculine innocence, and if anyone tries to hurt you, I'll defend you with my life against her! My life. Yes—ma'am! But you owe me a little something in return. [*Picks a meatball off the floor and wipes it on her cuff.*] Because, as the song goes, 'you give me the gift of your tears as a reward for my love...'

STYOPKA [*picking up the meatballs and putting them on the dish. The* ORDERLYETTE *helps by wiping the meatballs on her sleeve*]. Oh, Lord, Solominida Fominishna! You know how we feel about you... Oh Lord, there's someone coming!

[*Runs with the dish into the dining-room. The* ORDERLYETTE *exits.* FATHER *comes rushing in from the dining-room.* AUNT MASHA *follows, then the rest in a crowd.*]

AUNT MASHA [*waving a bottle of champagne*]. No, Shurochka, stop fussing. It's a time-honoured Polish custom. When we were stationed in Poland, we did it at every single dinner. Before dessert, someone always proposed a toast, to be drunk from the host's little bootee.

FATHER. But we're not in Poland... I'm not sure that I like this...

OMNES. Nonsense! You must! What a ridiculous fuss! It's such fun! What a good idea! It's the custom!

MOTHER. No more false modesty! You're dying to do it really! Come on, take your bootee off! What are you waiting for?

[*Father sits down and slowly removes his top-boot.*]

AUNT MASHA. That's the way! Now give it here! Good! [*Pours the bottle into the boot.*] Styopochka, my love, bring another bottle, will you? No, two! Two, do you hear? Hang on, though, you'll never manage two all by yourself—Katya, you go and give him a hand!

[*Pours out two more bottles. The boot starts bulging outwards.*]

AUNT MASHA. And another two!

MOTHER [*anxiously*]. Are you sure one's not enough? You must have gallons there in that one little boot...

AUNT MASHA. Pour all the bottles in! Right, that's enough! Let me give you the toast: to the health of all fair gentlemen! Hip, hip, hooray! I'll be the first to drink to that!

PROFESSORESS. No, let me! I can't possibly drink after you have... think of the molecules there might be, swarming about in your mouth... Help, I can't lift this... Give me a hand there... Hold my back...

[AUNT MASHA *gives the boot a shove under the heel, and champagne pours all over the* PROFESSORESS]

PROFESSORESS [*gasping for breath*]. Help, help, I'm drowning! My glasses have been washed away! Save me! I'm dying!

[PYOTR NIKOLAEVICH *is clutching the* PROFESSORESS'S *shoulder and sobbing.*]

MOTHER [*to* MASHA]. What on earth have you done?

FATHER. It's dreadful! All that wine!

AUNT MASHA. I'm sorry, I'm sorry. The Professoress did ask me to give her a hand, after all, heh heh. A propos of that, let me tell you a story. Well, not a story: it's Gospel truth, actually. You see, there was this brigadieress who swore like a trooperess, she swore so much, in fact, that...

FATHER. Marie, *les enfants*!

AUNT MASHA. Ah! Pardon me, pardon me! I'll stop!

PYOTR NIKOLAEVICH [*wiping down his wife with a handkerchief*]. Let's go home, my dear. You should rest.

PROFESSORESS [*wiping her eyes and moaning feebly*]. Never mind that! My glasses, my glasses! And cold showers after dinner are so unhealthy. I might even have been grateful had they made the offer before dinner, but now... And not even time to take off my dress! Why did they have to pour it over my dress? They should have given me time to take it off...

AUNT MASHA. Ha! Ha! Ha! You know, the other day in the regimental stables. ...

FATHER. Just come and sit down here by the stove—you'll be dry in a few seconds.

PROFESSORESS. No, no... It would make more sense to pour ethyl alcohol over me, so as to facilitate the evaporation of the water droplets... What? You do not have any by you? Well, in that case I shall go and lie down. I beg your pardon, gentlemen and ladies; I cannot presume to depend upon your company after this unfortunate incident.

PYOTR NIKOLAEVICH. Lili! Lili! We're at their house, they're not at ours.

PROFESSORESS. Yes, yes, indeed, my sweet! In any case, I am most grateful, gentlemen and ladies, for the honour which you have shown me, and I trust that you will not neglect us in the future... What *is* the matter, Petrushka? ...in the future. Please forgive the modesty of our hospitality, and let me assure you that I made every effort to see that things were done as they should be; if I have not succeeded, then I do beg your pardon. What is it, Petrushka? Yes, yes! We are in their house, so my husband says; accordingly, we shall certainly visit *yours* in our turn. Good evening. [*Makes an elaborate bow, and moves off in the direction of Vanya's bedroom*]

VANYA. Oh, no! Not that way!

KOLYA. Madame Professoress, that's Vanya's bedroom.

[PYOTR NIKOLAEVICH *and* STYOPKA *take the* PROFESSORESS *by the arms and lead her away*].

MOTHER. What a mind!

FATHER. A brilliant woman!

KATYA. But what a scatter-brain!

AUNT MASHA. Hmm... yes. Oh, apropos of that, I just remembered...

MOTHER. Now children, off to bed. We're going to have a little woman-to-woman talk here. Shurochka, make us some coffee, there's a good boy. [*Exit* FATHER, VANYA, *and* KOLYA.] Well, now we can let our hair down. [*They light cigars.*]

AUNT MASHA. What's the matter with your Kolya? He seems awfully down-in-the-mouth.

KATYA. That's because he and Andrei Nikolaevich are all taken up with the man question.

AUNT MASHA. You mean all this nonsense about equal rights for men? Is that it?

MOTHER. Well, yes. They've gone completely soft in the head. They go running off to lectures, they grow their hair; Andrei, the little fool, has been stuffing his head with lots of nonsense out of books, and now he's leading my Vanya astray. Oh, to marry them off as fast as possible to good wives...

ADJUTANTESS. I would never have made an offer to a young man like that, who rode horses, let his hair grow long, and went running round to lectures!° It's just not modest, it's just not manly! But, Ekaterina Aleksandrovna, I gather that you are not entirely indifferent to the charms of Aleksandr Nikolaevich?

KATYA. Hmm... I suppose not. I'm counting on being able to re-educate him. He's still young. Doing the housework, having children—it's bound to steady him.

AUNT MASHA. These young men are such fools! Wanting to be women! What on earth for? We respect them, we adore them, we feed them and we buy them shoes... And it's an impossible dream, even in a physical sense! Even scientists recognize that man's brain is heavier and more dense than woman's, that the convolutions and whatnot are—whatever they are. No-one's going to stick them in parliament with those convolutions of theirs, are they? Ha, ha! But I would vote for Vanka the Canary! Why not? Ha, ha! Equal rights are equal rights, after all!

MOTHER. And who is supposed to take care of the children?

AUNT MASHA. Oh, that's obvious, you and I are. Ha, ha, ha! It's obvious, we'll have to. So what? I'll hang up my sword, and the orderlyette can beat her drum so the children don't cry. Ha, ha, ha! And then bye-bye to evening meetings, Shurochka. What about that, eh? Ha, ha, ha!

MOTHER. All these innovations recently, they make your head spin. Fancy, men are going to be lady doctors now! Well, judge for yourself: would *you* send out for a young man when you were ill?

AUNT MASHA. Ha, ha! In our regiment...

MOTHER. Just a minute! You wouldn't, would you? That shows what nonsense it all is! Some offices have started giving jobs to boys now, you know. Even to husbands. The children are abandoned at home, left to the mercy of fate... and they're lowering women's wages as a result.

ADJUTANTESS. And the most important thing is, they're all losing their charm, their refinement, their manliness!

FATHER [*at the door*]. Coffee's ready.

MOTHER. Let's go, chaps. [*They exit*

A bell is heard. Enter STYOPKA and ANDREI NIKOLAEVICH.

ANDREI NIKOLAEVICH. No, thank you, Styopka, I won't take off my coat. I've only dropped in for a minute. Do you have guests? My, how embarrassing. So Vanichka's at home... Hmm... Wait a minute, Styopka... Be a good boy, could you, and bring Ekaterina Aleksandrovna out here for a minute? Wait a moment, wait a moment! You see, I have a secret... Be sure no-one sees, would you? Call her quietly.

STYOPKA. Delighted, sir. After all, we men must stick together. [*Goes to the door and shouts.*] Miss! There's someone here ask... Whoops! Psst, over here if you please, in secret!

KATYA [*running out*]. What's all this? Have you gone soft in the head? Oh, is that you Andrei? Do come in! Why haven't you taken off your coat?

ANDREI NIKOLAEVICH. No, no, *merci*. I've just dropped by for a moment. I wanted to find out whether Vanya was well... Papa sent me out for some dress patterns...

KATYA. You shouldn't be out alone so late in the evening. Some woman might get the wrong impression, and treat you impertinently.

ANDREI NIKOLAEVICH. I ought to... I must... tell you something...

KATYA. Styopka, go to the kitchen. [*Exit* STYOPKA

ANDREI NIKOLAEVICH. I've come... to release you from your offer... I can't...

KATYA. Then you don't love me! My God, my God! Tell me, for God's sake! I'm going crazy!

ANDREI NIKOLAEVICH [*in tears*]. I can't... We'll get married and the very next day you'll ask, 'Andryusha, what's for dinner today?' I can't. I'd be better off shooting myself... Slavery...

KATYA. You don't love me! You don't love me!

ANDREI NIKOLAEVICH. Vanya and I have agreed... We're both going to study... I'll become a lady doctor... then I'll support you, and you'll do the housework...

KATYA. Are you out of your mind? What me, a woman, to be kept at your expense?

ANDREI NIKOLAEVICH. Yes, yes! I love you so much, I can't manage otherwise. Power has driven women insane... We'll wait... until I myself can support... I love you so much, so much... the housework... [*Puts his arms round* KATYA *and hugs her.*]

[*A loud bell is heard. The stage grows completely dark. Then it is illuminated again immediately. A lamp is burning on the table.* KATYA *is asleep on the couch. The bell rings again.* KATYA *jumps up. A half-dressed maid runs across the room and opens the door.* FATHER *enters.*]

Scene 3

KATYA [*jumping up*]. Eek! [*Rubs her eyes.*] Papa? Is that you? Ha, ha! How wonderful! Dear Papa, do you know that we're good-for-nothings just like you? We women, that is, Aunt Masha and I, we're exactly the same as you are! Oh, I'm so happy!

FATHER. Have you taken leave of your senses? Who are good-for-nothings? What are good-for-nothings?

KATYA. Oh, you don't understand anything! I'm going to marry Andrei Nikolaevich. Nothing matters now, because we're all exactly alike anyway. Vanya! [*Pounds her fist on the door.*] Vanya! Get up! I'm going to marry Andryusha! What joy! We're all exactly alike! Dear Papa. Ha, ha! Aunt Masha became a general, and she became exactly like Uncle Petya. We'll have to wait for a new breed of humanity! [*Pounds on the door.*] Vanya, wake up!

FATHER [*pathetically*]. The Devil knows what's going on! Father works all day like a pig, not a moment to himself... but they... no respect at all...

[*Takes off his hat and throws it to the floor; reaches for his handkerchief, and pulls a long lady's stocking from his pocket, with which he then wipes his forehead.*]

CURTAIN

[*c.*1907]

Translated by Elizabeth Neatrour

◆ NADEZHDA TEFFI ◆

Walled up

The Easter loaf° was a disaster. Standing skew-whiff, with its crust bulging at the top and plastered in split almonds, it looked like an ancient, rotten fly agaric swollen by autumn rains. The blowsy paper rose which had been stuck in at one side lent it no elegance whatever. The rose's head hung down as though it were scrutinizing the big patch stitched prominently to the off-white tea-cloth, an attitude which still further emphasized the irregularity of its pedestal.

Yes, the loaf was a disaster. But there seemed to be an unspoken agreement not to pay the matter any attention. And no wonder. Madame Schrank, the hostess, had little to gain by pointing out the deficiencies in her own hospitality; whilst Madame Lazenskaya, the guest whom she had invited to share her Easter meal, had naturally to find everything perfect, out of plain good manners. As for Annushka, the cook, she certainly had no reason to draw attention to a failure for which she herself was directly responsible.

For some minutes now, Madame Lazenskaya had been feeling that it might be no bad thing to begin on the hors d'œuvres. In deference to propriety, she was doing her best not to stare at the table, but there was a look of tense expectation on her little pointed face, which was surrounded by scanty waves of hair, and set on a neck creased by wrinkles, and encircled by a dirty lilac choker. Every now and then she would raise her brows, whose deficiency of hairs had been made up with the end of a matchstick, and study the crochet covering of the whatnot intently, though she had been looking at it every day for the last ten years. Or she would lower her eyes and screw up her toothless mouth, dabbing at it delicately with a handkerchief edged in torn lace.

The hostess, a stout brunette with a bulldog's jowly cheeks, walked to and fro about the table, smoothing her grubby embroidered apron over her bulging stomach. She could tell what state Madame Lazenskaya was in, knowing that she had eaten nothing but baked potatoes without butter all Lent; but her guest's affected indifference irritated her, and she was resolved to spin the torment out.

'Not time yet,' she said in her sonorous bass voice. 'They haven't rung the bells.'°

She spoke with a strong German accent, pushing out her upper lip, which was graced by a dainty black moustache, to articulate the words.

Her guest went on dabbing at her mouth in silence. When she spoke, it was to change the subject.

'I shall get a letter from Mitenka tomorrow, I am sure. He always sends me a little money at Easter.'

'Lot of idiocy. You'll spend it all on scent, as usual. You're nothing but a silly old flirt.'

Madame Lazenskaya laughed ingratiatingly, flaring out her lips to hide her toothless gums.

'Tee-hee-hee! What a joker you are, Madame Schrank, to be sure!'

'It's quite true,' the hostess boomed, annoyed by this reaction. 'Can't miss it. Hits one in the face soon as one walks in the door of your room. All vials and phials and eau-de-toilette and that—it looks like a laboratory.'

'Tee-hee-hee!' squealed her guest, glancing coquettishly at the whatnot. 'A lady must keep herself smelling sweet! Perfumes do soften the gentlemen's hearts! And I have a fancy for a delicate perfume myself. One must bear in mind, however, that *verveine* is a light, sweet scent, and *ambre royale*° a heavy, thick one.° Take two drops of *ambre royale*, one of *verveine* and you have a perfume that's really... really...' She chewed her lips, searching for the word, 'a mixture of earth and heaven, really. Or you might take three drops of *trèfle incarnat*,° now that's got a spicy smell, a sort of cinnamon one, and, anyway, to three drops of the *trèfle* you add one drop of white iris... Oh, that is a scent that is enough to drive you insane!'

'Why should I want to go insane?' asked Madame Schrank sarcastically. 'Be better off dropping in to Ralle's° and buying some of their flower-scented cologne.'

'Or you may take a quantity of sweet ixore,'° Madame Lazenskaya rambled on, 'and add to that a drop of the heavy *fougère*...'°

'Prefer lily-of-the-valley in any case,' the thunderous bass tones of her hostess interrupted her; Madame Schrank had decided that it was time to show off her own knowledge of scents.

'Lily-of-the-valley?' cried her guest, startled. 'You like lily-of-the-valley? Tee-hee-hee! Oh, but for Heaven's sake don't tell anyone that, though! Oh! deary me! You'll be teased quite unmercifully! Tee-hee-hee! Lily-of-the-valley! How terribly bourgeois!'

'Charming!' said Madame Schrank, offended. 'And as if it all mattered, in any case! I don't see much sense in starving yourself to buy scents. You're no beauty, after all. You may be able to smell your scent three rooms away, but that doesn't stop you looking like the back of a bus, does it?'

Madame Lazenskaya drooped her head, leaving only her big crimson ears in sight, and picked a spot off her blouse.

'Right,' the hostess said at last, sitting down at the table. 'Annushka! Bring the coffee in!'

Madame Schrank had no use for bells when she wanted to call servants. Her voice, thundering like a Chinese gong, reached without difficulty to the furthest corners of the little flat. She could often be heard grumbling at Annushka from the hall, whilst the cook bawled her own replies from the kitchen in return. In order to converse with Madame Schrank, one had no need at all to be in the same room as she.

'Be quick, will you!'

From far away came the sound of a poker crashing to the floor, followed by the yowl of a dog, and then Annushka's substantial figure appeared in the doorway, dressed in a scarlet blouse nipped in at the waist with an army officer's leather belt. Her cheeks, which she had dyed with beetroot in honour of the holiday, were very nearly as bright crimson as the hard-boiled Easter eggs lying piled on the dish. Her dirty grey hair was thickly pomaded, and caught up in a high bun crowned with a rosette of gauffred green paper taken from the top of a jar of medicine. Bashfully lowering her eyes as though she were embarrassed by her own finery, Annushka put down the tray with the coffee-service on it.

'So where's your apron, you scarecrow?' Madame Schrank boomed angrily. 'And who told you to make your hair into a bird's nest? Will you look at the woman, Madame Lazenskaya, she's scratched her cheeks to ribbons!'

'Tee-hee-hee!' Madame Lazenskaya squeaked in her high, bird-like tones.

'Don't talk nonsense, I never did scratch them,' Annushka protested, gingerly wiping her face with her sleeve. 'Swear to God... by that icon there... It's the heat got to it. What with baking the Easter bread there and roasting the chicken... You might as well sit in the oven yourself as work in that kitchen.'

She walked out, slamming the door behind her crossly.

'Well now!' the hostess cried indignantly. 'Can't tell her anything! That's the kind of service you get these days! Paints her face, plays with her hair, but one's never to make any observations! It's the same thing every Sunday. As soon as the flat's empty, she smears that stuff on her cheeks, puts on that officer's belt, and starts singing Mass all by herself. You know, I make a point of coming in when she doesn't expect it and standing in the hall to listen. She'll keep it up two hours or more, singing "Lord have mercy! Lord have mercy!" at the top of her voice. Bawling like a bull. My nerves can't take the strain. Suppose some idiot neighbour thought it was me singing...'

'It's a pity about Dasha,' Madame Lazenskaya put in, 'she was so much less forward.'

'Less forward! What, with a new gentleman friend for every day of the week? None of them can think of anything else!'

Madame Lazenskaya squirmed in her chair, but she said nothing.

'It's astonishing,' the hostess went on as she carved the chicken. 'Every one of them has to have strings of gentleman friends. Well, at least Annushka never tries going out...'

'I'll give in me notice tomorrow,' came a wail from the kitchen. 'If it kills me I will... Can't hold me head up before folks! And the janitor won't leave off. When are you ever going to start going out, you old hag? he says. First time I seen anything like it, he says, never once known that Annushka go out.'

'What's this, Annushka?' her mistress asked, taken aback. 'Don't think you're going to start that. After all, you've got nowhere *to* go to.'

'There are plenty of places I can go to. Maybe I'll go and visit the cemetery. That's what we all do in the village whenever there's a holiday. What do you think I am—saying I don't know where to go! I've got a better idea than most!'

'Will you stop yelling, woman! My nerves can't take the strain!'

Madame Schrank turned her back on Madame Lazenskaya, and walked over to the sideboard. She opened it, reached inside it, and starting moving some things around. There was a faint clink, then Madame Schrank's head jerked backwards for a moment; she locked the sideboard and returned to her place, coughing discreetly. Her guest stared fixedly at the whatnot all the while.

She knew this little routine very well, and she also knew that when Madame Schrank had gone through it she would suddenly become intensely patriotic and start talking about Germany, a country which she had never actually seen, since she had been born and brought up in St Petersburg. Madame Lazenskaya would always become a little offended on Russia's behalf, and would try to terminate the conversation so soon as she was able. She did not dare contradict her moustachioed hostess directly; the fact of the matter was that she was beset by feelings of guilt towards her. To her own discomfort, Madame Lazenskaya could not often afford to pay the rent for her tiny room on time, and Madame Schrank was gracious in allowing her extensions.

'There are no servants like that in Berlin,' the hostess said reproachfully, putting a big bit of ham in her mouth.

Her guest silently loaded her fork with rice.

Madame Schrank paused, giving herself time to think of something unpleasant to say.

'Nothing to say for yourself, eh? Expect you're thinking of the perfumes you'll buy with Mitenka's money, eh? Well, it's his money to send if he wants to, I suppose! Some people's sons certainly are fools! He won't get anything when you're gone, after all. You got through what his father left you quick enough...'

Madame Lazenskaya's face had gone blotchy.

'Imagine, Madame Schrank,' she broke in. 'I saw such a pretty fabric today, just like the one in which I had a riding habit made up in once. Do you remember me showing you? This was exactly like, exactly...'

'Well, I'm sure you're right! After all, you could hardly be expected to forget that riding habit, could you? Not when you galloped about in it for, what, twenty thousand miles with all those officers like you did! And you only three years old yourself at the time, eh?'

'Tee-hee-hee!' her guest sniggered, making a desperate attempt to regain the hostess's favour.

'What's that you're sniggering at?'

'I've remembered something rather funny,' Madame Lazenskaya said, anxious to please. 'Do you remember telling me about that old man a day or two ago...'

Madame Schrank wrinkled her eyes, and the corners of her mouth shrank back into her fat cheeks. Her face spread into a slow smile.

'Ho-ho-ho! "Might I offer you my arm, madam..." I turned round! Lordy! I see this gent there! With little skinny legs he can hardly stand up on, gripping the brim of his hat with both hands... Nose bright blue, everything else grey, even his eyebrows... "What you?" I say. "Is that your arm you're offering me? Get away with you—high time you ran along home!" He looks at me with these great goo-goo eyes of his, he doesn't understand what on earth I'm getting at... So then, "Run along now," I say, "you look like you're going to peg out soon, make sure you get back home to your bed first!" Ha-ha-ha! You should have seen him spit on the pavement when he heard me say that! Ha-ha-ha! He didn't like that at all!'

'Ooh, Madame Schrank, stop it! Hee-hee-hee! You'll be the death of me! Hee-hee-hee! There's my Madame Schrank! What amazing things you do say!'

'"Get a move on home," I said. "After all, you don't want to die on the street, do you?"'

'Oh! Tee-hee-hee!'

'Take a hold of yourself, Madame Lazenskaya! Your powder's all dropping off your face!'

Although the two ladies had lived together for the last ten years, they never used one another's first names. Once, one of Madame Schrank's relatives had asked her what her lodger's name was; rather to her own surprise, Madame Schrank had been forced to confess that she had never troubled to enquire it.

'Ah, those men!' Madame Lazenskaya gave a languid sigh. 'Lizaveta Ivanovna told me...'

'Your Lizaveta Ivanovna talks a lot of hot air,' the landlady exploded. 'After all, what else can you expect from her, when she only talks Finnish? This morning she foisted her company on me at the butcher's, if you please. You should have seen her waving her arms about and yelling, making a spectacle of us both in front of everyone. Then later, we were crossing the street and I said, "Will you try and hurry up, I haven't got all day" and she said, "I can't go any faster, the horses have stepped in me!" I ask you! You'd think she'd at least have been able to say, "I beg your pardon, Madame Schrank, I am in middle of beeg crowd of horses." She's lived in Petersburg for how many years now? And she still can't speak proper Russian. She ought to be ashamed of herself!'

Madame Lazenskaya was eager to try some of the salami, but she was afraid to say so with her hostess in this mood, so she changed the subject again.

'Ah, those men! They're so... so...'

Madame Schrank stiffened like a caged thrush which has just recognized a tune.

'Do have some salami! Why aren't you eating anything? Yes, men certainly are strange customers. I had a paying guest once, a very handsome young fellow, an admiral's son as it happens. He was from Kharkov, and he'd come up to town to take his exams so that he could get promotion to a general in the Civil Service.° "You've got cheeks like rose petals, Madame Schrank," he told me...'

'I don't think he's visited you since I've been here, has he?'

'No, it must have been a year or two before you arrived. Ha ha! Rose petals!'

'They are a most excellent anti-wrinkle treatment,' Madame Lazenskaya put in—not quite tactfully, it must be admitted. 'You should try using them yourself, Madame Schrank. It's amazing the effect they have on one's skin. Mind you, of course, I would not use anything now myself but Crème Simon. You put a little on cotton wool and rub it in—so. You know, you really should...'

'Ha ha ha!' Her landlady was shaking with indulgent laughter. 'If you hadn't told me *you* used it, I really might have given it a try. But thank you kindly for the warning. I never in my life saw so many wrinkles as I see on your face.'

Her guest blushed and gave a crooked smile.

'And what a squander-bug you are, in any case,' her hostess went on. 'You shouldn't spend money on all your cream Simons and Timons. You should save your copecks. When my husband was still alive, and I used to wear great big diamonds on every finger, and more hanging from my ears, I used to get treated very different, I can tell you. People did nothing but talk of my brains. I can't say anyone thinks much of them now, and I don't think I ever said anything so very clever then either. Money's a wonderful thing. If you had it, everyone would tell you that you were brilliant, and colonels would start paying calls on you, and you'd get all the prizes for beauty too.'

Madame Lazenskaya's face broke out into a bashfully flirtatious smile, and she straightened her lilac choker; Madame Schrank went to the sideboard once more, and there was another clink of glass.

'They know how to look after money in Berlin. They know everything in Berlin. Where do the electric lights on Nevsky come from? From Germany, of course! What about all the big buildings? The Germans built 'em. Fabrics, silk, all the arts and sciences—they're all German, the Germans invented them all!'

Madame Lazenskaya went red and pale by turns. She was dying to object to this, but didn't know how; and besides, she hadn't had any *paskha*° yet, and decency demanded that she withdraw to her room when these ideological disputes reached their climax.

'How lifelike that rose on your Easter loaf is; I almost feel tempted to smell it,' she said, lips trembling.

After an ominous silence, Madame Schrank observed:

'Lizaveta Ivanovna read in the newspaper just recently that there was a big earthquake in Germany. A really big earthquake. Russians never have earthquakes.'

This was too much even for Madame Lazenskaya. She began to tremble all over, then she broke out in a fresh crop of red blotches.

'Not true! Not true!' she cried in a high, unsteady voice. 'There *have* been earthquakes here. Several times. Why, in Verny° just recently there was...'

'Verny doesn't count,' said her hostess in tones of studied calm, 'Verny's on the far side of the Balkan Sea,° it's not part of Russia proper.'

'Not true!' Madame Lazenskaya waved her fist in a frenzy. 'You're saying that on purpose to spite me... You think that because I've no money, I've no right to a fatherland either. Shame on you! Everyone knows the Russians did have their own earthquake! You're so dishonest! You do nothing but tell lies! You've told me that same story about the old man dozens of times in the last five years, yet you keep pretending it happened two days ago! Shame on you!'

Leaning heavily on the chair, she got to her feet, and ran off, with a quick clatter of heels, into her little bedroom. Once inside, she latched the door.

All was quiet there. Through the open window came the intense, damp smell of the spring; the soft tolling of the Easter bells shook the air with deep heavy waves of sound, stirring and troubling the soul like the echo of someone else's happiness far away.

On the other side of the window was a high wall. It began somewhere far below, and rose up into the dim sky, so endless, so smooth, so grey...

It was quiet there, and Madame Lazenskaya could weep without restraint. For a long time she stayed weeping, head drooping, and elbows propped on the window-sill. Then, when her tears were dry and the sharp feeling of injury had been blunted, stilled, she got up. She walked over to the chest of drawers and, pulling out the top drawer, took out a little bottle wrapped in a scrap of silk. Carefully she pulled out its cork, then sniffed deeply, inhaling the contents with trembling nostrils. Then she gently wrapped up the bottle once more, and softly, tenderly laid it back in its place, as though laying down a swaddled child to sleep.

Slowly, with a hand that still shook, she reached for the box of powder and powdered her face with the puff, then hung her handkerchief on the back of the chair, carefully pulling its lace edging flat.

'Annushka,' Madame Schrank's voice boomed in the background, 'tell Madame Lazenskaya that she can come and have some coffee when she gets over her little turn. I can't wait up all night for her. Here's a piece of *paskha* for you; I'll put the rest in the larder. I'm going to bed. My nerves can't stand the strain of this.'

Madame Lazenskaya's heart beat loudly. She knew that Annushka had gone to bed ages ago; her landlady was saying all this for her own benefit.

She crept to the door and stood listening, waiting for Madame Schrank to leave the dining-room so that she could creep in there herself.

The wall outside the window began to glow pink with the sun's first rays. The brisk dawn wind rattled the window impudently; at last a thin current slipped in under the pane, and twitched at the handkerchief as it hung drying on the chair.

[1910]

◆ ADELAIDA GERTSYK ◆

Gertsyk, who came from a Russified Polish noble family, was born in 1874 and brought up on her parents' estate near Moscow. After studying language and literature, she worked for a while as a teacher, but after 1900 became increasingly active as a writer. A gifted, original, and influential poet, she was one of the first Russian women writers to appropriate a lexicon coloured by archaic and dialect forms to the representation of a 'magical' feminine persona. Gertsyk was also the author of interesting essays, combinations of fictionalized memoir and literary commentary, which in some senses prefigure the late writings of Marina Tsvetaeva. A direct connection between the two writers' work is, in fact, more than likely: Tsvetaeva and Gertsyk, who had met through the poet and painter Maksimilian Voloshin, were in regular contact during 1914–15. However, Gertsyk's tone is quite different from Tsvetaeva's, hovering between an effusiveness that can occasionally border on the mawkish, and a humorous sense of the ridiculous aspects in her own behaviour. After the 1917 Revolution, Gertsyk remained in Russia, but had to endure very difficult circumstances; her material hardships were exacerbated by her complete inexperience in practical and domestic matters, and she rapidly became terminally ill, dying in 1925.

Spring

(Russian text p. 426)

Vanish, deceiving veil,
Draw in, misty haze,
Watch over still sleepers!

(Vyacheslav Ivanov)

to V.G.

A woman sat on the mountain,
Divining by the somnolent grass—
Have you not heard? Was that mutter
The wind, as it flattened the stalks?
  A sea of corn flowing wide,
  Or a woman's hair, spreading in waves?

Have you not seen?
See her whisper ... was she raising her hands?
Or lifting her burning heart?
Was she knocking on the dreaming earth?
She was bewitching something...
Perhaps calling green shoots to start growing?
Smoke hovered, heat smothered,
Dew twisted, Spring floated...
Did you not hear?
Can the wind know the secret,
Know the words that she whispered?
The wind rocks the words here and there—
I heard what they were.
'Go on, go on past,
Tear the frail threads,
Sail on, deceiving veil!
Embrace me, misty haze!
Here on the hill
A grave waits for the filling,
Time has woven and sewn
Me a shroud for the Spring. —
I shall nurse, I shall carry the clouds...
No need for miraculous green,
I shall be true to the sky...
Go on, go past,
Frail, but eternal, threads;
The sun shall not deceive me,
Neither the heart mislead me...'
The wind swept away the rest.
Peace thinks that silence is best.
Spring has arrived at last.

[1907/1910]

♦ ADELAIDA GERTSYK ♦

(Russian text p. 428)

To Evgeniya Gertsyk

Silent, draped in the garments of sacrifice,
You once more draw out beautiful sadness,
Once more, in the gold autumn garden
Your white vestment freely flows,
Then freezes, misty as dreams...
  How can I drug your heart's
    sleeplessness?
  How can I ease your heart's richness,
    fruitfulness?
You carry time's brimming vessel,
The drops are blended, yet each one's distinct...
  Forget, o forget!
Tear these white petals,
Lay these lilies upon your own breast!
  There, by the spring,
  in a grove of pale olives,
  were not you sitting, bright lady,
Dipping your slender hand
    in the transparent spray?
Your desires were curly-haired maidens
That flocked to their faces in mirroring water...
You are the same, bright-eyed lady,
  Yet you are never the same.
You have not suffered parting,
you have never known loss,
yet you *are* separation,
are nothing but loss...
You carry your final greeting,
    wordlessly slipping
in white vestments, and never fading...

Yet fate confounds me, whispering:
Hush! Learn to see
  sadness beyond consolation,
  sadness beyond response.
Hold back your frantic heart.
And silently learn
The indifference of eyes
    struck mute.

[1910]

◆ ADELAIDA GERTSYK ◆

My Loves

When I look back on my past, I see a line of staging posts that mark the way I have come, torches whose light has illumined and guided my path: these are the enthusiasms which set fire to my soul, which moulded new forms within it.°

My 'loves' are these staging posts: love affairs with books and their authors. These episodes have been no less vivid than my meetings with real people; they have done as much to decide my fate, to beat out my soul like silver.

Or perhaps even more: it is these loves which have weighed heaviest in my life, and the best part of my strength, my warmest feelings, have been given to them.

I am sure that many others have shared the sense that the pages of a book open up a new undiscovered country, and the recognition that your reading of it is the most important thing that can happen to you; there will never be anything like this again.

The startling novelty of this new world tears you from your ordinary surroundings, you are plunged into its special atmosphere. Body, mind, and spirit are forced to submit to the demands, to the laws of this new world—and real people float away, melt to nothing, become pale and superfluous as phantoms...

Such are the loves which I now recall.

I
Ruskin°

It was a day late in autumn, in town; the streets were soaked and dreary, days crawled one after the other slow as clouds in the sky. People hurried, grimly dreamless, through the streets, carrying their packages and briefcases. Everyone had something to do; it would be dark by four. Work, white-hot mental activity, was all that made life worth living.

I lay on the sofa, indolently turning the pages of a new catalogue of

English books which I had just picked up in a bookseller's, and reflecting mechanically that I had better order something new to read. On the last page, where the cheap shilling editions are listed, these words passed before my eyes:

Mornings in Florence—Ruskin. (New edition.)

Where had I, when had I been reading about Ruskin? Ruskin? The name glimmered faintly in my mind; scattered shreds of thoughts, memories began to heap round it. My heart knocked impatiently; I knew there was no time to waste.

The next morning I read an announcement in the paper. A new 'journal for criticism and the arts', *The Ensign*,° editor and publisher Stalaktitov, was preparing to publish articles about 'writers from abroad'.

The editor's name was curious, the advertisement ill-phrased—there was nothing that should have inspired my confidence in the enterprise. It was precisely for that reason that I set off to visit the *Ensign* office.

A narrow staircase to the second floor, rising into a minuscule dark hall. I felt amused and embarrassed by turns. Then a table in a big empty room, with a man at the table. A quire of blank paper, a long, shinily new accounts book, a box of sand—everything ready for the new journal, and everything brand new. It was like a children's game.

I sat down opposite the editor and offered to write an essay about Ruskin for his new journal.

He frowned at me suspiciously, and fiddled with his new fountain pen (there wasn't a trace of ink on the nib).

'Short pieces, that's what we need. We haven't the space for essays.'

'As you wish. But if you really are interested in foreign writers, you must start with Ruskin. No one in Russia knows him. He has been translated into every other language there is, but here most people haven't even heard his name.'

I became more and more heated, accusing the Russian public both of ignorance and of indifference.

He was acting the editor quite well, but I acted the contributor better. Eventually he gave way.

'Send your essay in, then, and we'll let you know.'

I got up and left.

Once I was outside, my excitement grew. Talking about Ruskin had made me realize his importance. I could not forgive myself for not having heard of him earlier, could not understand *why* I had not heard of him.

That evening, I went into Gautier's bookshop to have a look at the English catalogues; and what should I see on the counter but a fat yellow volume, Sizeranne's new study, *Ruskin et la religion de la beauté*.°

My hand shook as I opened it. Inside was the profile portrait of a handsome, stern, distinguished elderly man. Fixing my eyes on it thirstily, I sensed that all my hopes had been transcended. I had been expecting to fall in love with a book; now here was a real person. I rushed to pay for the book, and hurried out of the shop, gripping it tightly, afraid to let it out of my grip for one minute. I wanted to get home as soon as possible and find out who this Ruskin might be.

That evening, when I went to bed, for the first time in many days I found myself looking forward to the next day, and feeling as though I had been given a gift. My boredom and loneliness had vanished.

That was how my love for Ruskin began.

I soon had all his most important books: *Modern Painters*, *Seven Lamps*, *Val d'Arno*, as well as the little shilling book that had seduced me first, *Mornings in Florence*. I even tried to translate this last work, struggling to understand the unfamiliar architectural terms, to distinguish one from the other.

But understanding was not Ruskin's most important gift to me. I had found a teacher, a friend, one that was living and real. I had fallen in love with everything about him: his neat grey beard, his lofty brow, his stern profile, his strong—though elderly—hands, which dealt so deftly and affectionately with every plant, every pebble, and could capture in his sketchbook the most complicated ornament, the most delicate vein on a flower-petal.

I grew to know his life: I learnt from his *Praeterita* how the toothed oak leaves had taught him about the everlasting beauty that lit the world. I learnt how an old canvas of Turner's had made him the friend and lover of art for ever.

From Sizeranne I learnt about Ruskin's life: how he lived in an old house° in England, and how visitors came to see him from all over the country. I imagined him walking slowly into his dining-room at breakfast, with a greeting, a question, a word of advice for everyone. He was wearing a soft grey suit, his voice was soft and low—except when it occasionally rose in an angry or reproachful crescendo; he would sit in his high-backed chair in the big bay window, whilst his visitors grouped themselves on the steps at his feet.

Soon the charm of his personality even overwhelmed the power of his books for me. From time to time, of course, I would go back to them, lying awake at night to think about Giotto's tower,° and the naïve paintings of Memmi° there, or falling in love with the Pre-Raphaelites and resolving to devote my life to studying them. But Ruskin's influence went far further and deeper than this; he became part of my own inner life.

For the first time, I learnt the joy of obedience, the beauty of pupillage; every moment of the day, I had this stern, noble, elderly man as companion. I could ask him whatever I liked, I could sit at his feet and listen, and believe all he said, uncritically, unquestioningly.

I learnt how thought can enliven a strange, damaged fresco in the courtyard of an old church, turning it into something as sparkling and precious as a diamond; I learnt how one can sit in a room in town during the winter and ponder with trembling joy on the silvery tiny stars of the saxifrage, growing way up in the English hills, understanding that they are the voices of the earth, calling from her sheltering womb to the heavens. Was this not a miracle? And who could bring such miracles about but this old man? Already he had lived such a long life; he was incapable of error, he knew and comprehended everything, this patriarch, like the silver-haired Moses. The keeper of secrets, he who had the ear of the Almighty.

At such moments I despised youth and young people.

I now had a favourite pose: I would sit on the floor, 'at his feet', arms round my knees and looking up at his face, every inch the diligent student.

So it was at the school of Pythagoras,° under the shade of the olives. People would often find me sitting on the floor of my room; but no-one ever saw the old man, although he had now become so real that I could feel his hand on my shoulder. His touch was not always gentle. On occasion the old man became despotic and demanding; sometimes he would even growl at me; but it was sweet to submit to his tyranny, muttering quietly to myself.

I loved Ruskin's habit of stopping in mid-description, so that he could utter a stern aside to his fellow-travellers (especially the ladies, who have a weakness for showy things of all kinds). 'I shall let you go now. You may leave the church if you wish, and take a tour around the fashionable shops, or join the jostling crowds on the square, where hundreds of other persons as idle as yourselves are staring into the shop windows. But remember! we shall meet again in Santa Maria Novella, tomorrow at eight sharp.°

The old man treated me just as he did them, chiding me, but never banishing me from his company for ever; his interest in me was stern, yet emboldening, and I felt it on my shoulders as a horse feels his harness. I had no love for Ruskin the moralist: it was tedious to read his homiletic excursions on the detriments wrought by the railways on nature and on man, the evils of factories, and the importance of craft industries. But I wanted the old man to demand that I be kind, that I concern myself with the welfare of the poor; in order to please him, I forced myself to read every single article on economics that *The European Herald*° could publish. My spiritual vocabulary, till then amoral, was supplemented by new words: responsibility, honesty, egoism. I began to work more industriously. My gait, formerly fast and uneven, became slower and more cautious, to match the sober walking pace of my favourite old man.

That winter, Ruskin died. That is, the real Ruskin, in his English manor house near London. I read about this in the papers, but the news did not particularly bother me. My own Ruskin was quite real enough; the death of his English original only made him seem more alive. He began to acquire new characteristics, which were no longer borrowed from Ruskin's own books. The appearance of a certain predilection for melancholy, of a distinct alienation from humankind, transformed the apostle of socialism and moralist into a solitary philosopher, dissatisfied with his own existence.

At the same time he seemed to become gentler; he began treating me more directly, more affectionately. I could tell that my devotion had softened him, and that he loved me in his turn; I sometimes even sensed a readiness in him to unburden his soul, to tell me about his unhappy youth, or some love affair of the distant past...

But by now he had become so real that his constant presence in our house or in my own bedroom sometimes made me feel a slight sense of claustrophobia.

In the next street along was a little house with three windows, where the blinds were always down. I moved my old man in here; as I passed, I would pause in the street and see in my imagination the room with its books, and its desk, where he was always sitting solitary, communing with beauty and goodness. I would stare at the wonderful Sizeranne picture, which I had cut out and placed on my own desk; at last, I began to write down the conversations I had with the old man.

The winter went by. Spring came; perfumed air began to seep through the open windows, and long rolls of thunder cut through the stuffy haze in town. Drops of rain still trembled on the acacia buds, the puddles shone on the streets in the lamplight, the air was fresh and heady as wine. I went to the three-windowed house, and called to my old man to come down.

We walked on and on, arm in arm, over the moist, echoing planks of the pavements in the quiet side-streets; clear drops fell from the scented acacias on our heads.

For some reason I began thinking of Mozart, perhaps because his music always reminds me of an acacia. I told my old man what I was thinking. In reply, he began speaking about the sufferings of mankind, but he was unable to finish. He seemed to have lost his train of thought.

'How much older he seems,' I thought.

And for the first time, both of us felt sad, as though we were far from home and from each other—though perhaps we had never been so close, so loving, in any case. Our dialogue had ceased; there was no teacher, no pupil, any longer. There was only the spring, and its scents, and the sense of how wide the world was.

At last I decided to go back home; as I rang at the door, I thought how little this fading, elusive, submissive, and sad old man resembled the wise, didactic aesthetician who had so enraptured me earlier...

I don't think we met again, after that.

II
Annie Vivanti°

The last part of my love affair was played out on Lago Maggiore, on one of those scorching hot, cobalt-blue, herb-scented Southern days. How clearly I see before me the azure lake, the narrow path fringed with cypresses, and the white marble villa with its roses behind the wrought-iron fence. On the gate is written in gold letters: *Villa Vivanti*.

But perhaps I should begin at the beginning, on that Moscow winter day when I was visiting friends, and saw an unfamiliar little book in red morocco; opening it, I read the words, *Lirica. Annie Vivanti*. I knew no Italian, but the softness of the leather, the elegance of the pages with their poems in fine print, were so appealing that I was reluctant to put the book down. It was strange how nearly I could understand it!

Just a little effort, it seemed, and my eyes would be opened to the meaning of every word...

'Io sono tanto stanca di lottare...'° The words, the name of the author, the book itself, were all so melodious that I asked if I might take the book away for a few days.

'She's an Italian poet, but not a very well-known one. I was sent the book from abroad. Would you like me to translate anything for you?' asked my hostess.

I refused this kind offer. Already I had begun to have jealous feelings about this Annie; I did not want her contaminated by other people's ideas, by their explanations. I shall work it all out for myself—who she is, and what she is, I thought, as I took the book away.

Something was pulling me to her irresistibly, and over the next few days I found it impossible to forget her. The secret of the strange language teased at me; so did the secret of Annie herself, this poetess whom no one knew; so, too, those occasional magical lines that had made their way through to my consciousness:

'Quando sarò partita—piangerai!'°

I felt a rising sense of wounded pride. A woman, another woman was experiencing something, was troubled by something near at hand, was calling me to her, but I could not understand her. I decided that something had to be done.

I sat down with a dictionary and a pocket Italian grammar, and began reading, launching straight into that very book. Every day I was rewarded by being able to work through one new poem.

Slowly I picked my way through Carducci's preface, from which arose a charming and astonishing image: an adolescent girl with a fiery, courageous, uncontainable soul.

It was all so unlike my own life: her ringing laughter, her jokes, her nomadic, gypsy ways, her abrupt shifts of mood, her celebration of youth and all life's joys, but above all her beauty! How wonderfully she wrote about her own black curls, her dark-blue eyes, her supple body...

She was the first to teach me that one has no need to be ashamed of oneself, that one has the right to expect affection and admiration... She was the first woman friend who had taught me this. I was astonished by her, I deferred to her in everything; at first, certainly, I did try resisting her, opposing my own earnestness, my gloomy view of the world, to her bold high spirits, her daring. But she was too strong for me. I could almost feel the warmth of her soft, dark-skinned hands, could almost see the mocking laughter in her eyes as I spoke, and her flashing white teeth—so I gave way... She revealed to me the secrets of a woman's charm, the secrets of her own native language, where every word still held the aroma of a first acquaintance, where the very sounds still glowed with living colours and had not yet faded to mere algebra. The language was so festive, so captivatingly indolent, that I could not imagine how one could use it on ordinary days, how one could talk in it of everyday things.

As I began to understand the poems with more and more ease, my love for Annie grew; now I did not attempt to criticize her, but followed the caprices of her feeling with enthusiasm. Here she is, bursting into a room where a schoolboy who is in love with her is sitting at his books, and pouring out a foaming flood of raillery. (From 'Vuoi tu'°): 'Let us go! there is no air here indoors... Put down your books, leave your studies—who needs them? I shall teach you everything you need to know. Look into my blue eyes, learn astronomy from them. We will learn arithmetic by counting our kisses. Let us go! Let us give free rein to our youth! Let the sun scorch us and the wind blow round us!'

To another lover, she addresses the following heartless words: 'Soon my love for you will fade, and I shall go back to my wandering life, frivolous and carefree, glad that I can forget you... Soon my love will fade; when I meet you, I shall walk by with a light heart and shining eyes, not bothering to greet you... To love today, to love again tomorrow, that is my fate!' (From 'Fra poco'°.)

I was bewitched by these and other, similar, lines in this melodious new language. Imagine being like that! Why had I encountered her, fallen in love with her, so late? Why had it taken me so long to find out that life can be like that, that a woman can be like that?

But Annie did not only teach me the surging inconstancy of a woman in love; she also taught me passion—bleak feelings of sorrow, jealousy, revenge, the readiness to die, to be destroyed.

Her short, powerful poem 'Appuntamento'° (The assignation), whose fractured rhythms resonate grimly and clearly as the first beats of a troubled heart, had me in its power immediately. 'I am waiting for him—uneasily. He will come in silence, his face handsome and pale, smiling his smile of brilliant cruelty. He will come. I am waiting. I remember my sister, my poor timid sister, with her quiet voice, her gentle gaze, her pale face... She loves him... He laughed. She lay in my arms and wrestled with death, and I looked over her russet hair at him, not weeping. He loves me. Terrible, terrible! Passionate, forbidden desire burns in me... That is why I am here. And in my pocket is a Catalan dagger!'

That *coltello catalano* gave me a start each time I read the poem. The closeness of death and love, of passion and cruelty reminded me of Carmen, but how deep, how close, the image of Carmen had now become for me! I learnt the poem by heart; I would lock myself in my bedroom in the evening and dress up in a bright short skirt, wrapping my head in a gaudy scarf; clenching a miniature bone-handled knife, I would recite the poem slowly, emotionally, hearing in my voice tragic cadences and whispers of passion which until now I had not known. How overjoyed I was! I knew that I was capable of love, of murder, of treachery. And when I was with my family I adopted a secretive, provocative pose; in my heart I despised their dull morality, their virtue, their books, their logic, their safe lives. Which of them knew what hot southern blood pulsed in my veins? Which of them knew about the bead necklace I wore, like a gypsy's, or could tell what madness was destined to overcome me? Who knew that my submissiveness would not last, that I might run away with a horde of gypsies or bandits at any moment!

Sometimes I would stare at my face in the mirror: could anyone who looked so ordinary actually be mad? But I did not waste much time thinking about myself—that was not the point. *She*, my chosen woman friend, would do all this for me! If only I could see her for a moment!

At last the strange, passionate winter I spent in Annie's company came to an end; and at the end of the summer, we unexpectedly paid a visit to Switzerland. We had got so cold in the damp, close, low-lying fir forests that we had decided to go south for two days before returning to Russia. In search of flowers and sunshine, we travelled to the nearest Italian lake, Locarno. Here we entered a different world, where the air smelled sweet, where the water pouring down from the looming mountains trickled over the cliffs and lingered in festoons of clear, heavy drops, before falling at last to the aromatic earth. ...

On the morning after we arrived, I went for a walk by the lake on my own, and saw the white marble villa with the name 'Vivanti' on it. My heart began to race, and all my former emotion, subsided for a while, surged up with full force. Of course it was unlikely, it was impossible, there must be some coincidence, no doubt Vivanti was just as common a name in Italy as Ivanov in Russia... But just suppose... Could I possibly walk on past? Would I ever forgive myself? If it turned out not to be her, perhaps relatives might be living there; if she *herself* were not there, perhaps I might see her portrait? Whilst I was still engaged in thought, my hand automatically went to the wicket-gate, and it opened up, showing a gravel path leading to a flight of steps, with statues on either side. Was I mad? But after all, I *had* chosen her for good reason, I had a right to her... A moment later I was ringing at the door.

A tall man in a velvet double-breasted jacket opened the door; his face was handsome, but there was something in it I found unpleasant, a slightly raddled look. All this brought home to me the absurdity of my situation. Seeing his eyes fixed on me with a look of surprise and puzzlement, I was seized with embarrassment; I felt not only my cheeks, but also my forehead and my neck, suffused by the most violent blush. I mumbled something in French. He heard me out; it was clear he had little idea what I was saying, but he smiled politely, and gestured that I should come in. When he had showed me into a cool light room, rather like an artist's studio, I once more stumbled into an explanation: I was a Russian visitor, a passionate admirer of Annie Vivanti; I had seen her name on the door and had not been able to resist finding out whether she lived here.

This time he did understand, and his face lit up with delight.

'Annie Vivanti! *Oh! sono il suo fratello!...*'°

I gave an excited exclamation. He began speaking rapidly in Italian, and to my embarrassment I was forced to interrupt him, since I found that I could not follow what he said. At last we discovered that we could communicate in German, and so we went and sat in two wicker rocking-chairs by the window.

Her brother! So fairy stories do sometimes come true! I had been brought here by Fate... I looked at him greedily, absorbing everything about his appearance. Now everything appealed to me, even the faintly bibulous tinge of his skin and the sarcastic set of his lips.

'But she herself... is not here?' This was an unnerving question, and I was rather hoping that he would say she was not. There is a limit to success and happiness, even to magic.

'Ah... No, she is in America, she has lived there two years now, ever since she was married.' And he began telling me all about it; my excitement had infected him too. By some strange twist of chance, my Annie had married an Englishman—a representative of that coldly rational nation which she had so often mocked in her poems, and whose ways were so inimical to her own temperament. She had settled with him in New York, where he was engaged in business of some kind; she had a daughter who took up all her time and attention.

'Does she still write?'

'Since she married, she only writes in English. She has learnt the language of her new homeland.'

He got up and took two volumes in English from a bookcase.

'You see, here is a novel of hers, *The Hunt for Happiness.*° A very convincing and lifelike study of American manners.'

'But what about poetry?'

'She writes no poetry now. But she has published critical essays on music and art.'

He took down an issue of some American journal.

'No doubt you have...' and my voice stammered to a halt.

'Her photograph?' he supplied the rest. He laughed and stood up. 'Just one moment, and I shall show you. I can bring you pictures of her husband and her daughter too.'

He went out. A minute later, and I had a little heap of photographs lying before me. With a shaking hand, I took them one by one and studied them.

It was a reasonably handsome young face, rather of the Hebraic type than anything else... But in any case, far more suitable to a drawing-room than a gypsy camp. You could see a certain likeness to her brother...

I soon came to terms with what I had seen, and accepted this strange new image, which had erased all that my fancy had found so mysterious, so bewitching. Yes, she looked exactly as one would expect...

I selected what I found most appealing in each photograph: yes, her eyes had come out well here, but her nose and mouth less so—and that was not a very typical expression... In one photograph (the last one) she was holding her little daughter on her knees and pressing her cheek to her head in a manner that had just the slightest touch of affectation about it. Her husband was a typical Englishman, the blond, classically handsome sort that so often figures in novels, with neatly combed hair and a cold, expressionless face.

The photograph I liked best showed Annie full-length, standing by a bookcase in a grand evening gown, head tilted back provocatively. I returned so often to look once more at this portrait that Annie's brother suggested I might like to keep it.

Just then, two ladies walked in, and began giving me curious looks. Annie's brother said that they were his wife and daughter, and we exchanged bows. It was clear that they could not understand a word of what we were saying; they sat down at the other side of the room, smiling politely. It was high time for me to take my leave.

I stood on the threshold of the house, portrait in hand, and thanked him for his hospitality. His parting words were, 'Yes, yes, you must tell all

Vivanti's admirers in Russia that she has become a model mother and housewife (*modelle Hausfrau*)!' He laughed. Once more I began to find him unpleasant.

A few minutes later, and I was back on the aromatic path by the lake, walking so fast that I could hardly keep from breaking into a run.

Before I reached the hotel, I turned off the path and rushed down to the water's edge, snagging my dress on the wire fence by the path and making it tear. I sat down, next to the blue rippling water, and took out her portrait again. I pondered on what had happened to her.

This was very important. The former Annie was no more. Everything which had enraptured me, which was so unlike *my* life about her life, was now vanished. Gone were the sudden whims, the secret meetings, the Catalan dagger, the raptures of self-love or uncontainable surges of feeling.

She was now a sensible, solid, citizen, a mother, a faithful wife, the author of critical essays on music...

Of course she no longer wrote poems. How could she? Her poetry had been a reflection of that other life, of a girl's innocent thoughtlessness. But I realized with dreadful clarity that I could not walk the path down which she had led me *alone*, that there would be no more nights when I would put on my gaudy scarf and lovingly recite the festive Italian words to my bedroom mirror... It was no wonder that Annie had also abandoned that language in which she had expressed all her youthful madness.

But *I* must walk a different path—no one would make such a passionate and convincing case for my right to freedom, passion, and beauty again. I would have to go on living severely, responsibly; I would have to find someone else...

Something warm rushed into my eye (was it a tear or the sun's reflection?) for a moment, and blocked my view of the portrait. For a moment I could not see.

On that morning I spent by the lake, I celebrated something very like the funeral rites for my miraculous friendship with Annie; I mourned my lost vision, my first glimpse of the joy of triumphant femininity. In the evening, we left for Russia.

III
The World of Words

In Potebnya's book *Thought and Language*, I came across the following words, written by Humboldt.° 'Language resembles a garden where there are both flowers and fruits, green leaves and dry fallen leaves, where death and eternal life stand side by side, so too growth and development.' I was delighted to discover this passage, which first taught me how to see and to hear the secret life of words, a life that I have gone on sensing ever since. I suspect that in fact similar thoughts about language had come to me even before that, though I do not recall for certain whether they had; at any rate, even before then, I had always taken a great interest in words. I always noticed new epithets, and remembered them; when I read a passage that was badly or clumsily expressed, I would become quite indignant.

And I remember that Humboldt's sentence acted for me as an impulsion, an illumination; it opened my eyes to many things for the first time.

I began to find the very existence of those verbal signs that come to our aid when we communicate, whose life depends on us alone, intensely involving and exciting.

And so I started to read more widely: chapters of Potebnya, of Ovsyaniko-Kulikovsky,° even sections of Wundt's extremely dry and academic *Psychologie der Sprache*.° From these books I learnt about the physiology and the characteristics of words. The more I learnt, the more convinced I became that every one of us has the most serious crime on his conscience. I realized how blindly words are treated by us, and how the 'living fruits and flowers' of that paradisaical garden are ruined by our careless hands. Every living flower is certain to wilt, to scatter its petals, to turn to dust and compost, mulch for the earth in which it grew—even so is every word destined to turn from a fragrant living image into something mechanical, a mere cipher for passing thoughts.

That is how words live, and that is how they die. But we so often speed up the process, like children tearing the petals of flowers or impatiently picking apart unripe buds. And yet it is we who should try to maintain their freshness and beauty. How well I could understand the words of that French aesthete who said that 'sometimes a drop of moisture is enough to freshen the driest style, a mere spark of inspiration will warm it into life' (Rémy de Gourmont, *Esthétique de la langue*).°

Having become a partisan on words' behalf, I began to hate everything which was inimical to them, which threatened to destroy them; I began to detest any treatment of them which was passive or unreflective, any attitudes to them which lacked love or artistry; the slipshod tastelessness that is so characteristic of articles in newspapers and magazines became repulsive to me. At the same time, I developed a passionate desire to protect some favourite words from destruction, to stop them losing their leaves and withering. On falling in love with some word that had not yet been trampled to pieces, that still smelt of the fresh spring soil, that suddenly made conversation bright and festive when it was introduced, I would start fretting about how to save it, how to keep it hidden for a while, so that its scent should not be dispersed, so that it should not be vulgarized, pawed too often by indifferent hands. I would search for some other word which might stand in a while for the first, so that it would have a chance to relax and recuperate; and I would plant this new word into my conversation ostentatiously, almost as though I were trying to prompt my companions, so eager was I to dissuade them from using my favourite; or I would change the subject abruptly, stopping others from reaching the point where, I was sure, my word would come up in conversation... What tricks did I *not* use!

For example, I felt like that about the word 'glade' at one time. This was the delightful name which someone had given to the clearing beside our dacha one spring; later, everyone had started calling the clearing that.

We began using it automatically whenever we went for a walk. Shall we go to the glade? The word soon lost nearly all its novelty, all its delights were gone. But how well it had captured the green grass, the sky, the first time it was used; the whole of spring had blossomed in it. You did not need to go there to feel it; you had only to say, 'the glade'.

Then another time someone said: 'She was extraordinary yesterday evening, behaving in this positively *vermilion*° way'—saying the word hesitantly, because it was so unusual.

But I was delighted, and I am sure that I was not alone in this, because people immediately started imitating the coinage, and soon you heard it being used constantly, without any good reason or justification. 'I feel positively *vermilion...*' It soon lost all its innocence, became degraded... I expect soon everything in sight would have been 'vermilion' in our family, had I not intervened to save the fresh young flower that still had so much life in it.

It caused me much anxiety and difficulty when I learnt about the life of words; once I was aware of it, I was forced to concentrate all my efforts and interest on it.

You listen intently to people talking; you can hardly grasp their meaning, but you see very clearly how they trample and destroy words—just as we stand on beetles or gnats without noticing it on hot June days. The frail verbal creations cannot even fly away; they have nowhere to hide; they grow before our eyes, and we must pick them carefully, and weave garlands of them lovingly, not tear them up by the handful, collecting them in rude bunches.

Having once taken an interest in words, I soon began to grasp their characteristics, their habits. I realized that their main vice was laziness, and that this made them prefer to walk ready-marked paths; one word would drag another behind it, blindly, unconsciously. They would all come along mechanically and stand in their usual places, like civil servants sitting in the same offices for decades, and drafting the same papers.

How could there possibly be any novelty in such routine work! Nothing goes blunt so rapidly as a word. Quickly, then still more quickly, it loses its living nature and turns into a pale, shadowy thing, which we unceremoniously push into any place that happens to be empty.

Not that we would notice words if they vanished. They die unmourned.

One of my friends has a phrase he uses constantly. 'Terrible business!' Whether it fits or not, he uses it everywhere. 'The church was packed—terrible business!' 'All the walls collapsed during the fire—terrible business!'

Why can't he say: 'it was a terrible sight, a terrible experience'? Because the word 'terrible' has fastened itself to the word 'business', the word itself is too lazy to do anything but follow. Words do not realize that they are rushing headlong to their own deaths. It is our business to hold them back; we should not encourage them to destroy themselves.

I began to shake when I heard clichés, banalities, the ready-made phrases that encrust ideas. You find plenty of them in literature, and in scholarly books too. 'Their lips fused in a passionate kiss.' 'This might be termed the worm in the bud of our social institutions.' Surely other people must shudder, surely they must realize that they were perpetrating a crime, a crucifixion, that they were sticking pins into things that had once been alive, but had now become as desiccated as mummies?

By determining the characteristics and the vices of words, I had also established how to fight with them. The best way was to transfer a word which had grown idle and atrophied to a new place; somewhere where it would feel uncomfortable and ill at ease, where it would have to live self-consciously, not stupidly, where it would have to behave responsibly, to live harmoniously with its new neighbours. So I eagerly began to read books by 'the decadents', as they were then called, searching for new and unheard-of combinations of words.

Often I could not have said what a book was actually about; its content escaped me entirely. Ideas, symbols, structures were unimportant.

But had words themselves been saved or destroyed by what I read? In fact, I found that these new books, for all their silliness, rather resembled hospitals for words, places whence they returned with new strength. And I was delighted to see them being cured; I was sure that the more radical the method, the better.

There are some words that are so well-born they are incapable of vulgarizing thought; vulgarity of any kind is foreign to them, they do not even know what it is (such are, for example, the terms that have come into ordinary language from science and scholarship). But like any noble family in decline, they have no creative powers, no life-force; they do their duties with a sort of pallid dullness, though they do them conscientiously enough. These elderly aristocrats need marrying off to commoners, so that a healthy propinquity to coarseness may revive and revivify them. Experimental marriages of this kind had proved successful, I found.

The things that had been done, for example, with that ugly and colourless word 'eternity'! Eternity had been hand-tinted: it had become 'turquoise', 'flecked with light'; it had started 'peering in at the window'—in short, it had become a living organism.

'Eternity flexed its muscles,' someone had written; someone else had said, 'eternity bared its teeth', and although that was said only once, never to be repeated, all the same eternity *did* have teeth for a moment, and that gave it new vigour.

All those 'splashes of anguish', 'sky-blue joys', 'drunken earths', 'looming cliffs', 'oaky winters' were no less than acts of mercy, *mésalliances* destined to restore dead words to new life.

The dry word 'transparency' became the title of a whole collection of poems, and so attained a new significance, gave birth to a living image.

Even mathematical terms might have new life breathed into them. Balmont° took 'circumference' as a lyrical motif, and the word burst into bloom like Aaron's rod.

Another poet made a dry sign-word take upon itself the role of shepherd ('gathered in by a purpose near to their heart')—and so he made 'purposes' feed a whole flock of thoughts, caressing these at one and the same time with the words 'near to their heart'. What could be bolder, or more logical? I often sensed how uncomfortable, how uneasy words felt in their new resting-place, how they struggled to bring their old tastes and customs with them; but their impassivity and facelessness had vanished, and now they had become expressive, become visible.

Epithets helped words along here, and so I applied particular attention to them. They were the garments for a word to wear; sometimes they could take years off its age. Sometimes an epithet would be like a toga, so grand and heavy that it overwhelmed the word, and the word disappeared like a violin in a case, or so that everyone looked at its clothes and not at it. Many writers concentrated on manufacturing such cloaks or cases for words, and I watched them do it with excitement. Andrei Bely° was especially assiduous in this, though his efforts were not always successful. You could see the seams on his clothes; they did not dissolve into new organic wholes, but instead looked as garish as a patchwork dress on a shop mannequin. Every word continued to live its own life, refusing to give up a scrap of itself so that a new image could be made, refusing to dissolve into other words.

Bely tried particularly hard to forge combinations out of 'wine' and 'world', but the two words fought with him bravely: 'wineworldly', 'winescarlet' (leaves), 'unworldlypale', 'worldlightly', 'dawnwinely'...

But other combinations made beautiful and sparkling new wholes: 'lightflooding', 'moonsilvered', 'firetwisting', 'lightfoaming', 'linenflowing'°—such new pairings really did decorate and enliven the word to which they were attached.

Some other writers brought forgotten archaic words back into the language, digging corpses from their graves and breathing new life into them.

Such old words as 'chirm, wallwort, weald, archil, mazard, cumberground...'° came into the language in a slow, stately procession, as festive as trumpet blasts.

I imagined them parading in long caftans and conical hats like boyars, careless of other people and of the impression they were making on them.

To descend to the very elements of language and rescue forgotten sounds, to warm what is frozen into life, to create something new according to old rules—that is the highest mission we can have.

Often I would sadly recall that blessed time when language was being invented, when people communicated in gestures and inarticulate sounds, that blessed time when concept and word, word and object, were the same. Every word was a poem, there was a myth in every word, everything was animate, and scented as flowers when they open. There were no prostitutes, no corpses. I tried to resurrect that primitive state in my own soul, to forget all I knew, to begin thinking as though it were the morning of our life once more. You had to push your own thirst for words so far that it became a command.

Let it be! And this act of will must select the sounds unconsciously, must combine them and then give them words as flesh. That was how I imagined the process by which the first words were created—the first name, the primitive stuff of speech. And I shut my eyes so as to annihilate the visible world, and imagined myself sitting on a tree in virgin forest, and conjuring up a world of sounds by my own volition, calling them forth from the dark element, making them into the images I needed. It was magic of a kind. When other people came upon me in this 'savage' state, they were astonished by my mutterings.

I created an odd impression at such times, and people found it hard to understand what I said—I spoke slowly and stumblingly as a woman with a speech impediment; now and again I would pause before uttering some quite ordinary word, and search for another. I did not speak well, for I was not concerned with myself nor with the content of what I said, but only with 'them'. My soul was filled with greed; I did not want to waste the riches which had so often been squandered by others.

I never lived so selflessly as then; I forgot about myself, my own tastes; I sacrificed the beauty to which I was so attached; I paid no attention to the impression I made on others; I renounced philosophical enquiry, my spiritual and aesthetic life, in the name of those miniature creatures which had become so dear to me—for when I heard the throb of their life, I felt that I was called to defend and nurture them.

I pondered everything from the perspective of their well-being. I remember that when someone suggested spending the summer on the Baltic, the first question that occurred to me was how it would affect my 'words'. I was delighted to think how beneficial the visit would be, as the steely grey colours of the northern sea seeped into them, as they were revived by the noble silence of those desert-like dunes and forests.

This was my first real and genuine experience of maternity. It is true that I noticed many other people thinking about such things, preoccupying themselves with them, but they did not give up their whole souls; they retained sufficient serenity and self-will to be able to follow and preserve their own processes of thought, to think about the content of what they were saying, to love ideas as much as words. But in my case everything else was taken away; my contemplation of words paralysed my abilities, drove me to torment, turned me into a maniac.

I realized that this meaningless speech, this cult of words without significance, was deadly threatening; I knew that I was on the edge of madness.

I could only be saved by another passion, one no less strong than the first, a passion which would not injure my love for words, but which would reinforce that love, and which would at the same time instil into that love a new, powerful beauty, forcing it into subordination. And I found my salvation—in Nietzsche.°

◆ ANNA AKHMATOVA ◆

Akhmatova (1889–1966), the most famous and respected woman poet in Russia, came from a large upper-middle-class family that had no particular literary leanings; she herself was later to remember that the only book in the house was a volume of Nekrasov (which has rather the same resonance as 'a volume of Tennyson' might in equivalent English circumstances). Born near Kiev, Akhmatova was, however, to spend much of her childhood and early youth in Tsarskoe Selo, the residence of the Russian Emperor near St Petersburg, and her later verse reflects the neo-classicism and restraint of the so-called Petersburg tradition. Akhmatova's earliest poems were published under her own name, Gorenko, but her reputation was first assured by the verse that she brought out under her pseudonym, and particularly by her first collection, *Evening* (1912). Though her early work is usually associated with love poetry, her second collection, *The Rosary* (1914) contained a number of poems about poetry, of which 'Sister, I have come to take your place' is one; this theme was to be still further developed in *White Flock* (1917), which also contained much religious and civic verse. Akhmatova is most famous in Russia for her love poetry, her addresses to the Russian nation, and (with an academic audience) for the poetry in which she celebrated her affiliation with the male poets whom she considered her predecessors and peers (for example, Pushkin, Dante, Blok, Annensky, Mandelstam and Pasternak). But, as the selection of verse here shows, she was, at least in the poetry that she wrote before 1925, also concerned to write herself into a 'feminine' tradition of verse composition, not only by introducing into her verses idiosyncratic refashionings of that most conventional of feminine poetic figures, the Muse, but also by filling her work with allusions to Russian nineteenth-century literary tradition, to folklore, and to the work of contemporary women poets, such as Adelaida Gertsyk and Zinaida Gippius.

(Russian text p. 430)

'Sister, I have come to take your place
At the high bonfire standing in the forest.

Your hair has long turned grey. Your eyes
Are dimmed, turned misty, by your tears.

You cannot understand what the birds sing,
You do not see the stars or summer lightning.

Time has stilled your rattling tambourine,
I know you fear the silence of the trees.

Sister, I have come to take your place
At the high bonfire standing in the forest.'

'Have you come to bury me, then?
But where is your shovel, your spade?
You have only a flute in your hands.
Yet you are not to blame.
I must lament that my voice
Fell silent for good, long since.

So clothe yourself in my dress,
Forget the disquiet I feel,
Let the wind play in your hair.
You smell like the lilac smells,
The path you have walked is steep,
You have stepped into radiance.'

The first sister walked away,
The second took the first's place.
Stumbling as though she were blind
She went down the strange narrow path.

She sees the flame still before her,
Feels the tambourine still in her hand.
For the one is a snow-white banner,
For the one is a lighthouse ablaze.

(*24 October 1912*
Tsarskoe Selo)

◆ ANNA AKHMATOVA ◆

Solitude

(Russian text p. 432)

So many boulders have been cast at me,
That stones have lost their power to terrify.
The entrapping walls have made a slender tower,
It rises high above all other towers.
The stonemasons who did this have my thanks;
May sorrow, and may trouble, pass them by.
My turret top bathes in an earlier light,
The sun's last fading rays shine festively.
Winds fly from seas that lie in the far North,
Right to the windows of my lofty room,
A dove comes to my hands to feed on corn.
The page of writing that I did not finish
Is ended by the Muse's dusky hand,
Serenely virtuosic, and divine.

(*6 June 1914*
Slepnyovo)

◆ ANNA AKHMATOVA ◆

(Russian text p. 433)

Fear turns objects over in the darkness,
The moonlight catches on an axe's blade;
Something taps behind the thin partition:
Is it rats, a burglar, or a ghost?

It splashes water in the stuffy kitchen,
It numbers all the floorboards that are loose,
Then a flash of shiny-bearded features
Through the garret window peers a face—

Quiet again. He's spiteful and vindictive,
Hiding matches, blowing out the lamps—
Better by far to watch the glare of sunlight
On rifle muzzles as the squad took aim,

Better by far to lie on a rough scaffold
On the green grass of a city square,
Whilst amidst the groans and jubilation
Scarlet life-blood poured, then poured no more.

I press my crucifix against my bosom—
Heavenly Father, let me rest in peace!
My head spins as the sour-sweet stench of carrion
Rises thickly from the clammy sheet.

(*27–8 August 1921*
Tsarskoe Selo)

◆ ANNA AKHMATOVA ◆

Memories of Aleksandr Blok

In the autumn of 1913, on an evening when a party in honour of Verhaeren's arrival in Russia was also to be held, the Bestuzhev Courses of Higher Education for Women° organized a large evening reception. The reception was open only to students of the courses, but one of the organizers took it into her head to invite me to attend it. I had been expecting that I should go along to the Verhaeren do; he was a poet for whom I had great affection, not on account of the urbanism for which he was so celebrated,° but because of a certain little poem that he had written, 'On a low wooden bridge at the end of the world'.

But then I imagined the pomposity of the promised festivities in a Petersburg restaurant, like a grand funeral, as such things always are, with their frock-coats, their good champagne, and their bad French—and decided that I should join the Bestuzhev women students.

Amongst the guests at the reception were the patronesses of the Bestuzhev courses, ladies who had spent their whole lives fighting for the cause of women's rights. One of them, Ariadna Vladimirovna Tyrkova-Vergezhskaya,° had known me since I was a child; after I had given my reading, she said, 'See, now Anichka has won her own sort of equal rights.'°

Whilst I was waiting in the artists' room, in came Aleksandr Blok.

I asked him why he was missing the Verhaeren celebration. His answer was winningly frank. 'They'll ask me to make a speech, and my French is awful.'

Then one of the Bestuzhev students came up, holding a list, and said that I was to read after Blok. 'But Aleksandr Aleksandrovich, I can't possibly read after you,' I pleaded. He answered gently but reproachfully, 'Anna Andreevna, let us not behave like two tenors.'

Blok was the most famous poet in Russia at the time. I had given a number of readings myself—at the Poets' Guild,° the Society of Lovers of the Russian Word,° and at Vyacheslav Ivanov's 'Tower' salon°—but that evening was something quite different.

If the stage acts as a mask for those who perform upon it, the platform could be said to strip performers bare; its role is uncomfortably close to that of a scaffold. I think that evening may have been the first time I sensed the resemblance. A poet who is about to read feels that there is a distinct connection between his spectators and the many-headed Hydra. It is very hard to make an impression upon one's auditorium: Zoshchenko was a genius in the matter, and Pasternak was not far his inferior.

No one here knew who I was, and when I came out on to the platform, I could hear whispers of 'Who's this?' on all sides. Blok had advised me to read 'We are all wanderers here'. 'But when I read "I put on a tight skirt",° they always laugh,' I protested. 'They always laugh when I read "And drunkards with their rabbit eyes"° too,' he replied.

I don't think it can have been that evening—it is more likely to have been some other literary occasion—when Blok, standing in the wings during Igor Severyanin's° reading, put his head into the artists' room and said, 'He has a greasy lawyer's voice.'

On one of the last Sundays of 1913, I took my copies of Blok's books along for him to sign. In each, beginning with the *Poems about a Beautiful Lady,*° he wrote simply, 'To Akhmatova—Blok'—except in the case of his third book, which he also inscribed with a madrigal in my honour: it begins with the line, 'They will tell you that beauty is terrible...' I never had the Spanish shawl in which he represents me, but Blok was delirious over Carmen at the time, and so he decided that I too should be in Spanish costume. It goes without saying that I never wore a red rose in my hair either. Not coincidentally, the poem also employs a Spanish metre. The very last time we met, backstage at the Bolshoi Dramatic Theatre in the spring of 1921, Blok came up to me and asked, 'But where is your Spanish shawl?' Those were the last words that I ever heard him say.

On the one solitary visit that I made to Blok,° I remember telling him a story about the poet Benedikt Lifshits:° I mentioned that Lifshits had been complaining that Blok was stopping him writing poetry: his very existence was an obstacle. Rather than laughing, Blok answered quite seriously: 'I understand him perfectly. I feel the same about Tolstoi.'

In the summer of 1918, I went to stay with my mother at Darnitsa, near Kiev. In early July, I went back to my own home at Slepnyovo. I had to travel via Moscow, where I caught the first available train; it happened to be a mail train. Wanting to smoke, I went out in to the gap between the carriages. The gap was open to the fresh air; at some stage during the journey, we reached a station, which was apparently deserted. The engine braked so they could throw out a mailbag; before my astonished eyes suddenly loomed Aleksandr Blok. I called out his name. Looking round, he asked a question that revealed him to be not only a great poet, but also a master of diplomacy.° 'Anna Andreevna! But whom can you be travelling with?' 'I'm alone,' I managed to say; and at that the train moved off.

And today, fifty-one years later, I open Blok's *Notebooks*, and find the following entry for 9 July 1914: 'Mother and I went to see round the Podsolnechnaya sanatorium.—My devil is tormenting me.—Anna Akhmatova on a mail train.'

In another entry somewhere else, Blok writes that Lyubov Delmas,° Elizaveta Kuzmina-Karavaeva, and I were all tormenting him on the telephone. I think that I can fill in some of the background to that comment.

I had indeed telephoned Blok, and he, speaking his mind as was his wont, had said: 'You must be ringing because Ariadna Vladimirovna Tyrkova told you what I had said about you.' At death's door from curiosity, I went along to one of Ariadna Vladimirovna's at-homes and asked her what Blok had said. But she would not be swayed. 'Anichka,' she said, 'I never tell my guests what my other guests have been saying about them.'

Blok's *Notebooks* bestow many tiny, but delightful, gifts upon the reader, as they snatch dates from the abyss of oblivion, and restore them to events one had half-forgotten. Once more the burning wood of St Isaac's Bridge is floating down the Neva estuary, and I and my companion stand transfixed as we watch this extraordinary spectacle, on a day which now has a date—11 July 1916—as noted by Blok.

And again I live through another day, after the Revolution this time (21 January 1919), when I went into the Theatre Section° canteen and met an emaciated Blok with mad eyes,° and he said to me, 'We all meet here as if we were in the next world already.'

And here are the three of us (Blok, Gumilyov, and I) having dinner (on 5 August 1914) on the Tsarskoe Selo Station during the first days of the First War (Gumilyov is already in uniform). Blok is visiting the families of men who have been called up to see whether he can do anything to help. When he has left, Kolya asks me, 'Surely they can't send him to the front? It would be like roasting a nightingale.'

A quarter of a century after that last meeting, in 1946, I find myself back in the Bolshoi Dramatic Theatre for an evening in memory of Blok, reading a poem that I have just written:

All is as he wrote°—the light, the chemist's,
The granite, silence, the Neva.
For us, who follow him, he stands
Like the nineteen-hundreds' monument;
Waving his hand in brisk farewell,
He walked away, past Pushkin House,
And took the poison that brought death
Like a rest that he had not deserved.

◆ ELIZAVETA KUZMINA-KARAVAEVA ◆

Even by the standards of her generation, Kuzmina-Karavaeva's biography was colourful. Born in Riga in 1891, she spent part of her childhood in the Crimea before moving to St Petersburg; she became involved in literary circles through her first husband, Dmitry Kuzmin-Karavaev, who was a cousin of Akhmatova's first husband Gumilyov. The first woman to study theology at the St Petersburg Theological Academy, Kuzmina-Karavaeva was also an active member of the revolutionary-populist Socialist Revolutionary Party (see note to Strogova below p. 292); after the Revolution, she was to spend some months as mayor of a town in the Crimea, before emigrating to Paris in 1919. Kuzmina-Karavaeva had become estranged from her first husband not long after their marriage; in 1932 she contracted an amicable divorce with her second husband, Daniil Skobtsov, whom she had married in Paris, in order to take the veil as an Orthodox nun. Rather than lead a cloistered existence, however, she dedicated the rest of her life to aiding the many poor and deprived members of the Russian emigration. When France fell to the Germans, Skobtsova gave active help to the French Resistance, but was betrayed by a Russian émigré informer to the Gestapo in 1942; she was to die in Ravensbrück Concentration Camp three years later. Apart from her several books of poetry, Kuzmina-Karavaeva was also the author of verse morality plays, and is one of the few Russian women to have produced works of theology.

Long-Barrow Princess ii

(Russian text p. 434)

The moon, a ring of crimson snapped in two,
Will drop beyond the fogged horizon's reach;
I have no strength to turn my face towards
The blackened waters of the putrid ditch.

O, guardians of custom, o, you barrows,
I fall before you, seeking forgotten paths;
In all the world without Morgana triumphs,
But fragments of the past are in those caves.

I stood upon the heights and saw the valley
Where once I galloped with my caravan,
So I could scorch the villages and meadows,
Then climb my native mound to make a banquet.

I drank a cup of blood spilt in the battle,
Becoming drunk upon my wild revenge;
They reaped more men than wheat upon that cornfield.
Think of your bride, friend sleeping in the mound!

His fallen bones are softly wrapped in purple,
The banquet's crimson drops go seeping down;
My dark-skinned tsar will smile a smile of radiance;
He lies dreaming in a coffin white as snow.

The moon, a ring of crimson snapped in two,
Will drop beyond the fogged horizon's reach;
I have no strength to turn my face towards
The blackened waters of the putrid ditch.

[1912]

♦ ELIZAVETA KUZMINA-KARAVAEVA ♦

Ruth

(Russian text p. 435)

I collected the ears in my apron,
I walked barefoot in alien corn;
Above the wood huts in the village
The cranes were flying in strings;

I slipped through the inky mist
Far away from the flatlands of Boaz,
I travelled through countries unknown,
Wrapped against frosts in my kerchief;

And the crane, as he flies to the South,
Will say to no one, no one
How Ruth takes the trampled stalks
And weaves them in sheaves that are golden.

When the short day breaks in the sky
And the reaper goes to his labour,
Ruth begins to glean for the gold
In the plains, the homelands of strangers.

She wears her scarf low on her brow
So her dark Southern braids may be hidden;
She gathers the scattered corn,
As she wanders the hills and the meadows;

As they went in and out the door
In the cold hard winter, the women
Would see at their feet in the snow
A sheaf of corn lying...

[*1916*]

◆ VERA MERKUREVA ◆

Merkureva was born in 1876 in Vladikavkaz, where she lived until 1917, when she moved to Moscow following the death of her mother. She began writing shortly afterwards; the stimulation for her literary activity seems to have been contact with the poet Vyacheslav Ivanov, with whose circle she was associated until his emigration to Baku in 1921, and whose views on the 'Dionysiac', ecstatic and irrational, sources of poetic creativity are frequently reflected in Merkureva's work. A handful of her poems were printed in almanacs during the early 1920s, but the bulk of her work remained unpublished, and she was forced to seek work as a translator, mostly of Turkic poetry, though she was also to publish a volume of Shelley's verse. Merkureva returned to the Caucasus for a few years after the Revolution, but spent most of her later life in Moscow, summering at Starki nearby, before being evacuated to Tashkent in 1941; she died there two years later. Her poetry only began to be published in quantity, long after her death, in the late 1980s.

The Grandmother of Russian Poetry: A Self-Portrait

(Russian text p. 436)

Hair half gone grey, half blinded,
Half dumb and half gone deaf,
Half sleepwalker, half crazy Jane,
She doesn't speak: she mewls in a monotone,
But smiles when melting into unction.

Fitting her clashing bells to the psalms' sounds,
She goes on foot to hear the service sung,
And wanders to the Zubovo hermitage:
But if she says a church is like a circus,
Then that's the devil tempting her to sin.

No matter who goes forth or who returns,
She hardly hears or sees all those around.
Loving stupidity, or stupefaction,
She smokes complaisantly with anyone,
Although she cannot stand the smell of incense.

She'll gladly put off strict caesura's girdle,
And free verse cuts the track of her toboggan.
She'll often rhyme you *have* and *half-wit*.
But since she has no sex, no gender,
Her *no*, her *not*, and *half* are barren.

(*June 1918*)

◆ MARIYA SHKAPSKAYA ◆

Shkapskaya (1891–1952) came from a poor family in St Petersburg; the opportunity to progress beyond elementary education was given to her by the private charity of one of her teachers, but she made good use of the chance, and was later to continue her studies in Paris. Like Anna Barkova (see below), Shkapskaya felt liberated by the class politics of the Bolshevik Revolution, though she was also disturbed by the violence unleashed as a result of the Revolution and the Civil War. The ideological and emotional upheavals provoked by this contradictory standpoint were expressed in the fine collections of poetry which Shkapskaya produced in the early 1920s. After 1925, however, she became convinced that Soviet cultural politics made it pointless for her to try publishing or even writing poetry, and turned to the composition of journalistic sketches for the Soviet press.

No Dream

(Russian text p. 437)

'You hear? Tomorrow, they say?'
'I thought it was today.'
'There'll be crowds out to see it.'
'In public, what is the world coming to?'
'But it'll be interesting, admit it.'
'They say the Swiss do it in public, you know.'

All round town they put posters up,
They fixed up a gallows in pride of place,
Next to a wall by the cathedral porch,
To give them plenty of space.
A swing like a cross with two ends,
With stooped shoulders underneath,
And if you got on tiptoe and stared,
You could get a glimpse of a tongue—well, just.

They worked hard and long to hang him,
Cursing on their mothers' graves as they grappled.
He helped them as best he could,
But his strength had vanished away,
And his whiskers were dripping with blood—
You should see their big hands,
Those officers in the squad from Bryansk,
And yesterday they beat him in HQ.

Whilst he was carrying it, whilst he was walking
Inside his head someone seemed to be singing:
  'Farewell to ye, pines and fir trees,
  Farewell to ye, Mam and Dad,
  Farewell to ye, pretty ladies,
  For ye and I must part.'

It would stop for a while, then start:
  'Farewell to ye, pines and fir trees,
  Farewell to ye, Mam and Dad.'

'Mam and Dad'—what was the sense of that?
And the crowd stretched on and on.
His wife stood to one side
With the baby,
And the little boy tugged at her skirts.
They'd said she could watch her husband's last dance,
She and the little ones.
'So long as there aren't any scenes, got it?'
So there she stood under the old acacia,
Still,
Silent.
But her lips were white,
Bloodless,
And her babe didn't pull at the empty breast.

All around they pressed like wolves,
They muttered on every side:
'What a nuisance, eh—someone's in my way.'

'Let the lady through.'
'Mum, mum, where've you got to?'
'You over there—can you see?'
'I say, ma'am! Pardon me!'
'Look at the mess he's in!'
'Anna Ivanovna, don't take on!'
'Don't mind me, don't mind me!'
'Some new officer, is he?'
'Now come on—they say you don't feel a thing.'
'Glad I brought my jacket—it's cold, with this
wind.'
'I brought Petya along,
So we could have a look what's going on.'
'That's right, let them swing!
They need a taste of their own medicine!'
'What did she bring her kids here for?
It's not right. They shouldn't be here.'
'They've got to learn, you know.'
'Look, look! He's in the air now!'
'Here, I can't see a thing!'
'Let the lady through, you swine!'
'You're standing right on my foot!'
'Well, say what you like... but, God! ...'

But then a voice rings on the air:
The child can't take any more:
'Mamma!
Mam!
Look, it's him doing it, him!
He gave them the rope himself!
Now they're putting it round his neck!
O, Mamma, O!
Put your hand over my mouth,
I can't bear it, I can't!'

She puts out her coarse, red hand,
Holds his little mouth closed.
'Hush, little Vanya,

Little one, hush.
Hush, my sweetheart,
Look good and hard,
And remember it all,
You hear me, remember.
Let this, your father's Passion
Be laid on your life, your memory
Heavy as a slab of stone.
How you saw him swing,
How they scourged his legs with a whip,
And how that crowd laughed,
And how they stood on tiptoe and leered,
Yet the crosses on the church have not
 tumbled.'

She whispered, soft in his ear,
Her eyes staring out.
God's powers may not do it—
Human powers can do it,
The terrible powers of man.
 See those there, and those,
 And those there again—
 We shall not forgive them,
 We shall not forget them.

It was the feast of St Peter and Paul.
And he hung there for three days and nights,
And God's own people walked by,
On errands, or to stare at the sight.
They came past and past,
As they went to morning and to evening mass,
And the bell tolled on and on.
 And he swung in the wind, and listened.
'Starting to stink now, with the heat.'
'Eh! Have a look at them filthy crows!'
'I've five mouths to feed, you know!'
'I've got nothing against the revolution,
I'm all for the constitution.'

'Look at him—the Messiah! Poo!'
'Save Russia, bash the Jews!'
'How skinny he is!'
'What brutes! Is that true about the whip?'
'What about the relics in Chernigov?'
'And the secret police in Kiev?'
'We'll be quits, you can be sure,
Not in the next world, before.'
'What about God?'
'Nothing to do with us, is it?
The powers-that-be will answer for it.'

And when the third day was ended,
And a dark summer night had fallen,
The doors of the church were opened,
The royal doors burst apart,
And through them came, marching in procession,
The whole company of saints,
All the holy men of Orthodox Russia:
  John the Baptist, the Preacher,
  Panteleimon the Healer,
  St Nicholas Whose Hair is Grey,
  The simple-minded Saint Aleksei,
  Ipaty with the three wrinkles in his forehead,
  St Kasyan, whose feast comes once in four years,
  The murdered Tsarevich Dimitry,
  And all the Mothers of God Most Holy,
  Of Smolensk, Vladimir, and Kazan,
  The Hodigitria, The Mother of Sorrows, of the Three
    Hands,
  And others without special names.
  Going sadly as new-made monks,
  To the carnival tree they went,
  Stared up at his blue bruised face,
  Bowed low at his twisted feet,
  Sprawled in the dust of the road,
  As the most terrible vow dictates.
  They lay there until first light.

In the morning, when God's people came there,
The hanged man still swung in the air,
His shoulders still stooped and humble—
But the crosses on the church had tumbled.

(1919
Romny)

◆ OLGA FORSH ◆

Forsh (1873–1961), who came from a distinguished military family, had a life that was by no means typical for a woman from such a background. Her mother died young, and she spent much of her childhood in the orphanage to which she had been dispatched by her stepmother; on leaving school, she trained as a painter, and after her marriage, she and her husband went through the spectrum of fashionable intellectual views, from Buddhism to theosophy to Bolshevism. The couple supported the Soviet regime from the start; after her husband was killed fighting for the Red Army in the Civil War, Forsh continued the struggle on the intellectual front, and between 1925 and 1953 she was one of the most prominent woman writers in Russia. Although she continued writing perfectly respectable historical fiction even in the 1940s, Forsh's most interesting work dates from the late 1920s and early 1930s, when she was experimenting with Formalist literary techniques and foregrounding the process of composition.

The Substitute Lecturer

Farce in One Act

DRAMATIS PERSONAE

LECTURER

COPERNICUS

MONK

OLD SERVING WOMAN

FIRST STUDENT

SECOND STUDENT

RHAETICUS°

DEVIL—doubling as LIKELY LAD

THEATRE MANAGER

MILITSIYA° OFFICERS

Tableau I

LECTURER. *enters, wearing cloak with hood thrown back, panting.*

LECTURER. Please excuse my lateness, comrades... This is my fifth lecture today... I feel more like a cart-horse than a lecturer. Well, what's it to be? [*Takes out a notebook.*] Aha, popular science:° Nicholas Copernicus and the earth revolving round the sun. Old stuff. Let's be frank, citizens, all that happened a very long time ago. We can't be bothered with it now, can we? The most important result of Copernicus's discovery, as you know, was the globe. What a remarkable object! You'll find one in any classroom today, extra large size, so all the schoolchildren can see it. And you can get miniature ones, too, like this one on my watch-chain. I do recommend them to you!

Mind you, don't get me wrong, I've got plenty of time for great discoveries—just so long as you can take them round with you, like this charm on my watch-chain. Ha ha, excuse my little joke.

If a lecturer's to go on collecting his wages, then it's not enough just to get through his compulsory two-hour stints. No, he has to do good as well. In this case, 'doing good' means finding something new and edifying to say about Copernicus's wretched discovery. The problem is, citizens, my tongue feels as if it's about to drop off. As I told you before, this is my fifth... yes, my fifth talk today. So I'm going to give you a demonstration. We'll leave the edification to speak for itself—as indeed it will, if you wait till the end of the demonstration.

I'm going to ask you to do a little work here. We've wiped out a lot of things lately; what I'm asking you to do now is to make a big effort, and wipe out your prejudices about time as well. Believe me, time's a fiction. The world has its own consciousness, and it keeps a record of every event that ever happened. Now we're going to get the time machine going and shoot off backwards—top speed! This machine is quite a machine—it just slips through the heart and lungs and liver too—as our comrades the sword-swallowers might put it. But that's quite enough chatter for now... [*making conjuring gestures*]

O time machine, reverse your whirling wheels,
And take us back, back to the Middle Ages.
To Copernicus' last days. I think we may
Do violence of some kind to history,
But gather, ye shades, to edify the masses.
Let me, the exhausted lecturer, take courage,

I shall become a frightful monk: I'll speak
With mighty voice, in bad, but five-foot, verse.
Do not condemn me: I am a lecturer,
And lecturers, you know, do what they like...
O time machine, into reverse... top speed!

[*The stage goes dark.*]

Tableau 2

[*At the back of the stage, as though in a huge frame, is Copernicus's room, lit by a floor-to-ceiling window. There are piles of books, scientific instruments, maps.* COPERNICUS *sits in an armchair, deep in thought. His right hand is bandaged: he has injured it badly when helping to rescue the town during a flood. The* MONK *stands behind him. The* OLD SERVING WOMAN *stands in the doorway.*]

MONK. Copernicus, listen to what I tell you:
I shall not try to reason with you twice.

COPERNICUS. I'm listening, speak on...

MONK. A straw-filled dummy,
Your effigy for burning, is being kept
In the cellars of the Holy Inquisition:
It bears these words: Copernicus the Heretic.
I am commanded to force you to recant
Your heresy, that troubles intellects.
[*Pause*]
When they have burnt the figure, they'll burn you.

OLD SERVING WOMAN. Doctor, they are not joking. You must recant!

MONK. Old man, repent your awful heresy:
What God himself has told to stand stock still,
You must not move in senseless arrogance,
You pay no heed to the Church fathers' words,
What Ptolemy and Aristotle taught.
It chills the heart to listen to your speeches:
So the earth, where Jesus Christ rose from the dead,
Is not the centre of the universe,
But some mere clod of muck, shrivelled and wretched?
Who can believe such things? And even if
Your teaching were the truth, even in such case

The Holy Church must damn your teaching, as
The root of blasphemy...

COPERNICUS. Monk, heed you this,
You teach the resurrection of the flesh,
But, though you've learnt the letters of your text,
You have not learnt to think; perhaps you fear
The profundities of free investigation.
Yes, that is it: for he is truly risen
Who bends the slave's chains by creative will—
Who stands with an archangel's flaming sword,
Defending the absolute freedom of perception.
Monk, one who is made of flame can never rot,
Only things that will not move can petrify...
How miserable you are, jailers of God,
The men who put the living God to death.

STUDENT [*running in*]. Teacher, I bring you word from Rhaeticus!

COPERNICUS. My faithful Rhaeticus. But where is he?

STUDENT. Your student Rhaeticus is battling for your book—
Snatching your life's work from the leaping flames.
A mob has gone to burn the printing press.
These people here provoked them.
[*Points at the monk*].

COPERNICUS [*reading out loud*]. The people have been incited by the monks to curse you. The Academy demands your expulsion. The University has ordered that your instruments be smashed, your works burnt, and the ash scattered to the winds. We your students will defend them to the last drop of our strength. A bonfire has been constructed on the town square, and a figure of you...

MONK. Believe me, they will burn *you* next.

OLD WOMAN. Do as they say, you see they are in earnest.

COPERNICUS. He who is meant to burn had better burn,
So let him crumble, like the earth, to dust...
A spirit that knows itself lives on for ever.

SECOND STUDENT [*running in*]. Your horse is saddled, standing at the gates.
My arm shall be fast round you as we ride...

We'll soon be free, if you can find the strength.

FIRST STUDENT. Our teacher...

SECOND STUDENT. The mob feels in its heart
Things that its darkened mind can never grasp.

FIRST STUDENT. They know you as a doctor, and their saviour!

SECOND STUDENT. The fire will wait for no-one: when they light it
The paper will flare up... The earth will never move,
Fixity will endure for ever, as the Church says,
And the glass firmament will not be smashed.

COPERNICUS. I broke the chains that held the earth immobile,
To break man's mental chains is not my task.
The learned man is quiet, his voice is soft,
Humble his look. But what their rage burns up,
In burning books, is but an outward sign:
A living thought is no man's prisoner
Once it has been embodied.

FIRST STUDENT. But your work...

COPERNICUS. What of my work? Though damned, it will survive,
Like a flower's pollen, floating on the wind,
It will engender wonderful new growths;
Now is the time for cosmic movement's laws
To be discovered. They *will* be recognized..
Books have their fates.

MONK. Doctor, collect yourself:
For the last time I offer you the choice:
Recant your heresy, or mount the bonfire.

COPERNICUS. What is a signature to time? Mere words.
A free man does not bind himself in chains,
A slave can't break his shackles.

MONK. You must burn!
It is time that I was with the Holy Judges.
[*Goes to the door, then returns and lays a paper on the table.*]
Here, take this parchment. I trust that you will sign it.
I shall return so soon as the clock strikes.
[*Goes out looking meaningfully at Copernicus, who says nothing.*]

FIRST STUDENT [*to* SECOND STUDENT]. We *must* make haste, or his efforts will be lost.

[*Exeunt. Stage lights dim. The* MONK *takes the* LECTURER*'s position at the front of the stage.*]

LECTURER. Well, you see, comrades, he's a tough old bird. But his heart works better than his head, just like with all great people. So let's see how things go when they try the 'heart torture' on him, shall we. You're going to take part too, comrades. Yes, you are, though you'll stay sitting right there in your seats.

[*The* LECTURER *makes more conjuring gestures. The stage lights go up again.*]

OLD SERVING WOMAN. The mothers and the wives of all your pupils
Have come to see you.

COPERNICUS. Let them be admitted.

The MOTHERS *and* WIVES *come in.*

FIRST WIFE. We have come to beg your aid, most honoured doctor.
Our husbands are in danger. It's your fault...

SECOND WIFE. You told them that the earth goes round and round.

THIRD WIFE. Now tell them that it doesn't. If you don't
Our menfolk will be burnt when they've burnt you.

FOURTH WIFE [*angrily*]. They ought to think what the Church tells them to,
No use them listening to what you tell them.

FIFTH WIFE. They've left their homes, they've left their families.

COPERNICUS. But, ladies, these men are human beings first,
Only then husbands. Let them make their choice.
Breeding is not our only end in life.

FIRST WIFE. A man who's married is no longer free.

SECOND WIFE. A husband must love his wife with his whole heart.

THIRD WIFE. And make a home as good as anyone's.

FOURTH WIFE. Franz will go down with you...

FIFTH WIFE. And Karl!

FIRST WIFE. And Friedrich too!

LECTURER. Just like *your* wives, eh, comrades?

COPERNICUS. Well was it said, that a man's relatives
Are his worst enemies.

WIVES [*chorus*]. Damn you and science! Go and recant

Your blasphemous heresies!

MOTHERS [*on their knees, arms outstretched*]. We do not curse you, we, the mothers, beg you:
Let Heaven have our sons back: let *them* not fall
Into Gehenna's fiery pit, let *them* be saved.
Recant for show, so others may follow you,
May dare to recant unpunished. Take off your spell,
Unravel your black magic, let them go.
Take pity on us, we do not curse you, we implore,
We beg you...

COPERNICUS [*putting his head in his hands*]. O, mothers...

CHILDREN [*running in*]. No, don't you smash the bright blue heavens to pieces,
Let the earth stay like we've been taught it is!
[*Knock at the door*]

COPERNICUS. Who's there? Come in!
The Workers come in.

FIRST WORKER. We've been picked out
To ask if you would sign this paper here.

SECOND WORKER. When the bell sounds, they'll get the bonfire going
And burn that dummy that they made of you.

FIRST WORKER. We need a doctor. What happens if you're burnt?

SECOND WORKER. Who'll mend the water pipes when you are gone?

THIRD WORKER. Leave the earth standing on its own two feet.
So it does move! Does that give us more bread?
[*The bell sounds*]

CHORUS. Recant this minute!
[*Copernicus stands silent*]

LECTURER. Well, comrades, you can hear that, can't you?
[*The bell sounds once more*]
[*The* LECTURER *pulls the* MONK*'s hood on and knocks at the door.*]

MONK. For one last time the Council of Holy Judges
Gives you the choice: your signature, or burn.
[COPERNICUS *says nothing.*]

[*Exeunt the* WORKERS

FIRST WIFE. We'll burn the figure...

SECOND WIFE. The signature will burn.

THIRD WIFE. Copernicus is a blasphemous heretic. [*Exeunt* WIVES

MOTHERS. We can only weep, and pray.

[*The bell sounds a third time. On the far side of the window, the bonfire with* COPERNICUS*'s figure bursts into flames.*]

CHILDREN. AAAh, we're frightened... [*They run out*

OLD WOMAN. I'd sin if I stayed longer. Fare you well. [*Exit*

[*The* MONK *and* COPERNICUS *are left alone.*]

MONK. We're here alone. I'll tell you now, in secret:
We value your mind, and your brave spirit, so,
We have determined to save you from the fire.
[*Looks around, then comes closer.*]
There is a lonely cloister far away
Where you can work in peace, free from restraint.
Your ideas will find admirers there, believe me,
Admirers worthy of you, ranking high
In a most holy Order. Write your books:
What you believe is your affair. We know the earth
May not be still, that it could be in motion;
The question's ages old. Pythagoras
Raised it before, Plato's *Timaeus*° too.
You must recant for the *mob*'s sake, not ours;
They think the earth is still; we do not know
How to make belief compatible with science.

[COPERNICUS *is silent. The sounds of a building collapsing are heard.*]

MONK. The printing press is dust. Your book is ash!
[*A funeral procession passes by the window*]
The figure has been burnt. They're burying it.
You'll hear that final chorus once again
On your own bonfire. You *will* hear it, unless...
Unless [*pushing the paper towards him*] you take this way: the earth is fixed,
It moves for us, but moves only in secret.

COPERNICUS. Truths are for all to share.

MONK. The flames await you!

[*The* MONK *comes to the front of the stage as the* LECTURER. *The stage lights dim. Darkness.*]

LECTURER. Citizens, with that 'Nicholas Copernicus', our demonstration of popular science, comes to a conclusion. In fact they didn't burn the old man in the end, but that was because he had the sense to die of a heart attack like an ordinary human being. Copernicus's pupil Rhaeticus managed to save just one copy of his book. By the time he got hold of it, though, Copernicus was dead. Naturally the old man said all kinds of interesting things before he died, as wise men generally do, but I stopped the time machine before we got to those. You've no idea how infectious spiritual grandeur can be, and there's no profit to be had from it at all. Grab what you can carry with you, is what I say... Charms for your watch-chains, comrades, let me recommend them! Ideas are just so much chatter. All they're good for is throwing under the wheels of progress, just you try it—they make an excellent braking system! Ha ha, my little joke! As for heroes, citizens, don't crucify them, don't burn them—just vulgarize them! If some idea puzzles you, don't worry—you can make the sea run in a ditch any day...

[*Sings, conducting an invisible choir*]

Copernicus spent his time until he died
Trying to prove the earth moved round the sun...

[*Drinkers surround him on all sides waving bottles, and join in the singing*]

If he'd had more wine, and thought less hard,
He'd have fretted less, and had more fun!

[*Fireworks go off behind the* LECTURER. COPERNICUS *looms up...*)

LECTURER [*alarmed*]. Here, this isn't part of the lecture. Time to stop, I said. Time machine, leave off! Copernicus is dead.

COPERNICUS. He's found a spirit, so he will live.

LECTURER [*collapses, waving his arms*]. Ghosts are strictly forbidden... [*Vanishes.*]

FIRST STUDENT. Run, quickly!

SECOND STUDENT. You'll be imprisoned.

FIRST STUDENT. He can't hear you.

SECOND STUDENT. His face is radiant.

COPERNICUS. You are my father, Mighty Cosmic Movement,
I was no slave to you, I was your son.

This early world, all worlds were temples for me,
Spirits burned in my censer, and the stars
Conducted me to Mighty Movement's throne.
Escaping from the vault, I looked for others,
People, my brothers, held captive in the darkness,
You cunning teachers, you have fastened fetters
On your timid pupils, you have blinded them...
Sorrow on you, confusing ends and means.

[COPERNICUS *staggers and looks faint. His* STUDENTS *catch hold of him and help him to the armchair.* COPERNICUS *recovers his senses and goes on, as though talking to himself.*]

Alone... Hating the Church, hating all science!
Alone, alone... Let madness be my guide...

[*Pause*]

A law protected me, like a knight's helmet:
A threefold law: desire, dare, and perceive...

[*Gets up.*]

I have perceived you, Mighty Cosmic Movement.

[COPERNICUS, *by now in his mortal agony, raises his hands in blessing.*]

The deeds of those who dare are celebrated
In ages past, in centuries to come.

[*Falls into the arms of his* STUDENTS. *As he dies, says quietly but audibly*]

You are my father, Mighty Cosmic Movement...

RHAETICUS [*rushes in with the surviving copy of Copernicus's work 'On the Earth's Revolution'*]. Teacher, I have your great work safe.

[*Music*]

STUDENT. Too late.

[RHAETICUS *falls to his knees, and puts the book into the hands of the dead* COPERNICUS.]

Tableau 3

[*Darkness. Music. Suddenly the music stops. Beautiful fireworks. The scene is the same room. In* COPERNICUS*'s armchair sits a medieval* DEVIL, *with horns and a tail.*]

DEVIL. I called Copernicus forth from the grave,

But the sly rascal tricked me, came to life.
What should I do? Good form dictates that I
Become a Devil, not a Lecturer. And so I've grown
Horns and a tail. Feels a bit odd, mind you:
I've long grown out of medieval ways.
Those were the days! I used to torture man,
I had to, so's to stifle his soul's fire,
But now we devils have quite other tasks:
We fan the most ridiculous small flames
So souls don't flicker out before they should.
We drag you to hell, like loads of damp green logs;
But you won't warm our furnace. So what good
Is that to hell? Our profit's down the tubes;
We can't get heat from you. Besides, they've found
All kinds of drugs and vaccinations now,
To give a man a rush of blood like Faust.
It's no joke for us devils—even me.
Quite soon, no doubt, you'll come back from the dead;
They say folks do already: your jugged supper hare
Is rushing round as large as life next day,
And someone's granny, buried yesterday,
Is dug up, soon as they want pancakes made.
All in good time, my friends! The things you think of!
I'll say this in a whisper: just remember:
If you succeed in burgling heaven's stores
And stealing the apple of eternal life,
That minute heroes will vanish like the bison.
You're not such fools, and this is what you think:
Each one of us is human, men are mortal:
A death from cholera or even typhus
Is worse than a death that comes from your own virtue.
Socrates and his coterie were right!
That man I conjured up, his boast was true:
'A soul that knows itself will never die.'
But if your reason happens to sniff out
An everlasting body for you, so what then?
What happens to your spirit? Ha ha ha!

THEATRE MANAGER. Comrade lecturer, stop this at once! [*Scrambles up stairs to stage.*] You know perfectly well that magic shows invoking obsolete superstitions are strictly forbidden!° Will you kindly take off your horns and tail this minute, and finish your lecture in the way you started it, in your normal clothes!

DEVIL. Comrade manager, you and I address one another through the veil of five centuries. However, I have access to the time machine, so I can spin forward to modern times, which allows me to dimly comprehend what you might mean. But since the only machinery which you have at your service is a pocket-watch, there's no chance of your believing that I am quite unable to take off what Nature has given me [*swishes his tail*].

THEATRE MANAGER [*pulling it*]. Kindly remove it!

DEVIL. Ouch! You can see very well it's real, not stuck on... Remove yourself instead!

THEATRE MANAGER. I shall be making an official complaint about this lecture. You ought to be struck off the list of approved lecturers! You've been trying to corrupt honest citizens with reactionary pantomimes! Here, officers, remove this man's tail!

MILITSIYA OFFICERS [*mount the stairs, feel the horns and tail, and say in chorus, expressionlessly*]. The comrade's horns and tail are his own.

DEVIL [*tears off his own tail and horns. Is unmasked, not as the Lecturer, but as some nameless* LIKELY LAD]. Comrades, these modern synthetic materials have their uses. Even two militsiya men together couldn't see through my disguise. Allow me to recommend these superb synthetics to you, citizens—so vital in everyday life! I invented them myself. [*Bows to all sides.*]

[*The audience whistles and hisses. Cries of 'Swindler! Charlatan! Dressed up as our Lecturer! Throw him out!'*]

LIKELY LAD. Citizens, keep calm, I can explain everything. Sssh... [*Audience quietens down.*] Citizens, we actors aren't swindlers at all; we're an avant-garde drama group. We're all playwrights whose plays the theatres 'can't use'. Try and put yourselves in our position: we do have to act somewhere, after all! Your lecturer was off sick, so I dressed up as him. All right, so I did put in an advertisement for myself at the end, but only at the end, and only because I'm a bit short of the readies. The cultural enlightenment bit was much more important. So, citizens, please don't hiss. You have to hand it to us, after all! I'll lay a large bet that you had a lot more mental and cultural stimulation out of the Substitute Lecturer than you ever would have had out of any real one.

CURTAIN

(1919/1930)

◆ SOFIYA PARNOK ◆

Parnok (whose real name was Parnokh) was born in 1885 in a Jewish family in Taganrog on the Black Sea, but spent most of her adult life in Moscow; in a further split with her origins, she converted to Christianity at some stage in her early twenties. She was briefly married, but from approximately 1909 began to live openly as a lesbian; her most famous lover was Marina Tsvetaeva, with whom she had an affair in 1914–15. Although Parnok showed independence of literary judgement from an early stage, she took time to find her true path in a poetic sense, and her aestheticizing early poetry is considerably inferior to the powerful laconicism and chiselled colloquialism of the work which she produced from the early 1920s, and which includes autobiography, erotic poetry, social and literary commentary. A poet of exceptional talent, Parnok also stood out because her self-questioning standpoint made her a modernist in the Western sense, rather than a mystical post-Symbolist or self-aggrandizing neo-Romantic. Unfortunately, however, few contemporaries were to have the chance to appreciate her work. After 1925, Parnok began to have difficulty publishing, and was forced on to the hard road of literary translation working, among other things, on Proust; in 1933, barely two weeks after her forty-eighth birthday, she died from consumption, accelerated by exhaustion and overwork.

(Russian text p. 442)

I shall not lie to find a lurid rhyme,
Honoured master, no harsh words from you:
Since the cot your choice has not been mine,
I can only do what I can do.

How heartily I thank relentless Fate
For the prickly Muse that I've been given:
The path we walk is ours, though it be strait,
She and I aren't fellow-travelling women.

(*17 March 1926* [*1923/4?*])

◆ SOFIYA PARNOK ◆

(Russian text p. 443)

To Khodasevich

A childhood memory: those pears,
wrinkled, little, tight,
and hidden inside
tart flesh that puckered the mouth:
exactly so my delight
in the bitter shards of your verse.

(6 May 1927)

♦ SOFIYA PARNOK ♦

Through a Window-Light

(Russian text p. 444)

With both knees pressed down on the sill,
Mouth fixed like a fish's to the pane,
I breathe, and then breathe in again:
So, clinging to life, a body will
Suck from a greyish sack: so the heart bounds
Insistently: it's time, it's time to go!
The firmament is heavy on the ground,
The night has turned a dirty grey like snow,
Grey like this cushion filled with oxygen.

But I'm not dying yet: I'm still
Stubborn. I think. And now again
The bullying, magic syllable
Demands its tribute from my life:
I push my head out through the light
—The moon is ringed with rusty cloud—
And, gazing on the ordered stars,
Address the distance in these words:

'As in a steam-bath dirt evaporates
From sweaty skin, so now above the soil
Dark thoughts and septic secrets, petty hates
Rise in a miasma dense and foul.
And though the window's wide for air
I none the less choke on despair.
Strange, don't you think? Ills of all kinds
Are treatable: sarcoma, age's slow decline,
Sclerosis... But find the place
That might slow down the germ of evil's race!
Kneeling, like this, I'd crawl down rutted lanes

Down cratered city streets, if I could go...
Go where? Where to? God only knows!
Perhaps to a hermitage somewhere,
Repent my sins in tears and prayer—
Where is Zosima, faith's defender,
Or is the world without end ended?'

It's light. The houses in the dawn
Are bare and thoughtful; high above the roofs
The Burning Bush church dome and cross
Give off a flat and meagre glint;
And somewhere in the West, in Paris,
In Rome or Hamburg—who cares where?
Pressing against the pane for air,
Forcing its sour slops past the larynx,
Breathing with last reserves of strength,
Another stands and weeps and thinks:
Not Red, White, Black: a woman or a man,
A human being and not a citizen,
Like me, perhaps: someone whose life now ebbs
In stagnancy, and not in happiness.

(*February–March 1928*)

◆ MARINA TSVETAEVA ◆

Tsvetaeva (1892–1941) is by general consent one of the five or six best twentieth-century Russian poets (her reputation is, if anything, greater in the West than in Russia). She came from a well-off family of the upper bourgeoisie in Moscow: her father was a classical scholar who helped to found what is now the Pushkin Museum of Arts; her mother, his second wife, was a talented pianist who had made no career of her own, and who expended all her huge energies on her daughters. After 1900, Tsvetaeva's mother's health began to fail, and in 1903 she and her sister Anastasiya were sent to a pension for young ladies in Germany; in 1906 their mother died. Not long afterwards, Tsvetaeva began to move in literary circles. She brought out her first collection, *Evening Album*, in 1910: it was privately printed, but received good notices from several influential reviewers. After 1913, and still more after 1916, Tsvetaeva dropped the *faux-naïf* personae and domestic settings of her early poetry, and began to produce leaner and more mature lyric verse, now underpinned by complex historical and literary allusion. Her greatest work, however, dates from the period after her emigration from Russia in 1921: it includes literary essays, plays, and above all narrative poems, as well as lyric poetry.

Staircase

(Russian text p. 446)

[I]

Quick embrace
On quaking staircase,
Quick lipstick slick

Below putty that cracks;
Tale quickly told:
Neither 'hallo' nor 'à bientôt'.

Quick grapple
On shuddering staircase,
On juddering staircase.

Here, where no one sleeps at all,
Every stair is a waterfall
To Hell—
            path paved with cabbage leaves!
As though each step were a downward slope,
And (living is burning!) as though
Partings outnumbered meetings.

So—rushing to rose-pink lips—
We sometimes forget a greeting,
But, leaving those same lips' edge,
Does 'farewell' ever get forgotten?

Quick joke
On stair that rings,
On stair that sings.

Sinners—she and he,
Swallow hastily
Bread—love's daily.

Have you heard
The house *Diktat*:
'Thou shalt work
If thou wouldst eat'?

Things are dear in shops:
Thin men live by their wits.
Leave tomorrow for sleeping,
Today you must eat.

In life's grim battle
The prince's politeness is this:
Leave tomorrow for taking,
Today you must give.

Need explodes like gas,
And now, sir—yes—
The man who once was rich
Will—give.

He will!
(The gas has fangs today!)
Yes, for our sake—
He—will (it's a tiger, a pard,)
Give (it's the devil, not Marx)!

Rubbish overflows.
They'll say—say it! 'Rot!'
But the service stairs
Also have a drugget.

(Tabby colour,
Mind you...) Garlic, mogs...
But the back stairs
Also smell of Muguet.

How the worms of closeness
Love their little treats!
Isn't it a classic—
Garlic, garrets' reek!

Perhaps they're attacking colds?
No: in garlic vengeance is:
Sweetening the blackened hole
Of the back staircáse.

Poet, terrorist, urchin,
The *bel-étage* is our one aversion!

Quick collision
On heaving staircase,
On leaking staircase—

Squeaking and shrieking
Like badly tuned fiddles—
And dribbling—the heating!

Quick spat
On spattered staircase,
On battered staircase.

We bash till we see black,
Till we're knocked out flat.
What do you want from us?
Be bashed by as you bash.

Gripped in their owners' hands,
Down dripping staircase,
Down slippery staircase,

Rush the cases,
Rush the cloth caps,
Rush the fiddles!

—Oh, to sleep, to sleep!
Chewed, putrefied, crushed,
Rush the coat-skirts,
Rush the coat-skirts,
The coat-tails rush.

Stagger! Shudder!
Prizes! Run!
They get muddled—
Where's up? Where's down?

A cough for every landing—
Each a perfect fit—
For our staircase
Has its upper crust—

Some cough till eyes start watering,
Some deep, some ho-ho—
For this service staircase
Has its groundlings, too.

'That chest should see a doctor!'
'A pick would do more good!'
Gamut of splutters
Right up to the roof—

And down to the cellar—
Heuch! with patches on!
Marx's sermon
Set to Stravinsky's tune.

Quick singsong
On spat-upon staircase:
(The groundlings' number, this).

Trills expectorate, not decorate,
Lungs, here, on the staircase—
Shot to pieces—perorate!

Not sung, but strung together,
But what energy!
Put your back in, eh!

Who cares what gets flung in,
Nothing goes to waste,
Anyone who's hungry
Loves to stuff his face.

Just have what we're having:
Eat up, plenty more:
A whole *carte* of dishes
Hangs up and down the stair!

Diets here in profusion,
Pots full to the top:
For this service staircase
Has its own Franzensbad.

Jacob's dream of heaven!
Things were better in the past!
Gamut of stenches
From the cellar up

To the roof—they're cooking!
Do-re-mi-fa-so!
Gamut of stenches!
Quickly, stop your nose!

Planned, surely, in Hell,
Forged there, is the twirl,

The thread, of this screw?
How many feet go downward
By this stair of firewood?

Last clothes got dry,
Last boiler lit,
Last laundry done.

Last grope—one pair
Of legs—all rags and bones—
And wobbly stair.

Last briefcase,
Last cloth cap,
Last fiddle.

All quiet. The coughs, even—
Ground, shaken, to a halt—
Even the back staircase
Has its witching hour

Of quietude...

Last and final scamper
Down the rickety stair—
The last cat runs.

The dark erases all things—
We're rubbed out with the dirt—
Even the back staircase
Has its witching hour—

Of cleanliness...

I'll tell you why!
One last tub of water
Flows from Alpine heights—
A Rhine—down to the courtyard

Tarmac...

The yard sky is decorated,
A bunch of grapes; a cross:
On the service staircase
Hangs a chart of stars.

[II]

Night—how shall I put it?
At night the thing tells all.
Yes. Sincerity comes flooding out,
As things lay bare their souls—

They know things are degraded,
Whether flesh or fish or fowl:
Immovables too. Pride has welled up:
They want to stand straight and tall.

The twist of back stairs hangs there:
Fixed for good, you like to think?
Night is the time for prayers:
The screw wants to unwind.

Height is so reliable:
There's an honour in the thing:
I see that the lie is friable,
And can turn to a stray-ight line.

The yard—a mass of potholes—
The yard—not dug for years!
The yard dreams it's an allotment
Thick with berries, flowers.

The thing casts off good manners—
Says: I am chalk! am steel!
I will be no convert!—
The Jew shakes straight his curls!

Nail or tile or shaving,
The thing feels its vitals move:
Ancestral powers in conflict
With the parodies of crafts.

Glass nestles in the cabinet,
Cries, 'I'm sand! I'll break apart!'
One in the eye from the elements!
Glass is sand and dust!

Out to lies and forgeries!
Pail-lasse! I am straw!
Mat-tress! I am water-weed!
It, she—is nature now!

At the hour that smells of gunpowder,
The rope—tow, at one time—
The fire in a heap of coal-cinders,
Say: I was, will be, divine!

And the tap—what happened?
Tumbled—I'll be a god!
I'd better say it snappily:
The thing wants to be healed!

[III]

We with our factories, we with our trades,
What have we done with the paradise we
Were given? First knife, first spade;
What have we done with the first day?

The thing was confiding as a woman—
It wasn't enough to grab the wood
And iron—size it up! weigh it out!
No, we had to have planks and screws—

Chip! small stuff that we could swallow!
What have we done, we who first walked,
Done with this planet that speaks of Him,
Made it a heap of dull spayed things?

We with our trades, we with our arts!
The thing is splayed out on the bed
Procrustean: lying damned on the lathe
The thing is writhing: it waits for death.

Glory was poured out in rivers,
Glory massed up in their banks,
Most animate world of any ever,
What have you done to it, O Man?

Do you suppose that the divinity,
A God you can see, a God who hurts,
Would have gone to the trouble of inventing
Inanimate things? Most damnable slur!

You with your objects, you with your concepts,
You with your (cheaper than platinum) iron,
You with you (grander than flintstone) diamonds,
You with your kettles, more useful than I am!

You with your 'stability', your 'immobility',
—You've fashioned a step right next to the ground,
And to a prison of closeness and grossness
You have banished thought and song.

(We have ways of bursting out, though!)
What have you done with that first equality
Of all things—in each place, everywhere—
Equal, because they are their own peers?

The tree, naïvely trusting the racket
Of brazen axes and whining saws,
Stretched out its fingers, holding an apple—
Man chopped them off.

The mountains then laid bare their veins
Once hidden (then 'metal' became the word)
Revealing a miracle to Man—
Man blew them up.

The thing has learnt from experience,
And now it gives as good as it gets.
The table has always said it's a trunk.
Did the chair break? No, it was the branch!

That crunch from your shiny varnished cages—
Was it the sound of your ancestors' ghosts?
No! The walnut has spied the planets
And is stretching out to a crack in the glass.

A sound like gunfire—you sit bolt upright—
Has the wardrobe warped? No, it's the *will*
Of the thing. A servants' ball in your house!
A gas explosion? A devils' dance!

Right on the hour the banisters moulder,
'Shot himself by mistake!' Not that!
No: the will of the firearm lies in wait,
This is *premeditated* murder—

By the thing, staunch in its hate—
No rock falls down on a building site
Just like that—no, this is the way:
'Off with his head!' a rock will say.

The vengeance of cliffs—wood's revenge on scaffólding!
The clutter of your theatrical sets!
What are they made of? Fabric, wood?
So you take out a policy—on your own heads!

You insure every stick, right up to the flashing!
Can this really be you, Man the thinking
Reed? Not so: a billiard cue!
With insurance against the rain and the snow!

Against Hephaestus—i.e. contents of house!
Against Poseidon (in the case of yachts)!
What a thought and what a gesture,
Insurance against the deities' measures!

Against Hephaestus? Is that miserable spire
Insured against *him*? No, raise the stakes higher!
And quietly say: it amounts to this:
House insurance protects against Zeus.

You'll be sorry—who's going to help *you*?
What do you want the gods to do?
See, on every—my tongue won't stutter!
On every roof—is a god-conducter!

Deals and wheels and coats and boats—
Only one kind of insurance has *not*
Been thought of till now—and this is the one:
Fire: insurance *against* having things!

[IV]

Paupers' things. So is that sacking
A thing? And is that board a thing?
Paupers' things are bone and skin,
Lack of meat, whatever is lacking.

Where do they get them? You can see far away,
You can see from the depths. Don't strain your eyes!
Paupers' things must come from their sides,
Hewn on a sudden from their chests!

A shelf? Mere chance! A hanger? Mere chance!
And chance, too, is that phantasmagorical
Armchair. Things? A thorn, a branch—
The whole October forest in glory!

Shy furniture owned by the paupers!
You are—(*of* what?) a third, or a quarter!
The rest went to heaven long ago,
Thing, it hurts to look at you!

It's as hard to tear one's eyes from
You, as from a festering wound;
A Viennese chair—made of veiny bentwood—
Some chance of Vienna! A terrible thing!

The best thing here would surely dishonour
What—your house? Come off it! Your
Attic. A thing is a thing only *now*—
When it makes your eyebrow shoot up *so*—

?—like this. At rags, at widows' dull weeds—
What?—you raise your brow. (Can brows not be
Lorgnettes?) An eye can begin
Making queries, like brows. It can be a thing.

Supposing it's empty and dried-up—
A woman's eye, beautiful, round—
Then—compare them!—a bowl seems a spirit,
And a tub full of wash-blue—a soul.

Exactly like a sieve or a bucket—
Aye—to the tsar! At the trial—aye!—
Everyone who is called a poet
Has been burnt by the acid of that eye!

Penury and its shared utensils!
Every knife is a *personal* friend,
Like a wild creature waiting for morning
You live less here than you live *beyond*

The pane—in emptiness—on the fringes—
For (have you read the *Police Gazette*?)
The purity of things, their honour,
Is measured like this: can't be sent by freight.

Because they have chips
And are falling to bits
And because they don't fit
In carts.
              You weep:

This is no table: it's a husband,
A son. Not a wardrobe, but *our*
Wardrobe.
Because souls, because hearts,
Don't go by freight.

Paupers' things are flatter and drier,
Flatter than bast, and drier than wood—
Paupers' things are *souls*, in a word.
That's why they easily catch on fire.

[V]

Rise, rise
Thin smoke!
Varnish, shine
With elbow grease!

The cinders—where?
Turned to ash
By the glare
Of elbow grease!

Straight, straight
The outskirts burn—
Hard labour is Ham,
But never Cain.

Our sleeve-cuff slides
The table's length—
Our varnish is
Resin and sap.

A surface—services things.
Elbows polish so bright:
Sharp elbows wax clean,
Wax is con-gealed sweat.

By this, by this, your bedrooms
Are waxed (but never smeared!)
By this, by this, are whitened
Your floors—*before* the fire!

[VI]

Paupers' things—a strange married couple
Of words—a volatile pair!
Thing and *poor*—an ill-fitting coupling,
Though the tongue makes worse ones by far!

A word won't get the sacristan bothered!
Thing and *poor* are split, not linked.
Nakedness longs to be covered—
Which is why garrets so frequently

Burn—so frequently and fiercely—
The scarlet cloak is ours for an hour!
Confinedness is searching for distance:
(Your author is trapped in a crayfish claw).

When a ceiling is fallen, it's the right size—
We'd all grown humps, and begun to creep.
Justice will out and find a platform:
The stake is a pulpit for the truth!

This place, now, has bunks in dozens:
Not a chink: a tallow stink.
Pale poverty wants to get sunburnt.
The fire remembers all these things.

[VII]

A link, the sounds paired:
Fire—and—stairs.

Life lives by flares
On the payroll of fires.

In your baggy working skirt—
Charwoman, don't scrub the dirt!

Relic of the rural past,
Cleaner, put your broom down fast!

If you haven't much to play with,
The matches are temptation.

Mother nipped out of the flat
To see the neighbour for a chat

And left the box...
                    Now see the glimmer
The floor has, brighter than a mirror!

Life after death has started, and
Living death is at an end!

The dirt is burning bright,
The house—a bush alight!

Honour is royally saved!
The house—a bush ablaze!

Your slavery, precedence—
See them all in decadence!

You had heaven trussed and bound!
Now see your world fall to the ground!

The past will be incinerated!
Castles will make a merry blaze!

Now the clouds are swept away!
And the washing's nearly dry!

A furnace at night? A meadow, now!
Should we be saved? Only from you!

Do not trample this golden pasture!
Why save those who save themselves faster?

See the ash with branches wide
Gazing at the morning sky!

Golden as rye the fragments burn,
The washing line is flax in bloom!

On the staircase—with its hot sleepers—
Up go flying, down go flying
Rainbows...

[VIII]

—Morning
Ruffles feathers.
Birds'? Mine? Who wit?
First door slammed by first morning
Tight shut.
The poem sleeps.

(July 1926
Vendée)

◆ EKATERINA STROGOVA ◆

Strogova's biographical details, like Mirovich's, remain a mystery. Her only published work is 'The Womenfolk', though an unpublished story is held in the Central State Archive of Literature and Art. The scantiness of information is partly attributable to the fact that the literary group associated with the journal in which Strogova published, *Pereval*, was purged during the Stalinist terror, its leader Artem Vesyoly being shot; documentary materials on all the *Pereval* writers are therefore extremely scanty, and citations in official Soviet reference sources more or less non-existent. 'The Womenfolk' reads as though based on first-hand experience, but the experience of a participant observer, rather than of a factory worker; it is possible that Strogova was a member of a Party women's section involved in consciousness-raising at the factory in the Moscow Region that she describes. Whatever her background, she was obviously a writer of some talent. 'The Womenfolk' is the best of several interesting neo-realist stories published by women in *Pereval*; Strogova handles the rapidly shifting, almost cinematic, perspectives and aggressively colloquial narratorial manner, that all the *Pereval* writers favoured, with a high degree of skill.

Womenfolk

Factory Sketches

The Baroness and her Maid

Baron Shtakelberg had married his kitchen-maid. This kitchen-maid, Nyushka, a brisk, swarthy girl with a tongue like a razor, came from a village in the middle of nowhere. Once ensconced as the mistress of the Baron's Petersburg mansion, Nyushka quickly got used to her position. She started to wear fashionable dresses and fancy hair-styles and to yell at her maid.

In just a few years Nyushka had become plump, dignified Anna Ivanovna, a Baroness accepted everywhere in society and respected by all who knew her. The Baron spared nothing on tutors to improve Anna Ivanovna's education and, even more important, her taste.

The more brilliant the young Baroness's society successes, however, the greater the hatred felt for her by that rich mansion's many servants. They could not forgive her her brilliant career; still less her rudeness.

'Just see what a swell she is now!' said the Baroness's senior maid, Klavdiya, who came from the same village and hated her shrewish mistress most bitterly. 'Fan her here, and powder her there. Seems to have forgotten running around the village with hardly a rag to her back and snot dripping off her nose, begging bits of bread from better folks. Now, if you please, it's '*Madame parle français*!' From rags to riches! She puts on airs with people right and left, but meantime at home she hollers at you-know-who worse than a carter. Pfah, a somebody!'

And plain-faced, cross-grained Klashka banged around furiously in the corner with her dustpan and her fancy little feather dusters.

There is an end to everything, though; and that included Nyushka's happiness. October° came, and the treacherous Baron, abandoning his young wife along with his pouffes and his Chinese screens, high-tailed it across the border.

Baroness Anna Ivanovna, now demoted to Nyushka once more, knew many bitter trials and tears; then at last she found herself back in her remote little village in Moscow Province. Six years later, when they started up the silk factory that had stood there idle for so long, the Baroness became a worker.

She didn't stop looking after herself, though. She was still curled and dressed up and thought of nothing but good taste. That's the Nyushka we see every day in the factory now. She works as a silk-winder: Comrade Winder Shtakelberg, Worker Number 563. And right next to her on the machine is Klavdiya Kryuchkova, a Communist since 1918, a Party bureau member, an active worker correspondent, but in the past—Baroness Shtakelberg's senior maid.

Soon after she arrived, the Baroness was 'sniffed out'° by a group under Klavdiya's command. Klavdiya wept at the insult to the *fabkom*.° She and the other womenfolk demanded:

'Out with her, the stinker! Run the bitch out of the factory! First they forget to shoot her, then she creeps out of the woodwork and worms herself in with the workers. As if she hadn't lorded it over me enough, now she has to be one of the girls. We aren't going to work with her!'

But the *fabkom* took a dim view of the whole matter, and Shtakelberg kept her job. A good many of the womenfolk° started fawning on the Baroness and asking her about her grand life in Peter,° which the Baroness was willing enough to talk about. Then she began attending the women delegates' assembly, listening silently and attentively, and in 1924, after Ilich° died, she applied to join the Party.

Everyone remembers those days. The club's huge hall full, the tension in the silent crowd of thousands, who had buried their grief far below the surface. The workers went up on stage one after another.

The womenfolk have a special feeling and love for Ilich. When they went out on stage and started talking about him and the Party, they choked on their tears and couldn't finish, they would toss their applications to join the Russian Communist Party down on the black crape laid over the boards. Shtakelberg came out on stage, too. She began whirling around hysterically, flailing her arms, crying and laughing:

'Comrades... my dears... Our bright sun has set! Our Ilich has passed away... Women, why are you wailing?... You've been wailing your whole lives long. Do you have to wail now, too? Rejoice, women, our Ilich is calling on us to act... Let us vow, women, my comrades, let us vow: let us stop our wailing and take up action. Let us join the Party in triumph!'

There were shouts in the crowd, everyone climbed up on stage, and bundles of applications rained down on the table. But when the Baroness's application fluttered down on top of the others like a crumpled leaf, Klashka jumped up on the stage. The room hushed, her face was so fearful. She began railing in a strange high voice:

'Comrades, what is going on here? We are defiling Ilich! Our enemy is sneaking into the Party... So a Baroness from the enemy class is trying to sully our vanguard?' And, grabbing the Baroness's application from the table, Klashka tore it to bits.

That's why the Baroness wasn't accepted into the Party.

A Day in Trimmings

'Hello, dearies.'

'Hi there, Panya. How's your Tamarochka?'

'Oy, don't ask! What kind of a life *can* a child have with a father like that? Last night he came home drunk as a skunk, to celebrate them putting out some eighty proof—may it rot in hell! Beat the girl and laid into me: "Where were you hanging around yesterday? Who're you mixed up with?" When yesterday I was at a Party meeting. The no-Party scum—you should hear his dirty talk about the Party. Call this a new life, I ask you! Whatever my boy manages to learn in Pioneers, his father just knocks clean out of his head, the leper! He was sick just now—had an operation—his whole inside nearly turned upside down. But he survived, to hell with him!'

Panya is pretty and petite, she has curly hair, and her eyes are big and green. She wears a stylish grey suit and high yellow boots. Even though she's 35 years old, she's still fresh-faced; every day she comes in so pretty and pink you wouldn't think she was more than 20. Her husband is a flabby drunk who's let himself go. No match for her at all. The womenfolk say she cheats on him lots.

'So, Buzlova's late again, eh. How many times this month already!'

A day in the trimmings shop has begun.

The chain-stitchers are chatting and gossiping, bent over the table. Their fingers are just flying through the air as they overstitch the raw edges of the scarves; fringe piles on fringe gaily. Their hands are working mechanically—with simple and practised movements—and their tongues are in thrall to gossip. The trimmers are driven to that, it's in the nature of the work.

You don't gossip like that at a machine: a machine absorbs the whole person.

'What can I tell you, dears! They say our Buzlova's a right tart. Dunka Frolova lives by her: every night men drop by her place, she says. And today she was late—had herself a high old time, I bet.'

'Sure, Balashikha, you go ahead and talk. Who's going to believe you? We haven't forgotten the Belova story, after all.'

Polka Balasheva and Katka Tsvetkova are the number one gossips and whisperers in the whole factory. They know all there is to know about every woman there. Polka is a dried-up old worker who's produced ten boys and girls, her face is wrinkled to folds, and her breasts hang to her belly like lumps of soggy dough.

This is the 'Belova story' that made her famous.

Belova, a stupid, chubby, ginger-haired girl, got taken on under-age. The womenfolk latched on to her the way they would with anyone new to the factory (probably to check up on whether she'd been hired properly):

'How'd you get in? Are you a Komsomol girl, or did you come through the exchange?'

The girl didn't understand what they wanted from her and replied any which way. It turned out, though, she was a neighbour of Polka's, and Polka said that her father was a rich man, her grandfather worked at the next factory, and there were only two children. But at the labour exchange we have a waiting list of under-age girls who really *are* starving, they've nowhere to turn.

So we decided to send Belova away from the factory. We set to work, but it was hard. People stood up for her at the *fabkom*, they said the Belova family was very poor. But Polka kept egging us on:

'The labour inspector's her friend, we know that dad of hers gave him a bribe. They even have five whole cows!'

Our cell went through the official procedure to get Belova laid off.

When the Komsomol sent the lawyer to Belova's house for the final investigation, this is what he found: horrible poverty and a cartload of kids, all of them in rags. Then they sent someone into the shop from the *fabkom*:

'Who was the information on Belova from?'

'It was her neighbour told us.'

But by now our Polka had her tail well between her legs:

'I don't know anything. Really and truly, I've never heard the least little thing about any Belova.'

'Well, that Buzlova sails close to the wind,' the womenfolk started nattering.

'So then, here's Marusenka,' Polya sang out in her sweet little voice, greeting the tardy Buzlova. Polya's face blossomed in a smile.

'Oh, dearie, we were just saying: our Masha must have fallen ill. Everyone was feeling so sorry for you. After all, we love you so much!'

'He-e-ey, Kafistka, there's more dirt around me again!' shouts Buzlova angrily, her face all creased and sleepy.

Poor little Kafistka, the funny, dark little Tatar cleaning girl, the womenfolk have completely ground her down. They lord it over her and order her around: sweep here, dust there.

'Did you hear what's happening? Lay-offs. They're letting thirty people go!' cried Katka Tsvetkova, a plump, red-haired young woman. No sooner was the foreman out of the shop than she ran from her ironing-board to gossip with the womenfolk.

'That means some of us will get moved to the machines, right? Bet I know who! Foreman Konstantinich's favourites, that's who. And no matter how much I beg and wheedle, they won't take me. You can see our bosses don't like hearing the plain truth to their faces!'

Katka is incredibly lazy. Because of that she doesn't stand a chance of being transferred anywhere, and in fact they are even planning to fire her from ironing. And speaking 'the plain truth' just means starting rows. Katka raises scandals in the shop over every little thing. Not a day passes that she isn't hollering or kicking up a fuss with the foremen and the womenfolk. She curses like a carter, a regular fishwife. But later on she's everyone's friend again, as if nothing ever happened. She and Balashikha squabble all the time.

'I'm going to ask to go to the tie shop,' cheeps skinny little Varka, with her short, birdlike little head; a Party candidate. She's pregnant: her huge belly rests on her knees. But pregnancy is not spoiling her looks.

'You're not going anywhere, big-belly! You'll most likely be going on leave in a month.'

'Oh, you swine!' Varka goes pale. She's a mean little bitch herself, when it comes to it. 'Soon as I'm pregnant I'm not a person to you any more, you want to peck me to death! Fling it in my face, see if I care: "Big-belly, big-belly". I don't want maternity leave, I'm a totally equal worker and I'm going to work right up until the birth. You'll see, I'll be standing by my machine.'

'Fool, you'll be the death of the child!'

A bitter sense of insult eats at Varka. It's tough enough being pregnant. All those months absent from the workers' ranks! But it's even worse when you discuss the changes with everyone and suddenly feel how helpless you are.

'It's all right, Varka dearie! We've all been through it, after all, we're womenfolk, too. But then what joy you'll have when you give birth, and the baby will be so healthy,' Panya consoles her.

Varka is 26. She's been married since she was 17. And she's given birth every year since, nine times in all. But her children don't survive: they live a few months and die. But she, ever the mother and mourner, hasn't lost hope: she doggedly keeps giving birth.

Now it's time for the midday meal, and the womenfolk pull out their bundles: it's raining outside and you'd get soaked running across to the canteen. They eat with zest, with feeling. They treat each other: one has brought candy, another jam, someone else marinated mushrooms.

Our womenfolk begrudge their comrades nothing, they share everything one and all. If you don't have money, they'll scrape the last coppers from their pockets and give them to you; nowhere to sleep, they'll take you home, put you to bed, and give you a nice warm blanket. Not to mention feeding you! Often new workers are fed by the entire shop until their first pay packet comes through, for a month or more.

'Oy, girl, look at you go for that sardine! Bet I know why.' Katka Tsvetkova looks straight in the eyes of the young woman greedily demolishing the sardine, pickle, and dried flounder all together.

The young woman blushes and lowers her eyes.

'Your very first, is it?' Katerina fawns and whispers her brazen woman-to-woman advice.

Varka is sitting in a corner gnawing quietly on a crust. She never eats anything but dry crusts. We've offered to treat her, but she refuses.

'My bloke gets by half-starved, too,' Varka brags, 'but last month we bought a sideboard, all walnut, and with such a sweet little green door, and another month we got this bed with all shiny knobs on. Oh, dearies, and this month I'm going to buy a tea service: I already have my eye on one. The cups are so tiny, with a thin pink rim, and these little speckles all over underneath.'

Varka's face lights up with joy and satisfaction.

The Foreman and the Forewoman

The women-winders are sunbathing in the factory yard. It's mealtime. Summer. And hot. The older womenfolk in their navy overalls are sprawled out across the grass, their faces covered with kerchiefs. The young girls are giggling together on the logs, showing off in their white blouses and nice shoes; they've left their work clothes behind in the shop.

Lots of Soviet and Komsomol girls still haven't shed their leather jackets, crumpled skirts, and patched shoes, in their naïvety thinking that this shows their indifference to worldly goods and their great devotion to the Revolution. They're utterly convinced that working women—who they imagine are always heroic and solid as rocks—dress in just that way.

But our factory girls (not that the womenfolk lag behind them in this) are all avid followers of fashion and primpers. Yes, when they had to wear leather jackets at the front, they wore them. But now there *is* no front, wages are decent, and you can think about yourself a bit. You'll see our girls wearing stylish checked caps, and coquettish yellow shoes, and beige stockings. At work everyone wears very simple and elegant light-coloured blouses. Even the poorest—the under-age workers (who only get twenty-eight roubles a month)—are neatly dressed: nice dresses specially made for them, and always carefully ironed. At parties you wouldn't recognize the factory girls decked out in all their finery: silk jersey blouses (our factory's own manufacture) in all possible colours with stylish trimming, fancy shoes, and extravagant hair-dos. The only thing missing, of course, is make-up.° We also have quite a few 'old ladies'—sharp dressers who pay for expensive costumes from good tailors. These 'old ladies' even come into the workshop in curls and powder.

The girls on the logs start kidding around with the passing workers:

'Hey, Kirillych. How come you go around unwashed and uncombed? Or has your wife run off? Come over here, we'll wash you.'

The men joke back awkwardly at the sharp-tongued girls. They rush by like big shots, across the grass.

'Vovka, come on over, come on over, we don't bite!' And the curly-headed Komsomol secretary, a man anxious to please the womenfolk, is knocked to the ground with one shove. A merry row begins in the grass.

Our winders are unruly, shrewish females. It's hard to get on with them. A whole lot of 'old ladies' have ended up all together in winding; they're stuck in the past and they swear at the Communists and stir up the young folk. The winders made their peace with their forewoman, Praskovya Voinova, only after a lot of water had passed under the bridge.

Praskovya, her hair cut short, parted skew-whiff, and greased back with a dog's lick, doesn't look anything like a woman. She speaks like a bloke and wears a shirt and tie. She's a Communist, a worker promoted from the ranks.

Here she is lying with the womenfolk, next to plump Sashurka Gribkova. It may have been Sashurka's imagination, or maybe something really did happen—but soon after that sunny, happy day a dark rumour started going round that forewoman Praskovya wasn't a woman at all, but a man, or 'half-way in between.' They said she had made a pass at Gribkova like a man would.

Rumours flew around the workshops. Voinova was put under surveillance, and here's the evidence that turned up. During work Praskovya sends Komsomol girls notes: 'I love you.' 'How pretty you are.' She often spends the night with the *fabkom* chairman's wife, and is often seen kissing her (everyone's seen it), and then winking at the Baroness—that means she's sleeping with *her*, too. The cunning womenfolk began trying to get Praskovya to go to the bathhouse. Praskovya replied that she'd washed at home. They set some menfolk to wooing her: she snubbed them. The whole factory started talking about the man-woman. The winders lived only for this story: they almost stopped eating and drinking, and many weren't meeting their quota. Finally, we heard about a scandal in the winding shop: the Baroness had a fainting fit—the womenfolk explained it by saying she was jealous of Praskovya over the chairman's wife. Then the chairman's wife came to the shop and shouted at the womenfolk, also out of jealousy, apparently.

The director stepped in, and the Party cell. Voinova was expelled from the

Party. Our secretary thought up a reason to put in the minutes—'repeated insubordination'—and the minutes went to the *ukom.*° Voinova was sent to the doctor, who issued a certificate stating that said Voinova was a woman in the full sense. But no one believed the certificate, they'd all gone mad, so to speak—and Voinova was fired from the factory as a 'socially harmful person'. After a very big scandal at the *ukom*, she was reinstated in the Party just six months later and sent back to the factory, not as a forewoman now but as a simple weighing machine operator.

That is how the women's wild, barbaric fantasy ruined number one winding forewoman and worker-administrator Praskovya. If those women once take against you, you may be the most wonderful person—but they'll still drive you out.

After Praskovya they sent a non-Party expert to be winding foreman, Ivan Semyonych. The womenfolk took an instant dislike to him. On the first day he showed up at the workshop during the evening shift for some unknown reason, when only the women were on. Elena had just got married, the woman had come in after the wedding, she had to be congratulated and the ceremony celebrated. They quickly finished off their quotas and stopped work; and right there, by the machines, they plaited the young woman's braids, broke dishes (an old custom: after the young people's first married night, you break crockery), and they danced on the fragments to the sound of facetious jokes and songs. Ivan Semyonych hollered at them, complained to the director, and there was a reprimand.

'Eh, you'll not forget Praskovya, be sure of that!'

After that, the womenfolk began treating the foreman cautiously, with suspicion. One word from him to a woman and she'd start howling her eyes out. Ivan Semyonych was a bit strict, it's true, but the womenfolk credited him with God knows what sins and exacted a harsh vengeance. Semyonych was never off the pages of the wall newspaper.° Many of the stories were made up from start to finish, and later, retractions would appear. They accused Semyonych of giving the best silk for winding to the young and pretty girls, while the 'old ladies' got the dregs, they said he was constantly threatening to get rid of the womenfolk, that he frightened them with talk of the bosses and purposely stirred things up between the womenfolk and the Red director. Semyonych didn't get a moment's peace, everywhere he went he heard whispering behind his back. Then he really did become bitter and often shouted at the womenfolk unfairly. In their turn they sobbed, wailed, and transferred to other sections. Taking advantage of the fact that the foreman wasn't in the Party, they conducted a frenzied campaign against him through the Party cell, the production conference, and the women delegates' assembly.

No matter how much people told the womenfolk that Semyonych was a real expert at his job, and even if he was a bit of a grumbler, it was no more than you could put up with, the womenfolk stuck to their guns—we're not going to work with him.

Because he was so good, Ivan Semyonych had been put in charge of the factory's three most important shops. But on the womenfolk's insistence, he was prohibited from setting foot in the winding shop and his deputy was sent to see him: forewoman, worker-administrator, and Party member Dusya Boikova.

Dusya is a marvellous person. Boisterous (as her last name suggests),° with an intense, blue-eyed face, smart, energetic, cheerful, always singing. She lives with her Communist husband seven versts away, in the village. Together with her husband they have taken the entire *volost*° in hand: they work from morning to night and from night to morning. They've set up reading-rooms in the villages, travelled everywhere, gone to a lot of trouble, got hold of money, brought in books, started up clubs, and got people to switch to the crop rotation system. Their house is always full of peasant men and women. The womenfolk love Dusya very much: she is their number one helper and adviser.

Through Dusya the womenfolk maintain contact with their bosses—our factory women delegates.

But then Dusya too fell out of favour with the winders:

'Why weren't any of us nominated, but only them from another shop, from the twisters? What, don't we have enough of our own or something?'

And they did everything possible in their work to make trouble for her: they didn't obey her instructions, the evening guard purposely didn't turn off the electricity, forgot to turn off the motor, and threw armfuls of silk scraps under Dusya's work-table.

So even Dusya can't get along with the womenfolk. A wilful mood has taken root among our winders, and until they disband the entire shop and take on new women, no foreman is ever going to make headway in the winding shop.

The Row

'This is it, comrades! You can forget all the talking we've done at these meetings, we have yet another row on our hands!' So Party Secretary Utkin opens nearly every meeting of the cell bureau.

Out of our 400 women, 50 are Communists.

They've all joined since Lenin died. Only five or six are old members of the Party. Our cell is all Leninists. Leninists look after themselves. And they don't differ much, hardly at all, from non-Party members. Is Varka from trimmings really a Communist? How could that tart Marusya Buzlova be a Communist? But then, she *is* a Leninist, after all. You can imagine the trouble it takes to pick out the ones in the squad the Party needs and make genuine Communists of them!

The womenfolk join the Party out of gut feeling, out of sentiment for the Revolution, and out of their womanly love and emotion for Ilich and October.

Discipline is alien to the womenfolk, and they have a very vague idea of how a Communist should behave. No believing in God, no drinking—that they've learned by heart—but when it comes to the everyday, to life in the shop, the little things—then they fall apart.

Our Leninists start all kinds of 'rows'. In winding, the womenfolk didn't want their beloved forewoman taken away. Our young Party girls, instead of acting through the *fabkom* and the cell, are collecting signatures from the womenfolk, writing a petition, and taking it to the director; they gossip in the shop about Party matters, blab about what happened in the bureau or at a closed meeting of the cell; agitate for their own candidates during the *fabkom* campaigns; they even start public fights and brawls with their own; with other Communists right there in the shop.

This is why they call two or three and sometimes even ten women into each Party bureau and shower them with reprimands and punishments. But the punishments don't do any good. It's as plain as plain that the womenfolk need a long training and a huge campaign of education for anything to come of them. The punishments just embitter them and push them away from the Party.

The main rowdy is a Pole, Yanka Chakhurskaya. She's quite a sight, flirtatious, with pencilled eyebrows and ringlets round her face, she wears jaunty little high-heeled shoes, she's a real coquette and chatters away in her Polish accent nineteen to the dozen. She's never off the bureau's agenda. No sooner does she leave a meeting where they've decided to switch her to another shop for correction than she lands right back there again.

'What's the matter with you now, Chakhurskaya? You just left the bureau and look at you, back already,' Utkin says, sweating in exasperation.

'What have I done so bad?' Yanka is outraged. 'I just said that I'd spit in Utkin's face before I'd go to work washing. I'll see the bureau boiled in with the washing itself first.'

'Have you no brains? You've discussed Party business with non-Party members, you've blabbed about the bureau's resolutions, and you've brought the bu-reau in-to dis-re-pute.' Utkin spoke those last words syllable by syllable.

'So what? I only said...' And off she goes again, a hundred words a minute, like a machine-gun.

Rowdies can make very energetic and sensible women. Drill them some and you'll have valuable workers. But for now the old female gossipy ways are still intact in many, and they entwine in the most capricious manner with the new Party way of life and the grave new cause.

'The Women Run Everything...'

At the textile factory, we often have women in charge of all the factory organizations: our woman textile worker has a new strength, a typically female fresh and sharp enthusiasm for work, and a devotion to the cause, and the patience, painstaking diligence, and honesty especially characteristic of womenfolk.

Our female half—400—has the men—600—completely beaten.

Our *fabkom* chairman, Olga Kozlova, shaggy-headed and loud-mouthed (a rather hoarse bass voice), is straight-talking and bossy to a fault. She's not afraid to get bruised and bumped over *fabkom* business, she fights over everything, even down to the last work glove, and she goes all the way up to the highest circle over run-of-the-mill conflicts. In company, when she's had a drink or two, she starts holding forth loudly and dogmatically about all kinds of *fabkom* matters—larding her speech with obscenities as she goes.

'So I say to the director—you're picking on the wrong person there. I was a weaver once myself. I was at Sverdlovsk University, went through the first accelerated courses.'

The *fabkom* has two other women on it: a fat Tatar who works with national minorities, and skinny Lomonosova—who's always running around shouting 'no time, no time!'—to deal with labour protection. Come morning, she's rushing off to Moscow, and a few hours later she's already helping the women delegates organize a first-aid kit in the shop, and in the evening she's sweating through interminable factory committee meetings.

The shop delegates are women, the commission members are women, the Party and Komsomol bureaus are half female. In the club nearly everything is the work of women's loving hands, the hands of our women delegates, that is; in the study circles you'll find the same women delegates, brows furrowed, stubbornly moving their lips, wiping out their illiteracy, and in the Party schools you'll see them mastering the politics their brains are so unaccustomed to.

'Pfah! Who the hell is there here to talk business? Spit where you like, it's all womenfolk.' A visitor to the factory was aghast.

'You'll have to talk to 'em. The women run everything here,' the workers replied, abashed.

But they have no call to complain about the womenfolk. When Kozlova was elected, one of the menfolk° grumbled, 'What could anyone ever expect from you! Do you and these womenfolk really have the brains to stand up for us?' But after Kozlova won a few major battles with the administration, even the worst sceptics started treating her with more respect, and Olga was re-elected to the factory committee unanimously.

You won't just find our women delegates on the factory floor. Female intervention has gone way beyond that. Stop by at the co-operative shop of an evening, and the plump faces of two tall, elderly women will smile at you from behind the counter—Chasovikova and Pankratova, good friends and our two probationer-delegates.

Here, standing behind the counter in neat aprons and weighing out pounds of sugar, salt, and soap for the workers, they are getting dug into the co-operative strongholds and learning all the skills of expert sales staff. From their side of the counter they see a lot on the other side. They've already started figuring out about price lists, stocks, shrinkage, and leakage. When the co-operative canteen once served the workers off meat, their sharp eyes were able to catch a major co-op swindler and embezzler—the cafeteria chief. Later a show trial was set up to deal with him.

In the clinic at the hospital you'll see another delegate—chubby, curly-headed Shurochka, wearing a blindingly white jacket. She goes from doctor to doctor, sits in, learns how to do simple bandages, but at the same time she quietly keeps an eye on the sick leaves the doctor gives (you should hear what goes on there: a perfectly healthy man gets leave, but a pregnant woman is kept by her lathe up to the very last contraction, so that she ends up giving birth right there, under her machine).

At the production conference womenfolk have lagged behind a bit. But not long ago Marfa Gruzdeva, an old working woman, amazed the entire factory. At the women delegates' meeting she submitted a plan to reorganize the winding shop, complete with technical details: which silk would go better a slow rate, which needs its spools changed, etc. The plan was discussed and brought before the production conference. The menfolk laughed at it, of course: we'd better give it to the technical bureau to check over, they said. They did—and all Marfa's suggestions but one were implemented in the shop: what's more, they yielded an improvement in quality and productivity too.

'Pretty soon we're going to have to open up a men delegates' assembly and drag you idlers along. You've been falling behind,' the womenfolk tease.

'Go on and work, go on, work loves fools. This is all a novelty for you. We're not going to get steamed up. We know we have a director who's a man and a secretary who's a man, so all's not lost, at least the production control is in reliable hands. As for the small change—sure, keep it, potter around all you like.'

Whenever we need volunteers—in the shop delegate elections, for the sponsor society, when Party obligations are passed out—the men are apt to decline, refuse to get involved, but as for the womenfolk—just pile it on, a woman will take on everything willingly, unless of course she takes fright and says, 'Ooh, no, I'll never be able to cope with that.'

The womenfolk sense their own backwardness and greedily grab at work—so as to catch up. And at work they are starting to grow out of the gossip and squabbling and pull their lagging comrades along behind.

'Leaders'

Our women 'leaders', the female organizers, change often. Two or three sent from the *ukom* couldn't take the womenfolk's pressure: one got sick; two fled. Then the factory chiefs tried to nominate one of our own delegates, but the fur flew at the delegate assembly.

'Look at them, trying to fob bad lots off on me. Why didn't they appoint Steshka, she can read at least, but this one can't string two words together, and she hides behind other people's backs!' The woman was hounded out very quickly.

It's not easy being the women's leader. The womenfolk are awfully demanding. This one's too quiet, that one's not too bright, and this other one—well! she's a jack-of-all-trades, all right, but she doesn't know much about women's affairs.

'You've got a problem, you come up to her after a meeting and she's as much use as a lump of dead wood, she doesn't understand the first thing about our affairs. If it's anything to do with your child or your man, don't bother asking her advice. She's so dried up—you might as well talk to a brick wall.'

And so a new organizer was sent over from Moscow, Nastasya Petrova. An uncommonly ugly woman: bulging, tin-pale eyes, a red nose like a gun barrel, warty skin, grey hair like a bundle of sticks, black teeth jutting out every which way. A stout figure, holds herself straight, walks with her belly out front—very commanding! In the Party cell they immediately stuck her with the nickname 'the bus', and the womenfolk say when they see her:

'Ba-ah! Do you see that mug the bus has on her: an orang-utan, really!'

As soon as she arrived, the 'orang-utan' started issuing orders at the factory.

'Why hasn't your newspaper come out yet? Today's already the fifth,' she said, taking the editor of the wall newspaper's breath away.

'All of you here aren't worth a damn!' she flew at the *fabkom*. 'Why haven't work clothes been issued in the knitting shop? A fine *fabkom*, I must say!'

'You're not a Party secretary, you're a miserable excuse for one,' she hurled herself at Utkin. 'I can see they don't bother to do what you say. Why? Why do you let them talk back? You should give the orders, full stop, no discussion.'

'But this isn't War Communism° any more.' Utkin was dumbstruck.

'Oh, so you're all stuck on the NEP° here! Well, I fought at the front, dearie, and I insist on military discipline.'

At first, her raids just amused everyone, gave them something new to talk about, but later this senseless ordering around began to get on people's nerves, and soon the entire factory élite was at daggers drawn with Petrova. She got on specially badly with Kozlova and the Komsomol.

But Petrova brought the womenfolk to heel right away, or rather, got them twisted round her little finger. When she thundered out her first speech to them at the women's meeting, the womenfolk sat back stupefied: Petrova does indeed speak beautifully, with tremendous fire, and the womenfolk prize this highly.

She managed to liven up the womenfolk's lives right away, shook up all the women delegates, talked with each one, ferreted out what most interested them, redid everyone's assignments to factory organizations, based on a genuine view of their own interests, not mechanically. And then—a first—she took the womenfolk out to the country.

Our factory is in the central town in a *volost*; all around, for five or six versts, are villages, three of them under our sponsorship. Our womenfolk, the district's textile workers, are far from being true urban proletariat. They live all around here in the villages (the factory has no hostel), and some even have smallholdings. True, hereabouts a 'village' isn't a real village: it's a half-village, half-workers' settlement kind of place. The female workers are constantly at odds with the real women villagers, who give them no peace: 'What's it to you: you live like pigs in clover. You work your eight hours, then you roll off to bed if you want. *We* toil our whole lives long without ever straightening up from the ground!'

Nastasya Petrova led her force in the village, woman to woman. The women delegates were going to work among the peasant women *en masse*. They spent part of their Sundays fitting up a hut for a village nursery. That autumn, they went from village to village in the slush, the dark, and the rain to agitate among the womenfolk for the elections to the Soviets. Nastasya Petrova spent three evenings teaching her delegates how to talk to the womenfolk.

The women felt strongly that they were involved in an important, responsible cause, and they came to respect Petrova very much because they saw how tough she was. They respected her, though they didn't like her. There was no softness or soulfulness in her, and without that you can't get close to a woman.

'A rail, not a human being.' That's what they said about Nastasya.

Petrova often quarrelled with her delegates; she wasn't above bearing a grudge either. If she didn't get along with someone, she thought up a punishment for her right away:

'On Thursday you aren't coming with us to campaign in Danilovka, you can sit at home.'

The womenfolk got the feeling that she was conducting some kind of underground campaign against the *fabkom* and the cell. She talked people into writing denunciations of the *fabkom* on the wall newspaper and bitched about Kozlova in the women's presence. And this they could not endure.

Right from the start, Nastasya and Kozlova hadn't got on. One factory was too small to hold them both. They developed an intense hatred for each other, and Petrova never let a chance slip to catch Olga out somehow at a meeting or in the shop. Their main bone of contention was who had more influence over the womenfolk. Petrova felt that the women would die for Kozlova, but only respected her. She couldn't forgive Olga this, so she tried to undermine her authority.

When Petrova's subterfuge was uncovered, an *ukom* representative was called in and a question was raised about Petrova at the Party bureau. They called to mind both her forays against the secretary and her criticism of the *volkom*° and the *ukom*. What's more, she had let no opportunity slip of lambasting those in high places, with or without just cause, believing that this was what Party democracy was all about.

It turned out that at one time she had been a Socialist Revolutionary,° and that the Soviet Party School she had come to us from had given her an 'unrestrained element' evaluation. And the bureau's decision, along with that of the *ukom* representatives, was to transfer Petrova to the *ukom*'s jurisdiction, 'since the comrade has SR leanings'.

When Nastasya heard this decision, she burst into tears and sobbed for a long time, stretched out on the bench at the *fabkom*. She sincerely loved the womenfolk and had thrown herself wholeheartedly into her work. She even slept on the table in the Party cell room (she didn't have a place of her own). She had waded many long autumn versts through the mud out to the villages—and were the results of her work really so bad?

It was strange to see our stiff-backed Nastasya writhing in tears on the bench. Somehow you didn't feel sorry for her, though.

By this time Kozlova, having completely exhausted herself in work for the *fabkom*, was on a month's leave. As soon as she came back, the womenfolk started demanding her for their organizer. They stood yelling at meetings and went in crowds to see Kozlova in her apartment.

'Come on, Olgushka, be our leader. Look, we've been left empty-handed again. We want you and only you!'

Everyone in the factory loves Olga, but the womenfolk think the sun shines out of her eyes. Even Parashka, the very worst gossip, who calls the women delegates cretins and strumpets and can't talk about the women Communists without swearing, even she said about Olga:

'Now Olga Kozlova, there's one who really is a true Communist, and I respect her for it. She worked an iron in our shop, she was just a presser, fourth-category.° All the womenfolk howl and fuss over what category they get assigned, but she got less than anyone and didn't ask for anything, even though she worked day and night without let-up for us, donkeys that we are.'

People love her way of speaking, which may be coarse and muddled but has a power that could break your back. People love her for her merry ways and her open nature; Olga can play a prank, and tell a saucy joke, she likes a drink with the best of them. And when she's drunk, she first becomes excessively merry, starts doing a country dance, and then singing some of the old factory songs. But then she gets sad, and starts crying, and becomes unusually feminine and soft. She seems like a little girl (despite her 32 years). She gets melancholy and talks about her loneliness, says that her beloved, the head of the secret police, laughs at her. Then Olga grinds her teeth and pines.

Olga is one of the women, she grew up with them, she comes from their world. She has been in the factory since she was 10. She never got a chance to study, so she's barely literate. At 15 she was forced into marriage, but she ran away from her husband and went back to the factory.

'Ooh, but I hated men then, when I was a girl!'

Yes, 'when she was a girl'. But now, at 32, Olga is so lonely she can hardly bear it. She would like a husband and a child. Often she'll throw off her awful side-fastened blouse, dress up in her pink top, and set her sights on someone from the factory, or one of the visiting instructors from the provincial office. She's not bad-looking (a bit unfeminine though). Her face is young and her eyes are black with a glint. She's very sharp and funny like all the womenfolk are.

Olga has attended the odd course at Sverdlovsk University. And even though it's tough for her, being only half-literate, working her way round the political-economic subtleties of it all, everyone appreciated her there and she graduated as a women's organizer.

Olga hasn't been separated from the womenfolk once since. She was an organizer for four years, then she went back into production, and then she ended up on the *fabkom*. But even when she was up to her ears in *fabkom* business, she would sneak off to see the womenfolk, to peek in at the women delegates' meeting and a have a chat about the labour code or about how to restructure daily life. Olga may know very little, but what she does know, mixed up and peppered with mistakes though it is, she does her best to put into the women's heads. And the womenfolk take it from her. Olga is so good at wounding women's soft hearts with her words that often at her discussions and reports the womenfolk weep copiously, they're all prepared to follow Olga to the ends of the earth.

Olga's misfortune is having so little education. So last autumn she had a brainwave: she'd join the workers' preparatory faculty° at the university. For some reason, the womenfolk are overcome with this mad lust to study and study every autumn. Olga got through all the commissions—at *ukom* and MK° level—nearly worrying herself sick in the process. She met all their requirements, but when she got to the very last hurdle, the workers' faculty commission, they turned her down: you're too old, they said, let the young study. Here Olga sensed her doom: soon young, educated kids would be coming along, then, ignorant and rough folk like her would be on the shelf.

She sent an indignant article to all the papers protesting; then she wept, then she pined, and then she took to her bed and stayed there for a month.

Despite all the women's entreaties, the Party cell held out against letting Olga be a women's organizer for ages. They wanted to make a supervisor out of her, they tried to make her the director's assistant (he needed one of his own people). But the womenfolk get whatever they want. They went to the *ukom* as a delegation and made their demands there. Olga herself cried and begged to go to the womenfolk, said she wouldn't stay on at the factory if they didn't make her an organizer, and anyway she didn't know the first thing about supervising. The cell hurried to appoint a women's organizer from among the women delegates. The womenfolk chucked her out of the meeting and out the door the very first time she appeared, then the whole gang of them went to the Party bureau to demand Olga as a replacement.

And so the cell had to give in, and the womenfolk carried an expostulating Olga away on their shoulders, to the women's common room, to the sounds of loud singing and irrepressible yelling.

[1927]

Translated by Marian Schwartz

◆ ANNA PRISMANOVA ◆

Born in Libau (now Liepaja), Latvia, Prismanova (1892–1960) was the daughter of a doctor. Little is known of her early life or education; the family moved to Moscow in 1918, and Prismanova and her two sisters emigrated thence to Berlin in the early 1920s. By 1924, Prismanova had moved to Paris, where she was to spend the rest of her life. She married the poet Aleksandr Ginger in 1926. Whilst Ginger took an active interest in literary life, working as a publisher and editor as well as a poet, Prismanova, much the more talented poet of the two, regarded literature as a private activity, though a full-time one: her two sons, born in 1925 and 1928, were left to look after themselves from a very early stage. Prismanova began publishing in the late 1920s, but her best work dates from *c.*1930–50. The most verbally inventive and determinedly non-referential member of the remarkable 1930s pleiad of women poets in emigration, Prismanova is outstanding also in her sensitivity to the history of women's writing, both in Russia and elsewhere. As 'On Guard and on Town Gardens' illustrates, she was also a talented prose writer, attractively combining an eye for the bizarre with a dead-pan wit.

Lomonosov

(Russian text p. 462)

Kantemir's muse, next the world's cant immured,
defended Petrine craft with northern gall;
secured above the Chud, a yellow truckle
pock-marked the orphaned vellum of his scrolls.

Not Kant's inimitable gallimaufry
nor even Gallileo's gallantry
was able to blot out the yellow contour
with tangled lilies of mentality.

Armies of heroes, to his limbeck rush to greet him!
He travels through the circle of the skies,
but trembles on a spade. Hordes have exploited
Earth's riches, and the stumps are left to die.

Only the wind—a scallywag—resists him,
methodically he pins the ether down,
zodiac signs surrender to persistence,
and as a sign the ciphers click below.

(1928)

◆ ANNA PRISMANOVA ◆

The Brontë Sisters

(Russian text p. 463)

The happy have no notion how time passes,
but the unhappy need a monument:
and so give gilded letters to the marble,
and let the angels have a brow of stone.

Flammable is the covering of the body,
within it coals are heaped to make a pyre:
factory smoke has made the village sooty,
unblunted, though, the black cross on the rise.

O Emily, O lily of the valley,
lavender juice, the nightingale is dead!
Hidden from all, you carried to the moorlands
the overflowing gifts of useless pride.

The sins of generations are unburied:
search for the fathers' vices in the sons.
But flying is a gift of suffering's spirit,
it gives a quill to those whom vultures rend.

And it was Charlotte, though her head was heavy,
who with her quill unsealed the wretched house;
three sisters sat and listened to the howling:
implacable the voice of northern winds.

See how she grips the feather's shaft so tightly:
this thing built of irregular bone lumps
keeps locked, unhappily, behind her closeness
gigantic passions and a smothered flame.

Hiding my passions under a frail cover,
Like her, I cling to the feather's inky edge;
a doctor's daughter, I was once a pastor's,
another Brontë sister I once was.

Alas for us, the end is the beginning,
our joys are bounded by an inner judge.
But inspiration, and the taste of suffering,
and time will save those whom success eludes.

(1939/1946)

◆ ANNA PRISMANOVA ◆

On Guard and on Town Gardens

It was a town of music shops and old spinsters. The spinsters were all musical, the shops old, and so one might just as well have said that it was a town of musical spinsters and old shops.

The town's oldest street was also its crookedest. It ran from a square lined, on fair-days, with the shafts of peasant carts, down to a harbour flecked with the funnels of ocean-going liners.

Sluggish bottle-green water lapped the cobbled embankment, where grain stores and coal sheds stood side by side. In summer, the whitish stone of the grain stores would be thickly powdered in black soot, in winter the sooty coal-yards wore snow-white mantles. Everything complemented everything else, everything walked hand in hand.

On one of those winter days when spring is in the air, and falling snow hits the ground as rain, a hearse swept by, carrying Rosalia Sontag, the town's number one corsetière, to her last resting place.

The lady's surname evoked the day of rest;° and indeed, only last Sunday, she had been busy at her kitchen table. Her nose was shaped like a potato, her cheeks were the colour of two nicely braised escalopes. And every Sunday she would duly purchase two identical escalopes in Frau Gertrude Adam's butcher's shop, at the brink of whose scarlet gorge two frivolous twins, Adam and Eva, would dance every day in summertime. Both twins were dressed in starched aprons with high collars; the only difference between them was that Eva had two carrot-coloured plaits hanging down her back. This heavenly pair were decidedly satanic of character, alas; whenever they spied tall, long-legged Malchen Sontag, the girl who always managed to take first place in class two at school, they would begin to chant: 'One two three four, run away: the vixen has come out to play.'

But now, Amalia was on her way to her mother's funeral. Wrapped in a wool velour coat edged with swansdown, with gold buttons as fastenings, she stepped primly over the sleet-spattered pavement. To Malchen's right paraded her great-aunt on her father's side, who worked as a lady assistant former drummer, now in retirement. As you see, Amalia Sontag had spent her childhood in an atmosphere imbued with music.

As a baby, she had fallen asleep to the sound of a musical box. In the spring, the odd-shaped windows had let in the sound of a barrel organ along with the scent of leaf-mould and pine resin. When Amalia was doing her homework, dressed in her uniform chintz pinafore, a pendulum clock had filled the fly-spotted dining-room with its rhythmical ticks. The house was plain, but respectable. And so in time, Amalia Sontag became a music teacher; and simultaneously, the heroine of a short story.

When characters fall in with an author who is richly endowed with imaginative powers, he leads them by the nose, fixing them up with complicated destinies, fates abounding in love affairs and suchlike. But woe to the heroine whose author has no imagination whatever. Instead of leading her to a place where something unusual might happen to her, he passively follows her, and only describes what really does happen.

Amalia herself has forced your author to abandon her for ever in a sand-strewn little Baltic town, the haunt of the Sandman,° to bestow on her eyes like Carmen, but a nose like a Lapp reindeer-driver's, to dress her in a muslin frock, and to place her on an oak window-seat with a view of the cobble-clad foundation and shingled roof of the chemist's shop opposite.

The bespectacled midwife, clutching the hem of her home-made skirt, was picking her way over the pock-marked pavement, which the rain had made many-eyed with puddles. At the window to the right of the shop's moss-covered porch stood three globular flasks, each one a different colour. At the window to the left bobbed the whitish conical head of the chemist's apprentice.

Whilst this lanky youth, who is so devoted to the service of his craft, grinds his life-saving pharmaceutical powders, the wife of his podgy employer lies in the little bedroom behind the stockroom, dying of a disease beyond any powders' help.

Past the rows of provincial houses walks a breaker of ladies' hearts—the gynaecologist. Past walks the glazier—the owner of a diamond and of a voice like a goat's. Past go the dockers. Past go the years . . .

Rain is falling once more on the streets of the musical town. Or not falling so much as pouring, in flat sheets from the round chimneys, in round drops from the flat façades. It forms oval puddles on the clay paths of the old town gardens. It helps children mix clay to make their square toy houses in the kindergartens. It links sky and pavement in a slanting net.

The inspector of the lunatic asylum walks in to the chemist's shop. Dead desiccated leaves, made moist again by the rain, drop from the trees in the garden behind. The bare branches are as angular as the arms of Fräulein Sontag, now resting after a day of music, and clicking away steadily with her smooth needles. Tomorrow will be her forty-third birthday; some relations are coming to visit. The saffron-coloured *krendel*° lying on the white table-cloth, and the green wreath hanging on the yellow chair, remind her of her rose-coloured childhood. Rhubarb compote is cooling on the sideboard. Drops like tears run down the window-panes. Rainfalls are the only thing that unite earth and heaven.

In the garden of the lunatic asylum lies a sign from heaven, a rainbow marked out in a bow-shaped bed by flowers in seven colours. Amalia Sontag is walking over to the so-called nut-house (though in fact it is built of red bricks), wearing her knobbly straw hat, on her way to visit her feeble-minded nephew. This gentleman, whose forehead is as low as his chin is prominent and his eyes squinting, is able to play ditties upon the violin, but he prefers to stay sitting upon his chair, giving free rein to his nefarious whims.

As the indolent sun starts sinking into the warm bath of the sea, and nicely brought-up children begin quitting their places on the cooling sand, Amalia Sontag leaves the lunatic asylum. At almost the same moment, out comes the piano-tuner.

One-armed pines cast webbed shadows on the shoreline. The music mistress, whose straight shanks are enclosed in white pumps and black stockings, tries to walk in step with the piano-tuner. His elements are air and water. His deep voice sounds like the tolling of a bell sunk beneath the ocean. Looking at his black sideboards and black coat with its winged collar in the gathering dusk, Fräulein Sontag seems to see the captain of an airship . . .

On Fräulein Sontag's cheviot° bosom trembles an undulating brooch made of ivory. It is formed from two dead-white human hands, clasped together for all eternity. But the two living beings are condemned by their possession of souls to solitude, and so they walk at a respectable distance from each other, talking of the ivory keys.

Of course, he could very well have talked to her of something else; he could have sat with her in the little pavilion in the town garden, or they could have strolled over the corrugated-iron and nail-strewn glade to the ill-favoured pink shack, run up for the miserable town circus to give its main performances in. She would have held his hat, he her waist.

But instead he wished her a formal farewell, clutching his umbrella and standing on the corner of two empty streets. For the man who spent his days putting down artificial chords was preternaturally shy.

Today, Fräulein Sontag had ended her week of music, as she did every Saturday, by giving a lesson to the deaf post master's grand-daughter. The red-faced girl in her blue sailor-suit had taken Fräulein Sontag into the icy drawing-room, and here, under the chilly gaze of her grandfather, who hung on the wall among a hand-coloured group of trumpeters from a naval wind-band, the child had industriously thumped every one of the monster's black-and-white teeth.

This *divertissement* concluded, Amalia Leopoldovna armed herself with her lilac leather prayer-book and walked down along the endless railings to the gates that she knew so well. It was raining, of course. The knot of plump old ladies waiting under a tree with their umbrellas up looked like a family of mushrooms just popped up after a damp spell.

The evening sky was slowly turning red. As the crows flew up to the bell-tower, and the shutters rushed down on the music shops, rattling melodiously, the gravel paths in the church garden crunched moistly under the desiccated legs of the musical spinster. Gently, regularly she breathed the damp air. The black-edged faces of the old women, whose malice was only thinly veiled by their humility, looked at her approvingly. No one in town could cast aspersions on her—throw stones in her garden, as the local saying had it.

However, the stocky market gardener who lived next door to Fräulein Sontag would often throw a few stones into her garden, as a signal for one of their not infrequent assignations. And at such times one could certainly not have said that Fräulein Sontag was on her guard.

[*c*.1935]

◆ ANNA KARAVAEVA ◆

Karavaeva was born in 1893 and came from humble origins in Siberia. She began writing in her late teens, when she joined the writers' group 'Siberian Lights' in Irkutsk. Her reputation was established by a series of novels that she wrote in the late 1920s and early 1930s, notably the factory novel *The Sawmill* (1927). She attained high office in the Union of Writers from its inception in 1934, and she embraced the dictates of Socialist Realism wholeheartedly. Her trilogy *The Motherland* (1944–50) was awarded a Stalin Prize in 1951. Although Karavaeva's prominence declined after Stalin's death, she remained in official favour right up until her death in 1979.

A Soviet Madonna and Child

(*Extract from* The Flying Start)

(*Mamykin, a painter, has been working in the Klenovsk tank factory, producing pictures of the workers. In the following scene, workers and officials in the factory, including the women welders in the brigade led by Olga Chelishcheva, come to look at his canvases.*)

'Will you have a look at thi-is!' Aleksei Nikonovich said, drawling his words indignantly. 'See here, he's painted us a real madonna and child!'

Pouting his red lips in a grimace, he read out the caption contemptuously: 'Nastya Kuzmina and her son'.

Anastasiya Kuzmina, the woman from Stalingrad, looked down from the wall at them, her eyes full of tears. The dark curly head of her baby lay against her left arm; with her right arm, the mother pressed the small body against hers. You could sense the fragility of the infant's form under the flowing folds of the bright blanket covering him. The mother's face was inclined towards him, every lineament breathing sadness and anguish; an anxious flush covered her face in an uneven red, for she had just come back to her baby out of the blazing heat of the electro-welding line. In the distance, black iron girders stood out amongst clouds of crimson smoke, and below them cascades of sparks from the arc welding electrodes shot into the air like fireflies. The mother was feeding her baby.°

The figures of the mother and child were outlined faintly, in pastel tones, which gave them an especial purity of expression. But Aleksei Nikonovich, paying no attention to this, continued:

'Look, there's a welder congratulating his comrade on work well done: he's painted the truth there. But this snivelling mum with her hair all over the place—that's not the kind of thing we want, surely? Who needs pictures like that, Mamykin?'

'We *do* need them. Pictures like that show the truth too, you know,' said Plastunov calmly, stepping to the front of the throng. 'After all, Comrade Terbenev, such things do happen. That woman feels great sorrow, but when she has fed her child she will go back to work and give her last ounce of strength to the task in hand. Millions of people live like that these days.' Making a dismissive gesture, Plastunov went off after the artist.

The last two to approach the portrait were Glafira Lebedeva and Anastasiya Kuzmina.

'Did you hear what Plastunov said? He believes in you: she'll always get on with her work, he said. We all feel for you, Nastya! Do cheer up! Look, here's Sonya Chelishcheva!'

'What's been happening here?' Sonya said, all concern immediately.

'It's our Nastya, she's not feeling happy...' said Glafira. 'You're still young, Sonechka, and you don't know what torments a mother can feel. That picture really does show Nastya as she is. She cries every day when she feeds her son, you know.'

'What, she cries?' Sonya repeated, lifting her eyebrows and gazing at Anastasiya for confirmation. 'But why is that, Anastasiya? After all, they bring him round on the dot for you at feeding-time, don't they?'

'Ah, Sonya... My heart just contracts, when I take him off the breast... He's not strong yet, he can't drink his milk quickly, and I'm always in a hurry... I worry you might be waiting for me... angry that I'm...' And Kuzmina, overcome with timidity now, hung her head.

'What on earth do you mean, Nastenka!' Sonya said warmly. 'How could we be possibly be angry with you on account of the child?' she added, motioning her head at the portrait.

But then a thought suddenly occurred to Sonya, making her blush to the roots of her hair.

'So that's why Nastya's work rate was so low! I never even thought! And it's such a simple human problem...'

'Nastenka, dear, I beg you,' Sonya said, embracing Kuzmina, 'never think things like that! Take as long as you like feeding the baby... What a silly girl you are! You know very well you'll feel much better as soon as you know he's having enough to eat.'

'And your work will go better,' Glafira added.

'Of course, of course...' Kuzmina said, heaving a sigh of relief, and lifting her clear eyes to Sonya's face in a shy smile.

'There's a good girl, Nastenka!' Sonya said, feeling an extraordinary sense of relief.

However, in private she was still rebuking herself.

'I couldn't even think of something so simple! What an idiot! Call yourself a brigade-leader!'

Then suddenly an impudent whistle rang round the shop. Sonya saw that the whistler had been Seryozha Vozchy. His foxy little face, bustling figure and high-pitched, sniggering tones all overflowed with malice.

'Look out, folks! Our celebrated Stakhanovite woman, Yulichka, has come to admire her own portrait!'

'Quiet please, quiet please!' came the silly voice of poodle-permed Verochka Sboeva; she was shouting and clapping her hands.

All around, people were laughing and joking. Then Yuliya Shanina came in sight; she walked smartly up to Sonya, trembling and pale, eyes moving restlessly.

'Leave me alone, you shameless lot!'

'What's going on here?' Sonya shouted, taking charge of the situation. 'Sergei, why are you whistling like a street hooligan? Why is Yuliya crying?'

'Because she's got ideas above her station,' Seryozha said, now in a markedly less aggressive tone, and pointed at the water-colour.

'So that's it!' Sonya said, looking at Yuliya's portrait: the face looked familiar, but somehow extraordinary.

There was beauty not only in her youthful features and the soft delicacy of her colouring, but also in the inner light which glimmered in her violet eyes.° Her pink lips, soft as rose-petals, seemed about to open any minute: they seemed on the point of expressing words and hopes which only she knew.

'Look at her, like some holy statue!' hissed Verochka, from behind someone's back.

'That's envy talking, envy and spite!' Sonya, who had taken an instant dislike to Verochka, joined battle straight away. 'What's happened to make you all start getting at Yuliya Shanina? Look, here's a picture of our brigade, the women apprentice electro-welders. We're hardly even independent workers yet, but the artist did a portrait of us. He believed in us, he saw the future we had. He be—lieved in us, do you understand? And he believed in Yuliya too; she will be able to become the woman he drew. She *will* turn into that woman. Isn't that right, Yuliya?'

'Yes! I will!' And Yuliya embraced Sonya, her courage rising every second. 'Yes! I will be like that, like Sonya says. Don't suppose you can get away with making fun of me for long!'

[*1947*]

◆ VERA BULICH ◆

Born in St Petersburg, Bulich (1898–1954) came from a large and distinguished family of academics; her father, Sergei, was a historian and musicologist of note. Bulich's own studies at university were disrupted by the aftermath of the Revolution; in 1918, her family moved to their dacha in Finland, and from about 1920 they lived in Helsinki. Here Bulich found employment as a librarian (at first in the University Slavonic Library), and made contact with literary circles. She was active in the *Svetlitsa* (Chamber) literary society, and wrote numerous essays, reviews, radio talks, and even ballet libretti, as well as poetry. Her early poetry was heavily influenced by the work of Akhmatova, but from the mid-1930s she produced work of much greater originality and technical accomplishment. Though underpinned by Neoplatonic dualism, Bulich's poetry was always very much of this world; in its careful referentiality and discriminating use of language, it typifies the best work of the second-generation Russian émigré poets.

From my Diary, iii

(Russian text p. 465)

...And once again Good Friday comes.
The cycle in the spring sky is complete.
What was, a year ago, no longer counts,
For here I now stand by the Deposition,
My sapling candle burning in the thicket.

To sounds both sweet and sorrowful,
To *Lord have mercy*'s lengthy vowels,
We leave the narthex and with care
Go down the stone steps by the church,
Using one hand to stop the draught
And shield the candle's trembling flame,
Heels sinking softly in the ground
Cut into furrows by the thaw.
Between the dark limes and the lamps
The sky is clear and green, and overhead

Now and again the bells' cracked voice
Laments the holy burial.
Swimming in roses, smoke, and light
The icon navigates the church.
And so the smell of incense, roses,
Smoke from the candles, melting snow,
The pain of palms scorched by hot wax,
The vernal softness of the soil,
The Deposition's tragic sign
Lifted on high, the limpid skies,
The choir's complaint, more muted now,
The muffled moaning of the bells—
This radiant grief sinks in the soul.

Feelings will pass, forgotten, cooled,
Pain will be numb, and joys will fade,
But these things here will always be:
Death and the spring. The thought of loss,
The spirit's looked-for resurrection.
The pomp of this eternal rite.
This truth, the same for everyone.

(1937)

◆ VERA BULICH ◆

The Omnibus

(Russian text p. 467)

The Sunday swallows edged the sky,
tearing the air with their shrill cries;
and sunlight baked the empty streets,
below the cheerful, vacant blue.
A bus stood in a city square,
holding imprisoned shafts of sun,
which laid thick heavy dust upon
the leather seats, upon the floor;
the smell of petrol, harsh and sweet,
mixed with the dust, the scorching seats,
the faint remembered scent of flowers.
Fat doves went promenading by,
then fluttered as the engine roared.
Off the bus floats. This ark holds, two and two,
sinful and sinless, some carried to salvation
away from the flood of forty working days,
the anguish of bedrooms hushed as cobwebs.
The suburbs spin along to meet it
with houses in gardens; wooden poles
hold up their warp of threaded wires
to stripe the pallid canvas sky.
And voices beyond our ears take wing,
to rush into lavender-coloured space,
and murmur above the firmament;
each leaves a body stranded in a box.

Beyond the window, houses, people, trees,
flash past. But one man has a gun
pressed to his shoulder. Frozen in a pose
of fierce intent, he aims at something. What?

And everything around him turns to stone,
held by the press of pent-up expectation,
in the fantastic silence of a drawing.
The tension sparks across to me,
a mysterious, a sudden charge,
right through my body. I hold my breath,
and wait, fearful and rapt, and wait—

—Now I shall hear the gun's loud snap,
the frightful silence will collapse,
the picture will be smashed to pieces,
a perpetuum mobile begin.
The bus pauses, turns a corner, then speeds on,
fences and walls go past and past;
I strain my ears, but cannot hear
a shot, not even an echo. My body's trapped,
held stiff and chained. A fog of dust
flies off the road and beats the glass;
the wheels start spinning in vacancy.
We'll never reach our destination,
like nomads, we're condemned to stray
within ourselves, captive and mute,
with silent voices in our heavy bodies.

A passenger by chance with strangers,
held prisoner by edgy fate,
I sit and wait for resolution
and for release. I sit and wait.

(1938/1954)

♦ ANNA BARKOVA ♦

Born into the family of a *gimnaziya* janitor in the industrial town of Ivanovo-Voznesensk in 1901, Barkova was educated at her father's school, and gained an entrée to creative writing via a local Proletcult group in 1918. In the early 1920s, she moved to Moscow, where, helped by the Commissar of Enlightenment, Anatoly Lunacharsky, her career took off. She published little after 1925, however, and in 1934, she was arrested and sent to the camps, where she was to spend most of the next thirty years. She died in 1976. Much of her mature poetry only began being published in the late 1980s.

A Few Autobiographical Facts

(Russian text p. 469)

In a common pit, without a headstone,
I shall finish walking my life's road.
The pages of my writings, rubbed and faded,
May be found by someone in the end;
Perhaps he'll be insane enough to like them,
To like the vicious prickles of my verse,
'Genius and power of prophecy suffice here',
He'll say, 'to make this stuff a name of sorts.
And by the verb and adjective agreement
I'd say it was a woman who wrote these texts,
She was a restless soul and nothing pleased her,
But she'd a sharp, a fierce intelligence.
I'll send my pupils round the dusty attics,
Yes, all the dusty attics in the town,
With luck they'll find, I hope, some other matter
That's written in the same, though unknown, hand.'
The students sift the heaped-up sheets of paper,
And grab assorted refuse by the ton,
Mixing the sins I actually committed
With other people's dull and trifling ones.

All in good time these pupils get to work and—
Enlightening themselves, enlightening others too—
They write their dissertations by the dozen
About my life, sunk in obscureness now.
Their style's by turn gushing, dull, or dogmatic,
From day to day hypotheses they mint,
So in my common pit I'm fit to vomit,
O, fit to vomit with the tripe they print.
'For reasons that the years have cloaked in mystery
(For who can map the darkness of those times?)
This poetess, we're loath to tell our readers,
Was flung into a labour camp, it seems.
Records allow us to make no suggestion
Of how and for what reason she transgressed;
Without a doubt her action was detestable,
A crime that would make the law-abiding gasp.
And whilst in prison, she was often beaten
(So, at any rate, we may suppose),
But her disciples all showed her devotion,
And her students loved her none the less.
From *Fragment Number Eight* we may construe that
A patron of the arts came to her aid;
But the paucity of evidence is such that
We cannot speculate on names and dates.
The other texts (q.v.) all have *lacunae*
So that the work of many future years
Is requisite if scholars are to pinpoint
The reasons why this poet suffered thus.
Oh! "Poetess", not "poet"! Please excuse me!
But wait a moment! Let us pause for thought!
Might it not be that there is some confusion,
Might my mistake not guide us to the truth?
This intellect, so bitter and unsparing,
Dear colleagues—surely it is masculine?
Cool clarity of spirit so unwavering,
The manner caustic, dry, as desert winds—
Yes, all quite foreign to a woman's nature:
Colleagues! We ought to track down all the facts,
And when the evidence is on the table,

We may determine character and sex.
How much there is in this that's truly touching!
How much of general interest in these themes!
Well, to the documents! Begin researching!
Gather the verse, prose, letters, all in reams!
It seems our poet attained the furthest boundaries
Of fame, poetic genius, and old age;
And every town in Russia wished to tender
For the chance to be his final resting-place;
But his bones were buried in deep secret
And proselytes in their devoted crowds
Walked to the place of burial beside him
Along a little path outside a town.
They were decked by the night in starry robes of mourning,
Torches were lit along the coffin's way...
But regretfully I must inform you
That we have yet to find the famous grave.'
But here my bones ring out in indignation,
Beating against a stranger's in the pit:
'What's this? I'm buried in a northern graveyard!
You filthy hack, you're lying through your teeth!
I know that your parade of erudition
Is meant to net you a professorship;
But readers who want to know what I have written
Won't find me in your fly-blown vinaigrette.
Beyond the grave they've given me a sex-change,
When all my life, each hour, I was a *she*!
Patrons—to hell with them. What use were patrons
In the days that I was forced to see?
And I never had a single pupil
And they didn't beat me in the gaol;
I was condemned by a ludicrous tribunal,
And my "crime" was just as laughable.
I lived amongst young women who were stupid
And old ones who were senile and ran mad;
And the watery prison soup they fed me
Made my flesh dry up, my spirit fade.
The funeral procession and the torches
Are all a figment of your clichéd brain—

In a common pit my body rotted,
Whilst alongside five others did the same.'

[*c*.1954]

◆ ANNA BARKOVA ◆

Tatar Anguish

(Russian text p. 472)

Tatar anguish, anguish of the Volga,
Grief from far-away and ancient times,
Fate I share with beggars and with royalty,
Steppe and steppe-grass, ages gallop by.

On the salty Kazakh steppeland
I walk, head bare beneath the skies;
The mutter of grass dying of hunger,
The dreary howl of wolves and wind.

So let me walk, fearless, unthinking,
On unmarked paths, by wolfsbane clumps,
To triumph, to shame, to execution,
Heeding no time, saving no strength.

At my back lies a palisade of barbs,
A faded flag, which once was red;
Before me, death, revenge, rewards,
The sun, or a savage, angry dusk.

The angry twilight glows with bonfires,
Great cities blaze, put to the flames;
Knowing slave labour's agonies,
They choke and putrefy with shame.

All is alight, all flies to ash.
Yet why should breathing hurt me so?
Closely you cleave to Europe's flesh,
Dark Tatar soul.

[*c.*1954]

♦ TATYANA ESENINA ♦

The daughter of the poet Sergei Esenin and the actress Zinaida Raikh, Esenina (1918–92) was brought up in Moscow, but was exiled to Tashkent in 1941, following the murder of her mother by the NKVD. Here she worked as a journalist, producing many articles and factual sketches (*ocherki*); she was also the author of a memoir of Esenin, 'The House on the Nikolsky Boulevard' (see *Soglasie*, 4 (1991)). *Zhenya, the Wonder of the Twentieth Century* was the only piece of Esenina's fiction to be published during her lifetime, though other material has survived in manuscript. (Information kindly supplied by N. I. Guseva.)

[Male Bonding Sessions]

(*Extract from* Zhenya, the Wonder of the Twentieth Century)

(Sergei Vasilevich, a vet in the town of N., has boasted that he is capable of producing a humanoid superman in his laboratory, who would be able to solve all the town's many crime problems. Rumours about his discovery have been flying round the town: Police Captain Nabov° has threatened to arrest the humanoid on sight, since he cannot issue identity documents to an individual who has no birth certificate, and it is illegal to reside in the town without them. There have been long arguments about whether the vet can be telling the truth: eventually all doubts are settled by the arrival of Zhenya, a handsome, well-built, blond, and blue-eyed young man, who takes up residence with the vet. Here the narrator, a would-be hardbitten journalist on the local paper, tells the story of the first few days after Zhenya's emergence.)

Word Gets round about Zhenya

Don't imagine for a moment that I'd forgotten about Police Captain Nabov's threat to arrest Evgeny Aleksandrovich the moment he appeared. No, I'd been on tenterhooks the whole time—not that I'd said anything to Zhenya himself, naturally. And in due course Zhenya did indeed receive a summons from the station.

The morning of Zhenya's appointment, I got Ekaterina Ivanovna to make some meatballs just in case he did get put in prison—we had to make sure we had something to put in a food parcel for him.° I was about to go off to work when the door opened and Zhenya came in. He sat down, munched his way through the meatballs, then told me what had been going on at the police.

'Well well well!' Nabov had said, staring hard at Zhenya as the latter came in the office. 'So *you're* Evgeny Aleksandrovich Smirnov, are you? Well now, sir, would you happen to have any proof of identity about your person?'

Zhenya got out his internal passport and his other bits of ID, also a few certificates and so on, and put them down on the table. The police Captain snatched them almost before they landed, stacked them in a pile, and started scribbling something in his notebook. Then he said:

'Now, sir, if you wouldn't mind troubling to jot down a few details about your life story on that piece of paper there.'

Zhenya didn't take long to finish, and handed over half a page. After all, his experience of life was not exactly extensive.

'No, no, sir, this won't do at all!' Nabov reproved him, screwing up the sheet of paper and flinging it in the bin. 'Look here lad, let's have it out straight away. I want you to put down absolutely everything you can remember about your, hem, so-called life. I'm not settling for less than ten pages, and I'm not letting you out of here until I get them.'

'He has a strange way of putting things, that Nabov,' said Zhenya. 'I haven't the faintest what he meant when he said "your so-called life". It was a sweat remembering enough to fill ten pages too. I had to put down all this real nonsense, like the time I hit my little sister on the mouth and made her lip bleed...'

But Nabov hadn't been shocked by any of this, apparently; on the contrary, he'd given Zhenya a friendly slap on the back.

'Well done, lad,' he'd said. 'With a life like that, you're safe enough hanging about in this town. However, hem, let me ask you to cast your mind back one more time and reassure me that you haven't got any crimes on your conscience. Not done anyone in by any chance, have you, stabbed them or drowned them, I mean? Ever been involved in any burglaries? Picked any pockets? What about forgery?'

'Now that really did get my goat,' Zhenya told me. 'I was so angry I grabbed a chair and went to smash it against the wall. But then he took out his gun and looked as if he was going to fire it in the air, so I put the chair down. Then he wagged his finger at me...'

I thought, my God, this is all we needed. Why on earth did that idiot

Sergei Vasilevich decide that he had to give Zhenya his own habit of losing his temper and playing round with chairs? What a stupid mess!

'But then Nabov apologized and said he'd only been pulling my leg,' Zhenya went on. 'Only that wasn't the end of it. Then he started asking me whether I'd ever caught any villains or exposed any criminals, any small fry would do. I told him about how these two gangsters attacked me once. One got away after shooting me in the leg, that's why I still have the limp, but I managed to hand the other one over to the police. Well, Nabov seemed really chuffed by that. He started sort of walking round me in circles staring at me, and rubbing his hands. So why don't you join up in one of the *druzhinas*° at the building site, he asked? I said I already had, of course. And then he says, "Well, in that case it shouldn't be any trouble for you to catch Venka the Spade,° and turn him in here next week, should it?" OK, I said. But then I said, there's one thing puzzling me, Captain: why haven't you arrested him yourself yet? But he wouldn't answer that, he just said, "That's none of your business: you've got special talents, I hear, so let's see what you can do with them." '

But how on earth *was* Zhenya to catch Venka the Spade all by himself, and without a gun, when an armed police officer had never managed to, after chasing him dawn to dusk for weeks? When I asked Zhenya this, though, he only winked.

'That's exactly the point, you see: we shouldn't be trying to catch him dawn to dusk, we'd be much better off working dusk to dawn. He's a night bird. I'll have a word with some of the lads and we'll work out a plan together. You can help too.'

I felt riled by Zhenya's certainty about that last point. Sure, I'd had plenty of experience dealing with all kinds of fools and con-men and petty-minded bureaucrats, not to speak of bent officials. I'd developed great skill in using my chosen weapon—to wit, the pen, which is mightier than the sword, as we all know. But I knew that Venka the Spade didn't give a damn for my cutting wit, my scathing sarcasm, my allegations, or my insinuations. As soon as we came face to face, he'd just get out his pistol, shove it right in my face, and make me hand over my death-dealing pen—and my watch into the bargain. I knew that for certain. He'd already done it once.

This was the sort of sobering thought that was going through my head as I went in to work on the paper. I was so worried about what might happen that I couldn't concentrate all day. To make things worse, I had to stay late that night. Usually I'd have enjoyed it, but that evening the sight of darkness outside the window gave me no pleasure at all.

It was Chugalinsky who'd kept me.

'Dima!' he'd said, looking at me in this hangdog way. 'Do me a favour, be a good lad. Just cast your eye over this, would you? I've done a story on that man you told me about when we were following that lead down at the state farm. If Konstantin Petrovich won't print it here, then I'll just have to try sending it somewhere else, won't I?'

I started reading the story. It was called 'The Wonder of the Twentieth Century'.

'A local group of scientists, headed by Comrade Engineer Grushnyak, has achieved a scientific breakthrough of world significance. They have invented nothing less than a prototype for twenty-first-century man. The artificial brain installed in the prototype—to which the scientists have given the name "Evgeny Aleksandrovich Smirnov"—has truly incredible capacities. At the moment "Evgeny Smirnov" is working as a master builder on the site of a new block of flats. The site director, Comrade Gurev, told our reporter, "Yes, Smirnov is a very good worker, very conscientious, he can lay around five thousand bricks a shift."° Our reporter also interviewed "Evgeny Aleksandrovich", who was able to supply him with the following information. The artificial man has read more than one thousand books, he knows over 300,000 Russian words, has met over one million people, has seventy-five friends but only one girlfriend (his mother). He also knows at least 175 words in German. One must bear in mind that these astonishing capacities have all been built in to him artificially by the talented team of scientists...'

I couldn't bear to read any more.

'Chug, for God's sake,' I exploded. 'Three hundred thousand Russian words? How do you expect anyone to believe that? That's twice as many as in the average one-volume dictionary! Where on earth did you get that figure from?'

'Evgeny Aleksandrovich told me that himself.'

'Well! And who in God's name told you that idiot Grushnyak was the head of a whole group of scientists?'

'Gurev did. That site director. He's the only one down there that knows who Evgeny Aleksandrovich is.'

'Well! And in any case, the whole story's a write-off, you know.'

'What do you mean, a write-off?'

'Exactly what I say, a write-off. If he's an "artificial man", he can't have a mother, can he? And in any case, it would be fatal to let him find out about where he really comes from.'

Don't imagine Chug caught on straight away. It took a whole hour before he twigged. Anyway, off he went in the end, tail between his legs. Just a few seconds later Zhenya himself burst in. He was in a great stew. He told me some reporter from the paper had been down asking him all sorts of questions. Zhenya didn't like that one bit—there were lots of blokes down there who were much better builders than he was, he said. He'd only talked to the reporter so as to get rid of him. Now Zhenya was begging me to stop the story getting published. He'd never live it down otherwise.

'Why don't you just tell me where on earth you got those figures from?'

'What does it matter? I had to tell him something. He kept pestering me to give him some figures. I was nearly going mad with him nagging, and in the end I started to feel sort of sorry for him too, he was such a cretin.'

I gave a start on hearing this. What, even Zhenya felt sorry for cretins, just like everyone else did?

'OK, Zhenya, you've got your way,' I said. 'I'll make sure they don't use that story. Anyway, it's high time we both went home. I'll see you to the door—it's on my way.'

'Sure, let's go!' Zhenya said cheerfully. 'It's getting quite late. Why, we might even run into Venka the Spade. That would be great—I might even get the chance to practise something really fancy on him...'

'Stop arsing about, for God's sake,' I snapped. 'If you're going to talk like that, you can walk home on your own. Leave Venka to the police, let them practise their fancy stuff on him if they feel like it.'

I could have killed Nabov. Fancy taking risks like that! With the Wonder of the Twentieth Century!

A Few Drinks°

I was dying to introduce the 'live robot' to my mate Vasya Golubev. It was a bit late for visiting in an ordinary sense, but Vasya's wife never lets up nagging him, so he doesn't get to bed before the small hours.

Vasya was tremendously curious about Zhenya: he sat there without taking his eyes off him. But when we got up to leave, Vasya gave me a pointed look, and said, 'So one more wonderful idea bites the dust.'

I kept my cool. Zhenya wouldn't understand anyway.

But it got to me all the same. What did Vasya mean by saying that one more idea had bitten the dust? Next day I asked him.

'They were going to manufacture the happiest man in the world, so I heard,' Vasya said. 'Well, that Zhenka certainly ain't him. Oh, he's happy enough, I'll grant you that, but that's because he's as thick as two short planks, I could see that soon as I'd talked to him for a few minutes. The world's always been full of cheerful morons. What *I* want to see is someone who's happy *and sharp*.'

I expostulated with him here, saying that I felt that actually Evgeny Aleksandrovich wasn't stupid at all: he simply had a very individual and interesting world-view.

'Why not have another chat with him,' I suggested. 'Don't leap to any hasty conclusions.'

So next day, after work, we both dropped in on Zhenya. When he opened the door, I was startled to see that he was wearing glasses. Zhenya said rather defensively that he'd only been trying on Sergei Vasilevich's glasses, and he'd forgotten to take them off afterwards.

'We've come to drag you out boozing,' Vasya said. 'It's my birthday today, so the drinks are on me. Here, you, get off my foot,' he snapped at me, 'the lad's quite old enough to make up his own mind.'

Zhenya watched me take my foot off Vasya's with innocent curiosity, and said he'd be right out, he just had to get his overalls off.

Whilst he was busy in the bathroom, I lammed into Vasya:

'What in God's name do you think you're up to? Taking the Wonder of the Twentieth Century out boozing? You'd think you'd have learnt by now, with your wife always on at you.'

'Oh, I get! He's a "Wonder", and I'm not,' said Vasya, smiling sourly. 'I expect that's why you never bother trying to stop me drinking. On the contrary: you're usually glad enough to join in when I ask you. Any case, your "Wonder" is just a bloke who doesn't take time making up his mind. That's all there is to him, if you ask me. It was one thing sorting that old bully Zhritsyn° out, but so soon as he gets any real trouble to deal with, that Zhenka of yours will just fall to pieces. It'll end in tears, you mark my words.'

I reflected that he was right, up to a point. Zhenya really didn't seem to have much sense of self-preservation. I began to suspect that his anonymous creators had saddled him with the idea that peace and quiet and order were the natural state of things, and that you could stick your nose in anywhere without pause for thought...

By now Zhenya had finished changing, but I wouldn't let him go off with Vasya. Vasya went off on his own, whilst I read Zhenya a lecture about how to behave. I said he should take more care where he pushed his nose, especially at work.

'So you always keep your nose out yourself, do you?'

'Look, Zhenya, I'm a journalist, I'm just not in the same position. I'm in the penalty area, if you like to put it that way. Anyone who fouls me up pays for it quickly. But you're right out there mid-field. It's much harder for you to score, and all kinds of things can happen without the referee noticing.'

'What on earth do you think I *have* been up to?' Zhenka asked, all bug-eyed innocence. 'I haven't done anything yet. I just lay my bricks, and that's it.'

But I soon realized that wasn't the half of it. The next Sunday I went round to Zhenya's again. The front door of the flat was open, and so was the door into the living-room. And what I saw through the second door was the kind of scene that made me wonder whether I should rush straight out and find a public telephone. Only I didn't know whether to call the police or an ambulance first.

The dining-table—the same one where Sergei Vasilevich's wife, Yuliya Semyonovna, had served us up that dainty tea a few weeks before—was covered with empty bottles. The room was full of people in torn, dishevelled clothes, each sitting motionless and gripping another empty bottle. They had reached the morose, silent stage of inebriation. The ringleader was sitting slumped by the table, head in his hands. Someone else was sprawled out on the couch, squashing it into horrible contortions. Head propped on his fists, he was gazing obsessively at the chess-board in front of him. A third man—a young lad, to be more accurate—was propped in an armchair, with Sergei Vasilevich's microscope on a stool in front of him. He was squinting down it with one eye. There wasn't a sign of Zhenya.

I went up to the man by the table.

'Where's Zhenya?' I asked.

'Whassat you saying?' he croaked.

'Whassat you saying?' bawled someone behind me.

I swung round. It was the young lad. He'd leapt out of his armchair and was waving his empty bottle over his head.

I went up to the man on the couch.

'Where's Zhenya?' I asked him.

Slowly the man turned his head towards me, tearing his gaze from the chess-board. Slowly, with immense difficulty, he squeezed the words from his mouth, like someone forcing the last drops of glue from a tube:

'Keep your... effing nose... out of my... bleeding business...'

'Over my dead effing body!' someone bawled behind me. It was the young man again, still waving his bottle.

Then there was dead silence again. I searched Sergei Vasilevich's laboratory; then I looked under all the tables and the couch. Finally I went into the kitchen. No sign of Zhenya anywhere. I wondered whether to get the neighbours in to help, but I decided to have one last check in the bathroom. I tried the door: it was locked. I knocked on it.

'Who's there?' It was Zhenya's voice, sounding quite calm and normal.

'Open the door,' I hissed.

I heard the door being unbolted. Zhenya was sitting on a stool by the bath and reading a book.

'Have you seen what's going on?' he asked. I nodded in reply.

'I thought they might calm down if I left them to it,' Zhenya said. 'They've stopped shouting since I went out.'

I asked him to tell me the whole story, from start to finish.

'Well, the start was fine,' said Zhenya. 'We drank toasts to friendship and all that. As for the finish, I don't think it's happened yet.'

'You do actually know them, don't you?'

'Course I do! The one over by the table's the site manager. The other's the foreman, and the bloke in the armchair's our driver. They wanted me to stand them a few drinks out of my first pay-packet. My old man did warn me off doing things like that, but I decided I'd have them round here all the same. I showed them how the microscope works, taught them to play chess, and all that stuff. Was that such a bad idea?'

'It would have been an even better one to have started the evening without quite so many bottles on the table. Then there'd have been more chance that your workers' education class would have been a success.'

'Well, I wasn't to know they'd bring their own drink with them too...'

'Look, Zhenya,' I said. 'Let's ask your friends nicely if they wouldn't mind leaving now, shall we? After all, you don't want them staying here all night, do you?'

'Suits me,' said Zhenya obediently.

The guests were sitting in exactly the same poses as when I had left. Zhenya went up to the site manager and stroked his head gently. The man tensed all his muscles and croaked:

'You just say that once more!'

'Say that once more!' the driver parroted, but at twice the decibel level. He was on his feet again.

Zhenya went over to the foreman and patted him on the shoulder. The man raised his eyes with exquisite slowness from the chess-board. Then he squeezed out two more words:

'I'll—effing...'

It was all getting beyond a joke. Then I noticed that the driver was grimacing and twitching constantly.

'What on earth is he looking at through that microscope?'

'A fly, I think.'

'Well, then for God's sake get it out of there then, and put something more wholesome in. What about a piece of bread?'

'Poof, no!' Zhenya dismissed this with a wave. 'It makes you sick whatever you look at through one of those things.'

I took the microscope away, and carried it back into the laboratory. The driver sighed with relief, and wiped his sweaty forehead with the tail of his shirt.

That wasn't the last of it though. By the time we had got the three of them off on their way (they'd reached the maudlin and querulous phase), it was very late.

I was dying for bed, so I left. But a few days later Zhenya rang me.

'I've got the sack. For turning up to work drunk. But for God's sake don't imagine it's true.'

What was I expected to think, then, after seeing him with those three piss-heads the other night?

But when I actually confronted Zhenya, and saw his blue eyes fixed on me in that steady, honest gaze (which was so like Sergei Vasilevich the vet's), I felt ashamed of my doubts. No, surely this wasn't right: I'd have to do something to rescue the lad.

'You see, the point is they're all on the fiddle,' Zhenya told me. 'They rip off everything: planks, bricks, doors, even door-catches. I saw that driver, you know, the one who was round here the other evening, flogging a whole lorry-load of wood to some fishy-looking character the other day. When they came round here, I told them I was going to tell the police what they were up to. So now they've cooked up some document to say that I came in to work drunk, and got a dismissal order issued.'

'The main thing is to keep our cool, Zhenya,' I said. 'You've been stitched up, and that sometimes has dreadful effects on a man. You mustn't let yourself fall apart, start whining about how there's no justice in the world and so on. Keep a hold on yourself: we'll get you out of this.'

'I don't propose to start whining,' Zhenya said with a shrug. His lips (which, by the way, were rather well modelled) gave a faint smile. An impish light danced in his eyes. I could only marvel at the scientists' virtuosity: that light looked so natural, it must have been some work to get it right.

No doubt there'll be hell to pay with that impish look in the end, I thought. But it's obvious that Zhenya's been given the right foundation. He hasn't let those bastards and scoundrels turn him into a miserable little moaner.

I thought that I'd only have to make a couple of telephone calls, and Zhenya would be all right. I remembered how once Nabov had had a complaint from four strapping young lads (Kolya, Tolya, Shurik, and Sashka were their names, I remember). They'd 'blown it' for very similar reasons to Zhenya. Well, that's what local papers are for. We sat down and rang round a few people. We didn't even need to print anything: we just put the story round, invoked glasnost° and appealed to public opinion, and bob's your uncle. They got their jobs back straight away.

Unfortunately, though, it turned out that the elusive Evgeny Aleksandrovich had put more noses out of joint than those four lads had. Gurev refused to go back on the dismissal order.

Well, you could see his point in a way. You never knew what to expect from an 'artificial man'. Best keep him at arm's length. That was what Gurev thought, at any rate.

And so Zhenya had to take his case to court.

[1962]

◆ BELLA AKHMADULINA ◆

Of mixed Italian and Tatar descent, Akhmadulina was born in 1937 and brought up in Moscow, where she graduated from the Gorky Institute of Literature in 1960. Her first collection appeared two years later, to high praise; since then Akhmadulina has established herself as one of the most talented Russian poets of the late twentieth century. Though Akhmadulina's name is customarily linked with those of other Moscow writers who came to the fore since the 1960s, such as Evgeny Evtushenko and Andrei Voznesensky, her work has little in common with theirs; she writes for a small circle of readers, rather than an auditorium, and does not pose as a political commentator; she is also more gifted in a technical sense than Evtushenko, if not than Voznesensky. Many of her poems, including the piece anthologized here, take the standard themes of Soviet women's writing (motherhood, city life, the successful writer's trip to the dacha or to exotic places) and turn them into rich and often threatening meditations on feminine identity and human existence.

Lines Written during a Sleepless Night in Tbilisi

(Russian text p. 473)

I, who leapt beneath the Mtskhetian white moon,
I, who wept with every muscle, every bone,
I, who became a shadow, a pale bar
slipping away from Sveti-Tskhoveli church,
I who was stretched and pulled like silver wire
then pushed, Tbilisi, through your needle's eye,
I, who till dawn came lived beneath a star,
whose blood was frozen in your hothouse blast,
I, who can never fall asleep at nights,
whose madness scorches up my friends,
whose eye has a pupil like a stallion's,
who recoil from sleep like a trapped animal,
I, singing on bridges with the rising sun,
'May our transgressions be forgiven us,
have pity on our scorched and famished bellies,

and make them golden with a gift of *hashi*,'
I, who writhed along the sheets, across,
contorted by insomnia's bad jokes,
Oh God in heaven, lying in that deep
bed, like a cradle, how I longed for sleep.

I longed for it, drifting to sleep or waking,
for sleep as leisurely as drinking;
I longed to suck on sleep like sickly sweets,
with my saliva melting its excess;

to wake late in the mornings, eyes tight closed
so I could make a secret for myself
out of the weather, indulging myself in bed
with promises hardly registered as yet.

My brain is eyeless as a burnt-out planet,
my pulse beats soft as sap in wintry trunks.
I want to sleep again, for ages. Sleep for ever,
wrapped and enclosed, a child in her mother's belly.

[1969]

◆ MIRA LINKEVICH ◆

Mira Linkevich, who was born in 1909, graduated from the Moscow Institute of Foreign Languages in 1931, and then worked as a translator and interpreter. In 1937, her husband, the German Communist Karl Weidner, who had been living in the Soviet Union for some years, was arrested; he was later to die in captivity. About six months later Linkevich suffered the customary fate of wives of 'enemies of the people', and was herself arrested; she then served a ten-year prison-camp sentence in the Komi Autonomous Republic. She now lives in Yaroslavl, just north of Moscow.

How the Cadres were Broken in

At one of my early interrogations I vaguely noticed that there was a young man in the office. He had the pleasant, open face of a lad straight from the village; I accepted his presence without question, knowing that he must be some kind of a trainee.

At first this lad treated me very kindly. If we were ever left alone together, he would immediately offer me a cigarette, warning me to drop it the minute I heard anyone coming down the corridor. At that stage of my interrogation I was still allowed to sit down; later, I was to be deprived of even that elementary comfort, and would be made to stand days and nights on end with only short and occasional breaks (they called it 'riding the conveyor belt').° The investigator and his young helper worked shifts.

During those first stages, my lad used to get visits from a colleague who worked in another office—he too was scarcely more than a boy—and we all used to chat together. I think the second lad was probably a townie; he seemed quite well-informed and sociable, at any rate. They seemed to assume I was a girl their own age,—though I was in fact 28—, and we talked quite naturally and unconstrainedly. It didn't last, though. Quite soon my 'friend' clammed up on me: he stopped talking, and broke off all contact of any kind, even when we were alone.

Later I gathered that the two lads were students from the Saratov NKVD° college. They were breaking the cadres in, and the schooling they were putting them through wasn't hard to work out. Phase One: Observation. Look and listen, use your eyes and ears. Phase Two: Getting Tough. Don't trust them, they know just how to take you in. Even more important, don't start feeling sorry for them. They're enemies of the people, you've got to chill them out.

We'd obviously got to the end of Phase One; now we were well into Phase Two. I was made to stand night after night. For the time being, my trainee was simply keeping guard. He never said a word to me, so he had absolutely nothing to do. I felt sorry for him, in a way. I'd hear him ring down to the buffet so he could have a word with the girl behind the counter. 'Eh, Klava, what've you got to eat today, then, love? Mmmm, that does sound good!' Well, what else was he supposed to do? But the course moved on inexorably, and soon we'd got to Interrogation Practice.

I could see my lad practising: he'd put a pile of blank paper on the desk and work on... signing his name. He'd sign a blank sheet, then stuff it in the waste-bin. Then another, then another, till the bin was overflowing. He'd pack it down and then go on with his work. That phase didn't go on very long either, though. Soon the teachers told them: 'You can have a go at cross-questioning them now. Don't lay it on too thick, but don't be soft on them either.' My lad would take a sheet of paper and intone: 'Record of Interrogation'. What followed reminded me irresistibly of a torture scene in a book by Mayne Reid° that I'd read when I was a child. I hadn't understood at the time why the water torture was considered such a terrible ordeal. After all, it didn't hurt, did it, dripping water on someone's head? But now I did understand. The poor lad had a terribly limited vocabulary; his whole repertoire consisted of a few phrases, which he kept repeating in an endless, monotonous, drone. His questions were stupid, meaningless, but I had to answer them somehow. And I did answer them, trying to speak as laconically as possible, so that I didn't run out of saliva. For hour after hour we would go through the same routine:

'Well, tell me about it, then.'

'I haven't anything to say.'

'Why not, eh? Why not?'

'Because I haven't.'

'Because doesn't mean nothing.'

And so on, and on, and on.

I tried switching off, thinking about something else, dipping into my memories, filling my mind with fantasies of all kinds. I'd imagine that the door of the office cupboard was covered in pictures, seeing all kinds of visions on the surface of the wood, or I'd think up huge lists of famous people whose names all began with a certain letter...

The poor lad: he was like a badly trained parrot, muttering the same half-dozen phrases all the time. How crude their training methods were: it was like something in the circus. Making a limited intellect go through the hoops; turning an unspoilt, good-natured lad into a robot: it was barbaric.

But now Phase Three had come along. Their masters had told them: 'Enough shilly-shallying! It's time for the real stuff now!' Obediently, my nice lad began to imitate his superiors: he started bawling at me and whacking his ruler on the table. It was all-out psychological warfare! What a poor show he put up, too: as stilted as he was clumsy. And coarse, to boot: every other word had four letters.°

Every so often his colleague, the same young lad who'd been so friendly earlier on, would drop in to see how his mate was getting on. It was clear, though, that this second boy was in a quite different class by now: he'd turned into a real star pupil.

'What's this? Haven't you cracked this beauty yet? You shouldn't be so nice to her, you know! If you keep the pressure up, she'll start talking right away! I worked mine over good and proper, you know, and he cracked on the spot!'

[*1970s*]

◆ ELENA SHVARTS ◆

Born in 1948 and brought up in Leningrad, Elena Shvarts began a course in literature at the University, but found studying there too boring for her to stand it for more than a year. Though she eventually did complete a course of higher education, graduating from the Theatre Institute in 1973, she considers herself to be entirely self-educated. Three collections of her poetry were published in the West during the 1980s, and a considerable body of her work has been translated into other European languages. Her first Soviet collection, however, appeared only in 1990, though readings and unofficial publications had made her work known to large numbers of Russian poetry lovers before that.

Sale of a Historian's Library

(Russian text p. 475)

See the man sit in the corner there naked,
wearing a shoe that's not his, with a diamond buckle;
the man with a pinched pale face, who never knew fame
and lived in the Pryazhka madhouse more than at home.

Stirrups flash real gold in another time,
their buildings, though solid, are larded with fancy;
but when you have to live in your own century
a Budyonny cap means no more than a cloth one might.

And so he walked away, away and over the bridges
down the spines of books—crackling and adrift—
to mantuasoys, to cheekbones bottled in spirit
where poison is served in a crackle-glaze dish.

Where Freemasons incubate chickens at night
from eggs boiled so hard the yolks are like slate:
but their plumage is glassy, and they cheep faintly
and their faces shine with a headless light.

Into another year he went, with a wave of pilgrims,
but who will drink the waters that midnight flecked?
When evening falls the child goes barefoot,
picking the dry dun carnations of Nazareth.

And everywhere, in fields and taverns, he looked for
the extravagant sweep of a poisoned sword:
but the blade cut into a heart that was fleshless
till his courage was gone and his reason fogged.

Man's countenance means far more than a sounding cymbal:
some people resemble ears, or nostrils, or teeth:
time was when his unshaved beard grew thickly,
not balding and wispy, as in our days.

All souls have black in the white, like a wood in springtime,
but then St Francis comes scattering light:
a solitary soul is enough, one single,
for the world to glow with an odalisque's shine.

But the wheel span round, tore his clothing to fragments.
The legions of doubles are fighting on every flank;
yet they cannot be found, it is hopeless to trap them
by joining up in the manuscripts' ranks.

The crop-haired Queen mounts the steps to the scaffold,
but the ends of the circle must be joined:
so the nape of a girl's neck shines in the distance
as she stands and fixes her gaze on the south.

Nearer and nearer she comes: from her corset
she draws out a knife, and closes in;
you look like a king for a moment, Marat,
though your slipper is running in blood as you dance.

The centre of the world is forever
the glint on my finger, in Socrates' eye,
in a tram, on the moon, in clouds grey-knotted,
in the ruptured maw of a slaughtered private.

Where Nero sings in garlands of flame
and pulls a face for the looking-glass,
where Caligula so loves the moon
that, weeping, he calls her to come to his couch,

where Cleopatra's a moth in the night
with a dusting of stars on her fragile wings;
the wooden fleet has been snatched by a magnet
that pulls whatever is *not* made of iron.

O, but he loved them all—he even loved Peter,
who split Russia in two with his new-whetted knife:
and spread the dark jam of his serfs on the streets—
but their souls skipped away as he swatted, like flies.

Perhaps it was he who took Paul the valerian,
and pleaded his regiment should not be expelled,
but the Tsar only raged at his shade, began cursing,
shouting and stamping his feet like a child...

He stands in an empty room—they have cleared it,
the coloured glass of his window is smashed;
his notes are erased, they have taken the needle
that fastened his shade to the vacuous earth.

What he loved still more was to find in the archives
a name that time had forgotten for good;
how strange it was to sit in the lamplight
and look on the blind, gummy eyes of the dead,

but he knew they were grateful.
There wasn't much chance
that he himself would survive the past;
a tide of souls eddies where we come in
and we pull our names from a hat, like straws.

(1970s)

◆ ELENA CHIZHOVA ◆

Born in Leningrad on 4 May 1957, Chizova studied English at the Herzen Pedagogical Institute and then taught English in secondary schools. She began writing poetry in the 1980s, but very little of her work has been published in Russia; however, the verse play *Mary Stuart* appeared in 1993.

Cassandra

(Russian text p. 488)

Whole-breasted as billows that break on a bank—unwilling!
Not a voice crying—a singing reed
at Apollo's lips I beat. It is painful
to bury my cry in the maw of this steed
of wood. For whom, for what reason
must someone prophesy shame and doom?
I am the black plague that eats Priam's city,
not a woman—a sting. The Erinnyes' choir
has no pity. The blind make our prices,
hope burns on the funeral pyre.
And this voice, this voice honed by treason,
strong and sharp as the claw of a kite,
dives for carrion, folding its wings
high above the strange tangles of enemies, friends.
So the gods sport with the tides of men,
plait them into the tail of a horse.

(1986–8)

◆ LYUDMILA PETRUSHEVSKAYA ◆

Born in Moscow in 1939, Petrushevskaya studied at the University there, before beginning work at Moscow Television as a scenario writer. She first became known as a playwright, and her dramas have been very widely performed in Russia and abroad. However, she is also one of the most talented prose writers of recent years, the author of powerful and original prose fiction that courageously confronts the disintegration of Soviet and post-Soviet society. The quality of Petrushevskaya's work was recognized when her most recent story, 'Time. Night' was short-listed for the first Booker Russian Novel prize in 1992; an English translation was published by Virago/Knopf in 1993.

Both the stories by Petrushevskaya here appear by permission of the author and of the publishers, Moskovskii rabochii and Almanakh Aprel.

Words

The first thing I heard out of him was: look, there's a girl sitting alone, wouldn't mind nuzzling up to *her*.

There were two of them, him and a young guy who sat down across from me. I could see from the young guy's face that he was counting on me paying attention specifically to him. He was acting embarrassed, haughty, expectant all at once, behaving as though everyone was staring at him: his looks, his haircut, his shirt. Maybe there was something he was good at—playing the accordion, or designing boxes at the souvenir plant. Or maybe it was something else, something he was keeping to himself for the time being so that he could amaze everyone later on.

The other, older one probably knew something about some of the qualities his junior was hiding for the moment and would let out when the time was right, little by little. It was clear he'd seen it all before, he was visibly bored by the whole thing. No doubt the younger one had been unable to hold in his talents indefinitely, and had already boasted about them to his friends, who had grown blasé about hearing them. And now the older man was waiting for the younger one to begin his routine of revealing himself to me little by little. He was a bit jealous of the young guy because of all this, so he asked me for starters himself, 'Hey miss, have a guess—which one of us two is the youngest?'

I said I wasn't going to answer that one.

My friend is always telling me off, she says I answer drunks back and let them draw me into long conversations. But I can't do anything about it. It's not because I think that all people are equally interesting, or that drunks are any more sincere than anyone else. It's not because I don't get enough human contact, or get hooked on the slightest sign of attention. Everything happens without my knowing it. They ask me, and I respond automatically. It embarrasses me that I'd rather not answer, that I'd prefer to stand there as though I hadn't heard the question or seen the person look me in the face. But in fact, even before it occurs to me that I'd rather not get caught up in some long conversation, I'm already responding to the first stupid word. They don't usually expect they'll get answered straight away, it fazes them, so they stand there helplessly themselves, wondering whether to go on talking or not. But they only hesitate for a moment; almost at once everything suddenly begins to seem all right, just as it should be, and then they really start to fancy themselves. They start to explain at length that they weren't thinking anything bad about a girl like me. They fall all over themselves trying to explain, to grasp the meaning of things which seemed so clear only a moment ago, when they knew that you're not supposed to hassle young women... but *why*? Suddenly this question rises up before them in all its enormity. They wrestle with it, since they've now lost hold of common-sense values, of rule number one: that you mustn't talk to strangers without good reason, which in their case they didn't have, they started talking to me just out of being social, and now they're trying to wriggle out of it as best they can. They feel terribly guilty for having begun the conversation; but now they've got a response and have to make excuses, apologize, explain what purpose the whole thing serves.

These two, the young guy and the older one, were slightly tipsy. But in fact neither of them, especially not the older one, had any need to explain why he had started talking to me; it was the sort of relaxed brief encounter you get on a train. While the young guy stared out the coach window, bracing himself on the seat of the bench with both arms, his head sunk into his shoulders, the older one chatted with me cheerfully. I liked him right away—not in the sense young girls mean when they say 'I like him as a person', but in a very relaxed, cheerful, and carefree way.

It was clear he was paying absolutely no attention to the kind of person I was, he was just wholly involved in our conversation. I don't mean he didn't notice what I had on, how my hair was done, how I talked, of course. But it didn't matter to him, just as it's never mattered to me how I look myself. The whole thing was following its own path, I wasn't having to think about it every second. And I'm certain he wasn't thinking about it either, perhaps because both of us understood so clearly that we were just having a brief, relaxed conversation. Nothing more. We were too different. He told me right away that he was a carpenter and joiner, a master plumber and electrician, he'd made everything in his apartment—everything, from the kitchen appliances to the shelving and even the floor lamp.

He told me his wife had died in childbirth, of a heart attack.

I didn't question him further about anything myself, but not because I was afraid he wouldn't want to tell me. After all, it does sometimes happen that people don't respond to questions because when someone asks them a question they suddenly realize that their secrets, till then no use to anyone, have indeed suddenly become just that, secrets, and now need to be guarded.

No, I wasn't afraid he wouldn't answer my questions. Everything was so simple and open with him that I didn't need to ask questions. Instead, I told him about my daughter, and he told me about the child he'd been going to have, but who had got cut up when they did the Caesarean section. I told him that my daughter lives in a dacha right out in the country—four hours on two different stopping trains and then eight miles on foot if you can't get a lift.

I told him that last summer I only went to work once a week, so I could spend the summer with my daughter. But now that I've transferred to a different institute, I have to be at work two days a week, and now my daughter lives in the country with someone else's grandmother, in my husband's brother's family, 4 years old, and all alone already.

He told me he'd been alone since then, and that his wife had died in his arms—he'd been in the operating room during the delivery...

And I told him about how every time I leave my daughter to catch the three o'clock bus, when I'm crossing the field alone, I'm walking away for another four days, about going the long way round to avoid the ravine, which I'm afraid to cross, about how I always very vividly imagine that war will break out when I get back to town, and my daughter will be stuck in the country...

It made no difference that he was lying to me, or that I was telling him the truth. I like it when a person tells lies about himself. I welcome lies, I'm glad to go along with them, to take them as the absolute truth, because they might, after all, turn out to be exactly that. It doesn't change in the least the way I think about him. It's much finer and easier to accept someone as he wants to present himself. I don't try to construct anything out of the fragments of truth that sometimes leak out, or force their way out, in spite of all his efforts. Leave well enough alone.

He told me that 20-year-old girls are all over him, but it's not what you might think—his two-room apartment plays a big role. And he never feels the way he did with his wife with any of those girls...

Every so often the young guy would get up, then take his seat again, and I began to get the impression that they were travelling with someone else, that there was a whole crowd of them in the coach. So when yet another person took the free seat next to me, across from the young guy, and immediately started talking to me, I answered him as well. But I wasn't so carried away I didn't notice that he began the conversation completely differently than the first man. Unlike him, this man wasn't open, direct, unobtrusive. The first man, the older man, hadn't tried to force anything out of me, he wasn't interested in me in such a crude, obvious way.

This new one, as soon as he sat down, picked up something I said, and kept on repeating it and shaking his head. 'Well I'll be...' Then he asked, 'You mean to say a girl like you doesn't have anyone to go home to?' Then he started sniggering, the numbskull. I should have cut him off right then, not talked to him at all.

But he kept on talking. The other two lapsed into silence, then suddenly lit up cigarettes, both from the older man's match, and began smoking right there in the coach.

And then something terrible happened. Everyone travelling in the coach began yelling at them. The other men especially. And it was obvious that they had been wanting to yell for a long time, that the smoking was only an excuse, a pretext. Then I said to the two men, 'Maybe they're right, you really shouldn't smoke?'

Then they both got up and left, and I didn't see them again, and that numbskull went on tormenting me the whole way back.

Maybe they went to smoke between the coaches, and then stayed there the whole way, or maybe they changed coaches, or got off the train altogether at some station.

But I was left feeling as though I had broken some kind of law, done something that no one should do.

[1988]

Translated by Brian Thomas Oles

◆ LYUDMILA PETRUSHEVSKAYA ◆

Medea

It's a terrible story to tell, but it all started with me getting a taxi. I started chatting with the driver—you know how it is. I was complaining that a taxi ordered this morning hadn't shown up, they didn't even call. So grandmother, who's 73, missed her train. We all got in an awful state, and by the time grandmother did get through on the train, no one was there to meet her, so she went off to the dacha on her own (in another taxi, mark you), but by then the kids had gone off into Moscow. It was a real mess: the whole day gone and fifty roubles down the drain.

'Well, write and complain, then,' said the driver.

'They didn't even call.'

'Once,' the driver said, 'I got stranded in a new part of town. I drove into a pot-hole, there isn't a public telephone in sight, so I'm running around like mad. It's five minutes before I have to be there, and there's no way I'm going to make it. I stopped another driver and asked him to call. Don't know if he did, even now.'

'The most awful thing was that grandmother got in such a state.'

'That's not such an awful thing,' the driver answered.

'You never know what it could lead to, at her age.'

'And once I ended up at Troparevo when the fare was in Izmailovo. That time, I floored the engine and made it.'

The taxi driver was about 40, a real weakling, in a checked shirt with frayed cuffs. A half-cock worker, as a gay film director used to say—a brilliant guy, by the way, he died not long ago. A half-cock worker, or a junior half-cock worker—the kind that makes you lick your chops: he won't put up a fight. Small, half-closed eyes, glazed and weak-looking. (You need the portrait for what follows.) Sunken cheeks, but there's no smell of sweat in the taxi. Half-cock workers usually only wash on Saturdays. They only have sex on Saturdays too, after they've been to the bath-house. So this one did wash. That's not the point.

The conversation flowed on. The driver kept urging me, in a kind of nagging undercurrent, not to complain about the other driver. Anything can happen, he said.

'Are you working tomorrow?'

'Yes,' he answered, his guard going up straight away.

'From when?'

'From one.'

'You see, I've ordered a taxi to take us to the airport at six tomorrow morning, and I'm afraid it won't come. That really will be a mess! I'll never pick one up on the street at that hour.'

He didn't take the hint. Instead, he said again that, judging by what I'd told him, our disaster was exactly nothing compared with what can go wrong.

'So it's nothing, is it,' I said sourly. 'Sure, everyone has a story to tell. Of course mine isn't the worst.'

'It isn't the worst,' he echoed. 'The things that happen!'

'Don't tell me! This woman I know told me one of her classmates took her two children to Siberia, to stay at her mother-in-law's. It was winter, freezing cold, the youngest—a little boy a year old—came down with pneumonia, and there's no hospital for miles around. She took the children to the station and got a train. The little boy died on the way. At the other end, out she gets, with the little girl, 5 years old, and the dead baby. The husband was waiting at the station, and when he saw what had happened, he hit his wife and broke her jaw. They sent him to prison for four years. His wife was left with the girl, and no job. She began to make a bit of money writing all kinds of nonsense for some newspaper. She earned next to nothing, forty or fifty roubles a month, something like that. One day, she went to the editorial office just before closing time to collect her money, taking her daughter along. The daughter was being a real nuisance. The woman had to drag her along bodily, then right there, outside the office, she gave the girl a slap in the face and hit her on the nose. The caretaker saw, and she called the police. They put the girl in care and prohibited access. That was that. The court found the mother psychologically abnormal, unfit. End of story.'

He looked at me in a kind of strange, suggestive way. A flasher once looked at me like that, in an empty coach on a local train at night. I got in and sat down near him in a dream, turned around, and there he is sitting and looking at me wearily but with meaning, and holding all God gave him in both hands. Horrible.

By now we were nearing my house, though. I'd grabbed the taxi on the Kalanchovka,° there's usually a crowd there, with the three main-line stations all together, masses of people at the taxi stand, enough to drive you crazy, tons of bundles and suitcases, yelling parents with their kids. The taxi drivers edge down the far side of the square, picking out fares. When he heard I wasn't going far, he agreed. A quiet half-cock worker, not too young. He didn't try to talk me out of complaining. In any case, I wasn't going to take it further, but he wasn't making a big show of standing up for his mates, not going for the jugular. He was so apathetic it rent my heart. I can see him sitting there now, weak, quiet, and remote. His rough hands with their big tough fingernails lay feebly on the wheel.

'I could use some sleep,' I say. 'Last night I packed for the kids, and tonight I have to pack again.'

'That's nothing. Nothing,' he answered. 'I haven't slept in a month.'

'The best medicine is valerian,' I said to him. Idiot—I don't know a thing about it. 'A woman I know went round trying everything there is, and settled on valerian.'

'It doesn't help,' he responded, still defending drivers' honour in his own peculiar way. 'I still can't sleep.'

'The main thing is,' I said—going on attacking drivers' honour—'is that grandmother finds it all so frightening. She's 73, after all!'

'It's nothing, really it's nothing.'

'You never know.'

He said, 'Well, I'm rotten with guilt. And I've reason to be.'

I sat there like a dummy, digesting this announcement. Then he said this:

'My 14-year-old daughter died.'

So that was it.

'Not long ago—June fifth.'

That's why he can't sleep then. Poor driver.

He looked at me with his poor suffering eyes.

For some reason I said:

'The worst is the first year. The first year is the worst.'

He answered:

'A month's gone by already. I'm to blame.'

I had totally lost my bearings—where, what, and when. We drove on.

'Perhaps it just *seems* like that.'

'No. I messed around a lot. I paved the way for it. I... what can I say...'

I answered:

'I know a man whose 12-year-old son hanged himself. He called his buddies: come on over, I'm hanging myself, but they didn't come. So he did it. His mother got home later, she couldn't even cry. And his father couldn't.'

'I'm already cried out, my eyes are dry. Dry.'

He looked at me with his dry eyes, half-closed from fatigue.

'I'm to blame.'

I couldn't ask any of the usual questions, the ones people ask out of curiosity, how it happened, why, and so on. I went on the offensive.

'You know, they waited three years, then they had another son. He's 10 now.'

'Yes, but when you're 44 years old...'

'How old's your wife?'

'She's 42.'

'My friend gave birth at 44. Her daughter's 7 now. Sweet little thing.'

'My wife is in *there*, you know.'

'In the nut-house, you mean?'

'*There*. The doctors say she's had it.'

'In a serious condition?'

'You bet.'

'That means it's still treatable. Extreme cases are the ones they *can* cure.'

His defence of drivers' honour had taken us a long way. What on earth had happened to him and his daughter? Fourteen years old—a terrible age. Didn't see it coming. He's to blame.

'You know,' I say, 'there's this fairy-tale by Hans Andersen. They don't put it in the kids' editions. A mother has a child, the child dies. So the mother goes to God and says: give me back my child. And God answers: let's go and see my garden. So off they go. There's a flower-bed with tulips growing in it. God says, "Look, these are the future lives of all the children who ever were born. One of them is your child's. Look at them: is that the kind of life you want for your baby?" She looked, and was overcome by horror; she said, "You're right, Lord."'

'I don't believe my daughter's in heaven. Have you ever lost consciousness?'

'Yes.'

'You don't feel anything at all. I was brought back from the dead. I don't remember a thing. There isn't anything *there*.'

'You'll meet up with her sometime,' I said.

'I had a friend who was a Buddhist. I don't believe it.'

'Someone will come and see you. Don't chase them away. It'll be her. One winter I was walking along late at night, and I saw this cat sitting down, pressing himself to the ground. An hour later I was coming past again, and he's still sitting in the same spot, all covered in snow. During the day they'd been selling meat pies and he was eating the scraps. That stuff's bad for cats. For people it's one thing, but cats can die from it. I took him home. Gave him a wash. Dried him by the gas stove.'

'I know some people do take in cats and dogs. I can't.'

'Then after a month and a half he disappeared. I was coming home one evening, and he bolted up the stairs after me. He used to hang out there in the evenings, on the stairs. I chased him away. I never saw him again. But I realized later who it was who had come to see me.'

'I'm to blame,' said the driver.

'Everyone's to blame.'

I can't remember exactly what I said next, what arguments I used. I tried to persuade him to wait the year out, then tried to persuade him to take a vacation.

'It's easier when I'm working. And I've had my vacation already. I re-roofed the shed at our dacha and put a window in. At our dacha... Everything was all right then. My daughter came, my wife too, and we all went back together. That was five days before she died. Later they did some sewing together, my daughter made some leggings, my wife made a dress. We talked things over, everything was all right. I'm to blame,' he said again.

We were still stuck in the same groove.

'I can't look at children—it makes me cry. No, I don't even cry now. I just look away. I can't.'

'Leave it a year. A year more,' I repeated.

'Once I was driving some people with their dog. It was all they had left of their daughter. The dog was 12, it was already having trouble breathing. They had it dosed, nursed it, fussed over it. Ten years she had been dead, the daughter. They still felt it.'

'Yeah, like one man I used to know kept shouting: "I don't want another boy!" His 18-year-old son was murdered.'

'Sure. I used to look at strangers' children and be jealous, now they're *all* strangers' children. I know I don't need them. I need her. She wasn't just a daughter to me, she was a friend. I'd be going out to do some shopping, say, and she'd be sitting there doing her homework. She'd say, "Dad! Where are *you* going?" "Shopping." "What about me?" she'd say. And she'd go with me, except if she had a lot of homework—then she stayed.'

And he played his record again—I'm to blame, I'm to blame, everything I've done has led up to this.

So here we were, stopped by my house. I just couldn't get out, he kept on talking. Anyway, I didn't want to get out, though they were waiting for me at home. I was very late, we had still to pack. Somehow, I had to find something to say to him.

'My daughter was murdered, you know. Brutally murdered.'

I answered that I did know, I'd guessed. God! What kind of guilt was this? Did he blame himself for not protecting her?

'Five days before her death, she came with her mother to visit me at the dacha. As soon as I saw her, I got so frightened. Why? I got so frightened, seeing her.'

He had had a premonition. Though usually people get frightened when people are after them. If he really did 'mess around with' other women, as he put it, then it would have been worse for the daughter than for the wife. It always is. But in any case, people are frightened of people when they feel guilty about them. You don't love someone who makes you feel guilty, you want to stay well clear.

'The look she had on her face! Then later we all went home together, I took them back.'

'You don't have anyone to love now?'

'No one.'

'There's only one salvation. Find someone to love. Learn to pity your wife. Do you visit her?'

'They don't let anyone in to see her. I've thought about things, and I don't want to start a new family. I love my brother, but that's different.'

'Don't abandon her.'

He gave me another strange look.

'They were both sitting there peacefully sewing five days before her death. I'm to blame. I didn't do what I should have done. Somehow I thought that things would be all right. You know...'

Silence.

'You know,' he said, 'it was my wife who killed my daughter. She's in prison, in Butyrki. There's a section there for crazies.'

Silence.

'She went to the police herself, she took them a knife and axe covered in blood, and said, my daughter's been murdered.'

'Did they arrest her right away?'

'On the spot. Four years ago a woman in our building was murdered, someone stabbed her in her apartment. Now they're trying to pin that business on my wife too.'

'What about her lawyer?'

'By law she's not entitled to a lawyer yet. They'll allow her one when charges are brought. They do the psychiatric reports then too.'

'Suppose she didn't do it? She's in shock, she's lost her memory. You need some kind of hypnotist. A hypnotist can find out everything once she's under hypnosis. Maybe your daughter died some other way, and she's in shock.'

'Oh, there was a long time before when she was somehow... I noticed things.'

'Like what?'

'Like she's sitting by the television and repeating every item from the nine o'clock news. Then giving me a commentary on it. I could hardly stand it.'

'Sure, I can see how that would get to you. But *that's* not the kind of thing I meant at all! Was she ever aggressive?'

'One time she really went for me, with her bare fists.'

'Once?'

'Once.'

'Are you kidding? You know what family life is! One time? Are you crazy?'

'I'm no angel either, when you come to it. I was being very distant with her this last year. I didn't love her at all any more, only my daughter. There was no real contact.'

'Now *that* sounds like something.'

'Our daughter was closer to me, really. And my wife had been out of work for a long time. She was fired, to cut a long story short. She got into an argument with someone. She and I were in college together, then I started the taxi-driving. But she was fired from the scientific research institute, then she couldn't find a job, with the cut-backs. She was depressed.'

'You bet! I've been through all that too.'

'She was depressed, and she couldn't find a job anywhere.'

'There you are again.'

'I'm to blame. I did pay for this psychiatrist woman to come over, she said I should send for an ambulance and have her put in hospital. But somehow I just... you know... didn't do it.'

'Did you feel sorry for her?'

'Oh no. Just somehow...'

So she sits alone in her madness in prison, waiting for her execution.

[*6 July 1989*]

Translated by Brian Thomas Oles

◆ NINA SADUR ◆

Sadur, who is partly of Tatar extraction, was born in 1950 in Novosibirsk, but studied at the Gorky Institute of Literature in Moscow, and has lived in the capital ever since. Like many of those without Moscow roots, she has had difficulty finding accommodation, and lives in a crowded communal flat in the centre; the squalid and claustrophobic conditions of life there form the background, or implied background, to many of her works. One of the best-known 'new-wave' dramatists, Sadur shot to prominence with the relaxation of theatre censorship in the late 1980s, when she began to be performed by Moscow fringe theatres. She is the author of short stories as well as plays.

Frozen

Play in One Act

DRAMATIS PERSONAE

MUM

NADYA

LEILA

UNCLE LEO

[*At Nadya's. Bright lights. Quiet*].

NADYA. I've had enough of this. You spend every copeck we have on men, when I haven't a rag to my back. I'm off to get a job.

MUM. Well, off you go then. Who's stopping you?

[*At work. Dark. A snowstorm*].

NADYA. Leila! Leila! What d'you think you're doing with that dirty water again? The supervisor's sure to catch you! You're supposed to run and put it down the drain. Eh, Leila, listen! You can't pour it out there, it'll freeze, then everyone'll start slipping over! You have to run and put it right down the drain. Run, I said. Like I do.

LEILA. Eh? Were you wanting to tell me something, Nadya?

NADYA. Oh, Jesus!

LEILA. Well, I want to tell *you* something—there's no point you struggling through that snow to pour the water out. The supervisor won't ever notice—it's quite wet enough here anyway. You see how wet that snow is? When she sees the dirty water, she'll think that's melted snow too.

NADYA. Will you look at this woman! She's a bleeding genius! Here, Leila, don't make me laugh. The only reason you talk like that is because you're from Dagestan, you've never seen real snow before. Can't you see that's old snow, it's all gone hard? And our water's lying on top, making a puddle. Can't you see?

LEILA. Eh, that's great!

NADYA. What's great?

LEILA. Yes, yes!

NADYA. Yes, yes, what?

LEILA. Fantastic!

NADYA. You know, you really could do with an ear trumpet!

LEILA. Now I see! Look, there's water dripping down from up there, buckets of it! That water'll cover up our water. It's melted snow.

NADYA. I said, you ought to buy yourself an *ear trumpet*. Then we could yell in it so you'd hear.

LEILA. Hey! Did you hear that? Is that a blizzard, or what?

NADYA. *I* can hear all right.° It's *you* who's got problems—you ought to go to the chemist's and get yourself a trumpet, *an ear trumpet*.

LEILA. Oh, a hearing aid. Yes, you're quite right, my hearing really isn't up to much.

NADYA. You must buy one, or else we'll all wear our throats out shouting.

LEILA. Throats? Well, no wonder you catch cold, leaving your top button open like that. Hang on, let's do it up for you!

NADYA. For God's sake! Stop fiddling round like that! You've got gloves on, remember? Rubber gloves! And they're all wet!

LEILA. You're not wearing a scarf, are you? So just you do up that button, or you'll catch your death.

NADYA. What difference does it make, anyway? None of us has a stitch on under these overalls. Only our bras and knickers. I suppose you think the overalls help?

LEILA. I have to do the foyer now. Make it shine. I hate that foyer, the parquet's all uneven.

NADYA. I wish the supervisor wouldn't make me do those stairs. It's not even part of the job, not of my job, that staircase isn't. Why should we do more cleaning than we have to?

LEILA. What?

NADYA. Cleaning, I said! Why should we! Should we?

LEILA. Goodness?

NADYA. Don't feel like cleaning. Cleaning!

LEILA. Meaning?

NADYA. Oh Jesus, you moron!

LEILA. Don't you swear at me.

NADYA. Well, you can piss off, for a start.

LEILA. I keep trying to tell you, don't I. Don't do that staircase. You don't have to.

NADYA. I know, but she makes me.

LEILA. Don't do it, though.

[UNCLE LEO *comes wandering over the snow.*]

NADYA. Look, it's him again.

LEILA. Oh, that's Uncle Leo!

NADYA. Keep your voice down!

LEILA. Eh? It's Uncle Leo, I said!

NADYA. Keep your voice down, nothing wrong with *my* ears.

LEILA. All the men give him their empty bottles.

NADYA. Nothing wrong with *my* ears, *I* do the yelling, not you. *You're* the one that's deaf.

LEILA. There's something creepy about him.

NADYA. Oy, he's started staring at us now. Don't look at him. Suppose he saw!

LEILA. He's some kind of a wrong 'un. You'll get used to him.

NADYA. What's he fiddling round there for? Keeping an eye on the snow, or what? Look, he's even got overalls on. Like a real workman. He can't even speak, you know. Just makes this mooing noise.

LEILA. I'm sort of used to him. His looks don't frighten me.

NADYA. Bet those men gave him a bite to eat, too. They felt sorry for him, I bet.

LEILA. Don't worry about him. Don't look at him. Just try and imagine he's not there.

NADYA. Not there, indeed! Not that I give a piss, mind you. I'll get enough saved up to buy a new pair of boots and then I'll get the hell out.

LEILA. Boots? Oh, I see you're still wearing them slippers! That'll never do, not with us having to go out in the snow all the time.

NADYA. Why did they call him Leo?° Le-o. What a waste. I can't stand it when they waste a name like that on a half-wit. Leo, Arkady, posh names like that. Why couldn't they call him Vasya or Kolya? Or some sort of musty old-fashioned kind of name, one that no one normal would use. But *Leo*, for God's sake! When he can only moo, not speak... What's he bobbing about by that wall over there for?

LEILA. He sits in the workmen's room all day, drinking their tea.

NADYA. So what's he doing over by that wall? Why doesn't he go and ask the workmen to make some tea? Why does he have to keep hanging round like that, in the snow? That wind's really cold, too. Makes me sick, looking at him. [*Exit* UNCLE LEO

Just have a look at that, now he's gone! What a coincidence, eh—I was talking about how he ought to go, and he did go! Incredible! He really is a right one!

LEILA. You know there are all sorts of old cellars under the floor here? Corridors, and that?

NADYA. That's all we needed!

LEILA. And that wall where Uncle Leo was hanging about, that's the wall of an old church they knocked down.

NADYA. Where did you hear all this, Dagestan, is that it?

LEILA. I've got a university education, you know. There's buckets of cellars down there. The whole place has a curse on it. Every inch.

NADYA. That's not proper Russian, buckets isn't. You can have buckets of paint, red paint, say, you can have buckets of all stuff like... well, tinned milk, for instance.

LEILA. I'm going to tell you something, but promise you won't be scared.

NADYA. Well, what is it?

LEILA. This place is haunted. By the ghost of an actress. With a revolver.

NADYA. Pull the other one.

LEILA. She put a curse on this theatre here,° that actress did, on this very place we're cleaning. She cursed every inch of it separately, the stage, the curtain, the chandeliers, the dress circle, the mirrors, the plaster friezes—all of it. This is what she said. 'You've made a mockery of art, you've trampled on it, you've dishonoured it. You've driven art mad and watched with your fish eyes whilst it dies in horrible agonies. I curse you for it, and this is my curse. Nobody with talent will ever work in your theatre. If anyone with talent ever gets a job here, you'll break their hearts.'

NADYA. Well, that makes a lot of sense! That doesn't hurt the theatre, does it? It only hurts talented people. Right?

LEILA. When she'd cried herself out, she shouted, 'I hate you all! All of you! You're all damned!'

NADYA. Here, Leila, how on earth do you know all this about that actress? Do you read that kind of thing in books, or what?

LEILA. We take curses very seriously, we Muslims do.

NADYA. Well, blow me down! Any case, how come you ended up in Moscow in the first place? Just look at you, doing a cleaning job for a living—in fact you're so scared they'll throw you out of that you're practically wetting yourself.° Deaf as a post, and nowhere to live but that dreadful hostel. Here, look Leila, you've got ever such nice eyes, you know that? Shame about your chin, though. Pardon me for saying so, but it is rather big. Sort of sticks out funny too—mind you, not so's you'd really notice.

LEILA. Ha ha ha, if you could see your expression! Oh, so you're staring at my face, are you? Yes, this bottom bit *is* a bit squint, I know.

NADYA. This bit, where the beard goes.

LEILA. Yes, my chin. My father used to beat us children, you know. All twelve of us, specially the girls. He made me deaf, he broke my jaw—look, you can still see the place, this crooked bit here. My sister, though, he did for her liver. When my mother died, we all got out as quick as we could. That's when I came to Moscow. You know why? It's because there are buckets of art and things here, everything all comes pouring in here from all over the place. Hey, give me your pail, and I'll fill it up. Get you some nice hot water. [*Exit*

NADYA [*jumps up and down*]. Hear that echo! They must be really old.

[UNCLE LEO *brings in a big prop crucifix and leans it against the wall.*]

Jesus, now we *are* starting, and all! [UNCLE LEO *starts wandering up and down.*] Look at him, making dirty footmarks on the bit we just washed. Cretin. Freak. Mum's no better, she spends money like there was no tomorrow. Buys all beads and rubbish like that. Making herself look pretty for the men. Not that they even *are* men, that'd be bad enough, they're no more than boys. Same age as me. What on earth does she see in them? Hanging on their every word! Boys! I know what they're worth! She's an idiot, mum is, an idiot!

[*Enter Leila, carrying steaming buckets of hot water.*]

LEILA. God, that supervisor! Yaps and snarls at you like a dog! Even I can hear her yelling! Best get on, it isn't long now till they open, and we've still got the whole lobby to do. And the foyer. Can't stand that foyer, it's those mirrors in it.

NADYA. My mum messes round with young boys.

LEILA. What?

NADYA. Messes round with young boys! My mum does!

LEILA. She's lucky she can. My mum's dead, you know.

NADYA. I bought myself this dress, and she went and nicked it. All she cares about is messing round with young boys.

LEILA. I dreamt my mum rang me up after she was dead. I picked up the telephone and heard her voice say, 'Is that Leila? Here, Leila,' she said, 'if you marry a Russian, you won't be a Muslim any more, you'll turn into one of them.'

NADYA. I hate my mum! No matter what I manage to earn, she'll just get hold of it somehow and spend it on earrings or junk like that. I know she will! I know!

LEILA. To be frank, it suited me better when our Muslim women used to go round in veils.° You could keep your own face to yourself. But they made us take them off. It's a pity, if you ask me.

NADYA. I can't stand my mum! She's got this long thin face like a horse. She nicked my crucifix, too!

LEILA. Oh, right, that crucifix! Yes, I know it's all big and black and everything, but there's nothing to worry about. They're doing *The Robbers*,° and they've brought it out so the paint can dry. It's all to keep the audience happy.

NADYA. Have you seen that? It's a disgrace! Look, his skin's all cracked, and the stuffing's coming out of him. Will you look at that, the lazy bastards, they've even put a patch on his belly there! Why couldn't they make a new god? He'll drop off the cross altogether before long! Looks half-dead as it is!

LEILA. Oy, don't walk on that bit, you'll get your feet wet! The floor slopes, all the water collects in that corner, you can see, there's a whole lake of it there! See the steam rise. Like the gates of Hell.

NADYA. You're a moron. So's Leo. You're all morons. You make me sick. I'll earn my seventy roubles and get the hell out.

LEILA. Our God's not like a man, you know. You can't see him. It's forbidden to see him, you can only make patterns of him.

NADYA. I can't stand any of that God stuff. I did go to church once, but just for a laugh. There was all gold and smoke everywhere, gave me the creeps, and they was all droning on. It was sort of like, I don't know, but it gave me the shivers, hearing them droning away like that. Alright, come on, let's get some work done before the supervisor skins us alive. She's a moron too, when you come to it.

LEILA. It's just as well we're both young. You're even younger than I am. We'll scrape around some more, whilst we're young, and then we'll settle down. Everything will come out right.

NADYA. Look at him trying to bend over! Looks like a rusty old hinge, doesn't he? Hey, bet we hear him squeak in a moment. The mug he has on him, too! With all those wrinkles hanging down, they're so big and heavy they look like they might make him fall flat on his face, drag him right down into the cellars. Ha ha! What on earth does he live on, do you think? What does he eat? What does he dream about? Well, what do you expect him to dream about? I wonder whether he can think? A little bit? Look, he doesn't feel the cold. We do, he doesn't. He feels something else. Look at him bobbing up and down. Shall we test whether he can think or not? Shall we give him a wave?

LEILA. What d'you think you're doing? You can't wave at Uncle Leo like that! You'll make him angry! I'm sure I saw him stamp his feet! Brrr, I'm going to get some water. [*Exit*

[UNCLE LEO *lets out a roar and chases after* NADYA, *then throws a stone at her head. She runs away.*

UNCLE LEO *stands groaning to himself and swaying about. Clouds of steam are rising from below, snow is dripping down from above.* UNCLE LEO *stands in the middle, groaning and swaying.* NADYA *and* LEILA *are standing at one side, peering out at him.*]

NADYA. He'll kill us.

LEILA. I told you not to make signs at him! You mustn't make signs at him, he'll see! Don't worry, though, he won't do anything to us cleaners. He never takes any notice of cleaners. Come on, let's get on with some work. But quietly! [*They pour out water.*] Let's clear up that snow there.

NADYA. What on earth for?

LEILA. Because the water will run away better if we do.

NADYA. Alright then. What I don't like is the way all this sort of gets to you, know what I mean? No, you wouldn't of course, not with you being deaf, and all.

LEILA. I know this is a daft idea, but I'd like my own house some day.

NADYA. What's this about a house?

LEILA. House? Oh good, you understand. That's right, a house and a little garden. And three children. Promise you won't laugh.

NADYA. Where have you ever seen a house like that in Moscow?

LEILA. You can get anything in Moscow!

NADYA. Why not a flat? Flats, now those you *can* get here.

LEILA. And big wrought-iron gates. We have them in Dagestan, you know, all over the place. The only problem is, people are spiteful there. The little kids and the girls are beautiful, only they all grow up in the end.

NADYA. Well, go back to Dagestan then, if it's all so wonderful.

LEILA. Why do you have to be so nasty all the time? I can't hear what you're saying, but I can tell it's nasty.

NADYA. How can you tell?

LEILA. You have this way of pushing your lips out. I can tell what you're saying is poison.

NADYA. Alright, I'll stop then! Hey, give over Leila! Come on lovey, don't get upset!

LEILA. We've got these big gardens. All stuffed with flowers. They put iron railings round the outside to squeeze them in, but the gardens spill over the top like they was boiling over, they pour down on people's heads.

NADYA. Amazing!

LEILA. Gardens like that eat a lot of soil. But they really *are* gardens! Phe-ew!

NADYA. Is it one like that you want?

LEILA. Not here! The earth's too flat here.

NADYA. What's that supposed to mean, too flat? What, with these old cellars here and everything? Go on, tell me... is it really true, about the gardens spilling over and that? Hey, do you get globeflowers° there, all golden? And mallows?

LEILA. Eh! What flowers *don't* you get! And then I want a house right in the middle.

NADYA. I get you! What furniture will you be having?

LEILA. Eh! The house will be a classic! Five rooms. White everywhere. A white table just here, for instance.

NADYA. No, you should get a gold one! One of them Arab ones, with fancy sides, and gold patterns all over. And them sort of low armchairs that look as if they're bending over, kind of, trying to scratch their own backs. And blinds to keep the sun out, all bubbling over the windows like foam.° They should be white too, like—well, like that window there, see?

LEILA. Oh! You mean the director's window, eh?

NADYA. Stuff the director! It's the blinds I'm interested in. I don't want that kind of window though, we'll have a nicer kind, the kind we really want, we'll put it just here...

LEILA. And little kiddy beds in the nursery, for the children. Three of them.

NADYA. This here'll be our nursery. With a wardrobe—so, and a corner for them to play in—so, and a climbing frame too, so the kiddies can grow up with nice straight backs. What shall we call them, by the way?

LEILA. Eh?

NADYA. I know! Deniska and Andryusha! But what about the girl... Oh yes, of course, Leila, after you. Hang on a mo! What are we going to do about a husband?

LEILA. That's the whole problem!

NADYA. Hang on, let me think! Oh hell, maybe we should just stuff the husband?

LEILA. Won't do at all, I'm afraid. A woman isn't allowed to do without a husband, not in Dagestan.

NADYA. OK then. In that case let's.... Hang on, though! We're running this, aren't we? So what about Uncle Leo? I know he's a moron, but he could sort of stand in for a husband, if we had him hanging round, couldn't he?

LEILA. No, not him, for God's sake!

NADYA. Hang on a moment! So it'll look right, I mean! You don't have to go anywhere near him, and he looks fine in the distance, nice and tall and all that. All you want is for things to look right—kids here, husband there. He's in a good mood now, so he won't get in the way. I tell you where we'll put him! Over there, staring through that window! Look, now he's even standing up straight. No! I tell you what, he's reading a book! You'll have lots of books, after all, what else is an education for? Hey, now he really is standing up proper, all straight and tall! You can even see him staring down at his hand, if you screw up your eyes.—Poof, no, he hasn't got a book after all. He really is just a moron. Anyway, we'll put your husband there by the window reading. You'll be in the garden, lying in a hammock...

LEILA. Oooh, a hammock, eh...

NADYA. Yes. And you can hear the sound of the sea, coming from behind the garden wall...

LEILA. The sea, eh? Whatever next!

NADYA. Yes, that's right. And there you are in the hammock, wearing your white dress. And your husband says, 'Darling, I'm just off to get you a few nice boiled crayfish...' Will you look at that! He's off again, Leo is! What a coincidence! Incredible!

LEILA. Crayfish, did you say?

NADYA. Yes, he wanted to get a nice present for you. Understand? It's dead simple really. He just nipped down to the beach... Oh Jesus, now that halfwit's gone and spoilt everything! Why did he have to poke his nose in? [UNCLE LEO *starts bobbing up and down.*] All he's fit for is throwing stones at people. Cretin.

LEILA. The crayfish you get in Dagestan are amazing, all fat and pink, like babies' ears.

NADYA. Give over, will you, it's time we got something done.

LEILA. You've pushed your lips out again, I can see.

NADYA. You leave off, and all... I'm terrified of that supervisor, or else I'd just tell her to get rid of that idiot Leo. What's he hanging round here for? Splashing around in the puddles. Making all groaning noises. But it's no good trying anything with her, she hates our guts. Did you know that?

LEILA. And the sound of the sea. Oh! I remember that now! When you go to sleep hearing that! Amazing!

NADYA. Eh, Leila! You know, I think I've worked out why the supervisor hates us. She's ripping us off! She makes us all do more than we should, and then she pockets the extra cash! I hate her, you know!

LEILA. Keep your voice down, for God's sake.

NADYA. She's light-fingered, too!

LEILA. Shut up, for Pete's sake! I know. She rips us all off. I know that!

NADYA. They ought to send her to prison!

LEILA. She's got no shame at all. She thinks she can get away with it because we work in a theatre, she thinks everyone's only interested in the plays, so they don't care how the cleaners get treated. No one wants to spoil their evening thinking about it. *I* can't say anything, though, because I've got no right to be here in the first place, I've got no permit to live in Moscow, they can throw me out any time.

NADYA. I could say something, but I won't. Let her rot. I'm going to leave soon in any case. Leave all of you, all this moaning and misery.

LEILA. I like Russian blokes, you know. I like their blue eyes.

NADYA. What do they think of you, then?

LEILA. Oh, they like me, at least I hope they do!

NADYA. How come you suddenly start hearing things perfectly well, when you're supposed to be deaf?

LEILA. It depends on the vibrations, of people's voices and things. Any rate, that's what I think. For instance, I can tell you're shivering a lot, Nadya.

NADYA. That fat cow of a supervisor promised us padded jackets, for all this work we're doing out of doors.

LEILA. I expect she nicked them herself. She would if this was Dagestan, any rate.

NADYA. You don't get snow like this there.

LEILA. Why do you keep looking round like that? Is that crucifix getting to you? It's only a pretend one, for the play. They do everything so badly here. They're big and powerful, but that crucifix is nothing. They do everything so badly.

NADYA. Shut up, you moron! Moron!

LEILA. Watch your mouth, Nadya. You're a silly bitch yourself.—You see them creeping round like toads, and you stand there shaking. They're so strong and powerful, but they do everything so badly. I was at university, you know, I wasn't born yesterday. They're stuck here for ever. For ever. That crucifix won't help them. It won't even see them punished. It's worth nothing.

NADYA. Hey, look, see that over there? Or have you gone blind as well?

LEILA. Is it Uncle Leo you're talking about? Never mind him, he'll stay where he is. You're not an actress, you've got no reason to be scared, you don't even do the lights or the costumes. You're no one, no one at all.

NADYA. What d'you mean, no one? And what difference does that half-wit make in any case? Can't you see he's just gone?

LEILA. 'On' what?

NADYA. Eh, what's that thing all made out of snow that just flashed past?

LEILA. Flasher, you say?

NADYA. What's that there, I say, that?

LEILA. Oh, that! Hey, look! Two huge puddles over there, like lakes! Look at them, steaming and eating up the snow. The War of the Lakes, eh!

NADYA. I saw a face!

LEILA. Race?

NADYA. There's a face, look, there! Aren't you scared?

LEILA. What on earth are you saying, Nadya? Eh, Nadya, love, you've made me scared now! You're shaking like anything!

NADYA. I could see something funny happening when we was playing houses. Look, it is a face, it is! That god of theirs has got a face now!

LEILA. Eh, Nadya, for God's sake don't go over there! Don't go, please don't! Not in those slippers, not over all that snow and wet!

NADYA. Get out! [*To* UNCLE LEO] Get out, you freak, you monster! You make me sick!

[NADYA *goes up to the cross, stares hard at it, then wipes the snow from the crevices with her fingers, and the face disappears.*]

LEILA. Ha, ha! Now I understand! It's the snow that did it! The snow's all white, and it filled up the crevices, so it made a face! Ha, ha!

NADYA. The half-wits, you'd think they could give him a lick of paint, wouldn't you? They banged a ton of nails in him, and then they couldn't spare a lick of paint. Couldn't even give him a nice pink face like they should of. Instead they went and smeared black everywhere, the idiots. Bastards! [*To* UNCLE LEO] What are you hanging round there for, eh? Bloody freak show!

[NADYA *comes back towards Leila over the puddle.*]

LEILA. We have these patterns on our mosques, you know. Patterns everywhere. They all have this sort of bulgy dome with all patterns on. The dome's so big, and the patterns are all, oh, like sighs. That's where our god lives, you know. Beautiful.

NADYA. I don't know what keeps them alive, freaks like that Uncle Leo. Look at that great ugly face all over snow, his wrinkles are full of it too. Yeuch, I can't look. Why do you have to keep breathing down our necks, you great half-wit? Don't worry, I'm not going to wipe your face for you. Wouldn't even touch it if I had gloves on.

UNCLE LEO. You watch out, I can have you sacked if I like.

LEILA. We've got patterns, but we don't have any faces. You're not allowed to know what God's face is like. Eh, what's this? Not scared again? Why do you keep getting so scared? What are you pointing at him for? That's only Uncle Leo. You mustn't worry about him. But don't touch him either, because he's dead spiteful. He writes denunciations all the time, you know, tells tales. Tries to get everyone sacked. But he doesn't bother with us. We're only the cleaners. Eh, don't stand in that water. It's boiling hot, and the snow's freezing. You'll catch your death.

[NADYA *starts screaming.*]

[*At home. Morning. Bright sky outside the window.*]

NADYA. He can talk. He has a work record, just like us. He works there. He works there. He can talk. He has a work record, just like we do. He works there. He can talk. Why is the sky like that, when it's winter? Here, someone turn off the sky. It's too warm. Thanks. That's so nice. Did that just fall out of the sky? All warm. Hey, that tickles! What's that called? A golden globeflower? How come it didn't break the window? How did it get through the window in the first place? All golden. All warm. Now I'm warm. E—eeh! It's still moving! Faster, faster! This never happens in winter, not usually. Look how blue it all is! Make it warmer! Turn up the heat! How does this stuff manage to land here? What makes it fall from the sky? So it landed here all on its own, did it? Is it warm, or a storm? I'll have to get a rag so it doesn't burn me. No, it is the warm. Flashes of warm. There's something pulling them down here, something in this room. It's a trick of nature. No, that's enough! I can't see, it's too hot! Don't throw things at me! There's plenty of room! No, not my stomach! No, don't aim at me, you'll scorch me! I'll have to open a window, let the air in. Look, they're getting in any rate, through the glass. I can't see, it's too hot! I can't go on living here. I can't even move. Oh, don't make that noise, stop throwing that, you're hitting me! There'll be no space left soon! Have a look at them, shining and burning in all the corners! Just as well they did land in the corners, there's little enough space here as it is. That's it now, that was the last of it! All quiet. I can't move, I'm all scorched where that stuff hit me. Where will we live now? Mustn't think about it. Must stay squeezed up, so I won't burn. The sun is splashing. That's all, there won't be any more now. Hey, now there's more of it! Scorchlighting! Such a big flash, such a... can hardly move... don't let go, hold on tight, stay there, you can't come here! You'll crush me! [*Runs to* MUM.] Mum, Mum, what on earth was that? I could have been burnt to death!

MUM [*powdering her nose*]. Pull yourself together. Take an aspirin, for God's sake.

[*And* MUM *goes flouncing off, out to her date, click click click.*]

CURTAIN

[1989]

◆ BELLA ULANOVSKAYA ◆

Ulanovskaya, who was born in 1948, was brought up in the Urals, and then studied literature at the university in Leningrad. After graduating, she spent some time as a reporter, collecting material in mineshafts and metro stations, before beginning work at the Dostoevsky memorial museum in Leningrad (see note to p. 363). She has been involved in creative writing since the 1960s; her other work includes the story 'Albinos', published in the Paris journal *Ekho*, 13 (1984), and the documentary sketch 'Voluntary Seclusion: The Life of an Old Woman in a Deserted Russian Village', *Russian Review*, 2 (1992).

Journey to Kashgar°

We marched to the Eastern mountains.

(*The Shitszin°*)

After a fire, when the earth has been left so charred that you would think nothing could live there again, or not for years afterwards, you can sometimes see strange toadstools sprouting, their long fragile stalks ending in small sooty caps. Condemned, by an extraordinary stroke of fate, to live in places of extinction, under impossible conditions, these blackened toadstools can only grow on scorched and burned soil; they cannot tolerate soft living. A whole generation of carbon-loving plants grows up on the ashes of catastrophe, preparing the soil and renewing it for the rush of life that will follow.

I have begun this sketch for a biography without knowing whether I shall manage to finish it, to draw events to their concluding point—a wall in Kashgar° with the dawn chill still on it. See, there I am, deliberately running ahead, saying the last words first—describing the morning of Tatyana Levina's execution in Turan.° But actually writing her life, making it into a whole, will be like growing tomatoes in the far north. You dig over the beds and plant out the seedlings, and all summer you water them carefully. Some wither and die, but the others grow into sturdy bushes and flower bravely. Every evening brings the chiming of buckets, and the whirling of crowds of mosquitoes, and the calling of the corncrake in a meadow nearby; you can see the fruits start forming, you even pick off the surplus flowers—you don't like doing it, but the plant needs to save its strength, one has to draw the line somewhere. Yet already you can see that this summer is going to be a disaster, just like all the other summers—even if we get some wonderful weather now the plants will never make up for lost time, and then there might be an early frost, you always have to reckon on those—and now the bushes are drooping under their load of scrawny green berries, they've not grown for a month or more, you can see your neighbours picking the wretched things before they rot completely, it's high time you picked yours as well. Didn't you know that this summer would be another failure when you bought the seeds and prepared the soil? Of course you did, but you hoped for the best—after all, the seed was the best you could get, the soil's wonderful. It was only the weather that let you down. Will you try it again next year? Of course you will.

So all the keen gardeners take their horde of two dozen or so knobbly green fruit; they stuff them into a thick sock, and put them on top of the stove to ripen, to go scarlet and juicy—fat chance—and forget them. But then suddenly, right at the end of September, someone does remember them, and out they come again, to be welcomed like the first fruits of spring.

After all, we were hardly to blame that the tomatoes turned out so pale and shrivelled, were we? We could hardly have put more hard work and effort into them.

I have the feeling that I may have wasted my chances with Tatyana Levina as well, that I may not be able to make up for lost time in writing the tale of her heroic death, any more than one can with tomatoes. But at the same time I have the feeling that I am destined to do something with her story. No, it's not a question of destiny: I just don't want to give up at this stage, when I have already collected all the material that I can about her life, when I know more about her than anyone else. More than that: I haven't the right to give up. I procrastinated over writing up what I had gathered, hoping that I would be able to hand it on to someone else and that they would use it to better effect than I could, that they would make a novel or story out of her life. But it turned out that no one else could do it, or would do it. Friends would stop listening the minute I started talking about Tatyana Levina. You can't still be fussing round with that, they would say, you must be sick to death of it by now, it's so boring, and isn't there enough of that kind of thing around anyway?

Should I change her name? If I did that I could make up imaginary conversations, describe the journeys she must have made, or the first time she fell in love—give me a free hand, and I could tell you just what was going on inside her head.

The new cement path—'*Tyutyushkin done this concrete*'°—has made a mark that will last for ever; a hand grips our heroine's chin gently. If you stare at an eye close up, it loses its colour, looks strange and sinister. She knows how important all this is, but she can't help thinking of an aquarium, those walls of glass, and behind them two fish mouths primly pursed, whilst their eyes goggle away, hugely magnified by the water. She drops her eyes in embarrassment, she mustn't spoil the delicacy of this moment, it's supposed to last a lifetime—and now here she is, going home, she'll keep that expression on her face all night, delighted and astonished at the same time—and in the morning she'll pretend to be asleep. She'll wait till everyone else has left, then she'll go out and walk down to the sea—she doesn't swim very well, but she always strikes straight out anyway, going way out from the shore. See? Now she's just a speck on the horizon, but we can see her trying to kiss her own elbow—is that like her? Not very; but in any case, it's time to swim back now. She can feel what happened yesterday reflected on her face, so she turns over and swims on her back to the shore, then staggers backwards out of the water, still staring at the sea.

Or imagine Tatyana Levina in the last days of the summer holidays, feeling the prickle of her school-uniform dress on her bare legs (there's nothing else quite like it), and feeling that happy sense of being ready for anything, submissive to whatever fate may throw at you. Yes, I will work harder next year, yes, I will help other people, I'll learn to respect them.

Or imagine the fun of causing a scene at a dull and proper wedding. The bridegroom is skinny and weedy, she's never met him before, but she can feel him holding her tighter and tighter whilst they dance, they're dancing more and more slowly, and her own escort—he's begun to bore her horribly—has no idea what to do. Eventually he comes in and turns on the main light, and drags the bridegroom out into the hall. The guests are all crowded round, the fat ugly bride is crying her eyes out on the landing. But the bridegroom takes Tatyana's hand and leads her back into the room, and puts his arms round her, and they begin kissing again. Serve them right. Serve them right, serve them all right—for what, she hardly knew herself.

Levina's official biographies don't include that story, of course, but it's exactly the sort of thing that you'll find in any half-way respectable novel about her. Just recently, though, in fact exactly at the stage when I was beginning to amass material about Tatyana Levina's life, something odd happened. People stopped talking about her; you read about her less and less often in the newspapers. Eventually she sank without trace.

We won't change her name, then.

The stuff that used to get trotted out about her, though! Her parents were the first culprits, with those awful speeches of theirs, and those visits to Young Pioneer meetings, and the like. Do all your homework, and then you'll get good marks, like Tatyana Levina did! Be brave, like she was, then you might grow up to be a heroine, like her! And when the children heard about the streets of Kashgar, they all burst out crying; but they held their heads proudly, and flashed their eyes, feeling their sandy hair blow in the breeze, feeling the rope noose tight round their necks. (A red-haired girl, leggy as a young goat, is led through town on the end of a rope—and not one European face, not one Russian face, not one European face in sight.)

But I keep leaping ahead, rushing on to the end. We have a long way to travel with Tatyana before that, and I know that we shall travel it in style. Yet I keep going back (if you can go back to what lies ahead), back to Tatyana's last hours. Not a face that she knew—did she think about that?

It's odd, that instinct to surround ourselves with familiar faces. At weddings, birthdays, important meetings, farewell parties, we gather them round us. Do we need people to chronicle our lives, is that it?

Whom would she have wanted to witness her last hours?

I'm not a blood relation of hers, but mine is the only face left that she knows. Suppose I had been fated to show my face for a second in that hostile crowd, amongst all those people with their bristly hair, like black wires? Perhaps Tatyana would have seen me, and turned away. It's pointless to think about that, though, that's like imagining what, say, Dostoevsky would have wanted. Imagine if he rose from the dead and visited the Dostoevsky museum,° imagine what he'd do to the lot of us then, when he saw us all goggling at the exhibits, why, he'd kick us all straight out for sure. And imagine how red our faces would be if he went round and looked at the memorial flat we'd tricked out for him, every stick of it bogus—what right did we have to do that? Imagine him reading what was written on the captions, let alone joining (heaven help us!) one of the guided tours...

None of us did have the right, or does have, and if you read the nonsense Lyuba,° or her daughters Zoya and Shura, say, come out with, it just curls you up.

So what is a poor chronicler° to do? Come on, get a move on, do your best—there's a lot to get through. We need as accurate an account as possible of what happened. I won't say as *good* an account as possible, because that way we'd just end up with flowers that would never set fruit, so we'd have to nip them all out in any case.

The Korean Atrocities

Forty-five black pinafores°—worsted, rayon, sateen—were squeezed together shoulder to shoulder, in four rows. The sateen pinafores were the ones that couldn't read at all, the rayon pinafores (this was the largest group) were the ones that muddled through somehow, but the worsted ones could rattle along at top speed, without pausing for breath.

When the photograph had been taken, the top row—who might have been picked out for their bad marks and for not having any collars as well as for their height—jumped down off the bench (it had been brought in from the music-room), and the bottom row got up off the sticky polished floor; the third row clambered out from behind the chairs—their chins would be masked in the photograph by the heads of the final row. Last to get up was Stalinka° the general's daughter, who'd been sitting at teacher's right hand. She was wearing a white band round her sleeve, with a red cross made out of a bit of old red felt hat stitched to it: her mother had sewn it for her.

A lot of the girls dreamt of making friends with Stalinka; they kept telling you how pretty she was, and how lovely her parents' flat was, really big, all full of wonderful German things, and with this huge dog wandering about all over the place, but the dog wasn't fierce with children at all, and one day they'd tied it to Stalinka's toboggan, and it had dragged her all down Baskov Lane,° Zhuraeva had seen it, the tall girl, she'd visited them several times and met Stalinka's father; he was a general in the MGB° you know—and although that sounded funny when Zhuraeva said it, smacking her lips over the unfamiliar sounds, no one laughed.

'Would he give us a ride in his car, do you think, if we asked nicely?'

'I don't know. He took me, though, a few times.'

When they were taking the photograph, Zhuraeva stood behind Stalinka's chair; when they said to keep still, you could hear her letting down her lower lip and blowing frantically at a disobedient hair that had escaped from Stalinka's plait.

Stalinka was health monitor, so she had the right to inspect your fingers and neck and ears and collar, to see if they were clean. She liked going through other people's cases, too, to check that everything was neatly wrapped in tissue paper, like the school rules said, and to see that you didn't have anything you weren't supposed to. She'd begun searching our cases after one girl, one with a rayon pinafore was caught with this whole room in her desk, a model one, with a miniature double bed, and a wardrobe with mirrors on the doors, and partitions made of postcards, all packed in a fancy chocolate box for an outside wall.

No one knew what had happened to the toy room after it was confiscated, but Stalinka lived in hope of finding another. However, the girls were scared to bring their treasures to school now—and perhaps they'd outgrown such things as well.

The model room was taken to pieces, pulled apart, and left naked on teacher's desk, then it was locked up 'until your parents choose to come and collect it'.

The girls formed up in a long line and then left the school hall in silence. They were to bring the money for the photographs tomorrow; sepia mounted on board cost the most.

'I woke up and heard the dogs barking in alarm...'

You had to write the rest of the story yourself.

Miss Sirotkina, the teacher's, copper-plate handwriting flowed neatly over the black board; the top classes had dark brown boards, that made you think of something solid and respectable, like the sepia-tinted photographs—not those vulgar coloured snaps, heaven help us!—that were appropriate to the status of our famous, highly respectable girls' school. Before the Revolution it had been a girls' *gimnaziya*;° Lenin's 'wife, friend and faithful helper'° had studied here, and won a gold medal in her leaving exam. We all detested anything gaudy. All the hair-ribbons wound round girls' bed-ends at night were brown or black. The ends got creased if you were too lazy to iron them, but it wasn't half so bad to have creased ends as it was to wear a blue ribbon or worst of all, a scarlet one. Any girl stupid enough to wear a scarlet ribbon might even find herself in for a thrashing from her schoolmates.

The sentence ended with full stops, three of them. The first full stop was an ordinary one, nothing to it. So the dogs were barking? Well let them bark, turn over and go back to sleep. But then came that dreadful second full stop, standing face to face with the first, just look at the two of them gossiping away, leastways they would have been if it hadn't been for the third full stop. The two of them were just about to cook up something together, the vulgar baggages, they'd have started dancing, for instance, if they'd only been left to themselves. But the third stop was shouting at them to come along, so they'd lined up and were following it, and there they all were, running off into the distance, like a line of street-lights in a lane, you can still just see the third one in the distance, but beyond are darkness and snow and wolves.

Of course, everyone was going to write a story about a wolf, about him coming running out of the forest and creeping up to the dark byre where the sheep were sleeping, and scraping off the thatch, leaping down, and snatching a warm soft lamb. Uncle takes his gun down from a nail on the wall, puts on his padded coat, and rushes out to the porch. He sees the fields white in the moon, and the forest dark in the distance, and a speck of black moving slowly towards the trees. In their pen, the sheep press closely together, and a dark track of blood runs across the snow-sprinkled field (time those gaps in the fence were stopped up). He takes a crust sprinkled with salt from his pocket—he left it there yesterday by mistake—then opens the lower door and goes in to the sheep. Their little hooves clatter on the frozen floor as they start backwards. In the narrow window the glass glimmers, white with hoar-frost. Dogs are still barking somewhere at the edge of the village.

Tatyana Levina looked round. Everyone was writing, listening hard to the barking of the dogs.

It was frightening waking at night on Baskov Lane, and Korolenko Street, and Artilleriiskaya, and Sapyorny Lane,° where Lyusya Kotova lives, the nicest, the best-brought-up, the most cultivated girl in the class. She even has a special pinafore, a silk one. Her grandmother and grandfather brought her up; she thinks they're her mother and father,° she doesn't know anything about her real parents. Nor does anyone else, but everyone knows you can't ask Lyusya about them. She's sitting on the front bench in her gold-rimmed glasses and writing a story about sheep.

At night you could hear alsatians barking, and the wind howled in the empty streets.

'Papa, what are they barking at? I'm frightened.'

'Turn over and go back to sleep.'

'Are *they* going to come here?'

In the distance you could here the sound of men singing in harmony. That was our soldiers, marching from the Nekrasov bathhouse,° guarding our sleep.

I'll write something bold and heroic, Tatyana Levina decided.

A sabattur° has just landed. He made a parachute jump in the night—see the silvery-white globe cascading down over his shoulders—and now he starts running, running over the potato-field, away from boring old uncle with his gun. That was what uncle said in his letter. 'I arested a sabattur and took him to the pollis in the morning.' Boasting.

That was the end of lessons, but they had to stay for an hour of political education. Miss Sirotkina was telling them about the American atrocities in Korea. The forty-four sateen, rayon, and worsted pinafores, and the one silk pinafore, froze in delighted horror and indignation. The Americans had burnt villages, stuck needles under people's fingernails, chopped their tongues out, and plastered them with napalm. Then they had dropped an atom bomb on Korea.

The leaving-bell had still to sound, but Form IB had already lined up and marched out of the classroom, and now they were going down the main staircase. You were supposed to walk as quietly as you could, 'like mice', in single file, as close to the wall as you could get without touching it, stopping at every landing as soon as you were given the word.

At last the orderly line of young ladies reached the cloakroom, breaking up by the wire coat-racks. Immediately teacher was surrounded by a throng of parents. She talked to them for a while, looking over her shoulder every now and again. Eventually the girls had all put their coats on and left, and all the parents except Stalina's mother had gone. Stalina's mother was the head of the parents' committee.

Tatyana Levina crept up behind the two and stood for a long time, not sure whether she should say anything. Eventually she asked:

'Did the Americans really drop the atom bomb on Korea?'

But at the same moment the general's wife said: 'I'd like you to show me Stalina's marks.'

Fat little Stalinka already had her coat on, and was waiting for her mother in the dimly lit passage outside. Just then the bell went; the noise from overhead grew louder and louder. Stalinka began pretending to be very interested in the huge memorial board with its names in gold letters. Tatyana Levina was still standing about, not sure what to do. At that moment some older girls, bold and fearless Amazons from the second form—or maybe even the third, some of them—came down the stairs. When they saw Stalinka, they all shouted at the tops of their voices, 'There she is! There she is! Tell-tale!' and went straight for her. Stalinka shot a glance upwards—no sign of her mother—and rushed outside. Run, Stalinka! They all went after Stalinka, the whole of Form 2A, not stopping for their coats, they chased her up Baskov Lane, tripping her up with their cases. Past the school she rushed, then straight across the road—the house where she lived was opposite. There was a bus just coming round the corner into the street, and all the girls shouted at her to wait, but too late! She'd reached her home front doorstep already.

The next morning Tatyana Levina went off to school, dragging her heavy briefcase behind her. She was late; Baskov Lane was deserted. Black flags hung from the poles at first-floor level; it was the anniversary of Kirov's murder.°

Tatyana Levina walked the length of the brick barracks, thinking about Kirov, the boy from Urzhum, and staring through all the windows. The gates where the sentry stood weren't completely shut, and inside she could see a narrow yard with a cannon standing inside it. The sentry stared after her and said, 'You got legs like a piano's'. She was astonished: how did he know that she was having music lessons?

She didn't like her music lessons. It wasn't just the lessons themselves, or the terror of playing at concerts, it was the sense that she was missing out on life. She had the feeling that there were only two sorts of people in the world, those who were forced to have music lessons, and those who were spared them. Most of the girls in her class, in the district where she lived, and the books she'd read, seemed happier and freer than her. Feeling that real life, in all its rough vitality, was passing her by, she became ever more obsessed with descriptions of life. She never left home, never went anywhere, she never even went to Young Pioneer camp, though she was often asked to. Instead, she became more and more addicted to reading. 'That's right, you go and get some fresh air,' her parents would say, seeing her going off to her music lessons—and she did, three gulps of it, between the door of the house where she lived and the door of the music school five yards down the street.

'I'm finished,' Tatyana Levina would often think, 'My goody-goody life is dragging along in the dust like a music case'. She enjoyed tormenting herself with thoughts like this, trailing the hated case along the ground as she walked.

One day at school, she said something so dreadful that everyone stopped speaking to her. For some reason she couldn't stop herself lying to the whole class, telling them that her father was Gaidar the writer.° In fact Gaidar had been killed well before she was born—indeed, before anyone in Form IB was born. Not that anyone did the sums; they simply walked away from her in silence.

It's an oddly significant incident. By substituting an imaginary life for a real one, Tatyana had moved deep into the territory of art; yet she had felt compelled to lean on a father's strong arm to do it, not trusting in her own frail fictions. Imagine saying that about your parents, though! You sometimes see something like that happen with a hunting dog: it suddenly leaves its owners and goes off with a visitor, as though it had sensed a real hunter in this total stranger.

There was almost no one around outside school, and lessons had started. A lame girl whom Tatyana Levina didn't know was rushing towards the doors as fast as she could. Her mother was with her, carrying her briefcase. Tatyana Levina made to run too, but then she stopped, not wanting to barge in front of the lame girl; she stepped back, staring fixedly at her from behind. The girl was in baggy trousers; they were tucked into felt boots that had become pink, from the school polish. What on earth were they thinking of? The headmistress, Miss Surepka,° had said that the girls were to wear shoes, not boots, to school.

'Stop, they won't let you in!' cried Tatyana Levina, rushing after them. 'Not in those felt boots!'

No one in Form IB had ever seen Miss Surepka; some people said that she always wore a yellow dress, but that was all anyone knew. She was as hard to spot as a single stem of charlock in a tidy, monotonous ploughed field.

But everyone knew, loved, feared, and respected Kseniya Alekseevna, the black-haired director of studies for the lower school. She was so tall and thin, so neat in her severe black dress, cut in the pre-Revolutionary way; the girls must have loved her just as much then too, and when she went up the main *gimnaziya* staircase they'd all greeted her politely, inclining their heads just so—like that.

When Tatyana Levina came into the classroom, she stood and waited by the door, expecting she'd have to apologize and make her excuses. But everyone ignored her, so she went and sat down.

Something strange was happening. Tall Zhuraeva had been standing at her desk and sounding off about something.

Suddenly she stopped speaking.

'Go on,' said Miss Sirotkina.

'Tatyana doesn't pull her weight, she doesn't make any contribution to the collective.'

'Don't worry,' Tatyana's neighbour whispered. 'It's not you they're arresting, only your parents.'

It was her that Zhuraeva was talking about. She was calling her by her full name, Tatyana this, Tatyana that, just as if she were some newspaper reporter. And suddenly she brought up Gaidar, and it was clear that had really done it, there was no saving Tatyana now.

The door opened, and a grown-up pioneer no one knew came in and said loudly, 'I'm to take Tatyana Levina to see the headmistress.'

Tatyana got up, walked along the rows of desks and out into the corridor, then down the stairs, following the pioneer girl, who walked in stony silence.

The huge mirrors of the former girls' *gimnaziya* glimmered in the half-light. A strange cleaner was scrubbing the steps. On the second floor, there was no mirror: a big picture in a frame hung there instead. The picture was of Stalin, with a little Central Asian girl called Mamlakat in his arms: she was holding out a bouquet to him, and had her other arm wrapped round his neck.

At that point Tatyana Levina's nerves gave way and she burst out sobbing. In stern indifference, the pioneer girl waited for her to stop crying, and then they walked on.

'There she is, that's the one, the one who made those big bullies push Stalina under the bus.'

It was the general's wife, sitting slumped on a sofa. Miss Surepka, in yellow, and Kseniya Alekseevna, in black, were sitting at a desk.

'They'd actually grabbed hold of her, you know,' said Stalinka's mother. 'Fortunately she managed to struggle free, but they tore a great lump of fur out of her coat first.'

She leaned against the oilcloth back of the headmistress's sofa, and dropped her voice.

'My husband shot twenty hares last autumn, twenty, so that our little girl could have a proper winter coat. Now they go and grab her by the coat. Here, I'll show you!'

She began rootling in a shopping-bag that was standing by her on the sofa; the black and dun fox tippet round her neck slid sideways, leering with its red glass eyes.

'What are her marks like?' asked Kseniya Alekseevna.

'Excellent, of course,' the general's wife replied immediately, tearing herself from her shopping-bag. 'But we don't know about next term yet, do we?'

After lessons were over, Tatyana Levina wandered back through the streets; for some reason, the cellar windows far below the pavement kept tugging at her consciousness. They'd call her parents into school and arrest them there. Why had she gone back to the classroom after the interview? Why hadn't she gone straight home? Galya Tsvetkova used to live in a cellar like that. Then she died. A lot of the girls went to the funeral, they said it was really beautiful, her parents had bought her a real worsted pinafore, just like the one she'd always wanted when she was alive. The girls who hadn't gone to the funeral had asked what the point of buying her that was, when she was dead, and that had offended the girls who *had* gone. Everything was new: Galya's brown wool dress, her black worsted pinafore, and the big puffy brown ribbon in her hair, and her dark-red shoes were new too.

There she is on the photograph, amongst the others in sateen pinafores, pale and blurred but still alive. An underground child, from the corner of Korolenko and Nekrasov Streets, the meeting-place between the seeds fallen on stony ground, and those who reap life's rich rewards.°

So I find myself acting as a chronicler for Tatyana after all. It's a thankless task, and I'd appreciate the chance to say something about it. To date, all the chroniclers that ever existed—in Russia and everywhere else—have been men. There isn't a female equivalent of the role, and I think that's a pity. Women chroniclers have some advantages, if you like to put it that way. I seem to remember that Tolstoy got his wife to dress his heroines—that is, to tell him about her own clothes, so he knew what to put them in. Conversely, we women chroniclers have no trouble in dressing the bride all by ourselves, but we have to consult some retired officer we know about whether a detachment's position was really all that hopeless, and how it got into the mess in the first place. The officer I consulted had served in the Far East; he could answer all my questions about Tatyana perfectly.

Whose advice carries more weight, then, Sofya Andreevna's or my friend the retired pilot's? I think both kinds are equally important; I also think they relate to similar questions, that is, to questions of kit. There are times when it's more important how you kit yourself out at a ball than it is on a battlefield. Comparisons between the two situations are by no means fortuitous: in both cases victory depends on well-designed and reliable equipment just as much as it does on a well-thought-out strategy. A battleship's effectiveness often hangs on the quality of its rigging, I can tell you.

Try eavesdropping on two women talking to each other, having a private conversation about the astonishing conquest that one of them has just made.

'What were you wearing?' the more impetuous sort of friend will ask. Her question may seem to interrupt the narrative at a wholly inappropriate point, but in fact it's meant to help her reconstruct circumstances for herself. Or if, on the other hand, the friend in question is rather more reserved, she'll say nothing, knowing that she's bound to get all the details in due time. Then the whole panorama of battle will be spread out before her.

Woman is a chronicler by nature. Name me one headmistress or schoolteacher who can resist telling her husband every detail of the latest staff meeting the minute she gets home. More: I am absolutely convinced that many Soviet families only stay together because the husbands indulge their wives, and let them chatter on about work. If a wife is deprived of this, she'll go straight off to wail to her friends about her miserable life. And what joy when harmony is restored once more, when her husband is back home, and sober, and listening to her again, and even asking every so often, 'And how's that colleague of yours, what's her name, Arsefeatures, or whatever you call her?'

What about women fetching water? And chats in the train? Remember your sisters-in-law? Your neighbours telling you the story of their lives? Suppose you ring your sister at work. You can be certain everyone in her office knows why you're ringing better than you do; you can bet they know the whole history of your marriage better than you do too.

In any case, you can say what you like: I'm not letting anyone else get hold of Tatyana Levina's story.

So you're wondering what women know about war? No one asked that when they were made to do military subjects as part of their university courses, when all language graduates were forced to do 'military interpreting' as a subsidiary, and women were given military rankings—not to speak of being made to serve in the armed forces, if you please. Tatyana Levina herself understood as much about war as anyone could be expected to, and when she rushed into the reeds to save 'everyone', then that's exactly what she thought she was doing, 'saving everyone'.

And that's how I saw it too, though I did have quite a few arguments with my informant about things; he insisted that she shouldn't have done what she did at all, she shouldn't have got stuck in those wretched thickets to start with. It was her commanding officer's fault that she got stuck. Well, we can all understand *that* much. If they were going to go chasing after the partisans into the forest, then they should have had at least two motor launches equipped with machine-guns, and half-a-dozen grenade throwers, and they should have been sure to keep in radio contact all the time. But the radio contact was the strangest bit of the whole story, and neither I nor my informant understand much of what was going on there. In time, though, more may be discovered, so that we have a clearer picture of that last tragic battle.

Well, if I live long enough myself, I'll get hold of that bastard on the lake-shore post who called out 'Keep left'. She did what he said; after all, she was the messenger, and how was she to know that the post was in enemy hands? And the bastard spoke to her in Russian, how did they get him to do that? He called out to her, 'Over here, it's OK'. Did they use force? Well, they may have done, perhaps he even thought they'd shoot him, but in that case, why did he have to shout out so cheerfully? Surely they can't have made him do that, after all, why should they have wanted to? What was so threatening in seeing some damn fool of a woman a few feet away, quite obviously lost? Say what you like, but I'm sure he could have managed to drop her a hint. Actually, what I really think is this. He did it on purpose. After all, he had some sort of a funny name, didn't he? Bavyka, or Bavyakin, something like that. Not a Russian name, anyway. A good man to leave as a guard, I don't think! I've even heard he went out to welcome the partisans himself; well, he'd had plenty of time waiting around to think of how he'd give them the hospitality treatment! Anyway, I hope that when this essay is published someone who knew him will come forward. They wouldn't give me his case papers—there must have been classified information of some kind in them. He had the radio, and when they asked him to pass a message on, he said it was broken. I'm sure he was responsible for what happened to Tatyana Levina—and for the fact that the whole detachment was surrounded, wiped out. No, it's a clear case of treachery, and I'm astonished that the responsible authorities, as they say, haven't dealt with it yet.

If I ever get to him, the bastard, I'll make sure everyone in the country knows who he is, and I'll put a curse on his whole family. Unto the seventh generation.

War isn't the place for delicate young girls and high-minded chroniclers. Quite true. But if people like us happen to get mixed up in it, what can we do? After all, we see what we see.

When the general mobilization was announced, we were all given three hours to reach base. We were given bowls, mugs, toothbrushes and a day's supply of food. Soon we were on our way east.

I don't need to go into the details of what happened next, it's all too well known. But in due course our unit was disbanded, and we all ended up in different places. I was sent to the capital, and Tatyana Levina, the heroine-to-be, ended up in a village in the provinces, way up in the mountains.

The district was notable for its associations with Shokan Valikhanov,° the famous traveller.

Earlier, before the war started, Tatyana had done some research on the history of Russian travellers in Asia. She'd taken a special interest in Eastern Turkestan, which Shokan Valikhanov, a junior officer in the Russian army, had managed to visit in the middle of the last century, disguised as an Adzhani merchant. Valikhanov, a Kazakh, was descended from the line of Genghis Khan; he was a great-grandson of the Khan of Kirgiz-Kaisatsk Ablai—from whom, by the way, Andrei Bely derived the pedigree of his fictional hero, Apollon Apollonovich Ableukhov, in *Petersburg*.

Few Europeans have visited Kashgar. Marco Polo and a priest called Benedict Goes passed through many centuries ago. In 1857 Adolf Schlagintweit,° the famous German Indiologist, arrived here from Kashmir. Shortly after his arrival, he vanished without trace, and all academic Europe waited with bated breath for news.

A year later, Valikhanov's caravan appeared on the streets of Kashgar, to find them lined with lopped-off heads stuck in wicker cages on long poles. Valikhanov realized that he was witnessing the aftermath of a rebellion by the Muslim town-dwellers, which had taken place not long previously. The rebellion had been led by a khoja,° during whose short period of domination the streets of Kashgar and its environs had been heaped with corpses.

It was at the moment of the rebellion that Adolf Schlagintweit had appeared; he had gone to pay his respects to the khoja. The latter, in an intoxicated and maddened state from hashish, had instantly given the order that Schlagintweit should be beheaded; soon the inhabitants of Kashgar were to see a tall, bareheaded, blond European, with bound hands, being led through the streets to execution.

It was customary in Kashgar to entice visiting merchants into marrying local girls. Upon completing his business, a merchant would make ready to leave, and his wife would accompany him to the city limits, weeping and lamenting. Kashgar law forbade her from following her husband out of the city. Not long afterwards, she would be married off again. As a marriage token, these Kashgar beauties would be presented with a fur hat by each husband in turn; a bride's status rose in accordance with the number of such hats on display in her home. Valikhanov was taken to see a girl who possessed no fewer than twenty fox-fur caps, which she kept stacked one atop the other like pillows on her bed.

Valikhanov's Uiguri wife had also seen the blonde German man; she had especially noticed how his golden curls floated on the wind.

On a certain river bank outside the town was a pyramid of human heads that had been raised in the days of the bloodthirsty khoja; the heads of execution victims were collected from wherever they had fallen and brought here to be added to the pile. But it was clear to Valikhanov that the brutality of the regiments that had put down the uprising had been no whit inferior to that of the khoja himself.

Our forces soon moved on to the far east, leaving the detachment with which Tatyana Levina was stationed far behind in the rearguard. She was given a billet in a mud hut on the outskirts of the village; her quarters were in the best part of the hut, and the large family to whom the hut belonged were left crammed together in one corner.

HQ was set up in what had been the local Party headquarters, at one corner of the village market square.

There was a lot to do in the first few days. The military commandant's address to the local people had to be translated. He told them that a government that genuinely reflected the wishes of the people would be introduced, and that the norms of Party authority would be restored. Then there was a bit about the sincere friendship that had always subsisted between fraternal nations, before the commandant rounded off by ordering that all firearms be surrendered within twenty-four hours, and decreeing that a curfew was to be instituted throughout the district.

Some of the old men did duly hand in their guns, ancient Soviet weapons of long obsolete design, and some of our men dragged in a heavy machine-gun which they had found lying in a thicket somewhere (now someone needed to check what the name of the place was).

One day a prisoner of war was brought in to HQ. The colonel himself acted as interrogator, and Tatyana as translator.

The prisoner had been wounded whilst the rebel forces were in retreat. The local teacher's daughter had found him a hiding-place somewhere over by Southern Mountain. He had a slim, fine-featured face, and spoke like a man with an education. His pronunciation indicated that he was from the capital; from the few things that he was prepared to say, it seemed likely that he had been exiled here, to the wilds of the country, as part of a 're-education programme'. He soon began refusing to answer any questions, though Tatyana tried to convey to him as gently as possible the colonel's assurances that the teacher's daughter had nothing to fear, and that the only sensible course was for the prisoner to co-operate, especially as no-one was going to rush him into a decision.

A few days later, Tatyana was asked to go out with a hunting party. The path into the hills led through orchards of green apricots and pomegranates that had just set fruit; beyond lay fields of flax, white with blossom, and plantations of opium poppy. I have not been able to establish in detail what happened during the hunt, but I know for certain that Tatyana shot a lynx, a splendid specimen, apparently—accounts are consistent on that. I also know that on the way back, Tatyana's companions let off a few rounds at some jackdaws which had been feeding on the poppy seeds, and which were perched on the poplars round about stoned out of their heads—some of them were so far gone that they had given up any attempt to perch, and were sprawling on the ground below the trees.

'An odd thing happened today,' Valikhanov wrote in his memoirs. 'We purchased a hen for dinner, a black one; the juice that ran out of the bird was black, and the bones of the beast turned out to be covered by a thin black membrane.' According to many other records, too, the black hens of Kashgaria really are black, with black meat whose taste is coarse and unappetising. Birds are always sold with their throats cut, and plucked ready for the pot. Kashgar pigs are black too, and their flesh is extraordinarily fatty. The Kashgar people are baffled by the surprise of visitors; it has never occurred to them that pigs could be any other colour.

I can't say whether Tatyana ever tried 'black soup', but the extraordinary dark colour of the local domestic animals, the odd, one might almost say the charred, taste of their meat, are matters of interest in their own right.

Tatyana had told Captain Tarasenko several times how awkward she felt that she should be occupying the greater part of the hut where she was billeted, whilst its owners slept crammed into one corner. Every time she made a cup of coffee or opened a tin of milk she was seized by embarrassment; she knew perfectly well that the locals were severely short of food, and had been for some time. Officers' rations included a generous supply of tins of sprat paste and sticks of soya meat; Tatyana would try to catch one of the children in the courtyard whenever she got the chance, and press a tin of food, or a sweet, on him or her.

But then came the Sunday morning when the real meaning of war came through to us all for the first time.

It was a wonderful morning in March. Tatyana was getting ready to go for a trip into the forest; she was waxing her skis, whilst Taipi, her setter, bounded around impatiently.

Did she sense, when she gave her dog that name (which means both 'decadence' and 'rebirth', I think), how soon she would be face to face with the people whose ancient culture she so respected?

'I sit indoors during the wine-making season'—this was the title which she gave to a tristich that she had composed in imitation of Far Eastern poetry:

> An autumn moon.
> Bubbles escape from the bottles.
> Time for a walk to the hay.

She was going down to the lake, by a path she had used often before. If she was lucky, she would get a glimpse of the quail, flying up from their roosting places under the snow, and on the way back she would be able to cross a broad glade in the woodland. It freezes hard in the mornings there, making a crust of snow you can ski over fast without fear of falling through, light and swift as a bird.

Her birthday fell in the winter, and she had always liked to see the signs of stubborn survival that winter brought: crossbills feeding their young in the hardest of frosts, quail nesting in the snow, bears asleep in their winter lairs. Sometimes, whilst you lie dozing in your hideout, dozens of tiny shrews get to work on your thick fur; when you resurface, you force your eyes open and stare blankly, then with horror, to see the bald patches; too late, the industrious creatures have long since dragged the stolen wool off to make their own nests.

The hot spring sun rises higher and higher, and beads of water form under your skis; soon the thaw will begin.

It's good sitting in the hay, lifting your face to the hot sunlight. The north face of the stack is still covered in snow, but to the south the white blanket is runkled, and bright drops are trickling down. The spoor of hares lies all around, and out there in the snow are the marks of an elk's broad hooves. From a copse comes the cry of a black woodpecker. Your ski-sticks are stuck in the ground, your gloves are laid on top, casting shadows like cropped ears. The tracks of a sledge, strewn with fallen hay, lead away from the stack.

Tatyana switched on the radio for the weather forecast. She needed to know what kind of wax to use on her skis, and the thermometer outside the window was in full sun, so that there was no relying on it. Suddenly the forecast was interrupted; first came the schoolmarmy voice of an announcer, then the calling signal, then a famous voice. Levitan's. 'Attention, all stations,' he said. She was expecting to hear that they'd just launched a new space-rocket or something like that, but instead she learned that war had been declared.

Outwardly nothing had changed; Taipi still leapt at her feet, and the smell of resin hung on the air; but she would be following different paths from now on.

Tatyana had long been trying to talk to the old man in the family where she was staying, but it was clear that he was avoiding her; if she ever did run into him and start talking about the old days—she was particularly interested in hearing about any antiquities there might be nearby—he would pretend that he couldn't understand what she was saying.

In HQ everyone was talking about one thing. Partisans had appeared up in the hills; they had attacked a shed where food was stored, and blown up a bridge.

That night Tatyana woke up, with the sensation that something had just run across her face. She sat up in bed. It was dark, and dogs were barking somewhere in the distance. She would have to get the torch. Usually she tried not to walk barefoot on the earth floor, but there was no use thinking of that now. She found the torch in the pocket of her uniform jacket, and flashed it at the bed; there, right on her pillow, was an enormous scorpion, long hooked tail upraised. She took one corner of the pillow and shook it gently, but the creature didn't even twitch; and so she placed the flat of her hand under the pillow, picked it up as delicately as a fresh iced cake, took it to the window, and flung it, and its marzipan decoration, straight out into the yard.

She lay down, head on the bare, damp, rice-straw mattress, from which a vile stink was wafting. The air was dense and thick.

She was remembering something that had happened at the beginning of her fourth year at university. When she was on her way back from the virgin soil regions in Karaganda—she'd been doing a stint of compulsory vacation work—a soldier on the train had given her a scorpion, buried in a lump of epoxy resin. There was a hole at one end of the lump so that you could wear it round your neck. It was rather like a fly, or some other kind of insect, fossilized in amber. But on the first day of lectures, someone had told Tatyana that wearing the amulet was certain to have dire consequences. Scorpio wasn't her astrological sign. She'd be putting herself at the mercy of alien powers. Not long afterwards, she had swapped the thing for a pair of real Chinese chopsticks.

Now here was a scorpion again. How ominous. She got up, put on her coat, and went out for a walk. Why was she letting that kind of nonsense get her down?

It was one of those close nights you often get in Turkestan. The geckos' nocturnal chorus rose into the air. Suddenly came the sound of footsteps and a woman's muffled laughter. Tatyana stepped back into the shadow of a tall elm, and a couple passed close by. It was the teacher's daughter, she knew her voice, and one of the officers. That girl was certainly up to something.

Tatyana managed to get back to sleep in the small hours. She dreamt that she had taken it into her head to go and look at a shamisen,° a kind of ancient Oriental instrument that geishas play.

So here she was, in the Hermitage. The lights were out, the shadows in the corners were growing longer, the vistas of worn marquetry floors down the halls shorter. Outside the huge chilly windows glimmered the dark-blue expanses of Palace Square and the Neva. There was no one about, and the air smelt faintly of New Year tangerines.

At last came a distant, capricious shine: the gold of pipes, the silver of flutes; she was walking past case after case of strange instruments when she suddenly heard the sound of a Chinese song.

In a corner at the other side of the room stood a piano; a musician was sitting at it and playing superbly (what, a Chinese song on a piano? From sheet music?) She went closer, and saw that the man was Chinese, and breathtakingly handsome. And he *was* reading from music, ordinary music, except that the word 'Sonata' was picked out in red. Who was he playing for? No one ever came to this room, it was too far off the beaten track; and in any case the whole Winter Palace was empty by now.

He had stopped playing. How could she show him how enraptured she was? She put her right hand on her heart and made a low, respectful bow. He kissed her hand.

'Comrade Lieutenant!' Someone was knocking at the door.

'What do you want?' Tatyana leapt from her bed, awake at once.

In a low voice the messenger told her: 'The commandant is asking for you. The sentry's been stabbed, and the prisoner has escaped.'

Tatyana threw on her clothes, and went with the messenger to the market square. It was just getting light. The whole village was still asleep, or pretending to be.

How could she ever pass on to anyone the sound of that music? It was still ringing in her ears. She would never see that face again, he would never take her hand, and she would never feel gratitude like that again.

Was he a famous pianist whose hands had been beaten to pulp? Was that his soul, finding a last audience?

From the poplars came the sounds of dawn stirrings. The crows were cawing faintly. The officers walked to HQ in silence. Outside in the corridor, Tatyana used a tin mug to scoop some tepid water from a bucket and drank it down quickly. Who had that been out with the teacher's daughter? What was going on? Who had killed the sentry?

Amongst Tatyana Levina's papers, I found some essays she had written about Valikhanov: on his excellence as a writer, and his links with some of the great Russian writers; on Dostoevsky's prophetic sense of Valikhanov's high destiny, and the sense of mission that had inspired Valikhanov himself. But there was nothing about the Russian Imperial Government's motivation in sending Valikhanov to Kashgar. It was clear that this side of things hadn't interested Tatyana. The prompting behind Valikhanov's long voyage, as she saw it, had more or less begun and ended with his desire to find out what had happened to Adolf Schlagintweit; or perhaps he had simply wanted to add his name to the long and glorious list of travellers to Kashgar, the first of whom had been Marco Polo.

But Tatyana had made herself familiar with a file of documents from the archive of the Ministry of Foreign Affairs (Asiatic Section), under the heading, 'Valikhanov, Lieutenant Sultan Shokan: Mission to Kashgar of'; indeed, like the conscientious researcher she was, she had even copied out extracts from these papers, including, for example, extracts from the then Director of the Asiatic section's copious report, 'The Situation in Kashgar and its Relevance for the Affairs of the Asiatic Section'. This dealt with the formation of an 'independent Khanate' in Kashgar, which was to be placed 'under the protection of Russia', leading to the assumption by Russia 'of overall control in Central Asia', and hence to an augmentation of her influence over 'routes further east'. In consideration of these last matters, the Director considered that it was imperative to 'make all possible efforts to gather information about the current situation in Kashgar, and also to verify such information as is currently available about the routes leading in that direction'; to this end, he recommended that 'an experienced and reliable officer be dispatched to Kashgar forthwith'.

Valikhanov, who was later to become a famous scholar and academic, with many geographical discoveries and ethnographical works to his credit, was then at the very beginning of his career; but the Minister of War, responding to 'a Sovereign Command of His Imperial Majesty', ordered the commanding officer of the Autonomous Siberian Corps to be ready for a possible request for aid on the part of the Muslim ruling house of Kashgar, which was independent of the Chinese authorities, and instructed him that any such request 'must receive his immediate co-operation'.

It is clear that Tatyana only copied out these extracts, as I said before, out of conscientiousness, not attaching any particular importance to them, and not reflecting on whether Valikhanov had recognized the role envisaged for him by the Tsarist administration. For Tatyana, Valikhanov was no more than a scholar who had been encouraged to make his trip by P. P. Semyonov.°

There could be no question of 'roles envisaged by the administration'. This was the time when the fashion for excursionism° reached its apogee; people made lists of famous places, then read up about them, and went to stare at them. They were excited by the colourful exoticism of what they saw, by its literary significance—or, conversely, by the fact that everything was 'so remote and desolate'. The expansion of excursionism infected not only individual places, but whole routes, whole regions; it led to an inexorable search for new places, and still more new places.

'He has left part of his soul here.'

Schlagintweit, his curls blowing as he follows the cutthroats with their sabres, has a kind of beauty; and so, in her way, does Tatyana, when they take her to the place of execution.

We are left to remember what they did, and the places that they visited.

We were having an ordinary lazy Sunday morning. No more than that.

The excursionist era's rallying call is that programme called 'Good Morning'.°

The most over-used word in the world is 'happiness'. Nothing is supposed to get in its way. Those responsible for fostering it are allocated special broadcasting times.

'Good morning, dear listeners, we're happy to see you, hope you're happy to hear us,' say the grating, mechanical voices, 'happy there at home with your families.

'First things first: you won't have forgotten it's Chemists' and Metallurgists' Day° today, so let's wish a really happy day to all the chemists and metallurgists among us. As for the rest of you, we've got something here that's going to make you all very happy: it's your favourite comedian. If you hang on a couple of minutes, you'll hear him do your two favourite characters, the plumber who drops his aitches and the snotty professor who can't say his Rs...

'Remember, all of you, this lovely Sunday, wherever you are, whatever you're doing, the Motherland is thinking of you, thinking of how happy you are, because it's Sunday morning, you've just had a nice breakfast, and there isn't a war on.

'Oh yes, and while we're on the subject, what about a nice after-breakfast trip abroad? Chunga-Changa Island's a happy place: what about a little visit there? Now, let's move on to Friends of the Russian Language.' That doesn't make us feel quite so happy, does it? Half the day gone already. A stern nannying voice tells us: 'You mustn't say so-and-so, you must say so-and-so else, so-and-so is ungrammatical. Now, here's something to work on in your spare time: queuing etiquette. Is it proper to say: "Eh, are you last?" No, it is not. Repeat after me: "Excuse me, is this the end of the queue?"'

It's hard to remember what life before the war was like.

'You know that new guidebook? Want me to get you a copy?'

'You haven't been there? Oh, but you really must.'

'Have you read the latest *Science and Life*?'°

Science *for* life, that is to say: how to go on existing, a course in do-it-yourself survival: if you haven't read the manual, you'll go under.

This was the time of sensational articles in the Young Soldier magazines about an amazing recent discovery: biofields next to department stores. Did you know that they make dried-up cheese go all nice and moist? The effect on roquefort is incredible, it starts to smell quite different. There's one woman who owns a clearing in a wood with a biofield in it, she only has to leave the room and the cheese goes hard immediately.

But the thing that got the excursionist era more excited than anything else was museum openings, and the preparations for them.

One interior designer (from a family of famous architects) was nearly torn to pieces, he got so many commissions for exhibition designs. You could see his insipid concoctions in any town you cared to name.

An ambitious new type of museum director started to be seen about the place: someone who knew the value of money. In time, this new type forced out the old type of museum director, a dry academic with no sense of self-interest, and still more important, no gift for politicking.

The new-style directors sniffed out immediately what was 'really it', and they talked about things they didn't know the first thing about in such confident voices, parroting this, that, the other expert. They were so good at seeming diffident, too, at concealing how pushy and sly they really were, that they took quite a lot of people in.

The next discovery was someone who could do incredible forgeries of famous people's handwriting.

He churned out pages and pages of manuscripts by Tolstoi, Dostoevsky,

Chekhov, in handwriting that looked as if it had been sandblasted: his manuscripts were more real than the originals he copied. It was odd, though: in the end all his wonderful productions faded, the ink got this sort of satanic light to it, blood red. And the master forger himself broke out in eczema everywhere, not just his hands, but his boiled-looking face with its lashless eyes. There was a red light in his eyes exactly like there was in the ink, everyone noticed it.

Enough of that, though. I can't remember anything else about those days. They seemed so prosperous, so cloudless, but in fact they were days of fading and decadence, as short of colour and strength as wallflowers come up for the third season.

You switch on the radio. Any minute now there'll be a weather forecast or something important like that. We may be enjoying ourselves, but our memory is atavistic: it never sleeps, and it's always listening out for the voice of a special announcer, the one they keep for emergencies.

No one told us we should listen out for him: we ourselves sit waiting, waiting, and imagining exactly what will happen. Every Sunday. Every Sunday of glorious weather brings with it the threat of hearing that velvety voice again.

His velvety voice goes with his velvet breeches, his badge of office as royal messenger. He knows better than anyone how to wrap whatever he says in dense soft velvet, in velvet blacker than midnight; not one spring in his clockwork inside will squeak or creak or give itself away; all of it is packed so carefully.

From our earliest childhood we have been terrified by every pause during a radio broadcast; the People's Artist of impending catastrophe° is always on hand; during every news bulletin he watches and waits; he will hear the last trump before we do, he will hear every news flash first. We are always, always there, by the loudspeaker; whatever we are doing, wherever we are, the tick of the metronome is always with us.

The Punitive Detachment

A few days later, Tatyana Levina is one of a group taking part in a special operation. The motor-launch chugs down the lake, patrolling down empty banks, nosing into winding creeks.° The occasional scattered villages have been deserted by their Muslim inhabitants. According to all available information, they are in the heart of partisan country.

One evening at sunset, when the patrol boat was in Shaidan creek, the look-out spotted some dots moving about on the bank to starboard side. On closer inspection, however, all that was found was a herd of horses; no sign of human habitation was visible nearby, at any rate from the boat.

The commanding officer gave the order to drop anchor beyond the peninsula and dispatch a search party from there once darkness had fallen, in order to establish whether there might be a nomadic settlement anywhere around, and if so, whether it was a large one. He also ordered that one of the locals was to be brought in for questioning.

The next morning, when she came out of the tent, Tatyana noticed the marks of bare feet on the sand by the lake shore. They were so small they could have been a woman's, even her own, had it not been for the fact that nothing would have induced her to go barefoot on this terrain. She was always wary of poisonous creatures, scorpions, phalanges,° and karakurts,° especially when she reached for her boots in the mornings—she had to leave them by the tent flap overnight, getting soaked through with dew. So if she hadn't been sleep-walking through the moonlit fields, the marks must have been made by a stranger.

She followed the tracks, and they went from the sand into the water—he had been walking through the shallows—and back again. The heel was touchingly round, the toes straight, with hardly a trace of instep between—this spy certainly didn't have flat feet. The traces vanished in the reeds, next to an inlet—here the walker had swum away.

So he'd swum away. Fine. Time for a wash. Tatyana scooped up a mugful of the salty water, and hung her towel on a tuft of salt reeds; she reached for the soap, but the dish slid out of her hands and went bounding over the scalloped sand, into a pool of lake water that had filled up during a recent storm. The dish rolled over and over, then floated away on a blue wavelet.

Two herons flew by. The sun was up; it was high time to be going back. But suddenly Tatyana heard an echoing splash, as though someone had just dived heavily into the water.

She froze. Was it a flock of geese settling on the lake? No, it was too loud for that—it was more likely to be wild boar taking their young for a splash. She imagined them all, screwing up their eyes and plunging in. In that case, though, better move on. She'd got used to seeing their narrow tracks on the sand, and the paths they battered down in the reeds, she'd even seen the hollows once or twice where they'd been lying, but she wouldn't exactly have liked to meet one close to. But then she stopped: best have a look after all. She crept up as quietly as she could. Not a boar in sight. Could it be that barefoot Chinese fox? Suddenly she heard another splash, and then saw spreading ripples in the water. A glossy black back showed for an instant above the water—what could it be? Then she saw another, this time in the shallows. Tatyana ran up: so that's what it was, a huge fish. The water was knee-deep, but the fish was stranded; it lay trapped, thrashing by her legs. She tried to pick it up, but it was impossible; each time it slipped from her hands.

Tatyana ran for her towel; the fish was still lying there when she returned, so she wrapped it gently in the towel, picked it up, and carried it in triumph back to the camp.

It was still too early for reveille. Tatyana opened the tent-flap quietly and threw the fish in. It thrashed about wildly in the small, close space; the soldiers woke up and leapt from their beds. *Allakh akbar!*° No, don't shoot! It's the Lieutenant!

The soldiers rushed to the water, and began catching the fish with anything that came to hand. It was a whole shoal of carp spawning, it turned out. A cauldron of water was soon boiling; now all that remained was to cook the gutted fish. Gulls and crows were wheeling overhead. Bubbles of fish's breath rushed over the lake surface; every ripple brought up more and more of them.

But there was no time even to taste the fish soup. The commanding officer divided the detachment in two. One group was to stay here, another to track along the channel.

'That channel's a maze, no sense in trying to follow it,' thought Tatyana. She'd noticed that even the local fishermen made marks so that they could take their bearings and find their way back. They'd bend a tuft of salt reeds or make a knot in one, or leave a stick standing upright on the tallest dune.

The captain studied the map. If they kept to the left of the channel all the way, they were bound to come back into Shaidan creek eventually.

Exactly as she had thought. They'd got lost amongst all those endless lakes, with their thousands of channels and inlets; not only had they not been able to keep track of the enemy, they hadn't even been able to find their way out. Now they were coming under hostile fire from the opposite bank, and their position was dangerously exposed. Strange whistling noises were coming from the radio: it looked as though it had packed up altogether. The radio mast was at base camp. Two launches had sunk.

Someone had to go back for help. Why shouldn't she do it? They didn't seem likely to need a translator at the moment. She'd find her way, of course she would.

'At least let me try, comrade captain.'

'Very well then, off you go. Be sure to take enough water, and a rifle. Leave the dictionary behind.'

This was a new adventure, the most interesting she had had so far. She would find her way back to Shaidan creek. What was the meaning of 'Shaidan', incidentally? It meant a martyrs' burial ground, or something like that. Not bad.

She saw herself as someone who found, not someone who lost. What hadn't she found? Knives on forest paths, lots of them, one a real bandit knife with a blade that sprang out the minute you pressed a red button on the handle. Once she had found a huge watermelon floating along a river, God knew from where. On Nevsky she'd found a piece of lapus lazuli—it had probably fallen out of somebody's ring. She'd been cutting up a Hungarian cockerel to make a celebration meal, and in its thawing giblets she'd found a big pink pearl. Either some woman worker in the food factory had dropped it in, or else the Hungarian cockerel itself had grubbed up the pearl at some stage during its free-range existence, on a river-bank somewhere.

She wouldn't get lost in this jungle either. All she needed was a cork helmet. The rest was in order. The more so since she'd already covered a lot of the way back. Maybe she'd even end up with a cork helmet. How? It would float to her downriver, that's how.

She walked the path to Shaidan creek convinced of her own invulnerability.

She'd soon be back at base camp, and they'd send out the helicopters. Congratulations, Lieutenant! She'd always known she was destined to do something extraordinary. Even if the detachment was surrounded, it would be possible to hold out for a long time, but breaking out would be much more difficult. They'd probably be ambushed: there was only one route through from the lakes, only one channel led back to deep water, the rest led nowhere. But she would save them.

If only someone could see her. This was what she had lived for, this was why she'd learnt the language.—How far had she got down the boar path, she wondered?

Every now and again she would come up against a huge spider's web, binding the panicles of the reeds so tightly that the fat stems had given slightly, leaning one towards the other. At one corner lurked the spider itself. At first she tried to skirt the webs, but she soon forgot them. Sticky strands clung to her sweaty face and damp neck.

A black column of smoke was blowing about on the horizon somewhere, and if you looked carefully you could see flames, though these were almost transparent in the bright spring air. It was perfectly normal, she assured herself. You often got fires. What a lot of game there was round here, and all paired off already.

A cormorant flew by, black as a cinder, looking like something you might find at the bottom of a careless housewife's frying pan. There was a smell of smoke. She was nearer the fire now. It was upwind of her.

So what was she to do when the fire reached here? Wade up to her neck in water, or climb out of the reeds and up on to high ground—on to one of those volcanic hills there? Hell, now it was turning, coming at her from the other side too—that barefoot fox would smoke her out like a hare.

Better make for the the high ground all the same. Damn, now she'd cut her hand, there was blood all over the yellow stalks.

Suppose those leaflets were right, the ones they had posted on the gates and walls of the village? We told the soldiers they were nothing to worry about, nothing interesting at all, prophecies, New Year greetings. They were messages from the partisans, though. They said the enemy forces were suffering heavy losses; soon the People's Army would liberate Sin-Kiang°

At last she had scrambled out of the steamy rushes and was up on the sandy bank. A fresh wind had dried her sweaty face.

Up here on the dune, that barefoot man could pick her off as easy as pie. Better lie down behind that bush and reconnoitre. She had a look round. Beyond the sea of rushes rose a line of sandy hills.

What huge expanses. The fire had scorched all the lower ground, circling all the hidden lakes and channels; now it was racing onwards, leaving a line of black smoking bristles behind it.

It couldn't reach this land beyond the dunes, though. There was nothing here but sand, and the odd bush, and clumps of Tangut rhubarb.° A broad leaf spread under her hand. She snapped off its stalk and peeled the pink skin. It tasted just like the ordinary stuff.

Below her, holes gaped black in the sand, and grey lizards were scuttling about. What were they called? Hang on, hang on—look at that one bending its tail, like a peeled rhubarb stalk. A huge open mouth. Hi, Big Ears. I got a real fright when I saw your slit-eyed mug.

She'd run from the fire, so had all the creatures that could. The ones that lived high up were safe, all the ones that nested lower down had been burnt. Better look what had happened to her brood, though: after all, they nested on the ground too. She could see a faint trace of smoke rising.

It all looked so tidy: only a few shrivelled leaves of rhubarb were left, like shreds of burnt newspaper.

A wolf ran by the shores of the lake, throwing up dust.

The fire had vanished behind the hills. Time she vanished as well. She must cross those blackened tracts of ground as quickly as possible and get back in the sheltering clumps of reeds. Quickly, quickly. The sun shone dully. She felt the heat seep through her boots, black clouds rose with every step she took, like exploding puffballs.° It had all changed in the space of minutes. As though there had never been rustling jungles of reeds and nests and herds of wild boar, as though she herself had never forced her way through. She was running as fast as the wolf—let the ground burn under the enemy's feet—she wasn't anyone's enemy, how could she be, she'd never hit anyone, she'd never had an enemy, she was kind and pretty and that was all, her face was covered in soot, so who did she think she was anyway, and she did have an enemy, a deadly enemy, oh now she was finished. She stuck out like a white winter hare on a black footpath.

Bloody hell, she'd left the water bottle over on the sand-hill, now she had nothing to drink, too bad, you can drink salt water if you have to. She was nearly at the end of her strength, but still she pressed on, going further and further north. She must be getting to the big lake by now, provided she hadn't got lost, of course. She had to skirt lake after lake. The sound of the shooting seemed no further away; the water made it carry, so you couldn't tell where it was.

Then she saw a pole on one of the dunes. Good, somewhere over there the channel goes into the Great Lake, that's where base camp is. She thought she could hear the waves, but it could just have been the air beating in her ears.

Another creek blocked her path, a small one. She didn't want to have to go all round it. She waded into the water: it couldn't be more than ten paces across. Couldn't she just follow the creek's winding bank? You could see the water vanish there into the thickets, and that narrow channel could perfectly well broaden out into another lake. There were white traces of salt on the banks, that meant the water level was low, so it must be shallow here.

She trudged through the water, scooping it up in her hands and splashing it on her face. Then suddenly her foot slipped and she fell flat in the water. She tried to get up, but her feet were stuck fast in the mud. She hauled out her boots and staggered backwards, sending a shoal of bubbles from the bottom.

She flopped down on her belly and tried to swim; every now and then one of her feet caught the treacherous bottom. Swirls of the mud she had disturbed rose into the water. At last she reached the bank, but she had struck a wall of reeds on which she could make no impression. She should never have left the boar path. She tried to edge along the fringes of the creek, but she soon lost her footing, her feet sank back into the sticky mud. She seized hold of the thick reeds and hauled out each foot in turn.

'Hey! I'm stu-uck!' she yelled, just in case. After all, camp should be quite close by now.

She heard a noise ahead, then the sound of someone moving. A voice called: 'Who goes there?'

'It's me! Lieutenant Levina!'

She could hear the voice shouting again, and she thought she caught the words 'Keep to the left, to the left!' She moved to the left, but the wall of reeds was just as thick there.

'I can't get out!' But now she could hear people forcing their way towards her, splashing through the water. The reeds next to her parted, and two men came out.

'Hans uh!'° they shouted, training their machine-guns on her.

When the allied forces liberated Kashgar, some refugees told them that they had seen a tall girl being led through the town with a rope round her neck. But whether that girl was Tatyana or not is hard to say.

(1973/1989)

♦ OLGA SEDAKOVA ♦

Born in 1949 into the family of a military engineer in Moscow, Sedakova was educated at Moscow University, where she also completed a postgraduate dissertation on death rites amongst the Eastern Slavs. She still lives in Moscow, where she now lectures at the Gorky Institute of Literature. Her first collection of verse, *Vrata, okna, arki*, was published in Paris in 1987. Sedakova's work has been acclaimed at home and abroad, but, like Elena Shvarts, she has only recently begun to be published freely in Russia. Sedakova is the author of academic articles and essays as well as poetry; she has translated into Russian many major Western poets, including Horace, Verlaine, Rilke, and Claude.

Fifth Stanzas

(Russian text p. 479)

1

A great thing is a refuge for herself,
a broad deep pond or Trappist's far-off cell,
a mythic fish that swims the hidden depths,
a righteous man, reading his Book of Hours
concerning the day that has no evening;
a vessel holding her own beauty in.

2

And as the ocean swims inside a shell—
a valve in the heart of time, a trap as well,
walking on velvet paws, a marvel in a bag,
a treasure hidden in a sleeping draught,
so in my mind, inside this creaking house,
she goes, and holds her magic lantern up...

3

But tell me, don't you think the verse above
is crammed too full? All right, it's well enough
for one who feels the pull, outside his dreams,
of images aslant with silvery gleams,
carrying us on pointed fins to where
we and all we have known are dust, no more.

4

The light (for let me note in brackets this)
is something we could call a mystery,
speaking at will of God knows what,
whilst speech, like a sunbeam's dancing motes,
spins slowly as the eddied fragments spin,
but means—the transparency of things.

5

A great thing is a refuge for herself,
a place where beasts can leap and the birds peck
music for food. But panting on the heels
of day comes night. And he who sees it fall
puts down his work, so soon as the stars appear
with their magnetic pull, and ready tears.

6

It's odd how old one's eyes have got!
for they see only what they can't,
and nothing else. Even so from one's hands,
sometimes, a cup may fall. My friends!
what we have kept, like life, will slide away,
and a star we cannot know rise in the sky.

7

Poems, it seems to me, are grown for all,
as Serbian nut-trees grow along the walls
of monasteries, that keep a scoop of honey,
a well, with stars floating like ice in springtime,
so for a moment someone in the world
sees fragile life, like the spring stars that whirl:

8

—O, that is all: I knew that I was doomed,
and that my reason cried for lack of food;
trapped like a mouse in chilly vaults, it pined;
I knew no one felt pity for a friend—
all is in flight, and all is drunk on joy,
for 'things must pass', as Horace used to say...

9

Why hurry, life, why chivvy on the hour?
You'll soon have time to sew my mouth right up,
stitching with iron threads. So humour me,
deign, then, to give my *sententia* a try:
'A great thing is a refuge for herself':
she sings when singing us to rest,

10

—they say, most beautifully. Now
at noontide, beauty's night-time door
is open wide, and high up in the hills
the constellatory fire, both monk and angel,
reads by the light of its own candle-ends
the exemplary lives of guilty men.

11

A great thing is a loss to end all loss:
a Mediolanian glimpse of paradise;
its hearing is attuned; on the tuned string
fear strums away; dust is an animate thing,
and like a flame-tugged butterfly, it cries,
'I will not be the thing that I will be!'

12

The future rolls into the spacious house,
the secret cistern, forcing its way at last...

[1992]

APPENDIX

Poems in Russian

◆ EKATERINA URUSOVA ◆

О Музы! Вы мой дух ко песням всплamените,
И пола вашего вы голосу внемлите!
Во древни времена, Российская страна,
В невежество была, во мрак погружена.
Жилища вашего тогда не досязали,
И тернием пути к Парнассу зарастали.
Парнасский огнь еще Сердец не всплaменял,
К составу песен дух восторгом не пылал:
Но в мрачности такой Россия озарилась,
И Лиры красота в пределах сих явилась.
Невежество у нас в презрении лежит,
Российския страны незнание бежит,
И просвещению Державу уступают,
Ваш глас, приятный глас, сердца у всех пленяет.
В кратчайши времена Россия процвела,—
Расинов, Пиндаров, она произвела,
ЕКАТЕРИНИН век те ныне воспевают,
Премудрые дела в бессмертие включают.
На Росскую страну вселенна мещет взор,
Прославь ее, прославь, прекрасных Муз собор!
Се в наши времена златые зрятся веки,
Кастальские текут с Парнаса к Россам реки;
И чтобы окружать священных Муз престол,
То начал воспевать у нас и женский пол:
Они ко нежностям во песнях прибегают,
И добродетелям венцы приготовляют.
С приятностью они веселости поют,
И действие страстей почувствовать дают.
В России видимы Сапфоны, де ла Сюзы,
За ними я стремлюсь: ... О вы, прекрасны музы!
К ободрению, для песен красоты,
Рассыпьте предо мной Парнасские цветы!
Врачебною водой вы Лиру окропите,

И мне ее теперь из ваших рук пошлите.
Потщуся мысль мою я с вами согласить,
Потщуся песнь мою пред вами возгласить.
С холмистых гор ко мне вы взоры обратите,
И глас, мой робкий глас, коль можно ободрите.
С великодушием внимайте песнь мою:
О Музы! я для вас, на Лире воспою.

◆ ANNA BUNINA ◆

Хоть бедность не порок
Для тех, в ком есть умок,
Однако всяк ее стыдится
И с ней как бы с грехом таится.
К иному загляни в обеденный часок:
Забившись в уголок,
Он кушает коренье:
В горшочке лебеда,
В стаканчике вода.
Спроси зачем?—«Так, братец! для спасенья!
Пощусь!—сегодня середа!»
Иной вину сухояденья
На поваров свалит;
Другой тебе: «Я малым сыт!»
У третьего: «Желудок не варит!
Мне доктор прописал диету».
Никто без хитрости и без затей
Не скажет попросту: «Копейки дома нету!»

Привычки странной сей
Между людей
Мы знаем все начало!
Так будет и бывало,
Что всяк таит свою суму.

Итак, прошу не погневиться!
Ну, ежели и тот стыдится,
Что кушать нечего ему,
Кто вправду голодом томится,
То как же я подложной нищетой
Родителей моих ославлю в позднем роде?
Не ведали они напасти той,
Но жили по дворянской моде!

Палаты с флигельми в наследственном селе;
Вкруг сада каменна ограда:
В одном угле
Качели—детская привада,
В другом различны теремки,
Из дерева грибки,
И многие затеи;
Лимоны, персики, тюльпаны и лилеи
В горшочках и в грунту,
С плодом и на цвету,
У батюшки мово считали как крапиву!
Орехи кедровы, миндаль,—
Ну, словом, все свое! Ни даже черносливу
Купить не посылали вдаль
На зимню трату!
Все в садике росло, хотя не по климату.
(Губерния Рязань, Ряжск город был уезд.)
Груш, яблок... точно в небе звезд!
И все как в сахаре наливны;
И даже патока своя,
Затем что были пчелы—
Что день, то два иль три роя!
А люди-то бегут и принимают в полы!
Голубчики! Как бы теперь на них,
Гляжу на пчелок сих!
Летит красавица! Вся словно золотая!
Тащит в двух задних лапах мед;
То липочку, то розу пососет,
Передней лапочкой из ротика возьмет
Да в заднюю передает.
Подчас их цела стая,
И каждая поет!
А я, поставя уши рядом с веткой,
Учусь у них жужжать,
И, мысля подражать,
Клохчу наседкой!
Сама же думаю: точь-в-точь переняла.
Ребенок я была!
Однако детская мне в пользу шалость эта:

От пчелок я и в поздни лета
Навыкла песнью труд мой услаждать,
При песнях работа́ть,
За песнью горе забывать.
Однажды, помню я, сорвать цветок хотела,
Под листиком, таясь, пчела сидела:
Она меня в пальчишко чок!
Как дура я завыла...
Уж мамушка землей лечила,
Да сунула коврижки мне кусок.
В ребенке не велик умишка:
И горе, и болезнь - все вылечит коврижка!
Умом я и поднесь не очень подросла:
Прилично ль, столько наврала,
От главной удаляся цели!
Простите!—на беду
Некстати пчелки налетели!
Теперь же вас назад сведу
На прежнюю беседу!
Отцу мому и деду,
И прадеду, и всей родне
Не как теперя мне,
По божеской всемощной воле
Назначено в обильи жить!
Себя, гостей и слуг кормить
Довольно было хлеба в поле.

Три брата у меня, сестрами самтретья,—
И всем меньшая я.
Мной матушка скончалась;
Зато всех хуже я считалась.
Дурнушкою меня прозвали!
Мой батюшка в печали
Нас роздал всех родным.
Сестрам моим большим
Не жизнь была,—приволье!
А я, как будто на застолье,
В различных девяти домах,
Различны принимая нравы,

Не ведая забавы,
Взросла в слезах,
Ведома роком неминучим
По терниям колючим.
Наскучил мне и белый свет!
Достигша совершенных лет,
Наследственну взяла от братьев долю,
Чтоб жить в свою мне волю.
Тут музы мне простерли руки!
Душою полюбя науки,
Лечу в Петров я град!
Заместо молодцов и франтов,
Зову к себе педантов,
На их себя состроя лад.
Но ах! Науки здесь сребролюбивы!
Мой малый кошелек стал пуст!
За каждый период игривый,
За каждое движенье уст,
За логические фразы,
Физически проказы,
За хлеб мой и за дом
Платя наличным серебром,
Я тотчас оскудела,—
И с горем пополам те песни пела,
Которые пришли по вкусу вам.
Вот исповедь моим грехам!

Остались у меня воздушные накосы,
Но были б ноги босы,
Когда б не добрый наш монарх,
Подобье солнца лучезарна,
Что в тонких нисходя лучах,
От былья до зерна песчана,
От мошки до слона
Вливает жизненные силы!
Так им мне сила вновь дана;
И музы вновь меня ласкают милы!

29 Февраля 1813

Разговор между мною и женщинами

ЖЕНЩИНЫ

Сестрица-душенька, какая радость нам!
Ты стихотворица! на оды, притчи, сказки
Различны у тебя готовы краски,
И верно, ближе ты по сердцу к похвалам.
Мужчины ж, милая... Ах, Боже упаси!
Язык—как острый нож!
В Париже, в Лондоне,—не только на Руси,—
Везде равны! заладят то ж да то ж:
Одни ругательства,—и все страдают дамы!
Ждем мадригалов мы,—читаем эпиграммы.
От братьев, муженьков, от батюшков, сынков
Не жди похвальных слов.
Давно хотелось нам своей певицы!
Поешь ли ты? Скажи иль да, иль нет.

Я

Да, да, голубушки-сестрицы!
Хвала всевышнему! пою уже пять лет.

ЖЕНЩИНЫ

А что пропела ты в те годы?
Признаться, русскому не все мы учены,
А русские писанья мудрены,
Да, правда, нет на них теперь и моды.

Я

Пою природы я красы,
Рогами месяц в воду ставлю,

Счисляю капельки роосы,
Восход светила славлю,
Лелею паствы по лугам,
Даю свирели пастушкам,
Подругам их цветы вплетаю в косы,
Как лен светловолосы;
Велю, схватясь рука с рукой,
Бежать на пляску им с прыжками,
И резвыми ногами
Не смять травинки ни одной.
Вздвигаю до небес скалы кремнисты,
    Сажаю древеса ветвисты,
    Чтоб старца в летни дни
    Покоить в их тени.
Ловлю по розам мотыльков крылатых,
    Созвав певцов пернатых,
        Сама томлюся я
    В согласной трели соловья.
    Иль вдруг, коням раскинув гриву,
    Велю восточный ветр перестигать,
    До облак прах копытами взметать,
    Рисую класами венчанну ниву,
    Что, вид от солнечных лучей
        Прияв морей,
    Из злата растопленных,
    Колышется, рябит, блестит,
        Глаза слепит,
Готовят наградить оратаев смиренных.
Природы красотой
Глас робкий укрепляя свой,
Вдруг делаюсь смелее!

ЖЕНЩИНЫ

    Эге! Какая ахинея!
Да слова мы про нас не видим тут...
Что пользы песни нам такие принесут?
На что твоих скотов, комолых и с рогами?
Не нам ходить на паству за стадами.

Итак, певица ты зверей!
Изрядно! ... но когда на ту ступила ногу,
Иди в берлогу,
Скитайся средь полей,
И всуе не тягчи столицы.

Я

Нет, милые сестрицы!
Пою я также и людей.

ЖЕНЩИНЫ

Похвально! Но кого и как ты величала?

Я

Подчас я подвиги мужей вспевала,
В кровавый что вступая бой,
За веру и царя живот скончали свой,
И, гулом ратное сотрясши поле,
Несла под лавром их оттоле,
Кропя слезой.
Подчас, от горести и стонов
Прейдя к блюстителям законов,
Весельем полня дух,
Под их эгидою беспечно отдыхала.
Подчас, к пиитам я вперяя слух,
Пред громкой лирой их колена преклоняла.
Подчас,
Почтением влекома,
Я пела физика, химиста, астронома.

ЖЕНЩИНЫ

И тут ни слова нет про нас!
Вот подлинно услуга!
Так что же нам в тебе? На что ты нам?
На что училась ты стихам?
Тебе чтоб брать из своего все круга,
А ты пустилася хвалить мужчин!

Как будто бы похвал их стоит пол один!
  Изменница! Сама размысли зрело,
    Твое ли это дело!
Иль нет у них хвалителей своих?
Иль добродетелей в нас меньше, чем у них!

Я

Все правда, милые! Вы их не ниже,
  Но, ах!
Мужчины, а не вы присутствуют в судах,
  При авторских венках,
  И слава авторска у них в руках,
  А всякий сам к себе невольно ближе.[1]

---

[1] Да простится мне шутка сия из снисхождения к веселонравным музам, которые любят мешать дело с бездельем, ложь с истиной, и невинной резвостью увеселять беседы. (*Примеч. авт.*)

К Диане

Приветствуем, Диана,
Тебя, сестра Аполла,
В твоих тенистых долах
И на холмах открытых!

Из тула золотого
Ты вынимаешь стрелы
Отмщенья, чтоб дубраву
Очистить от чудовищ,

То от волков голодных,
Всегда хотящих крови,
То от клыкастых вепрей,
Всегда готовых к бою.

Земля от их паденья
Дрожит ужасным гулом,
Стонает вся дубрава
От смертного их воя.

Но лань младая, робко
К тебе прибегнув, лижет
Твои могущи длани;
И ты ее ласкаешь.

Она вслед за тобою
Идет до Дельф, где праздный
Колчан и лук сложивши
У врат святого храма,

Порой со звуком лиры
Аполловой ты пляску
Охотно начинаешь
В толпе Камен гласистых.

С высокого Олимпа
Латона златокудра
Неуклонимым взором
Тебя лишь созерцает.

Спешим мы—робки девы
На праздник твой залесный;
Будь нам в огромной роще
Защитою, Диана!

◆ EVDOKIYA ROSTOPCHINA ◆

Недоконченное шитье

Freudvoll
Und leidvoll,
Gedankenvoll sein . . .

(Klächens Lied, aus *Egmont*)

Нет! прочь с работою! ... нет! более ни шва!
Нигде и никогда мой коврик не дошьется,
Трудолюбивая игла не прикоснется
К работе прерванной, и белая канва
Шитьем узорчатым вовек не облечется!
Затейливый развод, блестящие цветы,
В иное время мной вы были начаты...
И много сладостных, живых воспоминаний
   Ваш вид наводит на меня,
   И много дум, событий, упований,
   С отделкой пестрой этой ткани
Во дни минувшие слила душа моя!...

   Для женщины час скромных рукоделий
Есть час спокойствия, молчанья, дум святых,
Самопознанья час вдали сует мирских;
То промежуток ей меж выездов, веселий,
То отдых от забот, от света, от людей,
Досуг, чтоб прозревать, читать в душе своей.
Когда над пяльцами, за столиком богатым,
Она склоняется, работой занята,—
Поверьте, тайная, любимая мечта
То тенью робкою, то призраком крылатым
Мелькает перед ней, зовет ее, манит...

Быть может, той порой в ней чувство говорит...
Быть может, сердце в ней волнуется тревожно
  И сон надежды невозможной
Она на дне души голубит и хранит...
Заветных тайн ее свидетель безопасный,
  Наперсник верный и безгласный,
Жизнь задушевную шитье проводит с ней
  И дорого и любо ей.
Былого памятник, мой коврик недошитый,
Когда тебе досуг я посвящала свой,—
Тогда видаемы бывали часто мной
Минуты светлые; и верною душой
  Они теперь еще не позабыты! ...
Но их блестящая, счастливая чреда,—
  Увы! ... она навеки миновала!
  Былых тревог, былых надежд не стало,
И думы милые не придут никогда
Мне в голову опять с их прелестью бывалой.
Теперь, работая, о радостном *вчера*
С волненьем и тоской уж я не вспоминаю...
Теперь, работая, о *завтра* не мечтаю,
Не жду; и мне пришла бесцветных дней пора! ...
С холодною душой, с напрасным сожаленьем
Свой труд неконченный брать в руки не хочу,
Его, блестящего, вотще не омрачу
Отливом мрачных дум! ... Тех дней поминовеньем
Пусть он останется! ... и глядя на него,
Забыв ход времени, вновь сердца своего
Услышу исповедь с унылым наслажденьем!

Октябрь 1839
Село Анна

♦ KAROLINA PAVLOVA ♦

Старуха

I

«Не гони неутомимо
По широкой мостовой,
Не скачи так скоро мимо
Ты, мой всадник удалой!

Не гляди ты так спесиво,
Ты не слушай так слегка:
Знаю я, как молчаливо
Дума точит смельчака;

Как просиживает ночи
Он, угрюм, неизлечим;
Как напрасно блещут очи
Всех красавиц перед ним.

Средь веселий залы шумной,
В тишине лесной глуши
Знаю бред его безумный,
Грусть блажной его души.

Усмехайся ты притворно,
Погоняй коня ты вскок;
Не всегда же так проворно
Пронесешься, мой ездок.

Хоть стучат коня копыта,—
Не заглушат слов моих;
Хоть скачи ты, хоть спеши ты,—
Не ускачешь ты от них

И взойдешь в мою лачужку,
Мой красавец, в добрый час;
Ты послушаешь старушку,
Не сведешь с нее ты глаз.

Пыль вдали столбом взвивалась,
Проскакал ездок давно,
И старуха засмеялась
И захлопнула окно.

И как только слышен снова
Звонкий топот бегуна,
Уж красавца молодого
Ждет старуха у окна.

Словно как стрелу вонзает
В глубину сердечных ран,
Взор за юношей бросает,
Как невидимый аркан.

И пришло то время скоро,
Что с утра до тьмы ночной
Ржал у ветхого забора
Быстроногий вороной.

Что творится у старухи
С чернобровым молодцом?—
Уж в народе ходят слухи,
Слухи странные о том.

2

Близ лампады одинокой
Он сидит, нетерпелив,
В сумрак комнаты глубокой
Очи жгучие вперив.

Что младому сердцу снится?
Ждет чего оно теперь?

Дверь, белея, шевелится,
И старуха входит в дверь;

Входит дряхлая, седая,
И садится, и опять,
Обольщая, возмущая,
Начинает речь шептать.

Юной грусти бред мятежный,
Сокровенные мечты
Одевает в образ нежный,
В непорочные черты.

Говорит про деву-чудо,
Так что верится едва,
И берет, Бог весть откуда,
Ненаслушные слова:

Как щеки ее душистой
Томно блещет красота
Как сомкнуты думой чистой
Недоступные уста;

Как очей синеет бездна
Лучезарной темнотой,
Как они сияют звездно
Над мирскою суетой;

Как спокоен взор могучий,
Как кудрей густая мгла
Обвивает черной тучей
Ясность строгого чела;

Как любить ее напрасно,
Как, всесильная, она
Увлекательно прекрасна,
Безнадежно холодна.—

А в покое темно, глухо,
Бьет вдали за часом час;

Соблазнительно старуха
Шепчет, шепчет свой рассказ.

Говорит про деву-чудо,
Так что верится едва,
И берет, Бог весть откуда,
Ненаслушные слова.

3

На коне неутомимо
По широкой мостовой
Уж давно не скачет мимо
Наш красавец удалой.

В зимней стуже, в летнем зное
Он и ночью, он и днем
В запертом сидит покое
Со старухою вдвоем.

Неподвижный, весь исчахлый,
Он сидит как сам не свой
И в лицо старухе дряхлой
Смотрит с жадностью немой.

Февраль 1840

◆ KAROLINA PAVLOVA ◆

Зовет нас жизнь: идем, мужаясь, все мы;
Но в краткий час, где стихнет гром невзгод,
И страсти спят, и споры сердца немы,—
Дохнет душа среди мирских забот,
И вдруг мелькнут далекие эдемы,
И думы власть опять свое берет.

Остановясь горы на половине,
Пришлец порой кругом бросает взгляд:
За ним цветы и майский день в долине,
А перед ним—гранит и зимний хлад.
Как он, вперед гляжу я реже ныне,
И более гляжу уже назад.

Там много есть, чего не встретить снова;
Прелестна там и радость и беда;
Там много есть любимого, святого,
Разбитого судьбою навсегда.
Ужели все душа забыть готова?
Ужели все проходит без следа?

Ужель вы мне—безжизненные тени,
Вы, взявшие с меня, в моей весне,
Дань жарких слез и горестных борений,
Погибшие! ужель вы чужды мне
И помнитесь, среди сердечной лени,
Лишь изредка и темно, как во сне?

Ты, с коей я простилася, рыдая,
Чей путь избрал безжалостно творец,
Святой любви поборница младая,—

Ты приняла терновый свой венец
И скрыла глушь убийственного края
И подвиг твой, и грустный твой конец.

И там, где ты несла свои страданья,
Где гасла ты в несказанной тоске,—
Уж, может, нет в сердцах воспоминанья,
Нет имени на гробовой доске;
Прошли года—и вижу без вниманья
Твое кольцо я на своей руке.

А как с тобой рассталася тогда я,
Сдавалось мне, что я других сильней,
Что я могу любить, не забывая,
И двадцать лет грустеть, как двадцать дней.
И тень встает передо мной другая
Печальнее, быть может, и твоей!

Безвестная, далекая могила!
И над тобой промчалися лета!
А в снах моих та ж пагубная сила,
В моих борьбах та ж грустная тщета;
И как тебя, дитя, она убила,—
Убъет меня безумная мечта.

В ночной тиши ты кончил жизнь печали;
О смерти той не мне бы забывать!
В ту ночь два-три страдальца окружали
Отжившего изгнанника кровать;
Смолк вздох его, разгаданный едва ли;
А там ждала и родина, и мать.

Ты молод слег под тяжкой дланью рока!
Восторг святой еще в тебе кипел;
В грядущей мгле твой взор искал далеко
Благих путей и долговечных дел;
Созрелых лет жестокого урока
Ты не узнал,—блажен же твой удел!

Блажен!—хоть ты сомкнул в игнанье вежды!
К мете одной ты шел неколебим;
Так, крест прияв на бранные одежды,
Шли рыцари в святой Ерусалим,
Ударил гром, в прах пала цель надежды,—
Но прежде пал дорогой пилигрим.

Еще другой!—Сердечная тревога,
Как чутко спишь ты!—да, еще другой!—
Чайльд-Гарольд прав: увы! их слишком много,
Хоть их и всех так мало!—но порой
Кто не подвел тяжелого итога
И не поник, бледнея, головой?

Не одного мы погребли поэта!
Судьба у нас их губит в цвете дней;
Он первый пал;—весть памятна мне эта!
И раздалась другая вслед за ней:
Удачен вновь был выстрел пистолета.
Но смерть твоя мне в грудь легла больней.

И неужель, любимец вдохновений
Исчезнувший, как легкий призрак сна,
Тебе, скорбя, своих поминовений
Не принесла родная сторона?
И мне́ пришлось тебя назвать, Евгений,
И дань стиха я дам тебе одна?

Возьми ж ее ты в этот час заветный,
Возьми ж ее, когда молчат они.
Увы! зачем блестят сквозь мрак бесцветный
Бывалых чувств блудящие огни?
Зачем порыв и немочный, и тщетный?
Кто вызвал вас, мои младые дни?

Что, бледный лик, вперяешь издалека
И ты в меня свой неподвижный взор?
Спокойна я; шли годы без намека;

К чему ты здесь, ушедший с давних пор?
Оставь меня!—белеет день с востока,
Пусть призраков исчезнет грустный хор.

Белеет день, звезд гасит рой алмазный,
Зовет к труду и требует дела;
Пора свершать свой путь однообразный,
И все забыть, что жизнь превозмогла,
И отрезветь от хмеля думы праздной,
И след мечты опять стряхнуть с чела.

Июль 1846
Гиреево

Автобиографический отзыв из глуши, в ответ на поздравительный билет, с букетом и новогодними приветственными пожеланиями

Посвященный С.М. Гогель

В просвет келейного оконца
Пустынной хижины моей,
Блеснул луч золота и солнца,
В один из года первых дней:
Златисто-палевая роза,
В кувшине синего стекла,
Чудесно вдруг, среди мороза,
С зеленой веткой, расцвела!
Чудесный дар во всем чудесен:
Цвет белый золотом горит,
И мне о строе новых песен,
О новых звуках, говорит...

«Мне не к лицу, и не по летам,
Пора, пора мне быть умней!
Но признаю, по всем приметам,
Болезнь любви в душе моей!»
Так, в ранний вечер жизни лета,
Бессмертный Пушкин говорил,
Когда в нем здравый смысл поэта
Волненья чувств не покорил.

Пора и мне о силах новых,
О звуках новых не мечтать,
Но, в зимний сумрак лет суровых,
Итоги жизни сосчитать!
Пора заржавленную лиру
На ветки северных берез

Закинуть,—пусть, по ветру, миру
Издаст свой стон последних грез!

Когда ребячьими перстами
Заветных струн коснулась я,
Уже не детскими мечтами
Звучала стройно песнь моя!
Свет дал мне чувство первой славы
Вкусить, отведать, ощущить,—
И мужи власти и державы
Склонялись юный дар почтить;
Поэты назвали сестрою,
Призывы, гимны мне несли;
Елисаветою второю,—
По Кульман,—смело нарекли;
Певец Светланы и Людмилы
Мне светлый путь предвозвещал,
И женский хор привет свой милый
Не раз мне вслед провозглашал.
И представители науки
На одобренье, на успех,
Мне в помощь подавали руки
И робость ставили мне в грех!

Но я—судьбиной роковою—
Была придавлена к стене,
И—с недовенчанной главою,
В тени осталась, в стороне...
В тот день, когда мой путь широко
Вдаль разостлался предо мной,—
В рассвете счастья, без порока,
Любви и радости земной,
За шаг до брачного чертога,—
Раздался, над челом моим,
Призывный глас Христа и Бога,
И—я, взяв крест, пошла за Ним!

Я отжила. Смежаю вежды
Моих заплаканных очей!

Но в том—что лучшие надежды,
И глас пророческих речей
Над горемычною цевницей,
Не совершились на земле,
Что не поэтом, а черницей,
Без лавров, с терном на челе,
Под крепом, мантией широкой,
Как в смертный саван обвита,
Сойду в могилу,—без упрека,—
Я неповинна и чиста!
Я ценный дар заветных песен
Полвека целых берегла:
Как мой удел ни сжат, ни тесен,
Их ни за *что* не продала!
И если он в глуши загинет,
Как часть зародыша в плоде,
И мир в меня свой камень кинет,—
Я оправдаюсь на суде!

Иная жизнь—иные песни!
Но я все пела и пою!
И вы—*одна* свое—«воскресни»!
Призывно шлете в глушь мою!
Вам дался ключ от тайны звуков,
И сила строй их возбуждать:
На ваших чад, на ваших внуков,
Да снидет Божья благодать!
В вас не утрачен вкус к святыне
Высоких чувств, и, чутко вы,
Глас вопиющего в пустыне,
Сквозь шума, говора молвы,
Неслышный свету, различая,
Задачи верные, на дне
Души поющей, в ней читая,
Познали, поняли вполне!
Иные песни глас приносит,
Из жизни замкнутой, иной:
Но этих песен мир не просит,
Ему язык их не родной!

Земные цели и задачи
Ему решат его жрецы,
И роковые неудачи
Заменят призраком льстецы.
Ему не нужно гласов с неба!
Пусть все, что вне земли, молчит!
Он только:—«зрелища и хлеба»!
Разноголосицей кричит.

Наш *лишний* в век в веках вселенной,—
Способен ринуть мир в хаос,—
Но, над землею обновленной
Свет лучший вызовет Христос!

♦ ZINAIDA GIPPIUS ♦

Швея

Уж третий день ни с кем не говорю...
А мысли—жадные и злые.
Болит спина; куда не посмотрю—
Повсюду пятна голубые.

Церковный колокол гудел; умолк;
Я все наедине с собою.
Скрипит и гнется жарко-алый шелк
Под неумелою иглою.

На всех явлениях лежит печать.
Одно с другим как будто слито.
Приняв одно—стараюсь угадать
За ним другое,—то, что скрыто.

И этот шелк мне кажется—Огнем.
И вот уж не огнем—а Кровью.
А кровь—лишь знак того, что мы зовем
На бедном языке—Любовью.

Любовь—лишь звук... Но в зтот поздний час
Того, что дальше—не открою.
Нет, не огонь, не кровь... а лишь атлас
Скрипит под робкою иглою.

1901

◆ ZINAIDA GIPPIUS ◆

Брачное кольцо

Над темностью лампады незаженной
Я увидал сияющий отсвет.
Последним обнаженьем обнаженной
Моей душе—пределов больше нет.

Желанья были мне всего дороже...
Но их, себя, святую боль мою,
Молитвы, упованья,—все, о Боже,
В Твою Любовь с любовью отдаю.

И этот час бездонного смиренья
Крылатым пламенем облек меня.
Я властен властью—Твоего веленья,
Одет покровом—Твоего огня.

Я к близкому протягиваю руки,
Тебе, Живому, я смотрю в Лицо,
И, в светлости преображенной муки,
Мне легок крест, как брачное кольцо.

1905
СПБ.

Заклинание

Расточитесь, духи непослушные,
Разомкнитесь, узы непокорные,
Распадитесь, подземелья душные,
Лягьте вихри, жадные и черные.

Тайна есть великая, запретная.
Есть обеты—их нельзя развязывать.
Человеческая кровь—заветная:
Солнцу кровь не велено показывать.

Разломись Оно, проклятьем цельное!
Разлетайся, туча исступленная!

Бейся сердце, каждое,—отдельное,
Воскресай, душа освобожденная!

Декабрь 1905
СПБ.

♦ ADELAIDA GERTSYK ♦

Весна

Вы сгиньте, обманы,
Укройте, туманы,
Храните глубокую дрёму!
(Вяч. Иванов)

Посв. В.Г.

Женщина там на горе сидела,
Ворожила над травами сонными—
Ты не слыхала? Что шелестело?
Травы-ли, ветром склоненные...
То струилось ли море колоса?
Или женские вились волосы?
Ты не видала?
Что-то шептала... ruku unimala?
Или сердце свое горючее?
Или в землю стучалась дремучую?
Что-то она заговаривала—
Зелье, быть может, заваривала?
И курился пар—и калился жар—
И роса пряла... i wesna plyla...
Ты не слыхала?
Ветер наверно знает,
Что она там шептала,
Ветер слова качает—
Я их слыхала.
«Мимо, мимо идите,
Рвите неверные нити!
Ах, уплывите, обманы!
Ах, обоймите, туманы!
Вырыта здесь на холме

Без вести могила,
Саван весенний мне
Время уж свило...
Ах, растекусь я рекой отсюда,
Буду лелеять, носить облака...
Ах, не нужно зеленого чуда—
Небу я буду верна...
Мимо, мимо идите,
Вечные, тонкие нити—
Солнце меня не обманет,
Сердце меня не затянет... »
Ветер развеял слова.
Хочет молчать тишина.
Это настала весна.

◆ ADELAIDA GERTSYK ◆

Посв. Е.Г.

Опять в тканях белых, жертвенных
Беззвучно влачишь прекрасную грусть свою,
Опять в золоте сада осеннего
Струится белая риза твоя
И стынет, как сон неясная...
  Чем сердце опоить
    недремное?
  Чем улегчить сердце богатое,
    плодное?
Все миги—слитно неслитые
С собой несешь ты в сосуде исполненном...
  Забудь! о, забудь!
Лилию белую сорви,
На грудь возложи себе!
  Там у источника,
  в куще оливы бледной,
  не ты-ли сидела, светлая,
Тонкую руку в прозрачной струе купая?
И желанья—девы кудрявые
Теснились, во влаге зеркальной
    собой любуясь...
Та-же ты и теперь, светлоокая,
  И не та.
Не изведав разлуки,
  не зная утраты—
вся ты разлука,
вся утрата...
Всем несешь свой привет прощальный,
    безгласно скользящая
в ризе белой, негаснущей...

И шепчет рок, меня вразумляя:
Тише! Учись видеть
  печаль неутешную,
  печаль безотзывную.
Сердце сдержи торопящее.
Молча смотри
в безбрежность немых
    очей.

◆ ANNA AKHMATOVA ◆

«Я пришла тебя сменить, сестра,
У лесного, у высокого костра.

Поседели твои волосы. Глаза
Замутила, затуманила слеза.

Ты уже не понимаешь пенья птиц,
Ты ни звезд не замечаешь, ни зарниц.

И давно удары бубна не слышны,
А я знаю, ты боишься тишины,

Я пришла тебя сменить, сестра,
У лесного, у высокого костра».

«Ты пришла меня похоронить,
Где же заступ твой, где лопата?
Только флейта в руках твоих.
Я не буду тебя винить,
Разве жаль, что давно, когда-то,
Навсегда мой голос затих.

Мои одежды надень,
Позабудь о моей тревог
Дай ветру кудрями играть.
Ты пахнешь, как пахнет сирень,
А пришла по трудной дороге,
Чтобы здесь озаренной стать».

И одна ушла, уступая
Уступая место другой.
И неверно брела, как слепая,
Незнакомой узкой тропой.

И все чудилось ей, что пламя
Близко... бубен держит рука...
И она, как белое знамя,
И она, как свет маяка.

24 октября 1912
Царское Село

◆ ANNA AKHMATOVA ◆

Уединение

Так много камней брошено в меня,
Что ни один из них уже не страшен,
И стройной башней стала западня,
Высокою среди высоких башен.
Строителей ее благодарю,
Пусть их забота и печаль минует.
Отсюда раньше вижу я зарю,
Здесь солнца луч последний торжествует.
И часто в окна комнаты моей
Влетают ветры северных морей,
И голубь ест из рук моих пшеницу...
А не дописанную мной страницу,
Божественно спокойна и легка,
Допишет Музы смуглая рука.

6 июня 1914
Слепнево

◆ ANNA AKHMATOVA ◆

Страх, во тьме перебирая вещи,
Лунный луч наводит на топор.
За стеною слышен стук зловещий—
Что там, крысы, призрак или вор?

В душной кухне плещется водою,
Половицам шатким счет ведет,
С глянцевитой черной бородою
За окном чердачным промелькнет—

И притихнет. Как он зол и ловок,
Спички спрятал и свечу задул.
Лучше бы поблескиванье дул
В грудь мою направленных винтовок,

Лучше бы на площади зеленой
На помост некрашеный прилечь
И под клики радости и стоны
Красной кровью до конца истечь.

Прижимаю к сердцу крестик гладкий:
Боже, мир душе моей верни!
Запах тленья обморочно сладкий
Веет от прохладной простыни.

27–8 августа 1921
Царское Село

Курганная царевна II

Половина обагренного кольца,—
Сгинет месяц за туманом горизонта;
К черным водам мертвенного понта
Сил нет повернуть лица.

Вы,—хранители заветов, вы,—курганы,—
К вам я припаду, ища забытой веры,
Мир живой, как явь фатаморганы,
А осколки бывшего спрятали пещеры.

Долго я держалась между скал залива,
Ночью набегала с диким караваном,
Чтоб предать пожару их дома и нивы,
Чтоб попировать над родным курганом.

Я пила из кубка кровь упавших в битве,
Я пьянела, предаваясь дикой мести,
Павших больше, чем колосьев в жнитве;—
Друг, в кургане спящий, вспомни о невесте.

До костей, обвитых багряницей,
Просочатся капли пиршественной влаги;
Дивно улыбнется царь мой темнолицый,
Средь кургана спящий, в белом саркофаге...

Половина обагренного кольца,—
Сгинет месяц за туманом горизонта,
К черным водам мертвенного понта
Сил нет повернуть лица.

Руфь

Собирала колосья в подол,
Шла по жнивью чужому босая;
Пролетала над избами сел
Журавлей вереница косая.

И ушла через синий туман
Далеко от равнины Вооза;
И идет сред неведомых стран,
Завернувшись в платок от мороза.

А журавль, уплывая на юг,
Никому, никому не расскажет,
Как от жатвы оставшийся тук
Руфь в снопы золотистые вяжет.

Лишь короткий подымется день,
И уйдет хлебуроб на работу,
На равнинах чужих деревень
Руфь начнет золотую охоту.

Низко спустит платок свой на лоб,
Чтоб не выдали южные косы,
Соберет свой разбросанный сноп,
Обойдет все холмы и откосы.

А зимою, ступив чрез порог,
Бабы часто сквозь утренний холод
На снегу замечали, у ног,
Сноп колосьев не смолотых...

◆ VERA MERKUREVA ◆

Бабушка русской поэзии
Автопортрет

Полуседая и полуслепая,
Полунемая и полуглухая,
Вид—полоумной или полусонной,
Не говорит—мурлычит монотонно,
Но—улыбается, в елее тая.

Свой бубен переладив на псалмодий,
Она пешком на богомолье ходит
И Зубовскую пустынь посещает.
Но если церковь цирком называют,
То это бес ее на грех наводит.

Кто от нее ль изыдет, к ней ли внидет,—
Всех недослышит или недовидит,
Но—рада всякой одури и дури,—
Она со всеми благолепно курит
И почему-то ладан ненавидит.

Ей весело цезуры сбросить пояс,
Ей—вольного стиха по санкам полоз,
Она легко рифмует *плюс* и *полюс*,
Но—ее *не*, *нет* и *без*, и *полу*—
Ненужная бесплодная бесполость.

Июнь 1918

◆ MARIYA SHKAPSKAYA ◆

Явь

«Слышали? Говорят—завтра?»
«А я думала, сегодня».
«Вот будет давка—»
«Да уж, как водится, на народе» ...
«А знаете—все-таки занятно» ...
«Говорят, вот в Швейцарии так же публично» ...

Объявляли по городу внятно,
И качели поставили у стены кирпичной
У самой паперти соборной—
Место самое видное и—просторно.
Качели как крест без двух оконечий,
А под ними сутулые плечи,
А если на цыпочки встать, да взглянуть,
Виден и язык—так, чуть-чуть.

Вешали долго, трудно, устали,
Часто мать поминали.
Помогал, как мог, сам,
Да только как-то ослаб
И кровь текла по усам—
Больно тяжел кулак
У офицеров прохожего эшелона из Брянска
(Били накануне в комендантской).

И пока нес, и пока шел,
В голове точно кто-то завел:
  «Прощайте, елочки-соселочки,
  Прощай, отец и мать,
  Прощайте, барышни веселые,
  Не буду с вами гулять».

Чуть отвяжется—и опять:
«Елочки-соселочки
Да отец и мать».

А какие тут отец и мать—
Народу—конца не видать.
Только жена в сторонке
С ребенком,
А другой, постарше, за юбку.
Разрешили взглянуть на последний танец
И ей, и маленьким—
«Только, знаете, чтоб у меня без демонстраций».
Вот и встала в сторонке под старую акацию,
Стоит,
Молчит,
Только губы белые,
Помертвелые,
И маленький грудь не теребит—пустая.

А там, около, точно волчья стая,
Только и слышно: «Экая обида,
Ничего не видно».—
«Эй, пропустите даму».—
«Мама, мама».
«Вам видно? А вам?»—
«Пардон, madame!»
«Ах, какой рваный».
«Не беспокойтесь, Анна Иванна».
«Ну что вы, что вы».
«Офицер-то какой-то новый».
«Отчего же... Говорят, смерть приятная... »
«Знаете, свежо с утра, я в ватном... »
«А я и Петю взяла,
Привела,
Поглядим».
«Они олово в горло, а вот и им».
«Детям-то не хорошо бы с таких лет,
Бог знает—какой в душе останется след».
«Ничего, пускай приучается».

«Глядите, глядите, качается».
«Эй, осади».
«Нахал, говорят—даму пусти... »
«Отдавили ногу... »
«Нет, это, знаете ли, ей-Богу... »

И вдруг голосок звонкий
Неперемогшего ребенка:
«Мамочка!
Мама!
Да ведь это он сам,
Сам веревку дает.
А они его—по плечу...
Ой, мамочка,
Зажми мне рот,
Я сейчас закричу».—

И рукой шершавой
Ротишко зажала.
«Молчи, Ванечка,
Молчи, маленький,
Молчи, ненько,
Гляди хорошенько,
Да запомни,
Слышишь,—запомни.
На всю свою жизнь и память
Положи как камень
Отцовские страсти,—
И как качался,
И как по ногам нагайкой—
И как вот эти смеялись,
И как вот те на цыпочки подымались,
И как кресты на церкви не зашатались».

Тихонечко, на ухо говорила.
И глядела, глаз не отрывая.
Божеских сил не хватало бы,—
Человеческих хватает,
Человечья страшная сила:

И те, и эти,
И какие-нибудь третьи,—
Никого не милуем,
Только—запоминаем.

Было это на Петра и Павла,
А потом еще три дня висел он,
И ходили мимо православные
Без дела и с делом,
К обедне, ко всенощной и к вечерне,
И бухал колокол мерный,—
А он качался, да слушал:
«Припахивает. Сушь ведь.
Ишь, воронье проклятое... »
«У самого пятеро... »
«Знаете, мы ведь не против революции.
Мы за конституцию»—
«Вот он—Мессия».—
«Бей жидов и спасай Россию».—
«Какой тощий».—
«Экие ведь звери. Верно нагайкой? ... »
«А черниговские мощи?»
«А киевская чрезвычайка?»—
«Рассчитаемся, пока можно,
На этом свете».
«А Божье?»—
«Ну, мы-то что же,
Начальство ответит».—

А когда третьи сутки кончились,
Летнею темною ночью
Церковные двери отомкнулися,
Царские врата распахнулися,
И пошел из них, словно в крестный ход,
Весь святой народ,
Русские православные святители:
Иван Креститель,
Пантелеймон Целитель,
Никола седенький,

Алексей простенький,
Ипатий с тремя морщинками,
Касьян—редкий именинник,
Убиенный царевич Димитрий
И все Пресвятые Богородицы
Смоленские, Казанские, Володимерские,
Скорбящая, Троеручица, Одигитрия,
И другие—без всякого имени.
Шли они—как приявшие схиму,
Подошли к веселой качели,
На синее лицо поглядели,
Да и пали ему в корявые ноги,
Прямо на пыльной дороге,
Как по самому страшному обету.
И лежали там до самого свету.

А когда утром пришли православные—
Все также качался удавленный,
Также плечи его сутулились,—
Только на церкви кресты пошатнулися.

1919
Ромны

♦ SOFIYA PARNOK ♦

Ради рифмы резвой не солгу,
уж не обессудь, маститый мастер,—
мы от колыбели разной масти:
я умею только то, что я могу.

Строгой благодарна я судьбе,
что дала мне Музу недотрогу;
узкой, но своей идем дорогой,
обе не попутчицы тебе.

17 марта 1926

◆ SOFIYA PARNOK ◆

В форточку

Коленями—на жесткий подоконник
и в форточку—раскрытый, рыбий рот!
Вздохнуть... вздохнуть... Так тянет кислород
из серого мешка еще живой покойник,
и сердце в нем стучит: пора, пора!
И небо давит землю грузным сводом,
и ночь белесоватая сера,
как серая подушка с кислородом...

Но я не умираю. Я еще
упорствую. Я думаю. И снова
над жизнию моею горячо
колдует требовательное слово.
И, высунувши в форточку лицо,
я вверх гляжу—на звездное убранство,
на рыжее вокруг луны кольцо—
и говорю так, никому, в пространство:

«Как в бане испаренья грязных тел,
над миром испаренья темных мыслей,
гниющих тайн, непоправимых дел
такой проклятой духотой нависли,
что, даже настежь распахнув окно,
дышать душе отчаявшейся—нечем! ...
Не странно ли? Мы все болезни лечим:
саркому, и склероз, и старость... Но
на свете нет еще таких лечебниц,
где лечатся от стрептококков зла...
Вот так бы, на коленях, поползла
по выбоинам мостовой, по щебню
глухих дорог—куда? Бог весть, куда!

◆ SOFIYA PARNOK ◆

Ходасевичу

С детства помню: груши есть такие—
сморщенные, мелкие, тугие,
и такая терпкость скрыта в них,
что едва укусишь,—сводит челюсть:
так вот для меня и эта прелесть
злых, оскомистых стихов твоих.

6 мая 1927

В какой-нибудь дремучий скит забытый,
чтобы молить прощенья и защиты—
и выплакать, и вымолвить... Когда б
я знала, где они,—заступники, Зосимы,
и не угас ли свет неугасимый? ... »

Светает. В сумраке оголены
и так задумчивы дома. И скупо
над крышами поблескивает купол
и крест Неопалимой Купины...
И где-нибудь на западе, в Париже,
в Турине, в Гамбурге—не все ль равно?
Вот так же высунувшись в душное окно,
дыша такой же ядовитой жижей,
и, силясь из последних сил вздохнуть,
стоит, и думает, и плачет кто-нибудь
не белый, и не красный, и не черный,
не гражданин, а просто человек,
как я, быть может, слишком непроворно
и грустно доживающий свой век.

Февраль–март 1928

♦ MARINA TSVETAEVA ♦

Лестница

Короткая ласка
На лестнице тряской.
Короткая краска

Лица под замазкой.
Короткая—сказка:
Ни завтра, ни здравствуй.

Короткая схватка
На лестнице шаткой,
На лестнице падкой.

В доме, где по ночам не спят,
Каждая лестница водопад—

В ад...
            —стезею листков капустных!
Точно лестница вся из спусков,
Точно больше (что—жить! жить—жечь!)
Расставаний на ней, чем встреч.

Так, до розовых уст дорваться—
Мы порой забываем: здравствуй.
Тех же уст покидая край—
Кто—когда—забывал: прощай.

Короткая шутка
На лестнице чуткой
На лестнице гудкой.

От грешного к грешной
На лестнице спешной
Хлеб нежности днешней.

Знаешь проповедь
Тех—мест?
Кто работает,
Тот—ест.

Дорого в лавках!
Тощ—предприимчив.
Спать можно завтра,
Есть нужно нынче.

В жизненной давке—
Княжеский принцип:
Взять можно завтра,
Дать нужно нынче.

Взрывом газовым
Час. Да-с.
Кто отказывал,
Тот—даст.

Даст!
(Нынче зубаст
Газ) ибо за нас
—Даст!—(тигр он и барс),
—Даст!—(черт, а не Маркс!)

Ящик сорный,
Скажут, скажите: вздор.
А у черной
Лестницы есть ковер.

(Масти сборной,
Правда...) Чеснок, коты,—
А у черной
Лестницы есть Coty.

Любят сласти-то
Червяки теснот!
Это—классика:
Чердаку—чеснок.

Может, лечатся...
А по мне—так месть:
Черной лестницы
Черноту заесть.

Стихотворец, бомбист, апаш—
Враг один у нас: бель-этаж.

Короткая сшибка
На лестнице щипкой,
На лестнице сыпкой—

Как скрипка, как сопка,
Как нотная стопка,
Работает—топка!

Короткая встрепка
На лестнице шлепкой,
На лестнице хлопкой.

Бьем до искр из глаз,
Бьем—в лёжь.
Что с нас взыскивать?
Бить—бьешь.

Владельца в охапку—
По лестнице каткой,
По лестнице хлипкой—

Торопится папка,
Торопится кепка,
Торопится скрипка.

—Ох, спал бы и спал бы!
Сжевала, сгноила, смолола!

Торопятся фалды,
Торопятся фалды,
Торопятся полы,

Судор'жь! Сутолочь!
Бег! Приз!
Сами ж путают:
Вверх? вниз?

Что этаж—свой кашель:
В прямой связи.
И у нашей
Лестницы есть низы.

Что до слез, кто с корнем,
Кто так, кхи, кхи—
И у черной
Лестницы есть верхи.

—Вас бы выстукать!
—Кирькой в грудь—ужо!
Гамма приступов
От подвала—до

Крыши—грохают!
Большинством заплат—
Маркса проповедь
На стравинский лад.

Короткая спевка
На лестнице плёвкой:
Низов голосовка.

Не спевка, а сплёвка:
На лестницу легких
Ни цельного—ловко!

Торопкая склёвка.
А ярости—в клохтах!
Работает—ох как!

Чтó ни бросите—
Всё—в ход.
Кто не досыта ест—
Жрет.

Стол—как есть домашний,
Отъел—кладут.
И у нашей
Лестницы—карта блюд.

Всех сортов диета!
Кипящий бак—
И у этой
Лестницы—Франценсбад.

Сон Иакова!
В старину везло!
Гамма запахов
От подвала—до

Крыши—стряпают!
Ре-ми-фа-соль-си—
Гамма запахов!
Затыкай носы!

Точно в аду вита,
Раскалена—винта

Железная стружка.
Короткая стопка
Ног—с лестницы швыркой!

Последняя сушка,
Последняя топка,
Последняя стирка.

Последняя сцепка
Двух—кости да тряпки—
Ног—с лестницей зыбкой.

Последняя папка,
Последняя кепка,
Последняя скрипка.

Тихо.—Даже—кашель
Иссяк, потряс.
И у нашей
Лестницы есть свой час

Тишины...

Последняя взбёжка
По лестнице дрожкой.
Последняя кошка.

Темнота все стерла—
И грязь, и нас.
И у черной
Лестницы есть свой час

Чистоты...

Откуда—узнай-ка!—
Последняя шайка—
Рейн, рухнувший с Альп,—
Воды́ об асфальт

Двора...

Над двором—узорно:
Вон крест, вон гроздь...
А у черной
Лестницы—карта звезд.

Ночь—как бы высказать?
Ночь—вещи исповедь.

Ночь просит искренности,
Вещь хочет высказаться—

Вся! Все унижены—
Сплошь, до недвижимых
Вплоть. Приступ выспренности:
Вещь хочет выпрямиться.

Винт черной лестницы—
Мнишь—стенкой лепится?
Ночь: час молитвенностей:
Винт хочет вытянуться.

Высь—вещь надежная.
В вещь—честь заложена.
Ложь вижу выломанной
Пря—мою линиею.

Двор—горстка выбоин,
Двор—год не выгребен!—
Цветами, ягодами—
Двор бредит за́городом.

Вещь, бросив вежливость:
—Есмь мел! Железо есмь!
Не быть нам выкрестами!—
Жид, пейсы выпроставший.

Гвоздь, кафель, стружка ли—
Вещь—лоно чувствует.
С ремесл пародиями—
В спор—мощь прародинная.

Стекло, с полок бережных:
—Пе—сок есмь! Вдребезги ж!
Сти—хий пощечина!
Стекло—в пыль песочную!

Прочь, ложь и ломанность!
Тю—фяк: солома есмь!
Мат—рас: есмь водоросль!
Всё, вся: пророда есмь!

Час пахнет бомбою.
Ве—ревка: льном была!
Огнь, в куче угольной:
—Был бог и буду им!

Чтó сталось с кранами?
—Пал—бог и встану им!
Чтоб сразу выговорить:
Вещь хочет выздороветь.

Мы, с ремеслами, мы, с заводами,
Что мы сделали с раем, отданным
Нам? Нож первый и первый лом,
Чтó мы сделали с первым днем?

Вещь как женщина нам поверила!
Видно, мало нам было дерева,
И железо—отвесь, отбей!—
Захотелось досок, гвоздей,

Щеп! удобоваримой мелочи!
Что мы сделали, первый сделавши
Шаг? Планету, где всё о Нем—
На предметов бездарный лом?

Мы—с ремеслами, мы—с искусствами!
Растянув на одре Прокрустовом
Вещь... Замкнулась и ждет конца
Вещь—на адском одре станка.

Слава разносилась реками,
Славу утверждал утес.

В мир—одушевленней некуда!—
Что же человек привнес?

Нужно же, чтоб он, сей видимый
Дух, болящий бог—предмет
Неодушевленный выдумал!
Лживейшую из клевет!

Вы с предметами, вы с понятьями,
Вы с железом (дешевле платины),
Вы с алмазом (знатней кремня),
(С мыловаром, нужней меня!)

Вы с «незыблемость», вы с «недвижимость»,
На ступеньку, которой—ниже нет,
В эту плесень и в эту теснь
Водворившие мысль и песнь,—

(Потому-то всегда взрываемся!)
Чтó вы сделали с первым равенством
Вещи—всюду, в любой среде—
Равной ровно самой себе.

Дерево, доверчивое к звуку
Наглых топоров м нудных пил,
С яблоком протягивало руку.
Человек—рубил.

Горы, обнаруживая руды
Скрытые (впоследствии «металл»),
Твердо устанавливали: чудо!
Человек—взрывал.

Просвещенная сим приемом,
Вещь на лом отвечает—ломом.
Стол всегда утверждал, что—ствол.
Стул сломался? Нет, сук подвел.

В лакированных ваших клетках
Шумы—думаете—от предков?

Просто, звезды в окно узрев,
Потянулся в паза́х орех.

Просыпаешься—как от залпа!
Шкаф рассохся? Нет, нрав сказался
Вещи. Дво́рни домашней бал!
Газ взорвался? Нет, бес взыграл!

Ровно в срок подгниют перильца.
Нет—«нечаянно застрелился».
Огнестрельная воля бдит.
Есть—намеренно был убит

Вещью, в негодованье стойкой.
В пустоту не летит с постройки
Камень—навыки таковы:
Камень требует головы!

Месть утеса.—С лесов—месть леса!
Обстановочность этой пьесы!
Чем обставились? Дуб и штоф?
Застрахованность этих лбов!

Всё страхующих—вплоть до ситки
Жестяной. Это ты—тростник-то
Мыслящий?—Биллиардный кий!
Застрахованность от стихий!

От Гефеста—со всем, что в оном—
Дом, а яхту—от Посейдона.
Оцените и мысль, и жест:
Застрахованность от божеств!

От Гефеста? А шпиль над крышей—
От Гефеста? Берите выше!
Но и тише! От всех в одном:
От Зевеса страхуют дом.

Еще плачетесь: без подмоги!
Дурни—спрашивается — боги,

Раз над каждым—язык неймет!—
Каждым домом—богоотвод!

Бухты, яхты, гешефты, кофты—
Лишь одной не ввели страховки:
От имущества, только—сей:
Огнь, страхующий *от* вещей.

Вещи бедных. Разве рогожа—
Вещь? И вещь—эта доска?
Вещи бедных—кости да кожа,
Вовсе—мяса, только тоска.

Где их брали? Вид—издалёка,
Изглубока. Глаз не труди!
Вещи бедных—точно из бока:
Взял да вырезал из груди!

Полка? случай. Вешалка? случай.
Случай тоже—этот фантом
Кресла. Вещи? шипья да сучья,—
Весь октябрьский лес целиком!

Нищеты робкая мебель!
Вся—чего?—четверть и треть.
Вещь—давно, явно на небе!
На тебя—больно глядеть.

От тебя грешного зренья,
Как от язв, трудно отвлечь.
Венский стул—там, где о Вене—
Кто? когда?—страшная вещь!

Лучшей всех—*здесь*—обесчещен,
Был бы—дом? мало!—чердак
Ваш. Лишь *здесь* ставшая вещью—
Вещь. Вам—бровь, вставшая в знак

?—сей. На рвань нудную, вдовью—
Что?—бровь наверх! (Чем не лорнет—
Бровь!) Горазд спрашивать бровью
Глаз. Подчас глаз есть—предмет.

Та́к подчас пуст он и сух он—
Женский глаз, дивный, большой,
Что—сравните—кажется духом—
Таз, лохань с синькой—душой.

Наравне с тазом и с ситом
—Да—царю! Да—на суде!—
Каждый, здесь званый пиитом,
Этот глаз *знал* на себе!

Нищеты робкая утварь!
Каждый нож *лично* знаком.
Ты как тварь, ждущая утра.
Чем-то—здесь, *всем*—за окном—

Тем, пустым, тем—на предместья—
Те—читал хронику краж?
Чистоты вещи и чести
Признак: *не* примут в багаж.

Оттого что слаба в пазах,
Распадается на глазах,
Оттого что на ста возах
Не свезти...
                    В слезах—

Оттого что не стол, а муж,
Сын. Не шкаф, а *наш*
Шкаф.
Оттого что сердец и душ
Не сдают в багаж.

Вещи бедных—плоше и суше:
Плоше лыка, суше коряг.

Вещи бедных—попросту—души.
Оттого так чисто горят.

Ввысь, ввысь
Дым тот легкий!
Чист, чист
Лак от локтя!

Где ж шлак?
Весь—золой
Лак, лак
Локтевой!

Прям, прям
Дым окраин.
Труд—Хам,
Но не Каин.

Обшлаг—
Вдоль стола.
Наш лак
Есть смола.

Стол—гол—на вещицы.
Стол—локтем вощится.
Воск чист, локоть востр.
За—стывший пот—воск.

Им, им—ваших спален
(Вощи́м, но не са́лим!)
Им, им так белы́
Полы—до поры!

Вещи бедных—странная пара
Слов. Сей брак—взрывом грозит!

Вещь и бедность—явная свара.
И не то спа́рит язык!

Пономарь—что́ ему слово?
Вещь и *нищ*. Связь? нет, разлад.
Нагота ищет покрова,
Оттого так часто горят

Чердаки—часто и споро—
Час да наш в красном плаще!
Теснота ищет—простора
(Автор сам в рачьей клешне).

Потолок, рухнув—по росту
Стал—уж горб нажил, крался.
Правота ищет помоста:
Все сказать! Пусть хоть с костра!

А еще—место есть: нары.
Ни луча. Лу́чная вонь.
Беднота ищет загару.
О всем том—помнит огонь.

Связь, звучанье парное:
Черная—пожарная.

У огня на жалованьи
Жизнь живет пожарами.

В вечной юбке сборчатой—
Не скреби, уборщица!

Пережиток сельскости—
Не мети, метельница!

Красотой не пичканы,
Чем играют? Спичками.

Мать, к соседке вышедши,
Позабыла спичечный

Коробок...
—как вылизан
Поп, светлее зеркала!

Есть взамен пожизненной
Смерти—жизнь посмертная!

Грязь явственно сожжена!
Дом—красная бузина!

Честь царственно спасена!
Дом—красная купина!

Ваши рабства и ваши главенства—
Погляди, погляди, как валятся!

Целый рай ведь—за миг удушьица!
Погляди, погляди, как рушатся!

Печь прочного образца!
Протопится крепостца!

Все тучки поразнесло!
Просушится бельецо!

Пепелище в ночи́? Нет—займище?
Нас спасать? Да от вас спасаемся ж!

Не топчите златого пастбища!
Нас? Да разве спасают—спасшихся?

Задивившись на утро красное,
Это ясень суки выпрастывает!

Спелой рожью—последний ломтичек!
Бельевая веревка—льном цветет! ...

А по лестнице—с жарко спящими—
Восходящие—нисходящие—

Радуги...

—Утро
Спутало перья.
Птичье? мое? невемо.
Первое утро—первою дверью
Хлопает...
Спит поэма.

Июль 1926
Вандея

◆ ANNA PRISMANOVA ◆

На канте мира муза Кантемира
петровский желчью защищала бот.
И желтый сыр, вися над Чудью сирой,
рябил черновики его работ.

Ни Кант, неотразимый головастик,
ни даже голенастый Галилей,
не в силах были желтый контур застить
извилинами мозговых лилей.

Ордой к баллону на поклон, герои!
Он, путешествуя в кругу небес,
дрожит на заступе. И роют рои
сырье, и пнями истекает лес.

Ему лишь ветер препонит, забияка.
Но он, отменно цепеня эфир,
без смены мерит знаки зодиака,
и в знак того—звенит внизу цифирь.

1928

◆ ANNA PRISMANOVA ◆

Сестры Бронтэ

О времени не спрашивай счастливых,
несчастным памятники приготовь:
дай мрамору—из золота курсивы
и ангелам дай каменную бровь.

Легко сгорает оболочка тела,
внутри которой угольный костер.
От близких труб деревня закоптела,
но черный крест над ней еще остер.

Эмилия, о дикий сок лаванды,
о лилия, о мертвый соловей!
Таясь от всех, ты уносила в ланды
избыток тщетной гордости твоей.

Живут грехи былого поколенья:
порок детей восходит к их отцам.
Но дух страдания, для окрыленья,
дает перо заклеванным сердцам.

И вот Шарлотта с грузной головою
пером гусиным вскрыла бедный кров,
где три сестры во мгле внимали вою
неумолимых северных ветров.

Перо она на редкость крепко депжит:
строенье из неправильных костей,
к несчастью, в тесноте своей содержит
притушенный огонь больших страстей.

Скрыв страсти под непрочной оболочкой,
держу и я чернильный край крыла.
Дочь лекаря, я пасторскою дочкой—
одной из Бронтэ—некогда была.

Увы, для нас, в конце как и в начале,
преграда счастью—внутренний наш суд.
Но вдохновенье, знание печали,
и время—неудачников спасут.

1939/1946

◆ VERA BULICH ◆

Из дневника III

... И снова Пятница страстная,
В весеннем небе год смыкает круг.
А главное не то, что было за-год,
А то, что вновь стою у Плащаницы,
И в чаще свеч горит моя свеча.

Под скорбные и сладостные звуки,
Протяжное взыванье «Святый Боже»
Выходим из притвора. Осторожно
Спускаемся по каменным ступеням,
От сквозняка рукою прикрывая
Испуганное пламя жарких свеч,
И вот уж каблуки уходят мягко
В разрыхленную оттепелью землю,
И между черных лип, над фонарями
Прозрачно зеленеет небо. Тяжко
Срываются над нами с колокольни
Надтреснутые, редкие удары
Колоколов святого погребенья,
И Плащаница огибает церковь,
Плывя в дыму, в сиянии и в розах...
И этот запах ладана и роз,
Дымка от свеч и тающего снега,
Ожог ладони от свечи палящей,
Весенняя податливость земли,
И скорбный символ темной Плащаницы,
Над нами поднятой, и ясность неба,
И жалоба стихающего хора
Под приглушенный стон колоколов—
Все входит в душу светлою печалью.

Пройдут, забудутся, остынут чувства,
Изменит радость, притупится боль,
Но навсегда останется лишь это:
Весна и смерть. И память об утрате,
И чаемое воскресенье в духе.
Торжественность обряда векового.
То подлинное, что одно для всех.

1937

♦ VERA BULICH ♦

В автобусе

Воскресный день тревожил и томил
неугомонным ласточкиным криком,
горячим солнцем, пустотою улиц
и неба праздничною синевой.
На площади томился автобус.
И солнце, запертое в нем, лежало
тяжелыми и пыльными пластами
на кожаной обивке, на полу
и на коленях пассажиров. Пахло
бензином сладковатым, душной пылью,
нагретой кожей кресел и—в мечтах—
прохладными цветами полевыми.
Вспугнув гулявших мирно голубей,
взревел мотор и, сотрясая недра,
поплыл тяжелый автобус-ковчег,
вместив в себя и чистых и нечистых.
И было в нем спасенье для иных,
спасенье от душевного разлада,
сорокадневного потопа будней
и паутинной комнатной тоски.
А пригород бежал ему навстречу
домами, огородами, столбами,
поспешно полосующими небо
прозрачными рядами проводов,
где голоса неслышно, окрыленно
скользили в голубеющий простор,
оставив тело в будке телефонной,
ведя под небом тайный разговор.

В окне мелькнуло: дом, деревья, люди.
Один из них, прижав ружье к плечу,

застыл в сосредоточенном упоре:
он целится в невидимую цель.
И все вокруг него окаменели
под гнетом длительного ожиданья,
в молчаньи заколдованном стоят,
как нарисованные на картине.
И напряженье мне передалось,
мгновенным и необъяснимым током,
пронизав тело. Затаив дыханье,
в тревоге нарастающей я жду———

Сейчас раздастся громкий, резкий выстрел,
как разрешенье страшной немоты,
и распадется на куски картина,
и все придет в движенье. Автобус,
качнув на повороте, мчится дальше,
мелькают палисадники, дома...
Напрасно напрягаю слух, не слышно
ни выстрела, ни эха. Странной мукой
все так же сковано все тело. Пыль,
с дороги поднятая, бьется в окна...
... И кажется, что мы летим в тумане,
вращаются колеса в пустоте,
и никогда мы не достигнем цели,
обречены на вечное скитанье
в самих себе, в плену и в немоте,
с беззвучным голосом в тяжелом теле.

Среди чужих, случайный пассажир,
томясь безвыходной судьбе в угоду,
я жду, когда откроется мне мир,
когда я выйду на свободу.

1938/1954

◆ ANNA BARKOVA ◆

Нечто автобиографическое

В коллективной яме, без гробницы,
Я закончу жизненный свой путь.
Полустертые мои страницы,
Может быть, отыщет кто-нибудь.
И придется чудаку по нраву
Едкость злых царапающих строк.
И решит он:—Вот достойный славы
Полугений и полупророк.
А по окончаниям глагольным
Я скажу, что то была *она*,
Беспокойна, вечно недовольна,
И умом терзающим умна.
Пусть ученики мои обрыщут
Все заброшенные чердаки,
И они, надеюсь я, отыщут
Письмена загадочной руки.—
И найдут, разрывши хлам бумажный,
Очень много всякой чепухи.
И к моим грехам припишут важно
И чужие скучные грехи.
Уж они сумеют постараться,
В поученье людям и себе,
Написать десятки диссертаций
О моей заглохнувшей судьбе.
Педантично, страстно и дотошно
Наплодят гипотез всяких тьму,
Так что в общей яме станет тошно,
Станет тошно праху моему.
—За таинственное преступленье—
Кто из нас проникнет в эту тьму?—
Поэтессу нашу, к сожаленью,

В каторжную бросили тюрьму,
Нет нигде малейшего намека,
Что она свершила и зачем.
Верно, преступленье столь жестоко,
Что пришлось бы содрогнуться всем.
А в тюрьме ее, как видно, били...
(Это мненье частное мое),
Но ученики ее любили,
Чтили почитатели ее.
Вывод из отрывка номер восемь:
Спас ее какой-то меценат.
Но установить не удалось нам
Обстоятельств всех и точных дат.
И в дальнейшем (там же) есть пробелы,
Нам гадать придется много лет:
За какое сумрачное дело
Пострадал блистательный поэт.
Не поэт,—простите! Поэтесса!
Впрочем, если углубиться в суть,
То и здесь какая-то завеса
К истине нам преграждает путь.
Едкий ум, не знающий пощады,
О, коллеги, не мужской ли ум?
О, душа, отмеченная хладом,
Нрав сухой и жгучий, как Самум.
С женственною это все не схоже.
Факты надо! Факты нам на стол!
А когда мы факты приумножим,
Мы определим лицо и пол.
Сколько здесь волнующих моментов,
Сколько завлекательнейших тем!
В поиски! Ловите документы,
Строчки прозы, писем и поэм!
Кажется, поэт достиг предела
Творчества, и славы, и годов.
И за честь покоить его тело
Спорили десятки городов.
Но его похоронила в тайне
Прозелитов преданных толпа.

Их вела по городской окрайне
К месту погребения тропа.
Ночь их звездным трауром покрыла,
Пламенели факелы в пути...
Только знаменитую могилу
До сих пор не можем мы найти.—
Тут с негодованьем мои кости
О чужие кости застучат:
—Я лежу на северном погосте,
Лжешь постыдно, наглый кандидат.
Знаю, что на доктора ты метишь,
С важностью цитатами звеня,
Но в твоем паршивом винегрете
Мой читатель не найдет меня.
В пол мужской за гробом записали...
Я всегда, всю жизнь была *она*.
Меценатов к черту! Не спасали
Меценаты в наши времена.
И учеников я не имела,
И никто в тюрьме меня не бил,
И за самое смешное дело
Смехотворный суд меня судил.
Я жила средь молодежи глупой
И среди помешанных старух.
От тюремного пустого супа
Угасали плоть моя и дух.
Факельное шествие к могиле—
Выдумка бездарная твоя.
В яму коллективную свалили
Пятерых, таких же, как и я.

◆ ANNA BARKOVA ◆

Тоска татарская

Волжская тоска моя, татарская,
Давняя и древняя тоска,
Доля моя нищая и царская,
Степь, ковыль, бегущие века.

По соленой Казахстанской степи
Шла я с непокрытой головой.
Жаждущей травы предсмертный лепет,
Ветра и волков угрюмый вой.

Так идти без дум и без боязни,
Без пути, на волчьи на огни,
К торжеству, позору или казни,
Тратя силы, не считая дни.

Позади колючая преграда,
Выцветший, когда-то красный флаг,
Впереди—погибель, месть, награда,
Солнце или дикий гневный мрак.

Гневный мрак, пылающий кострами,
То горят большие города,
Захлебнувшиеся в гнойном сраме,
В муках подневольного труда.

Все сгорит, все пеплом поразвеется.
Отчего ж так больно мне дышать?
Крепко ты сроднилась с европейцами,
Темная татарская душа.

Стихотворение, написанное во время бессонницы в Тбилиси

Мне—пляшущей под мцхетскою луной,
мне—плачущей любою мышцей в теле,
мне—ставшей тенью, слабою длиной,
не умещенной в храм Свети-Цховели,
мне—обнаженной ниткой серебра
продернутой в твою иглу, Тбилиси,
мне—жившей под звездою, до утра,
озябшей до крови в твоей теплице,
мне—не умевшей засыпать в ночах,
безумьем растлевающей знакомых,
имеющей зрачок коня в очах,
отпрянувшей от снов, как от загонов,
мне—в час зари поющей на мосту:
«Прости нам, утро, прегрешенья наши,
Обугленных желудков нищету
позолоти своим подарком, хаши»,
мне—скачущей наискосок и вспять
в бессоннице, в ее дурной потехе,—
о Господи, как мне хотелось спать
в глубокой, словно колыбель, постели.

Спать—засыпая. Просыпаясь—спать.
Спать—медленно, как пригублять напиток.
О, спать и сон посасывать, как сласть,
пролив слюною сладости избыток.

Проснуться поздно, глаз не открывать,
чтоб дальше искушать себя секретом
погоды, осеняющей кровать
пока еще не принятым приветом.

Мозг слеп, словно остывшая звезда.
Пульс тих, как сок в непробужденном древе.
И—снова спать! Спать долго. Спать всегда,
Спать замкнуто, как в материнском чреве.

◆ ELENA SHVARTS ◆

Распродажа библиотеки историка

Вот тот нагой, что там в углу сидит—
на нем чужой башмак с алмазной пряжкой—
он бледен, жалок, не был знаменит
и жил он дома меньше, чем на Пряжке.

Это в веке чужом золотят стремена,
так причудливо строят и крепко.
Но когда ты живешь-то в свои времена,
и буденовка кажется кепкой.

Потому он ушел, он сошел по мосткам—
корешков—по хрустящим оторванным—вниз—
к фижмам, к пахнущим уксусом слабым вискам,
где для яда—крапленый сервиз.

Где масоны выводят в ночи цыплят
из вареных вкрутую яиц,
но их шепот так слаб, так прозрачен наряд,
так безглаво сиянье лиц!

С волной паломников он шел в другое лето,
кто темные их воды пьет?
За желтой и сухой гвоздикой Назарета
дитя босое в сумраках бредет.

Он повсюду—в полях и в трактирах искал
полета отравленной шпаги,
но бесплотное сердце клинок протыкал,
только разум мутя и лишая отваги.

Лик человечества—не звук пустой—
есть люди-уши, люди-ноздри, зубы.
В те дни он был небрит, весь в бороде густой,
не то, что в наши дни—тончал и шел на убыль.

Все души с прочернью, как лес весной,
но вот придет, светясь, Франциск Ассизский.
Чтоб мир прелестен стал, как одалиска,
довольно и одной души, одной!

Но закрутилось колесо, срывая все одежды—
повсюду—легионы двойников,
их не найти, нет никакой надежды,
зарывшись в легионы дневников.

Идет, острижена, на плаху королева,
но чтоб замкнулся этот круг—
вперед затылком мчится дева
и смотрит пристально на юг,

Когда она подходит ближе,
из-под корсета вынимая нож,
хоть плещешься в ботинке с красной жижей,
Марат, ты в этот миг на короля похож.

Повсюду центр мира—странный луч
в моем мизинце и в зрачке Сократа,
в трамвае, на луне, в разрыве мокрых туч
и в животе разорванном солдата.

Где в огненной розе поет Нерон
и перед зеркалом строит рожи,
Где в луну Калигула так влюблен,
что плачет и просит спуститься на ложе.

Где Клеопатра, ночной мотылек,
с россыпью звезд на крылах своих нежных,
флот деревянный—магнит уволок,
дикий, он тянет—что не железно.

Ах, он всех—он даже Петра любил,
что Россию разрезал вдоль,
черной икрой мужиков мостовые мостил,
но душ не поймал их, вертких, как моль.

Ах, не он ли и Павлу валерьянку носил,
Просил—не ссылай хоть полками—
но тот хрипел, и тень поносил,
и как дитя топтал ногами...

Он в комнате пустой—все унесли,
его витряж разбили на осколки,
пометы стерли, вынули иголку,
что тень скрепляла с пустотой земли.

Но больше он любил в архивах находить,
кого напрочь забыто имя—
при свете ярком странно так скрестить
свои глаза—с смеженными, слепыми,

но благодарными.
А сам он знал,
что уж его наверно не вспомянут.
У входа, впрочем, душ един клубится вал,
А имена как жребии мы тянем..

1970-е

◆ ELENA CHIZHOVA ◆

Кассандра

Как волны о берег всей грудью—невольно!
Не глас вопиющий—поющий тростник
у губ Аполлоновых бьюсь я. И больно
в утробу коня деревянного крик
упрятать. Кому и зачем это надо,
чтоб кто-то пророчил беду и позор?
Я—черная немочь Приамова града,
не женщина—жало. Безжалостный хор
Эриний. Слепцами назначены цены:
надеждой горит погребальный костер.
И голос, пронзительный голос измены,
как коршуна коготь могуч и остер,
летит на потраву, склоняясь крылами
над порослью дивной врагов и друзей.
И боги, играя людскими делами,
их судьбы вплетают в хвосты лошадей.

1986–8

◆ OLGA SEDAKOVA ◆

Пятые стансы

1

Большая вещь—сама себе приют.
Глубокий скит или широкий пруд,
таинственная рыба в глубине
и праведник, о невечернем дне
читающий урочные Часы.
Она сама—сосуд своей красы.

2

Как в раковине ходит океан—
сердечный клапан времени, капкан
на мягких лапах, чудище в мешке,
сокровище в снотворном порошке—
так в разум мой, в его скрипучий дом
она идет с волшебным фонарем...

3

Не правда ли, минувшая строфа
как будто перегружена? Лафа
тому, кто наяву бывал влеком
всех образов сребристым косяком,
несущим нас на острых плавниках
туда, где мы и всё, что с нами,—прах.

4

Я только в скобках замечаю: свет—
достаточно таинственный предмет,
чтоб говорить Бог ведает о чем,
чтоб речь, как пыль, пронзенная лучом,

крутилась мелко, путано, едва...
Но значила—прозрачность вещества.

5

Большая вещь—сама себе приют.
Там скачут звери и птенцы клюют
свой музыкальный корм. Но по пятам
за днем приходит ночь. И тот, кто там,
откладывает труд: он видит рост
магнитящих и слезотворных звезд.

6

И странно: как состарились глаза!
им видно то, чего глядеть нельзя,
и прочее не видно. Так из рук,
бывает, чашка выпадет. Мой друг!
что мы, как жизнь, хранили, пропадет—
и *незнакомое* звездой взойдет...

7

Поэзия, мне кажется, для всех
тебя растят, как в Сербии орех
у монастырских стен, где ковш и мед,
колодец и небесный ледоход—
и хоть на миг, а видит мирянин
свой ветхий век, как шорох вешних льдин:

8

—О, это всё: и что я пропадал,
и что мой разум ныл и голодал,
как мышь в холодном погребе, болел,
что никого никто не пожалел—
все двинулось, от счастья очумев,
как «все пройдет», горациев припев...

9

Минуту, жизнь, зачем тебя спешить?
Еще успеешь ты мне рот зашить
железной ниткой. Смилуйся, позволь
раз или два испробовать пароль:
«Большая вещь—сама себе приют».
Она споет, когда нас отпоют,—

10

и говорят, прекрасней. Но теперь
полуденной красы ночная дверь
раскрыта настежь: глубоко в горах
огонь созвездий, ангел и монах,
при собственной свече из глубины
вычитывает образы вины...

11

Большая вещь—утрата из утрат.
Скажу ли? взгляд в медиоланский сад.
Приструнен слух; на опытных струнах
играет страх; одушевленный прах,
как бабочка, глядит свою свечу:
—Я не хочу быть тем, что я хочу!—

12

и будущее катится с трудом
в огромный дом, секретный водоем...

NOTES

The Notes that follow give information on points that readers might find puzzling, and which fall outside the scope of standard one-volume dictionaries, readers' handbooks, or 'what every schoolchild knows'. (To take two instances, I feel that to gloss 'Medea' would be an insult to my readers' intelligence, but that 'Ptah' does require a brief note.) In some cases I have also provided a little background information on a text, where this seems to be necessary, without entering into full-scale bibliographical details. As mentioned in the Introduction, renderings in the poetry translations which significantly deviate from the original are also glossed here.

Ekaterina Urusova (1747–after 1816)

1. '*Invocation*': the opening piece of Urusova's *Heroides* (Iroidy), a collection of verse epistles in the manner of Ovid (St Petersburg, 1777).

2. l. 17. *CATARINA*: Catherine the Great: the Latin form is used here because it would have been standard in English heroic poetry of the day: cf. Pope's employment of it in the following lines from *The Rape of the Lock*: 'Here Thou, great Anna, whom three realms obey | Dost sometimes counsel take, and sometimes tea.'

   l. 22. *Castalian waters*: the waters of the Castalian spring near Delphi, a metaphor for poetic inspiration since classical times.

   l. 29. *De La Suzes.*: Henriette de La Suze (d. 1673) was a salon beauty, *précieuse*, and author, with Paul Pellisson, of *Recueil des pièces galantes en prose et en vers* (1663). The 'Russian De La Suze' was Elisaveta Kheraskova (1737–1809).

Anna Bunina (1774–1829)

3. '*Though poverty's no stain*' (Khot' bednost' ne porok) is taken from the first publication, in Yu. M. Lotman and M. G. Al'tshuller (eds.), *Poety 1790–1810 godov* (Leningrad, 1971). The editors of this edition note that the poem was sent by Bunina to Shishkov in a letter dated 29 February 1813; the survival of numerous manuscript copies indicates that it became quite popular.

   l. 5. *luncheon*: here in its early nineteenth-century sense of a snack meal.

   l. 11. *It's Wednesday, I must fast*! Wednesday actually was a fast-day in the Orthodox Church; but amongst the Russian upper classes, only the impossibly pious would have observed it as such by the early nineteenth century.

4. l. 28. *Then how may I, by feigning penury*. The occasion of the poem had been Bunina's embarrassment at her citation for a pension as 'a woman who had educated herself, though having no means of her own'.

l. 51. *sweetmeats*: Russian *pátoka*, usually translated as 'treacle', which is, however, a by-product of sugar rather than of honey.

5. l. 72. *I've learned to sweeten labour with a song*. The use of bees as a metaphor for the poet's labour is a *topos* of neo-classical poetry; the charm of Bunina's poem lies in her employment of this standard reference as a vehicle for concrete biographical *realia*.

7. l. 136. *for our good Sovereign*: i.e. Alexander I, who had granted Bunina a small pension.

8. *'Conversation between Me and the Women'* (Razgovor mezhdu mnoyu i zhenshchinami): taken from Bunina's *Sobranie sochinenii*, iii (St Petersburg, 1821). Bunina had made a similar humorous assault on the giddiness of upper-class Russian women in the introduction to her translation of Abbé Blatieu's *L'art poétique* (1808).

l. 10. *madrigals*: i.e. a polite formulaic tribute such as might be written in a lady's album.

l. 18. *few of us, in truth, have Russian educations*. A more than likely situation, in the case of aristocratic women brought up before 1840. (Compare the Soboleva story below.)

9. l. 21. *I sing all nature's beauteous hues*. What follows is supposed to indicate Bunina's competence in the neo-classical pastoral style.

10. l. 67. *At times I've hymned the deeds of mighty men*: Here Bunina expands on her abilities as a composer of formal odes.

Elisaveta Kulman (i.e. Kul'man; 1808–1825)

12. *'To Diana'* (K Diane): the text is taken from Elisaveta Kulman, *Piiticheskie opyty*, ii (St Petersburg, 1833).

Diana. In common with most early nineteenth-century neo-classical poets, Kulman does not distinguish between Greek and Roman tradition: here the Greek goddess Artemis, whose shrine was at Delphi, is identified with her Roman counterpart Diana.

13. l. 26. *Camenae, sweet-voiced maidens*: Roman goddesses of springs and sources, who were frequently identified with the Muses.

l. 29. Latona: Latinization of the Greek Leto, the mother of Artemis and Apollo.

Zinaida Volkonskaya (née Belosel'skaya-Belozerskaya, 1792–1862)

14. *'The Dream: A Letter'* is taken from *Galateya*, 5 (1829). A contribution to the early nineteenth-century passion for all things Egyptian, Volkonskaya's story is of more considerable significance as a celebration of the irrational 'feminine' imagination, as opposed to the classifying 'masculine' intellect.

14. *my dear Gulyanov*: Ivan Alekseevich Gulyanov (1789–1841), who served in the Foreign Ministry, but is best known as the founding father of Russian Egyptology. Elected a member of the Russian Academy in 1821, he was a follower of Champollion (see below), and the author of diverse studies on the hieroglyph.

15. *opposite a noisy city*: i.e. Memphis, the religious and secular capital of Ancient Egypt.

    I never saw the person who gave me life: Volkonskaya's own mother, one might note, had died when she was a small child.

16. *the fearful god*: presumably Ptah, on whom see below.

    epitrachilion: the Orthodox Christian term for the stole, the strip of cloth placed round a priest's shoulders during Mass.

17. *Ptah* (spelt 'Phtakh' in Volkonskaya's transcription): the Egyptian architect of the universe, whose shrine was at Memphis. Volkonskaya's invented theology and symbolism diverge significantly from what is now academically accepted: it was in fact Ptah's wife Sekhmet who was charged with exacting vengeance on the gods' enemies.

18. *Champollion*: Jean-François Champollion (1790–1832), the first great modern Egyptologist, who was inspired by his study of Chinese to make the first scientific attempt to decode the hieroglyphs: see *Lettre à M. Dacier relative à l'alphabet des hiéroglyphes* (Paris, 1822). Also the author of various works on the Egyptian pantheon.

Evdokiya Rostopchina (née Sushkova, 1812–1858)

19. *'The Unfinished Sewing'* (Nedokonchennoe shit'e) is the final poem in Rostopchina's collection *Stikhotvoreniya* (St Petersburg, 1841).

    Freudvoll | Und leidvoll, | Gedankenvoll sein: i.e. 'Whether joyful, or painful [love is] always meditative': the opening lines of a love song sung by Klärchen, the heroine of Goethe's historical drama *Egmont*, in Act III of the play.

Karolina Pavlova (née Jänisch, 1807–1893)

22. *'The Crone'* (Starukha) first appeared in *Moskvityanin*, 12 (1841); the text here is taken from Pavlova's *Polnoe sobranie stikhotvorenii* (*PSS*; Moscow and Leningrad, 1964).

26. l.1. *'Life calls us'* (Zovet nas zhizn') was not published during Pavlova's lifetime; it first appeared in the Symbolist almanach *Severnye tsvety* in 1901, under the title 'Meditations' (Dumy). The appearance of this major work by Pavlova was an early illustration of the enthusiasm for women's writing amongst male Russian Symbolists which was to shape the course of women's poetry for the next twenty years. The text here follows *PSS*.

27. ll. 25–42. *lady, of whom I, weeping, took my leave*. It has been plausibly conjectured that these lines refer to one of the wives of the Decembrist rebels, who had been exiled to Siberia in 1826. One possibility for an exact identification may be Aleksandra Grigorevna Muravyova, née Chernyshova (1804–1832) who was a Muscovite of a similar age and social class to Pavlova. Muravyova, the wife of Nikita Mikhailovich Muravyov, died and was buried in Siberia; her daughter was allowed to return to Moscow only after the death of Muravyov himself, in 1843.

ll. 43–60. The subject is Kiprian Dashkevich, a friend of Mickiewicz and a Polish patriot, who died in Russia of consumption in 1829.

l. 47. *the futile dream*; Dashkevich had been passionately, and unreciprocatedly, in love with Pavlova herself.

28. ll. 59–65. *The cruel lessons . . . hope's destiny was dust*. Dashkevich had died before the abortive Polish rebellion of 1830–1, which was savagely crushed by the Tsarist forces, put paid to any immediate hopes of Polish independence.

l. 69. *Childe Harold, alas, was right*. Pavlova has in mind the following lines from Byron's *Childe Harold*, canto iv, stanza 24:

this lightning of the mind . . .
When least we dream of such, calls up to view
The spectres whom no exorcism can bind,—
The cold—the changed—perchance the dead—anew,
The mourn'd, the loved, the lost—too many!—yet how few!

ll. 73–7. *How many are the poets . . . had triumphed*: an oblique allusion to the deaths of Pushkin, in 1837, and Lermontov, in 1841.

ll. 78–86. A reference to the poet Evgeny Baratynsky, a friend and patron of Pavlova's, who had died in Italy in 1844, and whose posthumous neglect allows Pavlova to claim for herself, in naming him, the title of an unrecognized genius.

ll. 91–4. *Why, distant face . . . here*: perhaps a reference to Mickiewicz himself.

30. '*At the Tea-Table*' (Za chainym stolom) is taken from the first publication in *Russkii vestnik*, 12 (1859). The story is a very late example of a 'society tale', a genre popular amongst Russian writers in the 1830s; the literary references in Pavlova's text suggest that she may have begun work on it about this time, though some aspects of the plot recall her short verse play 'Scene' of 1855. Generically unusual at the time of its publication, 'At the Tea-Table' was also an unusual, even an inflammatory, treatment of the 'woman question' at that time, since the established emancipatory orthodoxy, expounded here by Pavlova's character Bulanin, was that women were inferior to men through educational and social disadvantage.

30. *Die Gräfin spricht wehmutig*. The Countess said melancholically | Love is a passion | And graciously handed the tea-cup | To the Lord Baron. The quatrain comes from Heine's poem, 'Sie sassen und tranken am Teetisch' (*Lyrisches Intermezzo*, 1819–27). Pavlova's use of the Heine poem as an epigraph is ironic. In Heine's poem, the speaker describes several aristocrats who sit at a tea-table, substituting good manners and decorum for true feelings. The poet's beloved is absent, apparently because she belongs to a lower social class. The speaker contrasts the aristocrats' inability to understand love with the warmth of his beloved, who, although not present, 'could have told so prettily | Of your love'.

I would prefer there to be... ratiocinations. Pavlova apparently wrote this epigraph herself.

Vae victis: Woe to the vanquished.

31. *Tant de choses en deux mots . . . c'est une belle langue que la langue turque*; so much in two words; what a fine language Turkish is! (proverbial).

deprives her of her patrimony. Under the 1835 Russian law code, a sister could inherit only one-fourteenth of her brother's share of immovable property, and one-eighth of her brother's share of mobile property.

33. *c'est un excellent garçon*: he is a fine young fellow.

c'est un rien du tout: he is a complete nobody.

34. *c'est un homme sans prétentions . . . et puis, il a une si haute opinion des femmes*: he is a man without affectations, and has such a high opinion of women!

36. *Je suis toujours chez moi dans l'avant-soirée*: I am always at home in the early evenings.

37. *vous n'êtes pas le pape*: you are not the pope.

38. *sans rancune*: no hard feelings.

39. *pour tout de bon*: once and for all.

guests à deux fins: lit. guests from two ends; here, guests from the two different spheres of élite society.

40. *the French word for the title of her novel*. The reference is to *Ennui* (1809) by the influential Anglo-Irish novelist Maria Edgeworth (1767–1849). Edgeworth's work also involves a cross-class romance, but the plot permutations that allow for the happy ending are less than convincing.

the Elskys. Perhaps an allusion to the Elagins, whose Slavophile salon, run by Avdotya Elagina, mother of I. V. and P. V. Kireevsky, Pavlova attended during the 1830s and 1840s.

raison de plus: still more reason.

41. *the Pythia*: the priestess of Apollo at Delphi, deliverer of oracles.

42. *our white stone capital*: Russian *Moskva belokamennaya*, a standard epithet for the city.

Tverskoi Boulevard: one of the sections of the 'Boulevard Ring' surrounding the old city of Moscow, this street, which has a strip of park bounded by trees running down the middle, lies at one end of Tverskaya Street; in the nineteenth century it was the heart of Moscow's most fashionable district.

46. *the terrible Marquise de Brinvilliers*. The whole of the Princess's narrative, including the references to *poudre de succession*, is taken from E. T. A. Hoffmann's 'Das Fräulein von Scuderi' (1821). Hoffmann was extremely popular in Russia during the 1830s and 1840s, and Pavlova could expect her audience to know this story.

50. *aiming at each other's breasts*. The conduct of Russian duels was rather different from that of duels elsewhere in Europe. A barrier was used to establish a minimum distance between the antagonists, who then stood facing each other at an agreed number of paces to either side. When the signal was given, each man approached the barrier, choosing to shoot at any point in his advance.

53. *Je vous salue*: I congratulate you.

nous sommes quittes: we are quits.

54. *There's no getting away from cleverness*: Russian *um*, a word that also signifies wit, and the intellect or mind, a faculty customarily contrasted to the 'heart' or 'affections' in Sentimentalist prose.

57. *Tout arrive*: all things come to him who waits.

59. *C'est tout simplement une envie de se jeter par la fenêtre; maladie de femme*: she is quite simply suffering from a craving to throw herself out of the window; it's a common affliction in women.

from a silk dress to a peasant sarafan: lit. from leather boots [i.e. the footwear of the urban working-class] to bast shoes.

Sand's Simon: another ironic citation of an idyll of cross-class love. Sand's novel, written in 1836, is set in 1825, during the French Restoration, and concerns a virtuous peasant, Simon, who falls in love with Fiamma, the daughter of a newly restored count. Fiamma helps Simon fulfil his potential by becoming a successful lawyer, and then marries him.

61. *guberniya*: the largest administrative division in pre-1928 Russia; usually translated 'government' but roughly equivalent to 'province'.

63. *Woe from Wit*: the famous play by Aleksandr Griboedov (1824). Pavlova's readers would have been aware that Khozrevsky, who compares himself with the play's hero, the aristocratic Chatsky, also has traits in common with Chatsky's anti-type, Molchalin (Mr Silent), an impoverished and seemingly obsequious secretary, who wins the love of his employer's daughter, but who is exposed as a self-interested schemer.

64. *the quit-rent from his three thousand souls*: 'quit-rent' is the tax due to their owners from serfs spared forced labour; three thousand souls, or serfs, was a most substantial holding.

66. *C'est bien possible*: that may well be.

Sofya Pavlovna Soboleva (née Lavrova [?], 1840–1884)

71. *'Pros and Cons'* (I pro, i contra) was first published in *Otechestvennye zapiski*, 6 (1863). The story's title refers specifically to the 'pros and cons' of education for women; book-learning, the narrator argues, is not enough in itself. However, this straightforward 'message' is undercut by layers of irony and ambiguity; though Soboleva, like other women writers, used fiction as a means of expressing the feminist ideas that she could not express in essays, her story is much more than a tract *manqué*.

    Madame Court Counsellor Lisitsyna (Russian *Nadvornaya sovetchitsa Lisitsyna*): one of this story's many ironies. The narrator refers to herself in terms of her husband's not terribly distinguished position in the civil service (he held the seventh rank of fourteen); as we are later to learn, their social prominence is in fact ensured by her own family's rank and wealth, and not by her husband's origins or career.

72. *fictions distinguished by a most exquisite refinement*. The story's chronology makes it clear that Lisitsyna was born in the 1820s; this passage must accordingly be satirizing the 'society tale' of the 1830s, as practised by Elena Gan and Mariya Zhukova amongst women writers.

    moujiks russes. The term pokes fun at what we can assume is the disgusted upper-class reaction to the work of Dal', Dostoevsky, and other early realists of the 1840s.

73. *Matryoshkas, Katyushkas, Varyushkas, and Dashkas*: i.e. the daughters of the narrator's parents' serfs, who all have stereotypical peasant names.

    guberniya: see note to p. 61.

75. *three bright angels . . . truth, sincere fellow-feeling, and rational labour*: the trio routinely admired by the mid-nineteenth-century Russian intelligentsia, with which the narrator allies herself.

77. *a life on the stage*. This would have been considered just as 'fast' for a Russian young lady of the 1840s as for her English equivalent.

    Academy of Arts. Founded in the late eighteenth century, this institution had since its inception furthered the social mobility of young Russian men of humble origins. Graduation with the top award, the gold medal, gave the recipient the right to set up as a painter; serfs who received it were automatically freed. It was not until the 1860s, however, that painting became an intellectually respectable activity, one comparable with literature. Lisitsyna's cousin, therefore, is an anachronistic character in terms of the 1840s, his supposed milieu, but contributes to a debate that was extremely lively in 1863, the year when the *Peredvizhnik* realists seceded from the Academy. (I am indebted for this information to Elizabeth Valkenier's *Russian Realist Art* (New York, 1977).)

80. *painters who lavished their labours on aping rich satins and velvets . . . the unshowy paintings of the Russian genre painters*: a contrast that could have been made in the 1840s, say between the work of Bryullov and Bruni on the one hand, and Fedotov and Soroka on the other, but which, like other aspects of Lisitsyna's discussion of art, relates more immediately to matters topical in the 1860s.

the methods by which drawing was taught. The course that Lisitsyna describes is in fact not far removed from the teaching of drawing in the Russian Academy of Arts throughout the nineteenth century; again, attacks on 'mechanical' art lessons were highly topical in the 1860s.

82. *awarded a gold medal . . . Academy*: see observations on the Academy above.

85. *village elder*: i.e. the elected representative of Russian serfs (or peasants after 1861), whose responsibilities included negotiating with the local landowner.

89. *Monsieur Michelet*: Jules Michelet, an anti-feminist French socialist, whose *L'Amour* (1858) and *La Femme* (1860) had attacked the 'interference' of women in public life. (The former tract had been the subject of an angry review by the Russian woman writer Evgeniya Tur, published in *Russkii vestnik* during 1859.)

90. *Unless, of course, a still worse fate overtakes her*. Soboleva's 1862 story 'Another Broken Heart', delineates this 'fate' in detail; the heroine, Varya, despairing of finding properly paid employment as a private teacher, allows a wealthy male acquaintance to set her up in a love-nest, with disastrous results.

91. *Newtons, Hegels, Copernicuses*. Like the 'three angels' above, this triad of two scientists and a realist philosopher is entirely in accordance with the tastes of the Russian mid-nineteenth-century intelligentsia in general.

94. *an institute of higher education were opened*. In 1859, Russian women had been granted permission to attend lectures at ordinary universities, but this arrangement had been stopped by government order in 1861. In 1869, however, something like Lisitsyna's 'experiment' came about, with the founding of co-educational 'Courses of Higher Education' in St Petersburg; these were succeeded, in the early 1870s, by the various 'Women's Courses' that existed, on and off, up till the Revolution.

gimnaziya: see note to p. 119.

95. *in a high solar . . . windows*: Russian *terem*, the women's quarters in pre-Petrine Russia.

97. *Zina had turned into a 'progressive'*. The description that follows gives an amusingly satirical description of 1860s radical chic for women.

99. *Souls*: see note to p. 64.

100. *a room not more than fourteen foot square*. As a description of poverty-stricken conditions, likely to raise something of a smile in today's Russia; and this space allocation by no means represented the deepest penury in 1860s Petersburg either, where the renting of beds, or even parts of beds, was a common practice.

101. *Ivanych*. This colloquial shortening of the patronymic Ivanovich is used to suggest affection or familiarity and is especially typical of non-educated Russian.

102. *such Tatar customs*: i.e. bullying guests into eating and, especially, drinking, more than they want, a habit which visitors to Russia have deplored since at least the sixteenth century.

112. *we should have travelled the world together . . . some far-off corner*. As the hero, Ralph, and eponymous heroine do in Sand's *Indiana*, a novel that enjoyed great popularity in Russia.

Elizaveta Shakhova (1821–1899)

114. '*Autobiographical Response from a Provincial Wasteland*' (Avtobiograficheskii otzyv iz glushi) was first published in *Sobranie sochinenii*, ii. The text is undated, but the editor's placing of it suggests a date of about 1865.

l. 8. *buffy*: Russian *palevyi*, from French pâle, a colour between yellow and pink, a fashionable shade for dress materials in the 1840s and 1850s and a favourite colour of Sentimentalist poets. (This and the following line read literally: A golden-pâle rose | In a jug of blue glass | Has miraculously, amidst the frost | With its green branch, burst into bloom!)

l. 13. *This does not . . . again*. These four lines are from Pushkin's lyric 'Confession' (1826).

115. l. 35. *Russia's most high and glorious sons*. In 1837 Shakhova was given a gold medal by the Russian Academy, in 1839 a diamond parure by Tsar Nicholas I.

l. 41. *The bard of Svetlana and Lyudmila*: Vasily Zhukovsky (1783–1852), one of the most prominent poets of the early nineteenth century. It is odd that Shakhova does not mention Vladimir Grigorevich Benediktov (1807–73), a popular poet of the 1830s and 1840s, who had addressed two poems of 1839 and 1840 to her; however, Benediktov's reputation had declined during the 1850s, and Shakhova was no doubt aware of this even in her 'wasteland'.

l. 43. *And the sweet chorus of fair ladies*. The editor of the 1911 edition states this to have been composed of the poets Poltoratskaya (an individual of whom no records exist); Korsakova (perhaps Ekaterina Korsakova, a minor early nineteenth-century poet); Karlgof (i.e. Elizaveta Aleksandrovna Karlgof, later Drashusova, née Ashanina, d. 1884, author of *The Bride from the Capital* (1838) and of other poetical works); Ishimova (i.e. Aleksandra Osipovna Ishimova, 1804–81, children's author and translator); Rostopchina (see biographical note p. 19 above); and Teplova (i.e. Nadezhda Sergeevna Teplova, married name Teryukhina (1814–48), whose *Poems* came out in 1833; one of the better-known women poets of the 1830s). On 'fair ladies' cf. also Shakhova's 1845 poem 'To Women Poets', published in *Sobranie Sochinenii*, and reprinted in *Tsaritsy muz*, ed. V. V. Uchonova (Moscow, 1989), wherein she speaks of herself as 'a newcomer' amongst established stars.

l. 45. *The scholars and the connoisseurs*. The 1911 edition lists these as follows: (Nikita Ivanovich) Butyrsky (1783–1848, one of the first professors of the St Petersburg University, a specialist in aesthetics); (Yakov Karlovich) Grot (1812–93), a famous translator, scholar, and member of the Russian Academy); (Osip-Yulian Ivanovich) Senkovsky, (an orientalist and journalist of Polish origin, and the editor of *Biblioteka dlya chteniya*, who had first brought Shakhova to the public's notice); (Petr Alekseevich) Pletnyov (1792–1862), a well-known critic, who had given Shakhova's second collection an encouraging notice in *Sovremennik*, 17 (1840)); (Aleksandr Vasilevich) Nikitenko (1804/5–77), philosopher, aphorist, and critic); and Cheslavsky (who has proved untraceable).

116. l. 83. *And now you, madam*: a direct address to the poem's dedicatee, Sofya Mikhailovna Gogel', née Stepova (1819–88), whose husband, General Grigory Fedorovich Gogel', was military commandant in Tsarskoe Selo during the 1860s.

117. ll. 109–12. *What seems superfluous . . . world for us*. These last four lines create an oddly feeble and uncomfortable impression in the original, perhaps because Shakhova felt compelled by her religious vocation to insert a devotional element into a poem whose main concern is an egocentric justification of her enduring genius to the world.

Olga Shapir (1850–1916)

118. '*The Settlement*' (V slobodke) was first published in the journal *Severnyi vestnik*, 6 (1893); the translation here is based on this edition. The story also appears, in identical form, in Shapir's *Sobranie sochinenii* of 1911.

Morals live on bread, not air. Russian *Chto za chest', koli nechego est'*: lit. What use is honour, if there's nothing to eat.

Settlement (Russian *slobodka*): refers here to a large village just outside the boundaries of a large town, whose occupants' social status was somewhere between that of peasants and workers. Cf. 'township' or even 'shanty town'.

119. *gimnaziya*: in full *klassicheskaya gimnaziya* (cf. German *Klassisches Gymnasium*) was the nineteenth-century term for the most prestigious type of secondary school administered by the Russian state. The *gimnaziya* curriculum was heavily biased towards the classical languages, and the teaching was both regimented and high-pressure; by the late nineteenth century, its pupils alone stood a reasonable chance of reading for a university degree in the humanities. By the 1890s, the *gimnaziya* was coming under criticism from all shades of the Russian left. The style of teaching was held to be unimaginative, and the long school day was felt to subject pupils to unnecessary stress; the emphasis on the classics was increasingly held to be irrelevant to contemporary life; there was also disquiet at the strict quotas of working-class (and for that matter Jewish) pupils which these schools maintained. The 'uniform' consisted of a miniature version of the military-style civil-service greatcoat and cap.

Easter. In Orthodox Christian countries, gifts are exchanged at Easter rather than at Christmas.

120. *'elder sister', as Fedya called her*: Russian *sestritsa*. In traditional Russian families it was customary for the younger children to address the older ones as '*sestritsa*' and '*bratets*', rather than by their full names.

121. *Avdotya Kuzminishna*: the full name and patronymic of Dunya, Fedya's sister. The use of Dunya's full name is unusually honorific, given her relative youth, and indicates the respect in which she is held in the Settlement. The use by villagers of the patronymic in its softened form, Kuzminishna (the standard educated pronunciation would be Kuzminichna) indicates that this story is set somewhere in southern or central Russia.

122. *dashing droshky*: i.e. *prolyotka*, a low open four-wheeled carriage. Tolstoi recalls in his *Youth* that his father gave him the use of such a carriage on his entering university; 'pony and trap' would be the approximate English equivalent.

examinations. The standard form of these in Russia was (and remains) an oral test, held at frequent intervals, in which candidates are allocated a short question paper (*bilet*) by lot. The marks run from a high of five (here translated 'top marks') down to one; the pass mark is three.

134. *matric*: i.e. matriculation, *attestat zrelosti*, the examination sat by those graduating from a *gimnaziya*, assessed across a broad range of compulsory subjects, including classics; only those successful in the 'matric' might proceed to higher education.

138. *kasha*: buckwheat groats, which, with cabbage soup, formed the standard daily diet of the Russian working classes.

145. *a real merchant, second guild*. The official Russian pre-Revolutionary social classification system was according to 'estates'. The merchant estate, the second-highest secular caste, was itself ranked into 'guilds', access to which depended on capital. Though the 'first guild' included some of the richest families in Russia, there was, by the late nineteenth century, little difference between some members of the 'second guild' and the better-off members of the next estate down, the *meshchanstvo* or petty bourgeoisie.

147. *go out herding*. The force of this insult depends on the low status of herding and shepherding in Russian villages, as the occupations of landless labourers.

Valentina Dmitrieva (1859–1948)

153. '*Round the Villages*' (Po derevnyam) was first published in *Vestnik Evropy* 10 and 11 (1896). This extract comes from Part I, pp. 554–65.

154. *gimnaziya*: see note to p. 119.

Rye all around. The quotation that follows consists of the opening four lines of Nekrasov's narrative poem 'Peace' (Tishina, 1857), a central text of Russian nineteenth-century radical populism, which, like Dmitrieva's memoir, intersperses recollections of a journey with ruminations on the state of things in the Russian countryside. Dmitrieva in fact misquotes slightly: Nekrasov's poem speaks of the Russian landscape's 'healing powers', not of its 'magic'.

Amelka: the familiar form of the peasant first name Emelyan.

just over a third of an acre (Russian *odna sazhen' s chet'yu*). A *sazhen'*, as a unit of land measurement, was equivalent to 80 ordinary square *sazhen's*, i.e. about 1,600 square yards.

156. *village elder*. See note to Soboleva's 'Pros and Cons', p. 85 above.

gummatous syphilis: a skin abnormality marking the early stages of syphilis, and characterized by the eruption of small tumours containing a sticky liquid.

157. *black houses* (Russian *topivshiesya po-chernomu*): heated without a chimney or flue, a system known as the 'black house' in western parts of the British Isles.

159. *auxiliary policeman* (Russian *desyatskii*): sometimes translated as 'peasant policeman': the village elder's deputy.

161. *packets of dried mint*. The interest in these would have been stimulated by traditional beliefs in the healing value of herbs, which were as widespread in Russia as in most other peasant cultures. Mint was particularly popular as a panacea because its ameliorative functions were believed to be accompanied by no side-effects. (I owe this information to Natalya Rumyantseva.)

164. *volost*: see note to p. 285.

zemstvo: local authority.

Zinaida Gippius (1869–1945)

166. *'The Seamstress'* (Shveya, 1901) is taken from Gippius's *Sobranie stikhov*, i (Moscow, 1904). The poem may profitably be compared with Rostopchina's 'The Unfinished Sewing'; it is also of interest as a decadent reworking of the subject-matter of Thomas Hood's poem 'The Song of the Shirt', which had been very popular amongst nineteenth-century Russian radicals.

168. *'The Wedding Ring'* (Brachnoe kol'tso, 1905) comes from *Sobranie stikhov*, ii (Moscow, 1910).

l. 3. *My soul is bare, stripped to the purest bareness.* An attempt to replicate the pleonasm of the Russian original (cf. 'empowered me with the power' in l. 11).

l. 5. *A man, I held desire.* A slightly awkward attempt to indicate in the English the fact that the Russian text employs masculine adjectival and verbal forms.

l. 12. *Your holy veil* (Russian *pokrov*): used to signify the protecting veil of the Mother of God, as well as 'covering' in a neutral sense. By combining this word with the 'flames' that signify active male spirituality, Gippius signifiies her aspiration to androgyny of the spirit.

169. *'Incantation'* (Zaklinanie, 1905) is taken from *Sobranie stikhov*, ii. The incantation, a type of magic spell, was a folkloric genre that was much imitated by Russian poets of the Symbolist and post-Symbolist generations. Gippius's poem imitates the conjuration formulas and insistent repetitions of the folkloric original.

Anastasiya Mirovich (*?c.*1880–?)

170. *'The Lizards'* (Yashcheritsy) and *'Elsa'* (Elza) are taken from *Severnye tsvety*, ii (Moscow, 1902). The second piece, with its woman revolutionary heroine, handles a theme that was treated 'straight' by many women prose writers of the 1890s and 1900s (for example, in Tatyana Shchepkina-Kupernik's story 'The Ball', of 1907).

Nadezhda Teffi (pseudonym of Nadezhda Buchinskaya, née Lokhvitskaya, 1872–1952)

174. *The Woman Question* (Zhenskii vopros) was first published in *Vosem' miniatyur* (St Petersburg, 1913); it had been performed at the Maly Theatre in St Petersburg in 1907; the play was also reprinted, and performed, in Paris during the 1930s. This publication is taken from *Vosem' miniatyur.*

179. *Deputy Ovchina was discussing the man question.* The arguments that follow parody and reverse *idées reçues* about women's mental capacities that were being much bandied about in early twentieth-century discussions of the 'woman question'.

if men work as cooks and nannies, why... Any early twentieth-century Russian spectator would have known that a defence of men's potential as doctors was certain to follow this opener.

180. *at one time it was quite different*. Another parody-reversal of clichés associated with 'the woman question', this time of the notion, propounded by Engels amongst others, that a primal matriarchal phase had been suppressed, in prehistoric times, as a result of the rise of patriarchy.

some firewoman. A further strand of Teffi's comedy is the mockery of conventional literary stereotypes, here, the cook who is forever having visitors in the kitchen, a favourite of late nineteenth-century realist writing.

181. *a real woman cook . . . budget*. In the real world of turn-of-the-century Russia, it was of course *male* cooks who were more expensive.

183. *gentlemen of easy virtue*. Russian *padshie muzhchiny*, lit. 'fallen men', from the customary euphemism 'fallen woman'.

184. *Coco, Vanka the Canary, Antipka*: masculinizations of typical names for music-hall singers in turn-of-the century Russia.

used to be a launderer. Russian *polotyor*, lit. floor-polisher: another *idée reçue* of early twentieth-century Russia was that music-hall singers were invariably former servants.

185. *Vasilievsky*: i.e. Vasilievsky Island, one of the constituent islands of St Petersburg; an obvious place for a professor to live, since the University is located there.

190. *rode horses, let his hair grow long, and went running to lectures*. Again, a parody of turn-of-the-century rebukes against young ladies, with the exception, of course, that the latter cut their hair rather than grew it.

193. '*Walled Up*' (Za stenoi) is taken from *Yumoristicheskie rasskazy* (St Petersburg, 1910).

The Easter loaf: the *kulich*, a form of enriched *brioche* baked in a shape rather like a solid chimney-pot with a rounded top. This opening also makes it clear that 'Walled up' is an 'Easter story', i.e. belongs to a genre which normally had the cosy sentimentality of Western European Christmas fictions such as Dickens *A Christmas Carol*, but which is very differently handled here.

194. *They haven't rung the bells*: i.e. to mark the end of the Lenten fast on Easter Saturday.

verveine . . . ambre royale: the French names for essential perfume oils derived from verbena and 'royal amber' (the latter probably a brand name for a variant of ambergris, a musky substance of marine origin).

trèfle incarnat: crimson clover.

194. *Ralle's*: A. Ralle and Co., a perfume and cosmetics company, by appointment to the Russian Royal Family, with branches at 8–12 Nevsky Prospekt and in many other parts of St Petersburg and Moscow. Evidently a manufacturer of reliable but not very glamorous goods, rather like Yardley of London; the more pretentious St Petersburg perfume shops, such as 'A la Renommée' of Bolshaya Konyushnaya, had French names.

ixore, exact information is elusive, but possibly an oil derived from Ixia, the generic name of a showy kind of South African iris.

fougère: i.e. fern.

198. *so that he could get promotion to general in the Civil Service*: a phrase indicating that Madame Schrank's visitor must have been a 'handsome young fellow' in his fifties.

199. *pashka*: the rich, sweet curd cheese mixture that accompanies *kulich*, the Easter loaf.

200. *Verny*: The pre–1917 name of Alma–Ata, site of a massive quake in 1887.

Balkan Sea; perhaps a mistake for Lake Balkash.

Adelaida Gertsyk (1874–1925)

202. '*Spring*' (Vesna) and '*Silent, draped in the garments of sacrifice*' (V tkanyakh belykh, zhertvennykh) are taken from Gertsyk's *Stikhotvoreniya* (St Petersburg, 1910). The dedication in the latter poem is to Gertsyk's younger sister Evgeniya (1878–1944), translator, essayist, and the author of important memoirs, to date published only in part (Paris, 1973). The dedication in the former is perhaps to another member of Gertsyk's family. The epigraph is taken from Part iv of Vyacheslav Ivanov's 'Mountain Spring' (Gornaya vesna), a cycle from his 1904 collection *Transparency* (Prozrachnost').

206. '*My Loves*' (Moi romany) was first published in *Severnye zapiski* 2 and 4 (1913).

When I look back on my past . . . forms within it. The Russian text employs a set of positively Tsvetaevan parallelisms, chiming on verbal suffixes and prefixes: '*Oglyadivyas'* na proshloe, vizhu ryad vekh, *otmechayushchikh* proidennyi put', svetochei, *ozaryayushchikh* i *napravlyayushchikh* v doroge.'

Ruskin Part I of the essay recounts Gertsyk's imaginary friendship with John Ruskin (1819–1900), a figure who had become fairly well known amongst the Russian intelligentsia by the turn of the century. Gertsyk's own essay on him, 'Religiya krasoty', appeared in *Russkoe bogatstvo* in 1899. The books which Gertsyk mentions are *Mornings in Florence* (7 parts; 1875–7); which Gertsyk herself translated into Russian in 1902; *The Seven Lamps of Architecture*

(1880); *Val d'Arno* (1882); *Modern Painters* (1888); *Praeterita*, his autobiography, (1889).

207. *The Ensign* (Russian *Vympel*): apparently an invented name, as too is 'Stalaktitov' (Mr Stalactite); the title may possibly veil a reference to *The Banner* (Znamya), a short-lived (1899–1901) Moscow 'political, scientific, and literary weekly', edited by N. D. Obleukhov. Gertsyk's first recorded publication was indeed an essay on Ruskin (see above), but this appeared in a mainstream literary monthly.

208. *Sizeranne's . . . la beauté.*: Robert de La Sizeranne's *Ruskin et la religion de la beauté* had been published in 1897.

old house: the house at Brantwood, near Coniston Water, in the Lake District, to which Ruskin retired in his last years.

209. *Giotto's tower*: i.e. the Campanile of the Duomo at Florence, begun in 1334, two years before Giotto's death, and built, at least in its earlier stages, to designs by him. Ruskin's own photographs of the tower were used as illustrations to Part VI of *Mornings* in later edns.

Memmi: Lippo Memmi (d. 1347), a pupil of Giotto.

the school of Pythagoras: i.e. the brotherhood at Crotona, southern Italy, to which the philosopher expounded his views on ethics.

I shall let you go now . . . eight sharp. Like the quotation from Humboldt (see below), this is Gertsyk's own invention, though similar chivvying comments do indeed lard *Mornings*: see e.g. the opening of 'The Second Morning': 'Today, as early as you please, and at all events before doing anything else, let us go to . . . Santa Maria Novella. . . . Do not let anything in the way of acquaintance, sacristan, or chance sight, stop you doing what I tell you.'

210. the *European Herald*: i.e. *Vestnik Evropy*, perhaps the most important literary and political monthly of the late nineteenth century, which did in fact carry many dull and worthy commentaries on economic affairs.

211. *Annie Vivanti*. Born in 1868 in London, the daughter of a German mother and Italian political exile father, Vivanti returned to Italy at the age of 19 to study as a singer. Failing to make a career on the stage, she turned to writing poetry; her first collection, *Lirica*, was published in 1890, with a foreword by the poet Carducci. In 1892 she married the Anglo-Irish (not English, as Gertsyk supposed) journalist John Chartres, and went to live in America. Apart from poetry, she was the author of large numbers of prose works, some of which ran into many editions. Returning to Italy in 1912, she remained there until her death in 1942.

Io sono tanto stanca di lottare: I am so weary of struggling.

212. *Quando sarò partita—piangerai*: when I am gone, you will weep.

213. *'Vuoi tu'* (As you wish), *'Fra poco'* (In a while), and *'Appuntamento'* (The assignation): the titles of poems from *Lirica.*

215. *sono il suo fratello*: I am her brother.

216. *The Hunt for Happiness*: i.e. *The Hunt for Happiness, being an Excerpt from 'Tales from Town Topics' no. 20* (New York, 1900) (Gertsyk gives the title in English in her original, spelling 'happiness' with one p).

217. *Humboldt*: Wilhelm von Humboldt (1767–1835), educationalist, humanist, anthropologist, and theoretician of language. Potebnya: i.e. Aleksandr Afansevich Potebnya (1835–1891), professor of Russian philology at Kharkov, and author of studies of comparative Slavonic grammar, histories of the Russian language, and of theoretical works, including *Thought and Language* (Mysl' i yazyk, 1862). Humboldt is extensively quoted in this volume, but the quotation to which Gertsyk refers does not appear—it would in fact be most incongruous in the context of Potebnya's abstract discussion of the communicative powers of language. It is possible that Gertsyk conflated two different Humboldt quotations, one referring to the fact that artistic representations are not inferior to real fruit, the other to the idea of language as a medium surrounding human beings; however, it is more likely that she simply misremembered the source of her citation.

218. *Ovsyaniko-Kulikovsky*: Dmitry Nikolaevich Ovsyaniko-Kulikovsky (1853–1920), a philologist and literary historian who had acted as a populist for Potebnya's ideas: see e.g. 'Ocherki nauki o yazyke', *Russaya mysl'*, 12 (1896).

Wundt's . . . Psychologie der Sprache: Wilhelm Wundt (1832–1920) was a German philosopher and psychologist; the study to which Gertsyk refers is in fact almost certainly *Die Sprache* (2nd edn.; Leipzig, 1904).

Rémy de Gourmont, Esthétique de la langue: the French poet's *Esthétique de la langue française, la déformation, la métaphore, le cliché, le vers libre, le vers populaire* (Paris, 1899).

219. *vermilion*: Russian: U neyo prosto *rdela* dusha (lit. 'her soul was simply blushing').

221. *Bal'mont*: Konstantin Balmont (1867–1942), whose early collections, especially *We Shall Be as the Sun* (Budem kak solntse, 1903) established him as a leading figure in the Russian Symbolist movement. I have not been able to trace a text in which the word 'surroundings' (*okruzhnost'*) is used; it is possible that Gertsyk has in mind 'Serenade', a poem of 1904 by Bely (see below), in which the similar word *okrestnost'*, environs, occurs: 'Sapphire, sapphire | Pours over the environs'.

222. *Bely*: Andrei Bely (real name Boris Bugaev, 1880–1934), now best known as a prose writer, but also the author of several fine collections of poetry, included

Gold in Azure (Zoloto v lazuri, 1904), *Ash* (Pepel', 1908), and *The Urn* (Urna, 1909).

wineworldly... (Russian *mirovinnoe, vinokrasnoe, bezmirnoblednoe, svetomirnoe, vinozarnoe,* and *iskrotechnyi, srebrolunnyi, ogneveinyi, svetlopennyi, lennostrunnyi*). Many compound adjectives of this type do indeed occur in Bely's early collections, including *vinnozolotistaya* ('Zakaty', 1902), *zlatomirnyi* ('Vechnyi zov', 1903), *fontanno-belye* and *pennozolotye* ('Predan'e', 1903), *tikhostrunnyi* ('Demon', 1908), but of those listed by Gertsyk I have only been able to trace *svetlopennyi*, a mistranscription of *svetopennyi potok* in 'Na gorakh' (1903).

chirm [i.e. noise], *wallwort* [dwarf elder], *weald* [wood], *archil* [red or violet dye], *mazard* [head], *cumberground* [useless object]: all archaic words of Anglo-Saxon or Old French origin, such as might have been used by some eccentric turn-of-the-century English poet: replacing the Slavonicisms *yarye peski, tekuchie reki, kladezi, ugor'ya, skatogoriya, pritiny* (lit. bright sands, flowing rivers, wells, estuaries, hillsides, currents) that are cited by Gertsyk.

223. *And I found my salvation—in Nietzsche.* Given that Nietzsche's own insanity was famous, one may assume that Gertsyk's tongue is well in her cheek here. Nietzsche's influence had been widespread, not to say ubiquitous, in early twentieth-century Russia, and Gertsyk herself had helped to translate *Götterdämmerung* (as *Pomrachenie kumirov*, Moscow, 1900), and *Unzeitliche Betrachtungen* (1905). The dates of these translations highlight a problem of chronology that is evident throughout 'My Loves'. Gertsyk asserts that her enthusiasm for Ruskin was replaced by a tenderness for Vivanti, and then by an abstract love of language, from which she was in turn 'saved' by her feeling for Nietzsche. However, her first Nietzsche translation, done in 1900, in fact predates not only her first article on language, 'Zhivoe slovo i klishe', *Russkaya mysl'* (1902), but also her visit to Italy (if her memory of being shown *The Hunt for Happiness*, published only in 1900, is correct). Factual accuracy seems to have been surpressed in favour of symbolic patterning: Gertsyk's progression from love of the masculine (Ruskin), to the feminine (Vivanti), to the 'it' of language recalls the structure of Innokenty Annensky's 1909 essay 'On Contemporary Lyricism', divided into 'Hes' 'Shes' and 'It' (though the last part was never completed). Gertsyk's final invocation of Nietzsche, in destroying the tripartite balance, seems, therefore, still more inappropriate.

Anna Akhmatova (pseudonym of Anna Gorenko, 1889–1966)

224. '*Sister, I have come to take your place*' (Ya prishla tebya smenit'). First published in *Apollon* 3 (1913). In this version, which was reprinted in *The Rosary* and in *From Six Books*, the last four lines of the poem are printed as one stanza. The version here follows these early editions, rather than *Stikhotvoreniya i poemy*

(Leningrad, 1976), in which the last two lines appear as a couplet; however, the clearer punctuation of the 1976 edition has been preferred. In its combination of references from Greek mythology and Russian folklore, and its use of metaphors hallowed by Russian Symbolist tradition ('flame' and 'whiteness' as markers of the spiritual world) in order to suggest women's powers of prophecy, Akhmatova's poem invites comparison with the two poems by Gertsyk included in this anthology.

224. l. 2. *bonfire* (Russian *kostyor*); a word which, like its English equivalent, is derived from 'bones' (*kosti*), and so can mean a funeral pyre.

225. l. 6. *lightning*: i.e. *zarnitsa*, summer lightning, lightning without thunder; one of an extremely important cluster of words describing different light phenomena, including *zarya* (dawn) and *zarenitsa*, a special bonfire lit around St Fyokla's day, 24 September.

l. 7. *Time has stilled your rattling tambourine*: lit. 'The tambourine's beats have long been inaudible'. Like the flute or pipe, the tambourine is one of the instruments associated in Greek mythological tradition with the train of Dionysus; such instruments had become, in the neo-classical poetry of Russian Symbolism, metaphors of 'the Dionysiac' in a post-Nietzschean sense, that is, of creation through ecstasy and excess. The reference points up the link between these 'sisters' and the composition of poetry.

l. 20. *lilac*: this plant is also associated with the Dionysiac, since by mythological tradition the bush had been metamorphosed from Syrinx, a nymph pursued by Dionysus' associate, the lewd god Pan—a myth which is preserved in the botanical term for lilac, 'syringa', which gives the standard Russian common name, *siren'*.

l. 29. *the one is a snow-white banner*: lit. 'And she, a white banner | And she, a lighthouse's light', which would sound impossibly clumsy in English, and lose the folkloric coloration of the original. The English, however, perhaps makes too apparent the symbolic connection between 'bonfire' and 'lighthouse', which brings the poem full-circle.

226. '*Solitude*' (Uedinenie): the version here is taken from *Belaya staya* (Petrograd, 1917).

l. 1. *So many boulders have been cast at me*: perhaps an oblique reference to the Gospel tale of the woman taken in adultery. Akhmatova makes the ritual of humiliation into a metaphor of self-assertion, as Christ had made the attempt to execute an adulteress into a parable of humiliation for the Pharisees ('Let he who is without sin amongst you cast the first stone').

l. 3. *a slender tower*: meaning both the tower in which the heroine of Western and Russian folk-tale lives, and, metaphorically, Akhmatova's own slender and lofty body.

l. 7. *My turret top bathes in an earlier light*: lit. 'From here I see the dawn earlier [than others, than from other places]'.

l. 11. *dove*: suggesting the messenger-dove dispatched from the Ark by Noah, whose return signalled the end of the Flood: here, the dove signals the poet's calm self-sufficiency, as she lives in retreat from the world, but not in complete isolation from it.

l. 13. *The Muse's dusky hand*: Darkness of complexion suggests both the Muse as Akhmatova's 'double', an idea explored in her 1914 narrative poem *By the Edge of the Sea*, and Pushkin, who is described in 'Tsarskoe Selo' as 'a dusky youth, wandering the avenues' of the Palace park.

227. '*Fear turns objects over*'; first published in the journal *Zapiski mechtatelei* in 1921. The version here is that of *Anno Domini* (1922). The date of the poem indicates that it was composed shortly after the execution of Akhmatova's first husband Nikolai Gumilyov for his alleged involvement in an anti-Bolshevik conspiracy.

l. 1. *Fear turns objects over*: lit. 'goes through its things', as the victims of political purges might, in order to rid themselves of potentially incriminating material.

l. 2. *an axe's blade*: A reference that simultaneously suggests: an object that might commonly be found in a Russian flat of the pre-central-heating era (for chopping wood); the public execution theme that is to figure later; and an oblique allusion to Dostoevsky's *Crime and Punishment*, a narrative that concerns the squalid murder of two women in a St Petersburg tenement block by an axe murderer.

l. 3. *Something taps behind the thin partition*: lit. 'Behind the thin partition comes an ominous tapping', 'ominous' being padding for metrics' sake, since the mood is already adequately suggested by the syntax.

l. 7. *shiny-bearded features*: i.e. those such as Dostoevsky's murderer protagonist Raskolnikov might be supposed to have; but also suggesting the characteristics of the *domovoi*, the malevolent Russian house spirit whose spitefully disruptive activities may be referred to in the next stanza; and the figure of Bluebeard, an important presence in Akhmatova's poetry, of the early 1920s: see e.g. 'A fearful rumour is going round town' (1922).

ll. 12–13: *rifle muzzles . . . rough scaffold*. Akhmatova juxtaposes two kinds of political execution, the firing-squad of the present, and the beheadings of the past (to which Russian political rebels of noble birth, like their Western counterparts, were occasionally subjected; the guillotine of the French Terror, set up in city squares, is another obvious association).

l. 17. *crucifix*: i.e. the small baptismal cross that is worn round the neck by all Orthodox believers.

228. *'Memories of Aleksandr Blok'* was first published in *Zvezda*, 12 (1967); the text, originally written for a 1965 television broadcast, is also available in Akhmatova, *Sochineniya* (Moscow, 1986). The text here is taken from the *Zvezda* publication. This late essay, written in 1965, is an excellent example of Akhmatova's sparely elegant prose style; it also exemplifies the manner of her late self-portraits, at once ironically self-deprecating with regard to her younger self, and authoritative in her association of that self with the great (male) Russian literary tradition—here present in the person of the most famous turn-of-the-century Russian poet, Aleksandr Blok.

the Bestuzhev Courses . . . for Women: the most famous of the private university-level institutes for women, founded in 1878, which was colloquially known by the name of its first director, the historian K. N. Bestuzhev-Ryumin.

not on account of the urbanism for which he was so celebrated. The manner of Émile Verhaeren's urbanism, evident in such books as *Les Villes tentaculaires* and *Les Campagnes hallucinées* (collected in vol. i of his *Œuvres*, Paris, 1912), had indeed been widely imitated in Russia, in the work of Bryusov, Blok, Gumilyov, and Mayakovsky, amongst others. I have not been able to trace the poem from which Akhmatova quotes; however, Verhaeren's *Toute la Flandre* (1904–6) and *Les Blés mouvants* (1912) do contain work in this manner.

Ariadna Tyrkova-Vergezhskaya: also known as Ariadna Tyrkova-Williams, from her second marriage to the British journalist Harold Williams; 1869–1962. Journalist, activist in the liberal Kadet Party, and one of the most prominent turn-of-the-century feminists; after the Revolution she lived in emigration, where she abandoned politics, turning to religious philanthropy, and wrote two interesting volumes of memoirs.

Anichka has won her own sort of equal rights: Not an impossible comment from Tyrkova, but still more characteristic of the dismissive attitude which Akhmatova, like most Symbolist and post-Symbolist women poets, felt towards institutional feminism, whose achievements they held pathetic compared with the true autonomy of literary activity.

the Poet's Guild: the society formed by young poets, including Mandelstam, Gumilyov, and Akhmatova, in 1912, out of which Acmeism grew.

the Society of Lovers of the Russian Word: a poetry society founded in 1909, and associated with the journal *Apollon*.

Vyacheslav Ivanov's 'Tower' salon: the *jours fixes* held by the important Symbolist poet at his flat overlooking the Tauride Palace in St Petersburg.

229. *I put on a tight skirt*: a line from Akhmatova's 'We are all wanderers here, or sinners'.

drunkards with their rabbit eyes: a line from Blok's famous poem 'The Strange Lady' (1906)

Igor Severyanin. The founder-member of the 'Egofuturist' group, and a very popular poet between 1913 and 1917, Severyanin was despised by many of his professional colleagues.

beginning with the Poems about a Beautiful Lady. At this point, during the television broadcast, Akhmatova held up a copy of the book in question (see note to Akhmatova, *Sochineniya*, Moscow, 1986).

On the one solitary visit that I made to Blok: i.e. in his flat; Akhmatova's emphasis on 'one' derived from her desire to scotch rumours that she and Blok had had a love affair.

Benedikt Lifshits: i.e. the minor Futurist poet (1887–1938), and author of the memoir *The One-and-a-Half-Eyed Archer*.

230. *a master of diplomacy.* Because Blok's observation at once absolved Akhmatova from the unladylike impropriety of travelling unchaperoned, and prevented her from asking what *he* might be doing at the station.

Delmas: i.e. Lyubov' Del'mas, an opera singer noted for her portrayal of Carmen; she and Blok had a passionate affair in 1914–15.

the Theatre Section. During the early years of Soviet rule, the state attempted a rapprochement with non-Communist artists. Many prominent writers managed to find employment in the various education and propaganda sections of the Commissariat of Popular Enlightenment, headed by Anatoly Lunacharsky. One of the most important of such sections was the Theatre Section; Blok was head of its Repertory Committee from the early summer of 1918 until his resignation in February 1919.

an emaciated Blok, with mad eyes. Blok was infected with syphilis, and had also become increasingly addicted to alcohol during his last years.

231. *All is as he wrote*: Akhmatova's tribute stitches together allusions to works by Blok, notably the famous short poem 'Night. A street. Gaslight. A chemist's' (1912).

Elizaveta Kuzmina-Karavaeva (i.e. Kuz'mina-Karavaeva; née Pilenko; also known by the name of her second husband, Skobtsova, and by her religious name, Mother Mariya, 1891–1945)

232. *'Long-Barrow Princess, ii'* (Kurgannaya tsarevna): the second poem of Kuzmina-Karavaeva's first collection, *Skifskie cherepki* (St Petersburg, 1912). The poem, like the rest of the collection, treats fashionable 'Scythian' themes from a feminine perspective; though the mask she adopts is original, Kuzmina-Karavaeva's imagery and metrics reveal the influence of Zinaida Gippius.

l. 7. *Morgana triumphs*: i.e. Fata Morgana; in the loose sense of magical illusion personified, rather than as a direct reference to King Arthur's sister.

234. '*Ruth*' (Ruf'): the opening poem of *Ruf'* (St Petersburg, 1916), Kuzmina-Karavaeva's second collection, indicates the poet's transition to a more sophisticated and internalized vision of self, which reveals a post-Symbolist concern with the fabrication of poetry, not simply with the extraordinary status of the poet.

ll. 1–6. *I collected the ears in my apron . . . Far away from the flatlands of Boaz.* A reference to the Old Testament account of how Ruth the Moabitess, who had of her own will returned with her mother-in-law Naomi to Judah after her husband's death, supported herself by gleaning in the fields owned by Boaz, until she was taken by him as his wife. Kuzmina-Karavaeva's poem uses only part of the biblical narrative, the gleaning motif. Ruth becomes a metaphor for the woman poet's serendipitous process of creation, turning the corn-stalks that have been 'trampled', or neglected, by others into 'golden sheaves'. Ruth's situation also suggests the strangeness of the woman poet in the sphere she has chosen; living in 'the flatlands of Boaz', her thoughts fly, like the crane, far away to the 'South'. Ruth/the woman poet's splintered identity is suggested also in the poem's shifts of tense, and in its shift of grammatical perspective, from first to third person (though it should be noted that the suggested change in identity is not quite so dramatic in the Russian text, where the unattributed feminine past tense can suggest *both* 'I collected' and 'she collected').

Vera Merkureva (i.e. Merkur'eva: 1876–1943)

235. '*The Grandmother of Russian Poetry*' (Babushka russkoi poezii): taken from M. L. Gasparov's publication 'The Grandmother of Russian Poetry', *Oktyabr'*, 5 (1989).

l. 3. *crazy Jane* (Russian. *poloumnaya*, 'half-witted'): the English version is chosen because 'crazy Jane', the popular name for Juana la Loca, the supposedly religious-maniac Spanish queen of the sixteenth century, has some of the ambiguous resonance of Merkureva's Russian allusions.

l. 5. *melting into unction*: the Russian *elei* means both 'chrism', i.e. consecrated oil, and 'obsequiousness'.

l. 6. *her clashing bells*: the original has *buben*, 'tambourine', avoided here because of its associations with the folk-mass Christianity of recent years, and also because the Russian word is closely allied with *bubenets*, a little bell such as might be sewn to a jester's costume. On the Dionysiac associations of the tambourine, see note to Akhmatova's 'Sister, I have come to take your place'.

l. 8. *Zubovo hermitage*: i.e. the flat of Vyacheslav Ivanov in Moscow, on Zubovsky Boulevard: but by word-play the reference suggests also the idea of the woman pilgrim with whose wandering and marginal religious existence Merkureva allies herself.

l. 9. *the church is like a circus*: a private reference to Merkureva's disputes with Vyacheslav Ivanov. By the time that Merkureva met Ivanov, the latter had cast off his earlier assertion of an ecstatically coloured, 'Dionysiac', religious mysticism, and had become an orthodox Christian believer. Merkureva, by contrast, had a marked distaste for ecclesiastical ritual, as she makes clear both here and in 'Vyacheslavu Sozvezdnomu' (To Constellatory Vyacheslav), an important cycle of poetry and prose addressed to Ivanov.

236. l. 19. *no sex, no gender*: ironic, since the poem gives Merkureva a grammatical gender, and a 'sexless grandmother' is an obvious contradiction in terms. The poem depends on a series of such paradoxes: as a pilgrim or holy fool, Merkureva exercises religious authority, yet cannot pretend to the authority of a priest (or of the priest-like Ivanov); in the terms of ordinary society, she is both 'complaisant' and repellent. The paradoxes are welded together, in the original, by an extended pun on *pol*, which means both 'half' and 'sex'.

Mariya Shkapskaya (née Andreevskaya, 1891–1952)

237. '*No Dream*' (Russian *Nayavu*, i.e. wakefulness, or reality as opposed to the world of a dream): taken from Shkapskaya's *Baraban Strogogo Gospodina* (Berlin, 1922); the text had earlier appeared in a separate edition, and also in the *Pravda* newspaper. The poem depicts a political execution during the Russian Civil War of 1918–21, probably of an officer in the Red Army by the Whites. However, the exact circumstances are deliberately left ambiguous by Shkapskaya, an ambiguity underlined by her ascription of the poem's composition to Romny, a small town in the Ukraine that was taken by both sides during the Civil War.

l. 6. *They say the Swiss do it in public*. Public executions in Switzerland were well known in Russia through the famous description in Dostoevsky's *The Idiot*.

l. 12. *With stooped shoulders underneath*: a personification of the gallows which is reflected later in the description of the man hanged on it. The 'tongue' (l. 14) refers to the noose.

238. l. 21. *Bryansk*: a sizeable town on the Desna, formerly in the Orlovskaya Government, but now the administrative centre of its own district; it lies about two hundred miles north-west of Romny.

l. 25. *Farewell to ye, pines and fir trees*. a snatch of a nineteenth-century 'prisoner's song', a melody sung by convicts.

240. l. 89, 91. *Let this, your father's Passion . . . heavy as a slab of stone*. These are amongst the many obvious parallels with the account of Christ's crucifixion in the Gospels. Cf. 'Three days and nights he hung there', l. 108.

l. 106. *the feast of St Peter and Paul*: i.e. 26 June, one of the major feasts in the

Orthodox Church, as in the Western; 'Peter's Day' was in popular tradition the first day of summer.

241. l. 120. *Save Russia, bash the Jews*! The political slogan of the 'Black Hundreds', a reactionary, and overtly anti-Semitic, national-populist movement that flourished in the unstable aftermath of the 1905 Revolution.

l. 123. *the relics in Chernigov*: i.e. the relics of St Feodosy (Theodosius) Uglitsky, Bishop of Chernigov in the seventeenth century, whose body was miraculously preserved after his death, attracting many pilgrims to his tomb in the Church of the Transfiguration; numerous incidents of miraculous healing led to his canonization in 1896.

l. 124. *the secret police in Kiev*: the Cheka, or 'Emergency Committee', the anti-counter-revolutionary organization set up by the Soviet government during the Civil War, which was later to form the basis of the Soviet secret police force.

l. 133. *The royal doors*: the two central doors of the iconostasis (icon screen), which are kept closed except when Mass is being celebrated.

l. 138. *St Panteilemon the Healer*: St Panteleimon of Nicomedia, a doctor and patron of doctors who was martyred in the year 305.

l. 139. *St Nicholas Whose Hair is Grey*. The reference could be to almost any of the many St Nicholases, most of whom are according to iconographic canon represented as greybeards; but the likeliest candidate is St Nicholas, Bishop of Myra, the fourth-century saint who is as much loved in Russia as he is in the West, being the centre of important popular cults. However, St Nicholas of Novgorod, a fourteenth-century 'holy fool' saint, was customarily honoured in the same chant as St Panteleimon, so that he, too, is implied by the formulation here.

l. 140. *The simple-minded St Aleksei*: St Alexis, by legend the son of Euphemianus, a wealthy citizen of Rome during the time of Pope Innocent I. Having fled to Edessa in Syria to escape the prospect of marriage, Alexis had the title of 'Man of God' conferred upon him by a vision of the Virgin; he then returned to Rome and, disguising himself as a beggar, went to live anonymously in his parents' own household. St Aleksei or Aleksy was one of the many saints honoured as a 'fool for Christ's sake' in Russian popular religious practice.

l. 141. *Ipaty* (Hypatius): several such saints are recorded. The reference here is probably to a fourteenth-century hermit saint of the Kiev Lavra (Cave) Monastery, who lived a life of fasting and self-denial, and who had the gift of healing by touch. This St Ipaty's feast was celebrated on 28 August; his relics were the centre of a popular cult, being credited, like the saint himself, with healing powers. In iconographic tradition, 'three wrinkles' are usually represented as two horizontal (the results of suffering) and one vertical, this last signifying happiness.

l. 142. *St Kasyan*: St Kas'yan, or Kassian, the Venerable, Hermit, a twelfth-century saint whose relics are interred in the Theodosian Lavra at Kiev, and whose feast-day falls on 29 February.

l. 143. *Tsarevich Dimitry*: the 10-year-old son of Tsar Ivan IV ('the Terrible'), whose murder at Uglich in 1591 led to the accession of Boris Godunov (traditionally held responsible for the murder), and provoked the so-called 'Time of Trouble'. Dimitry is significant in terms of Shkapskaya's own personal symbolism, where he stands, like Louis XVII and Aleksei, son of Nicholas II, for the innocent victims of political upheaval; but he cannot be said to be one of the most important saints of Russia. It is likely that, as in the case of St Nicholas, Shkapskaya is fusing a lesser-known saint with his better-known namesake, who in this case would be St Demetrius of Thessalonica, a fourth-century martyr whose cult was, and is, enormously important in Orthodox Christendom, and who is most commonly represented as a warrior-saint, mounted on a horse and riding to the defence of Byzantium.

ll. 144–6. *the Mothers of God . . . Three Hands*. The *Hodigitria*, from the Greek *hodigos*, guide, or way, is a very ancient icon of the Virgin, whose first version is by tradition ascribed to St Luke. A rather formal and forbidding image, it represents Mary with Jesus seated upright on her knee; the child is held with her left arm, whilst she points to him with her right hand. The Smolensk Mother of God is a variant of this icon, whose original was brought to Smolensk from Byzantium in 1103. The Vladimir Mother of God is a variant of the Mother of God of Tenderness (Eleoussa), in which Mary holds Jesus on her right arm, his face pressed against hers; the prototype of the icon was brought to Russia from Byzantium, and is associated with Russia's salvation from the incursions of Tamburlaine in 1395. The Mother of God of Kazan differs from all these others through being head-and-shoulders only, rather than half-length; the representation combines the Eleoussa and Hodigitria models, since the child is shown with his face next to his mother's, but face-on, rather than in part-profile. This icon was miraculously discovered in 1579, not long after the conquest of Kazan by the Russians. The Mother of the Sorrows (usually referred to as 'Joy to those who Sorrow') customarily represents the Mother of God full-length, carrying Jesus in her arms, and surrounded by representations of those for whom she intercedes. This icon is one especially venerated amongst Russian women. The Mother of God of the Three Hands shows the Virgin holding Jesus upright on her right arm; his face is turned slightly towards hers and he is making a sign of blessing. The icon commemorates the restoration of St John of Damascus's hand after this had been cut off by the iconoclast Emperor Leo in the eighth century. John had prayed to an icon of the Virgin that his hand might be restored, and when this miracle was granted, he had an additional hand painted on to the panel.

241. l. 149. *the carnival tree*: Russian *vesyolyi*, which for all its literal meaning of 'cheerful' 'full of fun' often has threatening or sarcastic undertones; it is the word used by Mikhail Bakhtin in his book on Rabelais in order to convey the vibrant but sadistic character of popular humour.

Olga Forsh (1873–1961)

243. *The Substitute Lecturer*, a reworking of an earlier, and much more conventional play entitled *The Death of Copernicus*, was first published in Forsh's *Sobranie sochinenii*, vi (Leningrad, 1930). Forsh's play transforms the life of the famous astronomer Nicholas Copernicus (1473–1543), author of *De revolutionibus orbium coelestium* (1543), into a fable about intellectual freedom in conditions of political repression. Forsh's interpretation relates more directly to her own era than to the sixteenth century, since in fact Copernicus, whose great work was dedicated to Pope Paul III, did not excite the disfavour of the Church; ecclesiastical suspicion of astronomy was only to be awakened by the later work of Galileo. The attempt to mask her play's direct relevance to Soviet cultural politics may be one reason why Forsh introduced self-consciously theatrical devices, such as the prologue, though these also have a certain absurdist logic of their own.

Rhaeticus. A genuine historical personage, Joachim Georg Rhaeticus (1514–76) was in fact Copernicus' student, and the author of *De libris Revolutionum N. Copernici, narratio prima* [1560].

Militsiya: i.e. the Soviet police force.

244. *Popular science*. The frame drama parodies a lecture on popular science in a workers' culture club, of the kind that were especially frequent in the Soviet Union during the 1920s and 1930s.

250. *Plato's Timaeus*: a dialogue dealing with the immanence of the ideal cosmos in the material world.

254. *Magic shows invoking obsolete superstitions are strictly forbidden*. Sanctions of this kind did indeed operate in Russia after 1917, and especially after 1925.

Sofiya Parnok (1885–1933)

256. *'I shall not lie'* (Radi rifmy rezvoi ne solgu). The date given on Parnok's manuscript is 1926, but following the observations of Sofya Polyakova, the editor of Parnok's *Collected Poems*, the piece is dated conjecturally here to 1923/4. The reason for the redating is that the poem's most likely addressee is Valery Bryusov (1874–1924), the former Symbolist poet turned Communist who exercised an enormous influence over Soviet literary policy in its early

days. Bryusov's 1922 article 'Yesterday, Today, and Tomorrow in Russian Poetry' had stressed formal innovation as the necessary path for Soviet poetry; his review of Parnok's *The Vine* in *Pechat' i revolyutsiya*, 4 (1923) had asserted that the metrical structure of her poetry could not be grasped 'unless you put yourself through contortions when reading it'. As Lev Gornung's memoir of Parnok, published in *Nashe nasledie* 2 (1989), indicates, Parnok had in any case disliked Bryusov heartily since the suicide of the young woman poet Nadezhda L'vova in 1913, for which she held him responsible. However, if the original date for the poem is accepted, then the addressee may perhaps be the in-house reviewer who vetted Parnok's collection *Music* for publication; this collection was published in early 1927, and is, therefore, likely to have gone for consideration in 1926.

l. 3. *Since the cot your choice has not been mine*. The Russian *my s kolibeli raznoi masti* would translate more literally as 'we have had different spots', *mast'* being the word for the colour of an animal's coat; the word also puns on *master*, and on *mastityi*, weighty, distinguished, here translated as 'honoured'.

l. 8. *Fellow-travelling women*: Russian *poputchitsy*, a feminization of the jargon term *poputchik*, 'fellow-traveller', applied in the early 1920s to writers who, whilst non-Communist, were also not considered hostile to the regime.

257. *'A childhood memory'* (S detstva pomnyu). The addressee is Vladislav Khodasevich (1886–1939), post-Symbolist poet and critic, a friend of Parnok's before his emigration to the West in 1922.

l. 6. *the bitter shards of your verse*: literally 'your angry, mouth-ulcerating verses'.

258. *'Through a Window-Light'* (V fortochku). One of Parnok's most important works, this impressive poem was written five years before she died, at a stage when she was already suffering from TB, and had become unable to publish poetry. Both circumstances are alluded to obliquely in the poem, which, however, transcends personal realia in its representation of the doubting, but resolute, modernist sensibility. The window-light (Russian *fortochka*) is the small casement in the top corner of a double window which can be opened for ventilation when the rest of the pane is sealed or closed.

l. 1. *both knees pressed down*: lit. 'with knees on the hard sill'.

ll. 3–4. *I breathe . . . clinging to life*: lit. 'to breathe, to breathe! So drags oxygen | from a grey sack a still living corpse'.

l. 8. *has turned a dirty grey*: lit. 'is whitish grey'.

l. 9. *grey like this cushion filled with oxygen*: i.e. the breathing apparatus used in cases of acute TB, alluded to in ll. 3–4.

l. 17. *address the distance*: lit. 'and speak, well, to no one, into the distance.' Polyakova has identified this as a reworking of a line by Pavlova.

258. l. 23. *I none the less choke on despair*: lit. 'there is nothing for the despairing soul to breathe with'.

259. l. 31. *Perhaps to a hermitage somewhere*: lit. 'to some dozy, far-flung hermitage'.

l. 32. *Repent my sins in tears and prayer*. Telescopes the original, which goes on to add *i vymolvit', i vyplakat'*, 'and weep them, pray them out'.

l. 33. *Zosima*: the saintly *starets* (monastic elder) of Dostoevsky's *Brothers Karamazov*.

l. 37. *Burning Bush church dome and cross*: The Burning Bush church, in full The Church of the Image of the Mother of God of the Burning Bush (see note to Tsvetaeva below): here, the church of that name in Burning Bush Lane (Neopalimovskii pereulok), just west of the Smolensky Boulevard, where Parnok was living at the time this poem was written.

l. 42. *Forcing its sour slops*: lit. 'breathing on the same poisonous slime'.

l. 47. *In stagnancy and not in happiness*: lit. 'too dully | immobilely [*neprovorno*] | and sadly living out [his] life'.

Marina Tsvetaeva (1892–1941)

260. *Staircase* (Lestnitsa) was first published in *Volya Rossii*, 11 (1926). In 1938–9, Tsvetaeva prepared a second version of the poem, altering the title and making other minor changes. The present text follows this second version, as printed in *Izbrannye proizvedeniya* (Leningrad, 1965). However, the fourteenth stanza, censored in 1965 for political reasons, is restored from the original, 1926, publication; one or two obvious misprints have been corrected; and Tsvetaeva's second title, *Poem of the Staircase* (Poema Lestnitsy) has been replaced by its less wordy earlier variant.

One of the most important works of Tsvetaeva's Paris period (1925–39), *The Poem of the Staircase* was begun in Paris in early 1926, and completed later that year in the Vendée, where Tsvetaeva spent part of the summer of 1926. It evokes a crowded tenement block where Tsvetaeva had lived for some months soon after her arrival in Paris. The poem moves from a description of the tenement staircase in terms of the senses, also playing on various literary associations (such as Jacob's Ladder) and on the link between the staircase and the 'gamut', i.e. the musical *scale* (which term is derived from Italian *scala*, 'staircase'), to a representation of the staircase as the place of a symbolic (and characteristically Tsvetaevan) conflict between consciousness and domestic enslavement. The central reference is 'the thing' (the noun *veshch'* is feminine in Russian), understood as not only the agent of female subjugation, but also as a metaphor for the subjugation of women. Tsvetaeva gives the poem a radical ending (the staircase is destroyed) suitable to the rebellious—and anti-revolutionary—history of the Vendée itself, which she had mentioned in a letter to Anna Tesková on 8 June 1926. *Staircase* has links to a number of other important works of Tsvetaeva's émigré period, for example the lyrics 'In Praise of the Rich' (1921) and 'The House' (1931), the narrative poem *Attempt at a Room*, and the section of the literary essay 'Natalya Goncharova' (1934) describing the staircase leading to Goncharova, the famous painter's, flat.

ll. 1–173. *Part I.* By far the longest part of the poem, this introduction is also one of the densest. It takes the reader through 'a day in the life of the staircase', from the brief encounters of lovers at the beginning of the poem, to the return of the inhabitants from work to supper, to the final household chores before sleep. The social paradoxes of life in a tenement are also represented: the staircase's 'upper crust' being near the bottom of the house, whilst its 'groundlings' are at the top (in a moral sense, too). The symbolic connotations of the staircase are also established: there are adumbrations of the conflagration that will engulf the structure, and ironic allusions establish both the religious connections of the staircase (Jacob's Ladder) and its revolutionary connotations (it is the dwelling-place of the proletariat).

l. 14. *living is burning* (Russian *zhit'—zhech'*), 'to live is to burn': introducing the idea of fire as the element of spiritual, rather than material, life.

l. 25. *Bread: love's daily.* This facetious allusion to the Lord's Prayer ('give us this day our daily bread'—also parodied in Mayakovsky's *Cloud in Trousers* (1914)) facilitates a transition from the opening theme, snatched love, to the second theme: eating.

ll. 28–9. *Thou shalt work . . . eat.* a rephrasing of 'Who does not work, does not eat', one of the key political slogans of the early Soviet days. The word *diktat* translates Russian *propoved'*, which appears as 'sermon' in l. 108.

l. 35. *the prince's politeness*: lit. 'the princely principle', which makes an ugly jingle in English; the translation also plays on the English saying, 'Punctuality is the politeness of princes'.

ll. 36–7. *Leave tomorrow for taking . . . give*: a reference to the hand-to-mouth existence on the staircase (where impromptu loans are the order of the day). The phrase, however, also reads like a parody of the Sermon on the Mount's injunction, 'Lay not up for yourselves treasures on earth' (Matthew 7: 20). This strophe encapsulates Tsvetaeva's ambivalent attitude to the poor, who both are, and are not, morally superior to their 'betters'.

l. 38. *Need explodes like gas.* A reference to a concrete event (the lighting of cookers and water-heaters for the evening domestic round), the phrase also points forward to the destruction which ends the poem. The reference to 'need', i.e. the 'need' for money to pay for the gas, initiates a description of the staircase inhabitants' mutual aid system over the next few lines.

261. l. 40. *The man who once was rich* (Russian *Kto otkazalsya*, lit. 'He who once refused'). The English makes explicit the connection between wealth and stinginess which is implied by Tsvetaeva: cf. the last two stanzas of 'In Praise of the Rich', which depict the hypocritical refusal of the rich to make a loan.

262. ll. 42–6. *'The gas has fangs today'*: suggests its rapaciousness; this is then transformed into the image of 'tiger' and 'pard', fanged wild animals who represent the 'law of the jungle' by which the staircase-dwellers live; their communal living has an edge of aggression on it, and it is the 'devil, not Marx' who will provide.

l. 54. *smell of Muguet*: a free translation, since the original has 'Koti', i.e. the brand name Coty, to rhyme with *koty*, the Russian for cats. Here 'Muguet' is an approximate rhyme with 'mogs', and also with 'drugget'; 'Muguet des bois', or lily-of-the-valley, was also the name of one of Coty's perfumes.

l. 59. *attacking colds*: i.e. curing or preventing them by eating garlic: the notion of food's curative properties looks forward to the idea of the staircase as Franzensbad (see l. 124).

l. 61–2. *Sweetening the blackened hole | Of the back staircase*: an attempt to convey by sound analogy the pun inherent in the Russian 'chernaya lestnitsa', 'black [i.e. back] staircase'. By stating that 'eating [garlic] is revenge', that sweetens the blackness [i.e. deprivation] of the staircase, Tsvetaeva is able to switch from food to a new theme, that of the staircase as the site of social conflict.

l. 64. *bel-étage* (Fr.). The first floor, traditionally the most prestigious in European blocks (also known as the *piano nobile*). This line reads literally: 'The *bel-étage* is our shared enemy'.

263. ll. 78–92. *Gripped in their owners' hands . . . down*: describes the evening return of the tenants; followed, 11. 93 ff., by the sounds in the flats on their return; and ll. 118 ff., the evening meal.

ll. 95–6. *Our staircase... upper crust*; ll. 99–100. *staircase . . . groundlings*: i.e. the upper and lower orders. For metrical reasons, these entities are cited in reverse order from the Russian.

l. 102. *A pick would do more good*. The meaning is that the average pair of lungs is too clogged for cleaning them to be efficacious; the reference to a 'pick' also suggests the manual labour by which some of those on the staircase live. The English translation also suggests nose-picking, a suggestion that is in tune with the many references to spitting in the Russian original.

ll. 104–5. *roof . . . cellar*: i.e. the attics and the basement, the dwelling-places of the poor. (The fact that spatial polarization does *not* reflect social polarization here undercuts the division between 'upper crust' and 'groundlings' in ll. 95 ff.).

264. l. 129. *Franzensbad*: a spa in Bohemia (now renamed Františké Lázne); probably chosen because of its location in Tsvetaeva's beloved Czechoslovakia.

265. ll. 143–74. *Last clothes... stars*. Night falls on the staircase; this is followed, in ll. 159 ff., by the beginning of its metamorphosis: note especially in l. 173 how the '*carte* of dishes' in l. 124 has now become a 'chart of stars'.

266. ll. 174–217. *Part II*. The metamorphosis of 'things' after nightfall is described, at first in terms of their desire to 'stand up straight' (both literally and figuratively), and then in terms of their determination to return to their natural sources.

l. 180. *Immovables too*. Referring to the staircase, but also punning on the legal term 'immoveable property'.

l. 185. *The screw wants to unwind*: i.e. the staircase wants to escape from itself, to 'stand straight' in its own way, an idea to be developed in the series of metaphors following.

l. 189. *stray-ight*: i.e. 'straight' (Russian *prya-moyu*). The English imitates Tsvetaeva's habit of splitting words, which allows a spondee to be used, and facilitates a punning second meaning (here 'stray': cf. pail-lasse and mat-tress below). The idea that distortion, or curving, is also a 'lie' is to be developed later on.

267. ll. 196–7. *I will be no convert . . . curls*. The Russian uses a term specific to Jews who have apostasized to Orthodoxy; the next line, conversely, sees the thing freeing itself as an Orthodox Jew (Russian *zhid*, a term which has a derogatory flavour, cf. Jew-boy) shaking free his 'peisy', i.e. Hasidic side-curls. The point being made is that identity should not be conferred by fanatical religious belief, of whatever coloration.

l. 206. *Out to lies and forgeries*. The original has *lomannost'*, 'brokenness', which begins a chain of association to '*lom*' (see l. 220 below). I have substituted a different vertical verbal tie, to the image of the 'forged screw' in ll. 139–40: the 'forge' as the place of mechanical manufacture is linked to the idea of 'forgery' as faking.

l. 215. *—I'll be a god*: in a neat reversal of the accustomed mythological pattern by which heroes and gods metamorphose to things (e.g. Zeus to gold in the Danaë myth), or, more broadly, an assertion of animist beliefs (each thing has its own soul, its own divinity).

l. 217. *The thing wants to be healed*: picking up the sickness motif from Part I.

ll. 218–305. *Part III*. We now shift from narrative to a meditation on the essence of the thing, which takes up the four central parts of the poem. The first part of this meditation deals with the history of man's inhumanity to things, the process which has turned the elements into the glass, mattresses, and taps of Part II; it also makes the vital connection between 'women' and 'things'.

267. ll. 220–1. *first spade*: Russian. *lom*, 'mattock'; the change was made in order to reflect Tsvetaeva's series of puns on associated meanings: *lom* as 'scrap', and *lomat'* 'to break': here rendered by the play on 'spade' and 'spayed' (l. 229), followed by 'splayed' (l. 231).

l. 222. *The thing was confiding as a woman*. Here Tsvetaeva makes explicit the latent connection between women and objects (suggested already in the reference to things' 'vitals' in l. 199). If women are 'things', then they, too, can revolt: and so is prefigured the theme of women's rebellion from domesticity which is to be introduced in Part VII.

268. l. 239. *A god who hurts*. The verb is used in its archaic/colloquial sense of 'to feel pain, grief', in exact rendition of the Russian, *bolyashchii bog*.

l. 247. *a step*: meant not only in its concrete sense of a place on this staircase, but also in the transferred sense of 'a step on the evolutionary ladder'.

l. 248. *closeness and grossness*: Russian. *v etu plesen' i v etu tesn'*, i.e. mould and claustrophobia; the change is made to allow the English to capture the Russian internal rhyme.

269. 1. 259. *Once hidden [then 'metal' became the word]*. Another central notion is introduced here: the process of naming is linked with that of forging 'things' from the elements (and so naming is, by implication, also 'masculine').

l. 266. *shiny varnished cages*: a metaphor for the wardrobes that are to be one of the most important things liberated in the poem. The motif of 'varnish' recurs in Part V.

ll. 282–5. *The vengeance of cliffs . . . heads*. The first line takes the 'rock on a building site' image of l. 279 back to its natural sources, cliffs and woods. The idea of the forests then suggests a visual progression to the image of a theatre stage and set (also built, like scaffolding, of wood.) The dangers raised by arousing the enmity of things provoke the apostrophized 'you', not to curtail the practices which have provoked the things, but to take out insurance against the consequences of their actions. The absurdity of insurance as a form of protection against the elements is to be the subject of mockery in the next five stanzas.

ll. 287–8. *the thinking | Reed* a quotation which to a Russian reader evokes less its originator, Pascal, than the borrowing of the phrase in a famous poem by Tyutchev. 'Billiard cue' is introduced as a parodistic parallel metaphor for man, the visual analogy to a reed enhancing the irony; it also introduces yet again the theme of wood distorted as bourgeois artefact, which for Tsvetaeva is the key instance of civilization as decadence.

270. l. 290. *i.e. contents of house*: lit. 'house, with all that is therein'.

l. 294. *spire*. The reader is to imagine one of the purely decorative variety, like an extended knuckle-duster, adorning the eaves of an early twentieth-century villa, rather than the type that crowns an English village church.

ll. 306–62. *Part IV* makes explicit a connection between things and the human body which had been implicit in Part I, where the staircase had had some of the functions of the human alimentary canal. The theme of 'things as women' is continued in a reference to Eve, made from Adam's rib: here there are subtextual parallels to *Staircase*'s companion piece, *Attempt at a Room*, in which the six surfaces of the room are simultaneously the various dimensions of the woman speaker's body. From 'paupers' things' as parts of the body, the poem moves on to paupers' things as tokens of love; by association, they are carriers of their own destruction (the idea of love as destruction having already been established). Hence, 'paupers' things' also enjoy the possibility of escape to the spiritual, elemental domain of 'fire'.

l. 313. *Hewn on a sudden from their sides*: i.e. as Eve was hewn from the side of Adam.

ll. 319–20. *You are [of what?] a third, or a quarter . . . long ago*. The rhetorical question in the first line is answered in the second: a poor person's thing shows only a fraction of itself in this world, the rest being 'in heaven', i.e. in the higher, spiritual, world.

271. l. 324. *A Viennese chair—made of veiny bentwood*. Somewhat tautologous, since *venskii stul* is a bentwood chair: but the original makes a sound-pun on Vena (Vienna) and vena (vein), which could not otherwise be conveyed, and which is important because of its place in the thing–body chain, a link back to l. 313, and forward to ll. 330–41. 'What chance of Vienna?' makes a rather different point: those on the staircase, and their things, could never hope to travel to Vienna; only journeys into the imaginative or spiritual world can be theirs. 'A terrible thing!' is meant quite literally (there *is* something disgusting about this veiny chair), but it is also intended as a conventional exclamation of horror ('how terrible!').

ll. 330–41: *At rags . . . acid of that eye*. Takes the analogy between things and bodies in a different direction: if poor people's things are like parts of the body, parts of rich people's bodies are like things. A brow raised at widow's weeds resembles a lorgnette, and a coldly vacuous eye has less 'soul' than a tub of washing blue; this eye-object in turn becomes a metaphor for the philistine's gaze, directed uncomprehendingly and scornfully at the poet.

l. 345: *You live less here than you live beyond*: A return to the 'fraction' idea of l. 319; the 'wild creature' image in l. 344 suggests one of the 'mogs' of Part I, trapped in a flat, and waiting to go out and live its real life outside.

271. l. 347: *the Police Gazette*: Russian *khronika krazh*, 'the list of thefts'; i.e. if you had, you would know that it is rich people's things, and useless things, which are the subject of greed.

272. l. 360. *Flatter than bast, and drier than wood*: i.e. more pliable, and so more useful, than the bast from which Russian peasants made their shoes and fences; but also more combustible than wood, i.e. more volatile. The second part of the comparison points forward to the fire which will destroy the staircase, and raises the tree–object dichotomy in yet a further context.

ll. 363–86: *Part V*: Another change of orientation, this time to a perspective understanding domestic labour, the care of things, as an enslavement to things and to their rich owners (here harangued as 'you'), but also as something which encapsulates the intense physical relation of poor people to things and nature ('our varnish is | Resin and sap'), and which raises 'smoke', i.e. threatens to provoke the life-giving blaze. As 'elbow-grease' is used, smoke is raised, and things start to 'shine' (because they have been polished, and because flames are produced).

ll. 373–4. *Ham | But never Cain*: i.e. a brute (Noah's son is a byword for boorishness in Russian) but not a killer.

l. 379: *Surface—services things*: Reproduces the internal rhyme *stol—gol—na veshchitsy*, lit. 'the table is bare for things'. The 1926 publication prints this as *stol—gol—ni veshchitsy*: 'the table—bare—not a thing', a reading restored by the editors of Tsvetaeva's *Stikhotvoreniya i poemy* (Leningrad, 1990); all other editions, however, print *na veshchitsy*. I prefer *na veshchitsy* because *ni veshchitsy* produces what is to my mind rather a banal tautology (heightened by the huge emphasis on 'bare').

273. ll. 387–406: *Part VI*: Here the focus shifts to the paradox 'paupers' things', with the idea of bad matching developed both through the image of the shaky marriage and through that of the shoddily made thing. The energy generated by this unsuitable pairing is, however, what will put an end to confinedness.

l. 389: *an ill-fitting coupling*: Russian *svara*, which could be more accurately translated as 'quarrel', but since *svarit'* also means 'to weld', I have preferred a term that conveys the notion of 'quarrelling' indirectly.

l. 391: *the sacristan*: Russian *ponomar'*, a word derived from the Greek *paranomonios*, i.e. one who lives in the vicinity of a church and does odd jobs there. In the Russian orthodox Church, the *ponomar* also has the tasks of ringing bells and of reading certain liturgical texts; in the latter capacity, he has become proverbial for dullness and insensitivity to language ('he reads like a *ponomar*'). This association cannot be conveyed in English, and so I have replaced *ponomar* by the word 'sacristan', since this clerical odd-jobs man could hardly be expected to bother himself about words.

l. 393: *Nakedness longs to be covered*: lit. 'longs for a cover'. The Russian *pokrov* means 'covering' in a neutral sense, but, as mentioned in my notes to Gippius above, it is also the word used for the Mother of God's 'Protecting Veil', which might cover spiritual nakedness. The English can convey only the second of these two senses, but has the advantage of communicating a third sense of *pokrov*, 'covering' in a sexual sense. (On the feast of the Protection of the Virgin, 1 October, Russian peasant girls would implore the Virgin to 'cover them quickly', i.e. with a sexual mate: see Julia Vytkovskaya's article on Slavonic mythology in Carolyne Larrington (ed.), *The Feminist Companion to Mythology* (London, 1992).)

l. 398: *Your author is trapped in a crayfish claw*: i.e. the claw of a freshwater crayfish.' Tsvetaeva underlines the paradox of 'fire' as both covering for nakedness and escape from confinement by continuing the visual image of something red and encircling, which here 'traps' rather than protects. This authorial intrusion looks forward also, in technical terms, to the self-conscious ending of the poem. *V kleshne* is also used loosely to mean 'in a tight place'.

ll. 399–402: *When a ceiling has fallen, it's the right size . . . truth.*: That is, once there *is* no ceiling, the inhabitants of low-ceilinged garrets can at last raise themselves, and look up at the sky. (Cf. the end of *Attempt at a Room*, in which the blasted ceiling is left 'singing like all angels'.) The hunched backs of the garret-dwellers also suggest a visual image of the rubble as a hunchbacked, slow-moving old man. Both characterization and personification are then refocused as an image of a righteous prophet on the bonfire (perhaps one of the Old Believers, who are Russia's most famous victims of burning).

l. 403. *bunks*: Russian *nary*, a word which is used for the communal berths of prison-camp huts.

l. 404. *tallow stink*: Russian *luchnaya von'*, from *luchina*, a primitive torch made of a rough splinter of wood; the word also suggests *luk*, onion.

ll. 407–45. *Part VII*. From the 'volatile marriage' of 'paupers' and 'things', Tsvetaeva goes on to a connection made in heaven: that between 'fire' and the 'staircase', as the locus and metaphor of poverty. From l. 411, there is a return to narrative, with a description of the fire in which the staircase is destroyed, transforming the burning house from something unnatural and ugly into something natural and beautiful: the glow of the fire is like 'meadows' and 'trees'. Part VII also brings together many strands in the poem's philosophical and discursive fabric. The link between women and domesticity amplifies the link between women and things which was stressed in Part III; the rebellion against domesticity brings back—in a quite different context now—the theme of poverty and revolution set out in Part I; the description of the fire as a tree in bloom reiterates a central metaphor of Parts II, III, and IV.

273. l. 407. *fire . . . stairs*: Russian *chernaya pozharnaya*, i.e. 'black [stairs]' and 'conflagrational' *or* 'firemen's' [i.e. as in 'ladder']. The original conveys an oxymoron which the translation does not, but the translation does reproduce the original's approximate internal rhyme.

274. l. 413. *Relic of the rural past*: Russian *perezhitok sel'skosti*: Tsvetaeva ironically borrows the Social-Darwinist vocabulary current in early Soviet Russia, so returning to her mockery of 'Marx' in Part I, and to the idea of 'steps on the evolutionary ladder' in Part III.

ll. 419–20. *see the glimmer | The floor has*: Picking up the 'elbow-grease' motif from Part V: the fire has made the floor shine more brightly than any effort ever did.

l. 424. *The house—a bush alight*. The Russian word used here for 'bush' is *kupina*, which is the word used in the Russian translation of the Bible for the 'Burning Bush' of Moses' vision, that 'burned with fire' yet 'was not consumed' (Exodus 3: 3–4). The 'Burning Bush' is understood in Russian Orthodoxy as a symbol of the Virgin; the 'Mother of God of the Burning Bush', an iconographic representation miraculously discovered in the late seventeenth century, whose holy day was 4 September, was kept in the eponymous church in the Convent of the Conception of St Anne (Zachat'evsky monastyr'), which was located just west of the Arbat, the district where Tsvetaeva was brought up. This reference to the Mother of God picks up the reference to her 'Protection' above (see note to l. 393)

l. 425. *Honour is royally saved*. Plays on the 'paupers as princes' theme which goes through the poem: cf. 'the prince's politeness' in l. 35.

ll. 429–30. *You had heaven trussed . . . to the ground*. Reintroduces the Christian motif of 'laying up treasure in heaven', and the idea that earthly prosperity is a block to happiness, through the metaphor of heaven abused on earth. (Something of a liberty, since the original reads, 'You gave a whole heaven for a moment of being stifled'; the translation gives an echo of Prometheus' fate, and of William Blake, whilst the original reads more like a travesty of the idea of 'a world lost for love' in Shakespeare's *Antony and Cleopatra*. But Tsvetaeva's exact wording cannot be concisely or memorably rendered in English.)

l. 431. *The past will be incinerated*. More accurate would be 'passions will burn in this stove'. Since English life is without ceramic wood-burning stoves, and the rituals that go go with them, I have substituted the image of leaves being 'incinerated' in braziers.

l. 432. *Castles will make a merry blaze*: Russian *kreposttsa*, the diminutive of *krepost'*, fortress or prison: 'dungeon' would be a possible translation in other circumstances, but the idea of a dungeon burning would tax credibility.

275. ll. 445–9. *Part VIII.* The coda interrupts the poetic 'rainbows' with the mundane 'morning' (note how the section-break is placed in mid-line). The narrative manner also puts an end to the apparent spontaneity of Part VII, as the poet signs off. By referring to the 'first morning', Tsvetaeva suggests the beginning of a new world; one in which possessions and parts of the body are no longer distinguishable; but she then leaves this world with the phrase 'the poem sleeps'—putting the poem to bed, as it were.

l. 447. *Birds'*: perhaps those of the nocturnal owl, whose cry is suggested, in the English, by 'who wit'.

Ekaterina Strogova (*c.*1900–?)

276. '*The Womenfolk*' (Baby) is taken from *Pereval*, 5 (1927).

277. *October*: the Bolshevik Revolution of 25 October 1917.

the Baroness was 'sniffed out': i.e., denounced as being from a 'hostile' class, according to the 'class war' politics of the time.

fabkom: a contraction of 'fabrichnyi komitet', factory (Party) committee.

Womenfolk: Russian *baby*, the plural form of *baba*, which in non-working-class speech signifies a woman of the lower classes, often with derogatory overtones ('a hussy, trollop'), but in working-class or peasant speech has no denigratory nuance, being simply the familiar term for 'woman'.

Peter. Russian, *Piter*: an affectionate nickname for St Petersburg, and later for Leningrad.

278. *Ilich*: the patronymic of Vladimir Ilich Lenin, use of the patronymic alone being the standard form of respectful or affectionate address to older people in villages or working-class communities.

282. *The only thing missing, of course, is make-up*. From the end of the New Economic Policy (see below) until the mid-1930s, when an indigenous Soviet manufacture was begun, make-up was not generally available in Russia, its use being limited to well-off women in large cities.

284. *ukom*: from *uezdnyi komitet*, 'district [party] committee.' Until 1928, when it was replaced by *raion*, *uezd* was the term for the administrative subdivision of *guberniya* (government: later replaced by *oblast'*, region).

the wall newspaper: a propaganda news-sheet for display in places of work, composed by some or all of the employees.

285. *boisterous* [*as her last name suggests*] Boikova being derived from *boikii*, 'lively, animated'.

volost: the subdivision of an *uezd* in Tsarist, and pre-1928 Soviet, Russia.

288. *menfolk*: *muzhiki*, the masculine equivalent of *baby*.

290. *War Communism*: the phase of early Soviet rule during the Civil War (1918–21), characterized by the imposition of authoritarian centralist directives.

NEP: New Economic Policy (1921–5) a phase of Soviet rule during which limited freedom was allowed to private enterprise, a toleration which had knock-on effects on pluralism of other kinds.

292. *volkom*: a Party committee at *volost* level (see above).

a Socialist Revolutionary: a member of the Socialist Revolutionary Party, a radical populist movement formed in the 1890s, whose wide support amongst peasants and to a lesser extent workers made it the target of the Bolsheviks' special enmity.

a presser, fourth-category. All Soviet workers were assigned to 'categories' of competence and achievement, ranging from 'first category' downwards; on these depended salary levels, privileges, and perks.

293. *workers' preparatory faculty*: the continuing education department of a Soviet higher education establishment, responsible for providing workers with a basic education, and for organizing courses leading to professional or other qualifications.

MK: the Moscow District Committee of the Communist Party.

Anna Prismanova (1882–1960)

295. The texts by Prismanova are all taken from her *Sobranie sochinenii* (The Hague, 1990), by permission of the publishers, Leuxenhoff Publishing.

'[To Lomonosov]' (1928). Although this poem is untitled, every Russian schoolchild would recognize its subject as the great Russian scientist, scholar, and poet Mikhailo Lomonosov (1711–65), who, amongst other discoveries, established the physical properties of the Northern Lights, exploding earlier theories of their ethereal origin (cf. Prismanova's phrase 'methodically, he pins the ether down'). Prismanova's poem encodes such well-known biographical realia in a dense network of puns and word-play (*na kante mira/Kantemira/Kant, golovastik/golenastyi Galilei*, etc.). The English translation attempts to reproduce Prismanova's sound-play, which is the most important feature of the poem, frequently predominating over strict sense.

l. 1. *Kantemir*: Prince Antokh Dmitrievich Kantemir (1709–44), scholar-poet, the most distinguished of Lomonosov's immediate Russian literary ancestors.

l. 2. *defended Petrine craft* (defended the *bot*). The Russian *bot* (a borrowing from the Dutch *boot*) signifies 'skiff', but the independent homonym *bot* is used for a type of net used on the Chudskoe Lake (see below). The reference links Lomonosov's life with Prismanova's: the eighteenth-century northern poet's celebration of Russia's seagoing power (Peter the Great's fleet) is assimilated to the fishing culture of north-western Russia, where Prismanova was brought up. The English subsitution 'craft' likewise evokes links with fishing and seafaring, as well as literature.

l. 3. *Secured above the Chud, a yellow truckle.* 'Chud' suggests at one and the same time a Finno-Ugric tribe of that name, which inhabited the far north (where Lomonosov was born), and the Chudskoe Lake which divides Russia from the Baltic (where Prismanova herself was born). 'Truckle', i.e. a large round cheese, is here a metaphor for the sun: the word 'cheese' in Russian, *syr*, chimes with the word *siryi*, 'orphaned' (Lomonosov had been orphaned at an early age), which the English pairs with 'vellum'.

l. 6. *gallantry*: here in its alternative sense of 'quick-witted'; playing on 'gall' and 'gallimaufry'.

l. 8. *tangled lilies of mentality*: a recurrent image in Prismanova's poetry, cf. her description of Emily Brontë as a 'lily' in 'The Brontë Sisters'. The budding lily's swollen head on its straggly stalk is indeed not unsuggestive of the shape of the brain.

l. 9. *limbeck*: i.e. an alembic, a spherical glass vessel with a long narrow spout at the top, used in alchemy and chemistry.

ll. 11–12. *Hordes have exploited | earth's riches.* Another of Lomonosov's achievements was to awaken Russian sensitivity to the vast mineral and natural wealth that lay hidden in the rocks and forests of the Russian far north: like Tsvetaeva in *Staircase*, Prismanova takes a rather 'green' view of the exploitation that followed.

296. l. 16. *and as a sign the ciphers click below*: probably a reference to the sound of the turning circular dials at the bottom of an astrolabe, or similar instrument.

297. '*The Brontë Sisters*' (Syostry Bronte) (first version 1939; this translation uses the second, shorter, version of 1946).

l. 2. *but the unhappy need a monument.* Prismanova plays throughout the poem on one of the most famous poems in Russian literature, Pushkin's 'I have built myself a monument', a reworking of Horace's 'Exegi monumentum', whose message is that poetry will live on to make a monument for the poet neglected in his lifetime. The 'monument' also suggests the 'cross on the rise', an allusion to the black iron crosses used to mark graves in Russian cemeteries.

l. 5. *Flammable is the covering of the body.* i.e. the flesh, as opposed to the 'flame' of the soul which scorches it: an image which then suggests the 'smoke' of ll. 7–8 (though 'smoke' is also a reference to the real, soot-blackened, appearance of Haworth).

l. 16. *those whom vultures rend*: a metaphorization of those who have 'tasted suffering', as Prismanova puts it later, in terms of the fate of Prometheus, chained to a rock so that vultures might tear out his liver again and again.

298. ll. 27–8. *a doctor's daughter . . . sister I once was*. Prismanova was indeed a doctor's daughter; she was also one of three sisters, and the interplay of fictional and real biography is facilitated by the fact that in Russian Anne Brontë becomes 'Anna', to go with 'Emiliya' and 'Sharlotta'. Prismanova also implies that 'Anna' synthesizes the spiritual qualities of 'Emiliya', and the physical qualities of 'Sharlotta' into a divided and contradictory femininity.

299. '*On Guard and on Town Gardens*' (O gorode i ogorode, lit. 'About the Town and the Vegetable Garden'): first published 1966, but almost certainly dating from the late 1930s or early 1940s.

lady's surname spoke of days of rest: a mock-derivation of Sontag from German *Sonntag*, 'Sunday'.

300. *a sand-strewn little Baltic town, the haunt of the Sandman*. By German nursery tradition, the 'Sandman' strews sand in children's eyes to make them sleep. (The English formulation approximates a pun in the Russian original, 'zasypaemyi peskami i zasypayushchii', lit. 'sand-strewn and sleepy'.)

301. *krendel*: a patisserie made of shortcake-like sweet dough, shaped like a capital B. (Often translated as 'pretzsel', but the latter is in fact savoury, and much smaller.)

cheviot: a fine wool fabric made originally from the fleece of the Cheviot hill-sheep (cf. 'merino').

Anna Karavaeva (1893–1979)

303. The extract here is taken from *The Flying Start* (*Razbeg*), first published separately in 1947. The novel, forming the second part of the trilogy *The Motherland*, and depicting the War and its aftermath in a small industrial town in the Urals, is a classic of high Socialist Realism.

was feeding her baby: a familiar icon of Socialist Realist art, an early example being Kozma Petrov-Vodkin's famous picture *The Petrograd Madonna* (1918). Karavaeva's fictional portrait, however, differs anatomically from Petrov-Vodkin's, since the mother she depicts is apparently able to breast-feed without a hand on her own breast—a remarkable feat. The traditional Orthodox icon of the breast-feeding Mother of God, the *Mlekopitatel'nitsa* (Greek *Galaktophousa*), is a great deal more naturalistic.

305. *her violet eyes*. This eye-colour—a most exceptional one in living humans—is a favourite of female Socialist Realist writers, as it is of their nearest Western counterparts, the authors of mass-market romances.

Vera Bulich (1898–1954)

307. *'From my Diary' III* (Dnevnik III) is taken from Bulich's second collection, *Plennyi veter* (Tallinn, 1938). It is one of a series of poems depicting the aftermath of an unhappy love affair. The English translations of this and the following poem do not always follow the Russian line division exactly, since to do so would mean either padding unnecessarily, or including lines whose short weight would not convey the rhythm of the original.

l. 4. *the Deposition*: Russian *Plashchanitsa*, 'shroud', the icon of the suffering Christ that is carried in procession in Orthodox countries on Good Friday.

309. *'The Omnibus'* (Avtobus) comes from Bulich's fourth and last collection, *Vetvi* (Paris, 1954). In order to make sense of the metrics of the original, it is important to note that Bulich used the now obsolete end-stressed pronunciation of the word *avtobus*.

ll. 14–17. *This ark . . . cobwebs*. The English abbreviates slightly at ll. 15–17, for the metrical reasons referred to above: the Russian (ll. 14–20) reads literally: the motor roared and, shaking [its] innards | the heavy bus-ark sailed away | holding inside pure and impure. | And in it was salvation for some, | salvation from spiritual discord, | the forty-day deluge of weekdays | and spidery bedroom anguish.

ll. 20–1. *hold up their warp . . . canvas sky*. The image of weaving is something of a liberty here: the Russian reads literally (ll. 23–4): hastily striping the sky | with transparent rows of wires.

Anna Barkova (1901–1976)

311. *'A Few Autobiographical Facts'* (1954). In this poem Barkova satirizes the Soviet archive industry in a manner that is far more vicious and far wittier than Pasternak's treatment of the same subject in his late poem 'Being famous is unattractive'.

l. 1. *In a common pit*: i.e. one of the mass graves in which inmates of Russian prison camps were buried.

l. 9. *the verb and adjective agreement*: i.e. because the gendered forms of these reveal the sex of a speaker or writer.

312. l. 41. *From Fragment Number Eight*. This, and some other references in the poem, such as the mention of 'proselytes' and 'students' suggest that Barkova is drawing a parallel between her own biography and Sappho's, the 'facts' of whose life have been reconstructed from fragments of her verse, just as Barkova imagines will happen in her own case here.

313. l. 70. *proselytes in their devoted crowds*. The description of the funeral that follows recalls the actual funeral of the famous liberal political thinker

Aleksandr Herzen, images of which occasion would certainly be imprinted on the consciousness of a banal Soviet academic of the kind that Barkova is mocking.

313. l. 82. *a professorship*: literally a 'doctorate', i.e. a qualification roughly equivalent to a D. Litt., awarded to prominent Soviet academics in mid-career.

l. 84. *fly-blown vinaigrette*. Though this translation makes its own kind of sense, the Russian *vinegret* in fact refers to the mishmash of chopped vegetables usually known as a 'Russian salad' in English.

315. '*Tatar Anguish*' (conjecturally dated by Barkova's Soviet editors to 1954, but in the manner of several poems which Barkova wrote in the 1930s).

l. 10. *by wolfsbane clumps*: Russian *volch'i ogni*, will-o'-the-wisps, with the idea of a fruitless chase for chimeras in boggy land. Wolfsbane is a striking yellow-flowered poisonous plant growing on damp soil, a subspecies of which, the Northern wolfsbane (*Aconitum septentrionalis*) subsists in eastern Russia. The English substitution has been made because of the importance of wolf imagery in Barkova's poetry (cf. 'In the Camp Barracks', in S. S. Vilensky (ed.), *Until this Day*, London, 1993). One resonance for the Russian reader lies in the expression *volchii bilet*, 'a wolf's passport', which is used to signify someone in disfavour with the authorities.

Tatyana Esenina (11 June 1918–5 May 1992)

316. *Zhenya: The Wonder of the Twentieth Century* was first published in *Novyi Mir*, 1 (1962); it appeared in book form in Tashkent that same year. The extract here is taken from the journal publication.

Nabov: Russian 'Poimakin', from *poimat'*, 'to catch'.

317. *a food parcel for him*: a fairly black joke in 1962. Only a decade earlier, mass arrests had still been in progress, and this kind of mercy mission had been all too common.

318. *druzhinas*: in full the 'voluntary people's *druzhinas*', part-time ancillary organs of the Soviet police force, organized through places of work, and charged with various public order and anti-sabotage duties.

Venka the Spade: Russian *Venka Bubnovyi valet*, 'Jack of Diamonds', a stereotypical villain's name.

319. *five thousand bricks a shift*. The whole passage, and especially this sentence, parodies the statistics-laden 'hero worker' articles that used to be staple fodder in the Soviet press, national as well as local.

320. *A Few Drinks*: Russian *magarych*, a slang term for a drinking-bout organized by a newcomer to a place of work for his workmates.

321. *that old bully Zhritsyn*. Zhenya's first heroic exploit had been to sort out an

army veteran who was causing havoc in a block of flats by playing his radio during unsocial hours.

325. invoked *glasnost*: i.e. open discussion of social problems, a buzz-word of the Khrushchev as well as of the Gorbachev days.

Bella Akhmadulina (full first name Izabella, 1937–)

326. '*Lines Written during a Sleepless Night at Tbilisi*' (Stikhi, napisannye vo vremya bessonnitsy v Tbilisi) is taken from *Uroki muzyki* (Moscow, 1969). Akhmadulina has translated from the Georgian, and many of her poems deal with visits to that country, which has, in fact, become a romantic space of desire and fantasy for Russian poets and writers generally during the Soviet period, and especially after 1960, having rather the same value that Italy has had for writers in Britain and Germany.

l. 1. *Mtskhetian white moon*: the moon at Mtskheta, the ancient capital of Georgia.

l. 4. Sveti-Tskhoveli church: i.e. the Patriarchal Cathedral of Sveti-Tskhoveli at Mtskheta, a church founded in the fourth century (the current building dates from the fifteenth), which served as the burial place of the Georgian kings.

l. 11. *a pupil like a stallion's*: cf. 'He, who compared himself with a stallion's eye', the first line of Akhmatova's poem 'Poet', which is addressed to Pasternak.

l. 15. *hashi*: Georgian thick spiced soup made of stewed entrails.

Mira Izrailovna Linkevich (1909–)

328. '*How the Cadres were Broken in*' is taken from S. S. Vilensky (ed.), *Dodnes' tyagoteet* (Moscow, 1989), by permission of the editor and John Crowfoot.

riding the conveyor belt: This method of torture, convenient in that it leaves no obvious physical evidence, is widely recorded in memoirs of the Purges.

the NKVD: the People's Commissariat of Internal Affairs, the forerunner to the MGB (see below) and KGB as monitor of state security.

329. *Mayne Reid*: Captain Mayne Reid (1818–83), the immensely popular author of dozens of books for boys, including *The Giraffe Hunters* and *The Headless Horseman*, which were translated into Russian in 1895 and 1896 respectively.

330. *every other word had four letters*: an indication not only of the paucity of the interrogator's vocabulary, but also of his espousal of an accepted interrogation technique, the use of abusive language to make the victim break down.

Elena Shvarts (1948–)

331. '*Sale of a Historian's Library*' (Rasprodazha biblioteki istorika) was first published in Shvarts's *Tantsuyushchii David* (Paris, 1985). It appears by kind permission of the author.

331. l. 4. *the Pryazhka*: a river in St Petersburg, a tributary of the Neva, on whose banks is the city's most famous mental hospital. Cf. 'spent more time in Bedlam than he did at home'.

l. 8. *Budyonny cap . . . cloth one*. A Budyonny cap is that worn as part of Red Army uniform during the Russian Civil War (1918–21; cf. the famous poster 'Have YOU volunteered?'); for a Russian reader, a cloth cap has the proletarian resonance of its English equivalent, but it is more immediately and significantly associated with Lenin, in whose informal official portraits it obligatorily figured.

l. 11. *mantuasoys*: Russian *fizhmy*. Usually translated 'farthingale', the Russian has in fact a quite different historical resonance, since it refers to a whalebone skirt-extender worn in Russia during the *eighteenth* century, the historical period to which most of the references here allude. Hence the substitution of 'mantuasoy', a type of silk used for formal wear during the eighteenth century, and also a puffed-out overdress or jacket made therefrom (cf. 'mantua').

333. l. 61. *Paul*: i.e. Tsar Paul I (1754–1801; ruled 1796–1801), who reorganized the Russian army, including its élite regiments, along harshly Prussian disciplinary lines, and whose reign was eventually brought to an end when he was murdered as the result of a conspiracy amongst his courtiers.

valerian: i.e. the herb of the genus *Valeriana*, whose essence is widely used as a herbal tranquillizer in Russia.

Elena Chizhova (4 May 1957–)

334. '*Cassandra*' is the opening poem of *Helen: A Game of Seers and the Blind*, a narrative cycle written by Chizhova in 1986–8. The poem has not been published previously; it appears by permission of the author.

l. 8. *not a woman—a sting*: perhaps meaning the sting of some fly that might bring the 'plague' referred to in l. 7. The Russian *zhalo* is taken up, though word-play, in the reference to the pitiless' (*bezzhalostnyi*) choir, or chorus of Erinnyes (the Fates).

Lyudmila Petrushevskaya (1939–)

335. '*Words*' (Slova) is taken from *Bessmertnaya lyubov'* (Moscow, 1988); it will also appear in *Immortal Love*, trans. Sally Laird, to be published by Virago/Knopf in 1995.

340. '*Medea*' is taken from *Aprel'*, 2 (1989).

341. *the Kalanchovka*: the old name, still in popular use, of Komsomol Square, where three of Moscow's most important rail termini (of the Kazan, the Yaroslavl, and the Petersburg lines) are located.

Nina Sadur (1950–)

347. *'Frozen'* (which also exists as a short story) was first published in Sadur's *Chudnaya baba* (VTO, Moscow, 1989). The play appears here by permission of the author. This short one-act play is typical of Sadur's work in its representation of apparently oppressed individuals whose power relationships are never quite so predictable as they seem, and whose language veers from tough streetwise cliché to flights of fancy and poetry, and then back again.

348. *I can hear all right.* A typical strategy of Sadur's is to take some well-worn theatrical device (here, the deaf scene, one of the oldest comic turns in the book) and exploit it to bizarre and absurd effect (a few exchanges further on, Leila is to mishear perfectly ordinary nouns as elevated abstractions).

349. *Why did they call him Leo?* Leo (Russian 'Lev') is not in fact an especially esoteric first name; Nadya's reaction is probably provoked by the fact that it was Tolstoy's first name (hence the rendition as 'Leo' here). 'Vasya' and 'Kolya' are, however, definitely more ordinary than 'Arkady' (cf. 'Ted' and 'Dave' on the one hand, and 'Marcus' on the other).

350. *She put a curse on this theatre here.* Such references to the supernatural powers of women are another characteristic of Sadur's work.

351. *you're so scared they'll throw you out of that you're practically wetting yourself.* As someone who is an illegal immigrant to Moscow from Dagestan, Leila is an obvious target for exploitation.

352. *it suited me better when our Muslim women used to wear veils.* An absolutely standard view in the contemporary (post-)Soviet world, but the opinion that Nadya then goes on to voice (i.e. that women can keep control of their own faces through the veil) is rather more unusual.

The Robbers: the famous historical drama by Schiller.

354. *globeflowers*: i.e. *Trollius europaeus*, a relative of the buttercup, with impressive large round yellow flowers on short to medium stems (Russian *zolotoi shar*).

Arab ones . . . like foam: cf. the Moroccan equivalents that would be brought back as souvenirs to British households. The 'blinds' meant are the sort made of ruched white net, left permanently down, that are ubiquitous in Soviet official buildings, and in genteel Russian homes.

Bella (i.e. Izabella Yur'evna) Ulanovskaya (1948–)

360. *'Journey to Kashgar'* (Puteshestvie v Kashgar) has appeared in *Sintaksis* 28 (1990), and also in *Neva*, 2 (1991).

Like all of Ulanovskaya's, writing, the story idiosyncratically combines fiction, memoir, sententious reflection, and reportage. Here, the tale of an imaginary heroine's voyage to Eastern Turkestan is set against general reflections on Stalinist and post-Stalinist Russia and on the character of women's writing, all refracted through the perspective of a woman narrator who shares some of Ulanovskaya's own experiences and opinions.

360. *The Shitszin*: an anthology of Chinese classical poetry from the eleventh to sixth centuries BC; the title dates from the twelfth century AD.

Kashgar: an ancient city in Eastern (Chinese) Turkestan, on the Kashgar River, near the Tian-Shan mountain range; the name Kashgar (or Kashgaria) is also given to the region where the city is located.

Turan: a region in South-Eastern Turkestan; also called the Turan Basin.

362. *Tyutyushkin done this concrete*. The phrase signifies that the workman who laid the path has scrawled his name in the wet concrete.

363. *the Dostoevsky museum*: i.e. the museum in the writer's former flat at 5 Kuznechnyi pereulok, just south of Nevsky; Ulanovskaya's own workplace.

the nonsense Lyuba: i.e. Lyubov' Dostoevskaya, whose lurid memoirs of her father were published in 1920.

chronicler: The term *khronikyor* is in fact used for a journalist who compiles brief news items to be used as filler or diary pieces. The less sexist nature of Western journalistic working practices means that the gender connotations of the term are lost in translation; hence the substitution of 'chronicler'.

364. *pinafores*. The uniform of Russian schoolgirls has, since well before the Revolution, been a woollen dress with detachable collar, worn with a pinafore whose variations indicate age and achievement.

Stalinka: the diminutive of Stalina, a first name derived from the Soviet leader's surname that was quite commonly given to girls in the 1930s and 1940s.

Baskov Lane: Russian *Baskov pereulok*, a side-street just east of Liteiny Prospekt and north of Nevsky, in the centre of Leningrad/St Petersburg.

a general in the MGB: i.e. in the Ministry of State Security, the Soviet secret police force (predecessor of the KGB).

365. *gimnaziya*: see note to p. 119.

Lenin's 'wife, friend, and faithful helper': i.e. Nadezhda Krupskaya, pedagogue and party activist, who had studied at the Princess Obolenskaya *gimnaziya* in the 1870s.

366. *Korolenko, Artilleriiskaya, Sapyorny*: all side-streets near Baskov Lane.

she thinks they're her mother and father: an obvious indication, to a Russian reader, that the girl's parents have been among those who perished in the Stalinist purges of the late 1930s.

the Nekrasov bathhouse: the public baths on Nekrasov Street, a long thoroughfare running east-west to the south of Baskov Lane.

sabattur: i.e. saboteur. What follows is a spy-story of the kind that were very popular in the Soviet Union during the late 1940s and early 1950s, the height of the Cold War.

368. *the anniversary of Kirov's murder*: i.e. the anniversary of the murder, at Stalin's instigation, of Sergei Kirov, the Leningrad party leader, on 1 December 1934.

Gaidar the writer: the pen name of Arkady Golikov (1904–41), a very popular children's writer, who was also (significantly for this story), a military hero. He joined the Red Army at 14, and fought valorously in the Civil War; he was killed in battle during the first months of the Second World War.

369. *Surepka*: probably a nickname (for some surname such as Surepina), since this is the common name of *Sinapis arvensis*, charlock, a straggly yellow-flowered weed belonging to the mustard family.

371. *the meeting-place of the seeds fallen . . . life's rich rewards*. Korolenko Street, at the western end of Nekrasov Street, is in the 'better' part of a socially mixed area that, roughly speaking, goes downhill as it goes east.

374. *Shokan Valikhanov*: properly Chekkan Velikhanov (1835–66), explorer and ethnographer, who visited Kashgar in 1858. He died too young to complete a major study of his voyage, but 'Studies of Dzhungaria' and other essays survive.

Adolf Schlagintweit: a famous German explorer, born in Munich in 1829, who accompanied two of his brothers on an expedition to the Indian subcontinent; returning via Kashgar, he was murdered there in 1857, just as Ulanovskaya describes.

a khoja: an Eastern title for a teacher, here referring to Wali Khan, leader of the last of many Muslim revolts against the Chinese; the *Encyclopaedia Britannica* describes him as 'a degraded debauchee'.

379. *shamishen*: a three-stringed, long-necked Eastern lute, usually played as an accompaniment to singing.

381. *P. P. Semyonov*: Pyotr Petrovich Semyonov-Tyan-Shansky (1827–1914), liberal thinker, statesman, geographer, and explorer, the first European to reach the Tian-Shan (in 1857–8). A meeting with Semyonov is said to have inspired Valikhanov to make his Kashgar voyage.

the fashion for excursionism. 'Excursionism' refers to a highly serious late nineteenth-century cultural movement, whose task was recovering the past. However, Ulanovskaya also plays on the fact that package holidays, with compulsory excursions, were one of the innovations of 1960s Soviet life; they were as much frowned upon by intellectuals there as in the West.

'Good Morning'. What follows is a vicious satire on the kind of material that used to be considered appropriate leisure listening for Soviet audiences: a

mixture of mindless entertainment and patronizing enlightment. Hostility to the radio is also evident in Ulanovskaya's other work, which may puzzle Western readers unaware that inane radio programmes were compulsory background listening in Soviet hospitals, trains, factories, and homes.

381. *Chemists' and Metallurgists' Day*. The Soviet calendar was peppered with such synthetic festivals: better-known examples included Soviet Army Day, Soviet Policemen's Day, Soviet Aviators' Day, etc.

382. *Science and Life: Nauka i zhizn'*, a popular science magazine, with material about inventions and discoveries, etc. The items on biofields and forged manuscripts that follow are a surreal parody of its contents.

383. *the People's Artist of impending catastrophe*: i.e. the famous announcer of Stalinist times, Yury Levitan (1914–83), whose voice brought news of the Second World War to Russians; the title 'People's Artist of the USSR or RSFSR' is a state honour comparable to the OBE.

the lake . . . winding creeks. The major rivers of Turkestan are surrounded by complex systems of salt lakes and reedy marshes, frequented by wild boar, corsac and black-eared foxes, and many other birds and animals.

384. *phalanges*: i.e. *Solpuga aranoeides* or *intrepida*, a kind of large, yellowish-brown, long-haired arachnid, with a poisonous bite.

karakurts: i.e. *Latrodectus tredecimguttatus*, a very poisonous black spider.

385. *Allakh akbar*: Great God (Arabic).

387. *Sin-Kiang*: the Chinese name for Eastern Turkestan.

Tangut rhubarb: a form of the familiar plant named from the Chinese province of Tangut, or Tangh-siang.

388. *exploding puffballs*: i.e. *pylevik* (*Lycoperdon*); the Russian common name refers to the dusty inside of the senescent fungus.

389. *'Hans uh!'*: Russian *Lyuki vel'kh*, in imitation of Chinese pronunciation.

Olga Sedakova (1949–)

390. '*Fifth Stanzas*', from 'Iambics', was first published in *Nezavisimaya gazeta*, 5 February 1992. The text appears by permission of the author. The poem is a long chain of images, with very diverse cultural and historical associations, generated from one central idea: the 'thing' as the repository of secret powers (contemplative and creative).

l. 3. *a mythic fish*: both the coelacanth, a mysterious survival from ancient evolutionary times, and the magic fish that rises from deep water, or the bottom of wells, to grant three wishes in Russian folk-tales.

l. 8–9. *a trap as well, walking on velvet paws*: a paradox which links the quality of the trap with the quality of its victim (a tiger or other fierce, but soft-pawed, feline).

391. l. 17: *carrying us on pointed fins*: repeats the fish image of l. 3 above, associating it here specifically with the idea of poetic creativity.

392. l. 39. *a scoop of honey*. The Russian for scoop, *kovsh*, has powerful associations with the culture of Old Russia (it refers to a utensil rather like a truncated ladle, but used as a drinking vessel, which is found in variants ranging from humble painted wood to richly decorated and bejewelled painted metal).

l. 40. *stars floating like ice in springtime*. Literally: 'the heavenly ice-breaker', but the line sets up a link with l. 42, which in the original reads 'the crackle of vernal icicles'; the tie has been retained in the English, but differently phrased, for metrical reasons.

l. 48. *'things must pass', as Horace used to say*. Literally: '"all will pass", the Horatian chorus'; see esp. *Odes* I. iv; I. xi; IV. vii.

393. l. 62. *a Mediolanian glimpse of paradise*. Literally: 'a glimpse into a Mediolanian garden'. Mediolanium was the original Roman city, a renowned centre of culture, that stood on the site of modern Milan. The reader is to imagine the lush green courtyard gardens, hidden behind high walls in southern cities, that may be glimpsed for an instant when their owners go in or out. There may also be an allusion to St Augustine's conversion, which took place in a Milan garden. (I am indebted to Stephanie Sandler for this suggestion.)

ABOUT THE TRANSLATORS

SIBELAN FORRESTER teaches Russian literature and language at Oberlin College, Oberlin, Ohio. She has published articles on the work of Marina Tsvetaeva, and translations from Russian, Croatian, and Serbian; she is now writing a book on the role of women's language in Russian poetry.

DIANA GREENE is a specialist on early nineteenth-century Russian women's writing; she is at present working on a critical biography of Karolina Pavlova.

CATRIONA KELLY's published translations include Leonid Borodin, *The Third Truth*, Sergei Kaledin, *The Humble Cemetery*, and work by Irina Povolotskaya, Elena Rzhevskaya, Anna Barkova, Elena Shvarts, and Olga Sedakova.

ELIZABETH NEATROUR teaches Russian literature at James Madison University, Virginia, and is the author of several studies dealing with the work of Nadezhda Teffi.

BRIAN THOMAS OLES is a graduate student in Slavic Studies at the University of Washington, Seattle.

MARIAN SCHWARTZ has published many translations from the Russian, including work by Nina Berberova (*The Tattered Coat* and *The Accompanist*), Elena Makarova, Dina Runova, and Lidiya Avilova.

MARY ZIRIN, a specialist on nineteenth-century Russian women's writing, is the co-editor of *A Bio-Bibliographical Guide to Russian Women Writers*; her published translations include Nadezhda Durova's *The Cavalry Maiden*.

INDEX OF TITLES AND FIRST LINES